THE TABLEAU WORKSHOP

A practical guide to the art of data visualization
with Tableau

Sumit Gupta, Sylvester Pinto, Shweta Sankhe-Savale, JC Gillet,
and Kenneth Michael Cherven

THE TABLEAU WORKSHOP

Authors: Sumit Gupta, Sylvester Pinto, Shweta Sankhe-Savale, JC Gillet, and Kenneth Michael Cherven

Reviewers: Siddharth Pawar and Murari Ramuka

Development Editor: Aditi Hinge

Acquisitions Editor: Sneha Shinde

Production Editor: Salma Patel

Editorial Board: Megan Carlisle, Heather Gopsill, Bridget Kenningham, Manasa Kumar, Alex Mazonowicz, Monesh Mirpuri, Abhishek Rane, Brendan Rodrigues, Ankita Thakur, Nitesh Thakur, and Jonathan Wray

First published: April 2022

Production reference: 1250422

ISBN: 978-1-80020-765-3

Published by Packt Publishing Ltd.

Livery Place, 35 Livery Street

Birmingham B3 2PB, UK

Table of Contents

Chapter 3: Data Preparation: Using Tableau Prep 113

Chapter 4: Data Exploration: Comparison and Composition

Chapter 5: Data Exploration: Distributions and Relationships   277

Chapter 6: Data Exploration: Exploring Geographical Data   345

Chapter 7: Data Analysis: Creating and Using Calculations   437

Chapter 8: Data Analysis: Creating and Using Table Calculations   503

Chapter 11: Tableau Interactivity: Part 1

PREFACE

ABOUT THE BOOK

Learning Tableau has never been easier, thanks to this practical introduction to storytelling with data. *The Tableau Workshop* breaks down the analytical process into five steps: data preparation, data exploration, data analysis, interactivity, and distribution of dashboards. Each stage is addressed with a clear walk-through of the key tools and techniques you'll need, as well as engaging real-world examples, meaningful data, and practical exercises to give you valuable hands-on experience.

As you work through the book, you'll learn Tableau step by step, studying how to clean, shape, and combine data, as well as how to choose the most suitable charts for any given scenario. You'll load data from various sources and formats, perform data engineering to create new data that delivers deeper insights, and create interactive dashboards that engage end users.

All concepts are introduced with clear, simple explanations and demonstrated through realistic example scenarios. You'll simulate real-world data science projects with use cases such as traffic violations, urban populations, coffee store sales, and air travel delays.

By the end of this Tableau book, you'll have the skills and knowledge to confidently present analytical results and make data-driven decisions.

ABOUT THE AUTHORS

Sumit Gupta is an analytics professional with more than 7 years' experience spanning across marketing, sales, and product analytics. As a consultant and trainer, he has utilized Tableau to build better data-driven teams for his organization. Sumit specializes in translating vast amounts of data into easy-to-understand dashboards which provide actionable intelligence. He is a Tableau Certified Associate and enjoys training data enthusiasts to become better Tableau developers and certified Tableau associates. This book is one such effort to reach masses.

I would like to thank my family for being incredibly supportive through this book-writing journey, especially my super-mom. Without her, I wouldn't be where I am today. I would also like to thank my friends (Piyush and Sheshnath, to name a few) and mentors/leaders/managers who have also pushed me to become better every day. Onwards and Upwards!

Sylvester Pinto has been using Tableau for almost a decade now for improving business performance for different industries. Sylvester has designed various business solutions using Tableau for different organizations leading to a huge impact to improve their businesses. He has a Tableau certification and as a consultant designs solutions for various organizations.

Shweta Sankhe-Savale is the co-founder and Head of Client Engagements at Syvylyze Analytics (pronounced "civilize"), a boutique business analytics firm specializing in visual analytics. Shweta is a Tableau Desktop Qualified Associate and a Tableau Accredited Trainer. Being one of the leading experts on Tableau in India, Shweta has translated her experience and expertise into successfully rendering analytics and data visualization services for numerous clients across a wide range of industry verticals. She has taken on numerous training and consulting assignments for customers across sectors such as BFSI, FMCG, retail, e-commerce, consulting and professional services, manufacturing, healthcare and pharma, ITeS, and more. She even had the privilege of working with renowned government and UN agencies. Combining her ability to break down complex concepts with her expertise on Tableau's visual analytics platforms, Shweta has successfully trained over 1,300 participants from 85+ companies.

Jean-Charles (JC) Gillet is a seasoned business analyst with over 7 years of experience with SQL at both a large-scale multinational company in the United Kingdom and a smaller firm in the United States, and 5 years of Tableau experience. He has been working with Tableau and SQL for multiple years to share his expertise with his colleagues, as well as delivering SQL training. A French national, JC holds a master's degree in executive engineering from Mines ParisTech and is a Tableau Desktop Certified Associate.

In his free time, he enjoys spending time with his wife and daughter (to whom he dedicates his work on this book) and playing team handball, having competed in national championships.

I'd like dedicate this work first and foremost to my wife and two children, who stand by my side every day, through thick and thin. But also to my parents, who taught me my core values, and my managers, especially my mentors and friends Robert and Miguel, who have meant so much to me.

Kenneth Michael Cherven is a Data Analyst and Visualizer based in Detroit, Michigan, USA. He has worked with Tableau for more than 15 years with a focus on making complex data easily understood through the of interactive dashboards and creative displays. Beyond his work in the automotive sector, Kenneth analyzes data and creates visualizations using open data sources from the baseball, government, music, and craft beer domains. Ken has previously published two titles for Packt – *Network Graph Analysis and Visualization with Gephi* and *Mastering Gephi Network Visualization*.

WHO THIS BOOK IS FOR

This book is for anyone who wants to get started on visual analytics with Tableau. If you're new to Tableau, this Workshop will get you up and running. If you already have some experience in Tableau, this book will help fill in any gaps, consolidate your understanding, and give you extra practice with the key tools.

ABOUT THE CHAPTERS

Chapter 1, Introduction: Visual Analytics with Tableau, teaches you the basic skills needed to understand data and its visual elements for reporting and creating dashboards.

Chapter 2, Data Preparation: Using Tableau Desktop, covers the essential skills you need to create reports in Tableau, such as loading, joining, transforming, blending, and manipulating data.

Chapter 3, Data Preparation: Using Tableau Prep, covers Tableau Prep and how Prep helps in cleaning and joining disparate data sources. You will learn how to perform data manipulation methods such as pivots, grouping, and aggregations, and finally, how to export the transformed data into Tableau.

Chapter 4, Data Exploration: Comparison and Composition, expands on your Tableau knowledge. You will start creating charts in Tableau, including line, bar, and stacked area charts. You will also learn how to create trend reports.

Chapter 5, Data Exploration: Distributions and Relationships, covers reference lines and advanced chart types such as Dual Axis and Quadrant charts.

Chapter 6, Data Exploration: Exploring Geographical Data, teaches you how to explore geographical data to perform location-based analysis in Tableau.

Chapter 7, Data Analysis: Creating and Using Calculations, covers calculations, including numeric, string, and date calculations. You will also learn how to write logical statements in calculated fields.

Chapter 8, Data Analysis: Creating and Using Table Calculations, touches on table calculations and how they differ from calculated fields, and when to use table calculations versus calculated fields.

Chapter 9, Data Analysis: Creating and Using Level of Details (LOD) Calculations, covers LOD calculations, with which you will learn how to control the aggregation level in your view.

Chapter 10, Dashboards and Storyboards, covers the basics of using a blank canvas to build interactive dashboards, including adding branding elements, filters, and web pages. Finally, we will also cover storyboards and how they differ from dashboards.

Chapter 11, Tableau Interactivity: Part 1, dives deeper into Tableau Order of Operations, Filters, Sets, and Parameters, while reinforcing the other charting and dashboarding skills.

This is part one of a two-part topic, the latter half of which is available online.

> ## NOTE
>
> There are also three bonus chapters (*Chapter 12, Tableau Interactivity: Part 2*; *Chapter 13, Distribution of Dashboards*; and *Chapter 14, Case Study*) which you can find at https://packt.link/SHQ4H.
>
> You can also find solutions for all activities in this Workshop online at https://packt.link/CTCxk.

CONVENTIONS

Code words in text form, database and collection names, file and folder names, shell commands, and user input use the following format: "There are also other **File**, **Edit**, **Flow**, and **Server** menu options at the top. The purposes of the **File** and **Edit** options are self-explanatory. The **Flow** menu can be used to run the flow and the **Server** menu has the option to sign in and publish the flow on Tableau Server."

Often at the beginning of chapters, key new terms will be introduced. In these cases, the following formatting will be used: "Understanding **aggregations** is the most fundamental concept you need to keep in mind when working with Tableau."

MINIMUM HARDWARE REQUIREMENTS

For an optimal experience, we recommend the following hardware configuration:

- Processor: Dual core or better

- Memory: 4 GB RAM

- Storage: 10 GB available space

MINIMUM SOFTWARE REQUIREMENTS

Unlike hardware requirements, software requirements can be challenging to list because Tableau releases new updates to their software every 3-6 months and there are new features added with these new releases. But considering the exercises/activities planned in this book, we expect the following to be required at minimum:

- Tableau Desktop 2020.1 or above

- Tableau Prep 2020.1 or above

This book was written and reviewed using Tableau versions 2020.1.x. Though new versions of Tableau are frequently released, the steps used for the exercises and activities in this book are unlikely to change with the version changes. Any known differences at the time of publication will be noted within the text as relevant.

DOWNLOADING THE BOOK/DATA SOURCES BUNDLE

GitHub link: https://packt.link/jqzD0

Download all the folders and data files from GitHub (as shown) or download individual chapter files separately as needed.

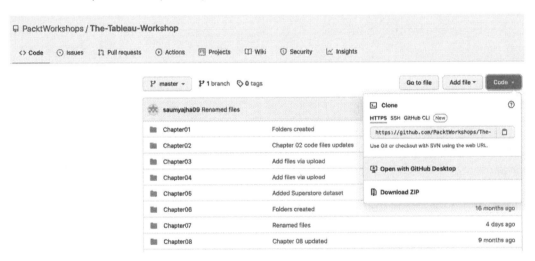

Figure 0.1: GitHub files

SETTING UP YOUR ENVIRONMENT

Before you begin the book, you need to set up both Tableau Desktop and Tableau Prep. In this section, you will see how to install Tableau Desktop. Once you have followed these steps and installed Tableau Desktop, you will also then need to follow the same steps to download Tableau Prep. The download links are as follows:

Tableau Desktop 2020.1: https://www.tableau.com/support/releases

Tableau Prep 2020.1: https://www.tableau.com/support/releases/prep

INSTALLING TABLEAU ON YOUR SYSTEM

1. From https://www.tableau.com/support/releases/, click on **2020.1** to expand the list. Click on any of the 2020.1.XX links as follows:

2020.1	Downloads and Release Notes
2020.1.20	Released Sep 2, 2021
2020.1.19	Released Jul 22, 2021
2020.1.18	Released Jun 24, 2021
2020.1.17	Released May 18, 2021
2020.1.16	Released Apr 22, 2021
2020.1.15	Released Mar 23, 2021

Figure 0.2: Tableau downloads/release notes page

2. Click on 2020.1.20 and on the new page which was loaded. Next, either click on **Download Tableau Desktop 2020.1.20** and Tableau will automatically detect your operating system, or else scroll down to the **Download Files** section and click on the appropriate download link for your operating system (Windows or Mac).

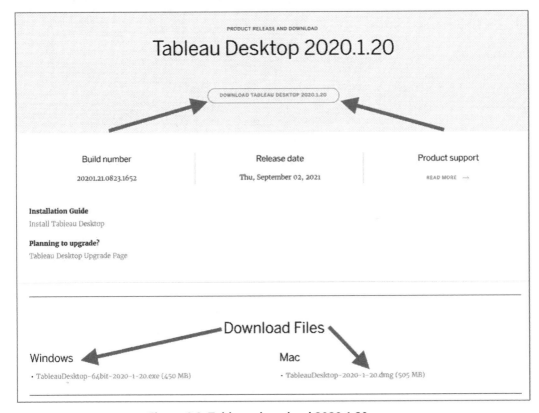

Figure 0.3: Tableau download 2020.1.20 page

3. Once you have downloaded the file, open your downloads folder, and double-click on the downloaded file. You will see the following screen if you are using a Mac (Windows will have a similar workflow):

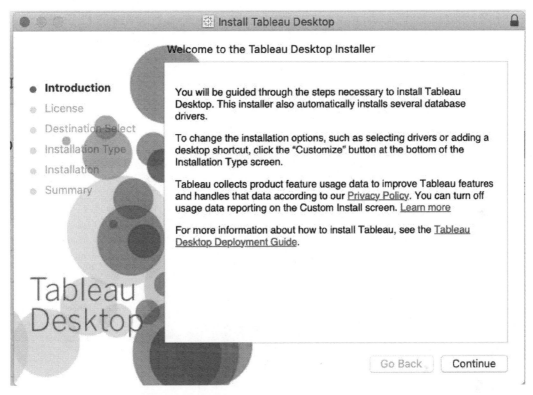

Figure 0.4: Tableau Desktop installer: introduction

4. Follow the prompt by clicking on **Continue** and agreeing to the terms and conditions of the software license agreement:

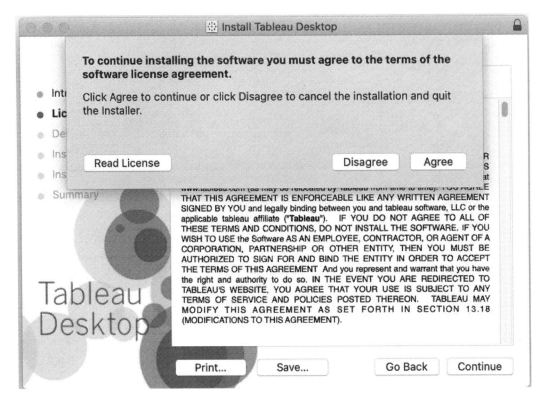

Figure 0.5: Tableau software agreement prompt

It might take a minute or two to install the software and you may be asked to restart your system, depending on your computer's configuration.

5. Once the files are written, you should see the following success message. Click on **Close** to finish the installation:

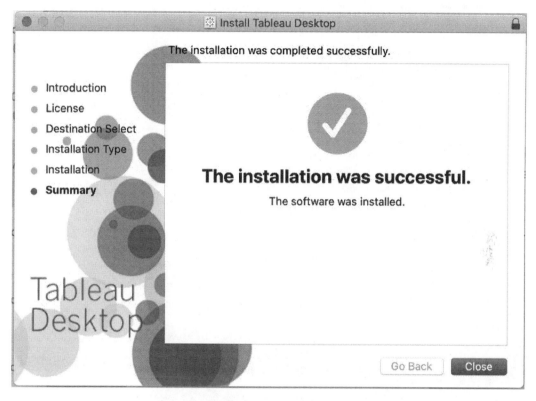

Figure 0.6: Tableau installation complete

6. To verify whether the software was installed, if you are using Mac, press *cmd* + *Space* to open spotlight search and type in **Tableau**. You should see the following on your screen. Similarly, if you are using Windows, click on the Windows button and type **Tableau** to open the application.

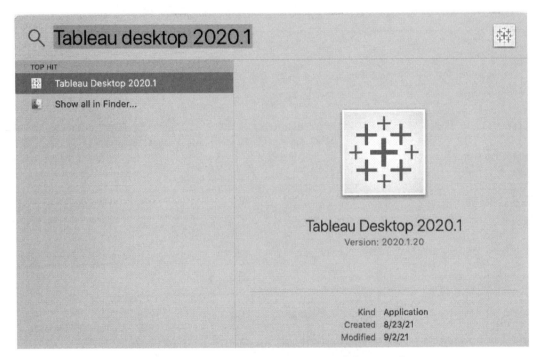

Figure 0.7: Searching Tableau in spotlight search

You can follow the same steps to install Tableau Prep by downloading the software from the download link above. When you load either Tableau Desktop or Tableau Prep for the first time, you might be required to register the software and enter the license key. Depending on your situation, either your organization might be able to provide the license keys, or you can start a 14-day trial to explore the software. Finally, if you are a student or teacher, Tableau offers free 1-year licenses; to learn more, visit https://www.tableau.com/academic/students.

GET IN TOUCH

Feedback from our readers is always welcome.

General feedback: If you have any questions about this book, please mention the book title in the subject of your message and email us at customercare@packtpub.com.

Errata: Although we have taken every care to ensure the accuracy of our content, mistakes do happen. If you have found a mistake in this book, we would be grateful if you could report this to us. Please visit www.packtpub.com/support/errata and complete the form.

Piracy: If you come across any illegal copies of our works in any form on the Internet, we would be grateful if you could provide us with the location address or website name. Please contact us at copyright@packt.com with a link to the material.

If you are interested in becoming an author: If there is a topic that you have expertise in and you are interested in either writing or contributing to a book, please visit authors.packtpub.com.

PLEASE LEAVE A REVIEW

Let us know what you think by leaving a detailed, impartial review on Amazon. We appreciate all feedback – it helps us continue to make great products and help aspiring developers build their skills. Please spare a few minutes to give your thoughts – it makes a big difference to us. You can leave a review by clicking the following link: https://packt.link/r/1800207654.

1

INTRODUCTION: VISUAL ANALYTICS WITH TABLEAU

OVERVIEW

In this chapter, you will learn about **Visual Analytics** and why it is important to visualize your data. You will connect to data using Tableau Desktop and familiarize yourself with the Tableau workspace. By the end of this chapter, you will be well acquainted with the Tableau interface and some of the fundamental important concepts that will help you get started with Tableau. The topics that are covered in this chapter will mark the start of your Tableau journey.

INTRODUCTION

At a very broad level, the whole data analytics process can be broken down into the following steps: data preparation, data exploration, data analysis, and distribution. This process typically starts with a question or a goal, which is followed by finding and getting the relevant data. Once the relevant data is available, you then need to prepare this data for your exploration and analysis stage. You might have to clean and restructure the data to get it in the right form, maybe combine it with some additional datasets, or enhance the data by creating some calculations. This stage is referred to as the data preparation stage. After this comes the data exploration stage. It is at this stage that you try to see the composition and distribution of your data, compare data, and identify relationships if any exist. This step gives an idea of what kind of analysis can be done with the given dataset.

Typically, people like to explore the data by looking at it in its raw form (that is, at the data preparation stage); however, a quick and easy way to explore the data is to visualize it. Visualizing the data can reveal patterns that were difficult to recognize in the raw data.

The data exploration stage is followed by the data analysis stage, in which you analyze your data and develop insights that can be shared with others. These insights, when visualized, will enable easier interpretation of data, which in turn leads to better decision making. In very simplistic terms, the process of exploring and analyzing the data by visualizing it as charts and graphs is called "visual analytics." As mentioned earlier, the idea behind visualizing your data is to enable faster decision making. Finally, the last step in the data analytics cycle is the distribution stage, wherein you share your work with other stakeholders who can consume this information and act upon it.

In this chapter, we will discuss all these topics in detail, starting with a further exploration of the value of the titular process.

THE IMPORTANCE OF VISUAL ANALYTICS

As mentioned earlier, "Visual Analytics" can be defined as the process of exploring and analyzing data by visualizing it as charts and graphs. This enables end users to quickly consume the information and, in turn, empowers them to make quicker and better decisions.

In this section, you will learn why data visualization is a better tool for evaluation than looking at large volumes of data in numeric format.

All of us have at some point heard the expression "A picture is worth a thousand words." Indeed, it has been found that humans are great at identifying and recognizing patterns and trends in data when consumed as visuals as opposed to large volumes of data in tabular or spreadsheet formats.

To understand the importance and the power of data visualization/visual analytics, let's look at one of the classic examples: **Anscombe's Quartet**. Anscombe's quartet is comprised of four distinct datasets with nearly identical statistical properties, yet completely different distributions and visualizations.

> **NOTE**
>
> This was developed in 1973 by an English statistician named Francis John (Frank) Anscombe, after whom it was named.

Let's take a deeper look at these datasets.

DataSet1		DataSet2		DataSet3		DataSet4	
X	Y	X	Y	X	Y	X	Y
10.00	8.04	10.00	9.14	10.00	7.46	8.0	6.58
8.00	6.95	8.00	8.14	8.00	6.77	8.0	5.76
13.00	7.58	13.00	8.74	13.00	12.74	8.0	7.71
9.00	8.81	9.00	8.77	9.00	7.11	8.0	8.84
11.00	8.33	11.00	9.26	11.00	7.81	8.0	8.47
14.00	9.96	14.00	8.10	14.00	8.84	8.0	7.04
6.00	7.24	6.00	6.13	6.00	6.08	8.0	5.25
4.00	4.26	4.00	3.10	4.00	5.39	8.0	5.56
12.00	10.84	12.00	9.13	12.00	8.15	19.0	12.50
7.00	4.82	7.00	7.26	7.00	6.42	8.0	7.91
5.00	5.68	5.00	4.74	5.00	5.73	8.0	6.89

Figure 1.1: A screenshot showing the datasets used in Anscombe's quartet

As you can see in the preceding figure, each dataset consists of 11 X and Y points. Now, if you were to analyze these datasets using typical descriptive statistics such as mean, standard deviation, and correlation between X and Y, you would see that the output is identical.

DataSet	Mean (X)	Standard Deviation (X)	Mean (Y)	Standard Deviation (Y)	Correlation (X,Y)
1	9.00	3.32	7.501	2.032	0.8164
2	9.00	3.32	7.501	2.032	0.8162
3	9.00	3.32	7.500	2.030	0.8163
4	9.00	3.32	7.501	2.031	0.8165

Figure 1.2: A screenshot showing descriptive statistics of the Anscombe's quartet data

Looking at the preceding figure, you can see the following:

- The mean of X for each dataset is 9 (exact accuracy).

- The standard deviation for X for each dataset is 3.32 (exact accuracy).

- The mean of Y for each dataset is 7.50 (accurate up to two decimals).

- The standard deviation for Y for each dataset is 2.03 (accurate up to two decimals).

- The correlation between X and Y for each dataset is 0.816 (accurate up to three decimals).

So, by looking at the above statistical inferences, you would assume that these datasets are identical until you decide to visualize each of them, the results of which are displayed below.

The images show how these datasets appear when visualized as graphs. Now, let's compare each of these visualizations side by side so that you can see how different each of these datasets really are.

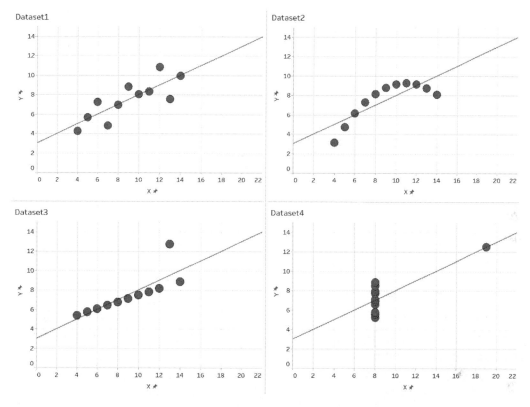

**Figure 1.3: A screenshot showing a graphical representation
of all four datasets of Anscombe's quartet**

The preceding example highlights how data visualization can help uncover patterns in data that it was not possible to see by simply looking at the numbers and/or just analyzing the data statistically. This is exactly why Francis Anscombe created his "quartet." He wanted to counter the argument that "numerical calculations are exact, but graphs are rough," which, back then, was a quite common impression among statisticians.

Next, take a look at one more example of how visualizing data helps us find quick insights. Refer to the following figure:

Product Type	Product	Market							
		Central Marketing	Profit	East Marketing	Profit	South Marketing	Profit	West Marketing	Profit
Coffee	Amaretto	1,776	5,104	368	1,010			2,514	-1,224
	Colombian	5,372	8,525	4,994	27,256	2,874	8,767	4,106	11,256
	Decaf Irish Cream	3,998	9,635	782	2,726	1,736	2,935	4,846	-1,307
Espresso	Caffe Latte					2,834	3,873	2,638	7,502
	Caffe Mocha	4,570	14,642	8,430	-6,232	2,264	5,202	4,422	4,066
	Decaf Espresso	3,142	8,859	1,044	2,411	1,868	5,930	4,058	12,302
	Regular Espresso			2,946	10,065				
Herbal Tea	Chamomile	5,332	14,435	292	764	1,566	3,178	4,976	8,854
	Lemon	3,760	6,253	4,400	7,902	3,420	2,593	4,300	13,121
	Mint	1,102	4,069	2,818	-2,243			2,188	4,328
Tea	Darjeeling	3,968	10,769	1,518	6,500			4,280	11,784
	Earl Grey	5,634	10,334	716	3,404			3,496	10,426
	Green Tea	758	1,227	1,134	5,654			5,234	-7,112

Figure 1.4: A screenshot of a grid view showing the marketing expense and profitability for products across markets

In the preceding figure, you can see a grid view of fields such as **Product Type**, **Product**, **Market**, **Marketing**, and **Profit**. In the data that you have used, **Marketing** is the money that is spent on any marketing efforts to promote products, and **Profit** is the profit generated after those marketing efforts. Further, these values are broken down by dimensions such as **Product Type**, **Product**, and **Market**. The idea is to evaluate how each product is doing in terms of **Marketing** and **Profit** across different markets.

Now, displaying this information in a grid format, as shown above, results in 84 numbers being shown in the view, and doing any kind of comparison across these 84 numbers is going to be very difficult. So, imagine you want to find out whether there are any products in any specific markets where losses are made even after spending significant money on the marketing efforts. Then you will end up comparing these numbers horizontally as well as vertically, which, honestly, is a bit tedious. However, let's see whether visualizing this data makes any difference. Refer to the following figure:

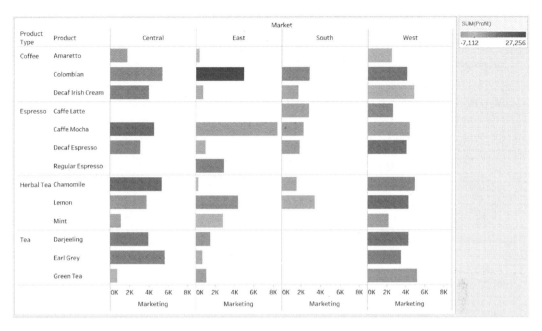

Figure 1.5: A bar chart comparing the marketing expense and profitability for products

In the preceding figure, you can see that the length of the bar is the money spent on **Marketing**, whereas the color of the bar represents the **Profit** value. So basically, the longer the bar, the more money was spent on marketing; the darker the shade of blue, the more profitable the product; and the darker the shade of orange, the greater the loss accrued.

Looking back at that figure, note that the longest bar is **Caffe Mocha** in the **East** market. This means that **Caffe Mocha** has the highest marketing spending, but because the color of that bar is orange, you also know that it is accruing a loss.

This is another example that demonstrates the power of data visualization.

Now that you have understood what visual analytics is and why it is important, let's look at some data visualization tools in the next section.

THE TABLEAU PRODUCT SUITE

There are a lot of tools available on the market offering various features and functionalities that you can use to visualize your data. When it comes to business analytics and data visualization, Tableau is one of the leading tools in this space because of its ease of use and drag and drop functionality, which makes it easier even for a business user to start making sense of their data. Tableau has different tools for different purposes, available in the Tableau product suite, which we'll explore in this section.

The entire suite can be divided into three parts: data preparation, data visualization, and consumption or distribution. Refer to the following figure:

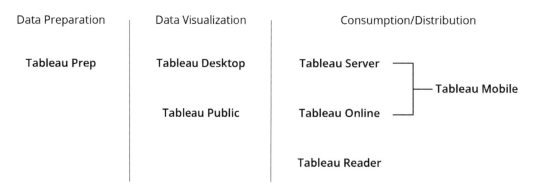

Figure 1.6: A screenshot showing the Tableau product suite

As shown in the preceding figure, you have *Tableau Prep* in the *Data Preparation layer*, which is used for cleaning, combining, reshaping, and enhancing your data. This tool helps get your data ready for analysis and visualization.

Now, once your data is ready and is in the right form and structure, you will start analyzing and visualizing it. For this purpose, you will use either *Tableau Desktop* or *Tableau Public*.

Tableau Desktop is where you create your visualizations, analytics, and dashboards. This is typically the tool you would spend your time on as most of your development is done using Tableau Desktop. Tableau Public can also be used for creating your analytics and visualizations. However, the catch here is that you cannot save your work locally or offline, and it will necessarily be saved to a Tableau Public server, which can be viewed by anybody. Tableau Public is a free version that is like Tableau Desktop and is typically used by bloggers, journalists, researchers, and so on who deal with public or open data.

Tableau Public is a great tool for anyone wanting to build visualizations for public consumption but is not recommended for anyone working with confidential data. When dealing with confidential data, it is best to use Tableau Desktop.

Once you are done building your visualizations, you can share your work with others using an online methodology with *Tableau Server* or *Tableau Online* or share an offline copy of your work, which can then be opened using *Tableau Reader*.

Tableau Server is an on-premises hosted browser and mobile-based collaboration platform used to publish dashboards created in Tableau Desktop and share them with your end users. It allows you to share and, to some extent, edit and publish dashboards, while also managing access rights and making your visualizations accessible securely over the web. It allows you to refresh your dashboards at a scheduled frequency and maintain live data connectivity to the backend data sources, which in turn allows users to consume the up-to-date dashboards online from anywhere. Tableau Server also allows you to view your dashboards on a mobile tablet through an app available on both iOS and Android. Tableau Online, on the other hand, is a cloud-hosted version (or SaaS version) of Tableau Server. It brings the server capabilities of the cloud without the infrastructure cost.

However, if you want to consume dashboards offline, you can use Tableau Reader. This is a free desktop application that can be used to open, view, and interact with dashboards and visualizations built in Tableau Desktop. So basically, it allows you to filter, drill down, view the details of data, and interact with dashboards to the full extent of what the author has intended. That said, being a reader, you cannot make any changes or edit the dashboard in any way beyond what has already been built in by the author.

The upcoming section, as well as the following chapters, will focus on Tableau Desktop. You will be familiarizing yourself with the interface of Tableau Desktop, to understand its workspace and see how you can create your visualizations and build your dashboards.

The point to note here is that Tableau Desktop is a licensed product and if you don't have the necessary license, then you can even use Tableau Public to try out the examples covered in the book. As mentioned earlier, Tableau Desktop and Tableau Public are the two main developer products offered by Tableau and the only difference between these two products is the range of data source connectivity offered, the ability to save files locally, and the security of your work. While Tableau Desktop offers all this, Tableau Public has limitations.

However, the rest of the functionalities and the look and feel of both these tools is the same. The next section explores how to use Tableau to connect, analyze, and visualize your data.

Please note that we are using a licensed version of Tableau Desktop in this book.

INTRODUCTION TO TABLEAU DESKTOP

Now, that you have identified and chosen Tableau Desktop for the creation of your visuals and dashboards, let's dive deeper into the product, its interface, and its functionality. So, once you have downloaded and installed the product, you will be able to use the products to connect to your data and start building your visualizations.

The landing page of Tableau Desktop is shown in the following screenshot:

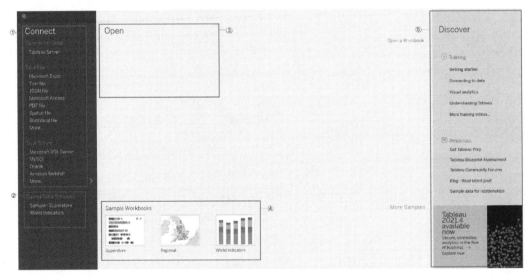

Figure 1.7: A screenshot of the Tableau Desktop landing page

Review the following list for explanations of the highlighted sections in the screenshot:

1. **Connect**: The list of data sources you can connect to. You can connect to data residing on Tableau Server (the **Search for Data** option); to flat files, such as Excel and CSVs (the **To a File** option); or to databases (the **To a Server** option). Tableau has native in-built connectors for a lot of the data sources, which makes the interaction with data from these data sources seamless. The list is quite extensive, and it keeps on growing. Note though that while Tableau Desktop provides an extensive list of data connectors, Tableau Public only allows you to connect to flat files (the **To a File** option). Refer to the following screenshot to see the **More**... option of Tableau Desktop 2020.1 version:

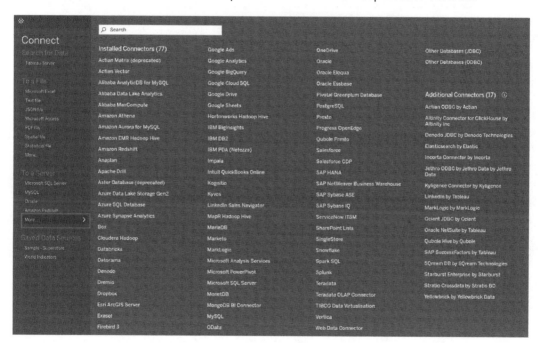

Figure 1.8: A screenshot showing the extensive list of data sources that Tableau Desktop can connect to

2. **Saved Data Sources**: While the top section allows you to connect to raw data sources, the **Saved Data Sources** option lets you connect to data sources that have been previously worked on and/or modified and then saved for later use.

3. **Open**: This section shows the thumbnails of the recently accessed Tableau files. This section is blank to begin with, but as you create and save new workbooks, it will keep on updating and will display the thumbnails of the most recently opened workbooks. This section can also be used to pin your favorite workbooks.

4. **Sample Workbooks**: This section shows some of the sample work already done in Tableau. Selecting any of the thumbnails here will open the relevant Tableau workbook. A quick point to note here is that a "workbook" in Tableau is a file that consists of multiple worksheets and/or dashboards and/or storyboards.

5. **Discover**: This section contains some shortcut links to the training videos and resources on the Tableau website.

6. Now that you are familiar with the landing page of Tableau, let's move on and see how to connect to data in the following exercise.

EXERCISE 1.01: CONNECTING TO A DATA SOURCE

In this exercise, you will connect to a data source for the first time, which is the very first step when analyzing data in Tableau.

There are many types of data sources that you can connect to, but for the purposes of this exercise, you will work with an Excel file—in this case, *Sample-Superstore.xls*, which comes in-built with Tableau and contains sales and profit data for a company.

Perform the following steps to complete the exercise:

1. Select the **Microsoft Excel** option from the **To a File** option under **Connect** on the left-hand side of the landing page. You should see the following screen:

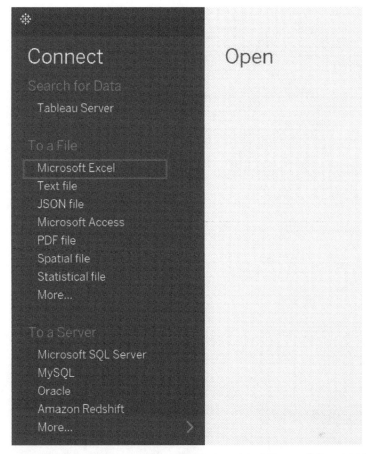

Figure 1.9: A screenshot showing the Connect to Microsoft Excel option

2. Once you have selected this option, it will ask you to browse the Excel file that you wish to connect to. To do this, connect to **Sample-Superstore.xls**, which can be found in *Documents>My Tableau Repository>Datasources*, or can also be downloaded from the GitHub repository for this chapter, at https://packt. link/7hnNH. Refer to the following screenshot:

Figure 1.10: A screenshot showing the Sample - Superstore.xls data under My Tableau Repository

This data is the sample dataset that comes along with the product. Once you have downloaded and installed Tableau Desktop, you will notice the **My Tableau Repository** folder being created under your **Documents** folder. This is where you will find this sample dataset.

3. Once you have connected to this data source, you will see the *data connection page* of Tableau Desktop, as shown in the following screenshot. Review the following notes to better understand what you're looking at:

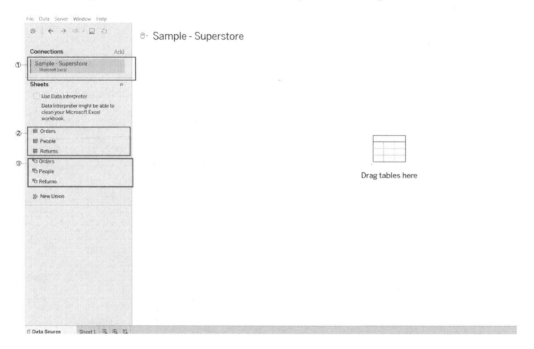

Figure 1.11: A screenshot showing the data connection page in Tableau Desktop

- **Section 1**: This highlights the *data source* that you have connected to. This is the **Sample - Superstore.xls** file that you just established a connection with. One point to note here is that just because you have established a connection to this Excel file does not mean that you have connected to the data.

- **Section 2**: These are the tables/worksheets in your **Sample - Superstore.xls** file, which is where the actual data resides. The **Orders** table contains the list of all transactions from this retail superstore and contains data at an order level. This order level contains details of the day, product, and customer levels. Refer to the following figure to take a glance at the **Orders** table:

Row ID	Order ID	Order Date	Ship Date	Ship Mode	Customer ID	Customer Name	Segment	Country/Region	City	State	Postal Code	Region	Product ID	Category	Sub-Category	Product Name	Sales	Quantity	Discount	Profit
1	CA-2018-152156	08-11-2018	11-11-2018	Second	CG-12520	Claire Gute	Consumer	United States	Henderson	Kentucky	42420	South	FUR-BO-10001	Furniture	Bookcases	Bush Somers	261.96	2	0	41.9136
2	CA-2018-152156	08-11-2018	11-11-2018	Second	CG-12520	Claire Gute	Consumer	United States	Henderson	Kentucky	42420	South	FUR-CH-10000	Furniture	Chairs	Hon Deluxe F	731.94	3	0	219.582
3	CA-2018-138688	12-06-2018	16-06-2018	Second	DV-13045	Darrin Van Huff	Corporate	United States	Los Angeles	California	90036	West	OFF-LA-10000	Office Suppl	Labels	Self-Adhesiv	14.62	2	0	6.8714
4	US-2017-108966	11-10-2017	18-10-2017	Standard	SO-20335	Sean O'Donnell	Consumer	United States	Fort Laude	Florida	33311	South	FUR-TA-10000	Furniture	Tables	Bretford CR4	957.5775	5	0.45	-383.031
5	US-2017-108966	11-10-2017	18-10-2017	Standard	SO-20335	Sean O'Donnell	Consumer	United States	Fort Laude	Florida	33311	South	OFF-ST-10000	Office Suppl	Storage	Eldon Fold 'N	22.368	2	0.2	2.5164
6	CA-2016-115812	09-06-2016	14-06-2016	Standard	BH-11710	Brosina Hoffman	Consumer	United States	Los Angele	California	90032	West	FUR-FU-10001	Furniture	Furnishings	Eldon Expres	48.86	7	0	14.1694
7	CA-2016-115812	09-06-2016	14-06-2016	Standard	BH-11710	Brosina Hoffman	Consumer	United States	Los Angele	California	90032	West	OFF-AR-10002	Office Suppl	Art	Newell 322	7.28	4	0	1.9656

Figure 1.12: A screenshot showing a glimpse into the Orders worksheet
of Sample - Superstore.xls

- The **People** table contains just two columns: **Region** and **Person**. The **Person** column is the list of managers for each **Region**. Refer to the following screenshot to take a glance at the **People** table:

	A	B
1	Person	Region
2	Anna Andreadi	West
3	Chuck Magee	East
4	Kelly Williams	Central
5	Cassandra Brandow	South
6		

Figure 1.13: A screenshot showing a glimpse into the People worksheet
of Sample - Superstore.xls

The **Returns** table contains the list of all the transactions/orders that were returned. So, again, only two columns: **Returned** and **Order ID**. Refer to the following screenshot to take a glance at the **Returns** table:

	A	B
1	Returned	Order ID
2	Yes	CA-2016-100762
3	Yes	CA-2016-100762
4	Yes	CA-2016-100762
5	Yes	CA-2016-100762
6	Yes	CA-2016-100867
7	Yes	CA-2016-102652
8	Yes	CA-2016-102652
9	Yes	CA-2016-102652
10	Yes	CA-2016-102652
11	Yes	CA-2016-103373
12	Yes	CA-2016-103744
13	Yes	CA-2016-103744

Figure 1.14: A screenshot showing a glimpse into the Returns worksheet
of Sample - Superstore.xls

- **Section 3**: This is the list of *Named Ranges* that were created on the aforementioned tables/ worksheets (that is, **Orders**, **People**, and **Returns**) of the **Sample - Superstore.xls** data source. *Named Ranges* are a feature in *Microsoft Excel*, and Tableau gives you the option of reading data from these predefined *Named Ranges*. To understand more about these *Named Ranges in Excel*, please refer to the following link: https://support.microsoft.com/en-us/office/define-and-use-names-in-formulas-4d0f13ac-53b7-422e-afd2-abd7ff379c64?ui=en-us&rs=en-us&ad=us.

4. So, at this point, you have made a connection to the **Sample - Superstore. xls** file; however, you are yet to establish a connection to the data to be able to read it in Tableau for your analysis. To do so, drag the **Orders** worksheet from the left-hand side list and drop it into the top blank section, which reads **Drag sheets here.** (If you are working with a version later than 2020.1, this may instead read **Drag tables here.**) Please note that you need to use the **Orders** worksheet and not the **Orders** named range since the data in the named range could be limited compared to the data in the **Orders** worksheet. Refer to the following screenshot:

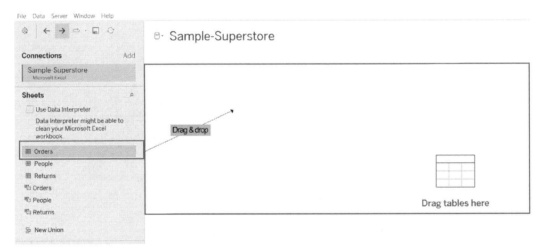

Figure 1.15: A screenshot showing how to read data from the Orders worksheet of Sample - Superstore.xls

5. Once you drag and drop the **Orders** worksheet into the **Drag sheets here** section, you will see the view update for you, as shown in the following screenshot:

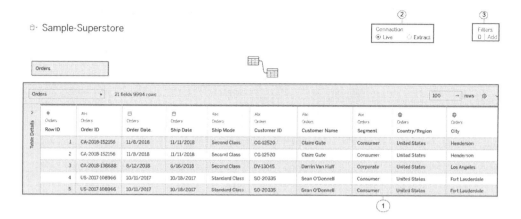

Figure 1.16: A screenshot showing the view after dragging and dropping the Orders worksheet

The preceding figure shows the view after fetching the **Orders** worksheet into the **Drag sheets here** section. Review the highlighted sections in the screenshot and the corresponding notes below to understand more.

- **Section 1**: This is the *preview section* where you get to see a quick preview (about 1,000 rows) of your **Orders** data. This is where you can quickly take stock of your data and make sure you have all the necessary columns to work with.

- **Section 2**: This is the **Connection** option. It has two options to choose from, **Live** and **Extract**. A **Live** connection is the option that you use when you want to connect to data in real time. This means that basically any changes at the data end will be reflected in Tableau. However, a quick point to note here is that the **Live** connection option relies on the data sources to process all the queries, and this could lead to performance issues in Tableau if the backend data source is a slow-performing data source. The **Extract** connection, on the other hand, is a snapshot of your data stored in a Tableau propriety format called **Tableau Data Extract**, which uses the file extension **.hyper**. Since the **.hyper** file only has a snapshot of the data, it will have to be refreshed if you need to see and use the updated data.

- **Section 3**: This is the **Filters** option, which is used to limit the amount of data that is read and used in Tableau. This works for both the **Live** and **Extract** options mentioned earlier.

Now that you understand the *data connection page* of Tableau, you can finally start using Tableau to analyze and visualize your data.

6. Connect **Live** to your **Orders** data from **Sample - Superstore.xls**. Refer to the following screenshot:

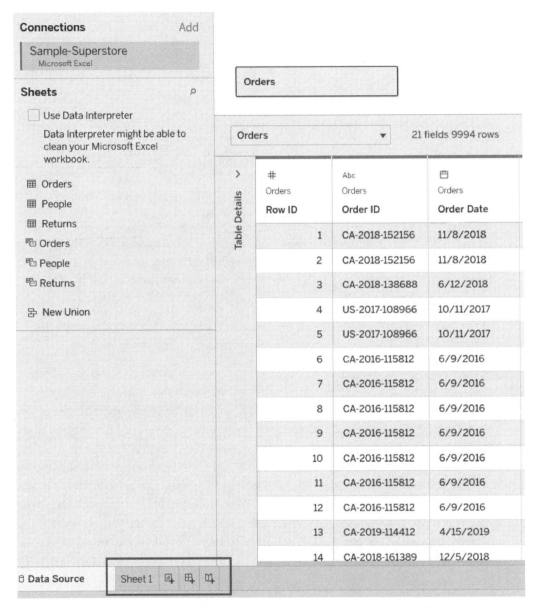

Figure 1.17: A screenshot showing the Go to Worksheet option

7. Now, the final step for fetching the data for your analysis is to click on **Sheet1**, and from there, select **Go to Worksheet**. With this, you will have read the data into Tableau Desktop and will now be able to start using it. Refer to the following screenshot:

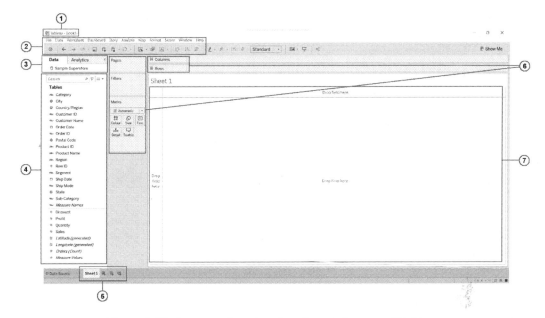

Figure 1.18: A screenshot showing the workspace of Tableau

The preceding screenshot shows the *Tableau workspace*. This is the space in which you will create your visualizations going forward. Let's quickly go through the highlighted sections in the screenshot to understand the workspace in more detail.

- **Section 1**: This is the *workbook name*. As mentioned previously, a *workbook* in Tableau is a file that consists of multiple worksheets and/or dashboards and/or storyboards. By default, it is named **Book1** (as shown in the image). However, you can assign any new name you like when you save the workbook.

- **Section 2**: This is the *toolbar section*, and this consists of various options that help you explore the various features and functionalities available in Tableau.

- **Section 3**: This is the *side bar* area, which contains the **Data** pane and the **Analytics** pane. The **Data** pane shows the details of the fields coming from the data, which are classified as either **Dimensions** or **Measures**. The **Analytics** pane, on the other hand, shows the various analyses, such as constant line, average line, median with quartiles, totals, trend line, forecast line, and clusters, that can be performed on the view that you create. To begin with, the **Analytics** pane is disabled or grayed out and will only start appearing when you create a view or visual.

- **Section 4**: This is the **Dimensions** and **Measures** section, which technically is part of the **Data** pane (and, if you are working with a version of Tableau later than 2020.1, it may not appear in the view). **Dimensions** are all the fields from the data that are categorical, descriptive, or qualitative in nature, such as **Customer Name**, **Product Name**, **Order ID**, and **Region**. These, when fetched in the view, will result in each data member of that field being displayed in the view. **Measures**, on the other hand, are fields from the data that are quantitative in nature and can be aggregated as either sum, average, minimum, maximum, standard deviation, variance, and so on. These, when fetched in the view, will result in aggregated values being displayed. Examples of **Measures** are fields such as **Sales**, **Profit**, and **Quantity**, which will be aggregated for the purpose of your analysis. Refer to the following screenshot for more clarity:

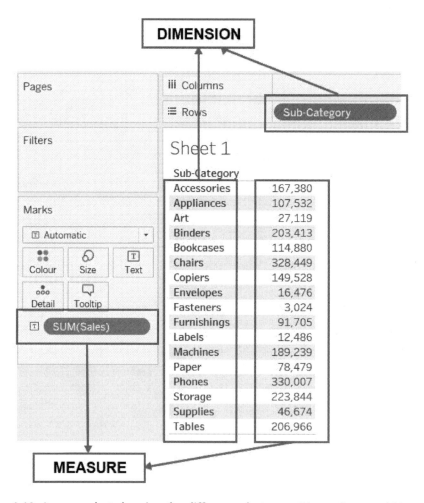

Figure 1.19: A screenshot showing the difference between Dimensions and Measures

- **Section 5**: This is the **Sheet** tab. Here you get the option to create either a new worksheet, dashboard, or storyboard.

- **Section 6**: These are the various *cards and shelves* available for use in Tableau. Here you can see various shelves such as the **Columns** shelf, **Rows** shelf, **Pages** shelf, and **Filters** shelf, along with the **Marks** card, which contains shelves such as the **Color** shelf, **Size** shelf, **Text** shelf, **Detail** shelf, and the **Tooltip** shelf. These shelves are used to change the appearance and details of your view.

- **Section 7**: This is the **View** section. This is where you will create your visualizations. It can be referred to as the canvas for creating your views and visualizations.

Now that you are familiar with the workspace of Tableau, you can create your first visualization. To create your views or visualizations, you can either try the **manual drag and drop** approach or the **automated approach** of using the **Show Me** button. Let's explore both of these options.

You will begin with the *manual drag and drop* approach and then explore the *automated approach* using the **Show Me** button in the following exercise.

EXERCISE 1.02: CREATING A COMPARISON CHART USING MANUAL DRAG AND DROP

The aim of this exercise is to create a chart to determine which ship mode is better in terms of **Sales** by **Region** using the manual drag and drop method. In this case, you will create one stacked bar chart using the **Ship Mode**, **Region**, and **Sales** fields from the **Orders** data from **Sample - Superstore.xlsx** and another by manually dragging the fields from the **Data** pane and dropping them into the necessary shelves.

Perform the following steps to complete this exercise:

1. Drag the **Sales** field from the **Measures** section in the **Data** pane and drop it onto the **Columns** shelf. This will create a horizontal bar.

2. Drag the **Region** field from the **Dimensions** section from the **Data** pane and drop it onto the **Rows** shelf. This will create a horizontal bar chart with labels for regions and bars showing the sum of **Sales**.

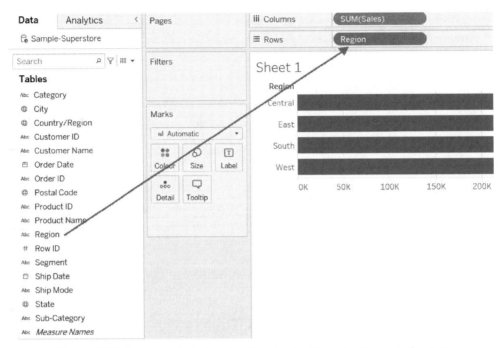

Figure 1.20: A screenshot showing the stacked bar chart created using the manual drag and drop method

3. Finally, to include the ship mode, drag the **Ship Mode** field from the **Dimensions** section in the **Data** pane and drop it onto the **Color** shelf available under the **Marks** card. This will update your view to show a stacked bar chart with ship modes as colors, as in the following screenshot:

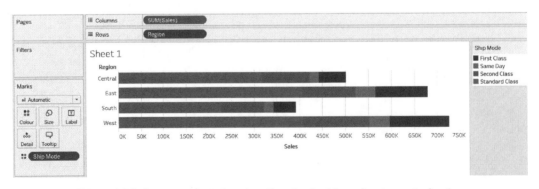

Figure 1.21: A screenshot showing the stacked bar chart created using the manual drag and drop method

In this exercise, you created a stacked bar chart to show which ship mode is better in terms of **Sales** across **Regions** using the *manual drag and drop* method. As you can see in the preceding screenshot, the **Standard Class** ship mode seems to be performing best by comparison to other modes.

In the following exercise, you will create another sales comparison chart—but this time with the **Show Me** button.

EXERCISE 1.03: CREATING A COMPARISON CHART USING THE AUTOMATED SHOW ME BUTTON METHOD

The aim of this exercise is to create a chart to determine which **Ship Mode** is better in terms of **Sales** by **Region** using the automated method via the **Show Me** button. Just like the previous exercise, you will create one stacked bar chart using the **Ship Mode**, **Region**, and **Sales** field from the **Orders** data of **Sample-Superstore. xlsx** and another using the **Show Me** button. You will then compare the resulting charts to determine which mode helps generate the highest sales.

In a new worksheet, perform the following steps to complete the exercise:

1. Press and hold the **CTRL** key on your keyboard and select the **Region** and **Ship Mode** fields from the **Dimensions** section and the **Sales** field from the **Measures** pane.

> **NOTE**
>
> You will need to keep the **CRTL** key pressed while doing *multiple selections*. Furthermore, if you are on an Apple device, use the **Command** key instead. Refer to the following link to find the list of equivalent macOS commands and keyboard shortcuts for both Windows and macOS: https://help.tableau.com/current/pro/desktop/en-us/shortcut.htm.

2. Once you have selected the necessary fields, click on the **Show Me** button, which can be seen in the *extreme top-right corner* of your Tableau workbook. Refer to the following screenshot:

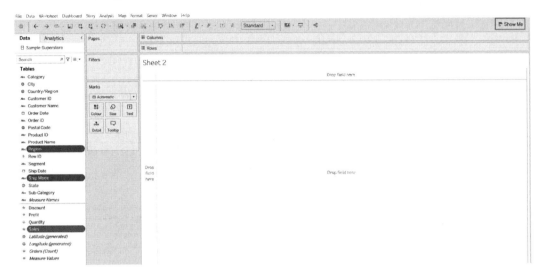

Figure 1.22: A screenshot showing the Show Me button

Once you have clicked on the **Show Me** button, you will see the list of visualizations that are possible with your current selection of fields, that is, *two dimensions* (**Region** and **Ship Mode**) and *one measure* (**Sales**). Further, you will also see that the horizontal bar chart is highlighted. The highlighted chart (this is highlighted by Tableau in version 2020.1 with an orangish-brown rectangular border in the following screenshot) is the result of the in-built recommendation engine that is based on the best practices of data visualization.

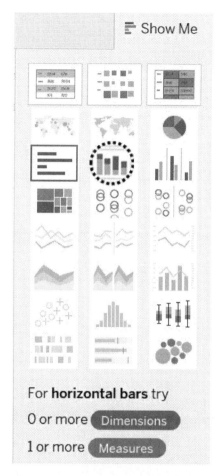

Figure 1.23: A screenshot showing the possible charts and the Show Me button

You now have two options: you can either go ahead with the chart recommended by Tableau, which will create a horizontal bar chart (which is not the aim here), or select some other chart that is available and enabled in the **Show Me** button (ideally a stacked bar chart like the one that you created in the previous exercise). So, select the chart right next to the recommended one (the one that is highlighted using a black dotted circular border in the preceding screenshot). This is the stacked bar chart option, which is exactly what you wanted.

However, when you go ahead with this option, you see two things that are different from the output that you created in the previous exercise. Firstly, it is a vertically stacked bar chart and not a horizontal one, and, secondly, you have **Region** in the **Color** shelf instead of **Ship Mode**. Refer to the following screenshot:

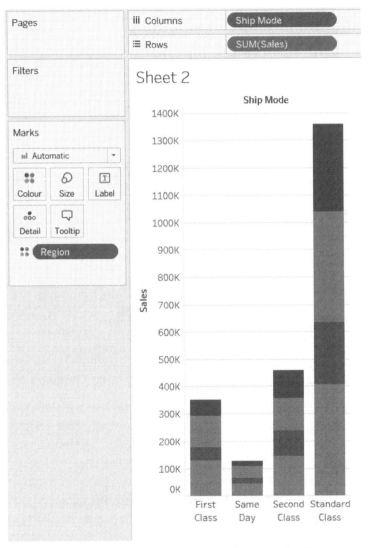

Figure 1.24: A screenshot showing the output of the stacked bar chart option from the Show Me button

Now, neither of these things are technically wrong, but they are not what you wanted in this case, and so you will need to change them.

3. Firstly, change the orientation of your stacked bar chart from vertical to horizontal by clicking on the swap button in the toolbar, as shown in the following screenshot:

Figure 1.25: A screenshot showing the Swap Rows and Columns button

4. Next, interchange/swap your **Region** and **Ship Mode** fields so that you have **Ship Mode** in the **Color** shelf instead of **Region**.

   To do this, press **CTRL** and select **Region** from the **Color** shelf as well as **Ship Mode** from the **Rows** shelf. Make sure the pills for these selected fields are now darker in color as the dark color indicates that the selection of these fields is retained.

5. Now, click on the dropdown of either the **Region** field or the **Ship Mode** field and choose the **Swap** option, as shown in the following screenshot:

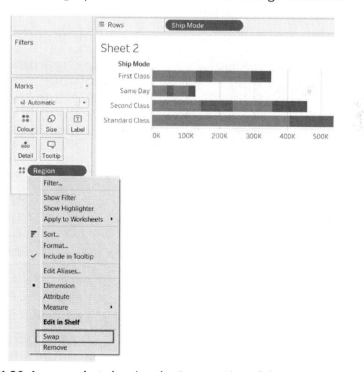

Figure 1.26: A screenshot showing the Swap option of the CTRL multiselect and drop-down method

This produces the following output:

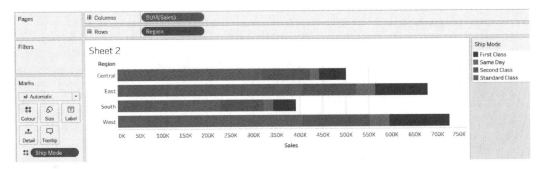

Figure 1.27: A screenshot showing the stacked bar chart created using the Swap options

In this exercise, you created a stacked bar chart to show which **Ship Mode** is better in terms of **Sales** by **Regions** using the *manual drag and drop* method. As you can see in the preceding screenshot, the **Standard Class** ship mode seems to generate more sales compared to the other ship modes.

DATA VISUALIZATION USING TABLEAU DESKTOP

In an earlier section, you familiarized yourself with the workspace of Tableau and learned how to create a visualization using the *manual drag and drop method* as well as the *automated* **Show Me** *button.* During the course of this book and across various chapters, you will get into more details of this workspace and learn about some more of the options available in the toolbar as well as the other shelves.

Now that you have some fundamental knowledge of how to create a visualization using the aforementioned methods, you will now explore some concepts of data visualization and how to use these in Tableau Desktop.

Ideally, when you present your analysis and insights, you want your end user to be able to quickly consume the information that you have presented and make better decisions more quickly. One way to achieve this objective is to present the information in the right format. Each chart, graph, or visualization has a specific purpose, and it is particularly important to choose the appropriate chart for answering a specific goal or a business question.

Now, to be able to choose the appropriate chart, you first need to look at the data and answer the question "What is it that you need to do with your data?".

To help you make your decision, consider the following:

- Do you wish to **compare** values?

- Do you wish to look at the **composition** of your data?

- Do you wish to understand the **distribution** of your data?

- Do you wish to find and understand the **relationships** between the various variables of your dataset?

Once you have addressed these points and determined what you wish to do with your data, you will also need to decide on the following:

- How many variables do you need to look at at any given point in time?

- Do you wish to trend the data?

With the help of this list, you will be able to figure out which chart is the most appropriate one to answer your business questions. To elaborate on this point, begin by first categorizing your charts into four sections—namely, charts that help you either compare, determine the composition, show the distribution of your data, or else the ones that help you find relationships in your data.

Comparison, composition, distribution, and relationships are often referred to as the four pillars of data visualization and are described in greater detail here:

1. **Comparison**: When analyzing your data, a common (if not the most common) use case would be to compare your data. Comparison is often done between two or more values. Some examples of comparison would be sales revenue in different regions, how the performance of a particular sales representative compared to their colleagues, the profitability of different products, and so on.

    Typically, you will see comparison being done across *categorical data*, that is, *data members of a dimension* (for example, comparison across regions wherein `Region` is a dimension, and `East`, `West`, `North`, and `South` are the data members of that dimension), but it can also be done across *quantitative data*, that is, *across measures* (for example, sales versus profit or actual sales versus budget sales).

    Another type of comparison that is very common is a comparison over a period of time (for example, evaluating your monthly sales performance or which months are better for your business and whether there are any seasonal trends that you need to look out for).

So, based on the preceding information, you will further break down *comparison* as *comparison across dimensional items or categorical data (for example, region-wise sales), comparison over time*, and *comparison across measures* or quantifiable data (for example, sales versus quota).

The following list outlines the typical charts that should be used for each type of *comparison*:

Comparison across dimensional items:

- Bar chart

- Packed bubble chart

- Word cloud

Comparison over time:

- Bar chart

- Line chart

Comparison across measures:

- Bullet chart

- Bar chart

2. **Composition**: Another common use case when analyzing your data is to find out what ratio or proportion each data member contributes to the whole. So basically, out of the total value, what is the contribution of each data member? This is typically referred to as a part to whole composition and it helps us understand how each individual part makes up the whole of something. For example, out of the total sales, which category is contributing the most? Or what is the breakdown of your total sales by region? And so on.

   Typically, you end up showing a static snapshot of the composition of your data (for example, your market share along with the market share of your competitors at a given point in time), or you may also want to trend this information over a period of time (for example, how is your and your competitor's market share changing over a period of time). Both these perspectives are important and can provide some very valuable insights regarding your performance.

   So, based on this information, you will further break down *composition* as *composition (snapshot/static)* and *composition over time*.

The following list outlines the typical charts that should be used for each type of *composition*:

Composition (snapshot/static):

- Pie chart
- Stacked bar chart
- Treemap

Composition over time:

- Stacked bar chart
- Area chart

3. **Distribution**: Finding the *distribution* of your data is important when you want to find *patterns, trends, clusters, and outliers or anomalies* in your data—for example, if you want to understand how employees are performing during the annual appraisal cycle (that is, which employees or how many employees are below par, which or how many employees meet expectations, and which or how many employees exceed expectations). Another example of distribution would be evaluating students' performance in an exam or determining the defect frequency in your manufacturing process.

So, based on this information, you will further break down distribution as *distribution for a single measure*, and *distribution across two measures*.

The following list outlines the typical charts that should be used for each type of *distribution*:

Distribution for a single measure:

- Box and whisker plot
- Histogram

Distribution across two measures:

- Scatter plot

4. **Relationships**: Finding and understanding relationships, dependency, correlations, or cause and effect relationships between different variables of your data is another method of data analysis. When analyzing your data, it is important to ascertain whether there is any dependency between variables of your data (does one variable have any effect on another variable and if so, whether it is a positive or negative effect, such as the impact of marketing expenditure on sales profit or the increase or decrease in warm clothing sales depending on temperature). So, based on this information, you will further break down *relationship* as the *relationship between two measures* and the *relationship between multiple measures*.

   The following list outlines the typical charts that should be used for each type of *relationship*:

   • Relationships between two measures: scatter plot

   • Relationships between multiple measures: scatter plot with size and color

Now that you understand these concepts of **Comparison**, **Composition**, **Distribution**, and **Relationships**, and which charts to choose for each of these scenarios, you will also try to see how to create these in Tableau. All these abovementioned scenarios and charts are explained in more detail in the upcoming chapters.

Apart from the aforementioned use cases or scenarios, you may also want to explore the *geographic* aspect of your data (that is, if you have any geographical information in your data). This could mean having data at a country level, state level, city level, or even postal code level. Creating geographic maps to show this geographic data is another way of exploring and visualizing your data since visualizing geographic data on a map can help us highlight certain events or occurrences across geographies and possibly unearth some hidden spatial patterns and or perform proximity analysis.

> **NOTE**
>
> For more information on choosing the right chart, see the following article: https://www.tableau.com/learn/whitepapers/which-chart-or-graph-is-right-for-you.

SAVING AND SHARING YOUR WORK

Another important point to discuss when working with Tableau is how to save your files and share them with others. As you know, Tableau is an interactive tool that allows users to filter, drill down, and slice and dice data using the features that are provided within the tool. Now, when it comes to saving and sharing your work with others, some people may want their end users to have the flexibility to play with the report and use the interactivity that is provided, while others may simply want end users to have a static snapshot of information that doesn't provide any sort of interactivity. Further, some may want to share the entire dashboard with their end users, while others may only want to share a single visualization.

All these scenarios can be handled in Tableau. The following list will go through these options in detail, breaking them into two parts: static snapshots and interactivity versions:

Static snapshots: The following is the list of options to choose from when you want to save and share a static snapshot of your work:

1. **Saving as an Image**: When saving your work as an image, you can either save just a single worksheet or an entire dashboard as either a PNG, JPEG, BMP, or EMF image. To do so, use either the **Worksheet > Copy > Image** option from the toolbar or the **Worksheet > Export > Image** option from the toolbar. Refer to the following screenshots:

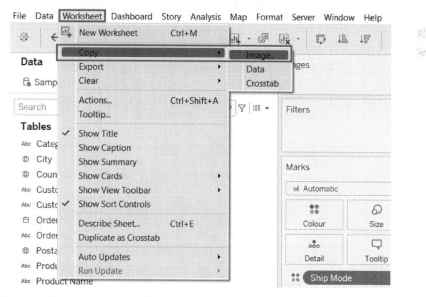

Figure 1.28: A screenshot showing the Worksheet > Copy > Image option
from the toolbar menu

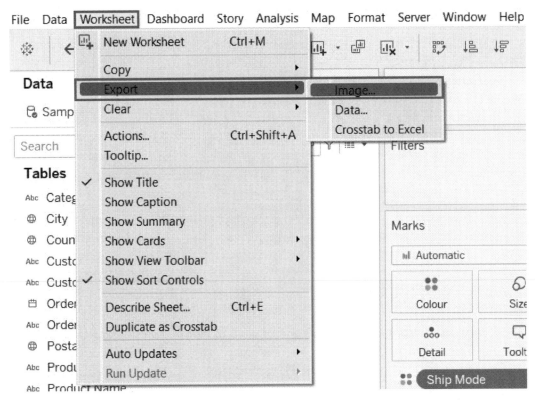

Figure 1.29: A screenshot showing the Worksheet > Export > Image option
from the toolbar menu

The **Copy > Image** option allows you to copy the individual view as an image
and then paste it into another application if desired, whereas the **Export >
Image** option lets you directly export the view as an image rather than doing a
copy and paste operation.

The preceding screenshots show the options of either *copying* or *exporting* just a single worksheet (that is, a single visualization). However, if you wish to save the entire dashboard as an image, then you will use the **Dashboard > Copy Image** or **Dashboard > Export Image** option in the toolbar. Refer to the following screenshot:

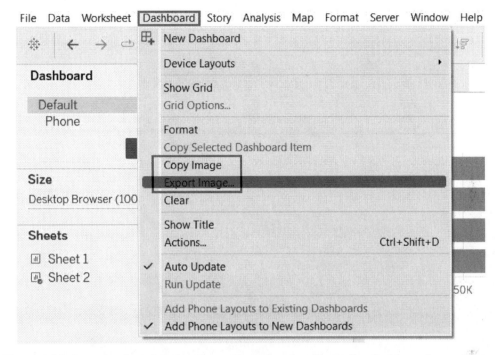

Figure 1.30: A screenshot showing the option of saving the entire dashboard as an image

2. **Saving as Data**: When saving the data that you have used to generate a view, you can either save the data as a **.csv** file by copying and pasting the data into a **.csv** file or export the data as a Microsoft Access file, using either the **Worksheet > Copy > Data** option or the **Worksheet > Export > Data** option from the toolbar menu. Refer to the following screenshots:

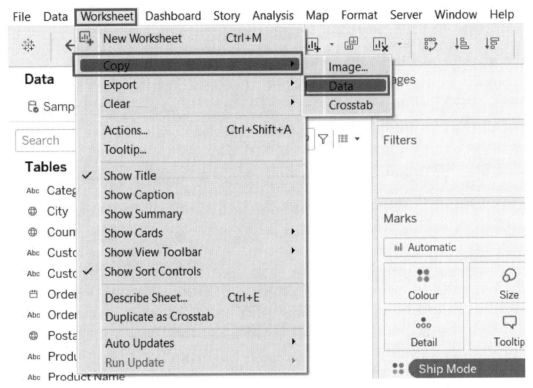

Figure 1.31: A screenshot showing the Worksheet > Copy > Data option

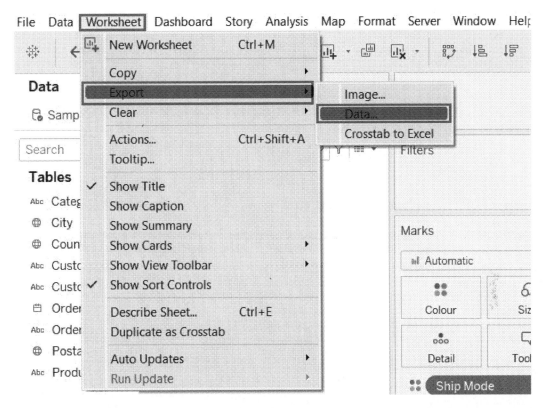

Figure 1.32: A screenshot showing the Worksheet > Export > Data option

3. **Saving as Crosstab**: Another way of saving the data that is used for building your view is to have it as crosstab Excel output. Earlier, in **Saving as Data**, the options were to save it as `.csv` or as `.mdb` files, which is the Microsoft Access format. However, when you want to have the data stored as an Excel output, you will either have to use the `Worksheet > Copy > Crosstab` option or the `Worksheet > Export > Crosstab to Excel` option from the toolbar menu. Refer to the following screenshots:

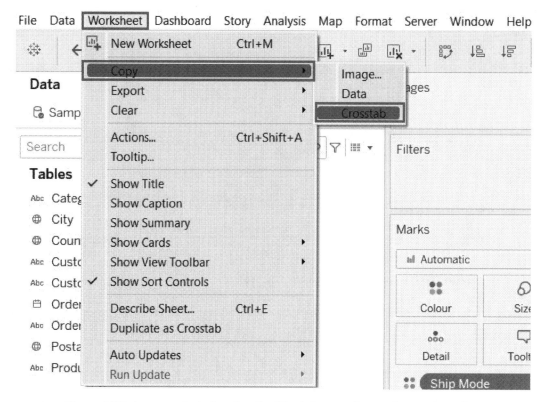

Figure 1.33: A screenshot showing the Worksheet > Copy > Crosstab option

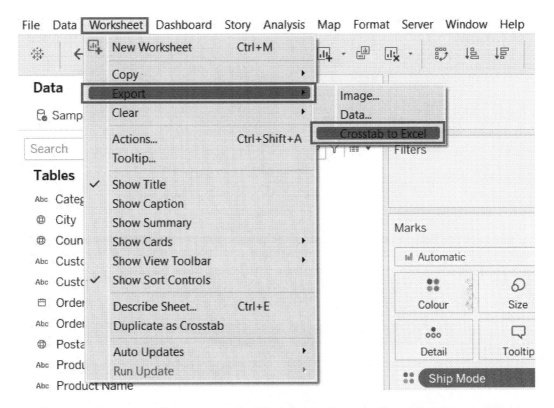

Figure 1.34: A screenshot showing the Worksheet > Export > Crosstab to Excel option

4. **Export as PowerPoint**: This option allows you to export your work into a PowerPoint presentation where the selected sheets are converted into a static **PNG** format and exported to separate individual slides. To export as PowerPoint, choose the **File > Export As PowerPoint** option from the toolbar menu. Refer to the following screenshot:

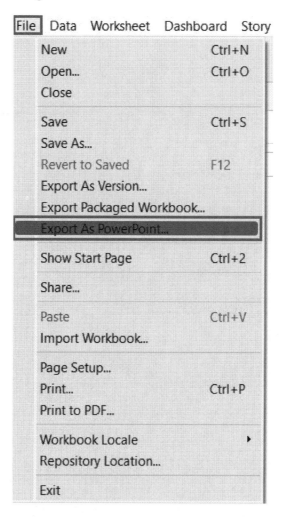

Figure 1.35: A screenshot showing the File > Export as PowerPoint option

5. **Print as PDF**: This option allows you to export your work into a PDF file. You can have a single or multiple selected worksheets, or the entire Tableau workbook saved as a PDF output. To export the view as a PDF document, choose the **File > Print to PDF** option from the toolbar menu. Refer to the following screenshot:

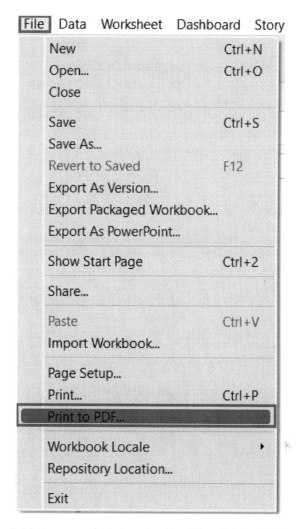

Figure 1.36: A screenshot showing the File > Print to PDF option

EXERCISE 1.04: SAVING YOUR WORK AS A STATIC SNAPSHOT-POWERPOINT EXPORT

In the previous section, you explored different options for choosing a static output of your work. In this exercise, you will export or save your work as a PowerPoint export. For this, you will continue using the stacked bar chart of **Ship Mode**, **Region**, and **Sales** that was created in the previous exercise. This exercise will help you see how you can save your analyses as interactive versions and publish these works to different platforms—something you'll need to do fairly often as a Tableau developer.

You will continue working with the Sample Superstore dataset for this exercise.

The steps to accomplish this are as follows:

1. Make sure that you have the stacked bar chart that you created earlier handy. If not, then please start by first re-creating the stacked bar chart by following the steps mentioned in the earlier exercise, *Exercise 1.03*, *Creating a Comparison Chart Using the Automated Show Me Button Method*.

2. Once you have the stacked bar chart ready, click on the **File** option in the toolbar and select the **Export As PowerPoint** option. Refer to the following screenshot:

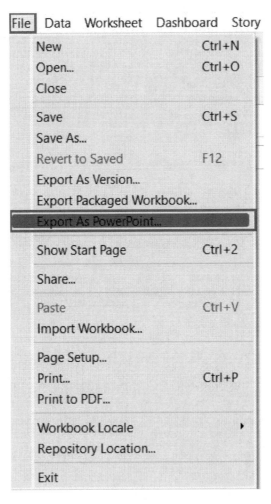

Figure 1.37: A screenshot showing the File > Export as PowerPoint option

3. Go with the default options in the pop-up window and then click on the **Export** button and save the file to your desired location. Finally, name the file **My PowerPoint Export.pptx**. Refer to the following screenshot:

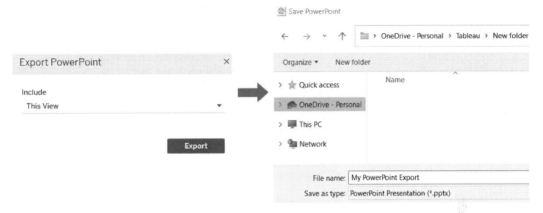

Figure 1.38: A screenshot showing the PowerPoint export

This will save your output as a **.pptx** file, which can later be opened in the Microsoft PowerPoint app.

Interactive versions: The following is the list of options to choose from when you want to save and share interactive versions of your work:

1. **Save the file as .twb or .twbx**: In order to save your views as interactive views, you will need to save your Tableau files in the following formats.

   .TWB: This is the file extension used to save a file as a *Tableau workbook*, which is a proprietary file format. **.twb** is the default file extension when you try to save any of your Tableau workbooks. These **.twb** files are kind of work-in-progress files that constantly require access to data and, since these require constant connectivity to data, it will not be possible to open the file unless you have Tableau Desktop and access to data that is used for creating this **.twb** file. So, if you wish to share this **.twb** file with anyone, you need to make sure they have access to the data; and if not, then the data source file will have to be made available to them. To save the file as **.twb**, choose the **File > Save As** option from the toolbar menu.

This will open a new window that allows you to save the file. Make sure to choose the **Tableau Workbook (.twb)** option. Refer to the following screenshot:

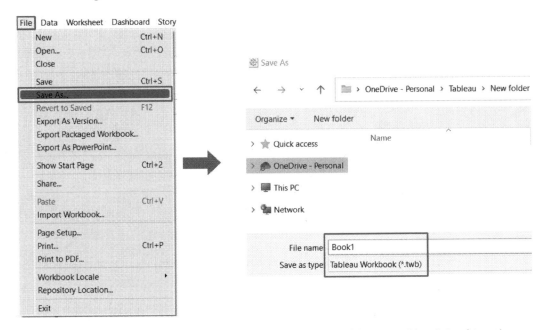

Figure 1.39: A screenshot showing the File > Save As > Tableau Workbook (.twb) option

TWBX: This is the file extension used to save the file as a *Tableau packaged workbook*, which contains the views as well as the copy of the data used for creating those views. Since the copy of the data is bundled along with the views that have been created, it allows the end user to access and interact with the file even when they don't have direct access to the raw data that is being used for analysis.

Further, since the copy of data is bundled along with the views, the data that is seen in the file is not the actual live data but a static snapshot of that data at a given point in time, which can be refreshed as and when required.

To save the file as `.twbx`, choose the **File > Save As** option from the toolbar menu. This will open a new window that allows you to save the file. Make sure to choose the **Tableau Packaged Workbook (.twbx)** option. Refer to the following screenshot:

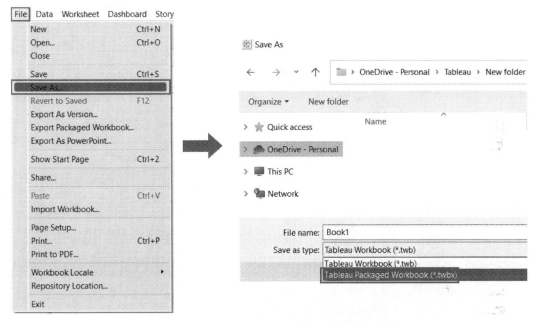

Figure 1.40: A screenshot showing the File > Save As >
Tableau Packaged Workbook (.twbx) option

To save the file as **`Tableau Packaged Workbook (.twbx)`**, you can even choose the **`File > Export As Packaged Workbook`** option from the toolbar menu. Refer to the following screenshot:

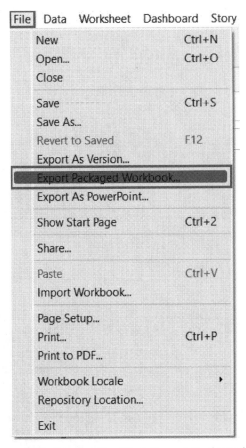

Figure 1.41: A screenshot showing the File > Export Packaged Workbook option

2. **Publish to Server**: This option allows you to publish your work on either Tableau Server or Tableau Online. You need to have permission to publish to Tableau Server, and when a file is published on Tableau Server, the end user will need to have permission to either view it or interact with it, or even modify it. So, in short, Tableau Server and Tableau Online are permission-based applications. To see how to publish to a Tableau server, choose the **`Server > Publish Workbook`** option from the toolbar menu. Refer to the following screenshot:

Figure 1.42: A screenshot showing the Server > Publish Workbook option

3. **Publish to Tableau Public**: This option allows you to publish your work to the Tableau Public server, which can be viewed and accessed by anybody. You do not need any special permissions to publish to the Tableau Public server. To see how to publish to the Tableau Public server, choose the **Server > Tableau Public** option from the toolbar menu. Refer to the following screenshot:

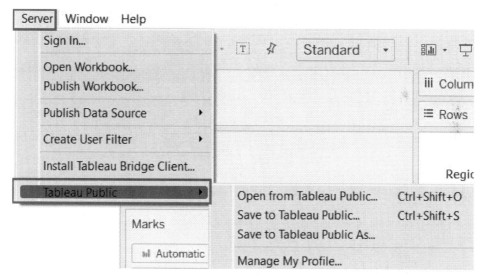

Figure 1.43: A screenshot showing the Server > Tableau Public option

In the following exercise, you will learn how to save your work in a packaged Tableau workbook.

EXERCISE 1.05: SAVING YOUR WORK AS A TABLEAU INTERACTIVE FILE—TABLEAU PACKAGED WORKBOOK

In the previous section, you saw different options when it comes to choosing an interactive version of your work. The aim of this exercise is to export or save your work as a Tableau Packaged Workbook (`.twbx`). For this, you will continue using the stacked bar chart of **Ship Mode**, **Region**, and **Sales** that was created in the previous exercise.

Complete the following steps:

1. Make sure that you have the stacked bar chart that you created earlier handy. If you don't have it handy, then first recreate the stacked bar chart by following the steps mentioned in *Exercise 1.03, Creating a Comparison Chart Using the Automated Show Me Button Method*.

2. Once you have the stacked bar chart ready, click on the **File** option in the toolbar and select the **Export Packaged Workbook** option. Refer to the following screenshot:

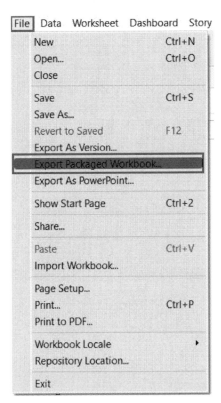

Figure 1.44: A screenshot showing the File > Export Packaged Workbook option

3. Save the file to your desired location and name it **My Tableau Packaged Workbook.twbx**. Refer to the following screenshot:

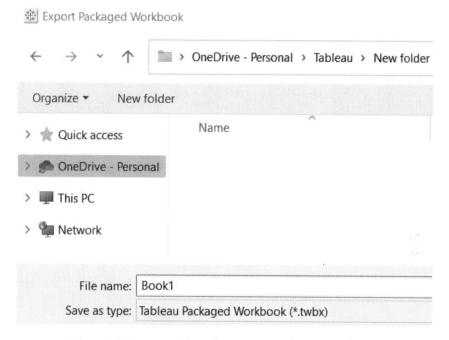

Figure 1.45: A screenshot showing the PowerPoint export

This will save your output as a **.twbx** file, which can later be opened in Tableau Reader or Tableau Desktop itself.

In the next section, you will practice your new skills by completing an activity using everything that you have learned in this chapter.

ACTIVITY 1.01: IDENTIFYING AND CREATING THE APPROPRIATE CHART TO FIND OUTLIERS IN YOUR DATA

In this activity, you will identify and create the appropriate chart to find outliers in your data. The dataset being used has two measures—namely, **Profit** and **Marketing**. **Marketing** refers to the money being spent on marketing efforts, while **Profit** is the profit that you are making. You need to compare **Marketing** and **Profit** across different products and across different markets (so, two dimensions and two measures).

The outliers to be identified are as follows:

1. High marketing and low profit

2. Low marketing and high profit

You will use the **CoffeeChain Query** table from the **Sample-Coffee Chain. mdb** dataset. The data can be downloaded from the GitHub repository of this book, at https://packt.link/MOpmr.

As the name suggests, the dataset contains information pertaining to a fictional chain of coffee shops.

Perform the following steps to complete this activity:

1. Select the *Sample-Coffee Chain.mdb* data using the *Microsoft Access* option in the data connection window of Tableau.

2. Use the *CoffeeChain Query table* from the *Sample-Coffee Chain.mdb* data.

3. Identify which chart would be the most appropriate to find your *outliers* in your data when looking at *two measures,* (that is, **Profit** and **Marketing**) across *two dimensions* (that is, **Product** and **Market**). The outliers that you are looking for are *high marketing and low profit* and *low marketing and high profit*. (Hint: Refer to the section that discussed the four pillars of data visualization and choose the chart that will help you find outliers.)

4. After identifying which chart would be the most appropriate, create that chart using the *automated* **Show Me** *button method*.

5. *Export* the view that you have created as a *PowerPoint* image.

6. Finally, *save* the workbook as a *Tableau Packaged Workbook (*.**twbx***)* on your desktop and give the file the following name: **My first Tableau view**.

> **NOTE**
>
> The solution to this activity can be found here: https://packt.link/CTCxk.

SUMMARY

In this chapter, you learned the definition and importance of visual analytics and data visualization. You were presented with several points for evaluation when choosing a data visualization tool and explored Tableau's product suite. Having identified Tableau Desktop as the best choice of platform for analyzing and visualizing your data, you looked at how to utilize it to connect to data and familiarized yourself with the Tableau Desktop workspace. You also considered various scenarios for data visualization and identified which charts to use for the given task and learned how to save and share your work with others.

In the next chapter, you will see how to build the various charts that you identified earlier. You will also learn how to prepare your data for analysis using Tableau Prep as well as Tableau Desktop.

2

DATA PREPARATION: USING TABLEAU DESKTOP

OVERVIEW

In this chapter, you will learn to use various tools for data preparation in Tableau Desktop and join different data sources using various options. This will equip you with the knowledge required to perform data manipulation activities, data transformation, and data blending, and provide options to manage various data sources. By the end of this chapter, you will be able to extract and filter data and use aliases for the clean presentation of data.

INTRODUCTION

Often, the data sources required for Tableau visualizations are stored in separate tables or files. A very common example is that of an online order on an e-commerce website. The order information and the customer information are stored separately within the website database. However, when suggestions are provided based on previous purchases, the website might combine the information to show a unified view. This is a very simple example of a data join, which is one of the most common scenarios that can be fulfilled using data preparation techniques. In addition to data joining, there is often a need to perform data manipulation activities such as grouping and adding calculations on the data being used. In this chapter, you will learn about using all such techniques to pull the data into Tableau for effective analysis and visualization.

CONNECTING TO A DATA SOURCE

For any visualization, you need to have an underlying data source that contains all the information you wish to show. This is the first step of any data visualization task.

The very first thing that you will see when you open Tableau Desktop is the **Connect** pane. Here, you can connect to a variety of data sources and perform various tasks related to data handling, which you will study in this chapter. The following figure shows the screen that comes up when you start Tableau Desktop:

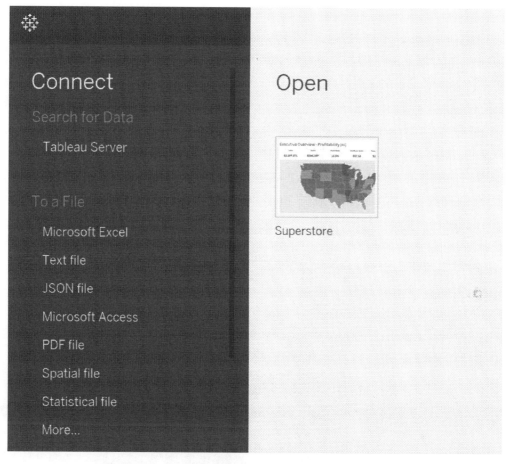

Figure 2.1: Start screen on launching Tableau Desktop

Depending on the version, this screen might look slightly different, but it should remain this way for the most part: you can observe that you can connect to multiple file options such as Excel, text, and JSON files. You can also connect to server-based data sources such as MySQL and Oracle. **Saved Data Sources** provides sample data sources that are available with Tableau Desktop.

In the following exercise, you will connect to an Excel file named **Sample - Superstore**, which is available with Tableau Desktop. This file contains an **Orders** sheet, which consists of information for various orders, based on attributes such as order ID, order category, ship mode, and customer details. It also has a **Returns** sheet, which consists of orders that were returned. You will use all of this data to perform various operations throughout this chapter, and visualize the data in Tableau Desktop.

EXERCISE 2.01: CONNECTING TO AN EXCEL FILE

In this exercise, you will connect to your very first data source in Tableau, the **Sample - Superstore** Excel file. This file is automatically accessible to you if you have installed Tableau as mentioned in *Chapter 1, Introduction to Tableau*. It contains three sheets, comprising order-level information stored in the **Orders** sheet, customer information stored in the **People** sheet, and order returns stored in the **Returns** sheet, and can be quickly downloaded from the GitHub repository for this chapter at https://packt.link/14u86. Make sure to download this file on your system before proceeding with the exercise.

Perform the following steps to complete this exercise:

1. Under the **Connect** pane, select the **Microsoft Excel** option.

Figure 2.2: Connecting to Microsoft Excel

2. This will open up the file menu where you can select the Excel file from the file explorer. Navigate to the location where you have saved this file locally and then select to open the **Sample-Superstore.xls** file. You will see the following screen once the file is loaded:

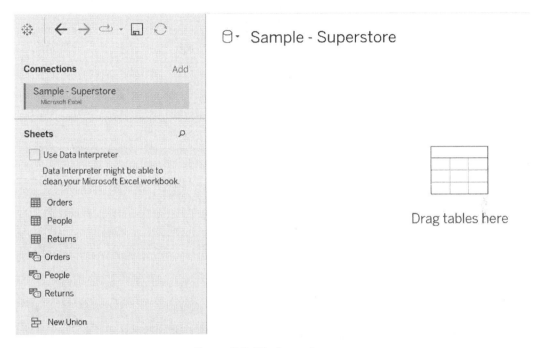

Figure 2.3: File import screen

3. Hover over the table to get the **View data** option (as highlighted in the following figure) and preview the data:

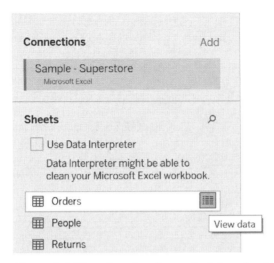

Figure 2.4: View data for the underlying sheet

The following figure shows the data preview:

Category	City	Country/Region	Customer ID	Customer Name	Order Date
Furniture	Henderson	United States	CG-12520	Claire Gute	08-11-2020
Furniture	Henderson	United States	CG-12520	Claire Gute	08-11-2020
Office Supplies	Los Angeles	United States	DV-13045	Darrin Van Huff	12-06-2020
Furniture	Fort Lauderdale	United States	SO-20335	Sean O'Donnell	11-10-2019
Office Supplies	Fort Lauderdale	United States	SO-20335	Sean O'Donnell	11-10-2019
Furniture	Los Angeles	United States	BH-11710	Brosina Hoffman	09-06-2018
Office Supplies	Los Angeles	United States	BH-11710	Brosina Hoffman	09-06-2018
Technology	Los Angeles	United States	BH-11710	Brosina Hoffman	09-06-2018
Office Supplies	Los Angeles	United States	BH-11710	Brosina Hoffman	09-06-2018
Office Supplies	Los Angeles	United States	BH-11710	Brosina Hoffman	09-06-2018
Furniture	Los Angeles	United States	BH-11710	Brosina Hoffman	09-06-2018
Technology	Los Angeles	United States	BH-11710	Brosina Hoffman	09-06-2018

View Data: Orders

9,994 rows

Figure 2.5: View Data window showing the data preview

4. Now, drag the **Orders** sheet onto the **Drag sheets here** area. This is also known as the canvas.

5. The sheet should now have been imported into Tableau. Preview the data, as shown in the following figure:

Figure 2.6: Data preview of the imported sheet

You have thus connected and imported the data in Tableau.

6. Hovering over **Sheet 1**, you can see the active **Go to Worksheet** option, which means that you can navigate to **Sheet 1** and start creating visualizations.

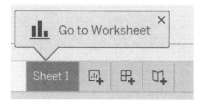

Figure 2.7: Go to Worksheet popup

Once the data is imported, you can start the visualization development by clicking on that option, as you will see later in the course.

In this exercise, you saw how you can connect to an Excel file. Tableau also allows you to connect to data that is stored on servers. In the next section, you will learn how this can be done.

CONNECTING TO A SERVER DATA SOURCE

Here, you will be connecting with Microsoft SQL Server, available under the server-based data sources. Note that the concept of installing and maintaining server-based data sources is beyond the scope of this chapter. However, ideally, in a business project, data would mostly be stored on servers. For this reason, it is important to know how to connect to these data sources.

The following steps will help you connect to a server-based data source:

1. Under the **Connect** pane, select the **Microsoft SQL Server** option, as can be seen in the following figure:

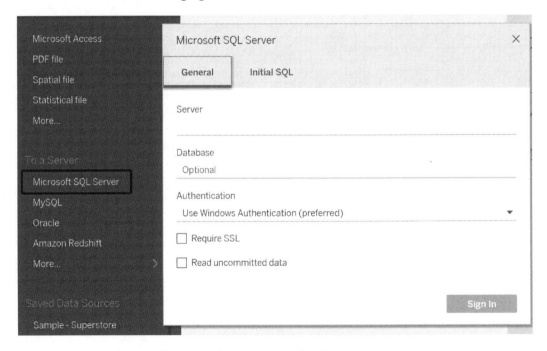

Figure 2.8: Server connection input screen

Here, you need to enter the information required, such as the server name and the authentication method. These details would be available from your database administrator.

2. Click **Sign In**. You will get a similar preview screen as you saw in *Figure 2.5*. All the steps afterward are the same as you do for an Excel-based connection.

> **NOTE**
>
> One of the most commonly occurring issues here is that sometimes the drivers to connect to the data source are not installed. This can be easily resolved by downloading and installing the drivers from https://www.tableau.com/support/drivers.

In this section, you connected to a server-based data source. The next section covers the different kinds of joins in Tableau to combine the data from multiple data sources.

VARIOUS JOINS IN TABLEAU

Quite often, the data that you're using will be stored as separate tables for efficiency purposes. There might be some fields that are common between tables and can be used to join the data sources together.

For example, suppose you, as a bank loan manager, would like to evaluate the best-suited customer profiles for granting a loan. Here, based on the customer-provided information, such as salary details and work experience, you would also need to access their financial history information, such as previous loans, outstanding loans, or any defaults. This kind of information can be fetched from their Experian score using the customer PAN as common information between the various data sources. This is how joins are commonly used in a lot of daily scenarios. You will learn about these joins and the different types in Tableau.

DIFFERENT TYPES OF JOINS

Tableau offers four types of joins, which are listed as follows:

- **Inner:** In an inner join between two tables, you can combine only the values that match among the two tables into the resulting table. For example, consider the following tables. When you join table A and table B using an inner join, only the common values will be a part of the resulting table:

Table A	Table B
1	1
2	
	3

Inner Join Result
1
–
–

Figure 2.9: Inner Join Between Tables A and B

- **Left:** A left join combines all the values from the left table along with only the matching values from the right table. If there are no matching values, those rows will contain null values in the resulting table. In the following example, when you join table A and table B using a left join, all the values from table A and only the common values of table B will be a part of the resulting table:

Table A	Table B
1	1
2	
	3

Left Join Result
1
2
–

Figure 2.10: Left Join Between Tables A and B

- **Right:** This is the opposite of the left join. A right join combines all the values from the right table along with only the matching values from the left table. If there are no matching values, those rows will contain null values in the resulting table. Consider the following tables. When you join table A and table B using a right join, all the values from table B and only the common value from table A will be part of the resulting table:

Table A	Table B
1	1
2	
	3

Right Join Result
1
–
3

Figure 2.11: Right Join Between Tables A and B

- **Full outer**: In a full outer join between two tables, you can combine all the values from the left and right tables into one resulting table. If values don't match in any of the tables, those rows will contain null values in the resulting table.

  Consider the following tables. Here, when you join table A and table B using an inner join, only the common values will be a part of the resulting table:

Table A	Table B
1	1
2	
	3

Full Outer Join Result
1
2
3

Figure 2.12: Full Outer Join Between Tables A and B

- **Union**: In a union, you combine two or more tables with similar column structures into a single resulting table. Union is performed when instead of joining you just want to append the data below other data with similar columns. A very common example of union is when you have two tables containing similar columns but maintained separately in different years, for example, combining order information for multiple years into a consolidated dataset.

- Consider the following tables, for example. Here, when you create a union of tables A and A1, you get a single table that will contain values for both A and A1:

A	A1
1	3
2	4

Union of A and A1
1
2
3
4

Figure 2.13: Union Between Tables A and B

You will learn more about these join types in detail in the following exercises.

EXERCISE 2.02: CREATING AN INNER JOIN DATASET

As an analyst, you might come across scenarios in which you need to display the common records between two tables. This exercise aims to show how to join two different sheets into a single data source in Tableau.

You will join the **Orders** table with the **People** table using an inner join. By doing so, you will be able to identify the customer records present in the **People** table along with the order information from the **Orders** table, which will help you to understand customers' buying preferences.

Perform the following steps to complete this exercise:

1. Load the **Sample – Superstore** dataset into your Tableau instance as you did in *Exercise 2.01*.

2. Drag the **Orders** table first, followed by the **People** table, from the **Sheets** area to the **Drag Sheets here** area. Alternatively, to add these sheets, you can double-click on them, and they will be added automatically to the canvas area. Tableau will auto-join the two tables using an inner join, as shown in the following figure:

Figure 2.14: Data joining using an inner join

3. Click on the **Join** symbol to open the **Join** menu:

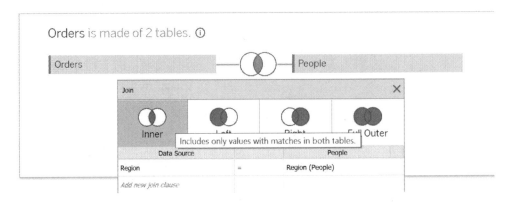

Figure 2.15: Inner join properties

Note the various ways to join data. By default, Tableau performs an inner join on the common field names:

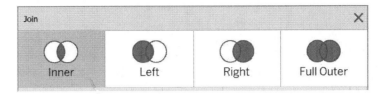

Figure 2.16: Various join options

> **NOTE**
>
> These instructions and images are based on Tableau version 2020.1. If you are using a later version of Tableau, such as 2021.4, this process may look quite different and even require an extra step. You can find additional guidance for this at the following URL: https://help.tableau.com/v2021.4/pro/desktop/en-gb/datasource_relationships_learnmorepage.htm

4. If there are no common names, select the columns manually to enable the join. Since you are joining the **Orders** and **People** tables, join on **Customer Name** from **Orders** and **Person** from **People**. First, de-select **Region**, which is auto-selected by Tableau. To do this, click on **Region** and select **Customer Name** from the dropdown, as you can see in the following figure:

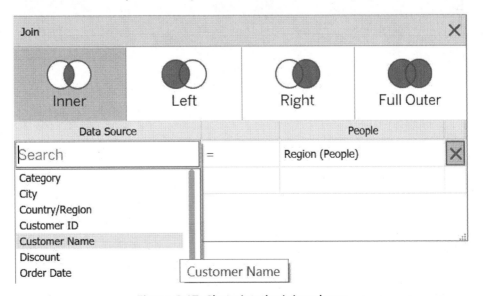

Figure 2.17: Changing the join column

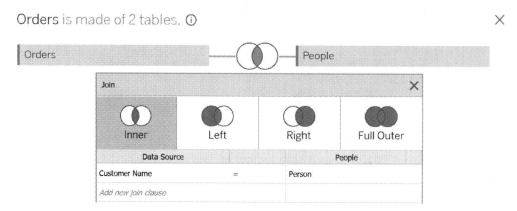

Figure 2.18: Final result of the inner join

5. Repeat the same for the **People** table and select **Person** as the joining column. Your joined columns should be as follows:

Orders ▼	23 fields 58 rows			58 → rows		
# Orders **Row ID**	Abc Orders **Order ID**	📅 Orders **Order Date**	📅 Orders **Ship Date**	Abc Orders **Ship Mode**	Abc Orders **Customer ID**	
196	CA-2016-1400…	21-03-2016	25-03-2016	Standard Class	CB-12025	
197	CA-2016-1400…	21-03-2016	25-03-2016	Standard Class	CB-12025	
660	CA-2017-146563	24-08-2017	28-08-2017	Standard Class	CB-12025	
661	CA-2017-146563	24-08-2017	28-08-2017	Standard Class	CB-12025	
662	CA-2017-146563	24-08-2017	28-08-2017	Standard Class	CB-12025	

Figure 2.19: Data preview of the Order and People tables

Now it's time to validate the results. This can be observed in the data grid screen in the bottom section.

You can see that you get only **58** rows in the joined dataset. Here, only the values from the **Orders** table's **Customer Name** column that match with values from the **People** table's **Person** column will be returned in the final dataset. Since the **Person** table has only four values, only those values from the **Customer Name** column that match these four are returned from the **Orders** table.

In this exercise, you used inner join and analyzed the results returned by using this join type. Next, you will learn about the left join type.

EXERCISE 2.03: CREATING A LEFT JOIN DATASET

In this exercise, you will join the **Orders** table with the **People** table in a left join. The objective of the left join is to verify how much customer information is present in the **People** table. This will help identify and update the **People** table so that you can expand the customer database, to drive better sales:

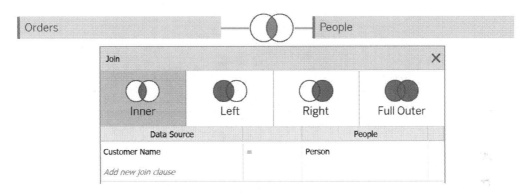

Figure 2.20: Join screen for the Orders and People tables

1. Repeat the same step from the previous exercise of dragging the **Orders** and **People** tables to the canvas. Once done, you should see the join options, as follows:

2. Change the join type to **Left**:

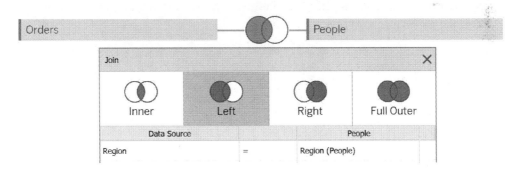

Figure 2.21: Selecting the Left join

3. Now, in the data preview (as shown in the following figure), scroll toward the right side. You will see two columns from the **People** table, **Person** and **Region**. Use the **Sort** icon to sort the values, as highlighted in the following figure:

Abc People **Person**	Abc People **Region (People)**
Cassandra Brando	People.Person
Cassandra Brandow	South
Anna Andreadi	West
Cassandra Brandow	South
Cassandra Brandow	South
Anna Andreadi	West
Anna Andreadi	West

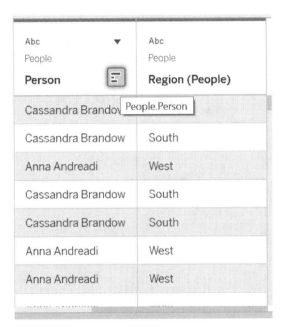

Figure 2.22: Analyzing the left join results

4. Scroll down to see what happens if the **Customer** names do not match any values in the **Person** column.

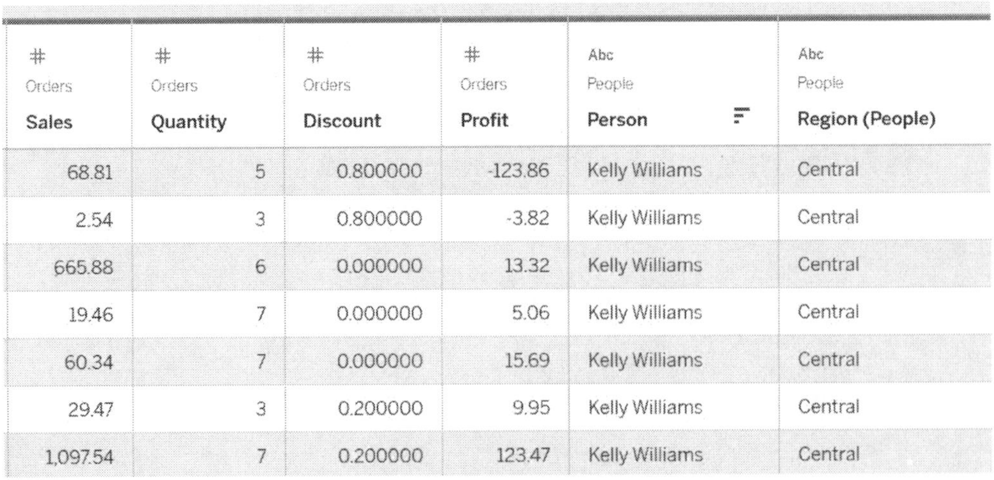

# Orders **Sales**	# Orders **Quantity**	# Orders **Discount**	# Orders **Profit**	Abc People **Person**	Abc People **Region (People)**
68.81	5	0.800000	-123.86	Kelly Williams	Central
2.54	3	0.800000	-3.82	Kelly Williams	Central
665.88	6	0.000000	13.32	Kelly Williams	Central
19.46	7	0.000000	5.06	Kelly Williams	Central
60.34	7	0.000000	15.69	Kelly Williams	Central
29.47	3	0.200000	9.95	Kelly Williams	Central
1,097.54	7	0.200000	123.47	Kelly Williams	Central

Figure 2.23: Nulls in the join result

You will observe that the rows where a match is not found are replaced by a **null** value, which means the **Person** table does not contain information for these customers. This means that you can add this customer information to the **People** table to improve the data quality.

In this exercise, you learned how to perform a left join and how data is matched between the two tables. Next, you will learn about the right join type.

EXERCISE 2.04: CREATING A RIGHT JOIN DATASET

In this exercise, you will join the **Orders** table with the **People** table in a right join. Consider a scenario wherein the **People** table consists of all the customers who have previously bought your company's products, and you want to fetch a complete list of the products a customer has bought, using information from the **Orders** table. This will help you understand the buying habits of customers based on their past purchases.

The steps to complete this exercise are as follows:

1. Drag the **Orders** and **People** tables similar to how you did in the previous exercises so that you can see the following on your screen:

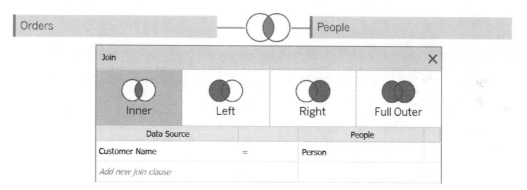

Figure 2.24: Join screen for the Orders and People tables

2. Select the **Right** join, as shown in the following figure:

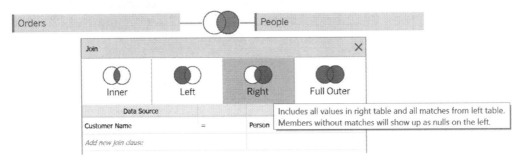

Figure 2.25: Selecting the Right join

3. Now, in the data preview, scroll toward the right side. You will see the **Person** and **Region** columns from the **People** table. Use the **Sort** icon to sort the values, as highlighted in the following figure:

# Orders Sales	# Orders Quantity	# Orders Discount	# Orders Profit	Abc People Person	Abc People Region (People)
69.22	6	0.200000	11.248	Kelly Williams	Central
106.50	6	0.000000	41.535	Kelly Williams	Central
28.40	4	0.000000	13.064	Kelly Williams	Central
212.94	3	0.000000	34.070	Kelly Williams	Central
32.04	3	0.000000	8.010	Kelly Williams	Central
7.36	2	0.000000	0.147	Chuck Magee	East

Figure 2.26: Analyzing the right join results

You will observe that the rows from the **People** table contain information about customers with past orders. This can now help you to analyze what products a person tends to buy often, and accordingly, you can suggest similar products to them, for a better-targeted sales strategy.

In this exercise, you performed a right join on two tables and saw how to use the right join results to analyze data. Next, you will learn about a full outer join.

A full outer join would combine the results of both the joining tables into a single dataset. To do that in Tableau, you can use the join properties and change the join type to **Full Outer**.

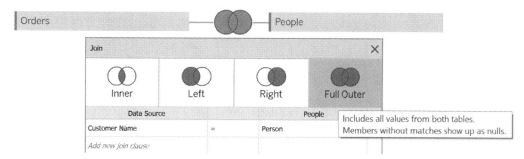

Figure 2.27: Selecting the Full Outer join

The next thing to cover is the union operation. In a union, the new table will be appended below the previous table in the final dataset. Usually, unions are used when you want to combine datasets with a common structure of columns. For example, order information for 2021 can be combined using a union with the order information for 2020 to get a unified dataset.

In the next exercise, you will learn how to implement a union in Tableau.

EXERCISE 2.05: CREATING A COMBINED DATASET USING UNION

Consider a scenario related to a large retailer such as Walmart or Amazon, operating in multiple regions. In such a case, it makes more sense to store the data at the regional level so that it can contain products customized to that specific region. If you were to compare how the different regions perform among each other, you would need to combine these different data sources into one. This is where the concept of a union comes into play.

In this exercise, you will use the **Orders** table, which is split by region. The files for different regions follow a similar column structure as the **Orders** table but are segregated into different sheets based on their regions, as you can see from the following figure:

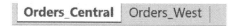

Figure 2.28: Input data for the Orders table preview stored as different tabs

You have the data for two regions: **Central** and **West**. You can implement a union to combine these two regions into a single dataset, as outlined in the following steps:

1. Save the files on your local machine. Load the **Union** Excel file using the **Connect** option from the location where the files are saved, as done for the previous exercises. Once the file is imported, you should see the following screen:

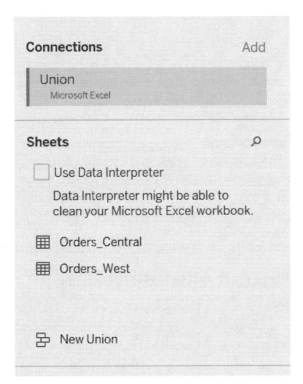

Figure 2.29: Orders table for the Central and West regions

2. Double-click on the **New Union** option to open the **Union** popup, as shown in the following figure:

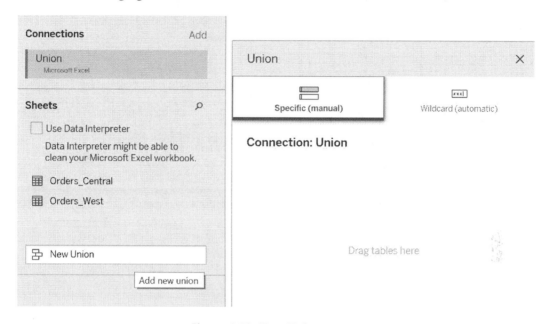

Figure 2.30: New Union popup

3. Drag the two order tables onto the **Union** popup, as follows:

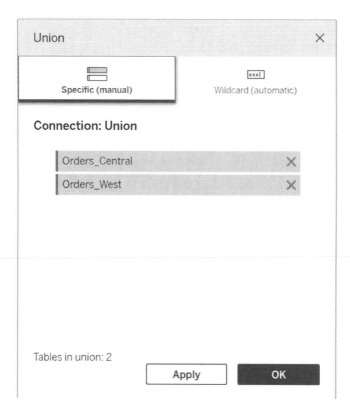

Figure 2.31: Adding tables in a union

4. Click on **OK** to add the union to the data grid.

   You can now preview the data in the bottom section. Tableau will combine the data from both tables into a single data source.

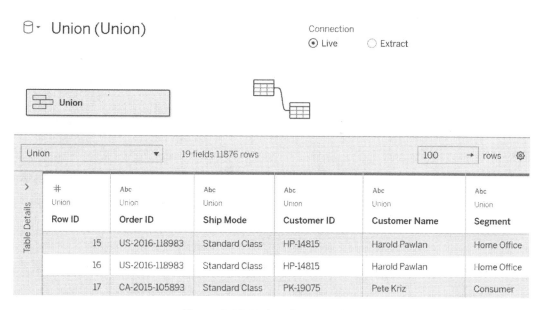

Figure 2.32: Union data preview

5. Scroll to the right side of the data preview. You will see two additional columns—namely **Sheet** and **Table Name**. **Sheet** signifies which Excel file sheet this data belongs to and **Table Name** refers to the table names in Tableau. This can be used to quickly identify which columns come from which sheets and tables.

Figure 2.33: Table identification columns in the union result

In this exercise, you learned how to perform a union of multiple data sources.

In all the preceding exercises, you joined on only two data sources. It is possible to add more than two data sources. You will just need to specify in the join connection how the tables join to each other.

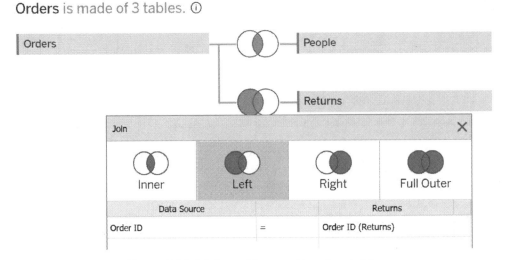

Figure 2.34: Joining with more than two tables

The preceding figure shows an example join on the **Orders** table with the **People** and **Returns** tables. If there were a common field between the **Returns** and **People** tables, you could also join these two tables as per your requirements.

This completes the various ways you can join multiple tables in Tableau and concludes the discussion on the various ways to combine data from multiple sources together. The following sections will deal with preparing your data for your desired task.

DATA TRANSFORMATION IN THE DATA PANE

Once you finish combining the data, you may also need to make some data adjustments, such as renaming certain columns or limiting the data to use in your visualizations. These are some common examples of data transformation.

Data transformations are a key step in preparing data for effective visualization. In this section, you will learn about some commonly used ways of transforming data. In particular, you will learn about the following:

- Data Interpreter

- Renaming data sources

- Live and extract connections

- Filters

- Data grid options

- Custom SQL

The following sections will define these one by one.

DATA INTERPRETER

Data Interpreter is an option available within Tableau that extracts only the actual rows and columns by removing titles, headers, and extra empty rows from the Excel data source.

You may sometimes add extra rows describing what kind of data the sheet contains, or some empty columns to improve the readability of the sheet. Consider the following example. Suppose you add certain comments to your **Sample – Superstore** file, as follows:

	A	B	C	D	E
1	Order Information				
2	This table contains the Order Information in the US for various regions				
3	Row ID	Order ID	Order Date	Ship Date	Ship Mode
4	1	CA-2018-152156	08-11-2018	11-11-2018	Second Class
5	2	CA-2018-152156	08-11-2018	11-11-2018	Second Class
6	3	CA-2018-138688	12-06-2018	16-06-2018	Second Class

Figure 2.35: Understanding Data Interpreter

From a data visualization point of view, rows 1 to 3 are meaningless as they don't belong to the actual data and are simply headers. Tableau can automatically remove these rows by using Data Interpreter.

Data Interpreter can be enabled by selecting the **Use Data Interpreter** option.:

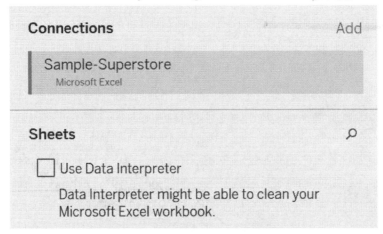

Figure 2.36: Enabling Data Interpreter

Once enabled, Data Interpreter will give you an option, **Review the results**. Clicking on **Review the results** will open up an Excel sheet of all the changes made by Data Interpreter, as can be seen in the following figure:

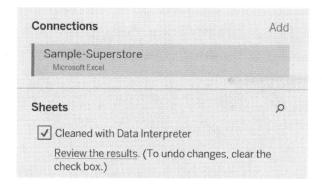

Key for Understanding the Data Interpreter Results
Use the key to understand how your data source has been interpreted.
To view the results, click a worksheet tab.
Note: Tableau never makes changes to your underlying data source.
Key:
Data is interpreted as column headers (field names).
Data is interpreted as values in your data source.
Data derived from an Excel merged cell is interpreted as value in your data source.
Data is ignored and not included as part of your data source.
Data has been excluded from your data source.
Note: To search for all excluded data, use CRTL +F on Windows

Figure 2.37: Reviewing the results of Data Interpreter

RENAMING THE DATA SOURCE

The data source can be renamed on the **Connect** screen just by clicking on it and entering the name of your choice.

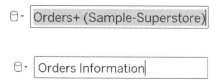

Figure 2.38: Renaming a data source

When working with data sources, you want to quickly identify the tables you are working with. Renaming tables allows you to give custom names so that it becomes easier to work with them.

LIVE AND EXTRACT CONNECTIONS

This is a very important concept for data visualization in Tableau. This option decides how the data is connected to the visualizations.

Live connections allow Tableau worksheets to be updated in real time based on any changes made in the underlying data sources. This may be a good solution when the data must be updated on a real-time basis, such as stock market data.

However, when developing the visualizations in a live connection, the database will be queried for any changes performed in the view related to the data. This may consume more time.

Tableau Data Extracts (TDEs), or **extracts**, are a compressed and optimized way to bring all the source data into Tableau's memory. TDEs improve the efficiency of the data query, which tends to increase the speed of executions while working with the data in the visualizations and performing user interactive activities such as filtering and sorting over the data.

When developing the visualizations in an extract connection, the database is also extracted into Tableau's local memory. Thus, any visualization development will be much faster compared to a live connection.

EXERCISE 2.06: CREATING AN EXTRACT FOR DATA

In the preceding exercises, you connected to the data using a live connection. Now, you will create an extract for it. The following steps should be performed to create a data extract for the **Orders** table:

1. Load the **Sample – Superstore** dataset in your Tableau instance as done in the previous exercises.

2. Drag the **Orders** table to the canvas.

3. Choose the **Extract** option, as shown in the following figure:

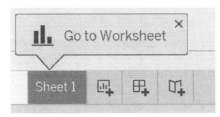

Figure 2.39: Creating an extract

4. Once done, click on **Sheet 1** at the bottom of the page to navigate to that sheet.

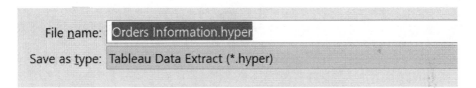

Figure 2.40: Navigating to a worksheet

5. This will open a popup to save the extract locally. Select a destination of your choice to save the extract.

Figure 2.41: Extract creation and save

Clicking on **Save** will create the extract and save it at the specified location. There is also the **Edit** option, which can be used to edit the properties of the extract. You will study these in the next section.

6. Refresh your extracts using the **Edit** or **Refresh** option if your data changes, as shown in the following figure:

Connection

◯ Live   ⦿ Extract │ Edit   Refresh

Extract includes all data. 03-01-2022 20:57:54

Figure 2.42: Extract Edit and Refresh options

In this exercise, you created an extract using Tableau Desktop.

EXTRACT PROPERTIES

To access the extract properties, you can click on the **Edit** option next to **Extract**, as shown in *Figure 2.42*, to open the following window:

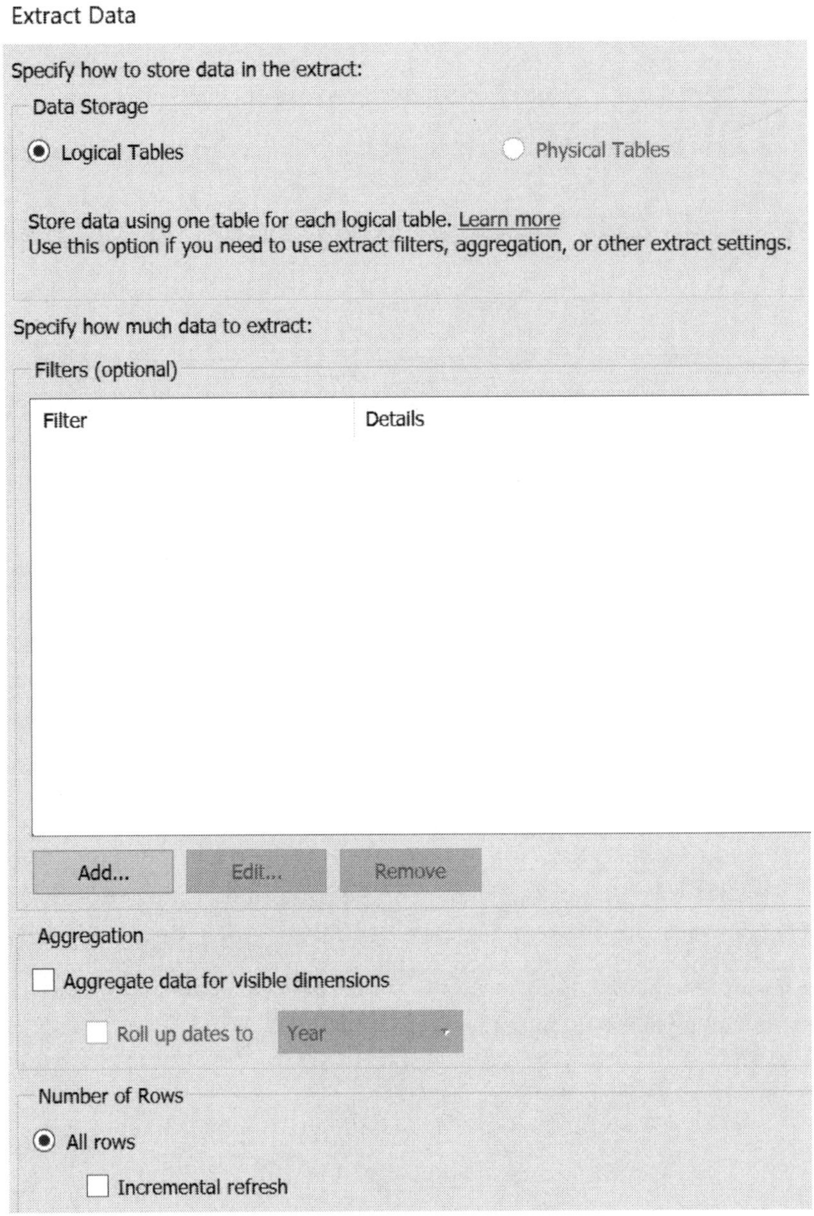

Extract Data

Specify how to store data in the extract:

Data Storage

(•) Logical Tables   ( ) Physical Tables

Store data using one table for each logical table. Learn more
Use this option if you need to use extract filters, aggregation, or other extract settings.

Specify how much data to extract:

Filters (optional)

Filter	Details

Add...   Edit...   Remove

Aggregation

☐ Aggregate data for visible dimensions

☐ Roll up dates to   Year

Number of Rows

(•) All rows

☐ Incremental refresh

Figure 2.43: Extract edit properties

The following sections will describe this window and its fields in detail.

THE DATA STORAGE FIELD

If you have multiple tables, the **Multiple tables** option will be enabled. For now, since you have a single table, the **Single table** option is enabled.

THE FILTERS FIELD

You can restrict the data in the extract using filters. For example, suppose you want only the data for the **Central** and **East** regions; you can easily do that using the **Add**... option. Select **Region** as the column to filter and select the **Central** and **East** values to add them as the filter condition.

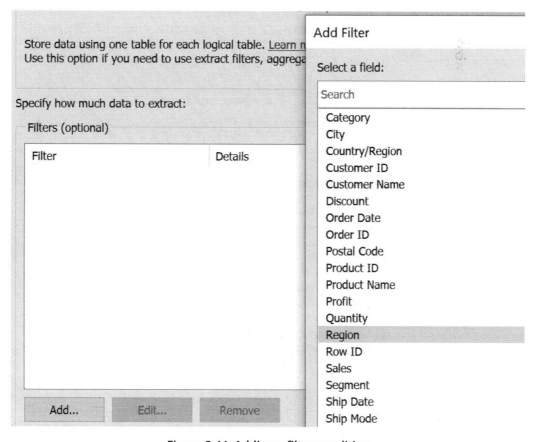

Figure 2.44: Adding a filter condition

As shown in the following figure, **Central** and **East** regions should be selected:

Filter [Region]

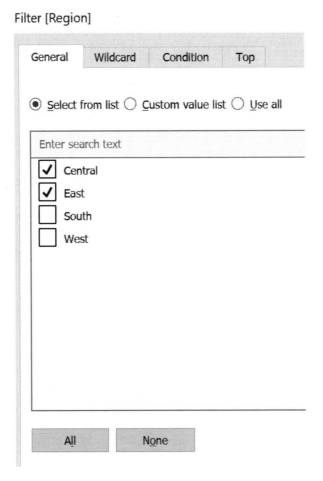

Figure 2.45: Selecting Central and East regions

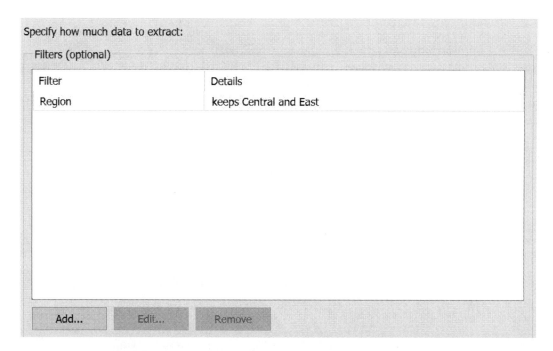

Figure 2.46: Creating extract filters using the Region column

You will learn more about these filters as you progress through this chapter.

THE AGGREGATION FIELD

You can also change the granularity of the data using this option. If you have dates in the dataset on a **Day** level, you can roll them up or aggregate them to a higher level using a different option, such as **Month** or **Year**. You will learn more about aggregations later in the book.

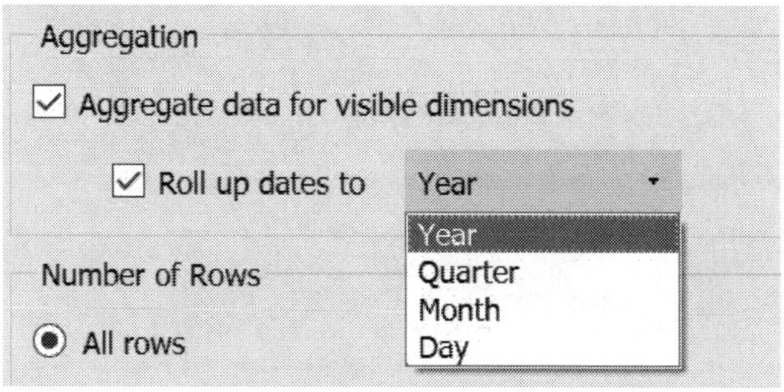

Figure 2.47: Transforming the data aggregation level

THE NUMBER OF ROWS FIELD

Using this option, you can choose the number of rows the extract should contain. **All rows** will include all the rows, **Top** will include only the specified number of rows, and **Sample** will contain a sample of specified rows. This is useful when you are working on a very large dataset, but for development purposes, you just need a sample of the data.

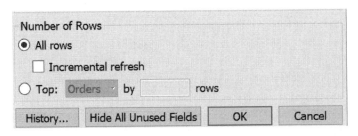

Figure 2.48: Sample selection using the number of rows

On selecting **All rows**, you will also get an option called **Incremental refresh**. Instead of refreshing the data every day, you can use this option to specify which field can be used to identify new rows so that only the specified section of the data is refreshed. This option is helpful when you have a very large dataset that updates at regular intervals wherein the old data does not change.

Consider the case of banking transactions. The bank will never modify the old data but would keep adding new data to maintain the historic data. In this case, an incremental refresh would be very helpful during extract refreshes.

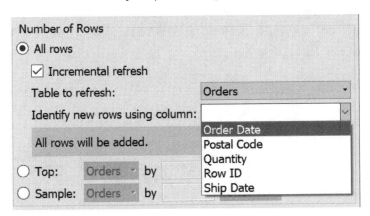

Figure 2.49: Identifying the column for performing refresh

Now that you understand what values to add in these fields, you'll review what factors to determine when choosing the type of connection.

WHICH CONNECTION IS BETTER — LIVE OR EXTRACT?

Ideally, in most projects, an extract is the ideal approach, but there may be a need to showcase live data as in the example you saw before. The following points should be considered before choosing an extract or a live connection:

- **Updated or delayed data**: If you have a requirement for which you need the most up-to-date information whenever you view the dashboard, you would need a live connection. Otherwise, if you are comfortable with some delay in the latest data, an extract is a better choice.

- **Data volume**: If your data volume is very large, it is ideal to use a data extract instead of a live connection as it might take a lot of time to develop dashboards on live connections.

With these points in mind, you can choose the right type of connection for your project.

FILTERS

This option is similar to the **Extract Filter** property you learned about before. These filters are also known as data source filters because they filter data at the source. You will further study various filters later in the book.

Consider the example of a large retailer such as Amazon, where the data has a large volume. Suppose you want to analyze the data for a specific region. In this case, it is not prudent to pull the whole data in Tableau as it would make the dashboard slower, and also, you would not have any use for the data other than that for your target region.

For such a case, you can use the **Data Source Filter** option. This would restrict the data at the source itself and only bring in the required data based on the filtering criterion specified.

EXERCISE 2.07: ADDING A REGION FILTER ON THE ORDERS TABLE

Consider that you want to add a **Region** filter on the **Orders** table, to bring the data for the **Central** and **East** regions only. You can do so by following these steps:

1. Load the **Sample - Superstore** dataset in your Tableau instance.

2. Drag the **Orders** table onto the canvas.

3. To add a filter, click on the **Filters | Add** option to open the popup:

Figure 2.50: Data source filter properties

4. Click on **Add**... to open the columns list. Select **Region** as the column:

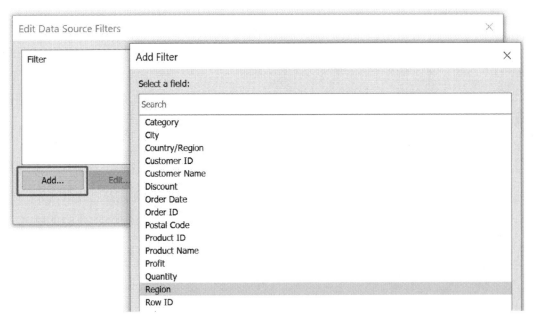

Figure 2.51: Column filter selection

5. Select **Central** and **East** as the regions that will be kept in the data. Click **OK** to add the filter, as follows:

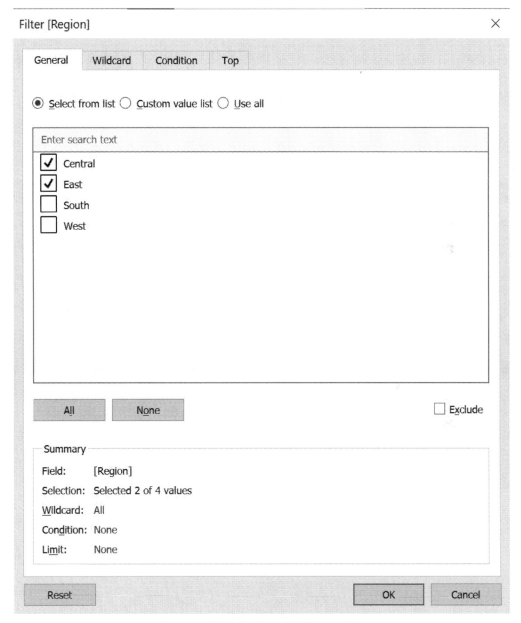

Figure 2.52: Selecting the filter values

You can similarly add more filters by clicking on the **Add**... option and repeating the previous steps.

6. You can also edit and remove the existing filters. To do that, select the filter you want to edit or remove and then select the required option, as shown in the following figure:

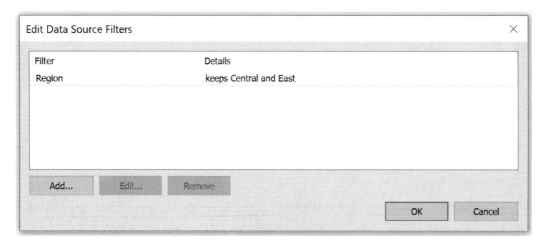

Figure 2.53: Filter preview

7. Once you have added the filter, preview the data in the data grid. You will observe that you only have data for the **Central** and **East** regions, as expected.

⊕ Orders City	⊕ Orders State	⊕ Orders Postal Code	Abc Orders Region
Fort Worth	Texas	76106	Central
Fort Worth	Texas	76106	Central
Madison	Wisconsin	53711	Central
Fremont	Nebraska	68025	Central
Fremont	Nebraska	68025	Central
Philadelphia	Pennsylvania	19140	East
Philadelphia	Pennsylvania	19140	East
Philadelphia	Pennsylvania	19140	East

Figure 2.54: Data preview post filter application

In this exercise, you learned how to apply a filter and the various properties associated with a data source filter. In the next section, you will learn how to transform data using the data grid.

DATA GRID OPTIONS

[handwritten: → transformation tool.]

The data grid allows you to preview data. You have been using it so far just to check the number of rows the data contains, but it also contains several other options to transform data before you start with the visualization development. In this section, you will learn about these options and how to use them to better understand the data transformations.

Data preview: You can use this to preview the data. You can also select the number of rows to be displayed, by specifying the number in the box on the right, as can be seen in the following figure:

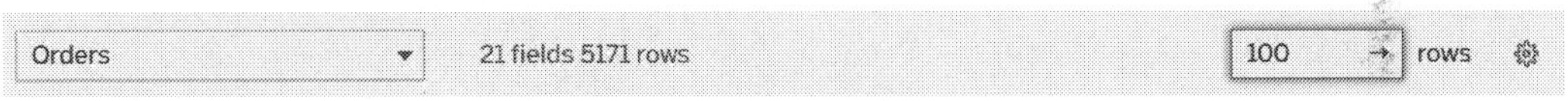

Figure 2.55: Data preview toggle

Metadata: Metadata provides information about the source, such as the table name. Toggling to the metadata view, you can see all the metadata about the data. You can view the various columns, the table they come from, and the remote field name.

If you rename a field here, the remote field name will show the original field name pulled from the data.

Orders ▼	21 fields 5171 rows

Name

Orders

Fields

Type	Field Name	Physical Table	Remote Field Name
#	Row ID	Orders	Row ID
Abc	Order ID	Orders	Order ID
📅	Order Date	Orders	Order Date
📅	Ship Date	Orders	Ship Date
Abc	Ship Mode	Orders	Ship Mode

Figure 2.56: Changing to the list view representation to show
input data source metadata properties

> **NOTE**
>
> In Tableau version 2021.4, the metadata is automatically available beside the preview, and you will not have to choose between these options.

The **Sort fields** option will sort the data as per the option you select. You can try changing these options and observe how the data preview changes.

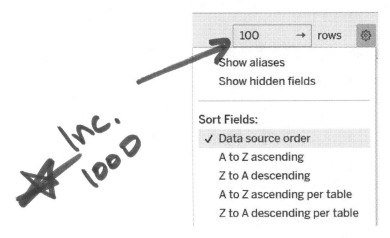

Figure 2.57: Sorting the data grid column values

Now, consider the following data transformation options.

Change data type: Using this option, you can change the data type of a column. By clicking on the **Abc** icon (see the following figure), you can select the required data type from the drop-down box for the column. A common example is the **Customer ID** field being stored as a number where you might want it to be a string:

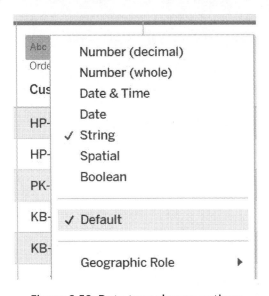

Figure 2.58: Data type change options

Data transformation: When you click on the drop-down icon, as shown in the following figure, you can see the options to transform the data, such as creating calculated fields on existing columns and creating groups. All these options are also available after you load the data. These will be covered in detail later in the book:

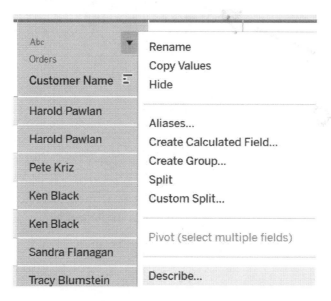

Figure 2.59: Data transformation menu options

The **Rename** option allows you to rename the column. You can also hide a column if it's not required in the data visualization. You can select the **Show hidden fields** checkbox to view any hidden columns. Hidden columns are grayed out in the view, as indicated in the following figure:

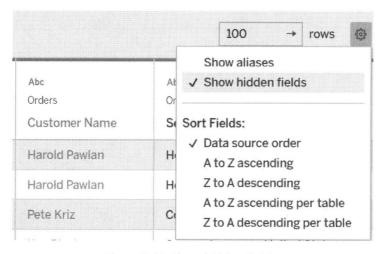

Figure 2.60: Show hidden fields

Hidden columns cannot be used in the visualization. If you want to use a column after hiding it, you need to first unhide the column to use it in the visualization. This can be done by clicking on the dropdown and selecting the **Unhide** option.

Figure 2.61: Hiding/unhiding columns from the input data source

Aliases: Aliases are a very effective way to present data in the visualization with a different name.

Observe the **Ship Mode** column in the data preview. You can see that the word **Class** is repeated for the different **Ship Mode** values, and it does not add any value; so you can exclude this word from all the values. This can be done using the **Aliases** option, which will help you to display the values as a different name. To add aliases on the column, click on the dropdown and select **Aliases…**, as shown in the following figure:

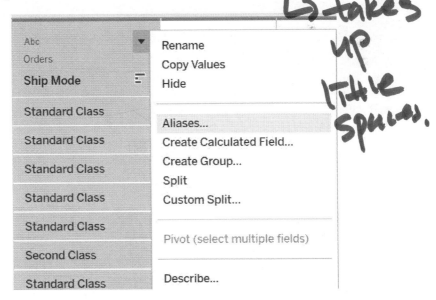

Figure 2.62: Setting a column value alias

This will open the popup to rename the values. Remove the word **Class**. Click on **OK** to add it to the data. You can also clear the aliases using the **Clear Aliases** option.

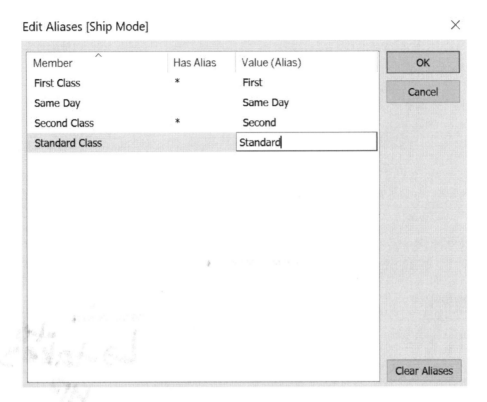

Figure 2.63: Edit Aliases properties

You can use the **Show aliases** toggle to switch between the original names and the aliases. Aliases are generally used to rename null records to blank or columns containing long value names.

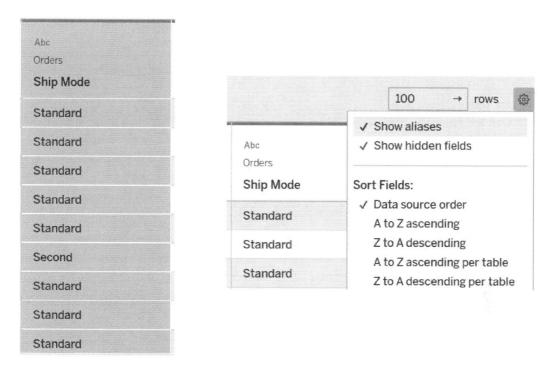

Figure 2.64: Enabling aliases in the data preview using the Show aliases option

All these options are also accessible after you load the data in the worksheet.

In this view, you learned how to perform data transformations before pulling the data in the worksheets.

In all the exercises previously, you just joined on two data sources. But it is also possible to add more than two data sources. You will just need to specify in the join connection how the tables join to each other.

This completes the various ways you can join multiple tables in Tableau. Next, you will learn about the custom SQL option.

CUSTOM SQL

Custom SQL, as the name suggests, is used for writing custom SQL queries to pull only the selected columns based on the conditions applied instead of pulling the entire database. This option is not available with Excel and text files, so you might not see this option.

This option will appear in the **Connect** pane once the database is connected. When you connect a database, you will see the **New Custom SQL** option below all the tables listed.

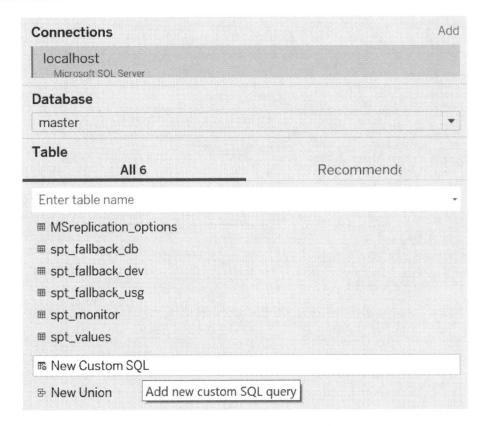

Figure 2.65: New Custom SQL option

You can drag this option onto the canvas, type in your query, and click **OK**. Once done, Tableau will pull the required data based on the query specified.

Custom SQL can be used to reduce the size of data by adding only the required columns in the data source, adding a union across the tables, and recasting fields to join multiple data sources together.

Until now, you have learned about the various data transformation steps that can be performed before pulling the data in the worksheet. In the next section, you will learn about data blending, which is another way of joining the data but with a difference.

DATA BLENDING

There might be times when the linking fields vary between the different worksheets. Also, if the data sources are too large, joining them with the conventional joins might be very time consuming. In that case, you can perform a data blend instead of joining the data.

In data blending, you query the data between the two data sources and then combine the result at the aggregation level defined in the worksheet of the primary data source. The primary data source will be the one from which the first dimension or measure is added in the view. Also, the results would be similar to a left join since all the records from the primary data will appear in the worksheet.

EXERCISE 2.08: CREATING A DATA BLEND USING THE ORDERS AND PEOPLE TABLES

In this exercise, you will learn how to create a data blend for the **Orders** table with the **People** table. The following steps will help you complete this exercise:

1. Load the **Sample – Superstore** dataset in your Tableau instance.

2. Connect to the **Orders** table and go to **Sheet 1**.

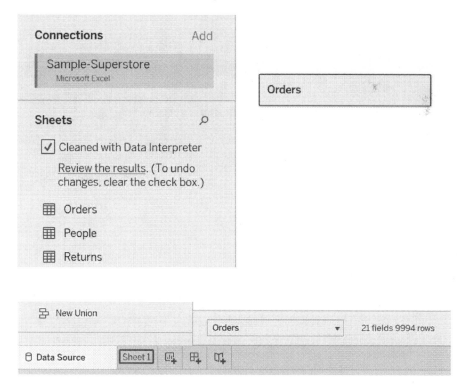

Figure 2.66: Adding the Orders table in Tableau

3. In a data blend, create the linking at the worksheet level and not at the data source level. Inside the worksheet, you will be able to see the **Orders** table and its columns. Add a new data source, as follows (see the highlighted option):

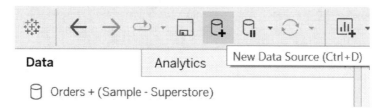

Figure 2.67: Adding data option inside a worksheet

4. This should lead to the same menu that you get for connecting to a data source. Click on **Microsoft Excel**, navigate to the location of the **Sample – Superstore.xls** Excel file, and click on **Open** to open the **Connect** pane.

Figure 2.68: Adding another data source in Tableau

5. Now, drag the **People** table to the canvas and go to **Sheet 1** like before:

Figure 2.69: Adding the People data to Tableau

Now, you will be able to see the two data sources, as follows:

Figure 2.70: Data sources listed inside the worksheet

6. Add a relationship between these data sources to use them. To do that, click on **Data | Edit Relationships**... to open the popup.

> **NOTE**
>
> If you are using a Tableau version later than 2020.1, this may be called **Edit Blend Relationships...** to differentiate between relationships made directly in the **Data Source** tab.

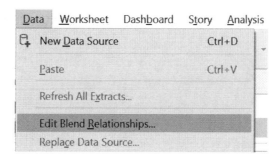

Figure 2.71: Edit data properties window

7. Based on the field names, the relationship can be set to **Automatic** by default. To change it, click on **Custom** and add the relationship. Edit the relationship to **Customer Name** and **Person**, as highlighted in the following figure. Select **Region** and then **Edit**... before making the selections in the popup. Click **OK** to add the relationship:

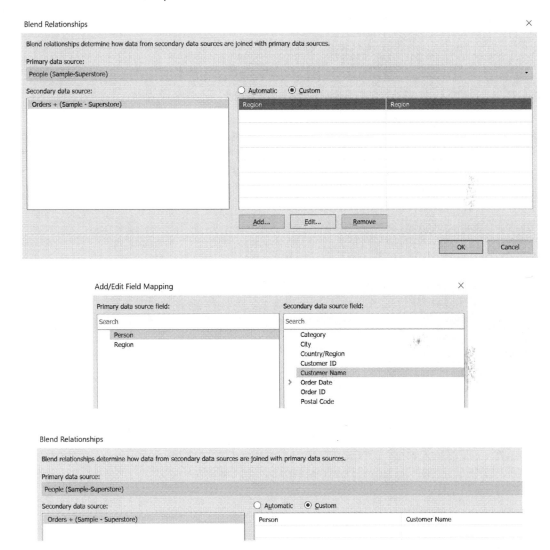

Figure 2.72: Selecting the matching columns between the two data sources

Thus, you have successfully blended the two data sources and can visualize your data in the next exercise.

EXERCISE 2.09: VISUALIZING DATA CREATED FROM A DATA BLEND

In the previous exercise, you learned how to perform data blending between two data sources. In this exercise, you will create a visualization on the blended data to understand the application of a data blend – again, you will continue using the **Orders** table and the **People** table for this purpose. Note that a blend will only be active if you use the fields from these two data sources; otherwise, it will remain inactive.

Perform the following steps to complete this exercise:

1. On the **Orders** data, click and drag **Customer Name** to **Rows**.

> **NOTE**
>
> Tableau versions later than 2020.1 may give a warning at this step that the field may contain more than 1000 rows. If this is the case, select **Add all members** to proceed.

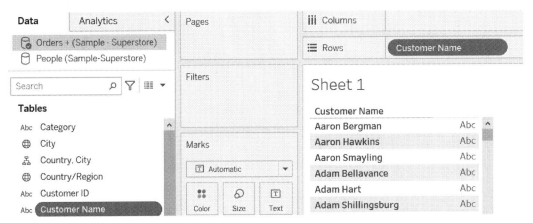

Figure 2.73: Adding the primary data source

This will now become your primary data source, indicated by the blue tick on the data source.

2. Repeat the step for the **People** data source.

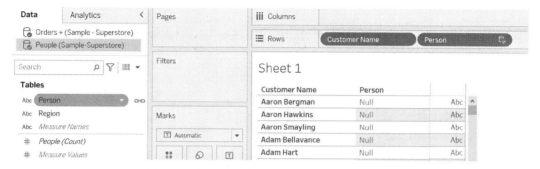

Figure 2.74: Adding the secondary data source

This will become your secondary data source, indicated by the orange tick on the data source. Also, notice the red linking icon that is used to link the two data sources.

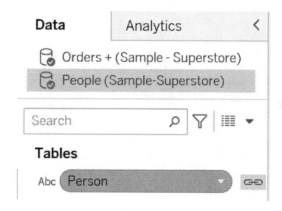

Figure 2.75: Primary and secondary data source icons

3. When you filter on **Person** for the four people that you have in the **People** data, you will see that you have linked these values between these data sources. Click on the **Person** column dropdown and then **Filter**..., uncheck the **Null** value, and click **OK** to add the filter.

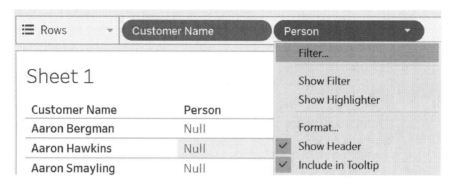

Figure 2.76: Filtering to remove unmatched values

You will get the following output, which shows the customer name matching **Person**:

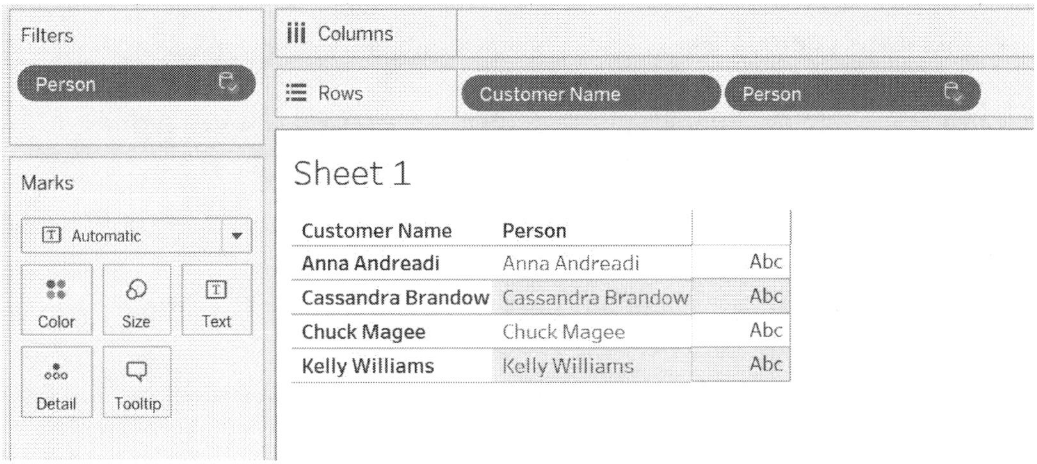

Figure 2.77: Data blend output

Using data blending, you can display data from various sources at multiple aggregation levels in different sheets. For instance, in one sheet, you can blend the data at the **Year** aggregation level, while in the other you can blend at the **Month** level.

This is possible because, in a data blend, the data sources are not joined at the input source. This provides the flexibility to have large data sources and blend only in certain sheets where required. This can help make the dashboard render faster.

LIMITATIONS OF DATA BLENDING

Data blending does not work with certain aggregation levels, such as **MEDIAN** and **COUNTD** (count distinct).

You cannot publish the blended data sources on Tableau Server directly. First, you need to publish the data sources individually on the server and then blend the published data sources in your Tableau Desktop instance. Publishing data sources means uploading your data and directly storing it on Tableau Server.

Another limitation is that the data used from the secondary data source must be at a higher aggregation level compared to the primary data source. If the aggregation level is not correct, an asterisk (*) will appear in the visualizations, indicating a one-to-many join aggregation level. You can swap the data sources to resolve this error.

This concludes the theory sections of this lesson. Next, you will put all you have learned into practice in the following activities.

ACTIVITY 2.01: IDENTIFYING THE RETURNED ORDERS

As an analyst, you may encounter a situation where you would like to assess business performance by sales. It is therefore important to understand how many orders are fulfilled and how many are returned. If certain products are being returned frequently, it is a point of investigation as it can have serious consequences on the business.

Usually, order information is kept separate from returns information. Hence, to bring this information together, you need to join the two data sources.

For this activity, you will use the **Orders** and **Returns** tables from the **Sample - Superstore** Excel file. You are already aware of the **Orders** table.

The **Returns** table consists of the **Order ID** and **Returned** columns. **Order ID** is the ID that would match with the **Orders** table. The **Returned** column indicates **Yes** for the order ID.

Returned	Order ID
Yes	CA-2016-100762
Yes	CA-2016-100762
Yes	CA-2016-100762
Yes	CA-2016-100762
Yes	CA-2016-100867
Yes	CA-2016-102652
Yes	CA-2016-102652
Yes	CA-2016-102652
Yes	CA-2016-102652
Yes	CA-2016-103373
Yes	CA-2016-103744
Yes	CA-2016-103744

Figure 2.78: Returns sheet columns

The objective is to identify the returned orders after combining them with the main **Orders** table so that you may determine which orders were both fulfilled and returned.

The steps are as follows:

1. Open the **Sample - Superstore** dataset in your Tableau instance.

2. Rename the data source to **Activity 1**.

3. Drag the **Orders** table onto the canvas.

4. Repeat the same steps for the **Returns** table.

5. You need to bring all the **Orders** and **Returns** table values into the combined dataset. Can you identify the correct join based on the requirement? Remember that for an order to be returned, it should always be completed first. What can be interpreted if you change the join types to left, right, or full outer in this case?

6. Identify how many products were returned from the data grid. (An order can have multiple products clubbed in it.)

Figure 2.79: Choose the correct join

In this activity, you strengthened your knowledge of various joins and their outputs. You also learned how to interpret the results by changing the join types.

> **NOTE**
>
> The solution to this activity can be found here: https://packt.link/CTCxk.

ACTIVITY 2.02: PREPARING DATA FOR VISUALIZATION

Now that you have joined the data, the next step is to make sure that the data is ready for visualization. This involves performing data transformation activities such as cleaning the data by removing the null values. You may also be required to rename certain columns or add aliases, split the columns, and so on.

In this activity, you will perform some data transformation steps based on the left join output of the previous activity.

This activity will help you to strengthen the concepts of data transformation in Tableau. This is a very important process in any Tableau project. Hence, it becomes crucial that you are well experienced in doing these in Tableau.

The objective of this activity is to transform the data into a cleaned form for visualization. You need to first create an extract for this data source. Then you need to display the data only for the **Furniture** and **Office Supplies** categories. Is there a way to do this using the extract properties? You will also clean up the final data by changing any nulls to blanks. Let's also remove repeated terms such as **Class** from the **Ship Mode** column.

Once done, your data should be ready for visualization.

Continuing from Activity 2.01, the following steps will help you complete this activity:

1. Open the **Sample - Superstore** dataset in your Tableau instance.

2. Create a data extract for this data.

3. Add a filter on the data to pull the **Furniture** and **Office Supplies** categories. Check the row count.

4. Transform the data by aliasing a few columns.

5. Alias the null values from the columns of the **Returns** table to blanks.

6. Remove the word **Class** from the **Ship Mode** column.

Once completed, you should get the following output:

Final Output Expected:

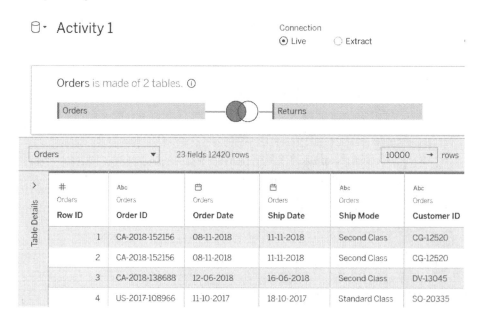

Figure 2.80: Final output for the activity

In this activity, you learned how to extract the data. You also added filters for the **Category** column to just pull the selected categories. Many times, you will work on projects that require the data to be segregated at the beginning, such as regional data. These filters help you to achieve exactly this. You also transformed the data using aliases, making it much cleaner by removing repeated words and nulls.

> **NOTE**
>
> The solution to this activity can be found here: https://packt.link/CTCxk.

SUMMARY

In this chapter, you learned how to connect to various data sources, which is the foremost step in data analysis in Tableau. Next, you learned about the various join options that Tableau provides and data transformation options to optimize the data for the final visualization. Joining tables is one of the most common requirements in practical data analysis. For instance, if you have two tables for employee details and department details, to find the number of employees per department, you would use a join key to get the required information.

You also learned about some advanced data joining options of blending and custom SQL. The key takeaway from this chapter is how to connect data most efficiently based on the requirements and also how to transform the data so that it becomes more suitable for the visualization activity. The next chapter continues with the topic of data preparation in Tableau Prep.

3

DATA PREPARATION: USING TABLEAU PREP

OVERVIEW

In this chapter, you will learn some advanced data preparation methods in Tableau Prep. You will learn how to use various Tableau Prep options to clean datasets, join different data sources using various options, and perform data manipulation activities such as pivots, grouping, and aggregations. By the end of this chapter, you will be able to export a cleaned data source to develop visualizations in Tableau.

INTRODUCTION

In the previous chapter, you performed some fundamental data transformations such as joins, filtering, and groups using Tableau Desktop. However, Tableau Desktop only performs basic data manipulation. It may not be able to handle raw unprocessed/unclean data, like data containing multiple entries, missing entries, or inconsistent formats. Now, you will learn about more advanced methods, better suited to these trickier scenarios.

Tableau Prep is a tool specifically designed to perform data transformation so we can use the data for our visualizations. It consists of advanced algorithms that help detect data inconsistencies and fix them. This can be done automatically as well as manually, depending on the requirements.

In this chapter, you will learn about the Prep interface, along with data operations like adding data sources, data profiling, and applying transformations such as cleaning, splitting, adding pivots, joining data sources, and applying unions. Finally, you will learn how to export this transformed dataset into Excel for data visualization.

PREP INTERFACE

In this section, you will look at the options available in Tableau Prep for data transformation. Tableau Prep can be downloaded from the Tableau website (https://www.tableau.com/products/prep) and installed like any other program. You can find detailed installation steps in the *Preface*. Once the installation is complete, navigate to your desktop and click on the Tableau Prep icon to open it.

When you open Prep for the first time, it will look like this:

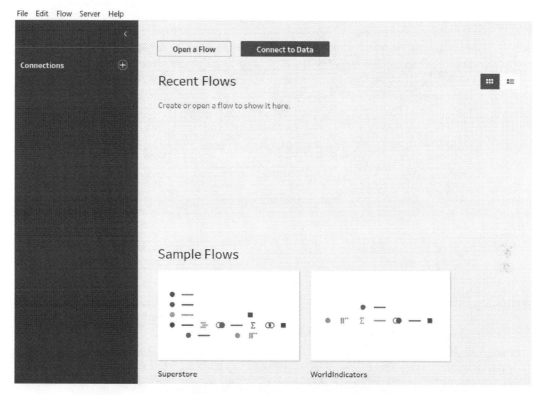

Figure 3.1: Prep start screen

The **Connections** tab (top-left corner), shows all data sources that can be connected in the prep. This is similar to the **Connect** pane in Tableau Desktop. (*Chapter 2, Data Preparation Using Tableau Desktop.*)

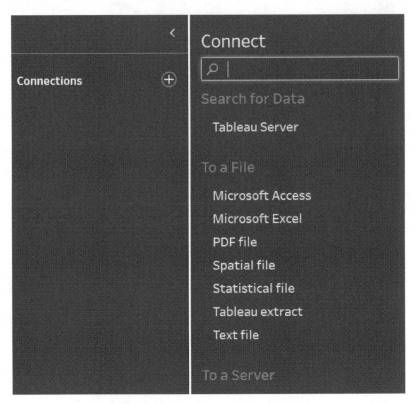

Figure 3.2: Data connections in Prep

Throughout this chapter, you will be working with file-based connections such as Excel spreadsheets and CSVs. First, let's look briefly at the other options available on the start screen (as shown in *Figure 3.1*):

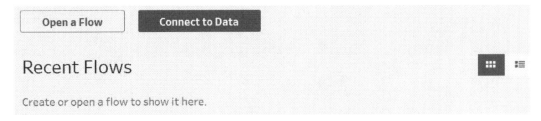

Figure 3.3: Options on the start screen

In the preceding figure, you can see the following elements:

- **Open a Flow**: This opens a workflow that has already been created. A workflow, or flow, is a series of data transformation activities that you perform on the input data in Prep. You will learn about creating different flows in the upcoming sections.

- **Connect to Data**: This opens the **Connections** menu, where you connect to data, as shown earlier.

- **Recent Flows**: All previous flows can be viewed here. You can toggle between card view or list view using the controls on the right side.

Other than these options, you also have **Sample Flows** provided by Tableau, and the **Discover** menu, where you can check out Prep-related content updates on the Tableau website.

There are also other **File**, **Edit**, **Flow**, and **Server** menu options at the top. The **File** and **Edit** options should be self-explanatory. The **Flow** menu can be used to run the flow, and the **Server** menu has the option to sign in and publish the flow on Tableau Server.

Now that you have learned about the various options, it's time to add some data in the flow.

ADDING DATA IN THE FLOW

As seen in *Chapter 2, Data Preparation using Tableau Desktop*, the first step of any data preparation activity is to add the data into your workflow. To do that in Prep, click on **Connections** and select the data source. In the following exercise, you will connect to file-based data sources, but the process is similar for server-based data sources.

EXERCISE 3.01: CONNECTING TO AN EXCEL FILE

In this exercise, you will connect with your very first data source in Prep. Follow these steps to complete the exercise:

1. After installing Tableau Prep Builder, find the files in the following location on your computer:

- Windows

```
C:\Program Files\Tableau\Tableau Prep Builder <version>\
help\Samples\en_US\Superstore Files
```

- Mac

```
/Applications/Tableau Prep Builder <version>.app/
Contents/help/Samples/en_US/Superstore Files
```

2. Click on **Connections** and select the **Microsoft Excel** option.

3. This will open the menu from which you can select the Excel file. Navigate to the aforementioned location and open the **Orders_East.xlsx** file.

Figure 3.4: Connecting to an Excel file using Prep

You will get the following screen once the Excel file has loaded:

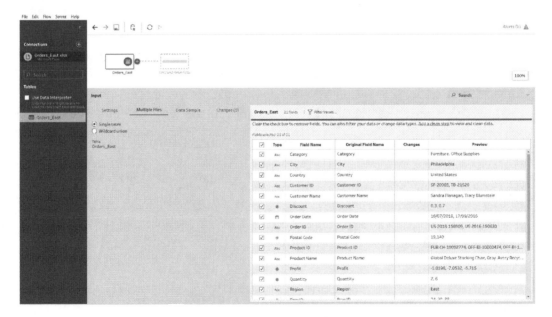

Figure 3.5: Data input properties

There are a lot of tabs and options on this screen. These will be covered in the upcoming sections.

4. Click the **+** icon (*Figure 3.6*) to see the steps that can be applied to this input data step:

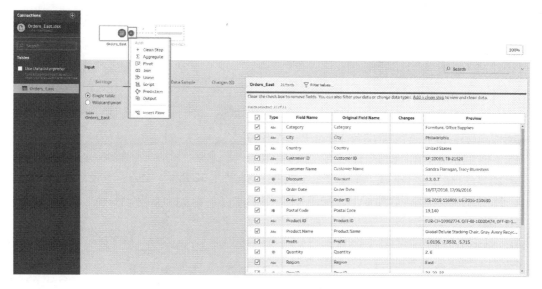

Figure 3.6: Adding steps to a workflow

Now it's time to add an output step. To do so, click on **+** and select **Output**. An output tab will open, and you can preview the data.

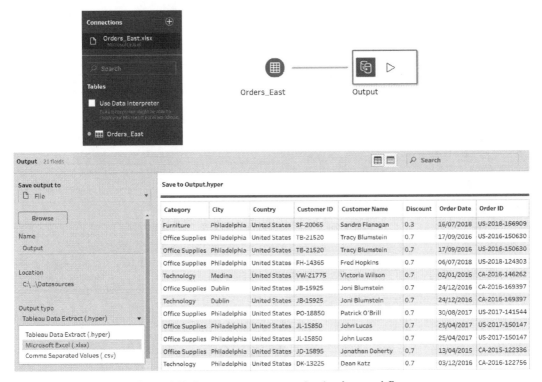

Figure 3.7: Output step properties in the workflow

Here, you learned how to connect to an Excel file. Next, you will learn about bringing multiple inputs into the flow.

EXERCISE 3.02: CONNECTING WITH MULTIPLE DATA SOURCES

Ideally, in a business project, data should be stored in separate sources. Thus, it is important to know how to connect to multiple data sources. In this exercise, you will try to add another data source to your existing flow.

You will be connecting the **Orders_South** data, as follows:

1. Continuing from the last step of the previous exercise, click on **+** and select the **Text file** option. This is because the required data is stored as a CSV file, which is a type of text file.

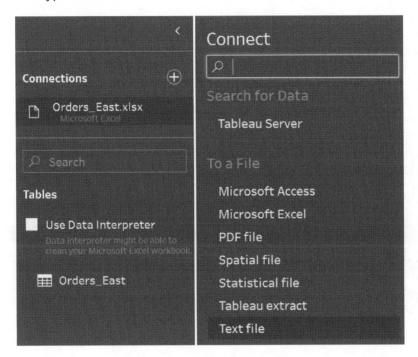

Figure 3.8: Connecting to a CSV file

2. Now, navigate to the **Order_South** folder under **Superstore Files**. Select **orders_south_2018.csv** and click on **Open** to bring the file into Prep.

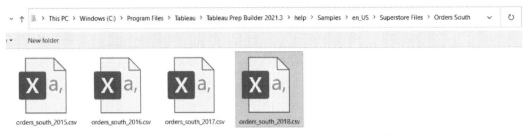

Figure 3.9: Data explorer window to view input files

You should get the following screen:

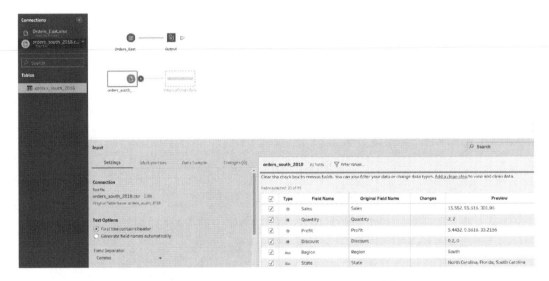

Figure 3.10: Adding multiple files to the workflow

The following steps will walk you through the various tabs in the **Input** pane shown in *Figure 3.10*:

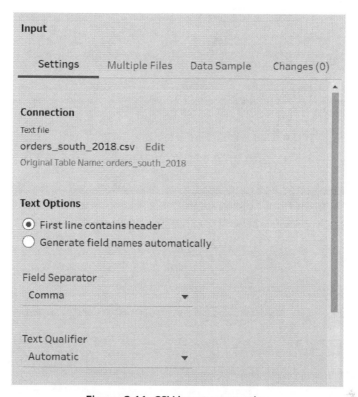

Figure 3.11: CSV input properties

3. The **Setting** tab is mostly related to the connection details of the data source, and might vary depending on the data source connection. You will find options here to edit connection details, select text options, decide which field separators to use, and more.

4. You also have options such as **Text Qualifier**, **Character Set**, and **Locale**. Prep is smart enough to recognize these configurations but, if required, configurations can be changed as per requirements. Finally, there is an option for **Incremental Refresh**. This is similar to Tableau Desktop, and can be used to load new data based on certain columns rather than pulling all data every time the flow runs.

5. Select the **Multiple File** tab to get the option to add multiple files together.

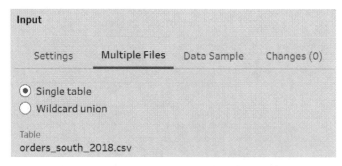

Figure 3.12: Options to input multiple files

6. Now, change the selection to **Wildcard union**. Suppose you want to get all the **orders_south** files from the folder. You can simply search it by a pattern (***south***) and get all the files you want to find (*Figure 3.13*).

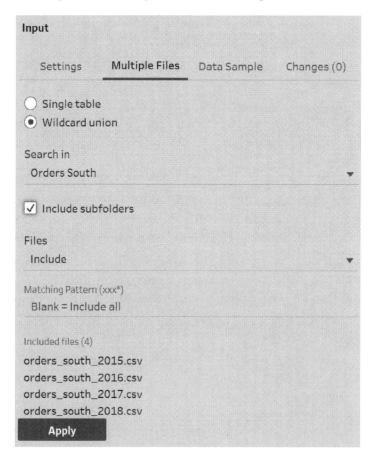

Figure 3.13: Wildcard search for multiple file input

You can search for files like this in the folders (or subfolders) as well. You can also include or exclude files that match a pattern. By including an asterisk (*****) you can selectively ignore all characters before and after a keyword.

7. Click on **Apply**, and all these sheets will be included in the flow. Prep also includes a new column, **File Paths**, which indicates the locations this data is coming from.

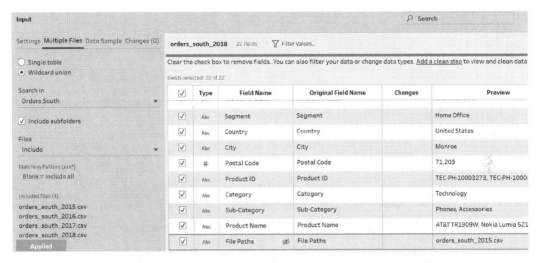

Figure 3.14: Identification of input file source using File Paths

8. Next, select the **Data Sample** tab. Here, you get the option to sample the input data, which is especially useful if the data is vast. Ideally, when working with a very large dataset, it is better to work with a sample to save time while developing the workflow, as the workflow will run faster if there are fewer records.

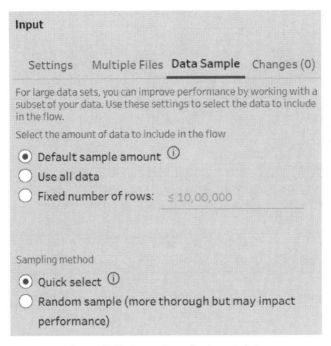

Figure 3.15: Sampling the input data

By hovering over the information icon, you can check how Prep samples the data.

9. Select the **Changes** tab. Any changes made to the data will be tracked here. A simple example is unchecking certain column names in the data. For example, if you uncheck the **Sales** and **Quantity** columns, these are immediately added to the **Changes** tab. The changes are also indicated by the annotations (small icons) in the **Changes** column, and on the data input icon as well. (Figure 3.16.)

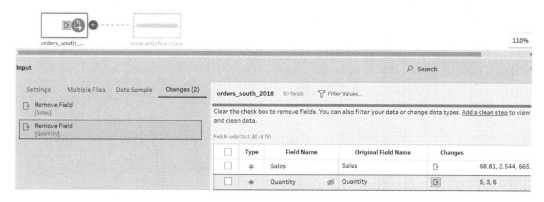

Figure 3.16: Tracking changes in the workflow

In this section, you learned how to connect multiple data sources in a workflow and their configuration properties. Next, you will learn how to profile data in Prep.

DATA SOURCE PROFILE

Until now, you have only connected to different data sources. But your main objective is to understand the data better. This can be done by observing the data distribution, the data types of various columns, the values that a column contains, and so on.

A data source profile gives you an understanding of the underlying data by allowing you to observe the data distribution and frequency, along with the various data types for the fields. This helps you make appropriate changes to the data to fulfill the requirements in the flow. Some common options include checking the data distribution frequency, the number of unique records, and the associations among various columns. You will first learn about some commonly used profiling steps, and then apply them in an exercise.

Data source profiling can be performed using a clean step. A clean step can be added by hovering over the **+** icon next to the data source and selecting **Clean Step**, as follows:

Figure 3.17: Adding a clean step in the workflow

Now, a clean step has been added to the workflow, which will open a new window for its connected input dataset. In this window, you can profile your data.

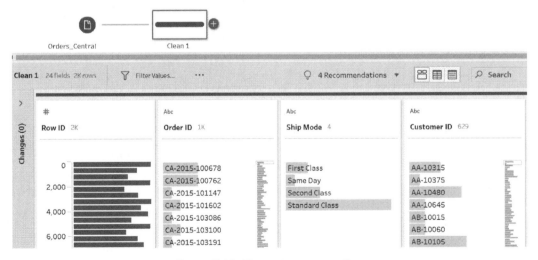

Figure 3.18: Clean step properties

The preceding screenshot shows the data profile pane. Each column will give a slightly different representation, depending on the data type.

For example, a string data type will give a distribution of the frequency with which it has occurred. If you observe the `Customer Name` column (as shown in the following screenshot) you will observe the number of orders placed by a customer. This is because the view is based on the customer order frequency.

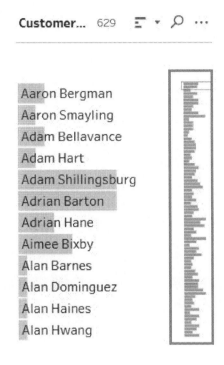

Figure 3.19: Observing Customer Name value frequencies

For a numeric column type, the profile would just give a histogram indicating the distribution of the values. Observe the **Quantity** column, which is a number. The data profile provides a histogram that can help you understand the range of the quantities sold.

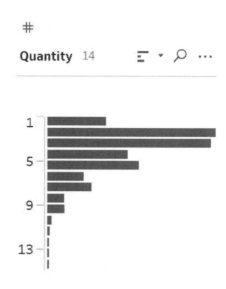

Figure 3.20: Data profile for a numeric column

Now that you have learned about the concept of data profiling, it's time for an exercise, to practice using the data profile of the **Orders** dataset.

EXERCISE 3.03: DATA PROFILE FOR THE ORDERS_SOUTH DATASET

In this exercise, you will learn how to better understand data using the data profile options in Prep.In the previous workflow, you connected to the **Order_South** dataset . This is a continuation of that exercise.

1. Perform the following steps:

2. Once the data is connected in Prep, click the **+** icon and then select **Clean Step**:

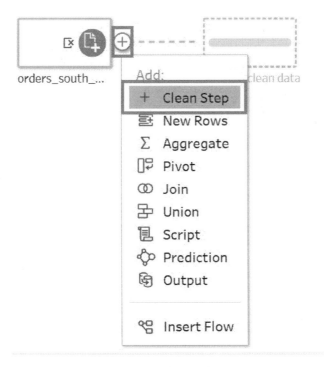

Figure 3.21: Adding a clean step

3. Click on the clean step to open up the details, as follows:

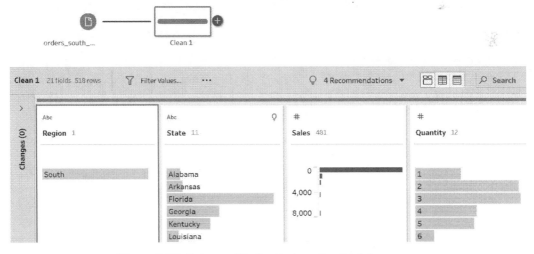

Figure 3.22: Data profile for Orders_South data source

4. Hover over the **Product ID** column to see the unique values it contains. You also have the option to change the data type, and sort, search, and perform a cleaning operation on it. Additionally, you also get a composition of the data using a histogram, as shown in the following screenshot:

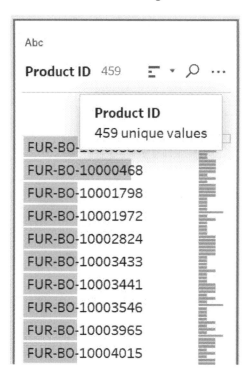

Figure 3.23: Observing the frequency of the values in the Product ID column

5. Select any value. Note that all associated rows are now highlighted. For example, if you select the state of Florida, you will see how the data is connected across the other columns. You will also observe that its profit trend is on the lower side, which indicates Florida is a low-selling state.

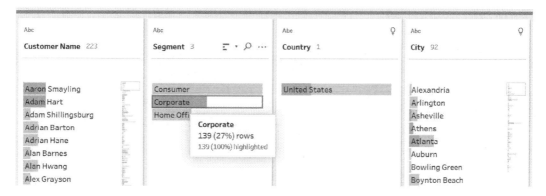

Figure 3.24: Associations across multiple columns in the data profile

Using data profiling like this, you can quickly see trends in data using the data distributions, which allows us to quickly spot and remove anomalies such as negative quantities sold.. These options will be covered in detail in the next section.

DATA PREPARATION USING CLEAN, GROUPS, AND SPLIT

Cleaning is a very important part of data preparation, because having the right data leads to proper and efficient data analysis.

For example, imagine the sales amount for an order in a dataset is blank, but an order is processed anyway. This cannot be right, and requires some action. The order in question should either not be included, or the sales amount should be replaced with an average.

Another example would be the same customer having multiple names, or more than one customer ID. You may need to combine the names into one to correctly analyze information. All such tasks can be done using data cleaning. Prep provides a variety of options to clean data. In this section, you will learn about them.

Refer to the **Orders_South** dataset workflow that was created earlier:

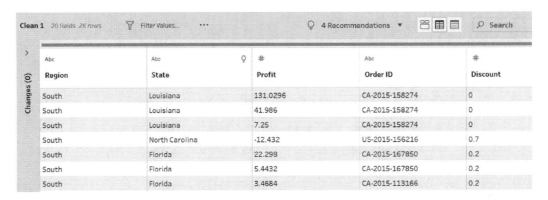

Figure 3.25: Orders_South workflow

Right-click on the **Clean 1** step to open the additional properties, as shown in the following screenshot:

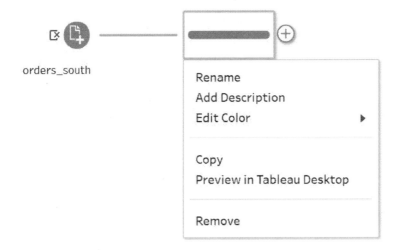

Figure 3.26: Step customization option properties

Here, you can perform operations such as renaming, adding a description and editing the color of the step, as explained in the following points:

- **Rename**: Double-click or *Ctrl + click* (if you are using Mac) on the field name. This opens a text entry box. Here, you can add a name of your choice to this step.

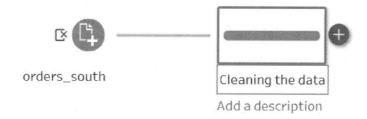

Figure 3.27: Rename the clean step in the workflow

- **Add Description**: Descriptions clarify the purpose of a step. This is especially useful if the workflow is being used by multiple people. To add a description, right-click on the step and select the **Add Description** option.

Figure 3.28: Adding a description to the clean step in the workflow

After you have added a description, the text appears under the step as follows:

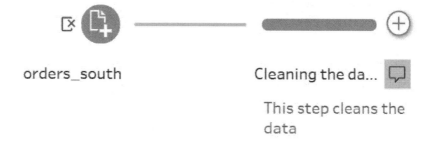

Figure 3.29: Toggling the description for the clean step in the workflow

You can choose to show or hide the description by clicking on the highlighted icon in the preceding figure. After you have added the description, you can also edit or delete it. To do that, right-click on the step again and you will see the **Edit Description** and **Delete Description** options (*Figure 3.30*):

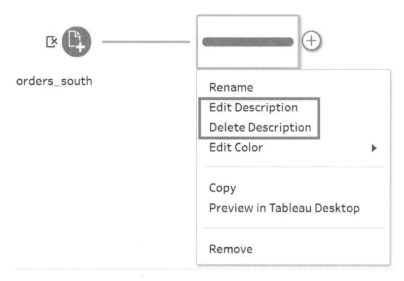

Figure 3.30: Description editing and deleting options for the clean step in the workflow

- **Edit Color** will change the color of the step. This is useful for visual identification in various steps of the flow.

You will now focus on the bottom pane. This is also known as the profile pane, which you saw earlier. Here, you will find the **Filter Values** and **Create Calculated Field** options. You will notice that Prep also gives recommendations related to the data. You can toggle between the three views using the view options.

Figure 3.31: Recommendations for data cleaning in the workflow

- **Change Data Type** changes the column's type to another data type. The following images shows the different data types in Prep:

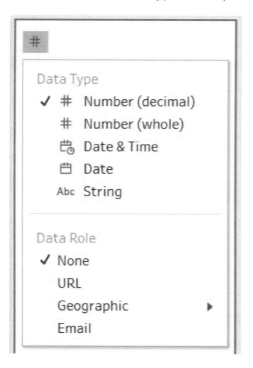

Figure 3.32: Changing the column data type

Currently, the column has the **Number (decimal)** data type selected. If required, you can select **String** to change the column's data type accordingly.

Number (decimal) and **Number (whole)** are numeric data types. **Date & Time** is used for columns consisting of date or time values. A **String** data type is used for columns consisting of character values. You also have **Data Role**. This is applicable to string data types, and further defines the type of string values a column contains.

Often, you will need to change the column data type for correct representation. For example, if a postal code is saved as a numeric data type, then it is not the correct representation. Although postal codes are numbers, their true representation is in the form of a **String,** with a **Geographic** role. You will now learn how to change the data types based on the following examples in Prep. Refer to the recommendations provided:

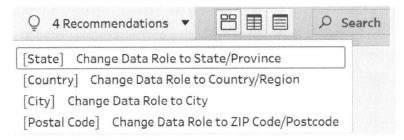

Figure 3.33: Changing the column data type using recommendations

As you can see, **State** is saved as a **String,** but no data role is assigned to it. To assign a data role to **State**, click on the **State** column, then change **Data Role** to **Geographic – State / Province**, as shown in the following screenshot:

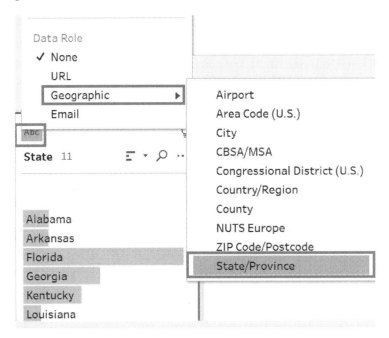

Figure 3.34: Changing the column data role

You can do the same for other columns as well, that is, for **`City`**, **`Postal Code`**, and **`Country`**. All the changes that we perform will be tracked on the **`Changes`** tab.

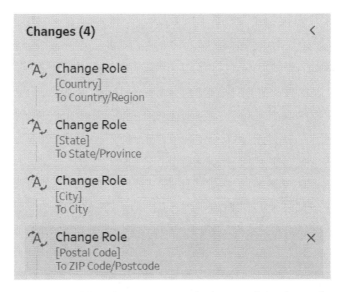

Figure 3.35: Applying the recommendations to the other columns

At any time, if you want to reverse a change, you can select it by hovering over the change and selecting the **Remove** option, as follows:

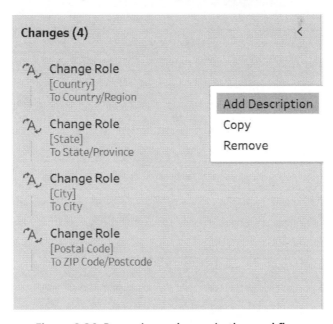

Figure 3.36: Reversing a change in the workflow

This is how the result looks after changing the data type and roles of these columns:

Figure 3.37: How the columns look before the changes

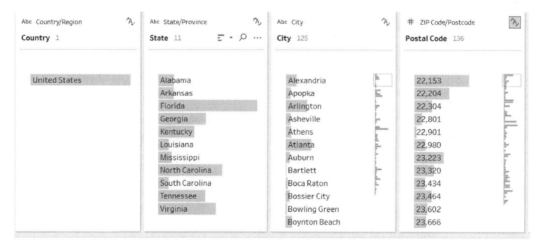

Figure 3.38: Columns after the changes are made

These changes help to create the right type of visualization to draw useful insights – for example, if these were simple string types, you would not be able to create geographical visualizations such as maps. This would restrict your visualization abilities to draw certain insights, such as which cities or which postal codes order most products or how they compare with other cities.

ADDITIONAL CLEAN STEPS

In the previous section, you learned how to add a clean step, and how to track changes using various options related to the clean step. You also saw how to change the data types and data roles. In this section, you will learn about some additional cleaning steps that are available at the individual column level. You will continue working in the same data profile pane.

To access additional cleaning steps, hover over individual columns and click on the ... icon to see the additional options, as follows:

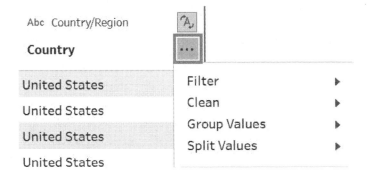

Figure 3.39: More cleaning options

Before proceeding, it is important to note that certain columns might have some unavailable options due to the different data types. For example, for **Country**, **View State – Summary** is disabled. However, it is available for the **Profit** column, as the following screenshot shows:

Figure 3.40: Available options based on column data type

With that in mind, it's time to learn more about the additional options you can use to clean your data.

CLEANING STEPS AT THE COLUMN LEVEL

In this section, you will learn about adding the filter and calculation options on the input data source. You will continue from where you left off, after changing the data roles.

Filter: The filter option allows you to select a subset of the data from the dataset. This option limits the data being pulled into the workflow. Quite often, it is useful to limit your analysis to specific subsets of the data to analyze it further. We can achieve this using the filter options. For example, you might wish to identify the **State** with the highest orders. This can be easily done by sorting the **State** column as follows:

Figure 3.41: Sorting the State column

EXERCISE 3.04: APPLYING A FILTER IN A CLEAN STEP

In this exercise, you will learn how to apply a filter in the clean step. You can see in *Figure 3.41* that Florida has the highest number of orders. You can now filter the data to show only the orders for **Florida**.

Follow these steps to complete this exercise:

1. Click on ... and select **Filter – Selected Values**.

Figure 3.42: Different filter types

2. Select **Florida** from the list and click on **Done** to filter the data:

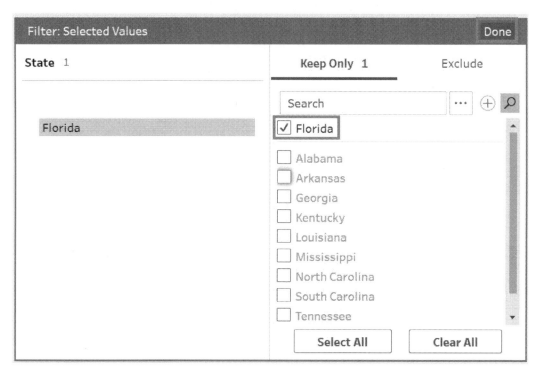

Figure 3.43: Selected Values filter properties

There are also other ways to filter the data using **Calculation...**, **Null Values**, and **Wildcard Match**:

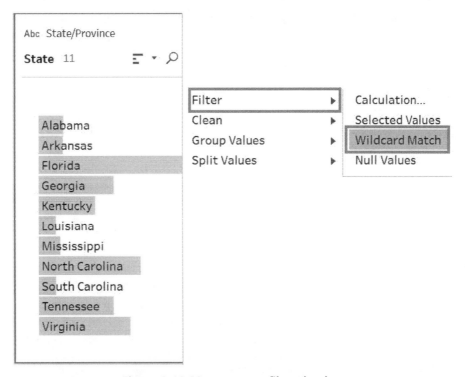

Figure 3.44: More ways to filter the data

3. **Null Values** filters the nulls in the data, while **Wildcard Match** filters based on a keyword.

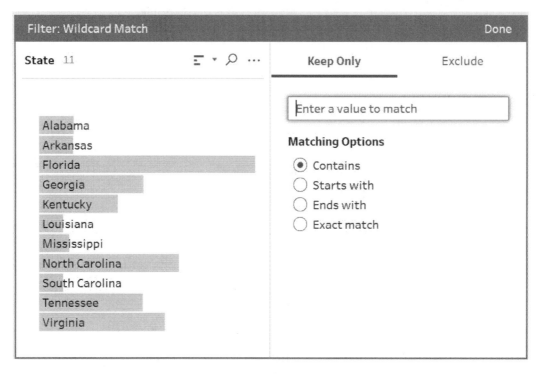

Figure 3.45: Calculation filter properties

As the name suggests, the **Calculation**... filter filters the data based on certain calculation conditions.

4. Now, create a calculation to check which month had the highest orders. To do that, click on the ... icon on the **Order Date** column, then find **Create Calculated Field** and **Custom Calculation**:

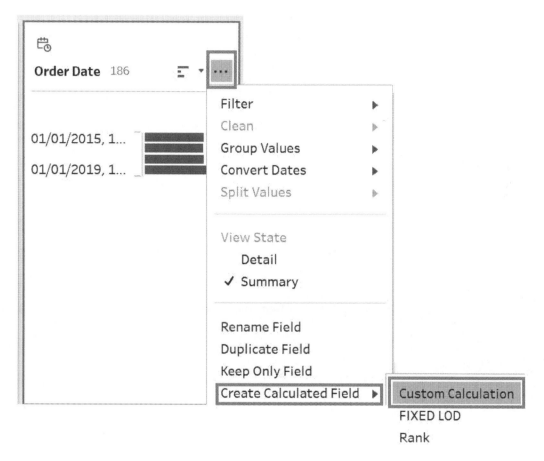

Figure 3.46: Creating a calculation in the workflow

5. This will open the calculation editor. Type the following expression in the editor and rename the calculation **Order_Date_Month**:

```
Month([Order Date])
```

Figure 3.47: Calculation editor properties

6. Sort the months and observe that the highest sales are in November, followed by June:

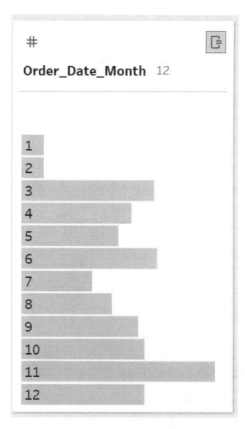

Figure 3.48: New column added using calculations

> **NOTE**
>
> Given timing and version variance, your calculation may result in a different month for highest sales. The step instruction to sort will be the same regardless.

Based on the conditions you specify, you can create calculations in a similar manner for filters. You will learn about calculations in more detail later as you progress through the book.

EXERCISE 3.05: CLEANING A COLUMN IN THE WORKFLOW

In the previous section, you learned how to filter data using various conditions. You also learned how to add calculations to this data source. In this exercise, you will learn about the **Clean** option.

The **Clean** option provides string operations that can be used to clean the column. Examples include removing punctuation marks or junk characters, making the character uppercase or lowercase, removing numbers from the strings, and more. The following steps must be executed to clean a column:

1. Continue with the same workflow from the previous section. Observe the **Product Name** column. It contains a lot of junk characters, such as **#** and **'**. You can remove these characters, as they are not very useful for analysis.

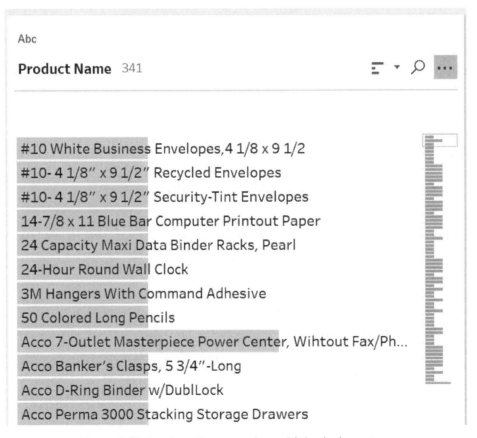

Figure 3.49: Product Name preview with junk characters

2. To access the **Clean** option, click on the ... icon. The **Clean** option will provide a variety of functions to clean the data, as you can see in the next screenshot:

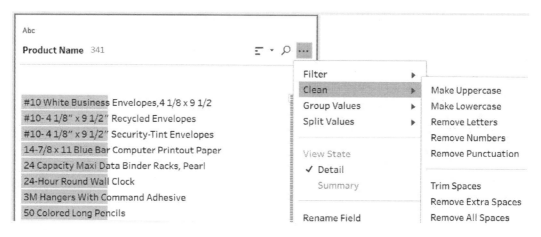

Figure 3.50: Various clean methods

3. Now, use the **Remove Punctuation** option for **Product Name**, as follows:

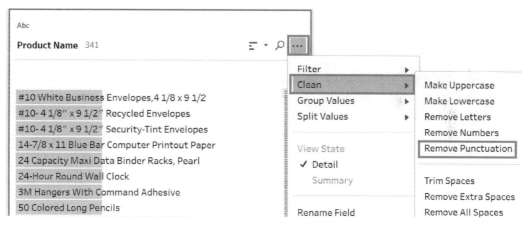

Figure 3.51: Using the Remove Punctuation option to clean the Product Name column

You will get a clean column without the junk characters:

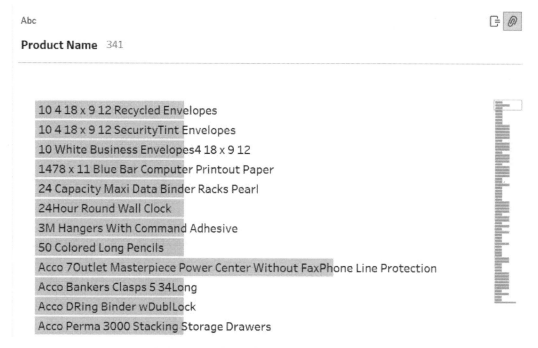

Figure 3.52: Cleaned Product Name column

There are also a few other options, such as removing numbers or characters, changing the casing, and removing spaces in the values. These options are self-explanatory and can be used as and when the project requires.

GROUPING VALUES

To group values means to combine two or more values into a single combined value so that they are represented as one value or group. This is generally used when the data contains spelling errors that result in the same value appearing in different forms.

Think back to our customer with multiple names being represented by different customer IDs. This data issue can be resolved using group values. We can combine the multiple customer names into one customer using group values.

Like the **Clean** option, the **Group Values** option can be accessed by hovering over a column and clicking the ... icon, as follows:

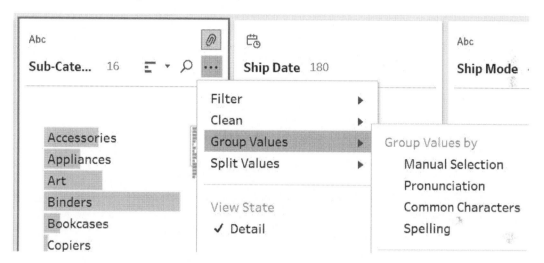

Figure 3.53: Various Group Values methods

You will learn how to use this option in a workflow in the next exercise.

EXERCISE 3.06: GROUPING VALUES INTO A GROUP

In this exercise, you will group the **Sub-Category** values **Chairs** and **Tables** into a group using the **Manual Selection** option. Follow these steps to complete this exercise:

1. Click the dropdown on the **Sub-Category** column, then select **Group Values** and **Manual Selection**:

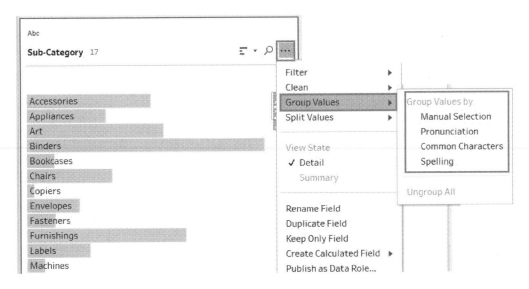

Figure 3.54: Group values using the Manual Selection method

2. Towards the left of the window, select the **Chairs** value, which should add a member group, also called **Chairs**, to the right. By default, the group will have the same name as the first member, which in this case is **Chairs**.

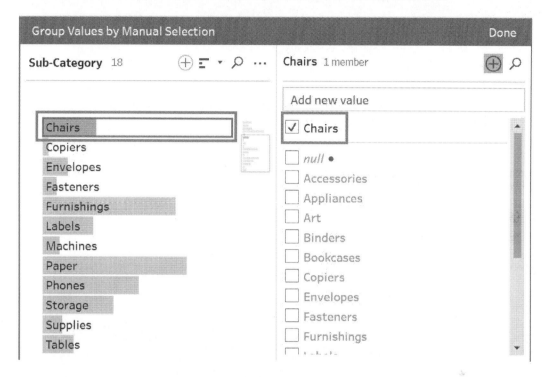

Figure 3.55: Adding members to a group

3. To rename the group to **Office Furniture**, double-click on **Chairs** and type in the new name, as shown in the following figure:

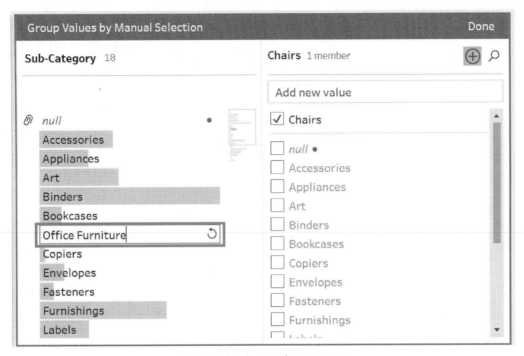

Figure 3.56: Renaming a group

Now the new group name should be visible as follows:

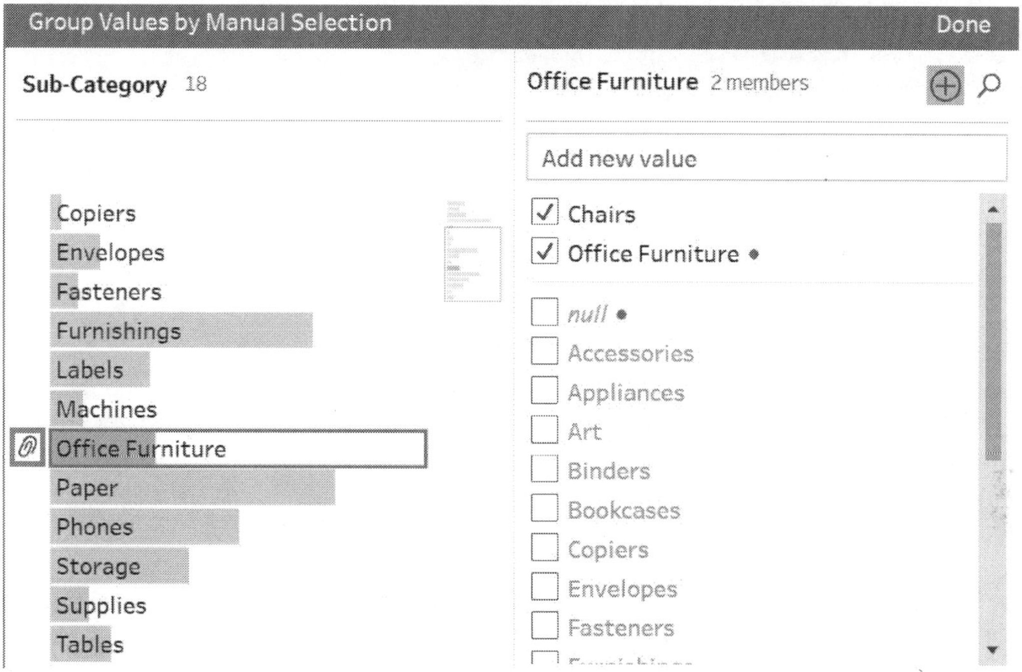

Group Values by Manual Selection	Done

Sub-Category 18	Office Furniture 2 members

Office Furniture

Add new value

- ☑ Chairs
- ☑ Office Furniture •

- Copiers
- Envelopes
- Fasteners
- Furnishings
- Labels
- Machines
- Office Furniture
- Paper
- Phones
- Storage
- Supplies
- Tables

- ☐ *null* •
- ☐ Accessories
- ☐ Appliances
- ☐ Art
- ☐ Binders
- ☐ Bookcases
- ☐ Copiers
- ☐ Envelopes
- ☐ Fasteners

Figure 3.57: Updated group name

4. Now you can add more members to the group using the right column. Add **Tables** to this group by selecting that value:

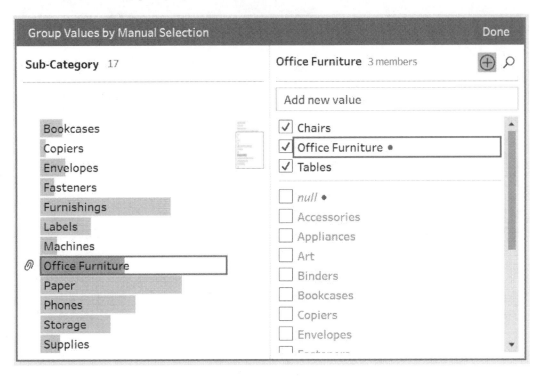

Figure 3.58: Adding additional members to the group

5. You can also add values that are not currently in the data but will be added in the future. To do that, click on the **+** icon and add the value in the textbox. You will see a red dot next to the value, indicating that it does not currently exist in the data. Note that this value should match the future expected value, or else it might not get automatically added to the group.

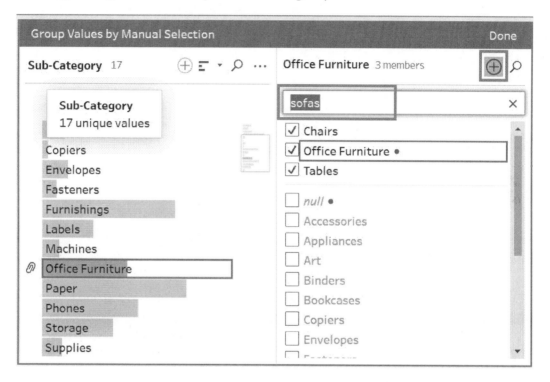

Figure 3.59: Adding future values to the group

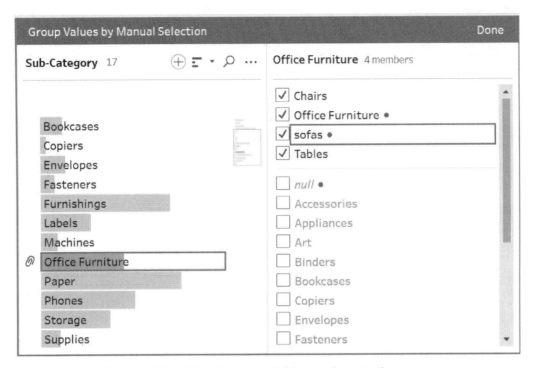

Figure 3.60: Adding future available members to the group

6. Next, click on **Done** to add the group. The new group will be added, indicated by a paperclip icon (*Figure 3.61*).

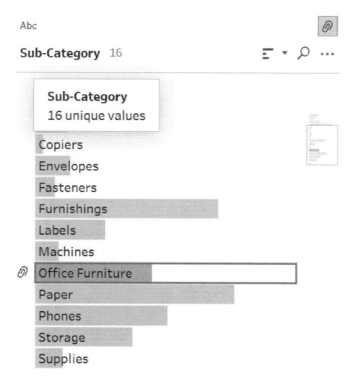

Figure 3.61: The grouped value replaces individual values in the Sub-Category column

This is an example of manual grouping. Another way to group data, is by using built-in algorithms that enable us to do this automatically using pronunciation, common characters, or spelling. A common example is the same phrase written in different ways, such as "Tableau Prep" and "Prep Tableau." These essentially mean the same thing but are written differently. Prep provides built-in algorithms that can identify such values and group them automatically.

SPLITTING VALUES

This option allows us to split column values into multiple sub-values. This can be useful in scenarios where multiple values are stored as a single value based on a delimiter such as , or |. Sometimes, to optimize data storage, multiple values may be stored as a combined column.

Consider the next example of **Product ID**, which contains a combination of **Category**, **Sub-Category**, and the actual **Product ID** fields:

Abc **Product ID**
TEC-PH-10002398
OFF-PA-10001937
OFF-PA-10001947
OFF-BI-10000773
TEC-AC-10002600
OFF-AP-10003914
FUR-FU-10004020
OFF-ST-10001490
FUR-FU-10001756
OFF-BI-10000773
OFF-BI-10001543
OFF-PA-10002120
FUR-FU-10004306
OFF-LA-10001613

Figure 3.62: Combined column value example

EXERCISE 3.07: SPLITTING COLUMNS

Imagine that due to storage size restrictions, you maintain a highly optimized database and make sure it does not consist of duplicate data. You only have the **Product ID** column available. , To obtain the **Category** and **Sub-Category** columns, you might split the **Product ID** column using the **Split Values** option. The following steps will help you complete this exercise:

1. The **Split Values** option can be accessed by clicking on the ... icon and selecting **Split Values**. There are two options available: **Automatic Split** and **Custom Split**.

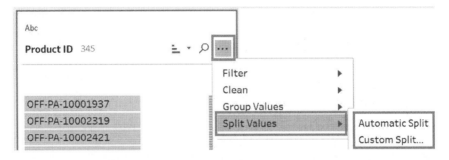

Figure 3.63: Various Split Values methods

2. **Automatic Split** can be applied when you need to split the entire column into multiple parts using a delimiter. If you require **Product ID** to be split into three parts, you can use this option. Select **Automatic Split** on this column and view the results:

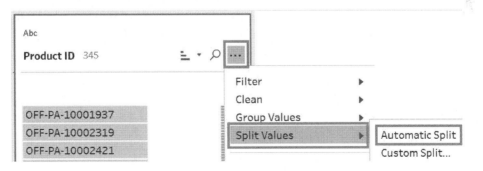

Figure 3.64: Applying automatic split on the Product ID column

You can see in the next screenshot that **Product ID** is now split into three parts using the hyphen (–) separator:

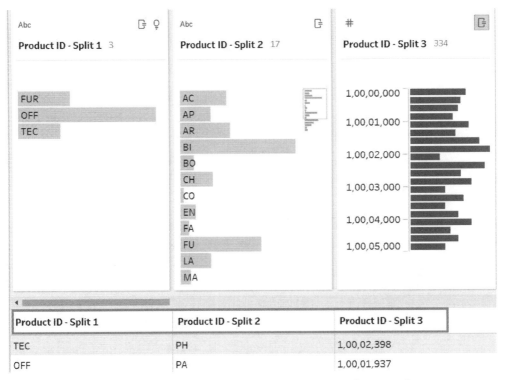

Product ID - Split 1	Product ID - Split 2	Product ID - Split 3
TEC	PH	1,00,02,398
OFF	PA	1,00,01,937

Figure 3.65: Result of an automatic split on the Product ID column

3. Now, suppose you want to have another column consisting of just **Product Category**. This is the first part of the **Product ID** column. Apply the **Custom Split** on **Product ID** to fetch the first part, which is the category. Use *Ctrl + Z* if you are using a PC (it's *Cmmd + Z* on a Mac) to revert to the original column and then apply **Custom Split**, as follows:

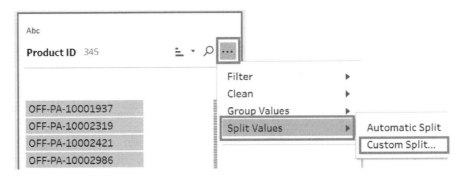

Figure 3.66: Applying Custom Split on the Product ID column

4. Enter the separator (-) along with the split number required, as follows:

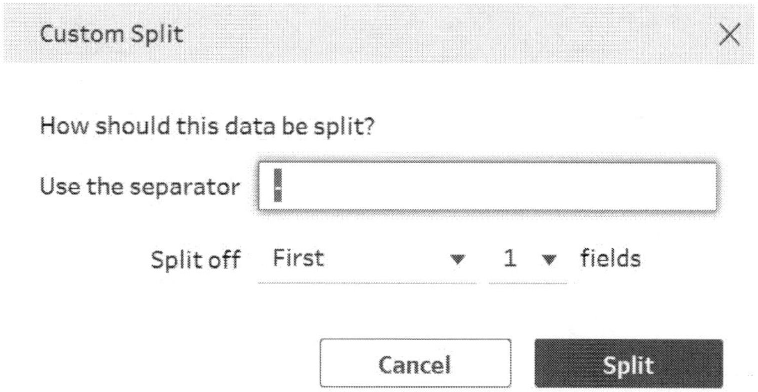

Figure 3.67: Custom Split properties

You will now see a new column that consists of the product category, as follows:

Figure 3.68: Custom split results on the Product ID column

This concludes the discussion on all the clean operations that you can perform on your data. You learned the various ways to clean the data using group, clean, and split. Next, you will learn about data transformation steps such as aggregation, pivot, join, and union.

AGGREGATION, PIVOT, JOIN, AND UNION

You will often encounter certain scenarios where the data might need to be adjusted to suit the visualization requirements. For example, if you are analyzing the monthly sales for your company, you don't need the data for every single day. In this case, you need to aggregate data to the monthly level. This also reduces the amount of data being used for analysis.

Another example, is when the data for all the past years is stored as standalone files, and the current year is stored as a separate file. All the files have a similar column structure. If you were to analyze all the data together, you may need to perform a union transformation to combine all these separate files into a single file.

Such data transformations can be done in Prep. You will now learn about how to do them.

AGGREGATIONS

Aggregations help to change the granularity of data. Granularity, in this context, means the level at which the data is available. For example, consider two files. One file consists of customer information such as customer ID, customer name, address, and joining date. The other table consists of transactional information that the customer has made, such as the number of orders of a particular product. The exercise explores this option in detail.

EXERCISE 3.08: IDENTIFYING HIGH-VALUE CUSTOMERS BASED ON PURCHASES

Suppose your task is to identify high-value customers based on their purchases. To do that, you need to first roll up the transactions file to sum the value of all purchases for each customer ID and then join it with the customer information table. In this exercise, you will connect with the **Orders_South** data and aggregate the **Profit** values in the **Category** and **Ship Mode** columns:

1. You will continue with the same workflow. Click on the **+** icon and select **Aggregate**:

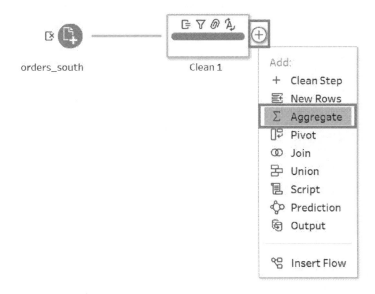

Figure 3.69: Adding an Aggregate step to the workflow

2. This will add an **Aggregate** step to the workflow. Click on it, and select the grouped fields and the aggregated fields. You will see the following on your screen:

Figure 3.70: The Aggregate step added to the workflow

The dimensions or text columns indicated by the **Abc** icon or date columns will act as the **Grouped Fields**, while the measures or numerical columns indicated by **#** will be the **Aggregated Fields**. You can only group text or date columns with numerical columns to form an aggregation.

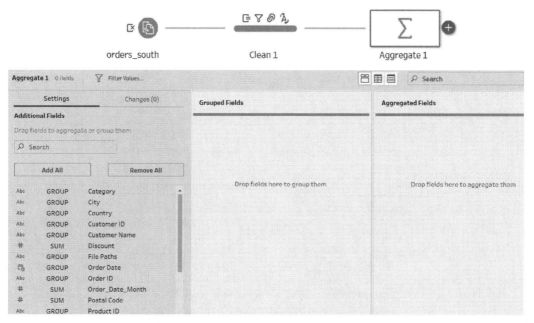

Figure 3.71: Aggregate step properties

3. Change the aggregation type by clicking on the field as follows:

Group by

Sum
Average
Median
Count
Count Distinct
Minimum
Maximum
Std.Dev
Std.Dev Pop.
Variance
Variance Pop.
Percentile   ▶

Figure 3.72: Various aggregation methods

4. Aggregate the data based on sales, grouped per **Category**. Since **Category** is a dimension, it will be under **Grouped Fields**, and **Profit** will be under the aggregated fields (since it is a measure). Double-click on **Category** to add it under **Grouped Fields** and, similarly, double-click on **Profit** to add it under **Aggregated Fields**:

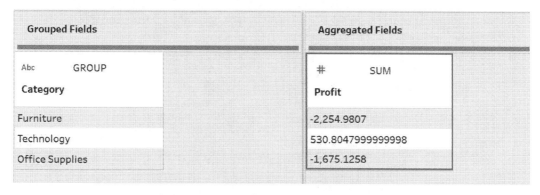

Figure 3.73: Adding grouped and aggregated fields

5. Now the data is grouped by the various **Category** values and **Profit**. To add another dimension to the group, you can double-click and add it to the grouped field section. Now, add **Ship Mode** to **Grouped Fields**:

Grouped Fields		Aggregated Fields
Abc GROUP **Ship Mode**	Abc GROUP **Category**	# SUM **Profit**
Same Day	Office Supplies	-25.9653
Same Day	Furniture	196.9368
Second Class	Furniture	115.1619
Standard Class	Furniture	-2,400.9874
Same Day	Technology	160.8302
Second Class	Office Supplies	-339.4644999999998
First Class	Technology	169.5712
Standard Class	Office Supplies	-1,222.4247000000005
First Class	Furniture	-166.092
Second Class	Technology	764.3715
Standard Class	Technology	-563.968100000001
First Class	Office Supplies	-87.27129999999987

Figure 3.74: Multiple grouped fields aggregation results

6. In addition to cleaning, the clean step also allows you to preview our data. Now add a clean step to this aggregation and preview the data. Toggle to display the data grid using the option highlighted in this screenshot:

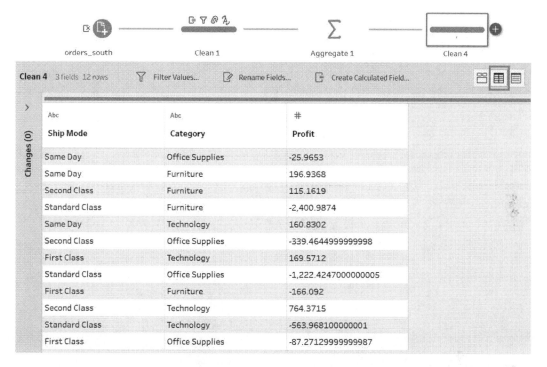

Figure 3.75: Full data preview based on the results of the aggregation step

You have aggregated the data at the **Category** and **Ship Mode** level based on the **Profit** values. In this section, you learned how to aggregate data based on the different levels of granularity. Next, you will learn how to pivot data.

PIVOTING DATA

Sometimes, data is stored in a wide manner as opposed to the tall manner required in Tableau. A wider manner indicates that the data is stored in a horizontal format. An example is the item category and the units sold for various years in Figure 3.76. Here, the data for a category is stored in multiple year columns, indicating a wide format.

Category	Year 1	Year 2	Year 3
TV	100	120	110
Tables	250	240	270
Chairs	320	350	380

Figure 3.76: Wide format

Data in tall format indicates a vertical spread. This means that the different values for an item category would be stored in the same **Category** column. As indicated in Figure 3.77, all the years are in a single **Year** column and all the units sold values are in a **Units Sold** column:

Category	Year	Units Sold
TV	Year 1	100
Tables	Year 1	250
Chairs	Year 1	320
TV	Year 2	120
Tables	Year 2	240
Chairs	Year 2	350
TV	Year 3	110
Tables	Year 3	270
Chairs	Year 3	380

Figure 3.77: Tall format

To use data for visualization, Tableau needs the tall format. In this case, you might have to pivot the data to be used in Tableau. You can do that using the pivot step available in Prep, as the next exercise shows.

EXERCISE 3.09: USING A PIVOT FOR DATA

In this exercise, you will connect to **ConsumerPriceIndices_E_All_Data.csv** and add a pivot on this data. Follow these steps to complete this exercise:

> **NOTE**
>
> Before proceeding with the exercise, make sure to download the CSV file from the GitHub repository for this chapter. You can find the data file at https://packt.link/LUsoU.

1. Connect to the **ConsumerPriceIndices_E_All_Data.csv** data source:

Area Code	Country/Region	Item Code	Item	Months Co	Months	Unit	Y2000	Y2001	Y2002	Y2003	Y2004	Y2005
2	Afghanistan	23013	Consumer I	7001	January							
2	Afghanistan	23013	Consumer I	7002	February							
2	Afghanistan	23013	Consumer I	7003	March							
2	Afghanistan	23013	Consumer I	7004	April							
2	Afghanistan	23013	Consumer I	7005	May							
2	Afghanistan	23013	Consumer I	7006	June							
2	Afghanistan	23013	Consumer I	7007	July							
2	Afghanistan	23013	Consumer I	7008	August							
2	Afghanistan	23013	Consumer I	7009	September							
2	Afghanistan	23013	Consumer I	7010	October							
2	Afghanistan	23013	Consumer I	7011	November							
2	Afghanistan	23013	Consumer I	7012	December							
2	Afghanistan	23012	Consumer I	7001	January							67.19627
2	Afghanistan	23012	Consumer I	7002	February							67.83596
2	Afghanistan	23012	Consumer I	7003	March						60.0775	69.05313
2	Afghanistan	23012	Consumer I	7004	April						61.00551	69.69442

Figure 3.78: Data in CustomerPriceIndices_E_All_Data

As you can see, the country data is stored for the different years in different columns (column **H** to column **X**). This is an example of wide format. To use this data for visualization and analysis, you need to convert it into tall format.

2. Click on **Add Connection - Text File**. Navigate to the **WorldIndicators Files** folder, where you can find this file. Click on **Open** to add it to the flow.

This will add the data to the flow. You can preview the data by adding a clean step. Once it has been added, click on **Clean 4** to open the data grid.

ConsumerPrice...   Clean 5

Figure 3.79: Adding a clean step

You will observe that the various year values are stored in different columns rather than different rows, as you saw in the Excel data preview in *Figure 3.78*. Also, the null values are the blank records where there is no data present:

#	#	#	#	#	#
Y2000	Y2001	Y2002	Y2003	Y2004	Y2005
null	null	null	null	null	null
null	null	null	null	null	null
null	null	null	null	null	null
null	null	null	null	null	null
null	null	null	null	null	null
null	null	null	null	null	null
73.243674	72.414202	76.917049	75.271271	79.945279	82.302032
71.69006	71.518899	76.021746	75.429266	78.565459	81.338265
71.729559	72.322038	75.52143	74.731456	79.53581	82.066357
70.439269	72.019215	74.257473	74.92895	79.03681	81.801716

Figure 3.80: Data preview for year values stored horizontally

3. Make sure it is similar to the **Months** column values (that is, in a single column):

Figure 3.81: Tall format representation by the Months column

4. Do that by clicking on **+** and adding a `Pivot` step:

Figure 3.82: Pivot step properties

5. Next, drag the fields that you want to pivot, that is, all the year fields. Do that by selecting all the year columns. Use *Ctrl* + click to multi-select and drag them to the `Pivoted Fields` area:

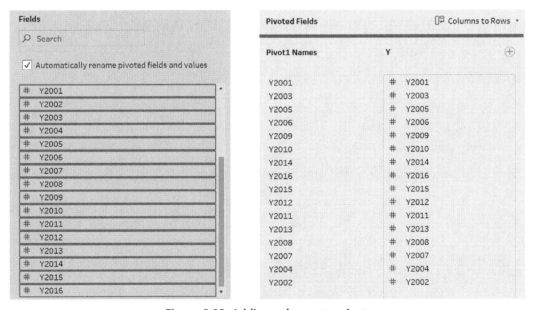

Figure 3.83: Adding columns to pivot

6. Rename these new columns. If you wanted to add one more pivoted field, you can do it by clicking on the **+** icon and adding another pivot to your data.

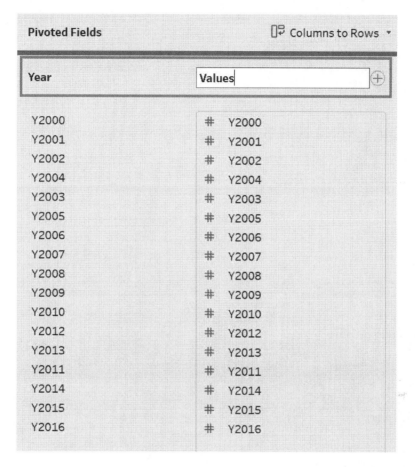

Figure 3.84: Adding additional columns to the pivot table

7. Now, add a clean step to this pivot, and preview the data. Scroll down the data preview window and observe the different values:

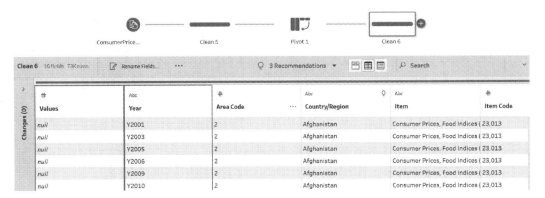

Figure 3.85: Data preview after completing the pivot transformation

You have pivoted data stored as years in various columns to years in a single column. Now you can compare the values for different years to understand the patterns – You will learn about this in further detail in the next chapters. Next, you will learn how to join and union the data.

JOINING AND UNION OF DATA

Joining and union of data is similar to that in Tableau Desktop, with some additional features that help to analyze the join results.

Joining is a way to combine two or more tables into a single table based on certain common fields. The result of this combination contains more columns than the original table, hence it gets extended horizontally. Tableau Prep supports the following join types:

Join Type	Description
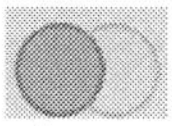 Left	For each row, values from the left table and matching values from the right one will be shown in the results. Unmatched values from the right table will be shown as null in the resulting table.
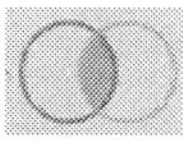 Inner	For each row, this join will include matching values from both tables.
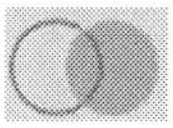 Right	For each row, values from the right table and matching values from the left one will be shown in the results. Unmatched values from the left table will be shown as null in the resulting table.
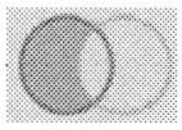 LeftOnly	For each row, this join will only include values from the left table that don't match any values from the right one. Field values from the right table will be shown as null values in the join results.
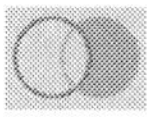 RightOnly	For each row, this join will only include values from the right table that don't match any values from the left table. Field values from the left table will be shown as null values in the join results.
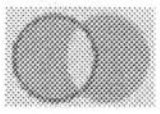 NotInner	For each row, include all of the values from the right and the left tables that don't match.
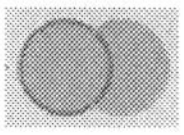 Full	For each row, include all values from the two tables. When a matching value is not found, a null will be shown in the resulting table column value.

Figure 3.86: Types of joins

You will now take a closer look at joins with the next examples.

EXERCISE 3.10: JOINING TWO DATA SOURCES

In this exercise, you will join the **Orders_Central** table with the **Return_
reason_new** table to analyze the order returns. Both the data sources are present
in the **Superstore Files** folder:

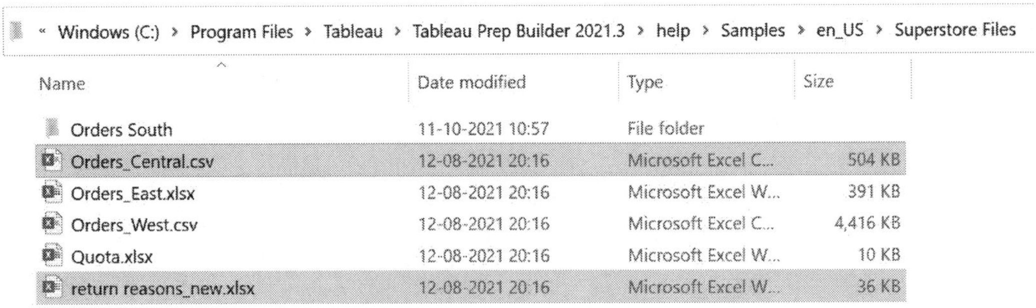

Name	Date modified	Type	Size
Orders South	11-10-2021 10:57	File folder	
Orders_Central.csv	12-08-2021 20:16	Microsoft Excel C...	504 KB
Orders_East.xlsx	12-08-2021 20:16	Microsoft Excel W...	391 KB
Orders_West.csv	12-08-2021 20:16	Microsoft Excel C...	4,416 KB
Quota.xlsx	12-08-2021 20:16	Microsoft Excel W...	10 KB
return reasons_new.xlsx	12-08-2021 20:16	Microsoft Excel W...	36 KB

Windows (C:) > Program Files > Tableau > Tableau Prep Builder 2021.3 > help > Samples > en_US > Superstore Files

Figure 3.87: Input file locations

Follow these steps to complete this exercise:

1. Add the **Orders_Central.csv** data source using **Connect – Text File**
   and select this file. Repeat the same for the **Returns** data. Use **Connect –
   Microsoft Excel** and select the **return reasons_new** file.

2. After adding clean steps for both data sources, you can observe that the **Order
   ID** column can be used as a common field to join these two data sources.

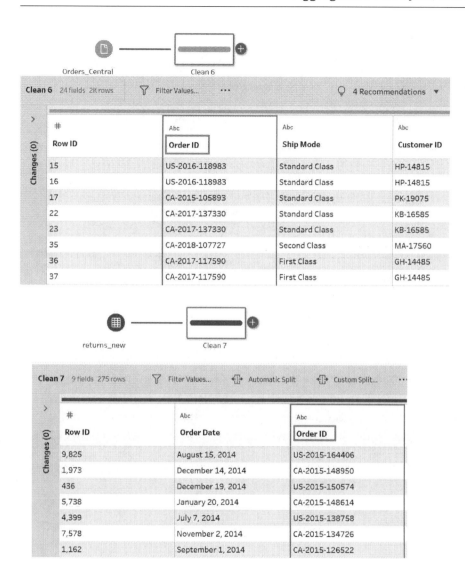

Figure 3.88: Finding the join column

3. Add a join step after the clean step for **Order_Central** as follows:

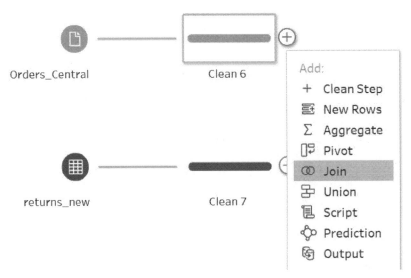

Figure 3.89: Adding a join step in the workflow

4. To do a join, select the step by clicking on it and dropping it on the **Join** icon. Select the **Clean 7** step and drag it on the **Join** step. When this is brought next to the **Join** icon, three options will pop up: **Add**, **Union**, and **Join**. Drop the **Clean 7** step on the **Add** option. Dropping it on the join will add another join step in the flow. You will study the **Union** option in the next section.

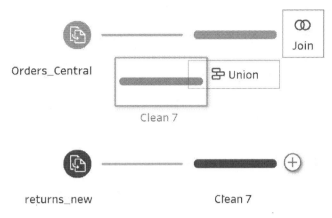

Figure 3.90: Join option preview

5. After adding the join, click on the **Join 1** window to open the properties:

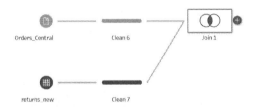

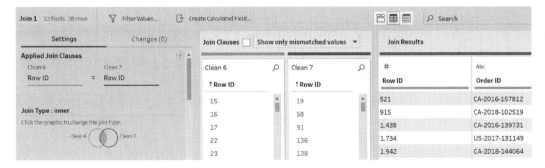

Figure 3.91: Analyzing the join results

6. As you can see in the settings, the default join is based on the **Row ID** column. This needs to be changed to **Order ID**. To change the join clause, click on the **Row ID** column to open a popup with the different columns and select **Order ID**:

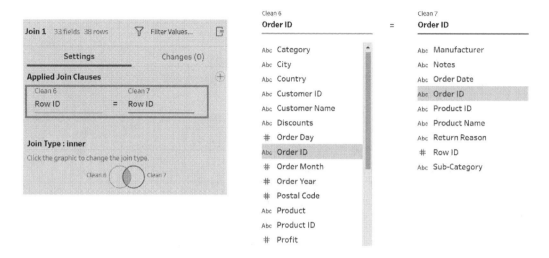

Figure 3.92: Changing the join clause

Once this is done, the workflow will reflect the join based on the **Order ID** column between the **Clean 6** and **Clean 7** steps:

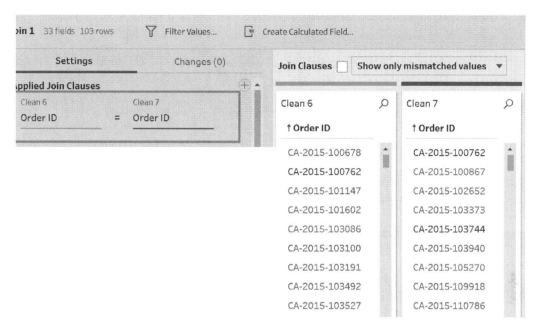

Figure 3.93: Join values preview based on changing the join clause

On your screen, you will see that some values are shown in red on the right-hand side. The red values are the ones that were not joined, and the black ones are the ones that were joined.

7. The default join is the inner join, but clicking on the various shaded areas of the join icon can change the join type. There are multiple join types, which will be discussed in detail after this example. Select the blank area of **clean 6** to change the join type to left, as follows:

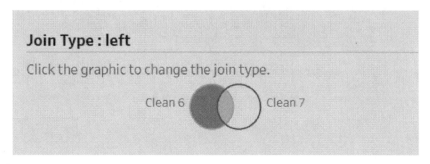

Figure 3.94: Changing the join type

In the **Summary of Join Results**, you can see additional information, such as how many records are included and excluded, along with the matched/unmatched records. Based on the join condition, these values will change. You can see that there are **2,341** orders that have been returned, as indicated by the **Join Results**:

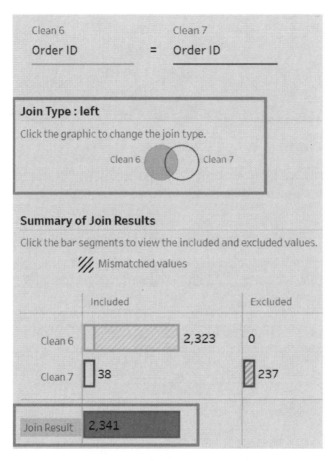

Figure 3.95: Analyzing the join results

8. Hover over the bars for more information in the tooltip:

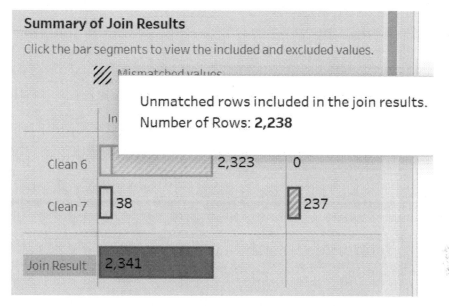

Figure 3.96: More details on hovering over the result bars

Finally, you have **Join Clause Recommendations**, which is a list of matching column names that can be used as potential joining clauses.

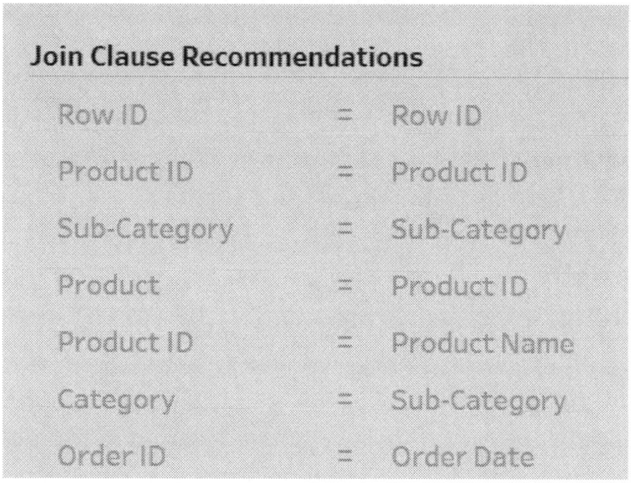

Join Clause Recommendations		
Row ID	=	Row ID
Product ID	=	Product ID
Sub-Category	=	Sub-Category
Product	=	Product ID
Product ID	=	Product Name
Category	=	Sub-Category
Order ID	=	Order Date

Figure 3.97: Join Clause Recommendations

9. As always, add a clean step to preview the joined data:

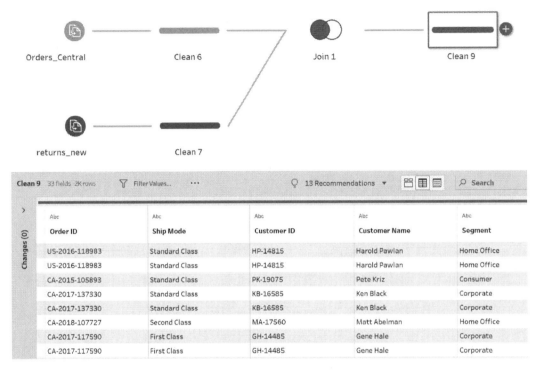

Figure 3.98: Data preview for the join results

You have now joined the **Returns** table with the **Orders_Central** table. You have brought in the records from **Orders_Central** and only the matching records from **return reasons_new**. This join has shown the number of orders that were returned. You can further analyze the returns based upon the customer names, product categories and products, and investigate the reasons for the returns.

UNION

A union is a way to combine multiple tables with similar column structures into a single table. Contrary to a join, in a union, you need to add the data rows vertically. A union is performed when instead of joining, you just want to append the data below another data that has similar columns. A very common example of union is when you have two tables containing similar columns but maintained separately to represent different years. For example, you may want to combine order information for multiple years into a consolidated dataset.

Consider the following tables. Here, the union of A and B results in a single table that contains values from both tables:

A	B
1	3
2	4

Union of A & B
1
2
3
4

Figure 3.99: Union of two tables

EXERCISE 3.11: UNION OF TABLES

In this exercise, you will connect the **Orders_Central** data with **Orders_East** to unite these tables into a single table. Both tables consist of similar columns consisting of order-level information, as shown in the following screenshot:

Row ID	Order ID	Ship Mode	Customer ID	Customer Name	Segment	Country	City	State
15	US-2016-118983	Standard Class	HP-14815	Harold Pawlan	Home Office	United States	Fort Worth	Texas
16	US-2016-118983	Standard Class	HP-14815	Harold Pawlan	Home Office	United States	Fort Worth	Texas
17	CA-2015-105893	Standard Class	PK-19075	Pete Kriz	Consumer	United States	Madison	Wisconsin
22	CA-2017-137330	Standard Class	KB-16585	Ken Black	Corporate	United States	Fremont	Nebraska
23	CA-2017-137330	Standard Class	KB-16585	Ken Black	Corporate	United States	Fremont	Nebraska
35	CA-2018-107727	Second Class	MA-17560	Matt Abelman	Home Office	United States	Houston	Texas
36	CA-2017-117590	First Class	GH-14485	Gene Hale	Corporate	United States	Richardson	Texas
37	CA-2017-117590	First Class	GH-14485	Gene Hale	Corporate	United States	Richardson	Texas
38	CA-2016-117415	Standard Class	SN-20710	Steve Nguyen	Home Office	United States	Houston	Texas
39	CA-2016-117415	Standard Class	SN-20710	Steve Nguyen	Home Office	United States	Houston	Texas
40	CA-2016-117415	Standard Class	SN-20710	Steve Nguyen	Home Office	United States	Houston	Texas
41	CA-2016-117415	Standard Class	SN-20710	Steve Nguyen	Home Office	United States	Houston	Texas
42	CA-2018-120999	Standard Class	LC-16930	Linda Cazamias	Corporate	United States	Naperville	Illinois

Figure 3.100: Data preview for Orders_Central

Category	City	Country	Customer ID	Customer Name	Discount	Order Date	Order ID	Postal Code	Product ID
Furniture	Philadelphia	United States	SF-20065	Sandra Flanagan	0.3	16-07-2018 00:00	US-2018-156909	19140	FUR-CH-10002774
Office Supplies	Philadelphia	United States	TB-21520	Tracy Blumstein	0.7	17-09-2016 00:00	US-2016-150630	19140	OFF-BI-10000474
Office Supplies	Philadelphia	United States	TB-21520	Tracy Blumstein	0.7	17-09-2016 00:00	US-2016-150630	19140	OFF-BI-10001525
Office Supplies	Philadelphia	United States	FH-14365	Fred Hopkins	0.7	06-07-2018 00:00	US-2018-124303	19120	OFF-BI-10000343
Technology	Medina	United States	VW-21775	Victoria Wilson	0.7	02-01-2016 00:00	CA-2016-146262	44256	TEC-MA-10000864
Office Supplies	Dublin	United States	JB-15925	Joni Blumstein	0.7	24-12-2016 00:00	CA-2016-169397	43017	OFF-BI-10002852
Technology	Dublin	United States	JB-15925	Joni Blumstein	0.7	24-12-2016 00:00	CA-2016-169397	43017	TEC-MA-10001148
Office Supplies	Philadelphia	United States	PO-18850	Patrick O'Brill	0.7	30-08-2017 00:00	US-2017-141544	19143	OFF-BI-10001524
Office Supplies	Philadelphia	United States	JL-15850	John Lucas	0.7	25-04-2017 00:00	US-2017-150147	19134	OFF-BI-10001153
Office Supplies	Philadelphia	United States	JL-15850	John Lucas	0.7	25-04-2017 00:00	US-2017-150147	19134	OFF-BI-10001982
Office Supplies	Philadelphia	United States	JD-15895	Jonathan Doherty	0.7	13-04-2015 00:00	CA-2015-122336	19140	OFF-BI-10003656
Technology	Philadelphia	United States	DK-13225	Dean Katz	0.7	03-12-2016 00:00	CA-2016-122756	19140	TEC-MA-10001681
Office Supplies	Philadelphia	United States	AR-10510	Andrew Roberts	0.7	23-05-2015 00:00	US-2015-105767	19134	OFF-BI-10000848
Office Supplies	Grove City	United States	CK-12595	Clytie Kelty	0.7	14-11-2018 00:00	CA-2018-138611	43123	OFF-BI-10002949

Figure 3.101: Data preview for Orders_East

You can see that both files have similar columns. The goal here is to combine these tables to get a single unified data file. Follow these steps to union these data sources:

1. Access both data files from the **Superstore Files** folder:

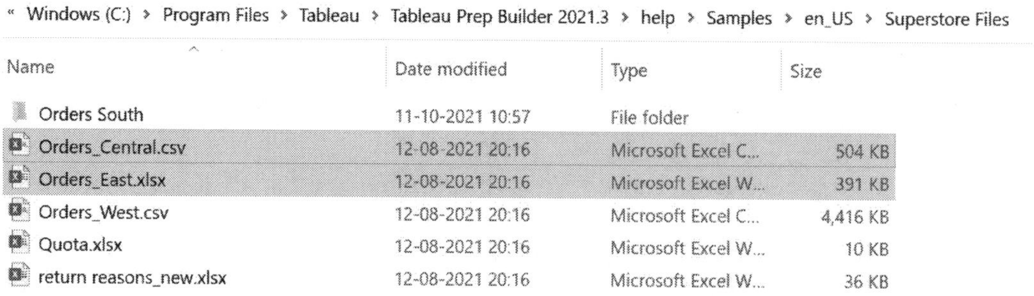

« Windows (C:) › Program Files › Tableau › Tableau Prep Builder 2021.3 › help › Samples › en_US › Superstore Files

Name	Date modified	Type	Size
Orders South	11-10-2021 10:57	File folder	
Orders_Central.csv	12-08-2021 20:16	Microsoft Excel C...	504 KB
Orders_East.xlsx	12-08-2021 20:16	Microsoft Excel W...	391 KB
Orders_West.csv	12-08-2021 20:16	Microsoft Excel C...	4,416 KB
Quota.xlsx	12-08-2021 20:16	Microsoft Excel W...	10 KB
return reasons_new.xlsx	12-08-2021 20:16	Microsoft Excel W...	36 KB

Figure 3.102: File location for the input files

You already have the data source **Orders_Central.csv** in the flow from the previous example.

2. Add the **Orders_East** data. Use **Connect - Microsoft Excel** and select this file. The flow should look like this after adding that step:

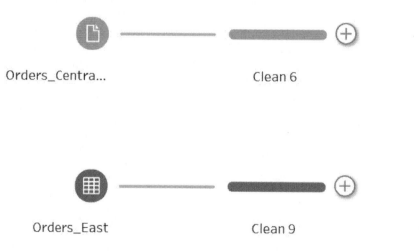

Orders_Centra...   Clean 6

Orders_East   Clean 9

Figure 3.103: Workflow after file the input step

3. Observe that the majority of the column names are the same, which means that you can unite these data sources. The ones that do not match are highlighted in both tables, as shown in the following screenshot:

Orders_Central	Orders_East
Category	Category
City	City
Country	Country
Customer ID	Customer ID
Customer Name	Customer Name
Discounts	Discount
Order Day	Order Date
Order ID	Order ID
Order Month	Postal Code
Order Year	Product ID
Postal Code	Product Name
Product	Profit
Product ID	Quantity
Profit	Region
Quantity	Row ID
Row ID	Sales
Sales	Segment
Segment	Ship Date
Ship Day	Ship Mode
Ship Mode	State
Ship Month	Sub-Category
Ship Year	
State	
Sub-Category	

Figure 3.104: Columns not matching in the two datasets

4. Drag the clean step from **Orders_East** over the clean step of **Orders_Central** and onto the union step:

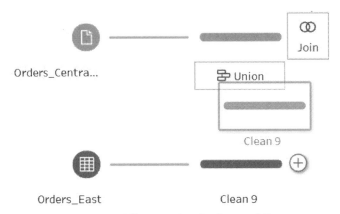

Figure 3.105: Adding a union in the workflow

5. A new union step will be added with the two data sources indicated by the colored columns:

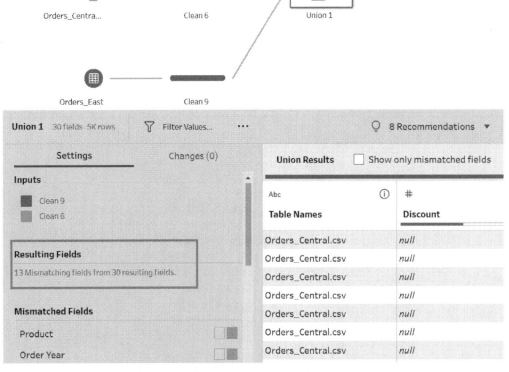

Figure 3.106: Analyzing the union results

You can see that there are 13 mismatched fields.

6. Certain columns, such as **Discounts (Orders_Central)** and **Discount (Orders_East)**, refer to the same column. Similarly, **Product (Orders_Central)** and **Product Name (Orders_East)** are the same columns. Merge them into a single column, as follows.

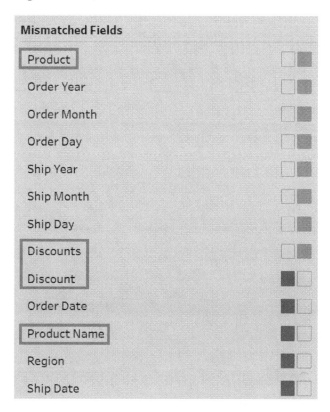

Figure 3.107: Identifying similar columns

7. Select **Discount** first and then hover over the **Discounts** column and click the **+** icon. This will merge the two columns into one:

Figure 3.108: Merging different Discount columns into a single column

8. Select **Product Name**. Prep highlights the other column with the matching word, suggesting a possible match. Now, repeat the same step for **Product** as well.

Figure 3.109: Merging different Product Name columns into a single column

9. The **Region** column is not found in **Orders_East**, so that can be excluded from the union result. To do this, hover over the **Union Results** section and remove the **Region** column, as highlighted in the following screenshot:

Figure 3.110: Excluding a column from union results

Further cleaning can be done by combining **Order Date**, **Order Year**, **Order Month**, **Order Day**, and **Ship Date** using the clean step.

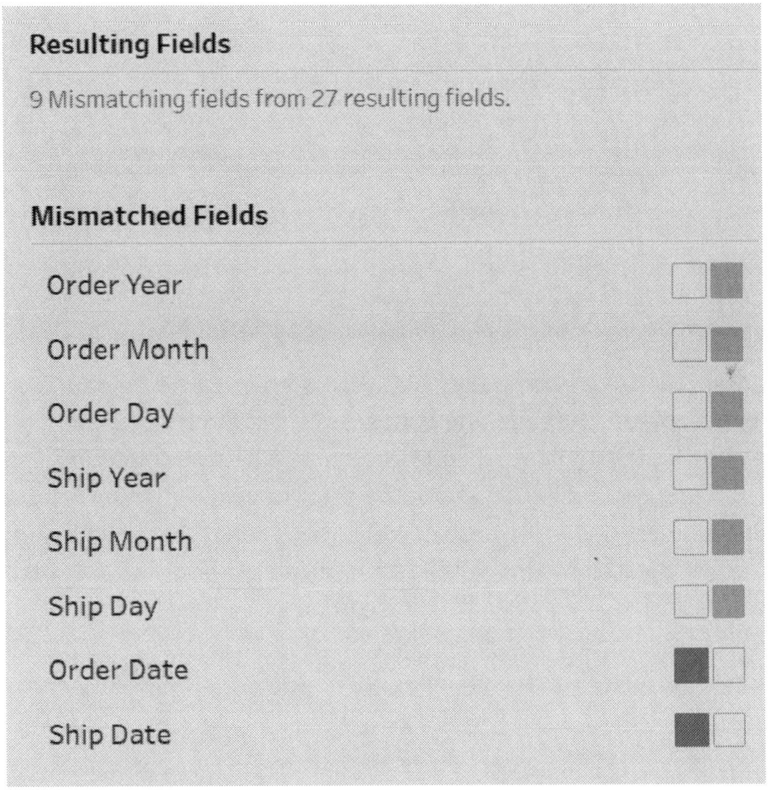

Resulting Fields

9 Mismatching fields from 27 resulting fields.

Mismatched Fields

Order Year

Order Month

Order Day

Ship Year

Ship Month

Ship Day

Order Date

Ship Date

Figure 3.111: Mismatched columns that can be merged using the clean operations

10. Once done, add a clean step to the union to preview the data. You can see that Prep has added a column named **Table Names** to indicate which table the data comes from:

Figure 3.112: Union workflow results

In this section, you learned how to use the union step to combine data from two sources. Once combined, the resulting data source can be used for performing comparative analysis through visualizations. You also saw how to merge mismatched column names. Next, you will learn about the script step. Note that this is not used very often as it is a very advanced step in which complex statistical programs are required to run on the input using R or Python scripts. Therefore, this will be a purely theoretical discussion.

SCRIPT STEP

A script allows you to run external programs written in R or Python. Sometimes, complex statistical computations on the data that cannot be done using Prep might be required. Hence, Prep allows you to integrate these programs into the workflow using the script step.

Before adding the script, you need to establish the connection for R or Python programs using Rserve or TabPy. You can do so using the **Help** menu and the **Settings and Performance** option by going to **Help** – **Setting and Performance** – **Manage Analytics Extension Connection**:

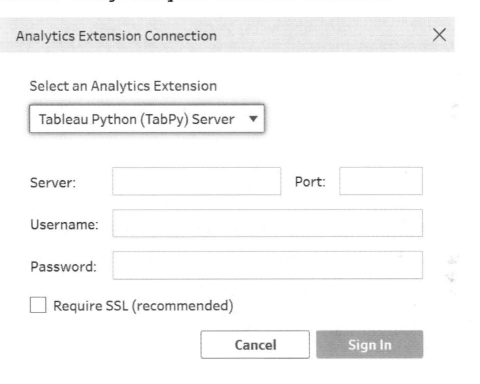

Figure 3.113: Script window properties

Now you can add the server details for R or Python. Once this is done, you can add the script step in the flow. This will open the following window:

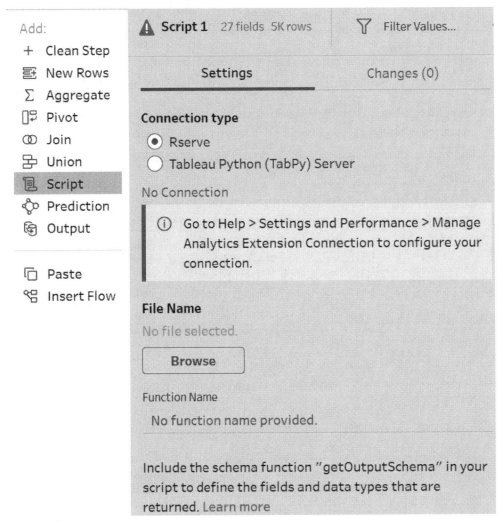

Figure 3.114: Script connection settings

Here, you can add the program file and specify which function needs to run on the data. For further details, you can click the **Learn more** link.

FLOW AND DATA EXPORTS

Once you have finished creating a workflow, you need to export the data or share the workflow so that it can be used in data analysis and visualization in Tableau Desktop. You will learn about the following exporting options in this section:

- Flow saving options

- Data export options

Flow saving options: The workflow can be saved in two formats: `.tflx` and `.tfl`. If you are working by yourself and have all the data in your system, you can save the flow in the Tableau Prep Builder flow (`.tfl`) file format. If you want to share the flow along with the data used in it, use the `.tflx` format, which will combine or package all underlying local files used in the flow, such as the Excel, text, or Tableau extract file, into a single flow file to be shared. Note that only local files can be packaged into a flow. Data from database connections isn't included.

To save a flow, click on the **File** menu, go to **Save As**, and select the format required.

Figure 3.115: Saving a workflow

The next exercise looks at data export options in detail.

EXERCISE 3.12: EXPORTING DATA

Once you have completed the data transformation steps in Prep, the last thing to do is to export this data so that it can be used to develop visualizations. The **Output** step allows you to export the data in multiple formats. In this exercise, you will export the data using the **Output** step.

1. Continuing from the previous example, add an **Output** step to the **Union** step by clicking on the **+** and then selecting **Output**:

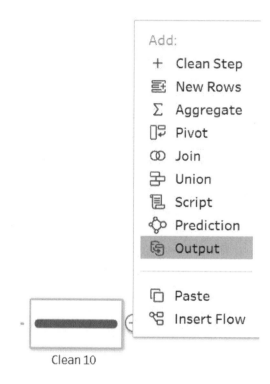

Figure 3.116: Adding an output step

Once this is done, you will see the following window:

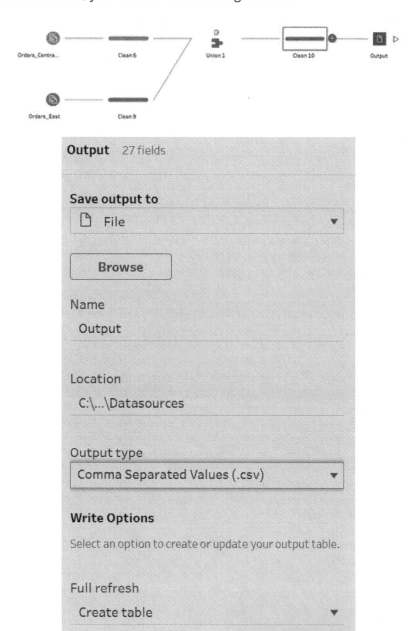

Figure 3.117: Output step properties

2. Save the output in various formats, as the following screenshot shows:

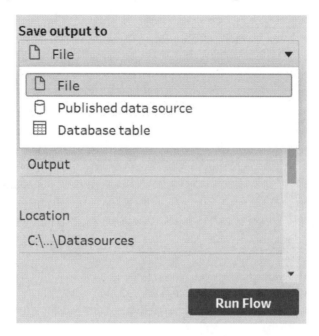

Figure 3.118: Formats for saving the flow output

Here, you will be saving it as the **File** format, but it's important to also know about the other formats.

3. Save it as a **Published data source** on Tableau Server, as a database table in a database such as SQL Server, or elsewhere, as follows:

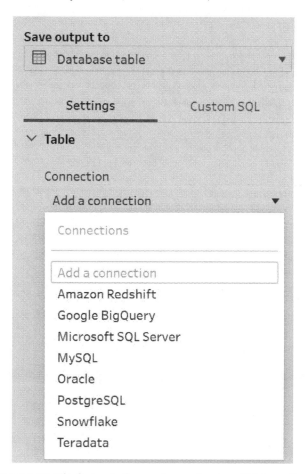

Figure 3.119: File formats for saving output on Tableau Server

4. Select **File** and then select the folder to save to. Enter the output name and set the output type to CSV. You will also see another option, **.hyper** format, which can be used in Tableau Desktop as an extract.

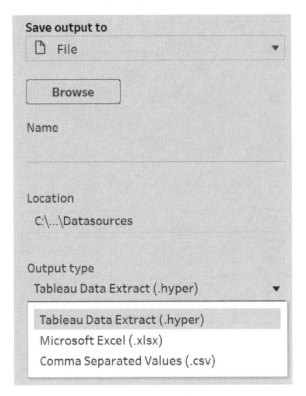

Figure 3.120: CSV file format for saving output

5. Click on **Run Flow** and save the output.

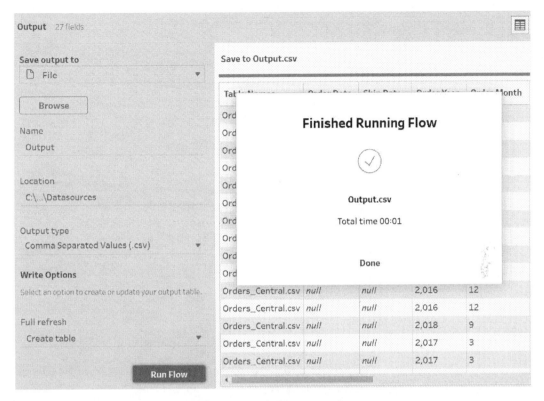

Figure 3.121: Running the flow

6. Once done, navigate to the folder location and check the file:

A	B	C	D	E	F	G	H	I	J	K
Table Names	Order Date	Ship Date	Order Year	Order Month	Order Day	Ship Year	Ship Montl	Ship Day	Row ID	Order ID
Orders_Central.csv			2016	11	22	2016	11	26	15	US-2016-1:
Orders_Central.csv			2016	11	22	2016	11	26	16	US-2016-1:
Orders_Central.csv			2015	11	11	2015	11	18	17	CA-2015-1(
Orders_Central.csv			2017	12	9	2017	12	13	22	CA-2017-1:
Orders_Central.csv			2017	12	9	2017	12	13	23	CA-2017-1:
Orders_Central.csv			2018	10	19	2018	10	23	35	CA-2018-1(
Orders_Central.csv			2017	12	8	2017	12	10	36	CA-2017-1:
Orders_Central.csv			2017	12	8	2017	12	10	37	CA-2017-1:
Orders_Central.csv			2016	12	27	2016	12	31	38	CA-2016-1:
Orders_Central.csv			2016	12	27	2016	12	31	39	CA-2016-1:

Figure 3.122: Workflow output preview

7. When the output type is CSV, the **Full refresh** option that you can see in *Figure 3.122* will overwrite the output file when the flow is run again. If the **.hyper** output format is selected, you can choose to append the new data to the existing extract as well.

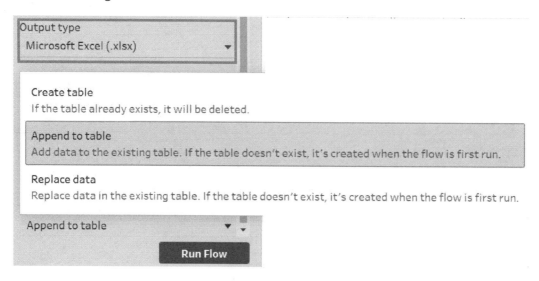

Figure 3.123: Adding new output to existing saved output

Now that you have learned about the different ways to transform data, it's time to get some hands-on practice on some project-based scenarios.

ACTIVITY 3.01: FINDING THE MONTH WITH THE HIGHEST ORDERS

As a store manager, you will have come across situations in which you would like to assess your store's performance by its sales. Hence, it is important to analyze patterns in the sales of the products. Further, you can also identify the products that sell more compared to other products, and this analysis can help to further increase their sales. Additionally, you want to know if there is a pattern in how the products sell in different months. If a pattern exists, then it can be analyzed and used to design strong marketing strategies to boost the store's sales and revenue.

Usually, the order information is kept separate from the product information. This is to keep the data optimized.

NOTE

The data that you will use in this activity is stored in **Activity File. xlsx**. The **Orders** sheet contains the **Order ID** and the **Product** categories. You can download the Excel file from the GitHub repository for this chapter at https://packt.link/iWtp4.

A	B
Order ID	Product Category
714997-12-2016	3
726827-7-2016	2
653442-11-2019	6
971353-6-2015	4
510196-1-2017	4
703859-5-2016	6
142007-10-2015	7
167157-5-2019	4
823162-9-2017	7
786924-10-2019	1
828138-3-2018	4
145954-1-2017	3
426894-10-2017	1
172293-12-2016	1
884933-1-2015	6
492691-9-2019	7
685568-12-2018	7
366616-1-2015	5
773281-5-2018	5

Figure 3.124: Orders sheet preview

As you can see, the **Order ID** column is a combination of the ID, month, and year of each order. **Product Category** is an ID column. Further details about this can be found in the **Product Category** sheet:

A	B
ID	Type
1	Accessories
2	Apparel
3	Books
4	Departmental
5	Health
6	Dining
7	Travel

Figure 3.125: Product Category sheet preview

To complete this activity successfully, you need to apply your knowledge of splits, joins, and cleaning to identify important sales trends. Specifically, you need to answer the following questions:

Which month and year combination has the highest orders?

Which product category has the highest orders?

> **NOTE**
>
> The solution to this activity can be found here: https://packt.link/CTCxk.

ACTIVITY 3.02: DATA TRANSFORMATION

Now you know about the trends for various products, it would be useful to analyze customer information to better understand customer behavior towards each product. With the results of this analysis, you can design customized offers and coupons that can enhance a customer's shopping experience. This will also help create brand affinity with the customers, which can eventually lead to an increase in sales. In this activity, you will combine customer information with the previous workflow to get a unified view of orders, products, and customers. You will continue using the same Excel sheet from the previous activity to complete this one.

The customer order information is stored in the **CustomerOrders** sheet, as shown in the following screenshot:

A	B	C	D	E	F	G	H	I	J	K	L
Order_ID	Customer_ID	Y2015	Y2016	Y2017	Y2018	Y2019	Q15	Q16	Q17	Q18	Q19
714997-12-2016	1738	0	6316	0	0	0	0	93	0	0	0
726827-7-2016	2075	0	0	0	0	0	0	22	0	0	0
653442-11-2019	2122	0	0	0	0	60847	0	0	0	0	845
971353-6-2015	2125	395	0	0	0	0	61	0	0	0	0
510196-1-2017	1772	0	0	13174	0	0	0	0	31	0	0
703859-5-2016	2004	0	0	0	0	0	0	99	0	0	0
142007-10-2015	1793	342	0	0	0	0	77	0	0	0	0
167157-5-2019	2023	0	0	0	0	58655	0	0	0	0	393
823162-9-2017	2139	0	0	8250	0	0	0	0	81	0	0
786924-10-2019	1668	0	0	0	0	27423	0	0	0	0	500
828138-3-2018	1836	0	0	0	10683	0	0	0	0	160	0
145954-1-2017	1974	0	0	5849	0	0	0	0	46	0	0
426894-10-2017	2009	0	0	12231	0	0	0	0	71	0	0
172293-12-2016	1905	0	0	0	0	0	0	97	0	0	0
884933-1-2015	1905	874	0	0	0	0	28	0	0	0	0
492691-9-2019	1760	0	0	0	0	75304	0	0	0	0	289

Figure 3.126: CustomerOrders sheet preview

You can see that the data is stored in a wide format, that is, it is spread horizontally across different years for each customer. You will need to pivot this data to use it in the workflow.

Next, you must join this information with the **CustomerNames** sheet, which looks like the following:

A	B	C
Customer ID	First name	Last Name
1738	Amber	Richards
2075	Tess	Campbell
2122	Isabella	Martin
2125	Ashton	Brown
1772	Dominik	Allen
2004	Cherry	Riley
1793	Amelia	Ellis
2023	Dale	Montgomery
2139	Oliver	Barrett
1668	Frederick	Myers
1836	Lana	Johnston
1974	Dominik	Harris
2009	Jordan	Wilson
1905	Maria	Wells
1760	Arnold	Fowler

Figure 3.127: CustomerNames sheet preview

In this activity, your goal is to identify the top five high-value customers, based on the number of orders.

You also need to export this data so that you can analyze it better using visualizations in Tableau Desktop.

Quantity	Sales	Customer Name	Month-Year	Month	Year	Order ID	Product Category	Order_ID	Customer_ID
0	0	Amber Richards	01-12-2016	12	01-01-2016	714997-12-2016	Apparel	714997-12-2016	1738
0	0	Tess Campbell	01-07-2016	7	01-01-2016	726827-7-2016	Accessories	726827-7-2016	2075
0	0	Isabella Martin	01-11-2019	11	01-01-2019	653442-11-2019	Departmental	653442-11-2019	2122
61	395	Ashton Brown	01-06-2015	6	01-01-2015	971353-6-2015	Apparel	971353-6-2015	2125
0	0	Dominik Allen	01-01-2017	1	01-01-2017	510196-1-2017	Apparel	510196-1-2017	1772
0	0	Cherry Riley	01-05-2016	5	01-01-2016	703859-5-2016	Travel	703859-5-2016	2004
77	342	Amelia Ellis	01-10-2015	10	01-01-2015	142007-10-2015	Travel	142007-10-2015	1793
0	0	Arnold Montgomery	01-05-2019	5	01-01-2019	167157-5-2019	Travel	167157-5-2019	2023
0	0	Oliver Barrett	01-09-2017	9	01-01-2017	823162-9-2017	Travel	823162-9-2017	2139
0	0	Frederick Myers	01-10-2019	10	01-01-2019	786924-10-2019	Apparel	786924-10-2019	1668
0	0	Lana Johnston	01-03-2018	3	01-01-2018	828138-3-2018	Departmental	828138-3-2018	1836
0	0	Dominik Harris	01-01-2017	1	01-01-2017	145954-1-2017	Dining	145954-1-2017	1974
0	0	Jordan Wilson	01-10-2017	10	01-01-2017	426894-10-2017	Apparel	426894-10-2017	2009
0	0	Maria Wells	01-12-2016	12	01-01-2016	172293-12-2016	Books	172293-12-2016	1905
28	874	Maria Wells	01-01-2015	1	01-01-2015	884933-1-2015	Accessories	884933-1-2015	1905
0	0	Arnold Fowler	01-09-2019	9	01-01-2019	492691-9-2019	Dining	492691-9-2019	1760

Figure 3.128: Activity 2 output sheet preview

NOTE

The solution to this activity can be found here: https://packt.link/CTCxk.

SUMMARY

In this chapter, you learned how to connect to various data sources. After connecting to the data, you learned how to analyze it using data profiling. Then, you learned to clean the data using various methods, such as filtering, creating calculations, groups, and splits. Cleaning data is a prerequisite for effective data analysis, and you will be using these methods throughout the remainder of this book.

Once you cleaned the data, you looked at ways to group data using aggregation, and then learned to transform it with pivots. You also combined multiple data sources using the join and union options. Finally, you learned about how to save, share, and export your workflow and the data.

The key takeaway from this chapter is how to transform data efficiently based on the project requirements so that it becomes fit for visualization. In the next chapter, you will use the skills you have learned in this chapter, such as aggregation, joins, and groups, to create charts in Tableau.

4

DATA EXPLORATION: COMPARISON AND COMPOSITION

OVERVIEW

In this chapter, you will create your first chart in Tableau and work through some basic and intermediate charts, such as tree maps, bar-in-bar charts, and stacked area charts. You will learn how to choose the optimal chart for a given scenario, look at the best ways to create a trend report, and explore comparisons across measures (using bar-in-bar and bullet charts). Then, in this lesson's final activity, you will put all you've learned into practice by analyzing data from Singapore's vehicle population audits over the past decade. By the end of this chapter, you will be familiar with working with bar charts, area charts, and **Marks** cards, which are used to add contextual detail to charts and views.

INTRODUCTION

Thus far, you have prepared, imported, and manipulated data for your visualizations. Considering that Tableau is a *business intelligence and visualization tool*, it is natural to now start creating your first charts. Before you can do this, however, (and certainly before you can create more advanced charts as you will in *Chapter 5, Data Exploration: Distribution and Relationships*), you must first learn the ins and out of creating charts.

For this reason, you'll only be creating some basic charts initially, and then eventually work through some intermediate-level charts, such as tree maps and bar-in-bar charts. The goal for this chapter is to be able to answer questions such as "*How much profit was generated in sales by each sub-category in a specific year?*," which is basically asking "*How much of your total sales was generated by each sub-category?*" In doing so, this chapter also teaches you how to remove complex terminology and communicate about data effectively.

Tableau is an intuitive and flexible tool. You can consider Tableau the Photoshop of business intelligence. In Photoshop, there are multiple ways for you to achieve the same result with an image; similarly, in Tableau, there is often more than one way to create the same chart. Tableau's **Show Me** panel comes in pretty handy most of the time, though the goal of this book is also to show you methods for creating these charts without the **Show Me** panel. This chapter will try to simplify most charts by describing when they should be used, why a chart is useful, and for what data type they are useful.

The whole chapter is designed so that, as a reader, you can follow along with detailed steps for each exercise and activity, including creating both basic and intermediate-level charts. But that does not mean you need to memorize these steps; instead, try to understand the reasoning behind why we are doing what we are doing. Although each step in the exercise of this chapter includes as many details as possible, you are encouraged to ask yourself questions such as, "*Why is this step being done, and can I improve the method?*" You might find that you can indeed obtain a given visualization using different means and, similarly, that the charts will get better as you unleash your creativity.

EXPLORING COMPARISONS ACROSS DIMENSIONAL ITEMS

Before diving into chart making, it is important to differentiate between dimensions and measures.

Every column that is present in some data has a data type associated with it, such as string, integer, or date. Also, every column that exists in some data is either a dimension or a measure. **Dimensions** are qualitative or categorical data, such as names, regions, dates, or geographical data, and the columns have categories of distinct values. Measures, on the other hand, are quantitative values that can be aggregated.

Consider the following: a `Country` column has country names such as Canada, India, and Spain. Can you sum the regions? Would a sum of Canada, India, and Spain make any sense? No, it wouldn't, so a region is a dimension. Similarly, data to which you can apply mathematical functions, such as sum, average, min/max, and so on, are measures. Hence, the rule of thumb is as follows: columns to which you can apply a mathematical function are columns of measures, and data you cannot apply functions to are columns of dimensions.

In this book, whenever measures are mentioned, it means that the chart will contain numerical/quantitative data in the view, whereas whenever dimensions are mentioned, we will be using qualitative/categorical data in the view.

BAR CHART

The bar chart is a versatile chart type that makes it easy to quickly understand data for spot checking or adding part of a total comparison for some categorical data. No other charts can beat the flexibility, ease of understanding, and usability of bar charts. The length of the bars in a bar chart represents the proportional aspect of the value for that categorical variable. The illustrative aspect of the bar chart makes it one of the most used charts; it gives accurate insights into our data. Bar charts in Tableau can use a combination of zero or more dimensions and one or more measures.

> **NOTE**
>
> Exercises in this chapter will use the sample **Superstore** dataset, which comes pre-loaded into each Tableau Desktop installation. Our version of Tableau Desktop contains another **Sample – Superstore** dataset, which has data till 2019; Tableau recently updated the data file to also include 2020 data, which you will have if you are using the latest version of Tableau Desktop. So, if your metrics/charts are not exactly the same as ours, do not worry. Our goal is to teach you the skills to develop these charts, reports, and dashboards instead of having you replicate our exact charts.

EXERCISE 4.01: CREATING BAR CHARTS

As a business analyst for your organization, one of the stakeholders has asked you to create a report displaying the total sales and profits across categories and segments using bar charts. You will be using the **Sample – Superstore** dataset to visualize the data.

Dataset: **Superstore**

Dataset download link: https://packt.link/cX32T.

> **NOTE**
>
> In Tableau, **continuous** fields are **green**, and when they're **discrete**, they're **blue**.

The following steps will help you complete this exercise:

1. Load the **Orders** table from the sample **Superstore** dataset in your Tableau instance.

2. Click on the **Show Me** panel in the top-right corner and hover over the bar chart. You will observe that it says **For horizontal bars try 0 or more Dimensions | 1 or more Measures**.

Figure 4.1: Bar chart in the Show Me panel

In this exercise, you will begin with no dimensions and only one measure, before moving on to adding dimensions to your view.

3. Drag **Sales** to **Rows** (for a vertical bar chart) or **Columns** (for a horizontal bar chart).

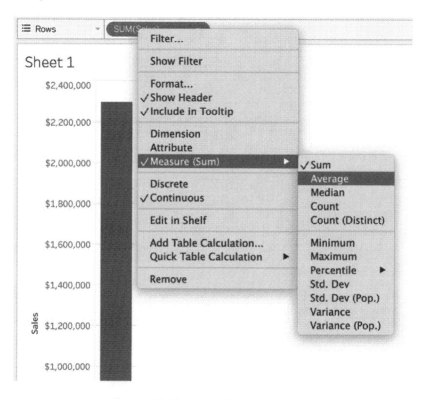

Figure 4.2: Changing the aggregation

When you drag Sales to the Columns/Rows shelf, the default aggregation changes to SUM(Sales).

4. Click on the **SUM(Sales)** capsule in the **Columns/Rows** shelf and change the aggregation from **SUM(Sales)** to any other aggregation average.

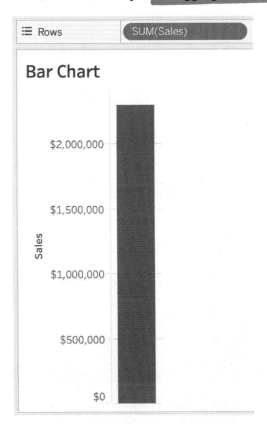

Figure 4.3: Bar chart for the sales figure

In the preceding screenshot, note that the total sales figure is around **$2.3M** for the whole store, which is the least granular metric in our sample Superstore dataset. Next, you will change the granularity of your bar chart.

5. To do that, add a dimension to your view. Add a **Category** dimension to our **Columns** shelf. When you add the **Category** dimension to the view, you get three bars to represent each category. Thus, you've just changed your granularity from the sum of sales for all the data to the sum of sales for each category.

    For better readability, also add **Sales** from the **Measures** data pane to the **Label Marks** card. As we can see, **SUM(Sales)** is now divided by category:

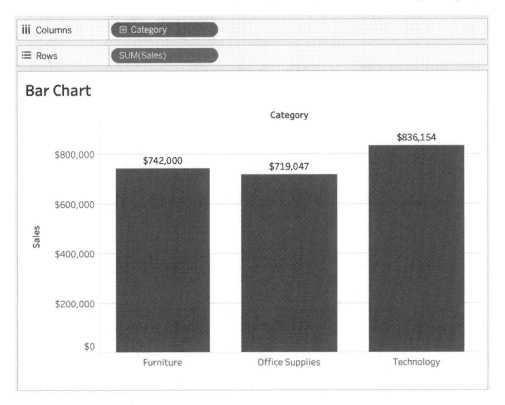

Figure 4.4: Sales by category

The preceding chart uses one dimension and one measure, so we can see that the total sales of Furniture, Office Supplies, and Technology are **$742,000**, **$719,000**, and **$836,000**, respectively. However, what if we want to study the total sales for each of these categories in more detail? We can make it more granular by adding more dimensions or measures. Let's explore our options in the next step.

6. Drag **Segment** to the **Columns** shelf.

You will notice that the sales by category are now divided into sales by segment and category. We just added another level of granularity to our view:

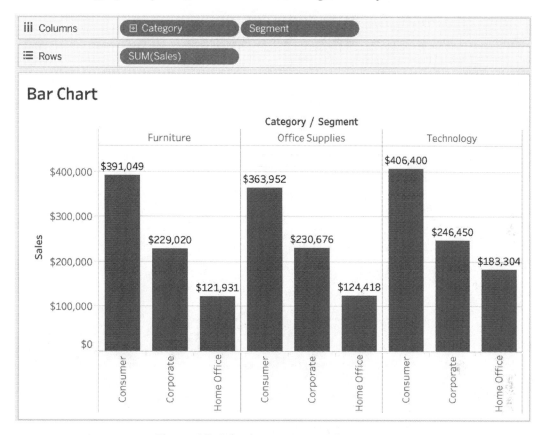

Figure 4.5: Sales by category and segment

In the preceding figure, you can see that even though **Technology** had the highest sales, the **Corporate** and **Home Office** segments of all three categories are not so performing well and will require attention. As the total sales of the categories are now bifurcated, it gives you more visibility as to how many sales you have in each of the segments (that is, **Consumer**, **Corporate**, and **Home Office**). Now that you know the sales values in greater detail, you can also find out the amount of profit gained in each of the categories and segments.

7. Add another measure, **Profit**, to the **Rows** shelf. As soon as you drop the measure onto the **Columns** shelf, you can see that a new row was added for profits:

Figure 4.6: Sales and profits by category and segment

As you can see, there is very little profit gained from **Furniture** and a huge amount of profit from **Technology**. This will help in making great business decisions as we now know that investing more in **Technology** and **Office Supplies** is more profitable.

When you create a bar chart one way, either horizontally or vertically, you will on occasion find that your dashboard design or storyboard design (a storyboard is where you use multiple visualizations/dashboards to convey a story) would be more aesthetically pleasing if the alignment was different—say, vertical instead of horizontal. There are multiple ways to change the alignment; the manual method is demonstrated in the next step.

8. Drag both the **Columns** dimensions to the **Rows** shelf and vice versa. Alternatively, Tableau makes it easy to swap things around by giving us a **Swap** button in our tool menu.

The final output is as follows:

Figure 4.7: Horizontally aligned bars

In this exercise, we explored how adding more granularity to our views can help add more context and data to our views without over cluttering.

This wraps up this section on bar charts for one or more dimensional items. Next, we will explore comparisons over time by using bar charts and line charts.

EXPLORING COMPARISONS OVER TIME

As an analyst, one of the most common requests that stakeholders will have is about comparing certain KPIs/metrics over time (for example, revenue quarter on quarter). In this section of the book, you will use date dimensions to create charts with which you can compare your KPIs over a certain time period. You will use date dimensions to compare metrics using a bar chart first and then move on to using line charts for KPI comparison.

EXERCISE 4.02: CREATING BAR CHARTS FOR DATA OVER TIME

Imagine you are a business analyst who is asked to provide a report about the total sales of your organization in different segments, namely, **Consumer**, **Corporate**, and **Home Office**, over a period of time. Use the sample **Superstore** dataset provided by Tableau to visualize the chart and display the output.

Perform the following steps to complete the exercise:

1. Load the the **Orders** table from the sample **Superstore** dataset in your Tableau instance.

2. Drag **Sales** to your **Rows** shelf.

3. Add **Order Date** to the **Columns** shelf. Tableau will automatically create a line chart (which will be covered in detail in the next exercise).

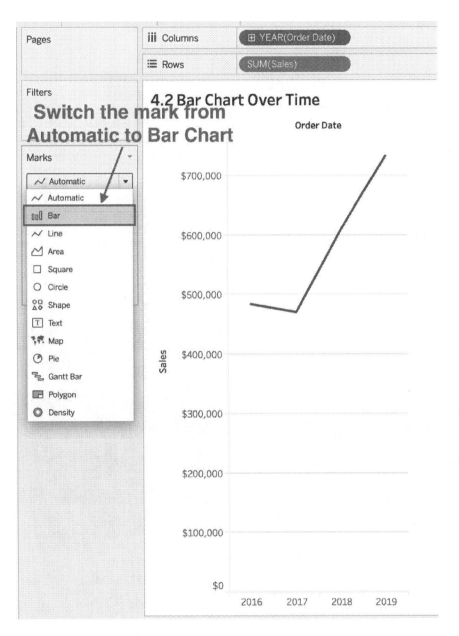

Figure 4.8: Bar chart over time as a line chart

The preceding figure shows the sales of the products on a yearly basis in the form of a line chart. To change the marks from line chart to bar chart, click first on the dropdown in the Marks shelf, then Bar as shown in the preceding figure. The view can be read as sales by year.

4. For readability, add **Label** to **Bars** by dragging **Sales** from the measures **Data** pane to the label in the **Marks** card:

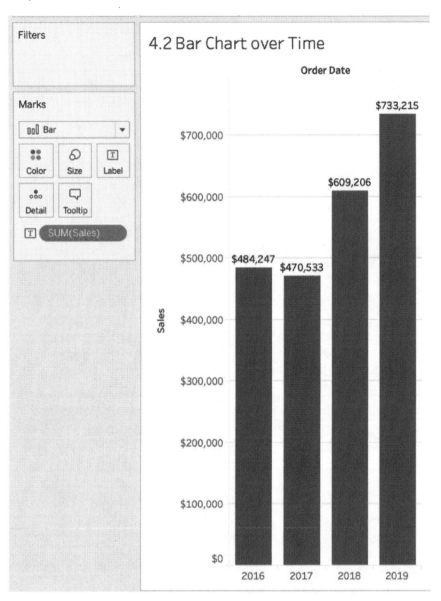

Figure 4.9: Sales by year (bar chart over time)

As you can see, by adding the labels, you have the exact sales values earned in the respective years. But you still don't know the value of sales earned over time for each of the segments. You will have to change the granularity of the view from sales by year to sales by year by segment.

5. To achieve that, drag **Segment** to the **Columns** shelf.

The view can change a lot depending on where you place your **Segment** on the **Columns** shelf. If you place **Segment** after **Order Date**, your view will read as sales by year by segment with the following view:

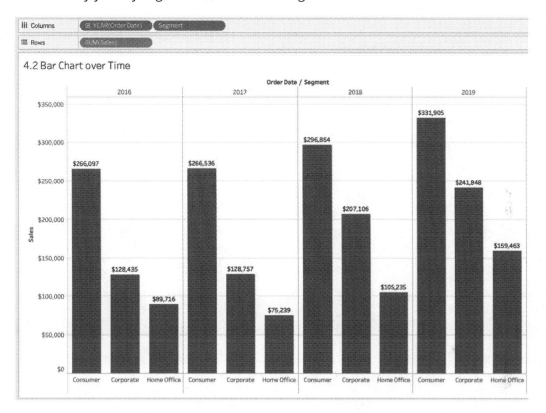

Figure 4.10: Bar chart over time by segment

From the preceding figure, it is clear that there has been progressive growth over the years, and you can also see the exact sales values for the segments. Although you got the data that you wanted, it is also important to present it in a formulated way. It will be more useful and understandable if you have the data for **Consumer** over the years together and the data for **Corporate** and **Home Office** together.

6. To do this, place **Segment** before **Order Date**. Your view will read as sales by segment by year with the following view:

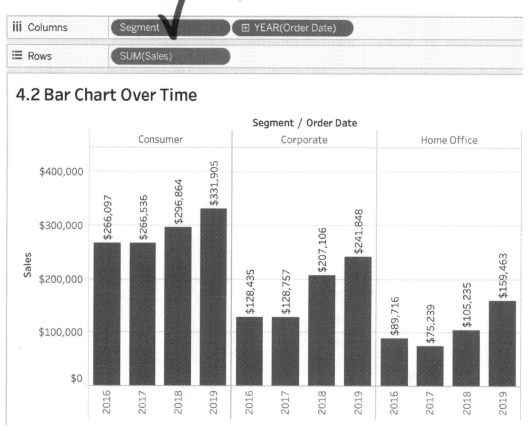

4.2 Bar Chart Over Time

Figure 4.11: Sales by year by segment

In *Figure 4.10*, you had sales by year by segment, whereas in *Figure 4.11*, you have sales by segment by year. This allows any stakeholder to take a quick peek at the sales trend for each of your segments. As you can see, **Corporate** saw considerable growth from 2017 to 2018, which was not easily understandable from the previous screenshot.

In this exercise, you reviewed bar charts over time and practiced adding more granularity and dimensionality to your data. Next, you will review comparisons over time using line charts.

LINE CHARTS

Line charts are another set of charts that are versatile, easy on the eye, universally understood. These have been used since the 18th century when William Playfair created them. They represent multiple data points connected with each other through a single line, usually signifying the trend of the data. In Tableau, you require at least one date, one measure, and zero or more dimensions to create a line chart.

DIFFERENCE BETWEEN DISCRETE DATES AND CONTINUOUS DATES

In the upcoming exercises, when you right-click the **Date** dimension in the view, you'll notice you have two options for selecting the quarter. The one at the top is the discrete date, where you will have discrete dates by year/quarter/month/day. If you observe the following screenshot, instead of 2016 Q2 to 2016 Q3 ..... 2019 Q1 data points, you just have four data points—one for each discrete quarter. Essentially, discrete dates are unique dates in the view. So, when you select discrete quarters, the view will only contain unique quarters without considering the year as part of the date.

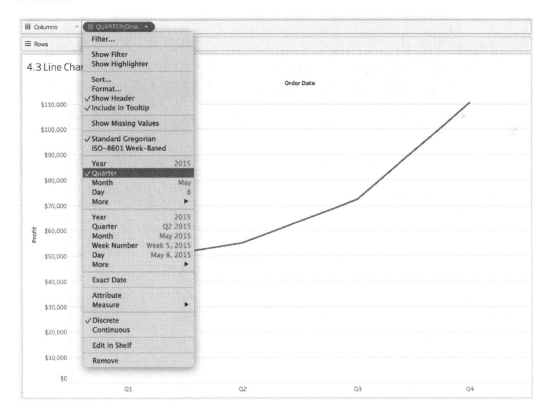

Figure 4.12: Discrete dates

The main difference between continuous dates and discrete dates is that continuous dates will give you more granular dates. So, instead of just Q1, Q2, Q3, and Q4, continuous dates will also factor in the year that the quarter/month/day is associated with. In most cases, you will want to use continuous dates because stakeholders often want to look at their metrics by month/quarter across multiple years.

Figure 4.13: Continuous dates

EXERCISE 4.03: CREATING LINE CHARTS OVER TIME

As an analyst, the category manager of your company would like you to create a chart so that they can look at the total profit across all the categories since 2016. They do not have a favorite chart type, but they do prefer a minimal look for their charts. In this exercise, you will tackle this stakeholder request as you go step by step in detail on how to make the best use of line charts and how adding color or changing the level of detail in the view adds incredible value to your charts.

Perform the following steps to complete the exercise:

1. Load the **Orders** table from the sample **Superstore** dataset in your Tableau instance, if you haven't already.

2. Similar to the steps for the bar chart, drag one of the measures to the **Rows** shelf. In this exercise, drag **Profit** to the **Rows** shelf.

3. Next, add **Order Date** to the **Columns** shelf. As soon as you add the **Date Time** dimension to your view, Tableau automatically creates a line chart (which you also saw previously in your bar chart view).

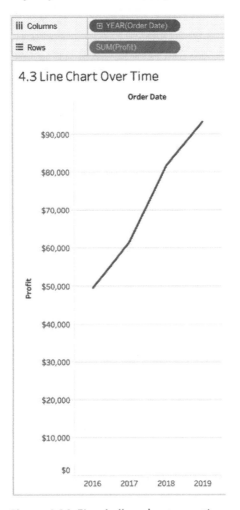

Figure 4.14: Simple line chart over time

In the chart, you have plotted profit by year and connected those points using a line. The profit grew from **$50,000** in **2016** to almost **$100,000** in **2019**.

That is a basic line chart for you, but as previously mentioned, the goal is to learn more than just the basics of Tableau. So, let's explore some of the options for more context or details for your line chart.

4. Add a **Profit** label to your line chart by dragging **Profit** from the **data** pane to **Label Marks** card in your view.

5. To have the line chart show your sales by quarter instead of by year so it is more granular and helps decision-making for your stakeholders, click on the **+** sign or click the arrow on the dimension in your **YEAR(Order Date)** dimension on the **Columns** shelf and change the granularity from **YEAR(Order Date)** to **QUARTER(Order Date)**.

6. To make your view even more granular, add **Segment** to your **Color** or **Detail Marks** shelf. Your data will be split by segment with a corresponding color for each segment, as observed here:

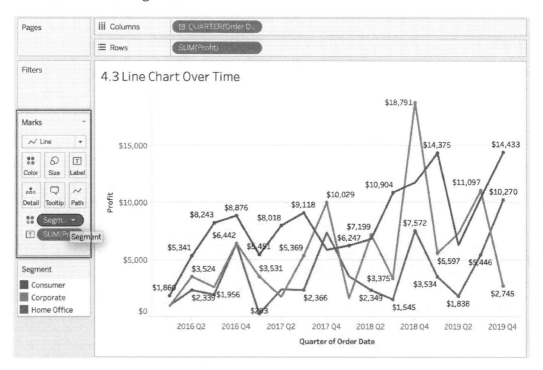

Figure 4.15: Line chart by segment

In the preceding figure, you can see that the profit for the **Consumer** segment has grown at a higher rate when compared to other segments. The line chart clearly illustrates the trend by segment across multiple years.

This wraps up our coverage of line charts. This section discussed line charts over time, the difference between discrete dates and continuous dates, and how you can add more color or contextual details to your line charts.

EXPLORING COMPARISON ACROSS MEASURES

Bullet charts are a type of bar chart that allow you to add target/goal comparisons to your charts/views. As much as bar charts are useful, more often than not when you are presenting data using bar charts, you will hear questions such as "*How does this compare to this KPI/metric?*" and "*So, what should we do with this data?*" because bar charts fail to add the additional context that stakeholders are looking for. This is where bullet charts shine as they add the required comparisons to goals/targets/thresholds. Think of bullet charts as bar charts with historical context or a baseline for comparison.

Say you are working on a project for which you are presenting sales figures for your SaaS products as bar charts. The first question you receive from your stakeholders might be "*How does this compare to our previous quarter's/year's results? Did we do well or underperform?*" If you had shown the same data with bullet charts, you could have also added a point of comparison for the period you want to compare your sales figures to. Here is a sample bullet chart:

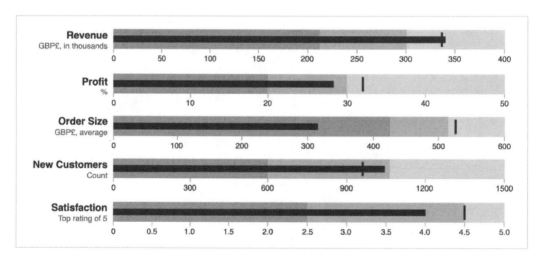

Figure 4.16: Sample bullet chart

In the following exercise, you will create a bullet chart that tackles that problem and learn about the impact that bullet charts can have on your reports/presentations.

EXERCISE 4.04: CREATING A BULLET CHART

You receive another request from the category manager: they now want to look at how each of the sub-categories trends toward the sales target for 2019. As an analyst, your job is to create a view with actual sales for each sub-category for 2019 while showcasing the target sales (the black vertical lines in the following sample bullet chart) for 2019.

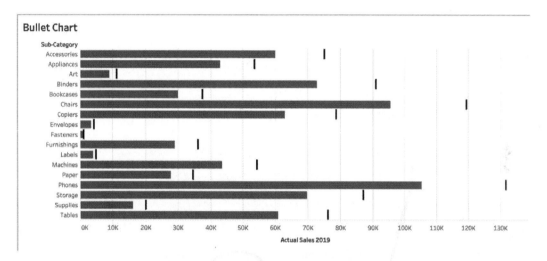

Figure 4.17: Sample bullet chart

NOTE

How to create a bullet chart using the **Show Me** panel could be studied here, but the book wouldn't do you justice if it didn't show you how to create a bullet chart using calculated fields, where you compare the sales of 2019 to the target sales of 2019 (which is a calculated field). We have not discussed calculated fields yet in the book, but we will be discussing them in depth in *Chapter 6, Exploration: Exploring Geographical Data*; for now, we will just try to explain each step of this exercise in as much detail as possible.

Perform the following steps to complete this exercise:

1. Load the **Orders** table from the sample **Superstore** dataset in your Tableau instance if you haven't already.

   Think of calculated fields as formulas that you can use to manipulate a field, create a subset of data, or extract information from rows/columns. In the following calculated fields, you will be creating two fields: **Sales Target 2019** and **Actual Sales 2019**.

2. **Sales Target 2019**: You are creating a dummy sales target for 2019 so you need a target field that can be used for comparing the actual to the target. Your **Sales Target 2019** field will be 125% of the 2018 sales figures. To create a calculated field using your **Sales** measures and **Order Date**, first, navigate to the **Order Date** dimension and right-click on it. Click on **Create | Calculated Field...**:

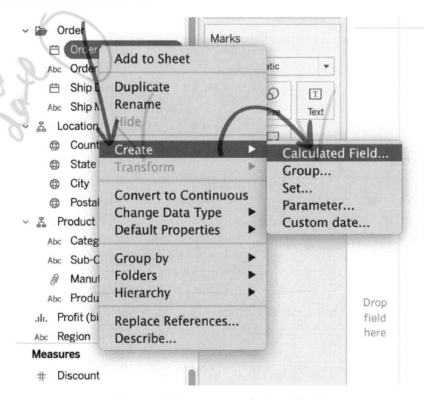

Figure 4.18 Creating a calculated field

3. Rename the field from "**Calculation1**" to "**Sales Target 2019**". In the calculated field window, type the following formula:

```
If YEAR([Order Date]) = 2019 THEN [Sales]*1.25 END
```

The formula is read as follows: if the year of order date is **2019**, make the target sales **125%** of the **2019** sales figures.

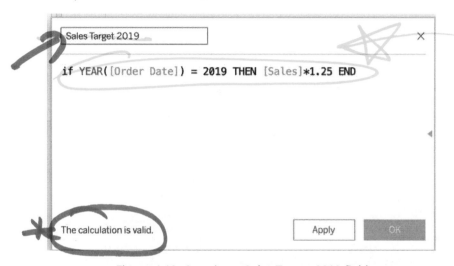

Figure 4.19: Creating a Sales Target 2019 field

4. Repeat the same steps for the **Actual Sales in 2019** calculated field with the following formula:

```
If YEAR([Order Date]) = 2019 THEN [Sales] END
```

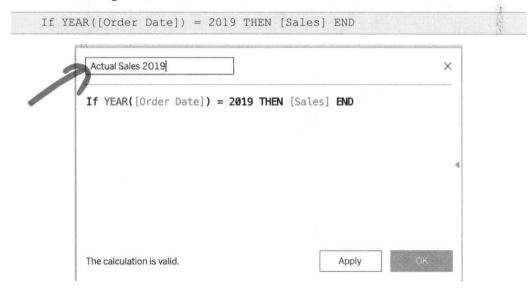

Figure 4.20: Creating an Actual Sales Target 2019 field

5. Drag **Sub-category** to the **Rows** shelf.

    The next steps will demonstrate both the **Show Me** and **non-Show Me** methods. You'll start with the **Show Me** panel method.

6. Drag the **Actual Sales in 2019** and **Sales Target in 2019** calculated fields to the **Column** shelf:

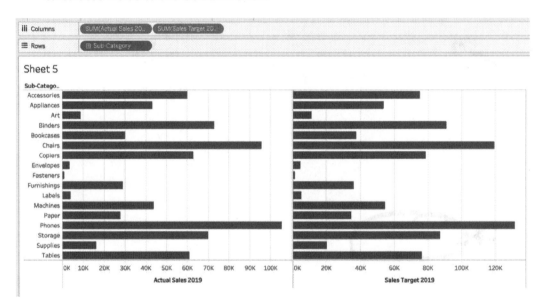

Figure 4.21: Side-by-side bar charts for actual versus target sales

In the previous figure, you have two charts: **Actual Sales** in **2019** and **Sales Target** in **2019** by sub-category. If you observe closely, you can see that Actual Sales 2019 for **Accessories** is **60,000** whereas **Sales Target 2019** is **75,000**, which is **125%** of **Actual Sales 2019**. In the next step, you will convert these two bar charts into a bullet chart.

7. Navigate to the **Show Me** panel and click on **Bullet Chart**.

    As soon as you click on **Bullet Chart**, you will notice multiple bars with a black reference line that has been added to each bar. The reference line is the target/goal line that adds the additional context:

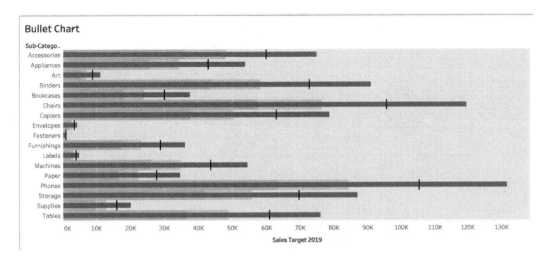

Figure 4.22: Bullet chart

You just created a bullet chart where the bars represent the sales targets in 2019 and the reference lines are the actual sales. But ideally, you want your sales targets in 2019 to be reference lines because that is the target that you want your sub-categories to aim for. You'll make those changes next.

8. If your bullet chart has **Sales Target in 2019** as bars instead of the target line, you can right-click on the **x** axis and click on **Swap Reference Lines** (this may be **Swap Reference Line Fields** in later Tableau versions) to change your reference lines to target sales instead of actual sales:

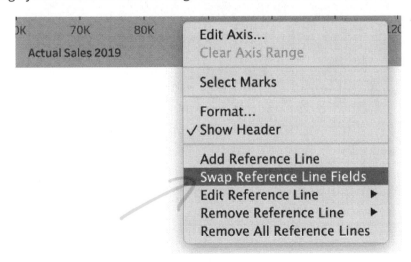

Figure 4.23: Swapping the reference lines

9. For the other method where the **Show Me** panel is not used, create a new sheet and drag **Sub-Category** to **Columns**, **Actual Sales 2019** to **Columns**, and **Sales Target in 2019** to the **Details Marks** card.

10. Right-click on the **x** axis and click **Add Reference Lines**. In the **Line** tab, click on the **Per Cell** radio button. In the **Value** dropdown, select **SUM(Sales Target in 2019)** and aggregate it as **SUM** in the dropdown right next to the **Value** dropdown. Change the **Label** dropdown from **Computation** to **None**.

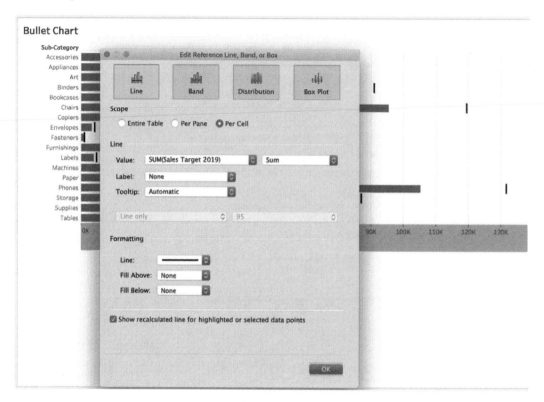

Figure 4.24: Editing the reference lines

After making the preceding changes, the final output of the bullet chart will be as follows:

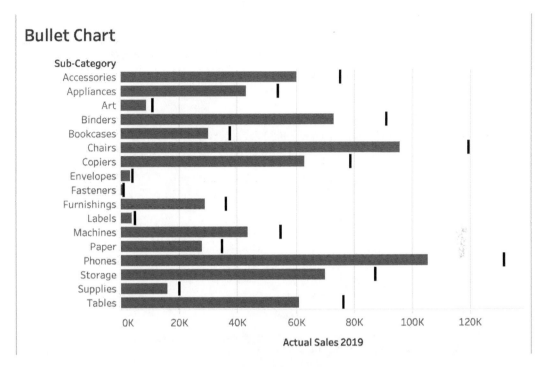

Figure 4.25: Bullet chart

In the preceding screenshot, the reference lines are now the sales targets for 2019, as opposed to the initial bullet chart where they were **Actual Sales 2019**, which was actually confusing. You want your stakeholders to understand how far off the target each of the sub-categories is.

In this exercise, you were able to create bullet charts using the **Show Me** panel as well as by manually adding reference lines to your view. We also briefly touched on calculated fields, which we will cover further in *Chapter 7: Data Analysis: Creating and Using Calculations* and *Chapter 8: Data Analysis: Creating and Using Table Calculations*.

BAR-IN-BAR CHARTS

Similar to bullet charts, this type of chart is used when you want to compare two measures or two values in the same row/column. Essentially, it adds the comparison/ goal/target context that every stakeholder is looking for in your report. It works pretty much like a bullet chart, the main difference being that instead of reference lines as comparison points, you will have another secondary bar embedded within your primary bar.

Think of a scenario similar to that of the bullet chart (for example, the US presidential election of 2019). As the electoral college votes were being counted, the Democrat and Republican vote counts were racing toward the target seat amount of 269. As the hours passed and more votes were counted, the actual number was updated and grew even closer to the target number of 269. That is a good example of where a bar-in-bar chart, such as the following, can be used.

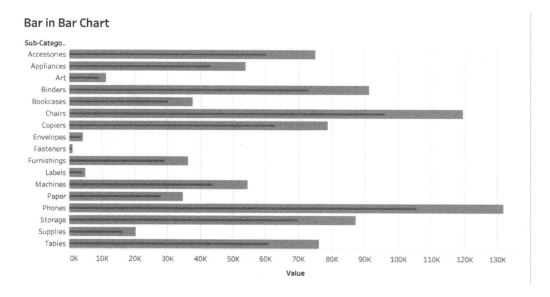

Figure 4.26: Sample bar-in-bar chart

[handwritten margin notes: "→ Similar to Bullet. Compared to value against each other"]

EXERCISE 4.05: CREATING A BAR-IN-BAR CHART

The previous view that you created for tracking actual sales versus target sales had a reference point in the view that, without additional helpful text and explanation, would have been confusing for stakeholders. The category manager has asked you to make the actuals versus targets comparison simpler. As an analyst, after researching potential chart ideas, you identify the bar-in-bar chart as a great chart for a simpler view. You will be re-creating the bullet chart view with same dimensions and measures but will be utilizing a bar-in-bar chart. You will be using the same **Superstore** dataset for the analysis.

[handwritten margin note: "business cases"]

Perform the following steps to complete the exercise:

1. Load the **Orders** table from the sample **Superstore** dataset if it's not already open in your Tableau instance.

2. Drag **Sub-category** to the **Rows** shelf and **Sales Target 2019** to the **Columns** shelf.

3. Drag **Actual Sales 2019** to the view and hover over the **Sales Target 2019** axis until you get two green stack bars highlighted in the axis, and then drop **Actual Sales 2019** on the **Sales Target 2019** axis as shown here:

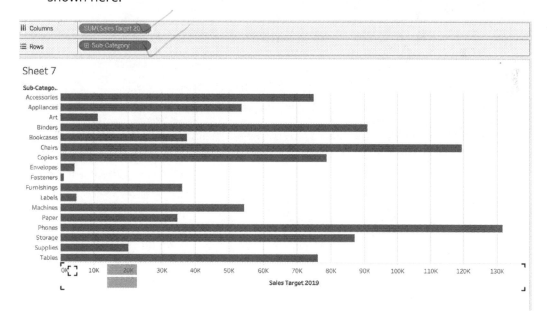

Figure 4.27: Sales by sub-category bar chart

In the preceding screenshot, you just plotted sales by sub-category, and in the next step, you will color-split these bars into actual versus target so that you can achieve your desired bar-in-bar result.

4. Drag **Measure Names** from the **Rows** shelf to the **Color Marks** card on the left. As soon as you do that, the two measures will be distinguished by different colors and will be stacked on top of each other:

Figure 4.28: Sales by actual versus target 2019

By adding **Measure Values** to **Columns** and adding **Actual Sales 2019** and **Sales Target 2019** to the **Measure Values Marks** card, you will see you were able to stack two bars on top of each other, with the orange bar being **Sales Target 2019** and the blue bar being **Actual Sales 2019**.

5. You'll also notice that both the measures are stacked on top of each other rather than starting at zero. Essentially, the **Actual Sales 2019** bar starts where **Sales Target 2019** ends, which is not how you want your data to be presented. To change that, navigate to **Analysis** in the menu, select **Stack Marks**, then choose **Off**.

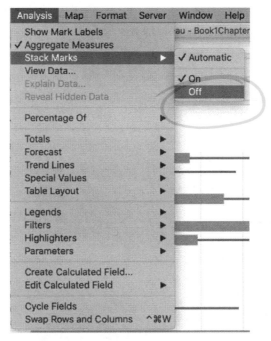

Figure 4.29: Turning off Stack Marks

6. As much as the current view looks good, you also want to differentiate **Actual Sales 2019** and **Sales Target 2019** by size too. Do this by dragging **Measure Names** from the **Dimensions** data pane and dropping it on the **Size Marks** card, as shown here:

Figure 4.30: Un-stacked bar chart

The preceding screenshot shows that **Measure Names** was added from the dimension pane to the **Size Marks** card.

7. If you want, you can swap the measure that is in the foreground. The current view is good as **Actual Sales 2019** is in the foreground and is racing toward **Sales Target 2019**, but if you want to change this, just swap the measures in the **Measure Values** card and play with the size, color, or width of the bar:

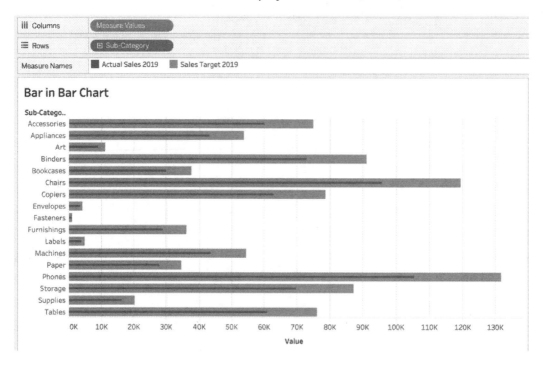

Figure 4.31: Bar-in-bar chart

In the preceding figure, the blue bar is **Actual Sales 2019**, which is racing toward **Target Sales 2019**, which is the orange bar. For example, the **Bookcases** sub-category has actual sales of **30,000** in **2019** and is racing toward the sales target of approximately **33,000**.

You could have also achieved the same bar-in-bar chart using dual axis, but we will be covering that in the next chapter. Here, we went with a standard approach and learned how to utilize **Measure Names** and **Measure Values**, which play an important role in Tableau report/dashboard building.

EXPLORING COMPOSITION SNAPSHOTS — STACKED BAR CHARTS

A stacked bar chart is nothing but a bar chart with an extra level of detail embedded in the bars, where each bar represents distinct dimensions/values. Stacked bar charts come in handy when you want to compare the whole to a segment of the dimensions/value, which are essentially smaller segments of the same bar. Think of the revenue generated by a car company: as an analyst, you want to show the revenue split by car/product type in a single bar graph without using too much space. By color-coding the bar chart with the car type, you can create a single graph with lots of contextual detail.

Think of stacked bar charts as showing **totals against parts**:

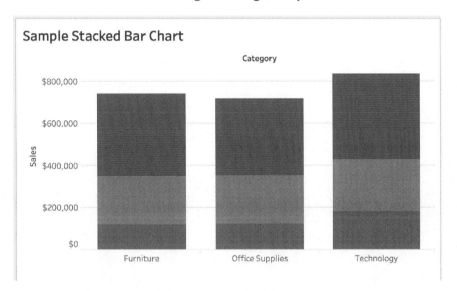

Figure 4.32: Sample stacked bar chart

Try your hand at creating a stacked bar chart with the next exercise.

EXERCISE 4.06: CREATING A STACKED BAR CHART

In this new request from your direct manager, they want to look at sales by sub-category in bar chart format, where the sales sub-categories are segments by color. Essentially, the manager expects a stacked bar for each sub-category, split into segments. You will continue to utilize the **Superstore** dataset for this exercise.

Follow these steps to complete this exercise:

1. Load the **Orders** table from the sample **Superstore** dataset if it's not already open in your Tableau instance.

2. Drag one of the measures to the **Rows** shelf. This exercise uses **Sales**, but you can use any of the measures in your own projects.

3. Drag **Sub-Category** to the **Columns** shelf, and now you shall have a simple bar chart for sales by sub-category:

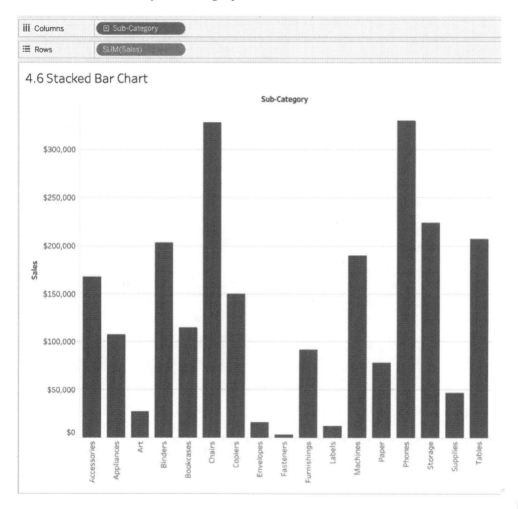

Figure 4.33: Stacked bar chart – sales by sub-category bar chart

4. To convert this bar chart into a stacked bar chart, select one of the dimensions (either **YEAR[Order Date]** or **Segment**) and drag it to the **Color Marks** card as shown here:

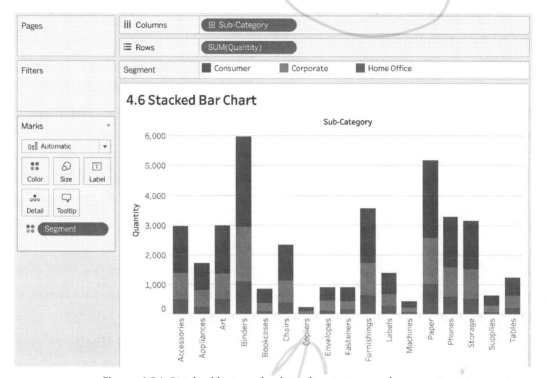

Figure 4.34: Stacked bar – sales by sub-category and segment

You have now essentially converted your simple bar chart into a stacked bar chart as you have color-coded or stacked multiple bars on top of each other by segment. **Chairs** and **Phones** were the highest-grossing sub-categories, but it is not clear which of those segments contributed more; so, next, you will add more elements to your stacked bar chart for readability.

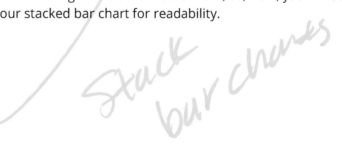

5. Add **SUM(Sales)** as a label for your bars. Drag **Sales** from the **Measures** data pane to the **Label Marks** card:

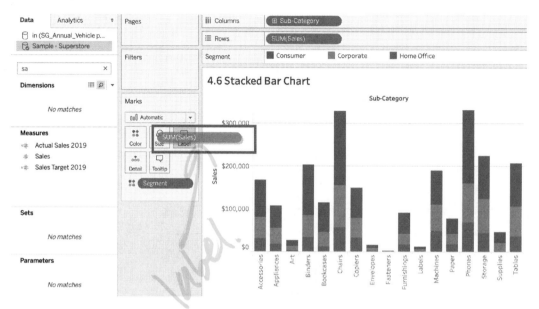

Figure 4.35: Stacked bar – sales by sub-category and segment

6. You might notice that the **Sales** label is taking a lot of space in our bars. The reason it is taking so much space is that the unit of **Sales** is tens, but considering that most of your sales are greater than 1,000, you can change the unit from tens to thousands so it is easier to read and saves you some real estate.

7. To change the unit for the **Sales** figures, navigate to **SUM(Sales)** in the **Marks** card. Right-click and select **Format**.

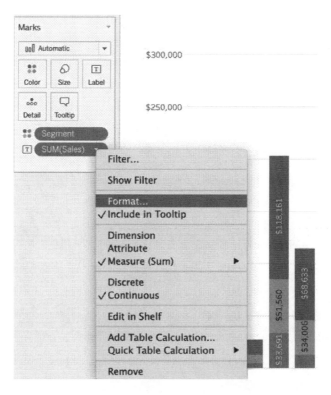

Figure 4.36: Formatting Sales

8. In the default section of the dialog box, click on the **Numbers** dropdown, select **Numbers (Custom)**, and change **Display Units** from **None** to **Thousands (K)**:

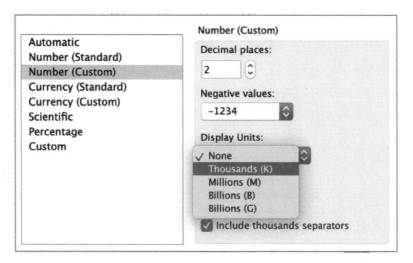

Figure 4.37: Formatting Sales

The stacked bar chart will now look as follows:

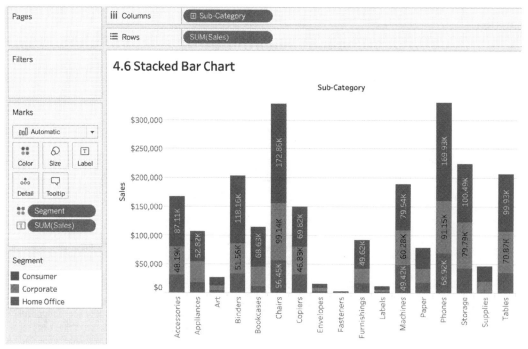

Figure 4.38: Final stacked bar chart

NOTE

In the preceding figures, you might notice that the smaller bars have no information embedded inside them. This is a limitation of Tableau. When you hover over the smaller bars, Tableau will display the information you need.

In this exercise, you looked at how to create a stacked bar graph. This is probably one of the easiest charts to build in Tableau, but it is an incredibly useful choice when you want to answer questions about parts against the total.

EXPLORING COMPOSITION SNAPSHOTS – PIE CHARTS

Although pie charts are quite often used, in the author's personal experience and the opinion of industry leaders in the field of data visualization, they are best avoided in reports/dashboards because it gets difficult to draw insights accurately from them. Pie charts often confuse even the best in the business. Notice how it is easy to trick people with the following pie chart (tricking people is not what we as data analysts/ visualizers are supposed to do):

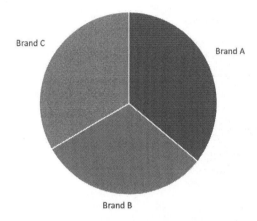

Figure 4.39: Sample pie chart

The goal of the pie chart is to display market penetration levels for brands A, B, and C. A simple visual inspection may cause one to believe that Brand A and C have equal market penetration, but in reality the difference between them could be several millions of dollars due to a couple of percentage points' difference. Therefore, it is recommended not to use pie charts. That said, if there is no way to avoid using them, keep in mind the following rule of thumb: if your pie chart has more than six labels, you are better off creating either a bar chart or a stacked bar chart.

EXERCISE 4.07: CREATING A PIE CHART

The VP of the company is going to be presenting in a board meeting today, and they are looking for your help to create a simple pie chart showing sales by segment. In this exercise, you will create your first pie chart and fulfill the requirement as requested by the VP. You will continue to use the **Superstore** dataset.

The following steps will help you complete this exercise:

1. Load the **Orders** table from the sample **Superstore** dataset if it's not already open in your Tableau instance.

2. Drag **Sales** to the **Rows** shelf and **Segment** to the **Columns** shelf, which creates your standard bar chart:

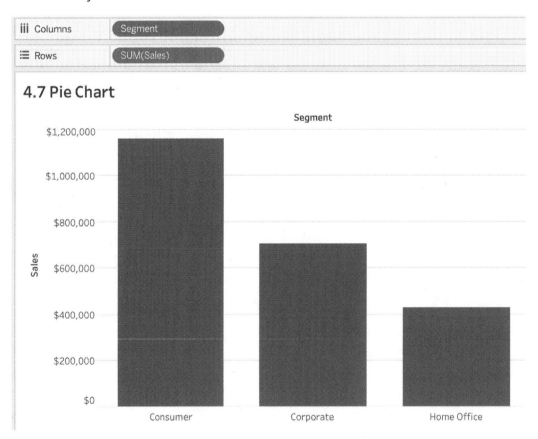

Figure 4.40: Pie chart – step 1

3. To convert the bar chart to a pie chart, open the **Show Me** panel and click on the pie chart icon:

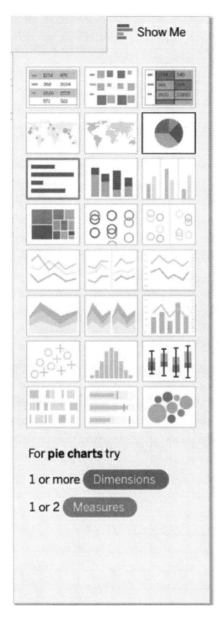

Figure 4.41: Adding a pie chart using the Show Me panel

When you convert the bar chart to a pie chart, the pie chart might be too small to read.

4. To increase the size of the pie, on a Mac, you can press *Command + Shift + B* to increase or *Command + B* to decrease the size of the chart. On Windows, press *Ctrl + Shift + B* to increase the size of the chart and *Ctrl + B* to decrease the size of the chart. Another way to increase or decrease the size of the chart is by using the **Size** tab in our **Marks** card:

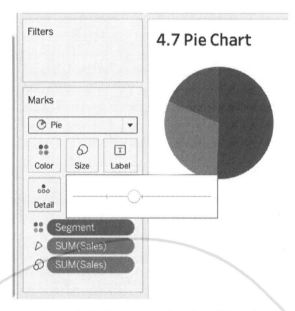

Figure 4.42: Increasing the size of the pie

5. To add labels to the chart, drag **Segment** as well as **Sales** to your **Label Marks** card. Increase the size of our label to 15 or higher. You can also change the units of the **SUM(Sales)** figure to thousands or millions as discussed in the previous exercise:

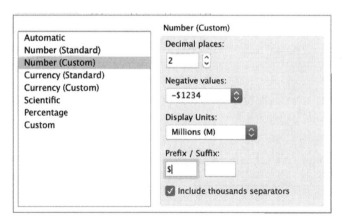

Figure 4.43: Adding the $ prefix

The final output after making the changes will be as follows:

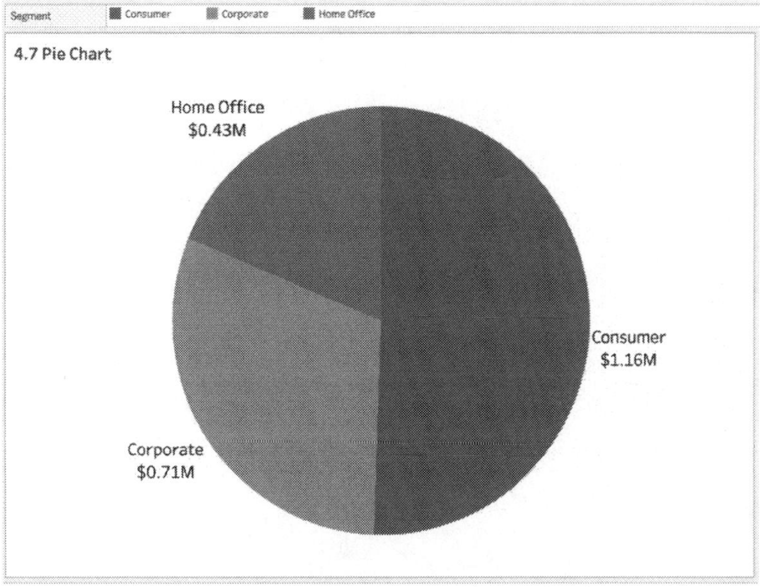

Figure 4.44: Final pie chart

In the preceding screenshot, you were able to show sales by segment in a pie chart. Although they have their drawbacks, pie charts can be really useful when the number of labels does not exceed 5-7 and the useable space on the screen is very limited.

TREEMAPS

Like pie charts and stacked bar charts, treemaps help you answer parts-of-the-whole types of questions, but the main difference is that treemaps and bar-in-bar charts show hierarchical relationships using rectangles. Using **Marks** card elements such as **Color** and **Size**, you can better analyze the data. When a rectangle is bigger or has a more concentrated color, it represents the highest value of the dimension in the view. Treemaps allow you to quickly measure contributions to the whole. Like pie charts, treemaps are not always the best choice, but depending on the analysis needed, treemaps can use contextual labels for better readability; they are also one of those chart types where you can plot hundreds of data points in a view.

Think of a case where the VP of delivery operations has requested a presentation on the total deliveries to each state as well as whether deliveries in those states were on time or not. Using treemaps, you can compare the delivery activity for each of the states, where the number of deliveries is communicated by the size of the rectangle for each state and the proportion of deliveries that were delayed is shown by color:

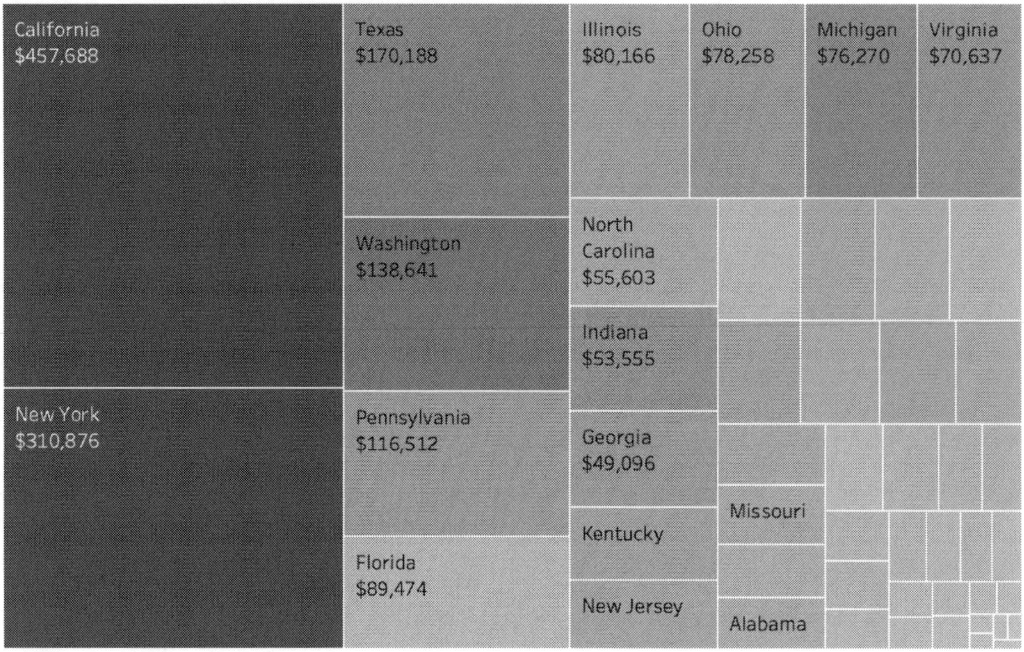

Figure 4.45: Sample treemap

EXERCISE 4.08: CREATING TREEMAPS

As an analyst, you want to create a view of profitable versus non-profitable states by category without using a cross-table in your view. For this exercise, you will use the **Superstore** dataset. You are required to color-code the states based on their profitability and sort the states in descending order based on total sales. The reason you are using treemaps for this is that you can use both size and color to convey information without sacrificing anything.

Perform the following steps to complete the exercise:

1. Open the sample **Superstore** dataset if it's not already open in your Tableau instance.

2. For this exercise, you have two measures: **Sales** and **Profit Ratio**. You will use **Sales** for sizing and **Profit Ratio** for coloring the treemap. Drag the primary measure (in this case, **Sales**) to the **Size Marks** card and the secondary metric, **Profit Ratio**, to the **Color Marks** card:

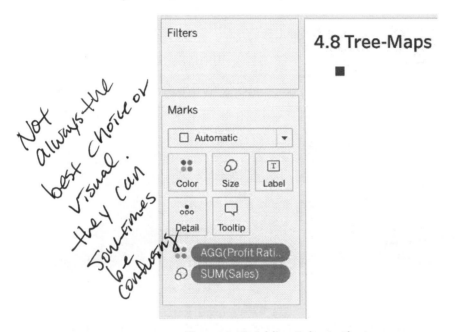

Not always the best choice of Visual. they can Sometimes be confusing

Figure 4.46: Adding Sales to the treemap

> **NOTE**
>
> If you are using a version of Tableau later than 2020.1, you may need to choose **Profit** rather than **Profit Ratio** for this step.

Parts of a whole.

3. Drag **State** to your **Detail Marks** card as it will make your data more granular and represent the states with sizes and colors.

When you add **State** to the **Detail Marks** card (in Tableau version 2020.1), you will see that **Country/Region** is automatically added as **State** is part of the hierarchy. Remove **Country/Region** from the **Detail Marks** card because it is not adding any value or detail to your view. While you are at it, drag **State** as a label:

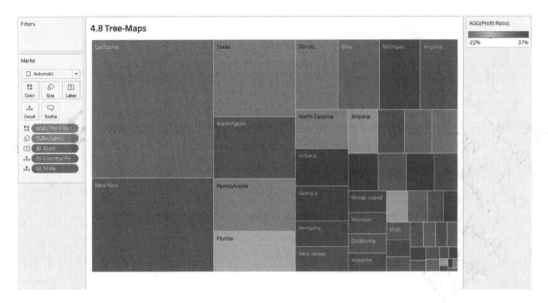

Figure 4.47: Color coding by profit ratio

In the preceding figure, you have represented sales and profit ratios by states. California and New York have the largest number of sales (larger rectangles means more sales), but states such as Michigan have higher profit ratios (darker blue means higher profits).

4. You could potentially stop the analysis/charting here, and this would be your treemap representing sales by each state and their profit ratios. However, in this case, you'll add another layer of detail to your view. Drag **Category** to the **Rows** shelf, and in the toolbar, change the view from **Standard** to **Entire View**, as shown in the following screenshot:

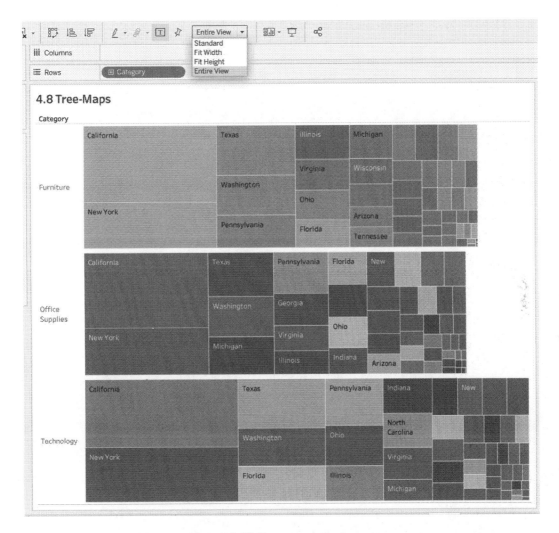

Figure 4.48: Treemap by category

You are just about finished, but the color range that you have used in the chart is a bit confusing because the stakeholders just want to know whether a state was profitable or not. They neither need nor want to know the exact profit or loss ratio for each of the states. You can add those exact **Profit ratio** details in a tooltip later.

5. Navigate to the **Marks** card and click on the **Color** tab. Check the **Stepped color** checkbox and enter its value as **2** steps.

> **NOTE**
>
> If you are using a version of Tableau later than 2020.1, you will need to select **Edit Colors** to find the **Stepped color** option.

6. Next, select the palette you want and click on **<< Advanced**. Check the **Center** checkbox and enter its value as **0** (green represents a profitable state):

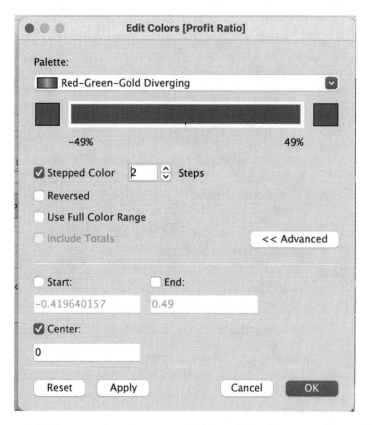

Figure 4.49: Treemap by category and state with red/green color coding

The final output is as follows:

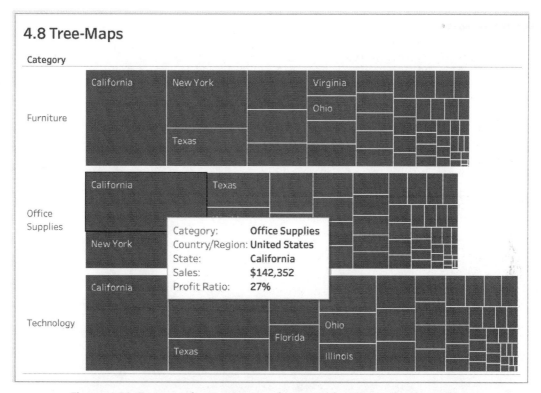

Figure 4.50: Treemap by category and state with red/green color coding

The main difference between this view of the treemap (*Figure 4.50*) and the default treemap you created in the previous step (*Figure 4.48*) is that in the latest treemap, instead of color-coding your profit ratio with gradient colors, you color-coded loss as red and profit as green, so it's easier for stakeholders to quickly view the most profitable and least profitable states.

If you look, you can see that California is the highest-selling state across all categories, and if you want to know the profit ratio of the state, all you have to do is hover over any of the states.

EXPLORING COMPOSITIONS FOR TRENDED DATA

AREA CHARTS

Area charts are among the most visually pleasing charts available and are used pretty frequently for reporting cadence. Area charts are essentially combinations of line charts and bar charts in that they show the relationships between the proportions of the total.

Think of a use-case wherein the branch manager of an electronics company wants to look at the total quantity sold in each television category by the series that they belong to. You can fulfill this requirement by using a stacked bar chart, but with an area chart, you can also add time trends, which is what you will explore in this

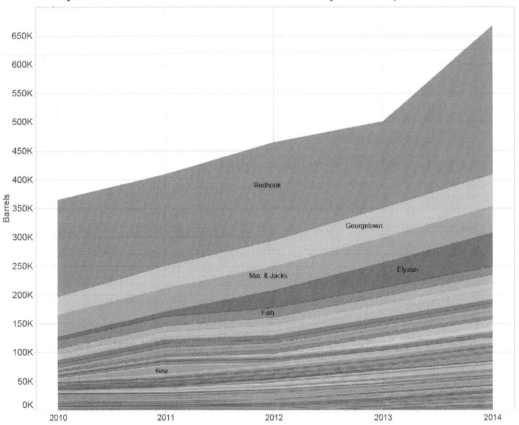

Figure 4.51: Sample Area Charts

> **NOTE: WORD OF CAUTION FOR AREA CHARTS**
>
> When you use an area chart as a stacked area chart, it can easily be misinterpreted—especially if you use stacked area charts for percentages. For example, say you are creating an email marketing report where you have conversion rates for different campaigns. Campaign 1 had a click-through rate (CTR) of 3%, campaign 2 had a 7% CTR, and campaign 3 had a 6% CTR for a particular month. The true CTR for that month was 5.3%, but using a stacked area chart, the CTR for all campaigns may show up as 16%, which is factually incorrect. Just be aware of the caveats here.

EXERCISE 4.09: CREATING AN AREA CHART

The director of financial operations reaches out to you, looking to understand how the sales for each sub-category trends across each month. The director wants to know whether they sell more in July or August. As an analyst, your job is to create a color-coded area chart showing sales by month of the year and how sales trend across the year. You will continue to utilize the **Superstore** dataset for this exercise. You will also explore continuous as well as discrete area charts in this exercise, utilizing **Order Date**, **Sub-Category**, and **Sales**.

Perform the following steps:

1. Open the sample **Superstore** dataset if it's not already open in your Tableau instance.

2. Drag **Order Date** to the **Columns** shelf and change the granularity from year to month by clicking the arrow on the **Order Date** capsule and selecting continuous **Month** (you will first create a continuous stacked area chart).

Figure 4.52: Continuous month selection

3. Drag **Sales** to the **Rows** shelf. As soon as you drop it onto the **Rows** shelf, a line chart is created.

4. Drag **Sub-Category** from data pane onto **Color Marks** card to and then change the **Marks** type from **Automatic** to **Area** using the dropdown:

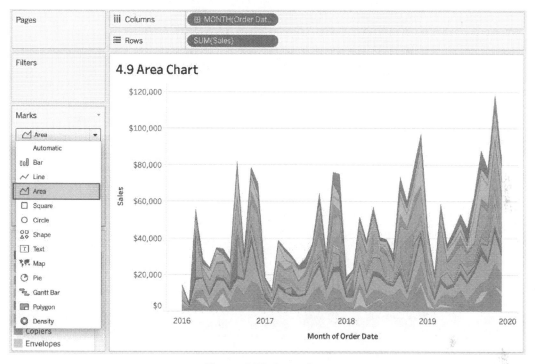

Figure 4.53: Area chart

The preceding chart represents the continuous stacked area chart. If you don't want the areas to be stacked on top of each other, you can turn off stacking.

5. Navigate to **Analysis** in the menu and click on **Stack Marks | Off.** Similarly, you follow the same steps to turn the stack marks back on:

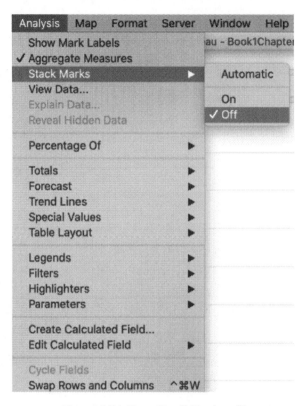

Figure 4.54: Turn Stack Marks off

The only reason that someone would want to turn off **Stack Marks** in an area chart is if they want to look at individual trends for the dimension in question (in this case, Sub-Category). The limitation of an unstacked area chart is that it carries a risk of hidden data points because what the background area represents is not clear:

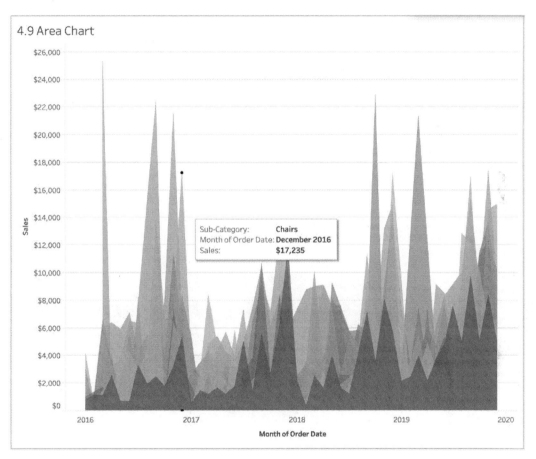

Figure 4.55: Area chart

6. To change the area chart to be discrete, change the type of **Order Date** from **Continuous** to **Discrete**:

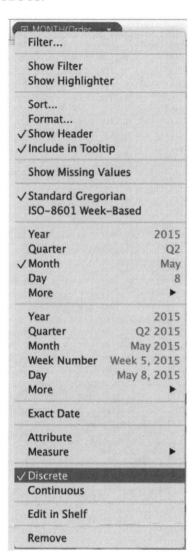

Figure 4.56: Discrete dates selection

With discrete charts, instead of **Month** for each year, now you only show discrete months without considering the year in the view. The view is a less granular view compared to that of the continuous stacked area chart. You will change the axis tick marks from $50,000 to $25,000 increments.

7. To change the axis tick marks, right-click on the **Sales** axis and click on **Edit Axis**....

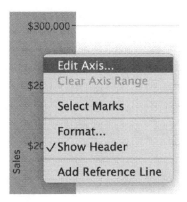

Figure 4.57: Editing the axis

8. In **Edit Axis [Sales]**, click on **Tick Marks** (this may be **Major Tick Marks** in later versions) and select **Fixed**, then set **Tick interval** to **25000**, as shown here:

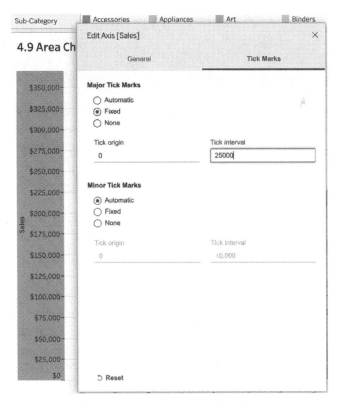

Figure 4.58: Setting Major Tick Marks

The final output is as follows:

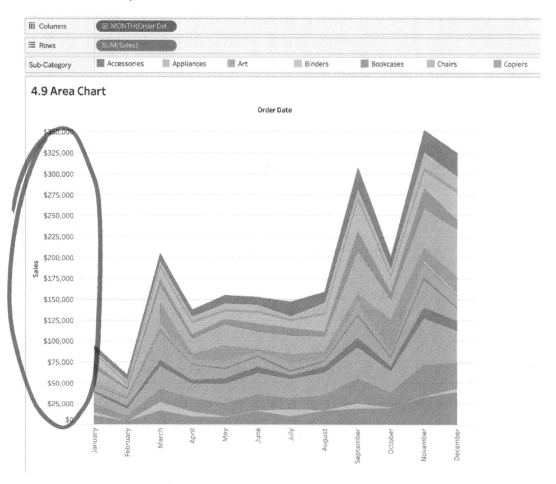

Figure 4.59: Final stacked area chart

In the preceding screenshot, each of the sub-categories is stacked on top of each other, while the sales trends are shown across months. From the given chart, you can easily make out that November is the highest-grossing month for the **Superstore** dataset.

In this exercise, you learned when and when not to use area charts, looked at stacked versus non-stacked area charts, and studied the best use cases for continuous and discrete area charts.

ACTIVITY 4.01: VISUALIZING THE GROWTH OF PASSENGER CARS IN SINGAPORE

Recently, the Singapore government appointed a new head of vehicle inspection. This newly created department will analyze vehicle sales over the past few decades, study growth/trends, and create policies and rules to further help the government reduce emissions. As part of the initial onboarding, the head of vehicle inspection has asked to look at sales trends for each vehicle category, including buses, taxis, cars, and goods vehicles. They expect an analyst to create a single view showcasing the trends for sales of these vehicle categories. As an analyst, considering that the head of vehicle inspection expects to see trends across multiple categories and years, you decide to use an area chart with color coding for easier readability.

In this activity, you will be showcasing the skills that you have learned in this chapter by creating multiple charts. You will be using the **SG_Annual_Vehicle_Population** data, which can be downloaded from https://packt.link/wLR2x.

Perform the following steps to complete this activity:

1. Import and open the data that was downloaded.

2. Drag **Category** to the **Columns** shelf and **Number** to the **Rows** shelf.

3. Drag **Year** to the **Columns** shelf.

4. Drag and drop **Category** to the **Color Marks** card.

5. Drag and drop **Year** to the **Label Marks** card.

6. Change the **Axis** title to just **Year of Audit**.

7. Edit the axis to change **Major Tick Marks** to **Fixed** and set the intervals to **1**.

8. Change the title of the worksheet to **Activity 4.1**.

The expected output is as follows:

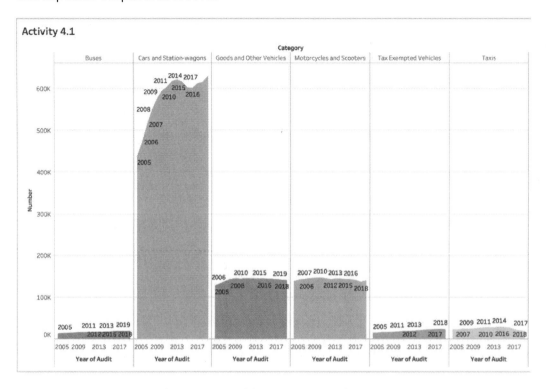

Figure 4.60: Activity 4.01 expected output

NOTE

The solution to this activity can be found here: https://packt.link/CTCxk.

SUMMARY

That wraps up this chapter. In this lesson, you created your first charts in Tableau, starting with bar charts, which are used for comparisons across dimensions, followed by line charts to show comparisons over time. You also looked at how bullet charts and bar-in-bar charts differ and the best use cases for them when exploring comparisons across measures.

You further composed snapshots, working through three major chart types: stacked bar charts, pie charts, and treemaps. When exploring treemaps, instead of using a standard treemap, you added an extra layer by utilizing multiple measures where the primary measure, **Sales**, was used for the size of the rectangle and a secondary measure, **Profit ratio**, was used for profit/loss using two different colors. The different colors made it easier for stakeholders to identify profit-making states across superstore categories.

Although we did discuss line charts for time series data, we also decided to work through an area chart problem and study the issues with stacked (*cannot aggregate percentages*) versus non-stacked (*risk of hidden data*) area charts. We briefly touched on continuous versus discrete stacked area charts. We wrapped up the chapter by working through a new dataset on Singapore's annual vehicle population audit and created an area chart for understanding the different trends of vehicle growth over the past 15 years in Singapore.

In the next chapter, we will take a step forward and work through dual axis, histograms, box and whisker plots, and scatter plots, as well as discussing some statistics related to reference lines and when to use different reference line models. Consider the next chapter as covering advanced charting in Tableau.

5

DATA EXPLORATION: DISTRIBUTIONS AND RELATIONSHIPS

OVERVIEW

This chapter builds on the basic charts you created in *Chapter 4, Exploring Comparison and Composition*. You will also cover the advanced topics of trend and reference lines, and will see some examples of where they are frequently used. By the end of this chapter, you will be able to create charts for distributions, show relationships across data points, and create advanced chart types such as **Dual Axis** and **Quadrant** charts.

INTRODUCTION

In previous chapters, you have learned about various charting methods that are reliant upon having both dimensions and measures in the view. However, there may be times, especially in business scenarios, where you only have measures to work with. In this chapter, you will learn how to create charts without dimensions, and also charts with multiple measures. You will learn to create relationships between measures, and will see how advanced Tableau skills like trend and reference lines can help better demonstrate insights to stakeholders.

First, you will explore distribution for a single measure using histograms, box plots, and whisker plots. Then, you will look at distributions across two measures using scatter plots, and scatter plots with trend lines (linear, logarithmic, and exponential). You will then look at advanced visualizations such as dual axis and quadrant charts for multiple dimensions/measures.

EXPLORING DISTRIBUTION FOR A SINGLE MEASURE

Distribution charts such as histograms and box plots are used to show the distribution of continuous and numerical quantitative data. However, bar charts, as discussed in the previous chapter, are used when plotting discrete and categorical data. In these sections, you will focus on discrete and categorical chart types.

CREATING A HISTOGRAM

A histogram represents frequency distribution. It shows the distribution of values and can help identify any outliers. Histograms take your continuous measures and splits the range of measurements. They are placed into buckets known as bins. Each bin is essentially a bar in a histogram representing the count of that range of values falling within that bin.

If you were to create a histogram of the salary of all the employees in a company, where the range of each bin is $10,000, your histogram would represent how many employees are earning $0-10,000, $10,001-20,000, $20,001-30,000, and so on.

It is straightforward to create a histogram in Tableau, as it is one of the 24 default chart types in the **Show Me** pane. Whenever you create a histogram in Tableau, bins/buckets of equal size are created, and Tableau creates a bin dimension (a local temporary dimension created for your bin ranges) for the measure you used while creating the chart.

The following figure shows a sample histogram. Here, you are looking at the distribution of the count of total order quantities with a bin size of 1. Essentially, from the following histogram, you can see that there were **899** orders with only 1 item, there were **2,402** orders with **2** items, and so on:

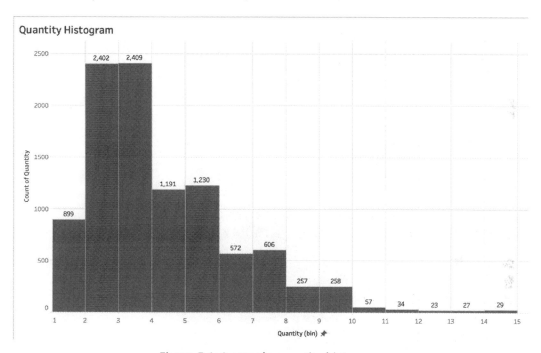

Figure 5.1: A sample quantity histogram

The following screenshot shows that the histogram option is part of the **Show Me** pane:

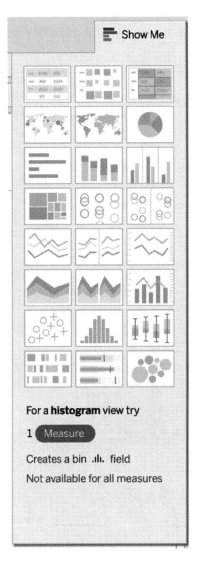

Figure 5.2: Histogram option as a part of the Show Me pane

While creating the histogram, Tableau automatically adds the **Quantity (bin)** dimension in the **Data** pane, as shown here:

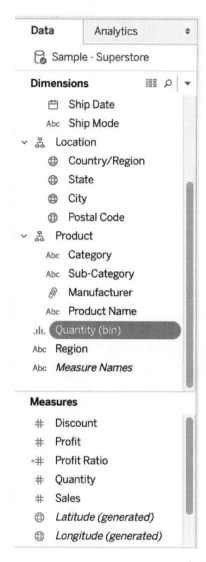

Figure 5.3: Quantity (bin) added to the Data pane

Now work through this Exercise 5.01 and see in practice how to create a histogram.

EXERCISE 5.01: CREATING A HISTOGRAM

As an analyst of an e-commerce store, your manager is looking to better understand the size of each order by asking you to create a chart that shows the count of orders by the quantity of orders. One of the better ways to represent frequency distribution is using histograms. In this exercise, you will use the **Sample - Superstore** dataset to create a view of **Counts of Orders by Quantity** distribution and in the process, learn the exact steps to create a histogram in Tableau.

> **NOTE**
>
> You can find the **Sample - Superstore** dataset at the following link: https://community.tableau.com/s/question/0D54T00000CWeX8SAL/sample-superstore-sales-excelxls?language=en_US.
>
> Alternatively, you can also find the dataset in our GitHub repository here: https://packt.link/21LCj.
>
> **Dataset Description**: The **Sample - Superstore** dataset is a dataset that comes loaded with Tableau Desktop by default. The dataset represents a fictional store that contains dimensions of orders such as **Order Dates**, **Ship Date**, **Country**, **Product Category/Sub-category/Manufacturer/Name**, **Segment**, and **Customer Name**, as well as measures such as **Discount**, **Profit**, **Quantity**, and **Sales** numbers.

Perform the following steps to complete this exercise:

1. Load the **Orders** table from **Sample - Superstore** dataset in your Tableau instance.

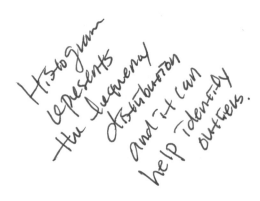
Histogram represents the frequency distribution and it can help Identify outliers.

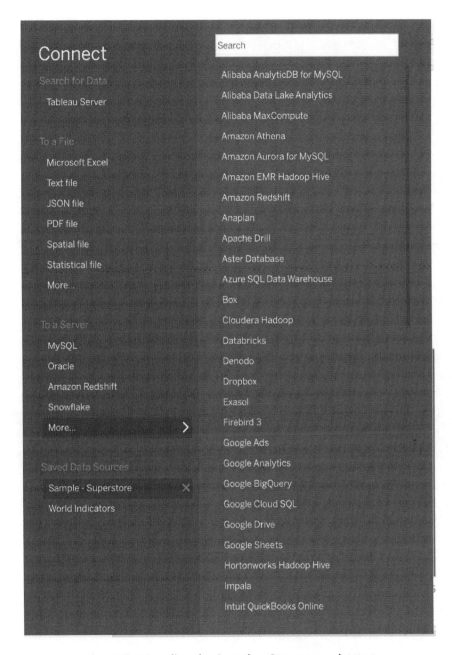

Figure 5.4: Loading the Sample – Superstore dataset

As mentioned, a histogram is used for continuous and numerical data, so in this case, you have **Discount**, **Profit**, **Quantity**, and **Sales**. In this example, you will use **Quantity** to create the histogram.

2. Double-click on **Quantity** or drag the **Quantity** measure to the **Rows** shelf. By default, Tableau selects horizontal bars as the preferred chart method, as seen here:

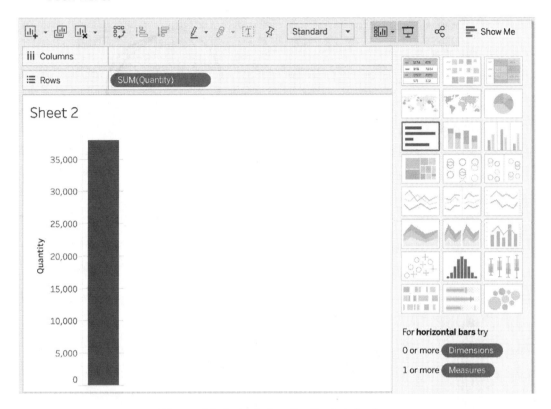

Figure 5.5: A single bar for the total sales

As you see, there are only two chart options for the **Quantity** measure available in the **Show Me** panel.

3. Select **Histogram** and you will get with the following view:

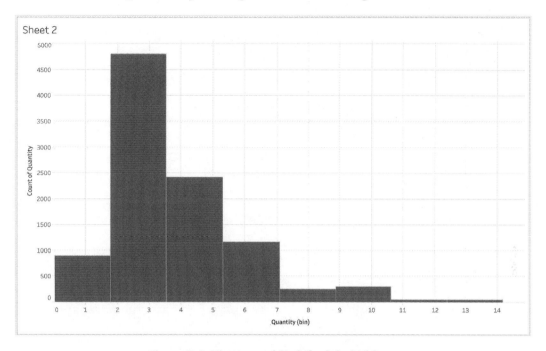

Figure 5.6: Histogram bin default by Tableau

As you see, Tableau has now created a Quantity (bin) dimension in the Data pane and has automatically decided the best bin size for the data. In your current view, it is unclear whether the first bin ends at **1.5** or **2.0**.

4. For better readability, edit the bin sizes to be integers. Right-click on **Quantity (bin)** in the **Data** pane and select **Edit...**:

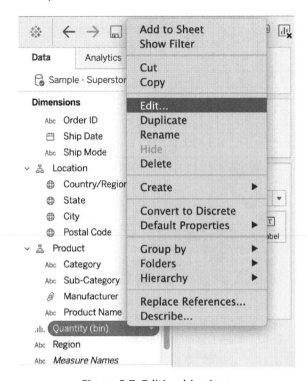

Figure 5.7: Editing bin sizes

In the Edit Bins [Quantity] window, the bin size is **1.77** for this dataset, which is less than **2**, making it unclear where our first bin ended.

5. Change the bin size to an integer value (in this case, to **1** for readability). This will show your end user how many orders included only one item in the invoice, two items, and so on:

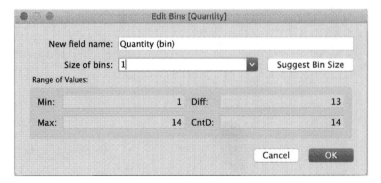

Figure 5.8: Changing bin sizes

Next, you will make some formatting changes. As you can see, the x axis starts from zero and ends at one bin past the maximum bin. Edit this to start the x axis from one and go up to the maximum bin size so that you have one continuous axis.

6. To edit the axis, right-click on the *x* axis and click on **Edit Axis**. Next, select **Fixed** range from the **Edit Axis** window, enter **1** for **Fixed start** and keep **Fixed end** as it is, as shown here:

Figure 5.9: Editing the axis for bins

7. Make one final edit by using *Ctrl* + drag (for Windows) or *Option* + drag (for Mac) the **CNT(Quantity)** pill from the **Rows** shelf to the **Label** shelf to add a label to individual bins. Finally, rename the sheet title to **Quantity Histogram** as shown here:

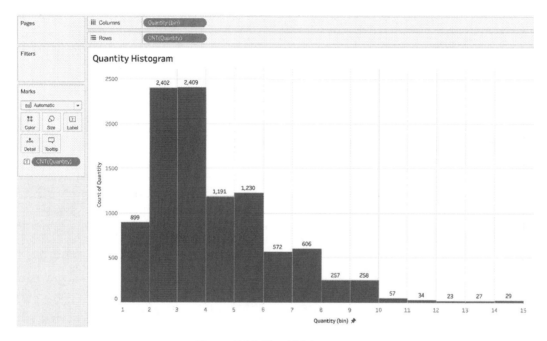

Figure 5.10: Final histogram

You have learned how to use frequency distribution to create histograms, and have answered the following question: *How many sales/orders included one item, two items, and so on?*

In the preceding screenshot, the histogram represents the count of orders with one item, two items, and so on. There are **1,230** orders with **5** items and **572** orders with **6** items.

Next, you will learn about the importance of **Box and Whisker** (**B&W**) plots and when to use them in your charts.

This label is a sum of the quantity. It might be better to have changed that to the count of quantity instead.

BOX AND WHISKER PLOTS

Whenever you want to illustrate distributions, apart from histograms, B&W plots are one of the other options you have. Box plots work really well when you want to compare two dimensions side by side where one of the dimensions is on the x axis and the other is on the y axis. For example, the batting average of hitters in major league baseball. Before learning to create B&W plots (also called box plots), it is important to understand their importance, how to read them, and when it's best to use them.

Here is what a B&W plot looks like:

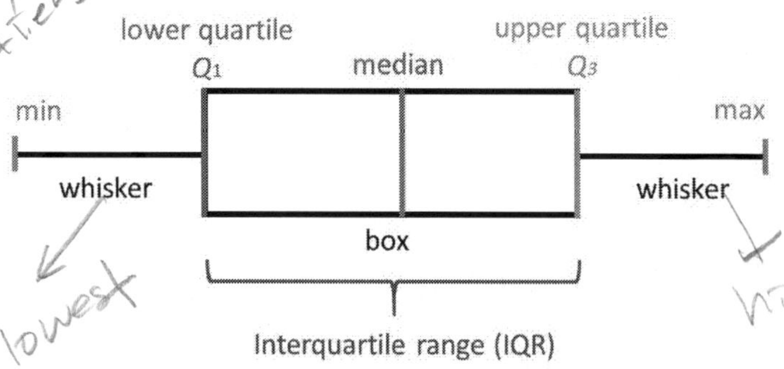

[handwritten annotations: "Identify the outliers", "lowest", "highest"]

Figure 5.11: Sample B&W plot

The box part of the image represents the first and third quartiles, also known as the **Interquartile Range** (**IQR**). The IQR is calculated as Q3 minus Q1 (Q3-Q1). The whiskers on the left and right represent the lowest value of the first quartile and the highest value of the fourth quartile respectively. The middle line in the box is the median (Q2), which is the middle number of the dataset. Data points to the left of the line are the numbers less than the median, whereas to the right side are all the numbers greater than the median. Next, you will start creating box plots with the superstore dataset.

B&W plots are particularly useful when you want your distribution to identify outliers. For example, the next screenshot shows the age distribution of two counties: the County of Philly and the County of Morago. The top plot represents Philly, the bottom Morago. The IQR for Philly is between 23 and 64, and for Morago is 15 and 43. But the screenshot also helps identify the outliers, as there is a section of the population in both counties with humans aged 100 and above. That is where B&W plots can be so useful.

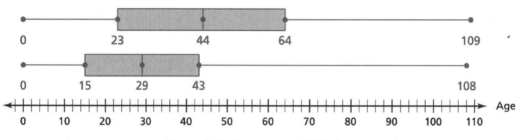

Figure 5.12: Two-county B&W plot

EXERCISE 5.02: CREATING A BOX AND WHISKER PLOT WITHOUT THE SHOW ME PANEL

Like a histogram, a B&W plot is part of the **Show Me** pane in Tableau, but in this case, you will learn how to create box plots using reference lines.

Perform the following steps to complete this exercise:

1. Load the **Orders** table from **Sample – Superstore** dataset in your Tableau instance.

2. Create a bar chart with one dimension and one measure (bar charts were discussed in *Chapter 4: Data Exploration: Comparison and Composition*). Select **Profit** as the measure and the product **Segment** as the dimension (looking at **Profit** by **Segment**).

3. Drag **Segment** to the **Columns** shelf and **Profit** to the **Rows** shelf as shown in the following screenshot:

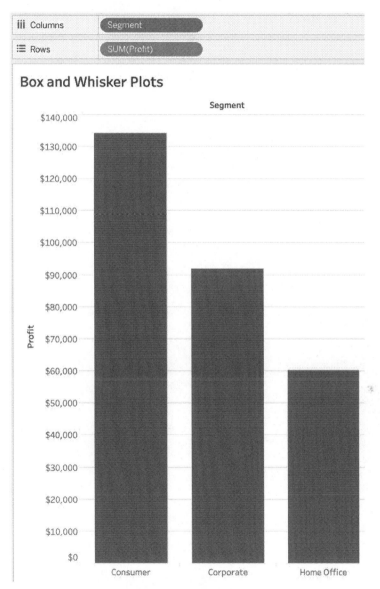

Figure 5.13: Bar Graph of Profit by Segment

4. Add the distribution dimension to the **Detail Marks** card. In this case, you are looking at **Profit** distributed by **Segment**, by year of order. Now, add *year of order* to the **Detail** card.

NOTE

Ctrl + drag (for Windows) or *Option* + drag (for Mac) the **Order** date to open the **Drop Field** window, which will allow you to select **YEAR(Order Date)** on the **Marks** card).

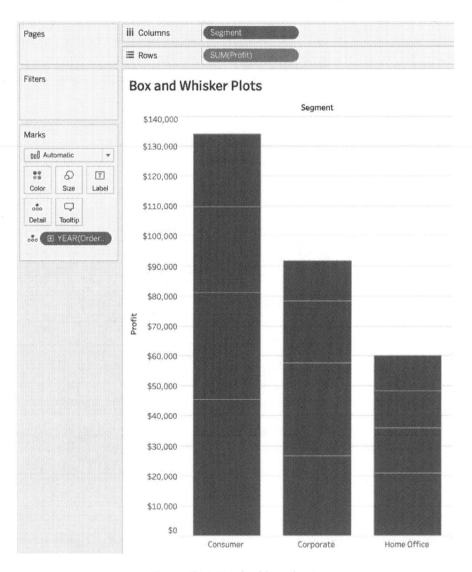

Figure 5.14: Stacked bar chart

Once you add **YEAR(Order Date)** to your **Detail Marks** card, a stacked bar chart is created, where each stack represents the year of the order date.

5. Convert this stacked bar chart into a dot plot for your B&W plots by changing the mark type from **Automatic** to **Circle** (from the **Marks** shelf):

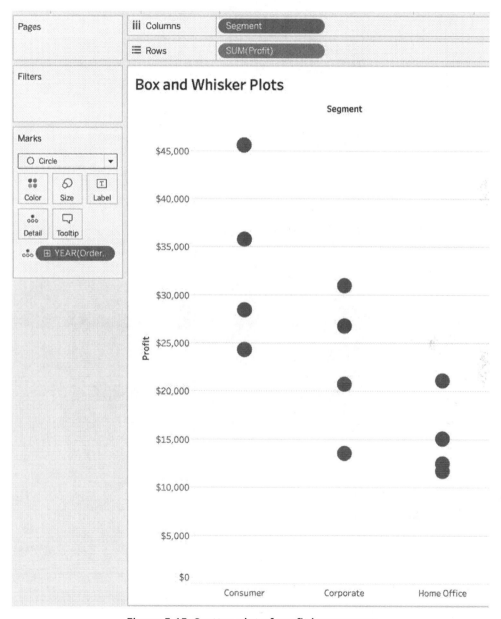

Figure 5.15: Scatter plot of profit by segment

If you don't convert the mark type to a dot plot, you won't be able to see the B&W plots as shown in the following figure:

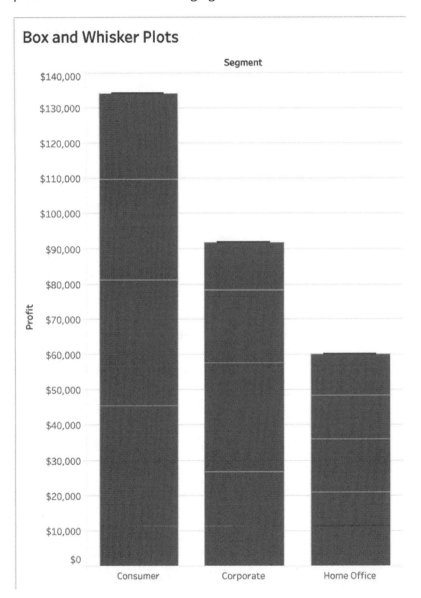

Figure 5.16: Issues with not converting the mark type from Bar to Circle

6. Now, to create the B&W plot, right-click the **y** axis and choose **Add Reference Line**:

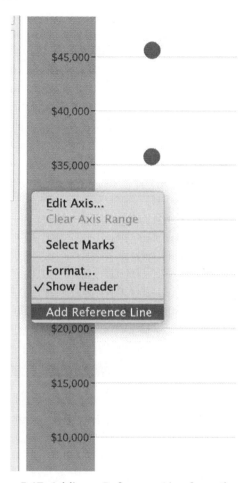

Figure 5.17: Adding a Reference Line from the axis

7. In the **Add Reference Line, Band, or Box** dialog box, select **Box Plot**. You can play with the options, maybe changing the fill color, style, or the weight of the borders and whiskers:

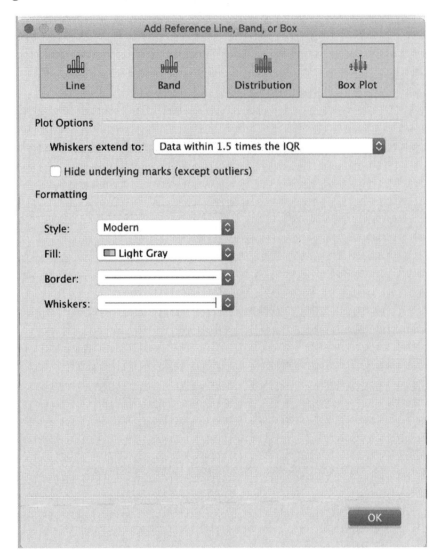

Figure 5.18: Reference line options

IQR, as mentioned previously, stands for interquartile range, which is all the data points between the first and third quartiles. In the **Box** Plot dialog option box, `Data within 1.5 times the IQR` essentially means we are asking Tableau to make all data points on the plot fit within 1.5 times the IQR. Any data point outside the range will be considered an outlier. You will explore this concept with your actual plot in the following figure:

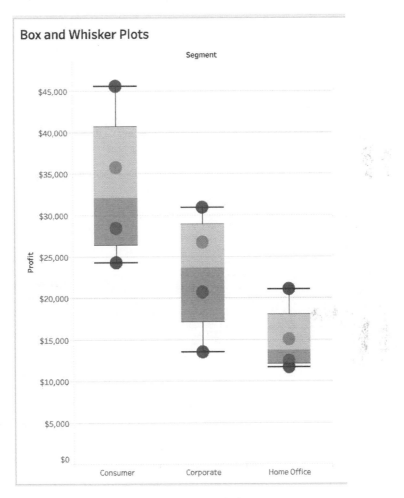

Figure 5.19: B&W plot for profit by segment

The middle line in the box plot, the intersection of light and dark gray, is the median. If you look across the view, you can quickly compare the medians of all the product segments irrespective of how big or small the median is. The upper whisker is 50% higher than the IQR and the lower whisker is 50% lower than the IQR. If data points are outside the box and whisker, those data points are considered outliers and this chart allows you to quickly identify them, which isn't so straightforward in histograms.

Next, you will see how to create a box plot using the **Show Me** panel, a more straightforward method.

EXERCISE 5.03: BOX PLOT USING THE SHOW ME PANEL

In this exercise, you will create a box plot from the **Show me** panel. You will be continuing on from where you left off in the previous exercise, but you may use a new sheet.

Perform the following steps to complete the exercise:

1. Drag **Segment** into **Columns** and **Profit** into **Rows**. This helps create the bar chart.

2. Drag the **YEAR (Order Date)** dimension onto the **Marks** shelf, which you want to use as your distribution dimension. In this example, use **YEAR (Order Date)** as shown here:

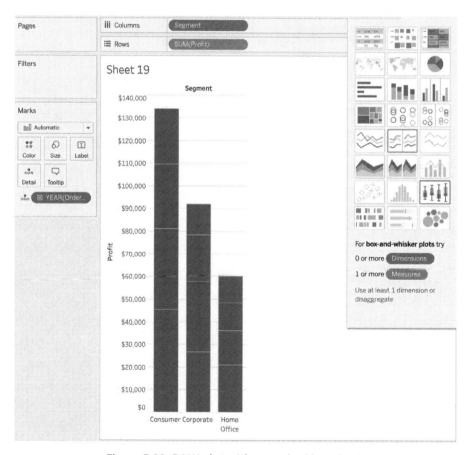

Figure 5.20: B&W plot with a stacked bar chart

3. Click on the **Show Me** panel (as shown in the previous step), and click on **Box and Whisker Plots**:

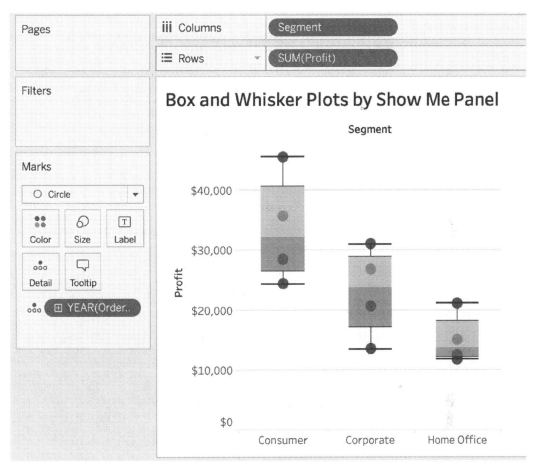

Figure 5.21: Final B&W plot

Consider the median (the middle line in the box plot) of the preceding screenshot. If you look across the view, you can quickly compare the medians of all the product segments irrespective of how big or small the median is. If a data point is outside the B&W, those data points are considered outliers.

Box plots can be incredibly powerful when the right data is in place. A box plot conveys a lot of information in a single chart.

This wraps up the histogram, box, and whisker plot activity using single measures. Next, you will explore scatter plots, which are useful when dealing with two or more measures.

RELATIONSHIP AND DISTRIBUTION WITH MULTIPLE MEASURES

In this part of the chapter, you will explore how to best represent two measures in the same view and how these charts can help build the relationship between two or more measures. You will initially look at scatter plots. Once you cover the distribution part of these multiple-measure charts, you will move on to the relationship between these measures by discussing dual axis charts and their uses.

DISTRIBUTION WITH TWO MEASURES

Scatter plots are two-dimensional graphs created with two to four measures and zero or more dimensions. The first two measures are used as the **x** and **y** axis, and the third and fourth measures, as well as the dimensions, are used for adding more formatting and context to the scatter marks.

Scatter plots are useful when plotting two quantifiable measures against one and other. This could be Sales versus Profit or Quantity versus Discount, for example. Scatter plots also help find patterns or clusters, which aids in decision making, by identifying outliers and groups of points that are related.

If you want to go a level deeper, you can also add reference lines to these plots, which can split the scatter plots into four quadrants (we will walk through an exercise later in the chapter explaining how to create a four-quadrant view). This makes it easier for the end user to call out the relationship.

CREATING A SCATTER PLOT

You will now create a scatter plot in Tableau. When doing this, one measure becomes the **x** axis and the second measure becomes the **y** axis. By default, when you plot two measures in your view, Tableau aggregates these measures to a single dot in the view. You then have to manually de-aggregate (make the more granular) the measure to create the scatter plot (as shown in the following screenshot).

Here is the final version of the scatter plot, which you will create with two measures and two dimensions:

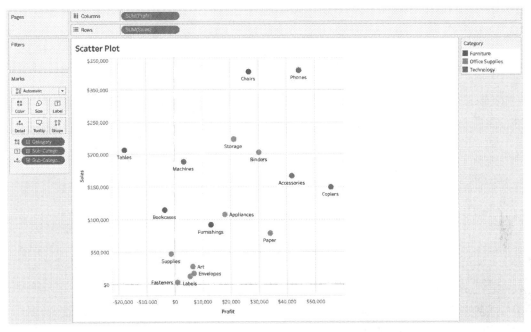

Figure 5.22: Sample scatter plot of Sales versus Profit for each sub-category

The following Exercise 5.04 will outline the steps to this in detail.

EXERCISE 5.04: CREATING A SCATTER PLOT

The manager of your store requests a report looking at total sales versus profit for each sub-category sold in the store. The chart must identify each sub-category, using color to represent the overarching category each subcategory belongs to. You will be using the **Sample – Superstore** dataset to fulfill the request.

Perform the following steps to complete the exercise:

1. Load the **Orders** table from **Sample – Superstore** dataset in your Tableau instance (if its not already open in your Tableau instance).

2. Select two measures for plotting data points. For this exercise, these are **Sales** and **Profit**.

3. Drag **Profit** to the **Columns** shelf and **Sales** to the **Rows** shelf:

Figure 5.23: Aggregated scatter plot of Profit versus Sales

As soon as you drag the second measure to the **Rows** shelf, you get a plot with only one dot in the view. By default, Tableau aggregates all measures whenever they are dragged from the **Data** pane to the shelf. The point here represents the intersection of **Sales** versus Profits for all records in the dataset. You have to specify the level of detail for the plot by de-aggregating the measures.

4. Next, you will de-aggregate the measures to break down your aggregate data point into multiple points. You do that by selecting **Analysis** from the menu bar at the top and de-selecting **Aggregate Measures**:

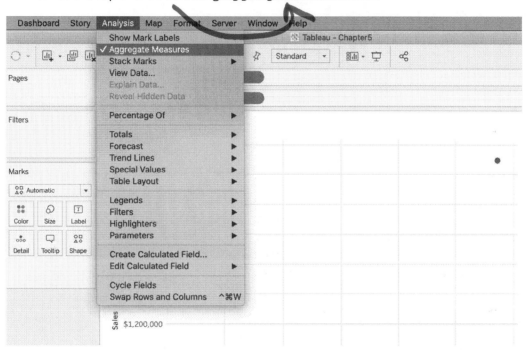

Figure 5.24: How to aggregate/de-aggregate measures

This changes the level of detail of the plot from one point for all the records in the dataset to one point for each record in the dataset.

5. Double-click the title to revise it, and your **Sales** versus **Profit** scatter plot is ready:

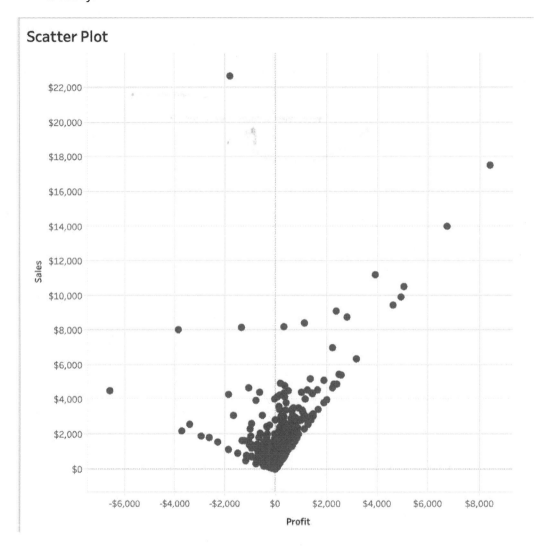

Figure 5.25: De-aggregated scatter plot of Sales versus Profit

In *Figure 5.25*, you see that after de-aggregation there is one point for every order in the dataset, rather than just one mark/point. The view represents every order in the dataset, and the sales and profit of each order ID.

6. Reselect **Aggregate Measures**. Change the level of detail to **Sub-Category**, so there is one dot for each **Sub-Category** in the data. Do this by dragging **Sub-Category** from the **Data** pane to the **Detail Marks** card. Next, drag **Sub-Category** to the **Label Marks** card so it is easier to understand the plot:

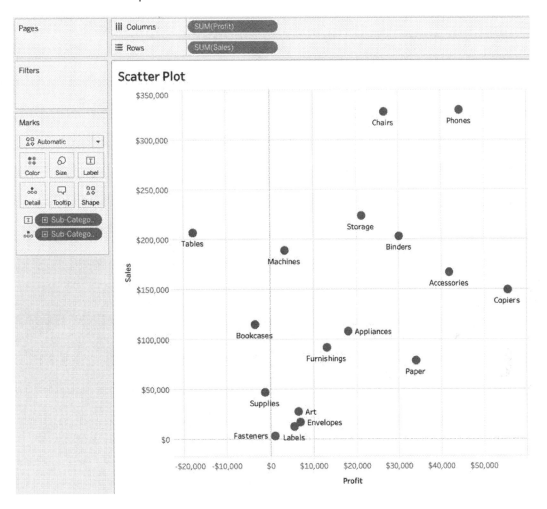

Figure 5.26: Scatter points of total sales versus profit for each sub-category

In *Figure 5.25*, you see that when the level of detail is changed from each order ID to each sub-category, the number of scatter points in the view reduces. There is now one mark representing each sub-category.

7. To add another dimension to the view, add **Category** to the **Color Marks** shelf, which allow you to identify the sub-category quickly. These category colors also act as highlighters. The final output is as follows:

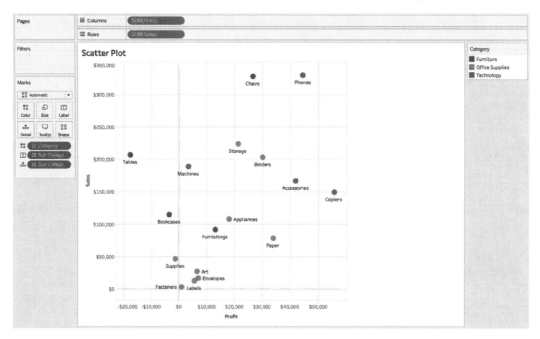

Figure 5.27: Color-coded sub-category scatter plot

Figure 5.27 clearly shows that the **Tables** sub-category brought in roughly $200K in sales, but was a loss-making sub-category, since **Tables** sales shows a loss of about $20K. **Copiers** on the other hand, shows sales of $150K and profits over $50K.

Considering how easy it is to observe these insights, scatter plots can be an incredible tool for plotting two measures against one and other. By adding more visual elements, it can transform into a powerful visual chart that is easily understandable as well as reasonably easy to create.

This wraps up scatter plots with two measures and two dimensions. Next, you will explore trend lines, and the options we have available in Tableau.

SCATTER PLOTS WITH TREND LINES

In this section, rather than focusing on the math that **trend lines** are dependent on, you will look at them from an analyst/data developer perspective, and will see some common use cases in business.

Trend lines are used to observe relationships between variables. For example, they could be used to see the relationship between force and acceleration, or to track the relationship between sales and profits over a given time period. They are statistical models that are useful in estimating future patterns or trends based on historical data points.

Adding trend lines in Tableau is fairly simple. In this section, you will explore the variations of trend lines available. *Figure 5.27* shows the five types of a trend line in Tableau. You will get a thorough definition of each as well as their most common applications a little later in this section.

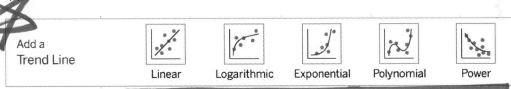

Figure 5.28: Types of trend lines in Tableau

In the next exercise, you will explore trend lines using scatter plots.

EXERCISE 5.05: TREND LINES WITH SCATTER PLOTS

You will create scatter plots (as before),   and will later add trend lines to your charts You will be using the **Sample - Superstore** dataset, and by the end of the exercise, you will have a good grasp of the different types of trend line that Tableau has available.

Perform the following steps to complete this exercise:

1. From the **Superstore** sample dataset, drag **Profit** to the **Columns** shelf in the view.

2. Drag **Sales** to the **Rows** shelf. Tableau automatically aggregates (sums) the measures as a default setting. To change the level of detail in the view or to de-aggregate the view, navigate to **Analysis | Untick Aggregate Measures**.

3. To make these trend lines clearer, add **Order Date** to **Color**. Also, format the opacity of the **Color Marks** to **70%** to make it easier to read.

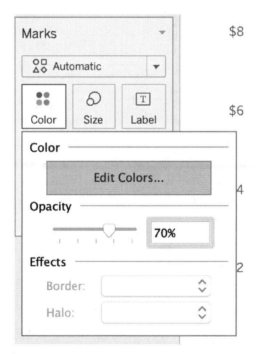

Figure 5.29: Changing Opacity for our Marks

There are three different methods to add trend lines in our views illustrated below:

4. **Method 1 – Using the menu bar**: Navigate to **Analysis | Trend Lines | Show Trend Lines**:

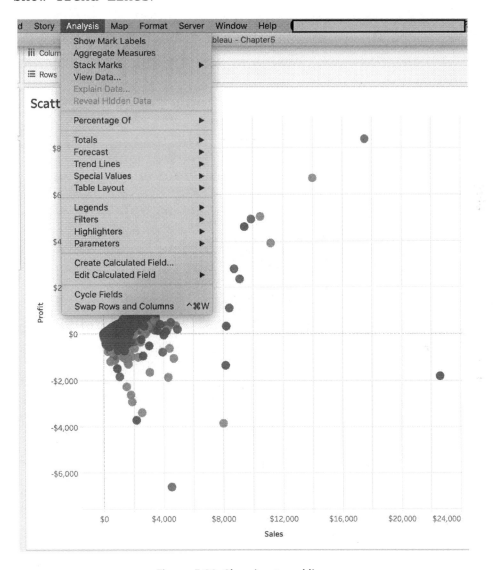

Figure 5.30: Showing trend lines

5. **Method 2 – Using the pane of the view**: Right-click on an empty area or any of the circular **Marks** and navigate to `Trend Lines` | `Show Trend Lines`:

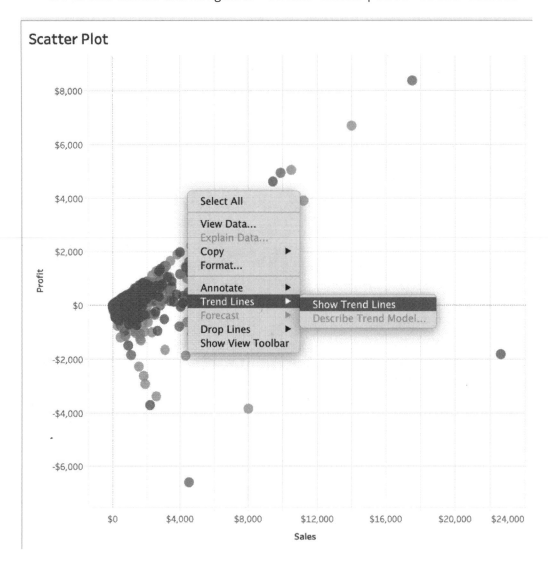

Figure 5.31: Showing Trend Lines – 2

6. **Method 3 – Using the Analytics pane**: If you have not yet explored Tableau's second pane in addition to the **Data** pane, it's about time. Navigate to the **Analytics** pane and drag a trend line into the view. Select any of the trend line options available to you.

> **NOTE**
>
> Depending on your Tableau version, you will either get four or five trend line options. Users with Tableau instances older than Tableau 10.5 won't be able to see the **Power** trend line. This book uses Tableau version 2020.X— hence, the **Power** trend line is available.

The final output is as follows:

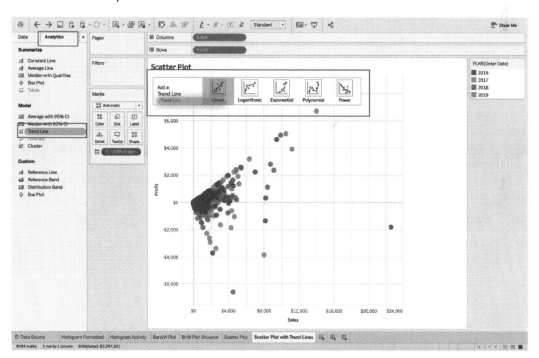

Figure 5.32: Types of trend lines in Tableau

In this exercise, you learned ways to add a trend line to the view. Next, you will explore each trend line in greater detail.

TREND LINES AND TYPES

As previously covered, trend lines help to show the overall trend in the view. They can also be used to predict the continuation of a trend in data. Additionally, they help to identify the correlation between two variables by analyzing the underlying trend.

You will now explore each of the five trend lines that Tableau has to offer, how they differ from each other, and when to use them.

LINEAR TREND LINES

When estimating the linear relationship between independent as well as dependent variables (for example, the exchange rate between US dollars and others currencies), linear trend lines are the best-fit lines. Linear trend lines help to estimate variables that are steadily increasing or decreasing. The formula for a linear trend line is as follows:

$$Y = mx + c$$

Figure 5.33: Linear trend line formula

Here, **Y** is the dependent variable, **x** is the independent variable, which affects the dependent variable. **m** is the slope of the trend line, and **c** is the constant (**y**-intercept).

In a linear model, it is assumed that as one of the variables increases, the rate of increase/decrease for the second variable will increase/decrease at a constant rate too. More often, the variables will fall close to the trend line plotted by the model. The following figure shows an example of a linear trend line:

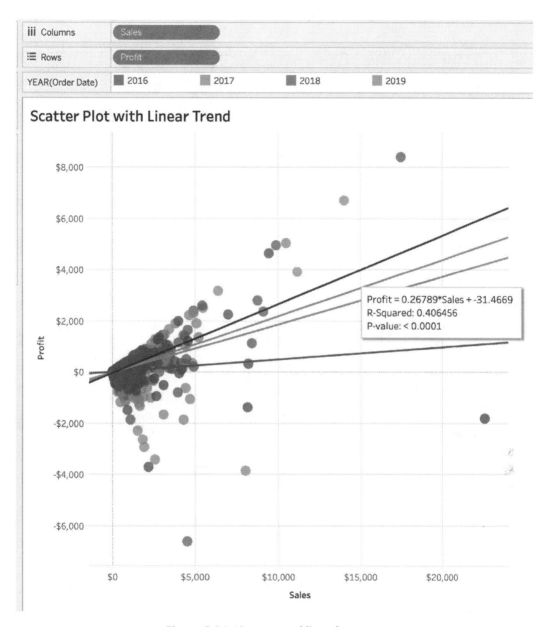

Figure 5.34: Linear trend line showcase

POLYNOMIAL TREND LINES

Polynomial, as the word suggests, means *multiple items*, and is best when there are a lot of fluctuations in your data. For example, it might be used when analyzing the gains and losses of stocks over a large dataset. The degree/order of a polynomial trend line is useful for determining the number of fluctuations or hills/bends in our data. The formula for a polynomial trend line is as follows:

$$Y = M_1 X_1 + M_2 X_2 + M_3 X_3 \dots M_n X_n + C$$

Figure 5.35: Polynomial trend lines formula

Here, *Y* is the dependent variable, *x* is the independent variable, which affects the dependent variable; *m* is the slope at a point, and *c* is the constant.

The following figure shows an example of a scatter plot with a polynomial trend line:

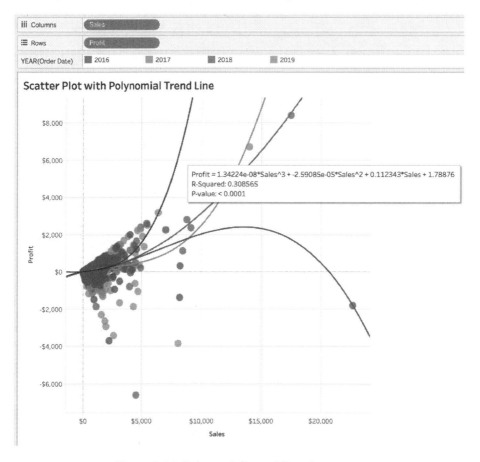

Figure 5.36: Polynomial trend line showcase

POLYNOMIAL DEGREE OF FREEDOM

In the following screenshot, the degree of freedom for the polynomial trend line is **3**, which means that, after analyzing the dataset, Tableau decided that the data should have three bends/hills depending on the fluctuations. A degree of **3** usually has either one or two hills and/or valleys. If you want the data to be more precise and sensitive to fluctuations, you can increase the degree of freedom to the maximum value of 8. Go ahead and play with it.

Figure 5.37: Polynomial degree of freedom edit

LOGARITHMIC TREND LINES

If variables increase/decrease quickly and the rate later flattens out, the best-fit lines are logarithmic trend lines. An example of a logarithmic trend line is inflation rate, where the inflation rate can increase/decrease quickly and eventually flatten as the economy starts to stabilize. Another example is the rate of learning for a novice versus an expert. When a novice starts learning a topic, the rate of learning is Very fast but as they master the topic, the rate of learning flattens out. Like a linear trend line, a logarithmic trend line can use both negative and positive values.

$$Y = m_1 * \ln(X) + C$$

Figure 5.38: Logarithmic trend line formula

Here, **Y** is the dependent variable, **ln(X)** is the log base, which affects the dependent variable; **m** is the slope, and **c** is the constant. The following figure shows a scatter plot with a logarithmic trend line:

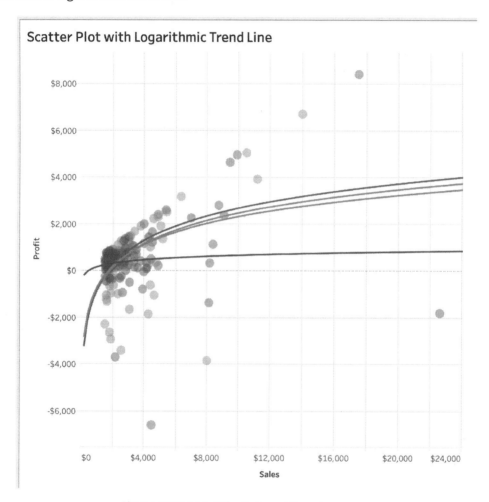

Figure 5.39: Logarithmic trend line showcase

> **NOTE**
>
> The opacity is reduced and some of the data is filtered to make it more readable.

EXPONENTIAL TREND LINES

The exponential trend line is the best-fit line that is most useful when the rate of the rise/fall of data is steep. The rate of spread of a virus is exponential, as an example from nature: COVID-19. The formula for an exponential trend line is as follows:

$$Y = M_1 e^{(m*X)}$$

Figure 5.40: Exponential trend line formula

Here, Y is the dependent variable, X is the independent variable, which affects the dependent variable; m is the slope of the line, and e is the mathematical constant. The following plot shows the execution of an exponential trend line:

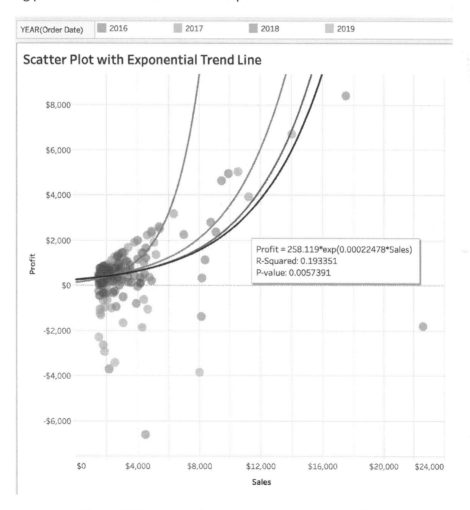

Figure 5.41: Scatter plot with an exponential trend line

POWER TREND LINES

A power trend line is usually a curved line that is best utilized when the dataset contains measures that increase at a specific rate. Think about the rate of interest every year, the rate of water flow from a dam every minute, or the acceleration of a train or car. Although the trend line looks like a linear trend line, it is not linear, but curved. The formula for a power trend line is as follows:

$$Y = M_1 * X^{(m_2)}$$

Figure 5.42: Power trend line formula

Here, **Y** is the dependent variable, **X** is the independent variable, which affects the dependent variable, and **m1** and **m2** are the slope. The following figure shows a scatter plot with a power trend line:

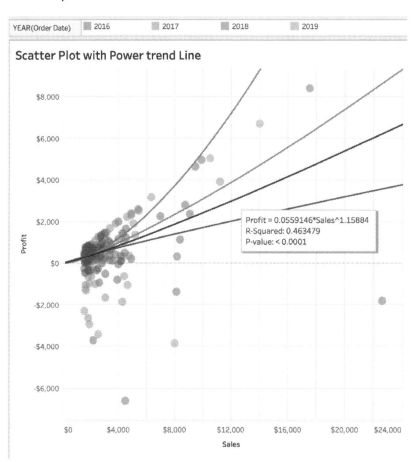

Figure 5.43: Power trend line plot

This wraps up the types of trend lines in Tableau. Next, you will explore the reliability of trend lines and the significance of R-squared values and p-values.

THE RELIABILITY OF TREND LINES

For each of the trend lines, you have a tooltip that includes the trend line formula, the R-squared value, and the p-value. For example, in a power trend line, **Profit**, which is the dependent variable, is related to the independent variable of **Sales** as seen in the following formula:

$$\text{Profit} = 0.5591 * \text{Sales}^\wedge 1.158$$

Figure 5.44: Power trend line result

The way to read the formula is that for every unit increase in *Sales*, *Profit* will be calculated by multiplying *Sales* by the *power* of *1.158* by *0.5591*. You will now explore the significance of R-squared values and p-values.

R-SQUARED

As end users of the trend line, it is important to understand the reliability of these predictions. The trend line is considered most reliable when the R-squared value is closest to 1. This signals that there is an extremely high likelihood that future data/variables will fall within the predicted line (or close to it).

P-VALUE

The **p-value** is a statistical function that quantifies how likely it is that a given prediction happened by chance. The lower the p-value, the more statistically significant. In the power trend line example, the p-value was very small ($p < 0.0001$), which means if you were to collect the data points for the report again, it is highly likely you would see a similar trend, . For most use cases, any p-value greater than $p > 0.05$ is considered statistically insignificant, which means if you were to repeat the same data collection, you would likely not get a similar trend, since there is a greater than 5% chance the results were due to randomness or chance.

This wraps up the section on trend lines, where you explored the five default trend lines Tableau and the importance of R-squared and p-value. In the next section, you will compare two measures with one another via dual axis.

ADVANCED CHARTS

In previous exercises, you have explored distributions and relationships across single as well as multiple measures, which allows you to answer essential business questions relatively well. But Tableau offers advanced chart types, which can help answer complicated questions such as *What are the trends of profit with regard to sales by year?* You can easily answer this question by utilizing a dual axis chart.

In this section, you will explore the following chart types:

- Quadrant charts

- Combination charts

- Lollipop charts

- Pareto charts

This is certainly not an exhaustive list of the advanced charting available in Tableau; there are other interesting chart types such as donut charts, sparkline charts, Sankey diagrams, and waffle charts. But the charts above are some of the essential ones that are most frequently used in business dashboards, and are generally well received by end users.

QUADRANT CHARTS

Quadrant charts are just scatter plots divided into four grids instead of two sections. In the scatter plots created previously (*Exercise 5.04, Creating a Scatter Plot*), you compared sales versus profits, but it was difficult to identify outliers, or marks that had high profit and high sales, or low profit and high sales.

Quadrant charts can help . In this section, you will create a quadrant chart, as you can see in the following figure:

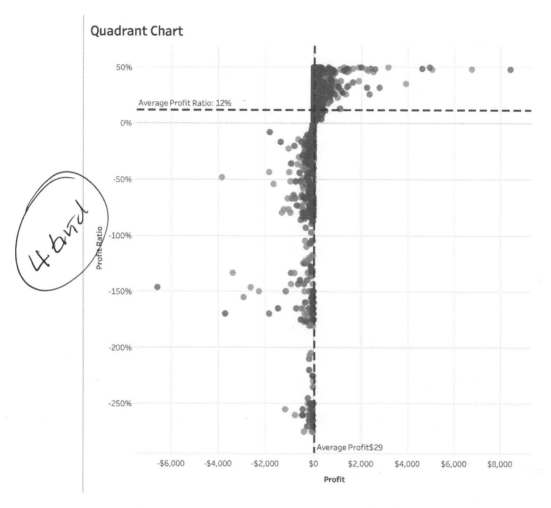

Figure 5.45: Power trend line result

Before creating your quadrant chart, it is important to talk about reference lines and the options available.

REFERENCE LINES

Reference lines do what their name suggests, adding a reference to our view. You can add reference lines either as constants or with calculated values of the axis. When you add a reference line with a computed value, the line is dynamic and adjusts depending on the specific field that the line is dependent on.

Apart from reference lines, you can also add confidence intervals to lines.

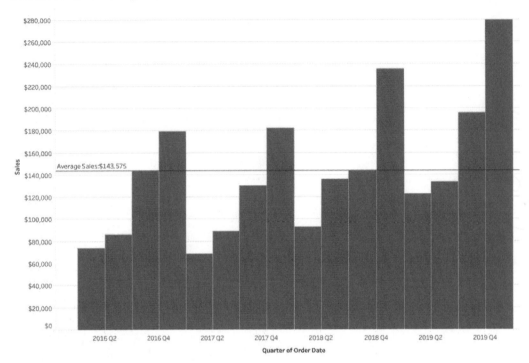

Figure 5.46: Reference line for average sales for the Superstore dataset

In the preceding screenshot, the reference line added in the view represents the average sales each quarter across the dataset. Adding reference lines helps to create a reference point where the reference point can be compared with the overall view.

UNDERSTANDING REFERENCE LINES

To better understand the importance of reference lines, you will now create a sample view of sales by year and explore the types of reference lines available in Tableau:

- **Entire Table Reference Line**: The scope of this type of reference line is the entire table.

- **Per Pane Reference Line**: This type of reference line is added to each sub-section of the view.

- **Per Cell Reference Line**: With this reference line type, you add a reference line for each individual cell in the view.

The steps to this are as follows:

1. Assuming you have the **Sample - Superstore** dataset open in Tableau instance, add **YEAR(Order Date)**, then drag **Category** (*Ctrl* + drag for Windows or *Option* + drag for Mac) to the **Columns** shelf.

2. Drag **Sales** to the **Rows** shelf and, to add color to the view, drag **YEAR(Order Date)** to the **Color Marks** card:

Figure 5.47: Sales by category and year

3. Navigate to the **Analytics** pane and select and drag **Reference Lines** to the view. As you do so, you get three options: **Table**, **Pane**, and **Cell**. These are the scope of the reference lines that you have to select for the view.

4. **Entire Table Reference Line**: The scope of the reference line in the entire table. In this case, you are adding a reference line for Average Sales for the entire table.

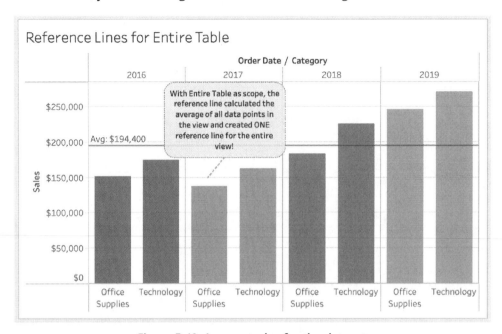

Figure 5.48: Average sales for the dataset

5. **Per Pane Reference Line**: In this type of reference line, the reference line is added to each category and the average or any other computation is calculated as required by each category.

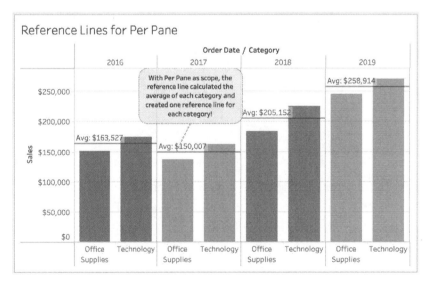

Figure 5.49: Average sales by year

6. **Per Cell Reference Line**: This is likely the least used reference line, because, in this case, it just adds a reference line for sales by category for each of the years in the view, which as you can see in the following figure is just a reference line at the top of the bar chart.

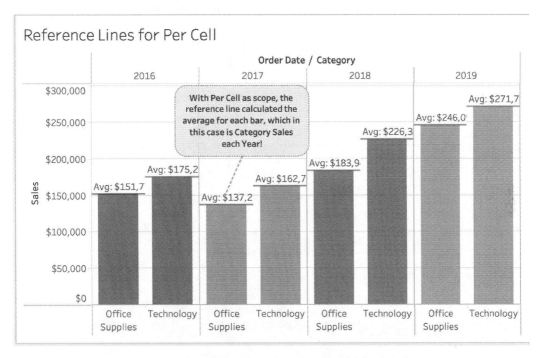

Figure 5.50: Average sales by category and year

7. In the preceding screenshots, you might have noticed that the reference line has the **Average Sales** label at the start of the line. You can add that either while adding the reference line to the view or by editing after adding the reference line to the view. Right-click **Reference Lines | Edit Reference Lines**. Navigate to **Label** and select **Custom** from the dropdown. Type your label name with **<Value>** (in this case, **Avg: <Value>**):

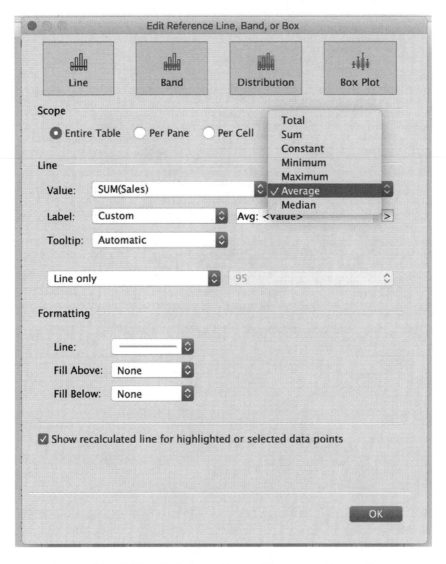

Figure 5.51: Editing Reference Lines with aggregation options

If you want to change the scope of your reference line, you can edit it from the **Edit Reference Line, Band, or Box** window that you saw in the previous step. You can also change the value of your measure to be count, sum, min, max, or some other aggregation as per your need.

EXERCISE 5.06: CREATING QUADRANT CHARTS

In this exercise, you will analyze store data to find both overall profit across all orders, as well as profit ratio. A reference point should be present in the view that allows anyone to quickly understand higher profit and higher profit ratio orders, as well as lower profit and higher loss-making orders.

The best chart to fulfill these requirements is the quadrant chart, because it allows for scatter plot-creation with vertical and horizontal reference lines, which will help create a reference point with regard to profit versus profit ratio.

You will be using the **Sample – Superstore** dataset. By the end of the exercise, you should be able to understand the different types of reference lines available in Tableau.

Perform the followings steps to complete the exercise:

1. Open the **Sample – Superstore** dataset in your Tableau instance.

2. Create a scatter plot of profit versus profit ratio. Drag **Profit** to the **Columns** shelf and **Profit Ratio** to the **Rows** shelf. De-aggregate the measures by navigating to **Analysis** and unchecking **Aggregate Measures**.

> **NOTE**
>
> If Profit Ratio is unavailable for you, use **Sales** instead.

3. Drag **YEAR(Order Date)** (*Ctrl* + drag for Windows and *Option* + drag for Mac) to the **Color Marks** shelf:

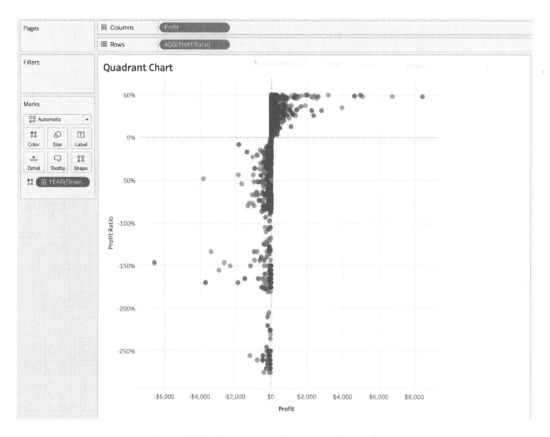

Figure 5.52: Scatter plot for a quadrant chart

As you can see, you have plotted all orders on the x-y axis where the **x axis** is **Profit** and the **y axis** is **Profit Ratio**. You also color-coded the orders by year.

4. To add quadrants, add reference lines to the view. Since a quadrant contains two lines intersecting in the middle, you will be adding two reference lines—one for **Average Profit,** and one for **Average Profit Ratio.**

5. Navigate to the **Analytics** pane, and drag **Reference Lines** to the view. First, you will create a reference line for **Profit**, which in this case is the vertical reference line. Right-click the reference line to edit the **Label** text and value as discussed in the *Understanding Reference Lines* section. You have added **Average Profit: <Value>** as the **Label Marks** card for the vertical line.

6. Repeat the steps for a horizontal reference line, which in this case, is the average horizontal reference line for **Profit Ratio**:

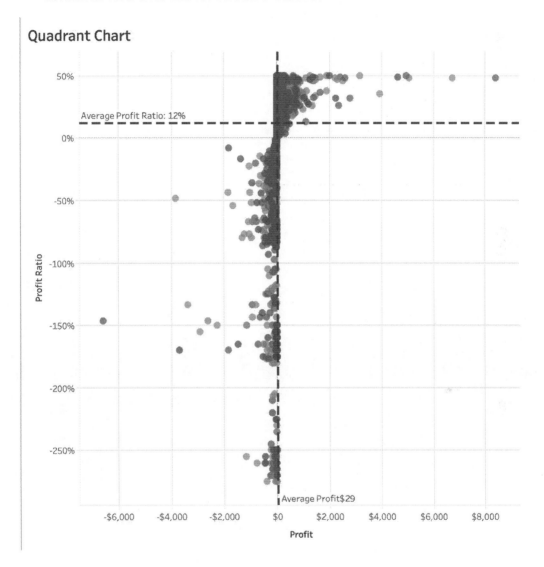

Figure 5.53: Reference lines on a scatter plot

In the preceding figure, you added two reference lines with aggregation set to Average. The *horizontal reference line* represents **Average Profit Ratio** across **Orders** and the *vertical reference line* represents **Average Profit** across **Orders**.

7. To make it easier for an audience, you can annotate the quadrants by right-clicking in the view and adding annotation text as shown in the following figure:

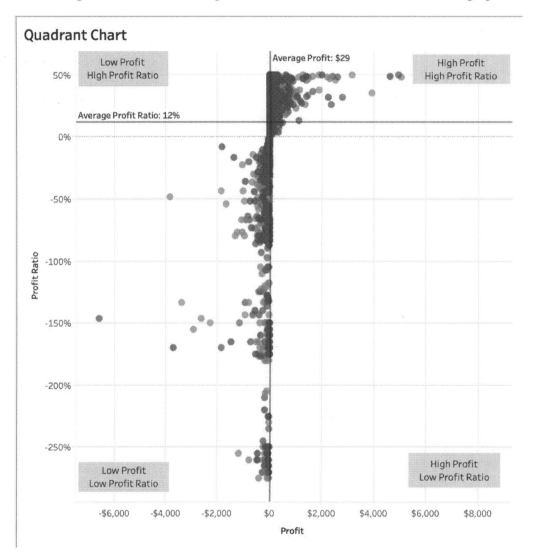

Figure 5.54: Annotated text quadrant chart

This wraps up this section on quadrant charts. You have now explored reference lines in combination with scatter plots and have also added annotations to the view, which is a great contextual tool for charts. Next, you will explore dual axis charts.

COMBINATION CHARTS — DUAL AXIS CHARTS

Combination charts (otherwise known as dual axis charts or combo charts) are one of the most popular chart types due to their flexibility and the value they add to storytelling. Dual axis chart types are essentially two charts merged into one with a shared axis. For example, a date dimension could be the **x** axis and you could have two separate **y** axes on the same chart representing two different measures. An example of a dual axis chart for our **Superstore** dataset would be the trends of profit with regard to sales by year. Here, **Year** will be the **Date** dimension (**x** axis) and Sales and Profit will be the **y** axis. You will create a dual axis chart with similar mark types as part of the section.

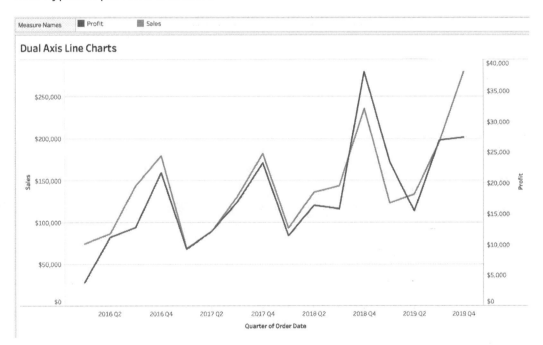

Figure 5.55: Sample dual axis line chart

As you can see in the preceding figure, there are two line charts in the same view. The blue line represents **Profit** by **Quarter** and the orange line represents **Sales** by **Quarter**.

EXERCISE 5.07: CREATING DUAL AXIS CHARTS

Now, you will create a view of sales versus profits, and will also show the trends of both these business-critical metrics in the view. The view has to be by quarter. You will be using the **Sample - Superstore** dataset to create the view.

Perform the following steps to complete this exercise:

1. Open the **Sample – Superstore** dataset in your Tableau instance.

2. Drag **QUARTER(Order Date)** to the **Columns** shelf and click the arrow on **QUARTER(Order Date)** in the **Columns** shelf and change the level of detail for the dimension to **Continuous** (you can also press *Ctrl* + drag for Windows or *Option* + drag for Mac to select **Continuous**):

Figure 5.56: Converting the date to Continuous

3. Add **Profit** as well as **Sales** to the **Rows** shelf. Create two bar charts as shown in the following figure. Add **QUARTER(Order Date)** as **Label** for better representation:

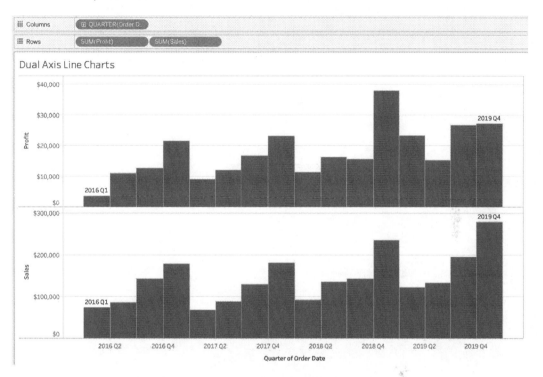

Figure 5.57: Profit and Sales bar charts by quarter

4. On the **Marks** shelf, there are three sections: **All**, **SUM(Profit)**, and **SUM(Sales)**. Having individual measures as **Marks** cards allows you to control each of these measures separately. On the **All** marks card (if applicable in your Tableau instance), change the **Marks** type from **Bar** to **Line**. The output is shown in the following screenshot:

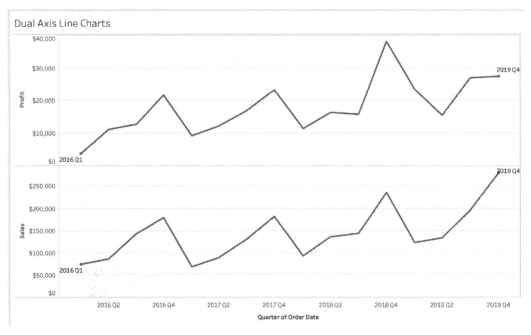

Figure 5.58: Sales and Profit line charts by quarter

5. The most important step is to right-click or click on the down arrow for either of the two measures (**Profit** or **Sales**) in the **Rows** shelf and tick to select **Dual Axis**.

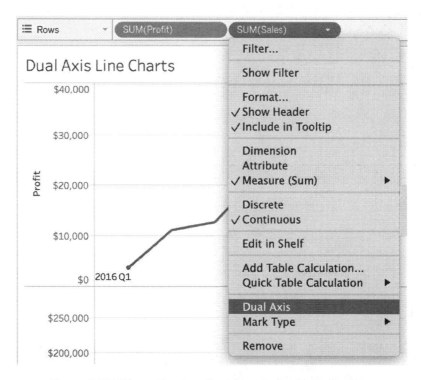

Figure 5.59: Converting two line charts to a dual axis chart

6. There are now two separate measures, **Profit** and **Sales**, sharing **Order Date** as a common *x* axis and two measure values as the *y* axis:

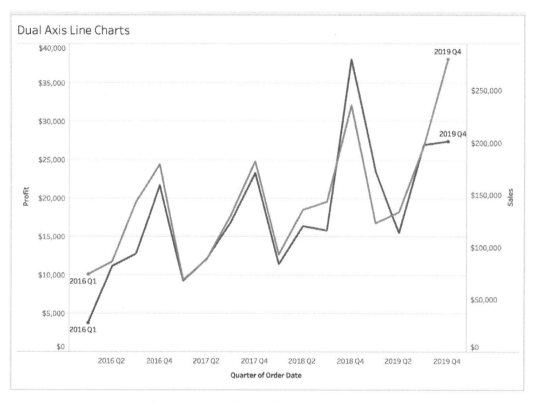

Figure 5.60: Dual axis chart – asynchronous

If you observe closely, the two axes have different **Marks**, with the **Profit** axis ranging from **$0-$40,000**, and **Sales** ranging from **$0-$250,000**. The chart portrays the completely wrong picture, because the two line charts have different axis ranges and could lead to incorrect insights.

7. To fix the asynchronous axes, right-click either of the axes and select **Synchronize Axis,** this will fix the issue and should now have two axes with the same ranges:

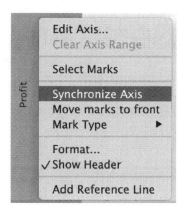

Figure 5.61: How to synchronize a dual axis chart

The final output will be as follows:

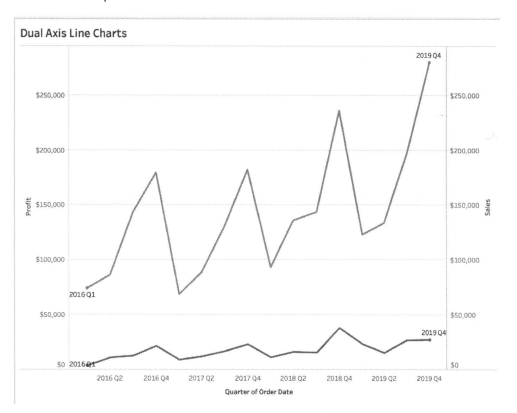

Figure 5.62: Synchronized dual axis chart

You have now created your first dual axis chart. The title or axes labels can be changed as per your requirements. In the preceding screenshot, after synchronizing the axes, you see that for **2016 Q4**, **Sales** were in the range of **$150-200K**, whereas **Profit** was in the range of **$0-50K**. If you had not synchronized the axes, it would have been difficult to understand what the sales or profit was for each of the line charts.

As you have observed, dual axis charts such as scatter plots can be *incredibly powerful charts to convey information in the most succinct, contextual way.* In *Figure 5.62*, you can see sales versus profit growth over the years, and can analyze the trend while doing so.

This brings to close the main body of the chapter. You will now complete some activities to build on what you have learned.

ACTIVITY 5.01: CREATING SCATTER PLOTS

Imagine you work as an e-commerce analyst and your manager has asked you to create a view of **Sales** versus **Profit Ratio**. (Use **Profit**, if **Profit Ratio** is unavailable for you.) They want to see the metric broken down by **Segment** and **Year**. You will use scatter plots to achieve this, and will fulfill the requirements using the **Sample – Superstore** dataset.

The following steps will help you complete this activity:

1. Open the **Sample – Superstore** dataset in Tableau instance.

2. Double-click or drag **Profit Ratio** to the **Columns** shelf.

3. Repeat the last step for the **Sales** to **Rows** shelf.

4. De-aggregate the measure by navigating to **Analysis** and unselecting the aggregate measures.

5. Add **Category** to the **Color Marks** card and **Segment** to the **Shape Marks** card.

6. Next, add **Segment** to **Filters** and show it in your view.

7. Repeat the same step for **YEAR(Order Date)**, by dragging **Order Date** to the **Filter** shelf.

8. Change both the filters shown in the view to **Single Value (List)** by clicking or right-clicking on the top-right arrow.

9. Double-click on **View Title** to change the title of the worksheet to **Scatter Plot by Segment and Year**.

10. Change the opacity of your color to **70%** for better readability.

11. You should have the following filters.

    The final output will be as follows:

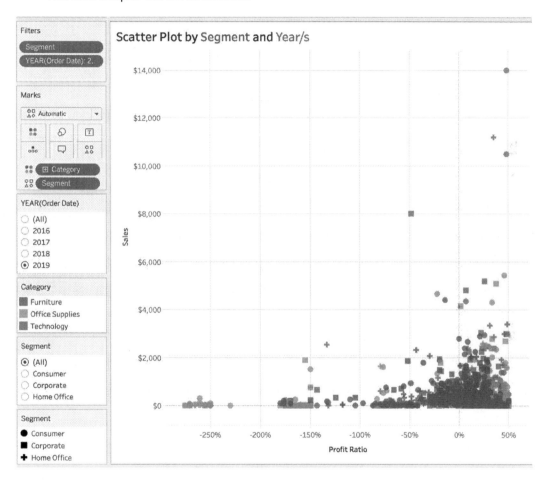

Figure 5.63: Activity final output

In this activity, you strengthened your knowledge of scatter plots and formatting options.

As a chart reading exercise, consider the circular (**Consumer** segment), red (**Technology** category) mark type at the top right of the chart. As you see, this particular point (order) has a high sales figure, and a high profit ratio for 2019. An observing category manager, will see such outliers, and can now take steps to replicate this success across the board.

> **NOTE**
>
> The solution to this activity can be found here: https://packt.link/CTCxk.

ACTIVITY 5.02: DUAL AXIS CHART WITH ASYNCHRONOUS AXES

This activity continues on from the last. After fulfilling the initial scatter plot requirements, you are now tasked with creating a dual axis chart, that shows how **Discounts** affect **Sales** month by month. Essentially, you are asked to create a view of sales versus discounts by month using a dual axis chart with an asynchronous dual axis.

The following steps will help you complete this activity:

1. Open the **Sample - Superstore** dataset in your Tableau instance.

2. Create the initial bar chart showing **Sales by Order Date by Month (Continuous)**.

3. Change the chart type from **Line** to **Bar** from the **Marks** card.

4. Drag **Discount** to the **Column** shelf.

5. Create a dual axis by right-clicking on any of the measures in the **Column** shelf.

6. Change the mark type of **Discount** from **Bar** to **Line** from the **Marks** shelf.

7. Don't synchronize your axes, because if you do, the **Discount** axis will have a range of 0-120,000%, which in reality does not exist.

8. Format the chart by adding the **Discount** label for **Discount**, and edit the color of the Discount line chart to blue, or any color you prefer.

The final expected output is as follows:

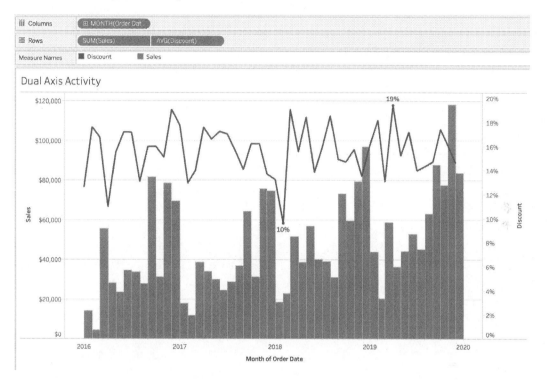

Figure 5.64: Final output of Activity 5.02

In this activity, you created a dual axis chart with different marks types for the measures, and explored why synchronizing the axes is not always a good idea, as it can lead to extrapolating or under-reporting the actual numbers.

The way to read the preceding dual axis chart is, say, for **April 2016**, the average discount was **11%** and **Total Sales** that month were **$28,295**.

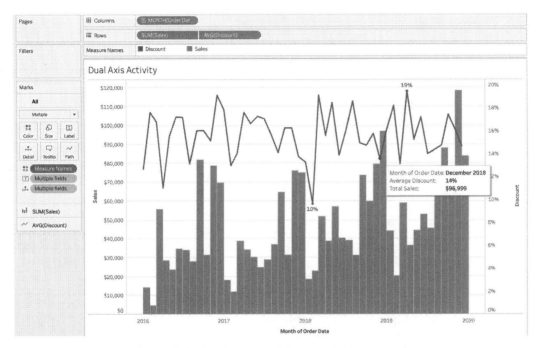

Figure 5.65: Dual axis final output of Activity 5.02

Similarly, for the month of **December 2018**, you should notice that the average discount was **14%** while **Total Sales** that month were **$96,999**. If you sync your dual axes, the average discount percentage would probably be in the thousands, as seen in *Figure 5.73*.

NOTE

The solution to this activity can be found here: https://packt.link/CTCxk.

SUMMARY

In this chapter, you explored distribution with one-measure histograms, box and whisker plots, and multiple-measure scatter plots. You also saw in detail the types of trend lines available in Tableau, why they are used, and which trend lines are most appropriate for given situations. Then, you learned how to check whether a trend line created by Tableau is reliable,   and touched on the R-squared value and p-value. Finally, you explored advanced chart types, where we interacted with dual axis and quadrant charts. Finally, you completed some activities on dual axis charts with asynchronous axes, as well as scatter plots with filters and shapes.

You are now at the stage where you can start to answer data questions using all the different types of you have created. You can start adding readability elements , and you can also create advanced visualizations if the view requires you to answer multiple questions at once (such as profit versus sales trend by quarter on a dual axis chart).

In the next chapter, you will move away from standard data and on to geographical data, where you will dive deeper into maps and the formatting options available.

6

DATA EXPLORATION: EXPLORING GEOGRAPHICAL DATA

OVERVIEW

This chapter reviews the geographic capabilities available within Tableau. Tableau provides an extensive set of options for working with location-based source data, which can help you design solutions using either point or polygon location data. By the end of this chapter, you will be able to effectively use geographic data in Tableau to perform sophisticated location-based analyses. You will gain a greater understanding of how to import multiple data formats and use your data to create polished, interactive maps. These skills will be developed through a series of exercises followed by an activity wherein you will create your own geographic workbook from start to finish.

INTRODUCTION

In the last chapter, you explored distributions and relationships in a dataset and learned how to identify patterns within a given dataset. This chapter will focus on the geographic aspect of data and how location affects those distributions and relationships.

Understanding geographic patterns is critical for many datasets, whether they are revenue patterns around the world for a global corporation or local purchase patterns for a small business. This type of data is especially useful for explaining patterns to internal or external customers with maps, in which you can show patterns at the region or country level all the way down to postal code or even smaller geographic levels, depending on how the data is collected. This can be highly useful for visualizing purchase, voting, or demographic patterns, as just a few examples.

One of the most powerful aspects of using geographic data and maps lies in the intuitive understanding of location data many users are likely to have. This helps to put patterns in perspective, allowing you to more quickly derive critical insights about the locations and interactions of customers, clients, donors, or other stakeholders within your organization.

Geographic data can be as simple as basic street address information or as complex as custom location-based hierarchies created by an organization, where multiple geographic levels have been defined based on a set of custom boundaries. Ideally, your work starts with data that has already been geocoded, making it quite simple to read the data into Tableau without further steps. In some cases, you will need to do some additional work so that your location data is accurately defined. It is very important to understand the level of geographic granularity you are working with in your data, as well as the type of location information that is captured in the data: do you have latitude and longitude coordinates in your source data, or will you use Tableau to automatically perform this process?

In this chapter, you will learn how to import geographic data and use it in your Tableau worksheets and dashboards. The chapter will also highlight when location data should be mapped and when it is best used within charts to tell the most effective story, as well as which level of geographic granularity (postal code, city, state, and so on) is appropriate for an analysis. By the end of the chapter, you will be proficient in using geographic data as a critical part of your Tableau toolkit.

In this chapter, you will work with a Madrid Airbnb dataset for your point data and a shapefile with New York City boundaries for your polygon data.

IMPORTING SPATIAL DATA

Before you can use the many capabilities Tableau provides for geographic datasets, it is important to understand the geographic data types that Tableau can utilize. Tableau can ingest geospatial data from many popular formats, including **shapefile**, **GeoJSON**, and **MapInfo** sources. The next section will cover some of the most common spatial formats and how to add them to your workbooks.

Spatial data is unique in how it defines geographic attributes. While typical spreadsheet or database data may contain geographic elements (city, state, country, postal code, and so on), it will not contain additional information about those entities. Most often, you will have a pair of geographic coordinates to work with: latitude and longitude. For common entities such as a country, state, or province, mapping software will recognize the codes and allow the use of choropleth (filled) maps.

Choropleth maps are shapefiles/**GeoJSON** data sources that not only contain simple latitude/longitude values corresponding to a postal code centroid, a store location, or even a city, but also include shape details as well as other geospatial details. You can create choropleth maps based on polygons in the data source. For anything more sophisticated or customized, you will typically rely on some type of spatial file that provides very detailed boundary information. Choropleth maps are synonymous with filled maps—the type often seen in displaying political or other preference data at a country, state, or county level. They differ from point-based maps, which are typically defined by a single latitude and longitude set of coordinates. In some cases, you can overlay points on a choropleth map to communicate a second layer of information to the viewer. Now that you have a basic understanding of what spatial, as well as choropleth, maps are, you can now proceed to learn about types of data files for these map types.

DATA FILE TYPES

This section will briefly discuss several types of spatial files that can be easily used in Tableau. Each of these data types represents specific spatial (geographic) data formats that may contain additional values at specific geographic levels. As previously noted, these types differ from typical databases or spreadsheet data that may also contain geographic fields such as city, state, or postal code. Those data sources will be addressed in the following subsection; your current focus is on several very specific spatial sources. Let's take a brief tour of each type.

ESRI SHAPEFILES

Shapefiles are commonly encountered when users are looking for boundary files defining specific geographic levels. This type of data is frequently viewed as polygons (or areas corresponding to specific geographic definitions) but may also contain point or line data. Shapefile data is contained in a set of multiple file types, and must contain at a minimum the `.shp`, `.shx`, and `.dbf` file type extensions. There are many other optional extensions providing additional information about the underlying geographic data.

Shapefiles are quite popular and are used especially for choropleth maps showing specific attributes about defined geographic areas, often based on administrative boundaries such as country, state/province, or county, such as official zoning maps from the city government, which you will explore later in the chapter.

GEOJSON FILES

GeoJSON is a format dating from 2008 and may contain geographic details at the point, line string, and polygon levels, as well as combinations of these three types. Files in this format can be more flexible than shapefiles as they use the JSON structure to include multiple levels of detail. Not all geometries can be represented in GeoJSON, but it is now recommended as a preferred alternative to shapefiles in many instances.

GeoJSON also enables geographic movement to be represented; for example, a driving route or a flight path can be tracked by a series of geographic coordinates in sequence, forming a `LineString`. Other geographic types include `Point`, `Polygon`, `MultiPoint`, `MultiLineString`, and `MultiPolygon`. These types may be used individually or in combination, making GeoJSON a flexible, powerful geospatial source.

KML FILES

KML is an acronym for **Keyhole Markup Language** and is in an XML type of format, always with latitude and longitude attributes as well as named geographic points (London, New York City, and so on). This has traditionally been the format used by Google Earth for plotting coordinates on a map.

MAPINFO INTERCHANGE FORMAT

MapInfo Interchange Format (**MIF**) files contain database and map information originating in the MapInfo software program, one of the oldest and most popular dedicated **Geographic Information System** (**GIS**) platforms.

MAPINFO TABLES

MapInfo tables (the `.tab` file extension) contain vector data formats for use in GIS software. As with shapefiles, there are multiple files used to contain attribute data, location data, and other related information.

TOPOJSON FILES

TopoJSON is an extension of GeoJSON that also includes topology information, which can be used to color maps based on topological features within an area.

DOWNLOADING THE DATA SOURCE FROM GITHUB

As has been previously mentioned, to complete this or any other chapter in this book, it is highly recommended that you use the data source uploaded to the official GitHub repository. The reasoning for this is that, by the time you are reading this book, the official data source or the link to that data source might have been changed. In addition, most times, the data source that is part of the GitHub repository for the book is cleaned to aid understanding of the concepts. Therefore, wherever possible, utilize the data from the official GitHub link, rather than downloading the data from official data sources.

The *Chapter 6: Data Exploration: Exploring Geographical Data* GitHub data source folder can be found at the following URL: http://packt.link/6fzj9.

- **NYC Zoning Data**: ESRI which stands for Environmental Systems Research Institute, is an organization which has supported in design, development as well as implementation of geographic based information management systems since 1969. In our data folder "New York City Zoning" folder, contains ESRI format spatial files which is a combination of .shp, .shx, .dbf, and .prj file formats. To connect to these spatial files, all the above files as well as .zip files should be included in the same folder.

  City of New York data source link: https://data.cityofnewyork.us/City-Government/Zoning-GIS-Data-Shapefile/kdig-pewd.

- **Madrid Airbnb data source**: InsideAirBnB.com was created by Murray Cox for his project on Airbnb and the dataset contains multiple files including listing details, reviews, as well as neighborhood details.

  InsideAirBnB data source link: http://insideairbnb.com/get-the-data.html.

- **SF buyout data**: This file is obtained from the City of San Francisco's public data repo, which contains a shapefile (.shp) of all the buyout agreements of the City of San Francisco from 2015. You will use this data source in the activity section.

  SFGov.org data source link: https://data.sfgov.org/Housing-and-Buildings/Buyout-Agreements/wmam-7g8d/data.

EXERCISE 6.01: DOWNLOADING THE SOURCE DATA

In this exercise, you will download and import a geospatial data source that can be used for filled (choropleth) maps.

Perform the following steps to complete this exercise:

1. Open a browser and navigate to the **Chapter06** GitHub repository: http://packt.link/6fzj9.

Figure 6.1: New York City zoning shapefile

2. Click on the **NYC Zoning Data** folder and download the ZIP file. Extract the ZIP file to the location of your choice:

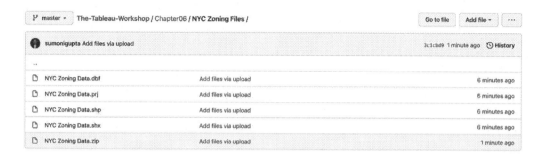

Figure 6.2: New York City data download formats

3. Locate and extract the shapefile you just downloaded.

4. Open a new Tableau workbook.

5. Add a new data source by selecting **Data | New Data Source**:

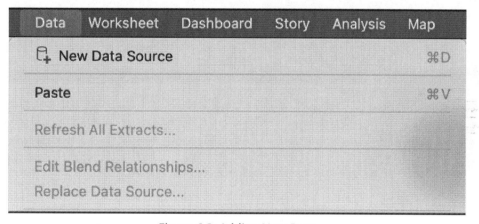

Figure 6.3: Adding New Data

6. Select **Spatial file** from the **Connect** menu:

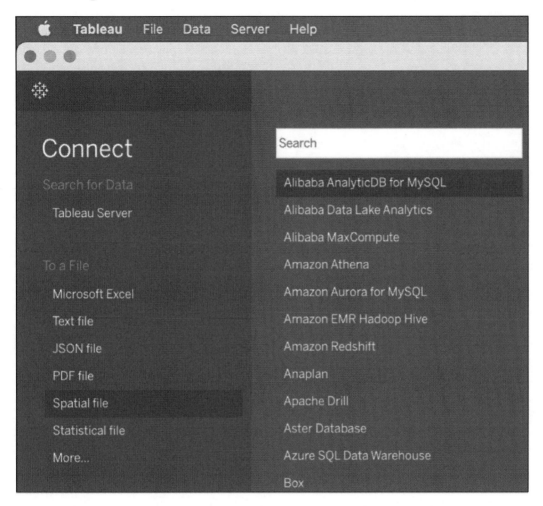

Figure 6.4: Selecting the Spatial file option

7. Open the downloaded file and import the `.shp` file into Tableau. When you add the .shp(spatial) file from the **NYC Zoning Data** folder, Tableau processes all the files in that folder including rest of four file formats and creates a polygon map of the data. ESRI files in Tableau gets processed when all the files are combined into one shape file and loaded onto Tableau:

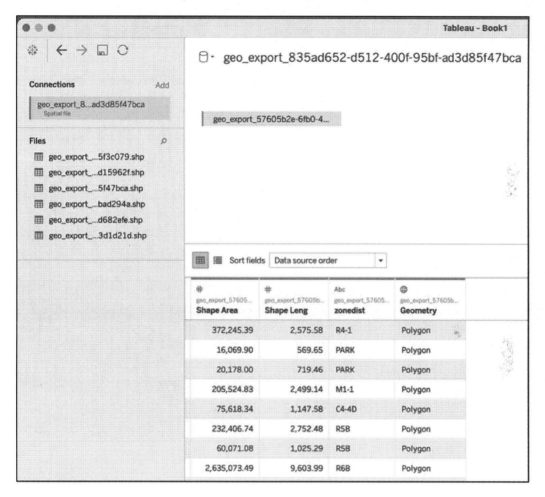

Figure 6.5: Importing the data source

8. Click on **Sheet 1** to create your first sheet.

9. Find the **Geometry** measure and drag it to the **Detail** card:

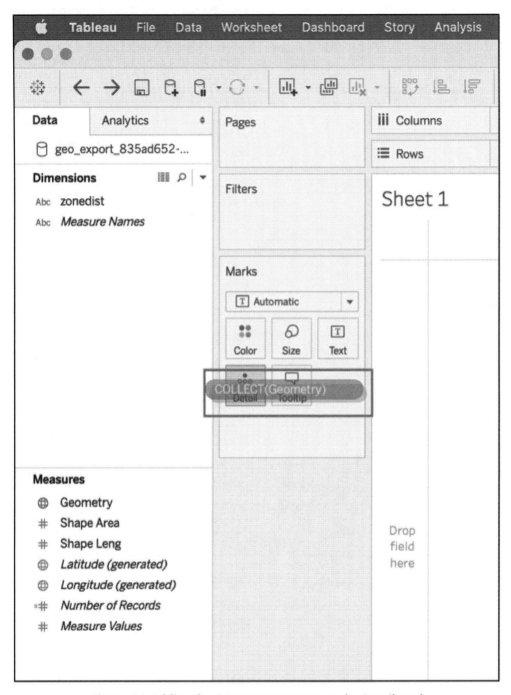

Figure 6.6: Adding the Geometry measure to the Detail card

Tableau will automatically create a map using the shapefile information, as shown here:

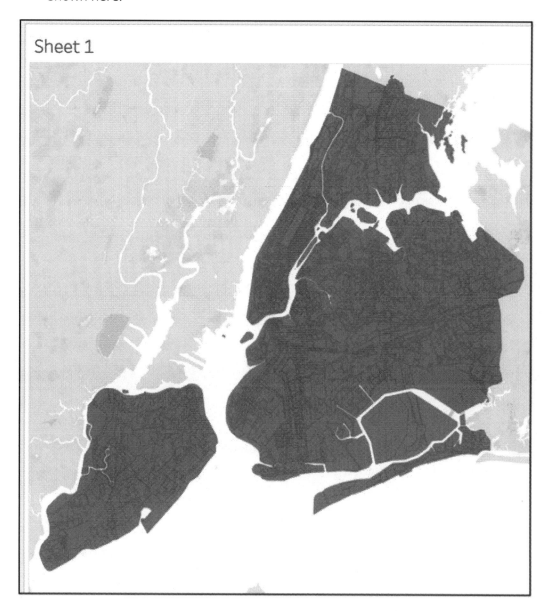

Figure 6.7: The default Tableau map output

The preceding screenshot shows a shapefile version of New York City and completes the goal of loading spatial data files into Tableau.

In this exercise, you downloaded the data source from https://www1.nyc.gov/ and imported a shapefile to display zoning districts for New York City. You can now view the information related to each of the polygon shapes in the file. In the next section, you will learn how to import non-spatial geographic data sources and join them for analysis later in the chapter.

IMPORTING NON-SPATIAL GEOGRAPHIC DATA SOURCES

Many geographic data sources are not specifically spatial sources but are instead found in spreadsheet or database formats as part of a larger dataset. These datasets will typically contain non-geographic data, such as customer information, time-period details, and assorted metrics. Geographic features such as country, state, and city will often also be included, making it possible to create maps displaying many data attributes.

Tableau makes it easy to create maps from these sources, although you may need to assist in the process, as you'll see shortly. Since many Tableau data sources will not reside in spatial formats, it is essential to make sure you can use general data sources to display geographic information at the appropriate level of detail.

Importing these sources is no different than the process for any general type of Tableau data. The only difference here is that you require one or more geographic fields to help you put your data in a map format. In the following section, you'll work through a quick exercise where you will import a non-spatial source.

Your first data source will be a detailed listing of Airbnb properties in Madrid. This file will contain information about the host, property location, ratings, reviews, and other property details.

EXERCISE 6.02: IMPORTING A NON-SPATIAL DATA SOURCE

In this exercise, you will import the detailed listings text file, which has already been downloaded. By the end of this exercise, you will have a Tableau data source with several attributes that can be used for mapping properties in a Tableau worksheet. If you have not already downloaded the `listings_detailed.csv` file, you can find it here: http://packt.link/Hh7ZL.

The steps to achieving this are as follows:

1. Select **Data | New Data Source** from the top menu:

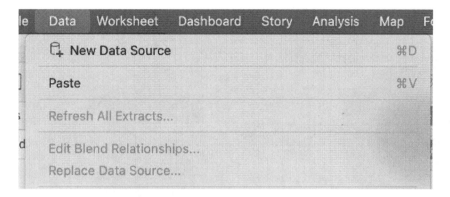

Figure 6.8: Creating a new data source

2. Select the **Text file** option:

Figure 6.9: Selecting the Text file option

3. Locate your downloaded file. It will be a `.zip` file probably, so extract the file in a folder and that folder should contain multiple files. To import the file (`listings_detailed.csv`), locate `listings_detailed.csv` and click the **Open** button:

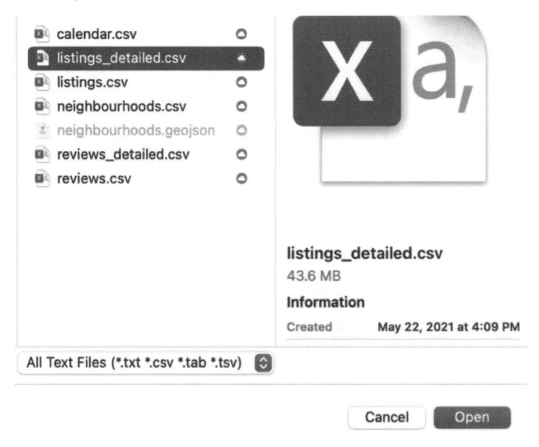

Figure 6.10: Adding the text file data source

4. For the purposes of efficient data performance, create an extract of this data instead of live data so that when you are developing your visualization, your data operations will be quick. Select the **Extract** radio button under `Connection` at the top right of the data pane and then click `Update Now`. This will populate your window with a subset of data:

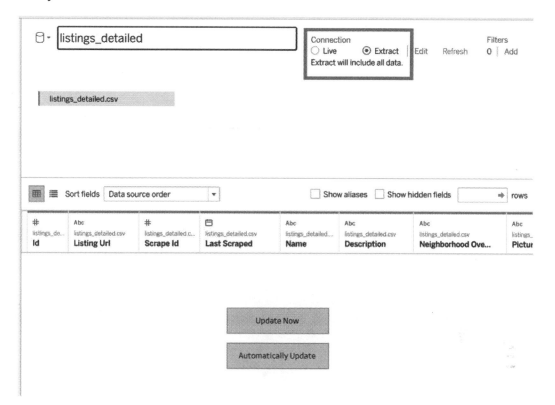

Figure 6.11: Selecting the Extract option

5. Rename the data source **bnb listings** and save your extract when prompted:

Figure 6.12: Renaming the data source

6. Select a sheet and let the extract run. You will now see all your data dimensions and measures, along with a blank workspace:

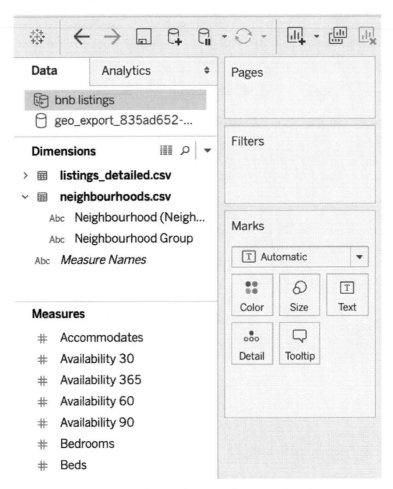

Figure 6.13: Viewing the workspace after creating the extract

In the previous exercise, you imported spatial data, and in this exercise, you've imported a non-spatial data source containing several geographic fields that will help you to create informative maps using the location of thousands of Airbnb properties. Next up are relationships between spatial and non-spatial data.

DATA RELATIONSHIPS

One Tableau feature you can use for geographic data (or indeed any data type) is joins, which allows you to create relationships at the data source level. Tableau has always permitted joins between multiple data sources added separately, but this was often useful only for smaller datasets where a simple join was sufficient. Using data relationships at the data source level takes a more robust approach, allowing multiple types of joins as well as unions of source datasets. This approach also leads to much better performance, especially when creating an extract.

Creating joins at the data source level allows connecting data from multiple sources (text, Excel, database, and so on), making it simple to combine data using a single key field within a join. This can be especially useful when different parts of an organization (that is, marketing versus finance) use different information systems, or when you require a simple lookup table to provide intuitive definitions that are not included in your source database information.

EXERCISE 6.03: JOINING TWO DATA SOURCES

In the following exercise, you will join two data sources to create additional possibilities for your analysis. The first (primary) source is the **listings_detailed.csv** file, and your secondary file is a simple neighborhoods file that will provide neighborhood names and was part of the data source you downloaded in the previous exercise. Keep in mind this exercise is for illustration purposes only. You can do much more with data joins, assuming your secondary file has additional fields. This topic will be covered in the subsequent chapters.

Creating your data join consists of a few simple steps:

1. Add a new data source or edit the existing source to be the **listings_detailed.csv** file if it's already been created:

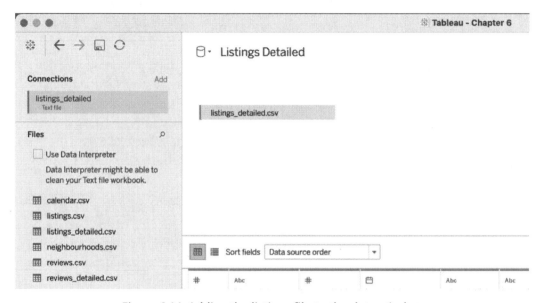

Figure 6.14: Adding the listings file to the data window

2. Add the primary data source to the window (if it's not already there) by dragging it from the **Connections** tab.

3. Drag the secondary source (the neighborhoods file) to the data source window from the **Connections** tab.

4. Create a join between the two sources using the **Neighbourhood** field from each data source in the drop-down menu for each source. Then, select the **Inner** join option. Your window should look like this:

Figure 6.15: Creating a table join between two data sources

5. Update the extract by selecting the **Update Now** button.

Your final output should be the following:

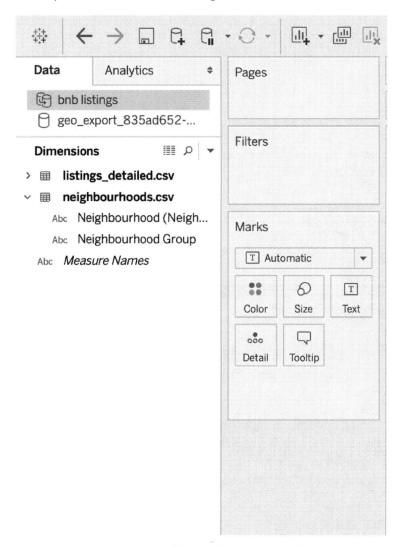

Figure 6.16: Creating a table join between two data sources

You will now have the new field(s) available from the secondary source. As mentioned previously, this is a very simple example, but you could also use the secondary source as a reference table to provide additional information about a neighborhood, such as the number of bars, restaurants, or tourist attractions. There are many other possibilities; all that is needed is a common field to create a join. In the next section, you will explore how to edit locations and their aliases and create custom geographies.

MANAGING LOCATION DATA

The key to producing maps and other meaningful geographic analyses is to have the necessary location elements (country, state, city, and so on) and to make sure they are classified correctly in Tableau. In many instances, Tableau will correctly identify these roles, making your job simple. In other cases, you will need to tell Tableau the correct role. This is often the case when your source field names do not correspond to the standard naming conventions used by Tableau. There may also be cases where Tableau incorrectly assumes that a non-geographic field represents location data based on the field name of the dimension, or where a value cannot be automatically identified.

This section will explore the various ways in which geographic data can be created and maintained in Tableau using three primary approaches—assigning roles, editing locations, and building custom geographic levels.

ASSIGNING GEOGRAPHIC ROLES

Tableau is quite adept at interpreting geographic levels based on source data naming conventions. For example, if you have a source field named `city`, then Tableau will assume you want to use this field to identify cities on a map. This may not always be the case—a field named `city neighborhood` may identify a different geographic level. In these instances, Tableau will require your guidance to match source fields to the correct geographic levels. Being familiar with your data sources will make this task simple.

Have a look at the following imported listings data to see how Tableau handled the data, and whether you need to make any modifications. You can easily locate the fields Tableau has determined are geographic by looking for a globe icon. In this dataset, you can see dimensions for city, country, country code, state, and ZIP code—each with a globe icon. Check to make sure each has the correct geographic role, starting with `city`:

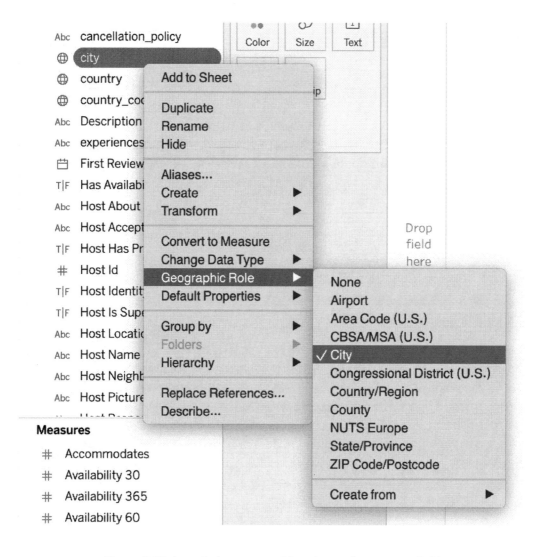

Figure 6.17: Associating geographic roles to data source fields

The **city** dimension has been correctly associated with a city geographic level. This is expected based on the naming convention; it might have required a manual linkage if the dimension were named **host city** or some other variation. You can then go through the same process and note that each dimension has been correctly identified with its geographic role. Also note that both the country and country code are associated with the **Country/Region** role; either field can be used to identify the country level on a map.

In a case where the geographic association has not been made or is incorrectly associated, you will need to inform Tableau of the correct category. This will often occur when a field name is unclear—for example, if **country** had been named **CTRY** in your source data, it is quite likely you would need to tell Tableau that this field is in fact referring to one or more countries. To make this correction, you simply select the **Geographic Role | Country/Region** option for this dimension and assign the proper value.

> **NOTE**
>
> *Figure 6.18* shows 13 unknown values below. Please note, however, that you may get different unknown values as the data gets updated constantly.

EDITING LOCATIONS

There will be times when Tableau is unable to recognize geographic data, often due to misspellings in the source data. This will result in null values when you attempt to map your data, leaving users with an incomplete picture of the information. Fortunately, you can provide more information on these values to help get them mapped correctly. See what happens when you attempt to map the state dimension:

Figure 6.18: Mapping the state dimension

Notice that in the bottom right of the preceding screenshot, there is a message that tells you that you have 13 unknown values. Tableau is not recognizing the states provided in your dataset. To find out what's happening, click on the **13 unknown** button, which opens a **Special Values** window:

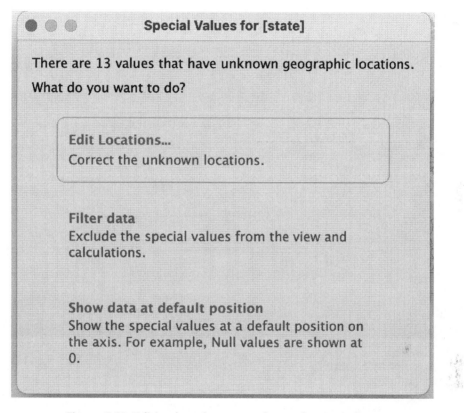

Figure 6.19: Editing locations to update unknown values

You then select the **Edit Locations...** option to open a window where you can begin the matching process. When this window opens, you quickly see the issue: your default **Country/Region** is set according to your location (the **United States** in this example), not **Spain**.

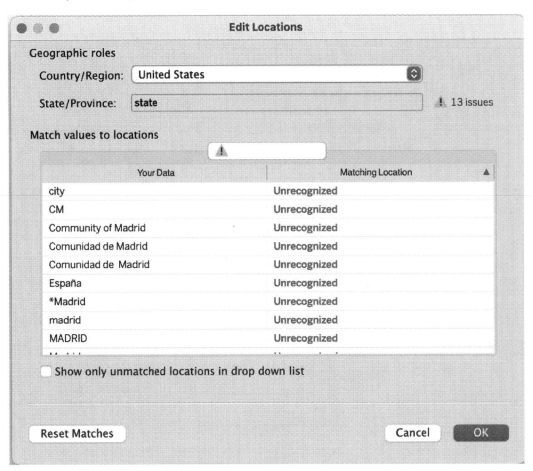

Figure 6.20: Identifying unrecognized geographic values

This is easily rectified by finding **Spain** in the drop-down list and setting it as your default. When you apply this change, you see that many of the entries have been automatically updated, especially any with Madrid as part of their name

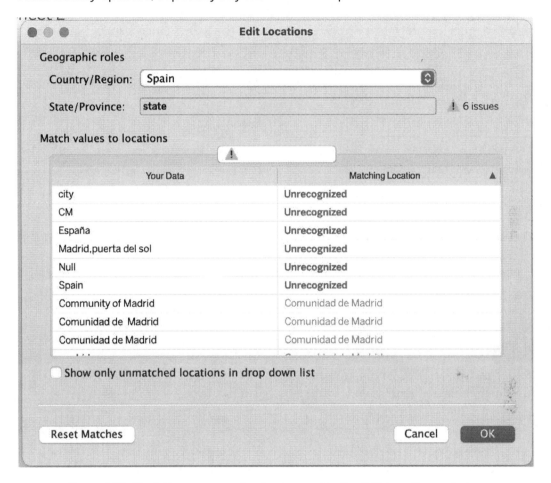

Figure 6.21: Updating unrecognized values using the Edit Locations window

There are others that have not been automatically updated, perhaps as a result of dirty data. You can now investigate these entries to determine the extent of the issue. Since you know that your dataset is entirely composed of Madrid properties, it is probably safe to update the remaining entries to the same **Comunidad de Madrid** entry. For each **Unrecognized** state in the **Edit Locations** window, simply double-click **Unrecognized** and select the **Comunidad de Madrid** entry from the drop-down list to make the manual updates.

BUILDING CUSTOM GEOGRAPHIES

In many cases, you will want to create custom geographic levels that are not already defined in your data source. This can be done quite easily in Tableau by specifying how you want the new level to be created, using an existing geographic attribute. You can also create custom geographies using calculated fields. Let's look at a single example for each approach.

CREATING A NEW GEOGRAPHY USING AN EXISTING ROLE

In some cases, you will create new geographic levels based on a level that already exists in the source data. This might be related to sales territories, neighborhoods, or some other aggregation where you don't have a formally defined geographic level in place. Let's look at an example using the Madrid dataset ZIP codes and neighborhoods.

You already have the ZIP code (postal code) data in the data source file, and you have neighborhood data as well, although only in text form. Your goal is to create geographic neighborhood definitions you can show on a map. To do this, right-click the **Neighbourhood** dimension and select **Geographic Role | Create from | zipcode**. This tells Tableau to build a geography at the neighborhood level using existing ZIP code data. Here is a view of the menu selections:

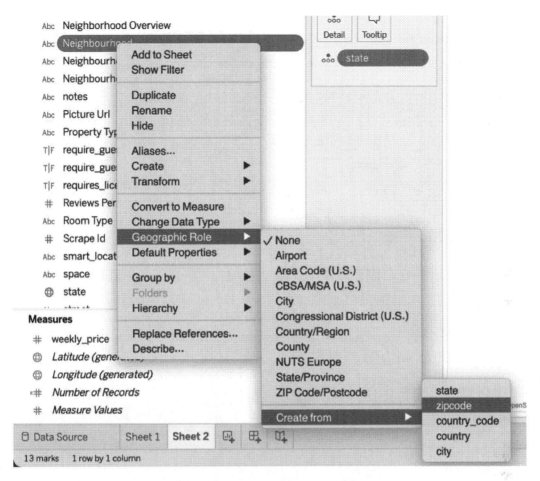

Figure 6.22: Creating a geographic role

You can see from the **Data** pane that Tableau does this by creating a hierarchy wherein **Neighbourhood** is the top level and `zipcode` is the lower level:

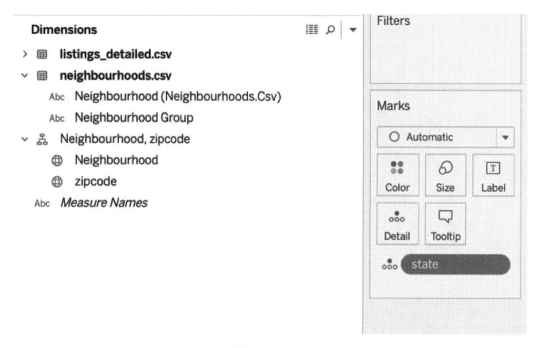

Figure 6.23: Building a custom geography level

What will this look like on a map? To display your new level, drag the **Neighbourhood** field from the hierarchy to the **Detail** mark, drag **Neighbourhood** to the **Label** marks card, and add **SUM(Number of Records)** to the **Color** mark, and then select the **Map** option from the **Show Me** menu, yielding this display:

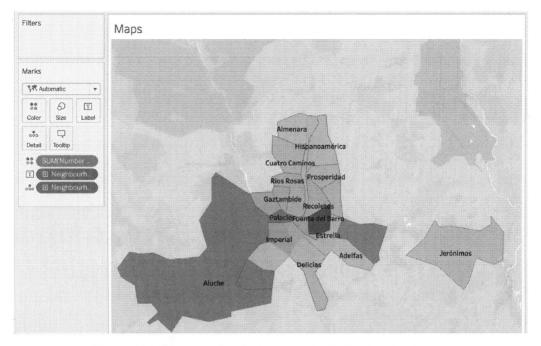

Figure 6.24: Mapping the newly created neighborhood polygons

You can see from the map that you again have an unknown issue with 66 values you were not able to associate with a neighborhood. This is most likely due to something in the source data—perhaps missing values in the **Neighbourhood** dimension or dirty ZIP code data. This sort of issue can frequently occur when there is not a strict standard for data entry; it is up to the Tableau designer to determine whether the issue is significant or minor and act accordingly.

CREATING A NEW GEOGRAPHY USING GROUPS

A second method for building a new geographic level is to create a calculated field, again using an existing geographic level as the base. You could do this again with a calculation based on ZIP codes (perhaps the first three or four digits), yielding an aggregate level similar to the neighborhood example. This assumes that the ZIP codes are assigned in a manner where this method makes sense.

Another possibility is to create a group in which you assign a name to each of your aggregate clusters, which can then be mapped accordingly. In the following example, a set of neighborhood clusters using the **Group** function have been created:

Figure 6.25: Creating groups based on neighborhood names

To create groups, follow these simple steps:

1.   Highlight one or more individual neighborhood values.

2.   Click on the **Group** button.

3.   Name the group by editing the default Tableau group name.

4.   Repeat *Step 1* to *Step 3* for each additional group.

5.   Click the **OK** button to save all groups.

Now you can add these clusters to a map by dragging the **Neighbourhood Clusters** dimension to the **Detail** mark; you can continue to use the **SUM(Number of Records)** measures for coloring purposes. Here's the result:

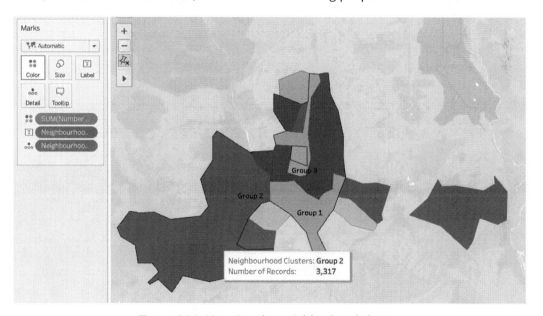

Figure 6.26: Mapping the neighborhood clusters

Note that there are 12 unknown entries; these can be addressed as detailed previously by clicking on the message and using the **Edit Locations** screen to update the entries.

Grouping geographic areas in this manner can help aggregate your data to meaningful levels for analysis, especially if you are familiar with the geographic attributes in your source data. In the next exercise, you will practice these concepts using the Airbnb dataset that you have been using.

EXERCISE 6.04: BUILDING CUSTOM GEOGRAPHIES

In this exercise, you will create custom geographies using both the existing role and group approaches. This will provide additional mapping options using these aggregate dimensions, starting with the role approach.

Perform the following steps to complete this exercise:

1. Open a new or existing Tableau workbook.

2. Import the listings and neighborhood files if you have not already done so.

3. Make sure you have a data source with the **listings_detailed** and **neighbourhoods** files joined. If not, create this relationship by joining them on the **Neighbourhood** field.

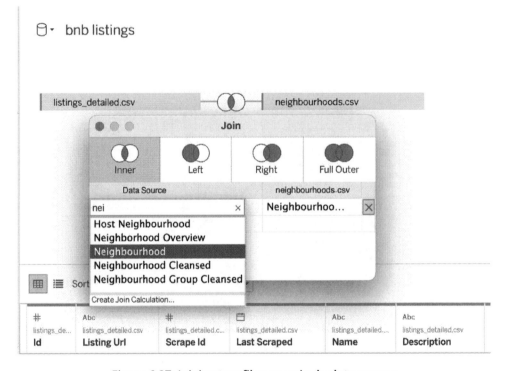

Figure 6.27: Joining two files as a single data source

4. Create an extract by selecting the **Extract** radio button. Save the extract and open a worksheet.

5. Create a geographic role for **Neighbourhood** by selecting the dimension and creating a role based on **zipcode**.

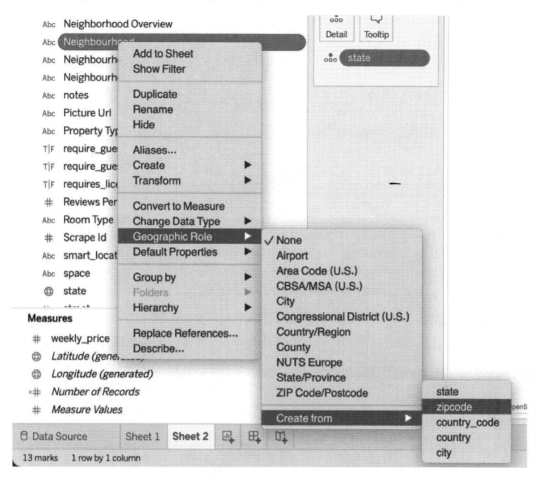

Figure 6.28: Assigning a custom geographic role

6. Right-click on the **Neighbourhood** dimension and select the **Create |**
   Group... menu item:

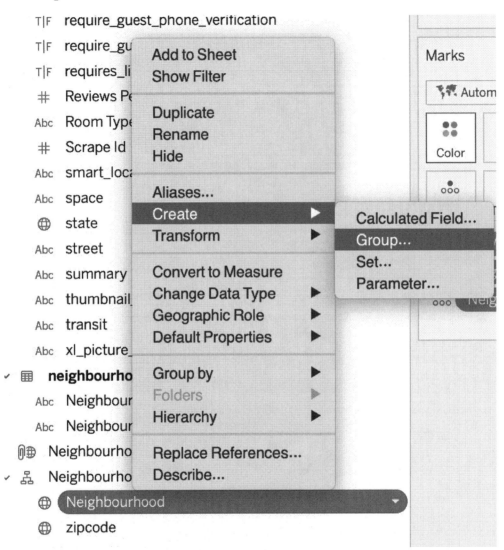

Figure 6.29: Creating a group from an existing field

7. Select the entries from **Acacias** through **Atocha** and click the **Group** button. Name this **Cluster 1**. Then, select some more entries through **Gaztambide** and click the **Group** button. Check the **Include 'Other'** checkbox:

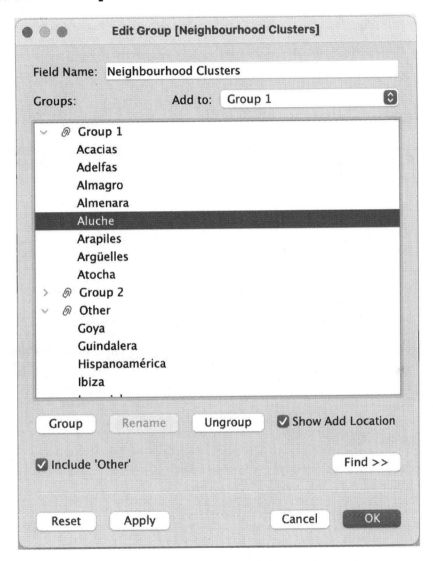

Figure 6.30: Results after creating groups from the Neighbourhood dimension

8. Click the **OK** button. You will now see a `[Neighbourhood Clusters]` `Group` dimension.

Figure 6.31: The Neighbourhood Clusters group as a new dimension

In this exercise, you created two new geographic fields using a pair of approaches. You can now use these dimensions to create filled maps, which is what you will be exploring in the next section, using a couple of options displayed in the **Show Me** menu.

CREATING MAPS IN TABLEAU

Tableau provides two distinct map options in the **Show Me** menu—one for symbol maps and a second for choropleth maps. If your data has simple latitude/longitude values corresponding to a postal code centroid, such as a store location (or even a city), then your mapping will be focused on the symbol map option. If, however, your data has more detailed data based on a shapefile or GeoJSON data source, you can then use the choropleth option to create filled maps based on the polygons in the data source. In some cases, you will have access to both types of source data and will be able to create a dual-axis map, which will be explored later in this section. The following is a simple comparison of the two types, with choropleth (filled) on the left and symbol on the right:

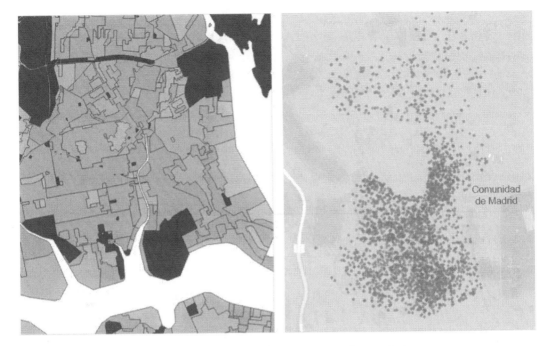

Figure 6.32: A choropleth (filled) map and a symbol map

GEOCODING

Geocoding is the process of assigning geographic attributes to a data field that may not be automatically recognized as a traditional geospatial field. In these cases, you need to assign values that correspond to these dimensions so maps can be created. This section will examine how this can be handled in Tableau.

In many cases, you will be presented with geographic attributes that Tableau will be unable to recognize without some guidance. Street addresses are a common example of this; unlike country, state, or even city, street addresses are too often duplicated across multiple geographies, making them very difficult to locate correctly on a map. Fortunately, Tableau enables custom geocoding, where you can use two distinct methods to provide more precise information. In both cases, you start with a .csv file.

The first case is where you wish to use existing geographic definitions and simply extend them to include new members. For example, if you need to add a new country, state, or county to your maps that is not recognized by Tableau, you can provide this information using a `.csv` file. You simply select the **Map | Geocoding | Import Custom Geocoding** menu option and direct Tableau to your directory where the `.csv` file has been created. The data field names must match the existing Tableau field names (**Country**, **State**, and so on) and should include latitude and longitude information so Tableau knows where to locate the new entries on a map.

The second type of custom geocoding involves information that may be specific to an organization (such as a regional sales hierarchy), or that may reference non-traditional point data such as lightning strikes or volcanic eruptions. In these cases, you create specific names for the new items, and then add a new field name that can be used in Tableau. For example, the field name might be called **Lightning Strikes** if you are attempting to map those events. Once again, latitude and longitude data must be included, as well as other appropriate geographic levels, such as **Country** and **State**.

Adding this custom geocoded information extends the mapping capabilities of Tableau beyond traditional boundaries and definitions.

> **NOTE**
>
> The steps to create the map shown in *Figure 6.33* are explained in *Exercise 6.05*.

SYMBOL MAPS

Symbol maps represent all maps where location data is provided in a point-based latitude and longitude format. Latitude represents the north-south location of a data point, while longitude provides the east-west location. Using these two measures in Tableau allows you to pinpoint the precise location of stores, offices, parks, museums, and many other entities with specific locations. These points may represent a central location within a large geographic entity (such as a park) or may have a higher precision level, depending on how detailed your source data is. For example, a latitude value of **45.37187** will be more precise than the same value rounded to **45.37**.

Symbol maps are quite simple yet very powerful in their ability to tell stories based on geographically positioned data. Let's explore the process for building effective symbol maps in Tableau. Everything starts with latitude and longitude measures, which may be included in your source data or can be calculated by Tableau for recognized attributes such as country, state, and county. As an example, using your Madrid locations data, here is a simple view based on the latitude and longitude data in the source file. You can select any point to see the supporting geographic coordinates:

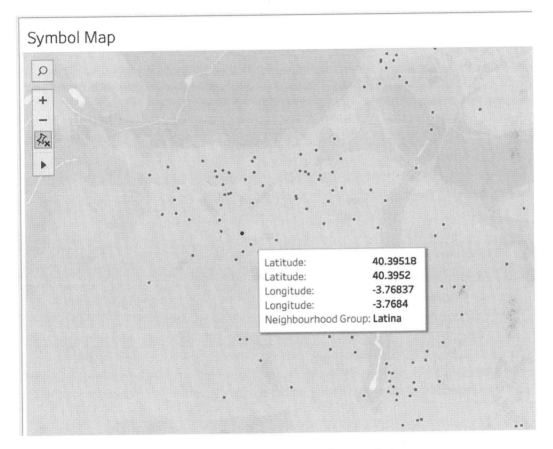

Figure 6.33: Details of a data point in a symbol map

Each point in the map is positioned based on latitude and longitude, as seen in the tooltip for the map. You can use additional map layers to provide more context, but for now, this is a good starting point.

ADDING DATA TO SYMBOL MAPS

While placing location points on a map can be informative, more often you will also wish to add data measures to those points—perhaps revenue for a store location or the number of visitors to a tourist attraction as two simple examples. This is easily done in Tableau using colors, sizes, or shapes to identify one or more features of a geographic point. You first need to determine which data fields will be most meaningful to display; this will allow you to build logic to display specific information based on user interaction.

When you add a measure to a symbol map, there are two commonly used approaches to display this data; the first is the use of colors or shapes, and the second is the use of the sizing of symbols. If you are adding dimensional information to the display, you will usually opt for colors or shapes to represent these categories. In some cases, both shapes and colors can be used to provide additional detail to the map viewer. If you are adding measures to your symbol display, sizing will often be the preferred approach, since it will help in identifying numerical differences across locations. Using colors or shapes is not as effective with measures, although either one could be used in tandem with size. In the following sections, you will see examples for each of these options.

COLORING A SYMBOL MAP

Colors can be used to provide insight into both categorical dimensions and numeric measures. This will give users a nice visual cue to help them see geographic-related patterns in the information. When using colors, it is important to recall that the human visual system has a limited range with respect to viewing colors; you typically would like to keep this to less than 10 distinct colors or shades. The Color Brewer website at https://colorbrewer2.org provides color palettes ranging from 3 to 12 distinct shades for mapping. Some users will be able to distinguish additional distinct colors, but it is best to err on the low side and minimize the number of map colors. You can also decide on colors based on your data distributions and find that you may need as few as 3 or as many as 9 or 10 colors to tell the story correctly.

Here, you can see an example of coloring using neighborhood groups in which you have nine colors:

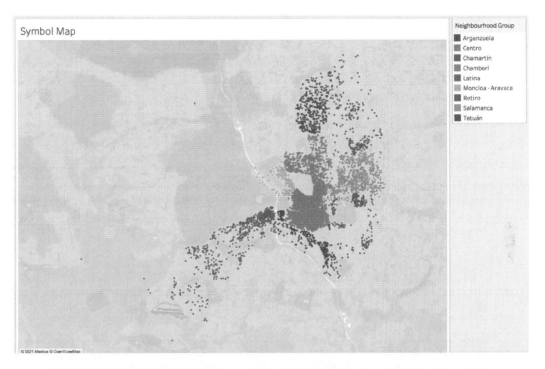

Figure 6.34: Coloring a symbol map using the Neighbourhood Group dimension

Notice how easily each neighborhood group is seen when you use distinct colors. Using a color palette with distinctly different colors is very helpful in this case, whereas a single color with shaded gradations would be more difficult to interpret. This same approach can be applied when you have distinct categories such as political districts or postal codes. On the other hand, if you wanted to see the percentage of voters voting for a political party or candidate, the best approach is to use shades of a single color to reflect percentages ranging from the minimum to maximum levels (perhaps 10% to 70% as an example).

To color the map, you perform the following steps:

1. Drag the coloring field (**Neighbourhood Group** in this case) to the **Color** card.

2. Select the **Color** card to edit colors if needed.

3. Choose an opacity level for optimal display; less than 100% opacity is recommended, especially when there are overlapping symbols on a map. This will improve data visibility.

SIZING A SYMBOL MAP

Individual points may also be sized based on values in the data, typically based on a single measure. For example, you may choose to display points sized based on revenue for each store location. Stores with higher revenue will have a larger dot (or another symbol) corresponding to their revenue relative to locations with lower values. This can be an effective approach, given that size differences are one of the more easily detected visual cues.

In the Madrid example, the dots are sized based on the number of bedrooms for each lodging. You can keep the colors already created so that your map will become even more informative for the viewer.

To do this, follow these steps:

1. Drag the **Bedrooms** dimension to the **Size** card in the **Marks** area of your worksheet.

2. Click on the **Size** card and adjust the symbol size using the slider tool.

Zoom in so you can see the effect more clearly:

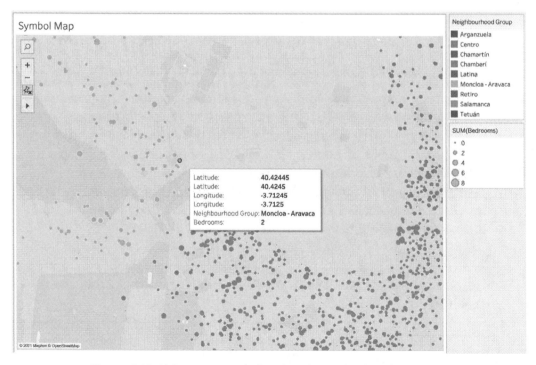

Figure 6.35: Sizing map symbols using the Bedrooms dimension

You now have points with anywhere from **0** to **8** bedrooms, with the differences quite noticeable at this zoom level. It may take a bit of work to distinguish between **6** and **7** or **3** and **4**; this is where tooltips can provide further clarity. You can easily adjust the size of your marks by selecting the `Size` card and dragging the bar to the left or right.

USING SHAPES IN A SYMBOL MAP

Let's continue exploring using the Madrid data. You have already used color and size to make your map more informative; now you can add shapes to provide one more level of detail to the map. At this point, you may wish to be careful by not adding too many shapes to the display, so a simple category is in order. Use the `Instant Bookable` field since it contains just two values.

To create this map, follow these steps:

1. Simply drag the `Instant Bookable` dimension to the `Shape` card.

2. Select the shapes you wish to display for each value by clicking on the `Shape` card and assigning a shape value to each data category.

Here is the result:

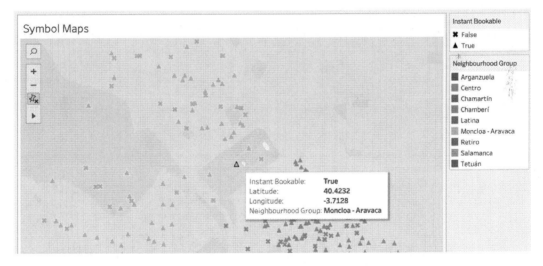

Figure 6.36: Using shapes to show the Instant Bookable value

Now you have a map that provides a wealth of information to the user, including neighborhood group, number of bedrooms, and whether a property is instantly bookable. To provide even more insight, you can customize tooltips so that users learn more about a property as they hover over a point.

ADDING MAP TOOLTIPS

Providing informational tooltips is a great finishing touch that helps users navigate maps and the underlying information they contain. While map labels can be helpful, there is a point at which they become visual noise that obscures the meaningful information contained in the map. This is where tooltips become especially useful as they can hold a lot of information without getting in the way of the map display.

Let's walk through a quick example of building a simple yet informative tooltip in your map. You've already seen tooltips in their simplest version, but they are capable of so much more, as you're about to see.

To add additional fields to a tooltip, simply drag dimensions or measures to the **Tooltip** card in the **Marks** pane. This will make these fields accessible even if they don't wind up being used in your text. Tableau, by default, will provide a functional tooltip containing information associated with the map, as seen in Figure 6.37 With just a little effort and the use of contrasting font colors, tooltips can become much more powerful. You can drag the **Host Name**, **Host Response Rate**, **Zipcode**, and **Summary** dimensions to the **Tooltip** card and continue to use the existing **Neighbourhood Group** and **Bedrooms** dimensions to tell a small story about the property, as seen in *Figure 6.38*.

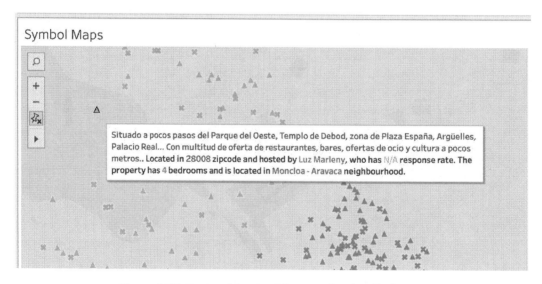

Figure 6.37: Customizing tooltips to tell a detailed story

As you can see, tooltips are a great way to include helpful information without the need to clutter a map with too much detail.

NAVIGATING SYMBOL MAPS

Tableau provides some simple tools for navigating maps. In the upper-left area of the **Map** window is a small toolbar with the following features:

- Search creates the ability to locate elements in a map.

- Zoom in is very useful for navigating a densely populated map.

- Zoom out can be used to display an entire map and provide surrounding context.

- Reset map will set the map to a fixed display size.

- Zoom area is an extension of zoom in that allows you to select a specific part of the map to zoom in on.

- Pan provides the ability to move the map up and down or side to side.

- The three selection tools (rectangle, radius, and lasso) enable highlighting elements within a selected portion of the map.

These tools make it easy to move the map within the map window, enlarge or shrink the data points, fix the display size (using reset map), and create custom selections using the three selection tools. Map data can also be filtered by using the map legends, as you'll see in the next section.

FILTERING SYMBOL MAPS

In an earlier section, you learned about the challenge of differentiating between places with three or four bedrooms, since the symbols are nearly the same size. This presents an issue for a user who may require four bedrooms but cannot easily see the difference based on symbol size. To address this, the user can simply click on the **4** in the **Bedrooms** legend and select the **Keep Only** option. Tableau will automatically add a filter to the **Filters** pane reflecting this selection.

The same can be done using the **Color** legend you have for **Neighbourhood Group**. With colors, you can click on one or more options and the data will be highlighted. In this case, both the **Centro** and **Chamberi** neighborhood groups have been selected, yielding this result:

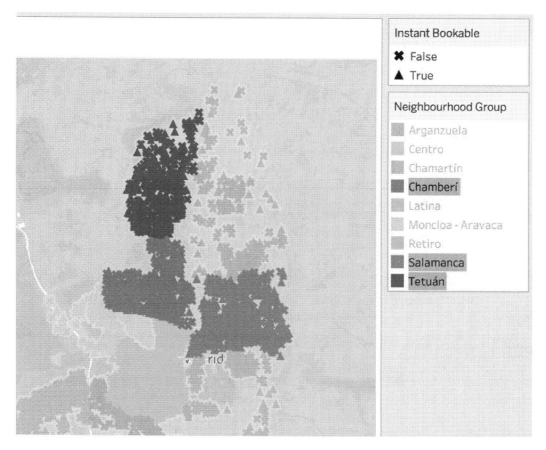

Figure 6.38: Filtering a map by selecting legend values

You could also select the **Keep Only** option and Tableau will add a filter reflecting your choice.

The shapes filter works like the size filter, allowing users to select the **Keep Only** option to set up a filter. Alternatively, users can choose the **Exclude** option if they wish to remove some locations from the map.

While these are very useful options, users can go one step further and build new groups and sets using map data. We'll visit those options in the next section.

CREATING GROUPS AND SETS FROM SYMBOL MAP DATA

One of the useful functions in Tableau mapping is the ability to create groups and sets based on a selection of points in a map. This is important because you won't always be aware of patterns until seeing them on a map. You can then grab a collection of data points using rectangular, radial, or lasso selections and create a group or set immediately. This is a powerful feature that allows users to take advantage of patterns revealed on a map to create meaningful aggregations of data.

Consider the following example using your previously created symbol map. Using the map toolbar, select the rectangular selection tool and highlight an area of points with it. (Notice the different colors for all the points in your selection area.)

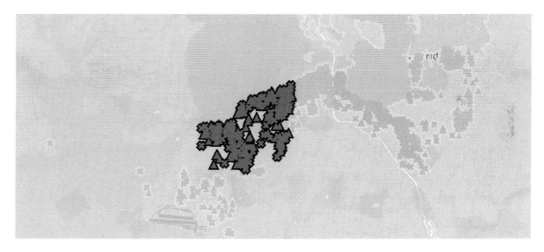

Figure 6.39: Selected points are displayed in a different color

You then create a group for the selected points by using the **Group Members** icon:

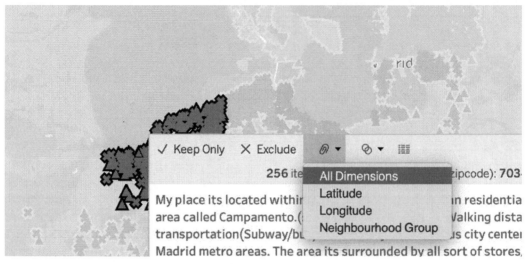

Figure 6.40: Creating a group dimension using the Group Members icon

Tableau has now created a group in the `Dimensions` pane that can be used in your analysis. This is a more intuitive, faster means to create groups rather than doing it manually using the group function.

The steps to do this are as follows:

1. Select the rectangular selection tool from the map toolbar.

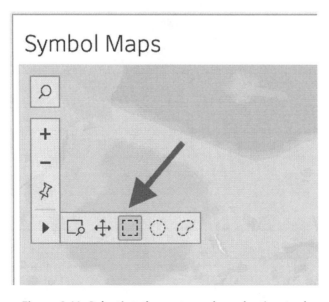

Figure 6.41: Selecting the rectangular selection tool

2. Highlight the area you wish to select within the map.

3. Hover over any of the selected data symbols.

4. Select the **Group Members** icon, as shown previously.

5. You can inspect your results to verify the group has been created:

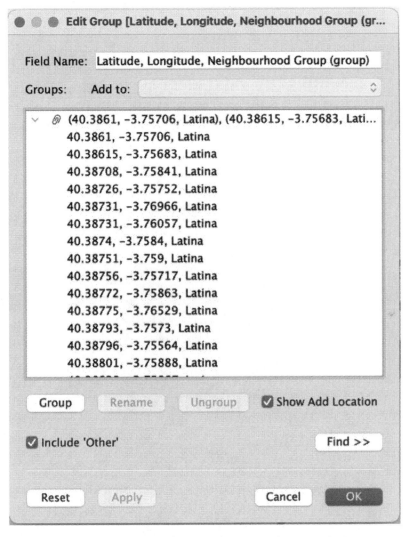

Figure 6.42: Viewing the values in the newly created group

This example illustrates another way you can use geographic data and maps to expand your analysis capabilities. You will now practice these concepts around the symbol map, including grouping locations and coloring them according to their groups.

EXERCISE 6.05: BUILDING A SYMBOL MAP

In this exercise, you will create a symbol map using data from the Madrid listings data. This will help provide insight into listing patterns across the city.

Perform the following steps to complete this exercise:

1. Import the **Madrid listings** dataset if you have not already done so.

2. Create a data source by joining multiple files as shown in previous sections/exercises.

3. Add a new Tableau worksheet.

4. Drag the **Longitude** measure to the **Rows** shelf and the **Latitude** measure to the **Columns** shelf. (Use these rather than the generated values provided by Tableau.) Change both **Longitude** and **Latitude** to **Dimension**:

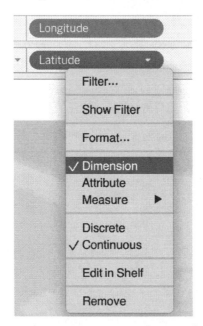

Figure 6.43: Setting Latitude values to Dimension

5. Drag the **City** dimension to the **Detail** card and the **SUM(Number of Records)** measure to the **Size** card and adjust the symbol size to better display all points. If for some reason you don't get a Map, click on "Show Me" card and manually select **Symbol Maps** from.

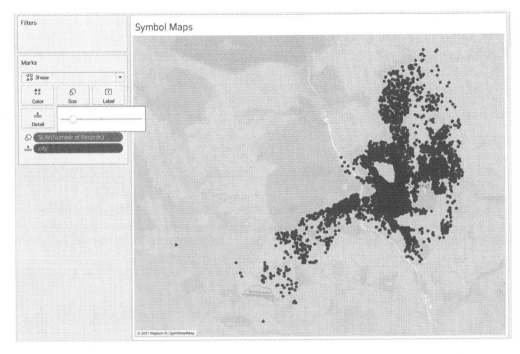

Figure 6.44: Adjusting the Size card for displaying symbols on the map

6. Replace **SUM(Number of Records)** with the **Accommodates** measure on the **Size** card:

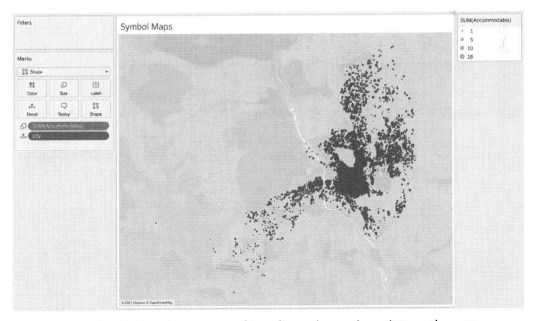

Figure 6.45: Using the Accommodates dimension to size points on the map

7. Drag the **Neighbourhood Group** dimension to the **Color** card and call this worksheet **Madrid Accommodates Map**. You will be using the same worksheet later in the chapter in *Exercise 6.07: Creating a Dual-Axis Map*:

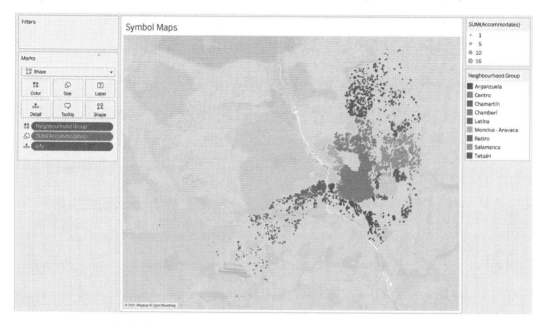

Figure 6.46: Coloring the map using the Neighbourhood Group dimension

It is now easy to identify the density of listings in the Centro neighborhood (displayed as the orange cluster in the lower half of the screenshot). Each of the surrounding neighborhoods has fewer listings scattered across the map due to their greater distance from the primary tourist attractions found in Centro.

In this exercise, you created a symbol map that details listing patterns across the city of Madrid. This map can form the basis for additional insights using multiple measures, parameters, and filters. In the upcoming section, you will review the second type of map that Tableau supports, which is choropleth maps, which you briefly learned about at the start of the chapter.

CHOROPLETH (FILLED) MAPS

Choropleth maps differ from symbol maps in one important respect: locations are now based on shapes (polygons, lines, or points) rather than on a single point using latitude/longitude coordinates. These maps will typically use officially defined geographic designations (country, state, city) as the basis for analysis, with colors as the primary method for displaying measures since size and shape are already defined. Filled maps may also be used with symbol maps to provide multiple levels of geographic analysis.

> **NOTE**
>
> For **Avg Area** measure creation mentioned in the topic below, if you are using any further version of Tableau than 2020.1, the field **Number of Records** does not exist. For creating **Avg Area** measure, you can explicitly create **Number of Records** on your own. Please refer to this link for more information: https://tarsolutions.co.uk/blog/number-of-records-missing-in-tableau/.

COLORING A CHOROPLETH MAP

As previously noted, colors will generally be the method used to display measure differences in a filled map. Distinct color sets are used when comparing dimension (categorical) values, while shaded palettes are the best approach for displaying measures.

Let's look at these two cases, first using a dimension, followed by a measure example. Both examples will use the previously downloaded **New York City zoning data**. For the dimension example, no new fields are needed; you simply drag the **Geometry** measure to the **Detail** card, allowing Tableau to use the shapefile polygon data, and then drag the **zonedist** dimension to the **Color** card. The result looks like this:

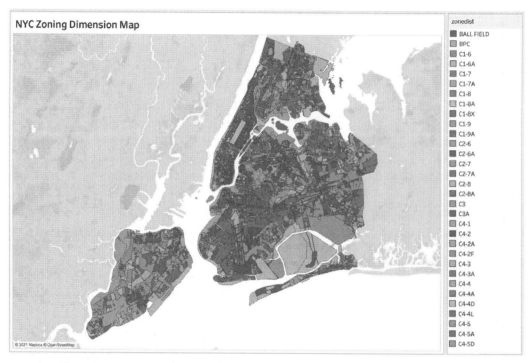

Figure 6.47: New York City zoning map colored by detailed zonedist values

Note that you have many detailed zoning types. These could probably be aggregated to present a similar map without unnecessary detail. To do this, you'll create a simple grouped field from the `zonedist` values, with very high-level groups in which zones starting with **C** are commercial zones, **M** are manufacturing zones, and **R** are residential zones; the others are self-explanatory. Let's revisit the map and drag the `zonedist (group)` dimension to the **Color** card. Here's your new map:

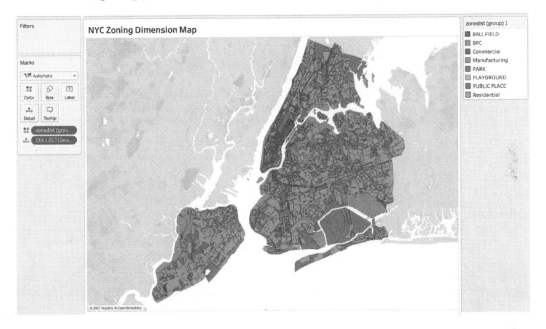

Figure 6.48: New York City zoning map colored by grouped zonedist values

Now you can see the more evident patterns between residential, commercial, and manufacturing areas, which were previously masked by the many subtypes within each designation.

You can use the same data to create a filled map based on measures, although you'll need to do a little work to create some new measures. Some datasets may have useful measures included (income, population density, and so on) but that isn't the case here. You'll create two measures you can use on the map (**Avg Area** and **Zone Counts**) using the following formulas.

The **Avg Area** measure can be created using the following steps:

1. Right-click in the **Data** panel and select **Create Calculated Field**.

2. Enter the **SUM([Shape Area])/SUM([Number of Records])** formula.

3. Name the calculation **Avg Area** and click the **OK** button to close the window.

   Zone Counts can be created in a similar manner:

4. Right-click in the **Data** panel and select **Create Calculated Field**.

5. Enter the **COUNT([Zonedist])** formula.

6. Name the calculation **Zone Counts** and click the **OK** button to close the window.

You can now create a filled map using either of these measures as the color. Drag **zonedist** on the **Detail** card and **Zone Counts** to the **Color** card to update the map, like this:

Figure 6.49: New York City zoning map colored by zone counts

You now see each zone colored by the frequency of occurrence (notice the highest count is represented by the darkest color). This is the type of color scheme to use when you have a continuous measure displayed on a map, as opposed to the dimension map where you used distinct colors. When numbers are below zero or an average value, a two-color scheme is useful to show low versus high values (red to blue, for example). Tableau has many native color palettes to choose from, making it easy to create compelling maps.

NAVIGATING A CHOROPLETH MAP

You can use the same map tools discussed in the symbol map section when navigating a map:

- Search creates the ability to locate elements in a map.

- Zoom in is very useful for navigating a densely populated map.

- Zoom out can be used to display an entire map and provide surrounding context.

- Reset map will set the map to a fixed display size.

- Zoom area is an extension of zoom in that allows you to select a specific part of the map to zoom in on.

- Pan provides the ability to move the map up and down or side to side.

- Three selection tools (rectangle, radius, and lasso) enable highlighting elements within a selected portion of the map.

FILTERING A CHOROPLETH MAP

You can also use the same filtering tools discussed in the section on filtering a symbol map, including the ability to create groups and sets using the selection tools. Note that when selecting areas on a filled map, you do not need to select an entire area to include it in your group or set. If you need more precision, then click on each desired area to build new groups or sets. Now, you will execute the following steps to build your own choropleth maps.

EXERCISE 6.06: BUILDING A CHOROPLETH MAP

In this exercise, you will create and populate a filled map using the New York City zoning shapefile you downloaded in *Exercise 6.01*:

1. Open your existing Tableau workbook or create a new workbook.

2. If you have not already done so, import the data source from https://data. cityofnewyork.us/City-Government/Zoning-GIS-Data-Shapefile/kdig-pewd.

3. Add the data source by navigating to the **Data | New Data Source** menu:

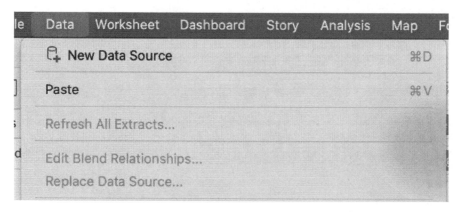

Figure 6.50: Adding a new data source

4. Select the **Spatial file** option:

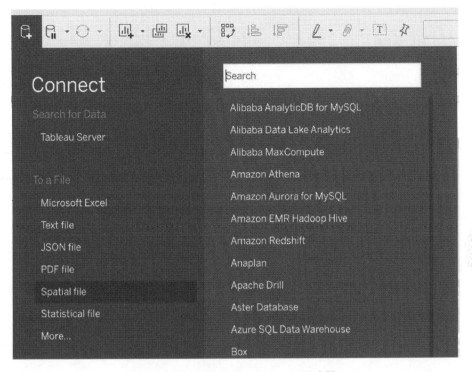

Figure 6.51: Connecting to a spatial file

5. Locate your downloaded file and select it. A sample of the data will appear in the import window:

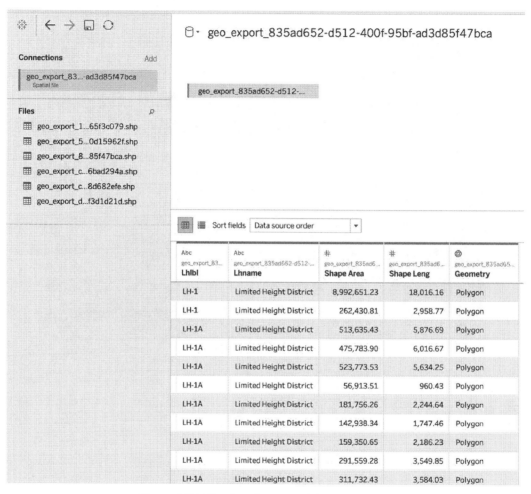

Figure 6.52: Viewing the spatial file attributes

6. Add a new worksheet and make sure it uses the spatial data source:

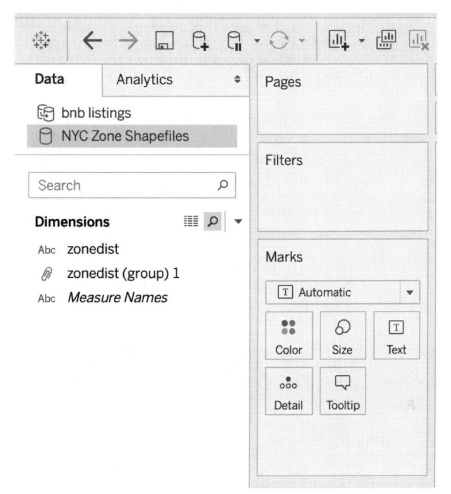

Figure 6.53: A worksheet with dimensions and measures from the spatial file

7. Drag the **Geometry** measure to the **Detail** card. Tableau will add **Latitude** and **Longitude** fields and create a map:

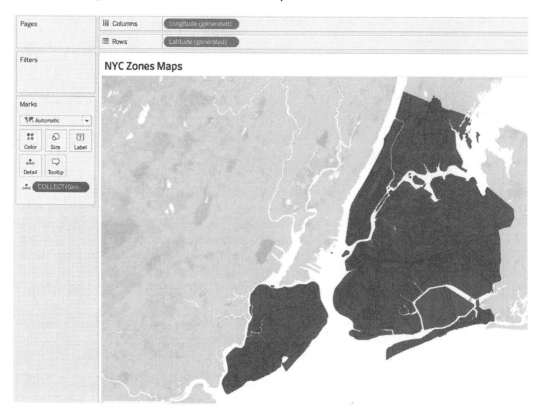

Figure 6.54: Adding the Geometry measure to the Detail card

8. Drag the **zonedist** dimension to the **Color** card:

Figure 6.55: Coloring the map using the zonedist dimension

9. Create a **zonedist (group)** dimension by summarizing all R, C, and M zones into **RESIDENTIAL**, **COMMERCIAL**, and **MANUFACTURING** groups. Click **OK** to save the group as a dimension.

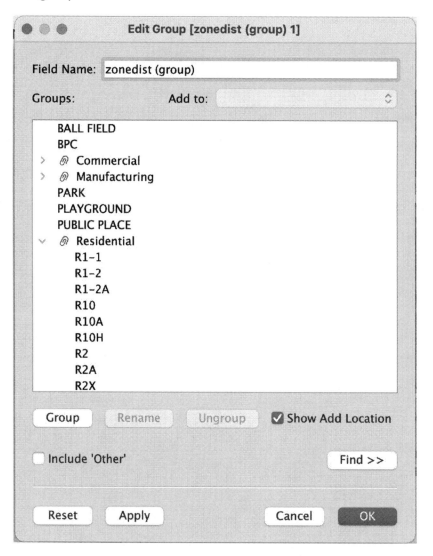

Figure 6.56: Creating a zonedist (group) dimension

10. Drag the **zonedist (group)** dimension to the **Color** card:

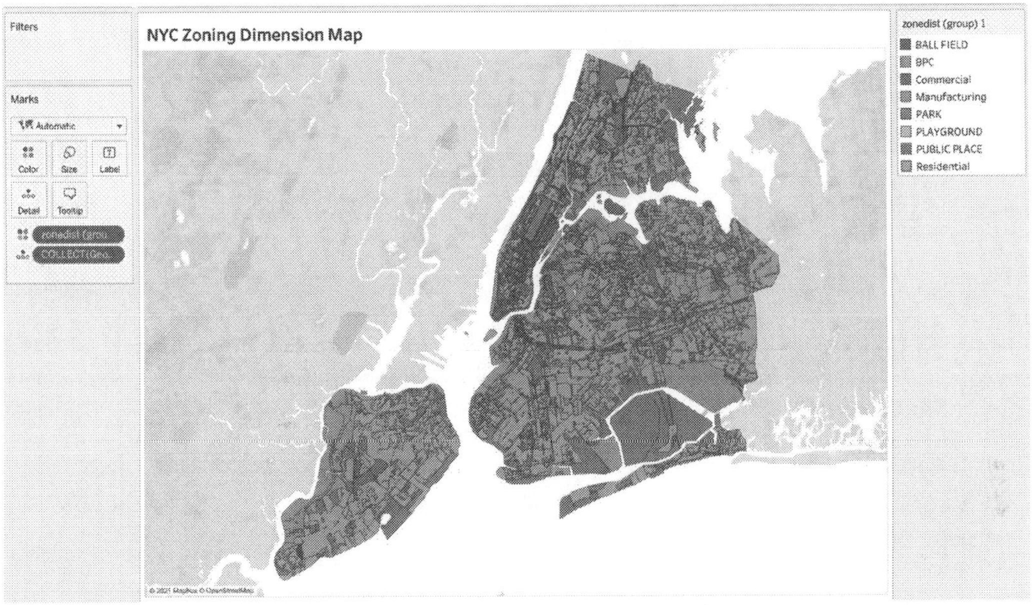

Figure 6.57: Coloring the map using zonedist (group)

In this exercise, you added a spatial data source and used the **Geometry** field to populate a map. You also learned how to color the map using both an existing and a newly created dimension. In the following subsection, you will gain an understanding of how to use dual-axis maps and when are they used.

DUAL-AXIS MAPS

Tableau allows you to create dual-axis maps so that you can overlay point data on a polygon map or simply use the second axis to display the data in a new way. This type of map could be used when you wish to overlay two data variables with different purposes for each, or even from distinct data sources. For instance, you could overlay a dataset based on geographic boundaries (states) with one using symbol data (latitude/longitude addresses), or you can simply create additional information from a single set of data points, as the following example will illustrate. In this example, you will use the second axis to create a density map to show areas within Madrid with the highest concentrations of Airbnb properties.

To do this, you start with an existing symbol map like the one built earlier in this chapter. All you need to do to create a dual-axis map is to drag the **Latitude** measure to the **Columns** shelf, placing it to the right of the existing **Latitude** measure.

Figure 6.58: Adding a second Latitude dimension

Tableau will create a second map by default; you need to use the drop-down menu from the new **Latitude** measure and select the **Dual Axis** option. You also need to tell Tableau to treat your new measure as a dimension by selecting the **Dimension** option from the same menu.

Figure 6.59: Setting up a Dual Axis map

Once you have the second axis specified, you can move to the **Marks** area, where a **Latitude (2)** entry has been added. In this case, you would choose the **Density** option for the display type and adjust the intensity and opacity levels to your preference. This will give you a map that retains the original elements from the map while adding the density markers.

The **Density** option will now display areas with a higher concentration of properties as blurred colors. The Centro neighborhood in the middle of the map will be especially dense at this zoom level. As you zoom in, the individual properties will gradually be revealed. In this section, you revisited a dual-axis chart but in map form. Now you will grasp these concepts in a better way by executing the next exercise.

EXERCISE 6.07: CREATING A DUAL-AXIS MAP

In this exercise, you will create a dual-axis map, using symbols for the base map and then adding a second axis that uses the density markers. You will use the Madrid Airbnb data source as you have in previous exercises.

Perform the following steps to complete this exercise:

1. Open the **Madrid Accommodates Map** worksheet that you created in *Exercise 6.05*.

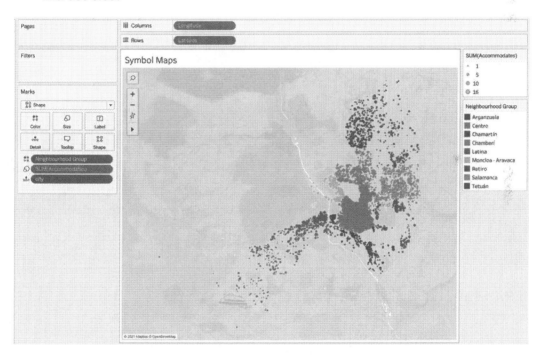

Figure 6.60: Symbol map colored by Neighbourhood Group

2. Drag the **Latitude** measure to the **Rows** shelf, next to the existing **Latitude** measure:

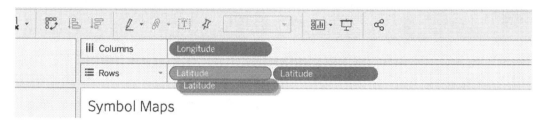

Figure 6.61: Adding a dual axis using two Latitude measures

3. Set the new **Latitude** measure as a continuous dimension and check the **Dual Axis** item to combine the elements into a single map:

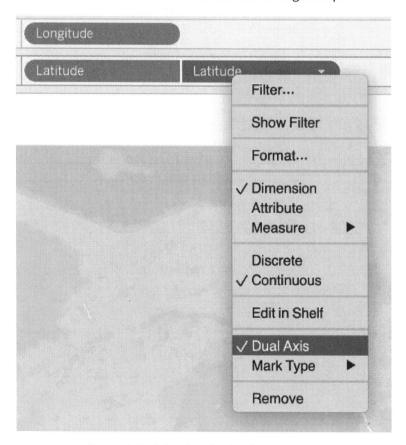

Figure 6.62: Selecting the Dual Axis option

4. In the **Latitude (2) Marks** area, choose the **Density** option:

Figure 6.63: Selecting a Density symbol

5. Adjust the **Density** settings by clicking on the **Color** card:

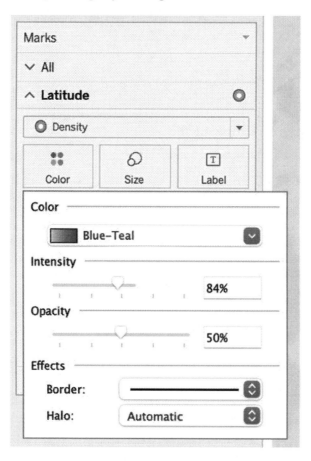

Figure 6.64: Adjusting the Density coloring

6. View the map to see the impact of the **Density** symbols:

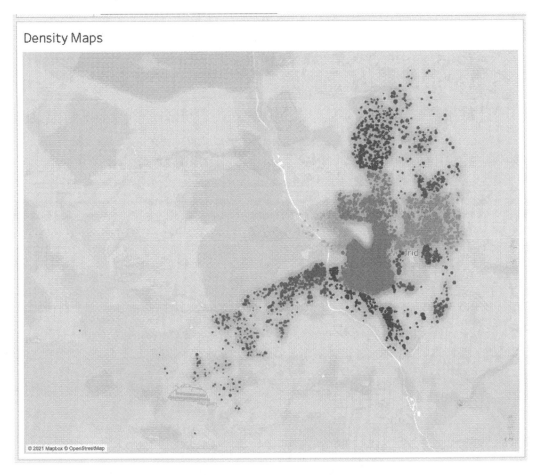

Figure 6.65: The completed dual-axis map with symbols and density

In this exercise, you created a dual-axis map using circle symbols on the first axis and density symbols on the second axis. You learned how to use them together to create a more complete map. The second level of density details that you added will now display areas with a higher concentration of properties as blurred colors. The Centro neighborhood in the middle of the map will be especially dense at this zoom level. These extra details on maps help end users/stakeholders to observe the map with extra context in one view instead of switching the view multiple times. In the next section, you will review what map enhancement options Tableau provides and how to best add/use them in your maps.

MAP ENHANCEMENTS

Tableau has multiple features you can use to upgrade your maps and make them effective for users. Some of these are native while others can be added quite easily. In this section, you will cover some simple ways to improve on the base maps used in Tableau.

SETTING MAP OPTIONS

Map options are simple selections that can be chosen to determine how a user can interact with a map. To set these options, select the **Map | Map Options** menu item, which will open a small window:

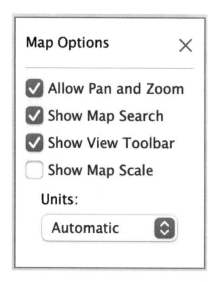

Figure 6.66: Map Options menu items

These options allow users to navigate the map using pan (to shift your map from side to side or up and down) and zoom, allow users to perform searches, and allow the functionality provided by the toolbar (radial selections, and so on). If you want your map to remain fixed with a single size and location, disable these capabilities.

USING EXISTING LAYERS

Default Tableau background maps provide numerous map layers that can easily be selected and deselected by users depending on their preferences. Map layers help you to add extra details such as highways, borders, terrains, coastlines, and county borders where these layers add minute details to the maps. To change the default map layer, click on **Map | Map Layers** from the menu. Tableau offers the following layer options:

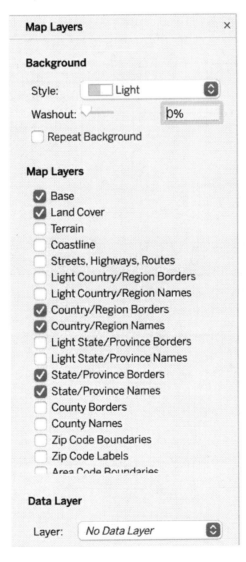

Figure 6.67: Map Layers menu options

These layers can be used to customize the appearance of a map. For example, in the Madrid listing example, if you select **Streets, Highways, Routes** as well as **Zip Code Labels**, you will notice how extra details are added to the map, as shown in the following screenshot:

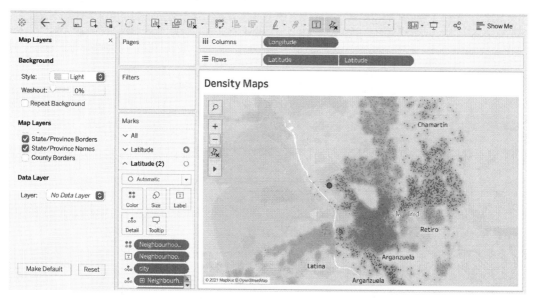

Figure 6.68: Map Layers menu options with added layers

Although aligning with data visualization best practices, you would generally try to minimize the number and visibility of these layers to not distract users from the map data. Using just enough layers to provide context is a smart approach.

In addition, more than 20 demographic layers are available as overlays for US-based data, which essentially allows you to add a data mask layer depending on the demographic you choose from the dropdown. But as mentioned previously, seldom do you have to use these extra layers in your maps because, more often than not, these layers confuse stakeholders rather than help them.

Layers are very easy to add or remove in Tableau, so it is wise to spend some time with the many options until your map is visually pleasing. As with most charts, less is often more on a map; make sure the focus is on the data and not on the map layers.

ADDING MAPBOX BACKGROUND MAPS

You do have options beyond the standard Tableau background maps. One of these is to embed Mapbox background maps in Tableau—an approach that enables the creation of uniquely styled maps. Mapbox is a popular map creation platform enabling users to customize maps for use in many applications. Tableau added Mapbox integration back in Tableau 9.2, so the ability to use Mapbox background maps is not new but should nonetheless be explored if you wish to feature maps beyond the native Tableau versions. You will need to create a free Mapbox account at https://www.mapbox.com/ to build these maps.

To export a Mapbox map for use in Tableau, navigate to Mapbox Studio, https://studio.mapbox.com/, and then simply create your own style by clicking on **New Styles** and choosing an option under **Choose a template** as well as **Choose a variation** from the popup:

Figure 6.69: Choosing a template and variation for Mapbox

Then, select the **Share**... icon at the top right of the map and view the **Third party** options to find the **Tableau** dialog:

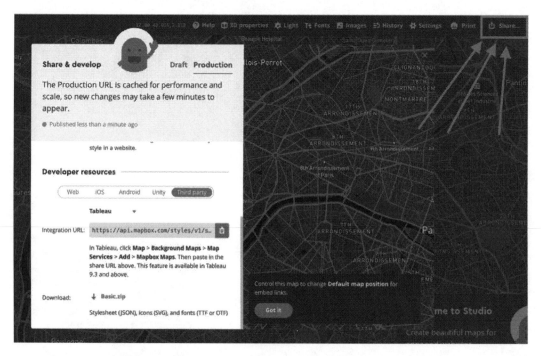

Figure 6.70: Exporting a Mapbox background map to Tableau

This provides you with a link to be used in Tableau as a background map style to provide a customized background to set your maps apart from the standard Tableau options. The link can be copied to the clipboard and then added as a background map. In Tableau Desktop, create a new sheet and select the **Map | Background Maps | Manage Maps** menu item, which will open a **Map Services** window. Clicking the **Add** button gives you two options: **WMS Servers**... (Web Map Server, similar to Mapbox) and **Mapbox Maps**.... Click on the **Mapbox** option and you will see a dialog screen:

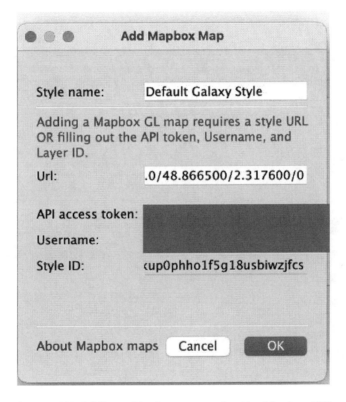

Figure 6.71: Adding a Mapbox map using the Mapbox URL

Here, you can add a style name of your choice, and then copy your Mapbox link to the URL text box. The remaining information will be automatically updated based on the URL link, and your background map will be ready to go. Multiple maps can be added using this same process, which will give you many options beyond the native Tableau map backgrounds. Now, use this Mapbox map style for your Madrid worksheet. Click on **Maps** | **Background Maps** | **Default Galaxy Style (or your style name)**. Here's a look at your data with a new background map:

Figure 6.72: A custom Mapbox map of Madrid

If you open the **Map | Map Layers** card, you will see the available layers from the selected Mapbox map. Note that each map style will have its own set of options. Here is what you have with your style:

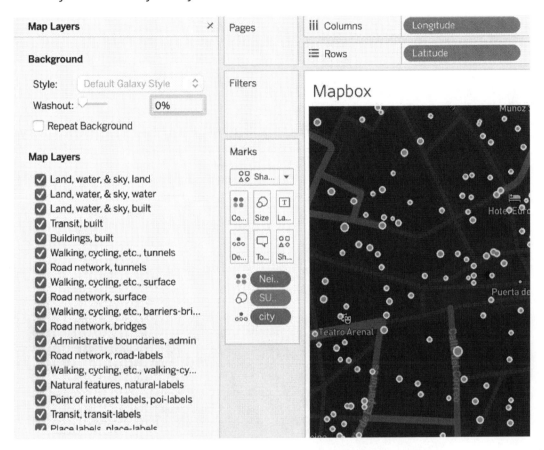

Figure 6.73: Selecting Map Layers for the Mapbox map

Using these checkboxes makes it simple to customize a map to work best with your existing point data. You can also use the **Washout** slider to add some level of transparency to the display.

As you have seen, Mapbox background maps can be used to add visual interest to your worksheets and dashboards and can be customized in Mapbox using an almost endless combination of colors and styling. To assimilate what you read in this section, you will now go through an exercise to add Mapbox and understand how to use it in Tableau.

EXERCISE 6.08: ADDING MAPBOX BACKGROUND MAPS

In this exercise, you will practice adding Mapbox data to the New York zoning data and apply a new Mapbox style for the GIS data that you have previously used.

Perform the following steps to complete this exercise:

1. Load the **New York City zone shapefile** if you have not already loaded the data into Tableau Desktop.

2. Drag **Geometry** to the **Detail** marks card and a **New York City map** will be created, which you have also seen previously.

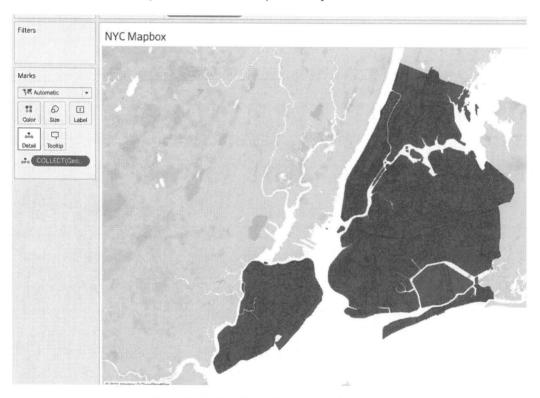

Figure 6.74: New York City zoning data map

NOTE

You can create an account with https://studio.mapbox.com/ and can continue to work on the exercise for free. Please make sure that you fill in the necessary credentials.

3. Now, go to https://studio.mapbox.com/ and sign in/sign up if you have previously not done so.

4. Click on the **New style** button at https://studio.mapbox.com/.

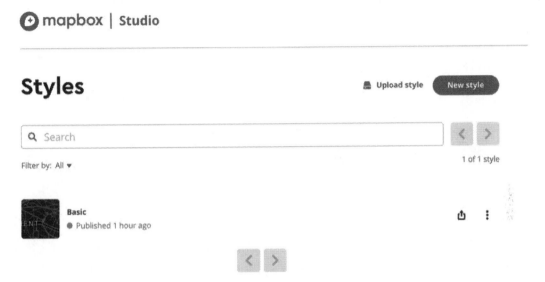

Figure 6.75: Creating a new style in Mapbox

5. Next, select the style you want to use. For the purposes of this exercise, select the **Streets** template as the style. Click on the **Customize Streets** button to create your own Mapbox style.

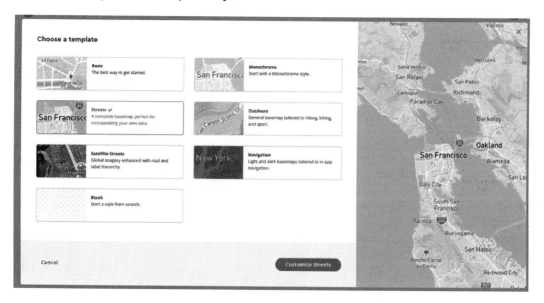

Figure 6.76: Choosing styles on Mapbox

6. On the new page that was loaded, click on the **Share** button in the top right-hand corner, scroll down the popup and click on **Third party**, then select **Tableau** from the dropdown, as shown, and copy the integration URL:

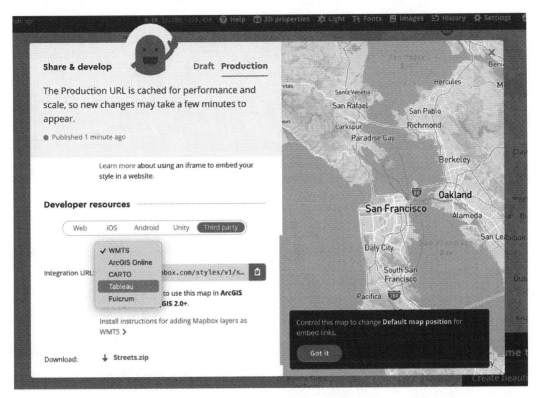

Figure 6.77: Selecting Tableau as the third-party service in Mapbox

7. In your Tableau Desktop instance, click on **Map | Background Maps | Manage Maps**, and in the popup, click on **Add**... and select **Mapbox Maps**..., as shown in the following screenshot:

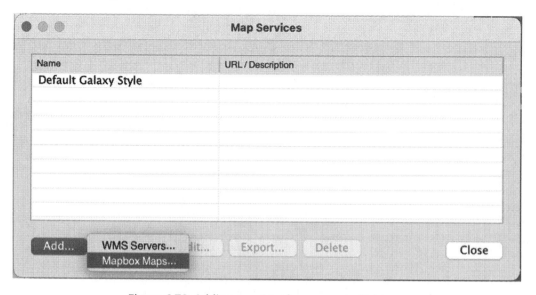

Figure 6.78: Adding new Mapbox maps to Tableau

8. Name your map style appropriately and paste your integration URL in the **Url** field. Other fields should autoload, as shown in the following screenshot. Click OK:

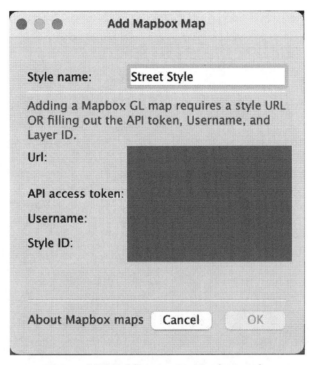

Figure 6.79: Adding a new Mapbox style

The New York City zoning map should have autoloaded the new Mapbox style with a lot more details than Tableau default map options, as shown in the following output:

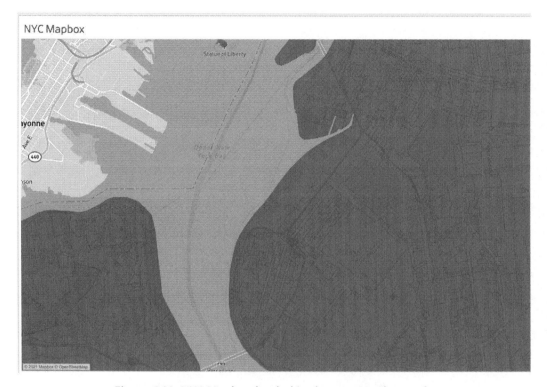

Figure 6.80: NYC Mapbox loaded in the new Mapbox style

As you can see, the Mapbox background map, when zoomed in, provides a lot more extra detail, including the city line and street names.

In this exercise, you practiced adding Mapbox to your Tableau maps with new styles with a shapefile, while previously, before the exercise, you only worked with ZIP code data. With Mapbox, you were able to add a lot more minute details to the maps, such as streets, neighborhoods, important attractions, coastlines, and highways. These newly added details have enhanced the map for end users.

This wraps up the theoretical aspects of this chapter. Next, you will go through a new set of data and a final activity to test the knowledge you have gained throughout the course of this lesson and the previous exercise by attempting to create useful and powerful maps.

ACTIVITY 6.01: CREATING A LOCATION ANALYSIS USING DUAL AXIS AND BACKGROUND MAPS

As a data developer for a San Francisco City Department, you are asked to create a report/visualization that will showcase the hotspots of house buyout agreements in the city from a high level and gather contextual information about the house, its neighborhood, its actual address, its buyout date, and its total number of tenants, as well as the buyout amounts for the houses. Stakeholders also want to be able to filter the map data points by buyout dates. You will be using the SF Buyout Agreement data provided in the GitHub link or by downloading the `.shp` file from the following link: https://packt.link/ojAf3.

Perform the following steps to complete this activity:

1. Locate the **SF Buyout Data.shp** file that you downloaded from GitHub and add that as a data source in Tableau.

2. Create a new worksheet named **SF Buyout Map**.

3. Add **Buyout Date** as a filter. Only include non-null values by selecting relative dates. Show the **Buyout Date** filter.

4. Before proceeding to the next steps, edit the title to **SF Buyout Map** and rename some of the column names for easier understanding. The mappings are as follows:

- **Case Number** – **Case Number**

- **Date Pre B** – **Pre Buyout Disclosure Date**

- **Date Buyou** – **Buyout Date**

- **Buyout Amo** – **Buyout Amount**

- **Number of** – **Tenants**

- **Analysis N** – **Neighbourhood**

5. Drag **Geometry** onto the **Detail** card.

6. Duplicate the **Latitude (generated)** column and create a dual axis.

7. Under the first **Latitude (generated)** marks card, change **Marks Type** to **Density**.

8. Add **SUM(Tenants)** to the **Color** marks card and add **Case Number** to the **Detail** marks card.

9. For the second **Latitude**, change **Marks type** to the **Circle** symbol.

10. Add **Neighbourhood** to the **Color** marks card and **Case Number** to the **Detail** marks card.

11. To add context to your map when you or a stakeholder hovers or clicks on the map, you will add **Address**, **Buyout Date**, **Buyout Amount**, and **Tenants** to a tooltip and edit the tooltip to look as in the following output.

   The expected output is as follows:

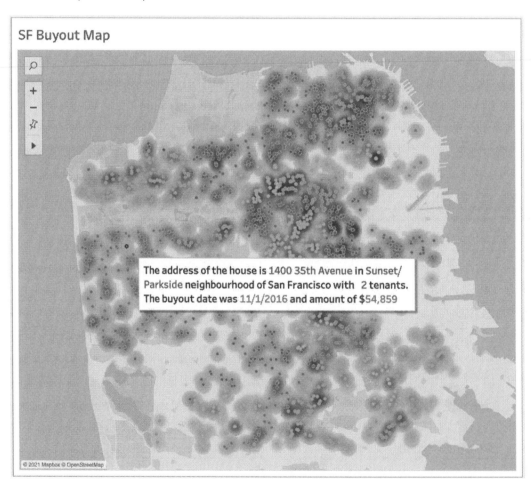

Figure 6.81: Activity 6.01 expected output

> **NOTE**
>
> The solution to this activity can be found here: https://packt.link/CTCxk.

SUMMARY

This chapter introduced you to many of the geographic capabilities and methods designers and users can employ in Tableau. The ability to take geographic data and create powerful, attractive maps that integrate with other displays is a critical skill in building visual insights. You learned how Tableau maps can incorporate size, color, shapes, and filtering so users can explore and understand geographic information more thoroughly.

You also learned that while Tableau is not a dedicated mapping platform, it can be used to replicate much of the functionality of traditional mapping and GIS software. Being able to map geographic data is an essential skill in developing complete Tableau solutions for users and can be incorporated into any analysis where geospatial data is available and interacting with external map files can add an additional layer of detail to maps.

In the next chapter, you will be moving into the analysis section of the course with *Chapter 7: Analysis : Creating and Using Calculations*. This next chapter will extend your ability to create many types of calculations that go beyond the few simple ones used in creating your maps.

7

DATA ANALYSIS: CREATING AND USING CALCULATIONS

OVERVIEW

In this chapter, you will learn to create and use various types of calculations, not just within an existing data source, but also across data sources. This chapter first describes the definitions and the differences between Aggregate and Non-Aggregate values. Then, you will learn about various types of calculations, such as numeric calculations, string calculations, and date calculations, as well as how to write logic statements in Tableau.

By the end of this chapter, you will be able to create and use various types of calculations in Tableau.

INTRODUCTION

Typically, the first step when analyzing data is to start with some questions or goals. It could be as simple as determining your most profitable customers, or more complicated, such as investigating which products are leading to losses despite high sales. After deciding on questions or goals, you would audit your data. This means identifying where data resides—whether the required fields are stored in a single or in multiple data sources and whether all fields are readily available for use. Then, you would check the integrity and validity of your data. This means checking whether the data needs any modifications in terms of cleaning, combining, or restructuring.

Once data is audited, the tools in Tableau Desktop allow you to explore it visually for more streamlined analysis. This can mean building charts, adding interactivity, separating data into groups, or creating calculations to derive more meaningful insights. Once analysis is complete, the insights you gather will be ready to share with others. This chapter aims to cover all aspects of the data analysis cycle.

In this chapter, you will later learn how to create and use Tableau's various types of calculation, which is an essential skill in data analysis. Differentiating Between Aggregate and Non-Aggregate

To work effectively with Tableau, it is vital that you have a thorough understanding of aggregation. When adding any data, Tableau quickly classifies the data in the **Data** pane as **Dimensions** and **Measures.** When a **Measure** enters the view, Tableau aggregates it (typically, using the **SUM** aggregation).

This can be demonstrated using the **Orders** data from *Sample-Superstore.xlsx*, which can be found at **Documents\My Tableau Repository\Datasources** or downloaded from this book's GitHub repository at the following link: https://packt. link/T9PeZ.

Once you have access to the data, drag the **Profit** field from the **Data** pane into the **Rows** shelf. Notice that the properties of the field have changed to **SUM(Profit)** and a vertical bar is generated. Refer to the following figure:

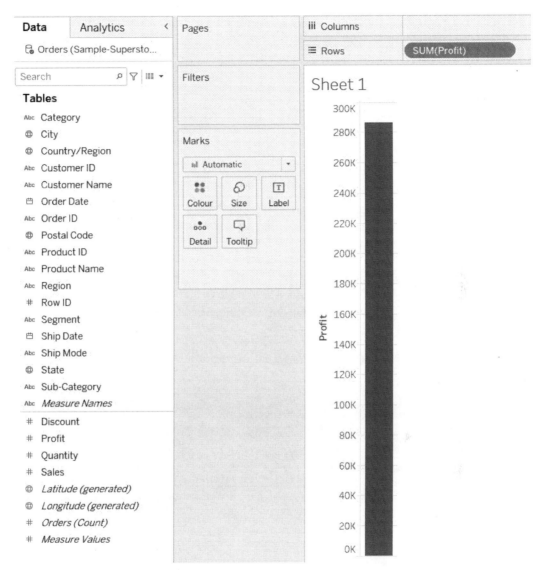

Figure 7.1: A screenshot showing SUM(Profit)

Look at the status bar at the bottom of the sheet. Notice there is only **1 mark** and the **SUM(Profit)** is **286,397**. This is the *total aggregated profit of the data*:

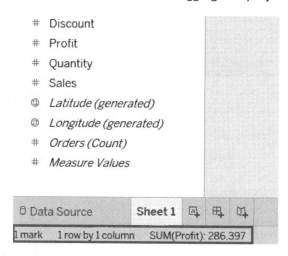

Figure 7.2: A screenshot showing SUM(Profit) in the status bar

Now, observe what happens when you disaggregate it. In order to disaggregate the **Measure**, uncheck the **Aggregate Measures** option, which is available in the *toolbar* under **Analysis**:

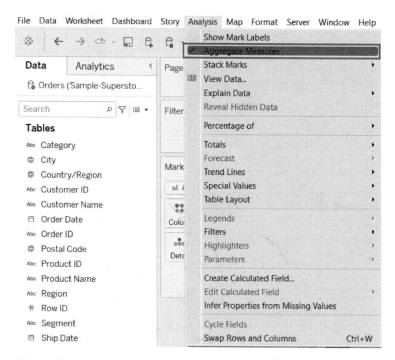

Figure 7.3: A screenshot showing the Aggregate Measures option

The **SUM(Profit)** field, which was in the **Rows** shelf, has now changed to show just **Profit**. Further, the bar chart is now broken into multiple bubbles; some bubbles are on the negative axis, and the status bar now shows **9994 marks**:

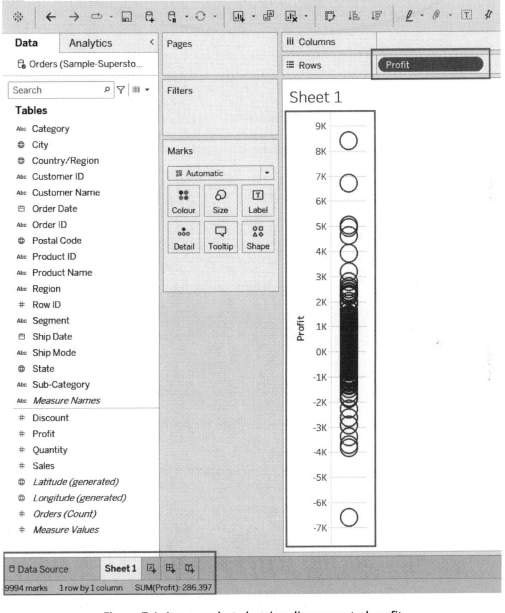

Figure 7.4: A screenshot showing disaggregated profit

When you uncheck the **Aggregate Measures** option, the **Profit** value becomes non-aggregated, which in turn breaks the aggregated profit bar showing the **Sum of Profit** in bubbles that represent *every transactional profit value in the data*. At any given point, you can right-click on a bubble to view the data and see the full details of a transaction:

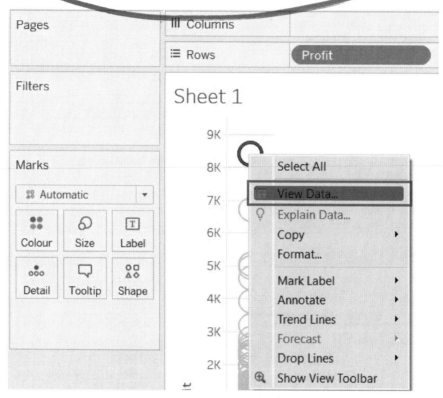

Figure 7.5: A screenshot showing the view data option

By default, the **Aggregate Measures** option is on, and all **Measures** will be *aggregated by default* (unless you choose to disaggregate them as explained above). Further, the default aggregation of **Measures** is **SUM** and this can be changed by right-clicking on a **Measure** in the **Data** pane and changing **Aggregation** under **Default Properties** from **Sum** to **Average** or **Minimum** to **Maximum, etc.**:

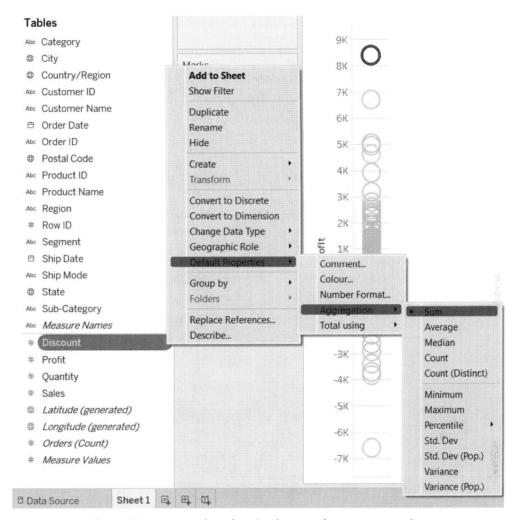

Figure 7.6: A screenshot showing how to change aggregation

From the previous example, you can conclude that when you see **SUM(Profit)** in the view, it means that Tableau is aggregating all transactional values. When you see **Profit** only, it means that Tableau is taking notice of the transactional values without aggregating them. This particular distinction is important, especially when creating calculated fields. You will further explore this point when diving deeper into creating and using calculations.

In the previous example, you looked at aggregating and disaggregating **Measures**. However, when dealing with **Dimensions**, which includes all categorical data, there are additional considerations. Specifically, you should be asking yourself: *Which/Who?* and *How many?*.

Taking the **Sample-Superstore.xlsx** file as an example, when analyzing **Sub-Category**, you might ask the following questions: *Which sub-categories are profitable?* or *How many sub-categories are profitable?* The first question is easy to answer as you are only concerned with data members from the **Sub-Category** field that are in profit. When you drag a dimension into the view, you will get the list of all unique data members of that field by default. So, dragging the **Sub-Category** field into the **Rows** shelf will result in the following view:

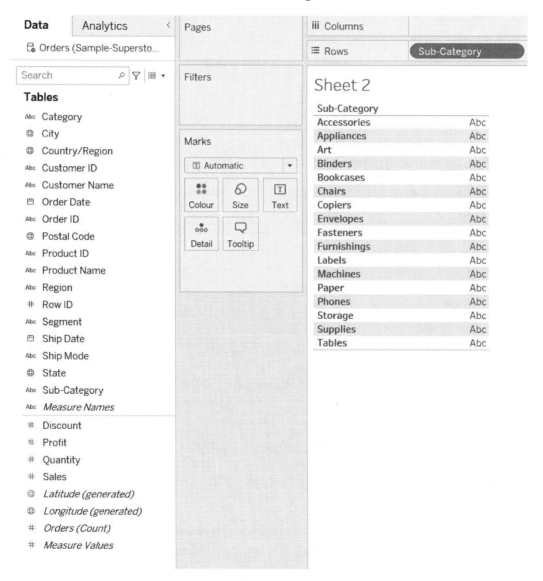

Figure 7.7: A screenshot showing the unique list of data members of a dimension

However, for the second question, you need to find the number of sub-categories that have positive profit. This means finding the number of data members for that dimension. This is achieved by clicking on the dropdown of the **Sub-Category** field, and selecting the **Count** or **Count(Distinct)** option, available under **Measure**:

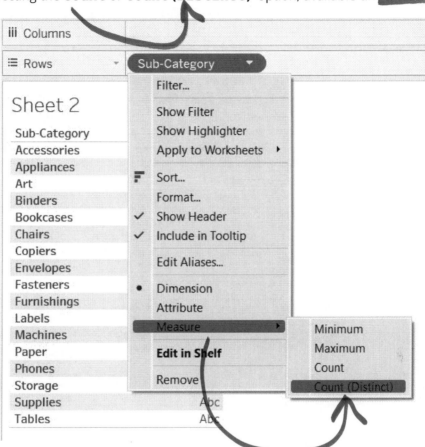

Figure 7.8: A screenshot showing the Count and Count (Distinct) options for a dimension in the view

When selecting the **Count** or the **Count(Distinct)** option, notice that the list of sub-categories changes into a bar showing that there are a total of 17 sub-categories in the data. This method will only make the count of sub-categories available in the worksheet where they were created. However, if you need to show the same information for other visualizations across your workbook, it makes sense to have the count in your **Data** pane, so you can drag it into the view as and when required. This can be achieved in two ways:

- The first method is to change the **Sub-Category** dimension into a **Measure**, which will change the original **Dimensions** field from showing a list of data members into a **Measure** showing a distinct count of sub-categories:

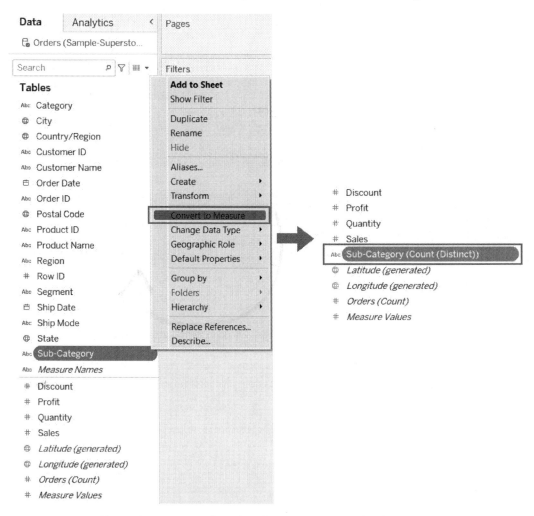

Figure 7.9: A screenshot showing aggregation of a dimension
by converting it into a measure

- The second way is to create a calculated field on the **Sub-Category** dimension. This will not only maintain the original dimension, but we will also have another field that can be used to get the desired output. You will learn more about creating a calculated field in the topics to come.

CREATING AND USING AD HOC / EDIT IN SHELF CALCULATIONS

Ad hoc / Edit in Shelf calculations are the quickest and easiest way to create a new calculated field in Tableau. Ad hoc calculations can be created in the **Rows**, **Columns**, and **Measure Values** shelves, as well as in the **Marks cards**.

Simply double-click on the existing field in your shelf of choice, or, alternatively you can use the **Edit in Shelf** option in the drop-down list of that field, as shown in the following figure:

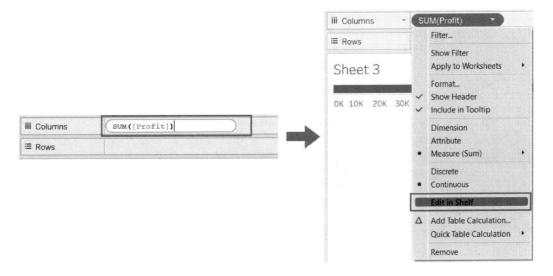

Figure 7.10: A screenshot showing how to create an ad hoc calculation

These ad hoc calculations are useful when creating quick, on-the-fly calculations that you may or may not want to save and reuse. You will explore this in the exercise below.

EXERCISE 7.01: CREATING AN AD HOC CALCULATION TO HIGHLIGHT LOSS-MAKING SUB-CATEGORIES

The aim of this exercise is to find out which sub-categories have negative profit and which ones have positive profit. Those with negative profit will be your loss-making sub-categories and will be color-coded orange. You will use the **Orders** data from **Sample-Superstore.xlsx** for this exercise.

Perform the following steps:

1. Start by creating a bar chart showing **SUM(Sales)** by **Sub-Category** with **SUM(Profit)** in the **Color** shelf, as shown in the following screenshot.

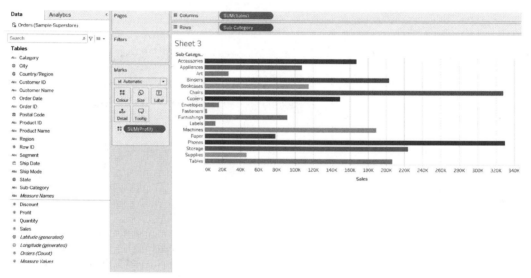

Figure 7.11: A screenshot showing a bar chart of Sales by Sub-Category with profit in color

The bars have a color palette of orange and blue, with shades of *orange indicating negative profit*, and shades of *blue indicating positive profit*. The shades indicate the intensity of **Profit**. However, the task at hand is to highlight the bars that are loss-making, which means those with a profit less than zero. The intensity of profit is irrelevant for this task.

To address this, either double-click or use the **Edit in Shelf** option in the dropdown of the **SUM(Profit)** field in the **Color** shelf and type the following formula:

```
SUM(Profit) < 0
```

2. Hit *Enter* to see the new ad hoc calculation. It now shows two colors instead of the previously seen diverging colors. In this case, the orange bars indicate subcategories are loss-making and the blue bars indicate subcategories are profitable. Refer to the following screenshots:

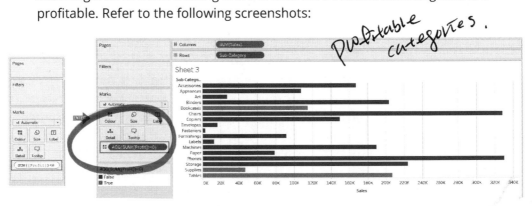

profitable categories.

Figure 7.12: Screenshots with an ad hoc calculation in the color shelf

Further, as mentioned previously, this ad hoc calculation is an on-the-fly calculation that may be used only in this specific visualization, in which case, there isn't any need to save this calculation.

3. So that you can reuse this in other visualizations, save the calculation in the **Data** pane by simply dragging and dropping, as shown in the following screenshots:

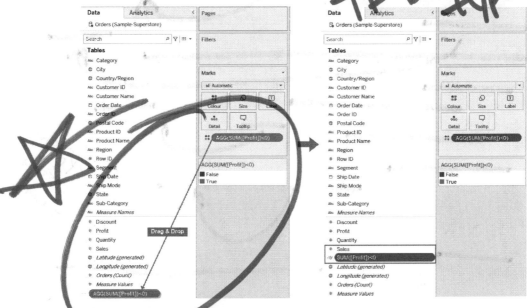

TF Data type.

Figure 7.13: Screenshots showing how to save an ad hoc calculation

CREATING AND USING DIFFERENT TYPES OF CALCULATIONS

Tableau is a simple yet versatile tool, and the ability to create calculations gives users the flexibility to perform powerful analysis, which can help with decision-making. Most of the time, creating calculations in Tableau is a fun experience, but sometimes it can be a little frustrating as well, especially if you are coming from a different platform to Tableau and are trying to replicate some functionality. The way these tools are structured and designed is different and trying to replicate the functionality from one tool in another can make the experience frustrating. The best way to avoid frustration while creating calculations in Tableau is to start small and get acquainted with the functions that Tableau has to offer. While writing a calculation in Tableau is easy, it is recommended that, if possible, you should try to use the built-in native features first, instead of creating a new calculated field. Some examples of these features are as follows:

- The **Split** or **Custom Split** function, available under the **Transform** option when right-clicking any **String Dimension** in the **Data** pane. This is used to split the string into smaller sub-strings. For example, splitting a customer name into, for example, the first name and last name.

- The **Group** function, which is available under the **Create** option when right-clicking any dimension in the **Data** pane. This is used to group the data members of that dimension into higher categories, for example, grouping the data members of the geographic state field into, for example, regions.

- The **Custom date** function, which is available under the **Create** option when right-clicking on a **Date Dimension** in the **Data** pane. This is used to truncate dates into different granularities such as month, month-year, etc.

- The **Bins** function, which is available under the **Create** option when right-clicking on a **Measure** in the **Data** pane. This is used to group **Measure** values into different range buckets, for example, age bins that range from, for example <10 years, 11-20 years, 21-30 years, etc.

- The **Combined Field** function, available under the **Create** option when selecting more than 1 **String Dimension** in the **Data** pane, and then right-clicking any selected string dimension. This is useful when combining multiple string dimensions into one field.

- The **Aliases** function, which is available upon right-clicking any dimension in the **Data** pane. This is useful when renaming the members of any dimension.

A point to note is that all objectives mentioned here can be achieved by creating a calculated field from scratch, but since these native functions are readily and easily available, it is best to avoid the hassle and make use of them. Over the course of this chapter and various other chapters in this book, you will explore these functions in a little more detail.

To understand the process of creating calculations, you will first create a basic calculation to find the distinct count of your order IDs. You can do this in many ways. You could change the **Order ID** dimension into a **Measure** or click the dropdown of the **Order ID** field that is shown in your view, and then click the **Measure | Count (Distinct)** option. Alternatively, you could even create an ad hoc calculation.

In an earlier topic, you saw how to save an ad hoc calculation in the **Data** pane. However, inexplicably, when attempting this after performing basic aggregations such as sum, average, or count, you'll find that the ad hoc calculation does not save. From testing, the drag-drop method appears to fix this issue. Try it with the calculation below:

```
COUNTD([Order ID])*1
```

You will now be creating a calculation in Tableau from scratch. To do this, you will continue with the objective of getting the distinct count of order IDs.

Right-click on the **Order ID** dimension in the **Data** pane and select the **Create | Calculated Field** option. This will open a new type in the box, as shown in the following screenshot:

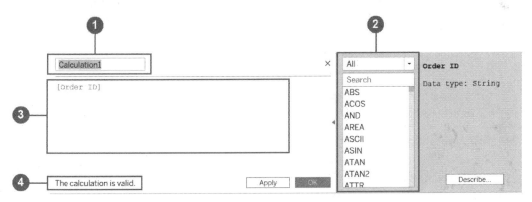

Figure 7.14: A screenshot showing components of a calculation box

Figure 7.14 shows the components of a calculation box. These are as follows:

- **1 – Calculation name**: This is where you can define the name of a calculation. It is always recommended to give meaningful names to calculated fields.

- **2 – List of functions / types of functions**: This is the list of all functions available in Tableau. The functions are listed in alphabetical order, and are classified as **Number**, **String**, **Date**, **Type Conversion**, **Aggregate**, **Logical**, etc. When clicking any of these functions, Tableau presents the syntax of that function, an explanation of what the function does, and an example. Refer to the following screenshot:

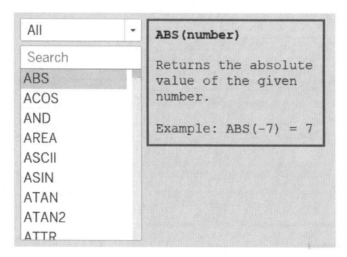

Figure 7.15: A screenshot showing details of the selected function

- **3 – Calculation editor**: This is where you will type your formula.

- **4 – Syntax validator**: This will validate whether your formula and calculation are syntactically correct. If there are any issues, the text will read as **The calculation contains errors** in red font, and the calculation editor box will display a red squiggly line near the text with the error.

Ever since you right-clicked on the **Order ID** field to create a calculation, Tableau has assumed you will be creating a calculation for that field, and because of that, it has already fetched the field into the calculation editor.

Start by typing the word **CountD** before **Order ID**. As you type, Tableau starts recommending functions, as well as data fields that share characters with what you type. Now, name the calculation '**Count of Orders**'. Your calculation box should look like the following screenshot:

Figure 7.16: A screenshot showing the formula for calculating the distinct count of Order ID

Once, you have valid calculation, you can click **OK** and proceed to use it. Clicking **OK** will save your calculation in the **Data** pane, as shown in the following screenshot:

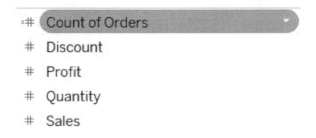

Figure 7.17: A screenshot showing the newly created calculated field

Now, that you have your calculated field available in the **Data** pane, you can start using it across the entire workbook. There are, however, a few important points to note:

- In the previous example, you right-clicked on **Order ID** and selected the **Create | Calculated Field** option, which opened the calculation editor box. This can also be made available by selecting the **Analysis | Create Calculated Field...** option in the toolbar, or by clicking on the dropdown in the **Data** pane and selecting **Create Calculated Field...**:

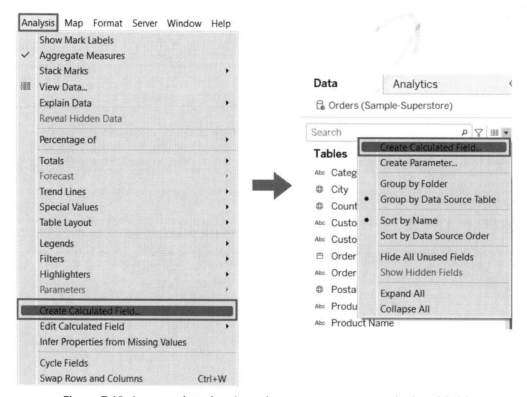

Figure 7.18: A screenshot showing other ways to create a calculated field

- Any field that is computed or calculated in Tableau will have **=** as a prefix, which indicates that the field was created in Tableau, and does not derive from the data itself. The = sign will be followed by either **Abc** or **#** (or something similar), which indicates the data type of that field. So, for example, **=Abc** is indicative of a computed field with a string output.

- To add comments to a calculation, you need to make use of two forward slashes, that is, **//. Tableau will ignore anything that follows the //**. Refer to the following screenshot:

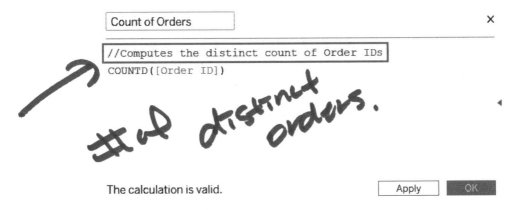

Figure 7.19: A screenshot showing how to add comments in a calculated field

- The functions (blue text in *Figure 7.19* in Tableau are not case-sensitive, but data fields (orange text in *Figure 7.19*) are, hence, you need to be extra careful about the case, as well as the spelling of the data field. If there are any issues, the syntax validator will give an error, and you will not be able to use the calculated field for further analysis. To overcome this, drag and drop the desired field from the **Data** pane into the calculation editor box instead of typing the text, as shown in the following screenshot:

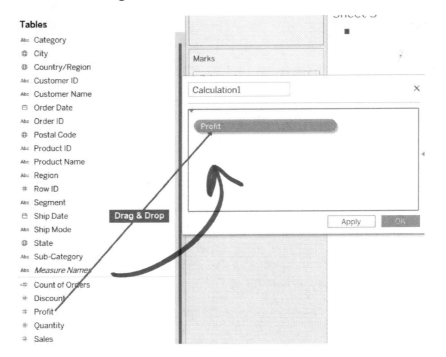

Figure 7.20: A screenshot showing dragging and dropping fields into the calculation editor

- Tableau supports all standard operators, such as multiplication (*), division (/), modulo (%), addition (+), subtraction (-), as well as all the comparisons, such as equal to (== or =), greater than (>), greater than or equal to (>=), less than (<), less than or equal to (<=), and not equal to (!= or <>). These operators must be typed and are not part of the list of functions in the calculation box.

- Since Tableau is a read-only tool, the calculated fields you are computing will not be written back to the data, thus keeping the integrity of your data intact.

- You can create a calculated field and use it in other calculated fields as well.

You will now work through examples of how some of these calculations can be created and used.

CREATING AND USING DIFFERENT TYPES OF CALCULATIONS: NUMERIC CALCULATIONS

Numeric calculations are used when performing mathematical/arithmetic functions on numeric data in order to return a numeric output. The **Number** functions supported by Tableau at this point in time (that is, in version 2020.1) are as follows:

- **Basic math functions** such as the **ABS** function, which is used to return the absolute value of the number; the **ROUND** function, which is used to round the number to the specified number of decimal places; **SQRT**, which is used to return the square root of a number; and the **ZN** function, which returns zero if there are null values, or returns the value itself otherwise.

- **Trigonometric functions** such as **ASIN, ACOS, ATAN, SIN, COS, TAN,** and others.

- **Angular functions** such as **DEGREES** and **RADIANS**.

- **Mapping functions** such as **HEXBINX** and **HEXBINY**.

- **Logarithmic functions** such as **LN** and **LOG**.

- **Exponential and Power functions** such as **EXP** and **POWER**, and others.

As mentioned earlier, when selecting any of these functions, you will see the syntax of that function, an explanation of the purpose of that function, along with an example. Further, with these numeric functions, as well as the arithmetic operators above, you can create some immensely powerful and useful calculations.

In the previous topic, you created a new calculated field called **Count of Orders**, which gave the distinct count of your order IDs. You will now use this computed field to create another calculated field to find the average order value for your sub-categories.

EXERCISE 7.02: CREATING A NUMERIC CALCULATION

The objective of this exercise is to create a numeric calculation to find the average order value of each sub-category. You will continue with the **Orders data** from the *Sample-Superstore.xlsx* file and, using the **Sales** field and the previously created **Count of Orders** field, create a new calculated field called **Average Order Value (AOV)** for each **Sub-Category** and display it in a bar chart.

1. First, drag your **Sub-Category** field and drop it in the **Rows** shelf. Next, drag the Sales and the **Count of Orders** field into the **Columns** shelf. Now enable the labels for your bar charts by clicking on **Show Marks Label** in the toolbar. See the following screenshot:

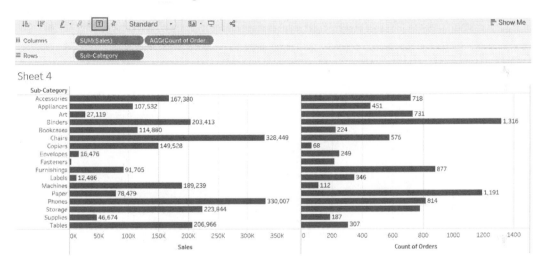

Figure 7.21: A screenshot showing a bar chart with Sales and
Count of Orders across sub-categories

2. Create a calculated field called **Average Order Value (AOV)** with the following formula:

```
SUM([Sales])/[Count of Orders]
```

You should see the following on your screen:

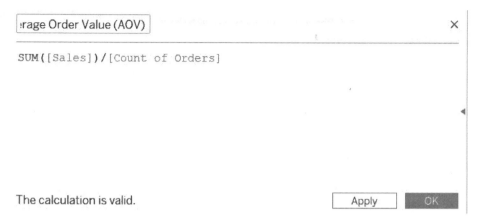

Figure 7.22: A screenshot showing the formula for
the Average Order Value (AOV) calculation

3. Drag and drop the **Average Order Value (AOV)** next to the **Count of Orders** field in the **Columns** shelf. Refer to the following screenshot:

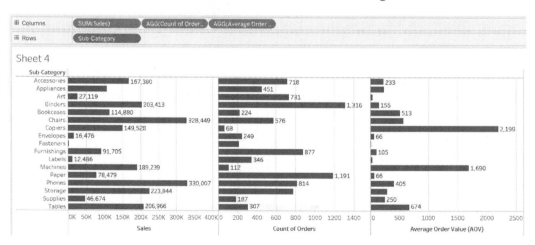

Figure 7.23: A screenshot showing the bar chart with
the Average Order Value (AOV) calculation

As you can see in *Figure 7.23*, the **Copiers** sub-category has the **highest average order value** followed by **Machines**.

Note that the prefix for **Average Order Value (AOV)** is **AGG**, which stands for **Aggregate**. This is Tableau's way of telling you that the calculation is pre-aggregated by the user (since you are using **SUM()** for sales and the count of orders field is using the **COUNTD()** function).

This exercise shows an example of creating and using a numeric calculation. You have created a new calculation called **Average Order Value (AOV)** using the **Sales** field and the **Count of Orders** field. Since this **Average Order Value (AOV)** field has a numeric output, the calculation is called a numeric calculation.

CREATING AND USING DIFFERENT TYPES OF CALCULATIONS: LOGIC STATEMENTS

Logic statements are typically used for criteria-based or condition-based evaluation. Some of the logical functions available in Tableau are as follows:

- Operators such as **AND, OR, and NOT.**

- Functions such as **IF, ELSE, ELSEIF, CASE, IIF, IFNULL, ISNULL, ISDATE**, etc.

IF...ELSE, IF...ELSEIF...ELSE, and **CASE** are the most commonly used logic functions and, typically, when using these logic functions, the **THEN** function is used to specify the value that needs to be displayed when the expression is true.

An important point to remember here is that when using the **IF** statement or a **CASE** statement for logical evaluation, you need to terminate your logical statement with the **END** function.

You have already seen an example of a logic statement in the **Creating and Using Ad Hoc / Edit in Shelf Calculations** section, where you found out which sub-categories were profitable, and which were not. You created a calculation to see whether **SUM(Profit)** was greater than or less than zero. The output of this calculation was a Boolean output, with the outcome being either **True** or **False**. Boolean calculations are a quick and easy type of logic statement. They get executed quickly and perform well compared to the other types of logic statement.

Although Boolean calculations have many advantages, they could confuse an end user if they are unaware of what **True** and **False** stand for. The meaning of Booleans depends on the criteria in your calculations. In the earlier example, the outcome **True** indicates either positive or negative profit, depending on what is specified in your calculation. If the end user is unfamiliar with these criteria, the Boolean outcome will be unhelpful.

#2 How many transactions for each product are Profitable?

#1 Which products are Profitable and which are unprofitable?

To avoid confusion, it is best to use a more elaborate logic statement incorporating user-friendly tags. You will explore this by following the steps in the following exercise.

> **NOTE**
>
> If you are using a version of Tableau later than 2020.1, you may need to create Number of records to match the output of *Exercise 7.03*.

EXERCISE 7.03: CREATING A LOGIC CALCULATION

In this exercise, you will create a logic calculation to find unprofitable products. as well as to find out how many transactions for each product are unprofitable. You will use the **CoffeeChain Query** table from the **Sample-Coffee Chain.mdb** dataset. This is a *Microsoft Access Database*. The dataset can be downloaded from the following link: https://1drv.ms/u/s!Av5QCoyLTBpnmkPL8Yx_0_2KtrG4?e=rWpksB.

First, you will connect to the **CoffeeChain Query** table from the **Sample-Coffee Chain.mdb** dataset and create a bar chart using the **Product** field and the **Number of records** field. You will then create new calculated fields, which will help find and highlight *unprofitable products*, and find out *how many of the transactions in each product are unprofitable*.

1. Connect to the **CoffeeChain Query** table from **Sample-Coffee Chain. mdb**. Create a bar chart by dragging the **Product Name** field into the **Rows** shelf. Then, drag **Number of Records** into the **Columns** shelf and enable the labels for these bars. Refer to the following screenshot:

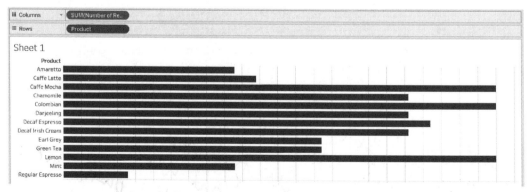

Figure 7.24: A screenshot showing the bar chart showing Number of Records by Product

Now, you want to find the profitability of your products. However, profitability (especially in this case) can be computed on two levels.

There is the overall profitability of a product, and there is how many transactions for a product are profitable. Both these requirements are useful to know. You will begin by finding the overall profitability of your products.

> **NOTE**
>
> Please replace the quotes around **Profitable Product** and **Unprofitable Product** after pasting the code in *Step 2* below. This will ensure the output is error-free.

2. Create a new calculated field called **Overall Profitability** using the **IF… THEN…ELSE…END** function. The formula will be as follows:

```
IF SUM([Profit])>0 THEN "Profitable Product"
ELSE "Unprofitable Product"
END
```

Refer to the following screenshot:

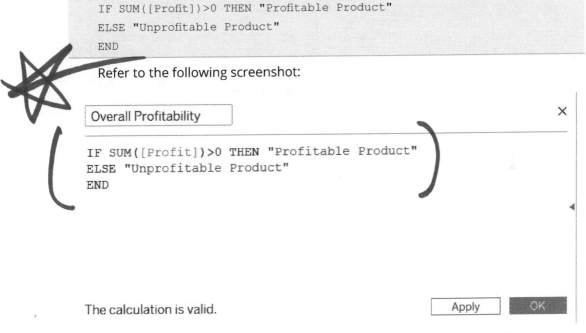

The calculation is valid.

Figure 7.25: A screenshot showing the formula for Overall Profitability

3. Click **OK** and drag this new field into the **Color** shelf. Your view will update, as shown in the following screenshot:

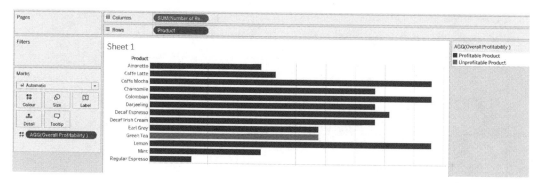

Figure 7.26: A screenshot showing Overall Profitability using color

As you see from the color legend, the *blue bars* are the *profitable products*, and the *orange bars* are the *unprofitable products*. In the preceding screenshot, you can clearly see that green tea is the only product that is unprofitable.

In the ad hoc calculation example (*Exercise 7.01, Creating an Ad Hoc Calculation to Highlight Loss-Making Sub-Categories*), when you saved the calculation in the **Data** pane, you had a Boolean output with a prefix of =T|F, whereas when you save this **Overall Profitability** calculation by clicking **OK**, you see that the output is a string with the prefix **=Abc**. Refer to the following screenshot:

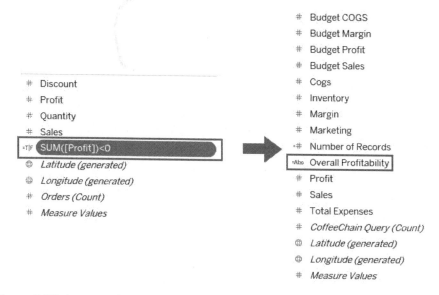

Figure 7.27: A screenshot showing the prefix for an ad hoc calculation and Overall Profitability calculation

Now that you have found which of your products are profitable, it is time to find out how many profitable transactions there are for each product.

4. **Duplicate** the **Overall Profitability** calculation and change the code.

5. Use the **IF**...**THEN**...**ELSE**...**END** function. The formula and syntax should be similar to the **Overall Profitability** calculation, except for a change in the aggregation of the **Profit** field and the displayed output string. Name this calculated field **Transactional Profitability**. The formula will be as follows:

```
IF [Profit]>0 THEN "Profitable transaction"
ELSE "Unprofitable transaction"
END
```

Refer to the following screenshot:

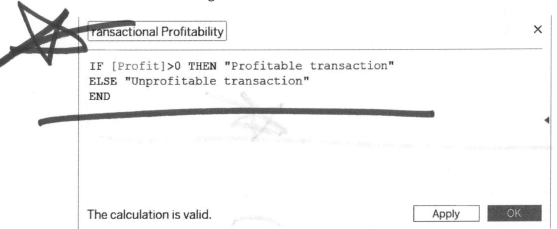

Figure 7.28: A screenshot showing the formula for Transactional Profitability

6. Click **OK** and drag this new field into the **Color** shelf. Your view will update, as shown in the following screenshot:

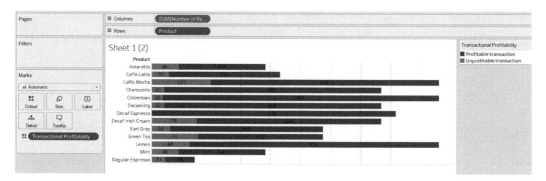

Figure 7.29: A screenshot showing Transactional Profitability in color

As you see from the color legend, the *blue bars* represent `profitable transactions`, and the *orange bars* represent `unprofitable transactions`. From this, you can find some interesting outcomes. For example, it shows that all **Decaf Espresso** transactions are profitable.

You have now successfully created and used logic statements to find the profitability, and profitable transactions for each of your products.

CREATING AND USING DIFFERENT TYPES OF CALCULATIONS: STRING CALCULATIONS

In Tableau, string calculations can be performed on any data type. Tableau converts and processes all such data types and yields a string output. You can create string calculations on **Integer** fields, as well as **Date** fields by first converting them into a string. You can use the type conversion function **STR()** in Tableau to achieve this. The various string functions supported by Tableau (in version 2020.1) are as follows:

- Functions such as **ASCII** and **CHAR** find the ASCII code of a character and the character based on the ASCII code, respectively.

- Case functions such as **LOWER** and **UPPER** change the casing of strings to lowercase and uppercase, respectively.

- Functions such as **CONTAINS**, **STARTSWITH**, **ENDSWITH**, and **ISDATE** check string or substring conditions.

- Functions such as **TRIM**, **LTRIM**, and **RTRIM** remove blank spaces.

- Functions such as **FIND** and **FINDNTH** find the position of a substring.

- Functions such as **LEFT**, **RIGHT**, and **MID**, return the specified number of characters in a string.

- Regular expressions such as **REGEXP_EXTRACT**, **REGEXP_EXTRACT_NTH**, **REGEXP_MATCH**, and **REGEXP_REPLACE** allow you to specify patterns to match, locate, and manage text.

- Some other string functions available in Tableau are **LEN**, which returns the length of the string; **REPLACE**, which searches for a specified substring and replaces it with a replacement substring; **SPLIT**, which returns the substring from a string based on the specified delimiter; and **MIN** and **MAX**, which return either the alphabetically minimum or maximum value for a string.

In this section, you will further explore some of these functions.

You will now continue with the **Orders** data from *Sample-Superstore.xlsx* and work with the **Customer Name** field. Currently, this field is a combination of the first names and last names of customers. First and last names are separated by a *space*. For this example, you would separate the first and last names of each customer, and then find the initial letters of the last names for your customers.

After that, you create groups for names starting with letters *A to I*, *J to R*, and *S to Z* to find out how many customers fall in each group.

You begin by dragging the **Customer Name** field into the **Rows** shelf. There should be 793 unique customers.

To find the last name, you have to create calculations on the **Customer Name** field. Right-click on the **Customer Name** field in the **Data** pane and choose the **Split** or **Custom Split** option available under **Transform**. Refer to the following screenshot:

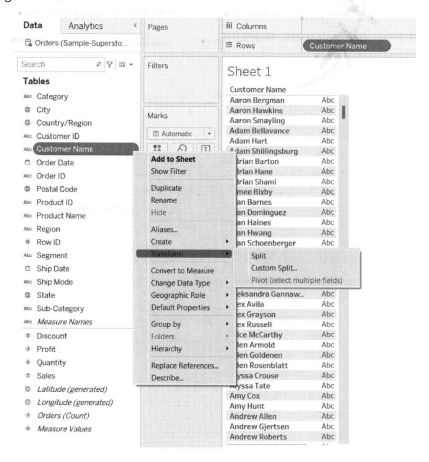

Figure 7.30: A screenshot showing the Split and Custom Split options

When using the **Split** function, Tableau automatically creates two calculated fields named **Customer Name – Split 1** and **Customer Name – Split 2**. When you edit these calculated fields, you will see the following syntax for **Split 1** and **Split 2** respectively:

```
TRIM( SPLIT( [Customer Name], " ", 1 ) )
TRIM( SPLIT( [Customer Name], " ", 2 ) )
```

This auto split targeted *delimiter*, which in this case was *space*, and on that basis, has split the field to give the *first column before the space*, which is customer *first names second column after the space*, which in this case is customer last names.

The **Custom Split** option allows for more control than the auto split option. Here, for example, only the last name is needed. The first name isn't of any use at this point. So, instead of using the auto split option, you can use **Custom Split**, which brings up the following screenshot:

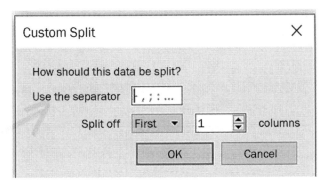

Figure 7.31: A screenshot showing the Custom Split option

Here, you can specify the separator/delimiter. You can decide whether you want the first column or the second column, and whether you want to split the columns. To get only the last name, choose *space* as the separator, and then **Split off** the **Last 1** column. You get one new calculated field called **Customer Name - Split 2**. The syntax of this field is as follows:

```
TRIM(SPLIT([Customer Name], " ", -1 ))
```

Split and **Custom Split** are shortcut options provided by Tableau to split strings. However, you could get the same result by creating new calculated fields from scratch using some of the previously stated string functions. You will now explore this further.

First, parse the string to find the position of the space. Next, ask Tableau to give the string that follows the space. To find the position of the space, use the **FIND** function in Tableau. The syntax of the calculated field should be as follows:

```
FIND([Customer Name]," ")
```

This gives the position of the space as a numeric value. However, you need the string after the space. To identify this, use the **MID** function. The syntax should be as follows:

```
MID([Customer Name],FIND([Customer Name]," "))
```

This formula gives you the string followed by the space, but this also includes the leading space. To remove this leading space, either use the **TRIM** function or the **LTRIM** function as follows:

1. **TRIM**:

```
TRIM(MID([Customer Name],FIND([Customer Name]," ")))
```

2. **LTRIM**:

```
LTRIM(MID([Customer Name],FIND([Customer Name]," ")))
```

Either of these two functions will remove the leading space and give only the string followed by the space. However, if you don't want to use the **TRIM** or **LTRIM** function, you could even modify the calculation to tweak the **FIND** function, as shown here:

```
MID([Customer Name],(FIND([Customer Name]," ")+1))
```

The **+1** in the preceding example finds the first position after the space, and thus will work similarly to the **TRIM** and **LTRIM** functions.

The point of discussing all these options is to show that many string functions can be utilized differently to get the same output. Now, choose any of the preceding formulae and save your calculated field as **Last Name**. Refer to the following screenshot:

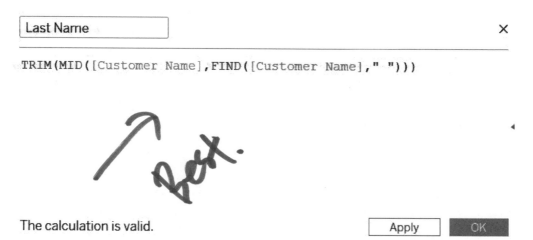

Figure 7.32: A screenshot showing the Last Name calculated field

Now, you have the **Last Name** of your customers, it is time to find the initial letter of **Last Name**. Here, again, you can use functions such as **LEFT** and **MID**. The syntax for both these functions is as follows:

```
LEFT([Last Name],1)
```

```
MID([Last Name],1,1)
```

The **LEFT** function will return the *specified number of characters (shown as **1** in the previous example)* from the start of the given string.

The **MID** function will return the characters from the middle of the string, giving a *starting position and a length (shown as **1**, **1** in the previous example)*. So, both the **LEFT** and the **MID** functions will give us the first character of the string.

Here, you will continue with the **MID** function, as shown in the following screenshot:

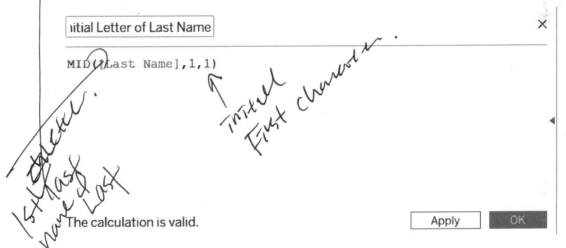

Figure 7.33: A screenshot showing the initial letter of the Last Name calculated field

Finally, it is time for you to create your groups. You can use the following formula:

```
IF [Starting alphabet of Last Name] <= "I" THEN "A-I"
ELSEIF [Starting alphabet of Last Name] >= "S" THEN "S-Z"
ELSE "J-R"
END
```

Name this calculation **Groups-Starting alphabet of Last Name**. Refer to the following screenshot:

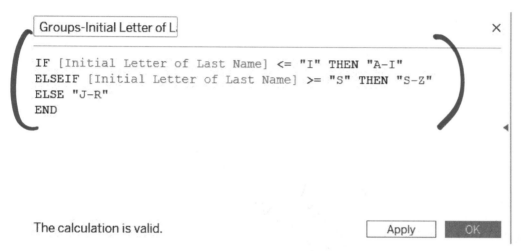

Figure 7.34: A screenshot showing the Groups-Starting alphabet of Last Name calculated field

Change the **Customer Name** field in the **Rows** shelf to show the distinct count of customers. Then, drop the new calculated field into the **Columns** shelf. Refer to the following screenshot:

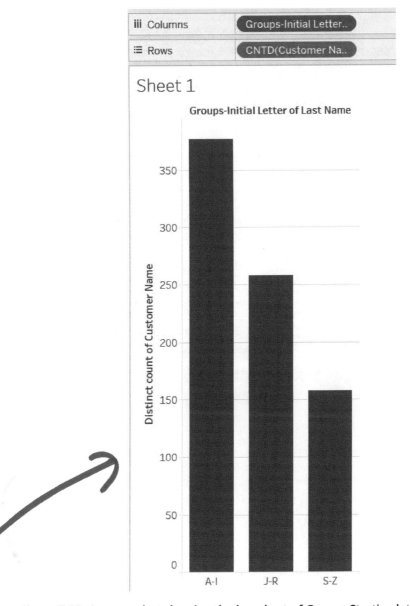

Figure 7.35: A screenshot showing the bar chart of Groups-Starting letter of Last Name

Figure 7.35 shows that there are more than 350 customers whose last name starts with a letter that is between **A** and **I**.

Typically, when dealing with string data, the two main operations you might perform are splitting a string into substrings or concatenating two or more strings to make one long string. You have now learned how to split strings. In the following exercise, you will be concatenating two strings together.

EXERCISE 7.04: CREATING A STRING CALCULATION

In this exercise, you will create a string calculation that will combine **Product Type**, **Product**, and the aggregated **Sales** value. You will continue using the **CoffeeChain Query** data from the **Sample-Coffee Chain.mdb** file. You will use the **Product Type** and **Product** fields, along with **SUM(Sales)**.

1. Start by creating a bar chart using the **Product Type**, **Product**, and **SUM(Sales)** fields, as shown in the following screenshot:

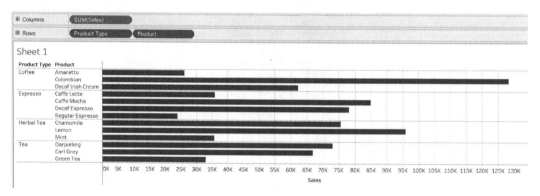

Figure 7.36: A screenshot showing the bar chart of SUM(Sales) by Product Type and Product

Once the bar chart is created, create a calculated field that is a combination of the first three letters of **Product Type** followed by the **Product** text and the **SUM(Sales)** value. So, for example, if **Product Type** is, **Coffee** and **Product** is **Colombian**, and if the total sales for this **Product** are **$90,000**, then the output should be **COF-Colombian: $90000**.

To achieve this, you must change the Product Type to upper case, then pick only the first 3 characters. You must append the Product labels, and the SUM(Sales) value, which needs to start with a $ sign and must be rounded off to show zero decimals. You also need to add some special characters such as space, **-**, and **:**. These can be inserted using either single quotes or double quotes. Follow along with this exercise to learn how.

Handwritten annotations: "AUpper case.", "+product.", "From Left.", "ED First 3 Letters", "II : $" +", "Round (Sum ((Sales)), 0)"

2. Begin by creating a new calculated field called **Concatenated string** and
    type the following formula:

```
LEFT(UPPER([Product Type]),3) + "-" + [Product] + " : "
```

This gives you the first part of what the desired string should look like. So,
for example, if the desired output is **COF-Colombian: $90000**, then the
preceding calculation gives an output of **COF-Colombian:**.

You are halfway there. Now, if you saved the calculation mid-way, you will have
to right-click on this new calculated field and edit it from the **Dimensions** pane.
However, if not, you can continue working in the same calculation box.

3. Now you must append the **SUM(Sales)** value, and this is where things start
    to get complicated. Firstly, **Product Type** and **Product** are *string values*, but
    SUM(Sales) is an *integer value*, so it is not possible to concatenate them, unless
    you convert **SUM(Sales)** to a *string value*. Further, you need the **SUM(Sales)**
    value to be *rounded off to zero decimal places* and it needs to have *$ as a prefix*.
    Keeping this in mind, amend the existing calculation as follows:

```
LEFT(UPPER([Product Type]),3) + "-" + [Product] + " : " +
STR(ROUND(SUM([Sales]),0))
```

4. You will see that Tableau doesn't agree with this formula and gives an error
    indicator. Refer to the following screenshot:

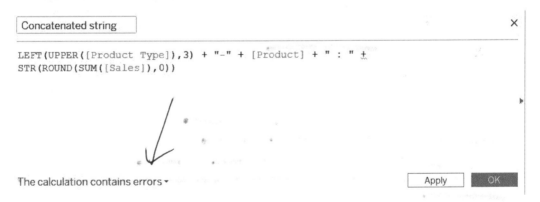

Figure 7.37: A screenshot showing the error in the calculation of Concatenated string

5. Click the error dropdown. You should see an error that reads **Cannot mix aggregate and non-aggregate arguments with this function**. Refer to the following screenshot:

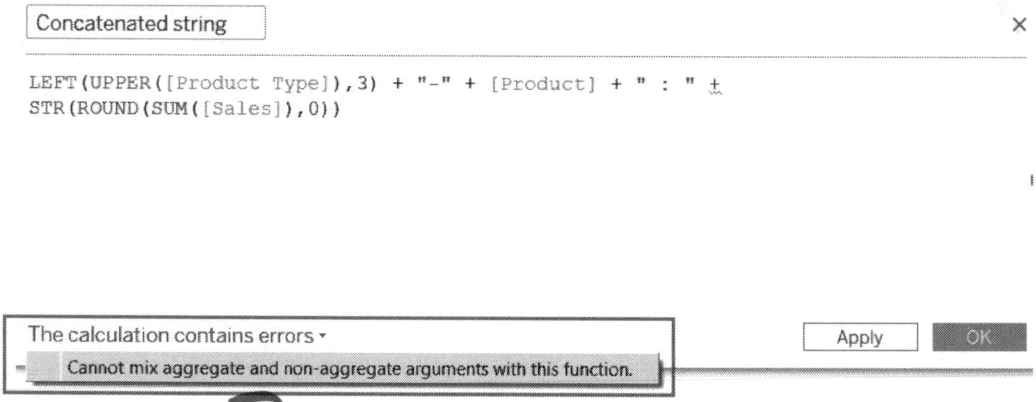

| Concatenated string | × |

```
LEFT(UPPER([Product Type]),3) + "-" + [Product] + " : " +
STR(ROUND(SUM([Sales]),0))
```

| The calculation contains errors ▾ | Apply | OK |

Cannot mix aggregate and non-aggregate arguments with this function.

Figure 7.38: A screenshot showing the "Cannot mix aggregate and non-aggregate arguments..." error

This is a *classic error* common in Tableau. It means that **SUM(Sales)** is an *aggregated field* whereas the **Product Type** and **Product** fields, being **Dimensions**, are *not aggregated* and, logically, Tableau can't work with aggregated and non-aggregated values in a calculation. So, to overcome this, you must aggregate the **Product Type** and **Product fields**. Since both the Product Type and Product fields are dimensions, you can use any of the following functions: **MIN, MAX, or ATTR**.

Save your existing calculation as it is and spend a little time understanding these three functions before amending it.

When aggregating the dimension using the MIN function, you get the *alphabetically minimum or lowest value*. The **MAX** function, on the other hand, gives the *alphabetically maximum or highest value*. The ATTR function gives the value of the field as is if it has a single value for all rows; otherwise, it will return an asterisk.

6. To demonstrate this, create a new sheet to show **Product Type** in the **Rows** shelf. Then, create a new calculated field called **Min of Product** with the following formula:

```
MIN([Product])
```

Refer to the following screenshot:

Min of Product	✕

MIN([Product])

The calculation is valid.   Apply   OK

Figure 7.39: A screenshot showing Min of Product calculation

Save the calculation. Notice that even though it has a string output, it is now part of the **Measures** pane. This is because it is now an aggregated field and, as discussed earlier, any aggregated field becomes part of the **Measures** pane.

7. Now, create another calculation called **Max of Product** with the following formula:

```
MAX([Product])
```

Refer to the following screenshot:

Max of Product	✕

MAX([Product])

The calculation is valid.   Apply   OK

Figure 7.40: A screenshot showing the Max of Product calculation

8. This calculation should also be in the **Measures** pane.

9. Finally, create a calculation called **Attribute of Product** with the following formula:

```
ATTR([Product])
```

Refer to the following screenshot:

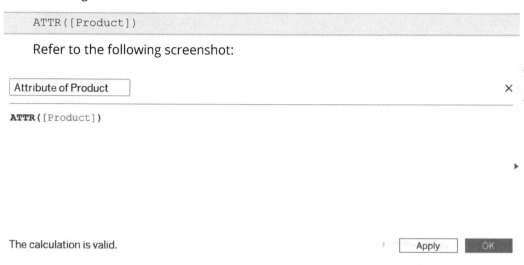

Figure 7.41 – A screenshot showing the Attribute of Product calculation

Now drop these three calculated fields into your sheet, right after the **Product Type** field in the **Rows** shelf.

10. First, drop the **Min of Product** field, followed by **Max of Product**, and finally **Attribute of Product**. You should notice that all three fields give different outputs. Refer to the following screenshot:

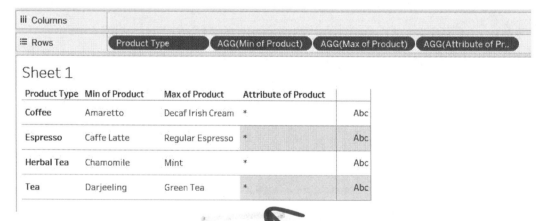

Figure 7.42: A screenshot showing the output of Min, Max, and Attribute of Product calculations at the Product Type level

As you can see, **Min of Product** gives you **Amaretto for Coffee**, **Caffe Latte for Espresso**, **Chamomile for Herbal Tea**, and **Darjeeling for Tea**. These are the *alphabetically minimum values* of our **Product** field within that **Product Type**. Similarly, **Max of Product** is giving **Decaf Irish Cream for Coffee**, **Regular Espresso for Espresso**, **Mint for Herbal Tea**, and **Green Tea for Tea**. These are the *alphabetically maximum values* of your **Product** field within that **Product** Type. Further, **Attribute of Product** is giving *neither the minimum nor the maximum*; instead, it is giving an *asterisk*. This means there is more than 1 **Product** under that **Product Type** and since Tableau can't display all the values, it is showing the asterisk to indicate there is more than 1 **Product** under each Product Type.

11. Now drag the **Product** field from the **Dimensions** pane and drop it after **Product Type** in the **Rows** shelf. Refer to the following screenshot:

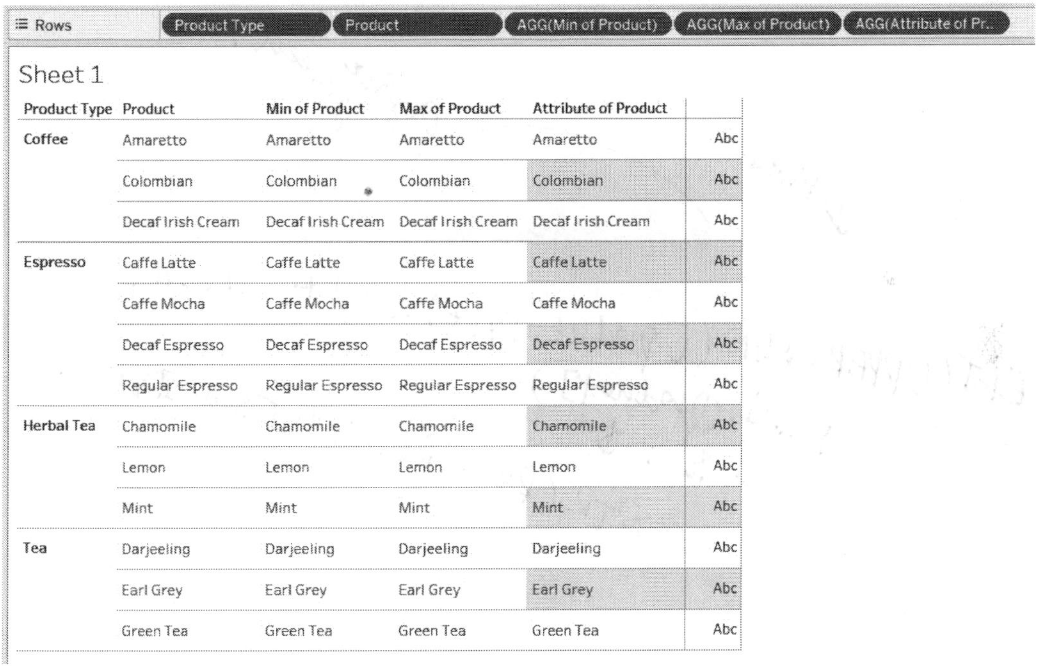

Product Type	Product	Min of Product	Max of Product	Attribute of Product	
Coffee	Amaretto	Amaretto	Amaretto	Amaretto	Abc
	Colombian	Colombian	Colombian	Colombian	Abc
	Decaf Irish Cream	Decaf Irish Cream	Decaf Irish Cream	Decaf Irish Cream	Abc
Espresso	Caffe Latte	Caffe Latte	Caffe Latte	Caffe Latte	Abc
	Caffe Mocha	Caffe Mocha	Caffe Mocha	Caffe Mocha	Abc
	Decaf Espresso	Decaf Espresso	Decaf Espresso	Decaf Espresso	Abc
	Regular Espresso	Regular Espresso	Regular Espresso	Regular Espresso	Abc
Herbal Tea	Chamomile	Chamomile	Chamomile	Chamomile	Abc
	Lemon	Lemon	Lemon	Lemon	Abc
	Mint	Mint	Mint	Mint	Abc
Tea	Darjeeling	Darjeeling	Darjeeling	Darjeeling	Abc
	Earl Grey	Earl Grey	Earl Grey	Earl Grey	Abc
	Green Tea	Green Tea	Green Tea	Green Tea	Abc

Figure 7.43: A screenshot showing the output of Min, Max, and Attribute of Product calculations at the Product level

As you see, when the **Product** field is in the view, all three calculations give the same value. This is because the **Min** or **Max** of a **Product** at the **Product** level is the **Product** itself (that is, the *Min or Max for Colombian will be Colombian itself*). Similarly, for the **Attribute** function, since there is only one row of **Product** under each **Product**, you get the output as that **Product** itself, and not an *asterisk*. However, the minute you remove the granularity of the **Product**, you start getting different results. So, keep in mind that if the dimension being aggregated is in the view, all three of these functions will give the same output.

12. Now you have seen the various options for aggregating dimensions, you will now go back and amend your **Concatenated string** calculation. Since you have two dimensions, namely, **Product Type** and **Product**, you must aggregate both. Since both dimensions are in the view, you can use any of the functions discussed. For this, use the **MIN** function. Your formula should update as follows:

```
MIN(LEFT(UPPER([Product Type]),3)) + "-" + MIN([Product]) + " : $" +
STR(ROUND(SUM([Sales]),0))
```

Refer to the following screenshot:

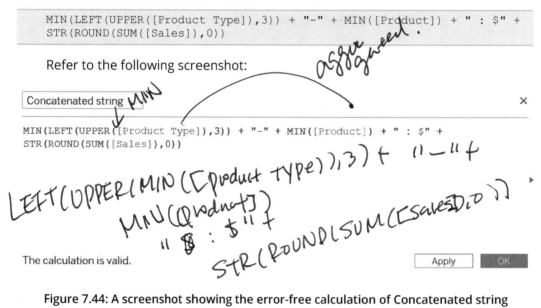

Figure 7.44: A screenshot showing the error-free calculation of Concatenated string

13. Click **OK** and go back to the sheet where you created a bar chart showing **Product Type**, **Product**, and **SUM(Sales)**. Drop this new field, which is now found under the **Measures** pane, into the **Rows** shelf just after **Product**. Refer to the following screenshot:

Figure 7.45 – A screenshot showing the output of the Concatenated string calculation

You have now created and used string functions in Tableau. You created a concatenated string using dimensions and aggregated **Measures**. You saw how to typecast an integer of a float value into a string, and how to aggregate a dimension using either the **MIN**, **MAX**, or **ATTR** functions to get rid of the `Cannot mix aggregate and non-aggregate arguments`... error. Now you know how to manipulate string fields, it is time to explore date functions.

CREATING AND USING DIFFERENT TYPES OF CALCULATIONS: DATE CALCULATIONS

When manipulating **Date** fields, you can use the various **Date** functions supported by Tableau. At this point in time (that is, in version 2020.1), these are as follows:

- `DATENAME`, `DATEPART`, `DATETRUNC`, `YEAR`, `QUARTER`, `MONTH`, `WEEK`, `DAY`, `ISOYEAR`, `ISOQUARTER`, `ISOWEEK`, and `ISOWEEKDAY`, which can be used to find the date part of the **Date** field.

- `DATEDIFF` and `DATEADD`, used to find the difference between two dates or to generate a new **Date** field based on an incremental interval.

- `TODAY` and `NOW`, which give the current date or date and time.

- `ISDATE`, used to find out whether a given field is a **Date** field.

You will now use a **Date** calculation to find out how many months it has been since your customers last made a purchase.

EXERCISE 7.05: CREATING A DATE CALCULATION

The objective of this exercise is to create a **Date** calculation to find the number of months since the last purchase for your customers. You will continue using your **Orders** data from **Sample-Superstore.xlsx** and use the **Customer Name** and the **Order Date** fields.

Perform the following steps:

1. Start by dragging **Customer Name** into the Rows shelf. Then, right-click drag and drop the **Order Date** field into the **Rows** shelf, which should create a **Menu**. Select **MDY(Order Date)**. Refer to the following screenshot:

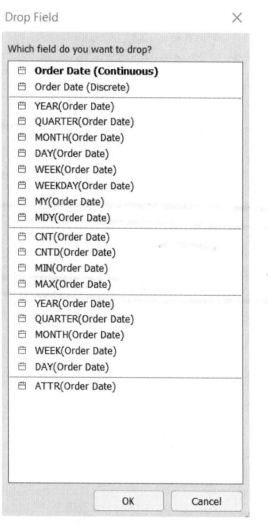

Figure 7.46: A screenshot showing the right-click drag-drop menu for Order Date

Now you can see all order dates at the customer level. There is no point looking at all transactional dates for every customer. You are only interested in the last purchase date, and how many months it has been since it occurred.

2. To achieve this, first create a calculation called **Last purchase date** with the following formula:

```
MAX([Order Date])
```

Refer to the following screenshot:

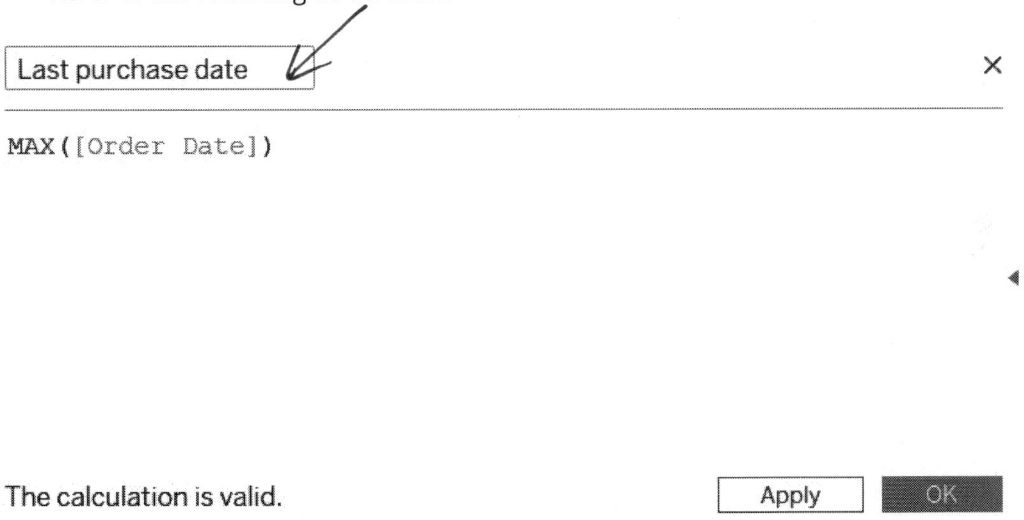

Last purchase date   ✕

MAX([Order Date])

The calculation is valid.   Apply   OK

Figure 7.47: A screenshot showing the Last purchase date calculation

3. Since this calculation will be computed on the fly, the **Max** date is dependent on the dimensions in the view. If you drag and drop this new field into your **Rows** shelf, you should notice that the values are the same as for the **MDY (Order Date)**. This won't work for you; you want the Max date for each customer, and hence you must remove the **MDY (Order Date)** granularity. This will update your view, as shown in the following screenshot:

Figure 7.48: A screenshot showing the Last purchase date for each customer

Now you have your **Last purchase date** field, it is time to find out how many months it has been since the customers last made a purchase. This can be achieved by finding the difference between two dates, that is, **Last purchase date** and, ideally, **Today**. However, since your data is not daily-updating, you will consider the end date as December 31, 2019, which is the last date in the data.

4. Create a new calculated field called *Months since last purchase* and use the following formula:

```
DATEDIFF('month', [Last purchase date], #2019-12-31#)
```

Refer to the following screenshot:

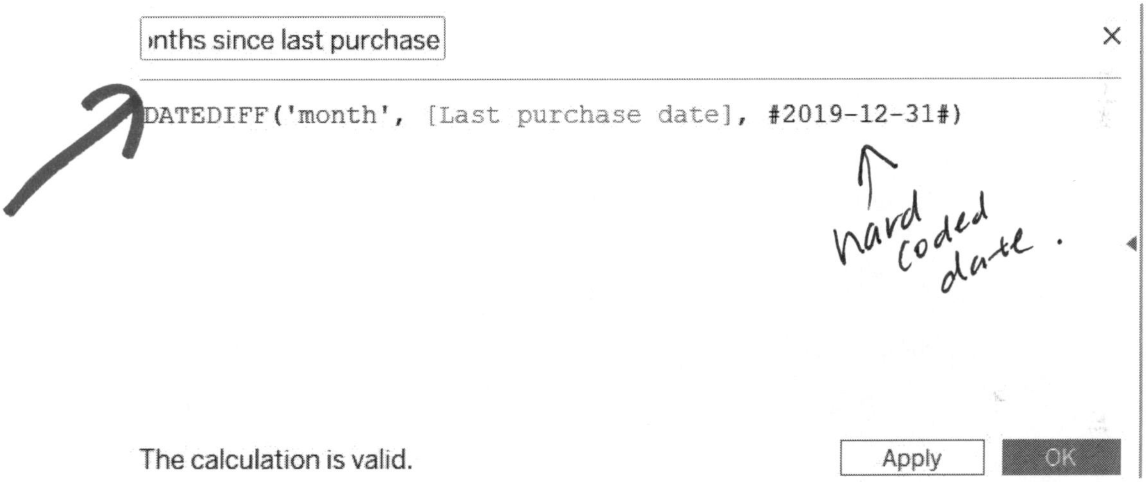

Figure 7.49: A screenshot showing the Months since last purchase calculation

5. After you save this calculation, you can drag it into the **Text** shelf, and should get the desired output. This calculation finds the difference in months between **Last purchase date** and December 31, 2019. A point to remember is that when you need to enter a hardcoded date, it will start and end with a *hash* (**#**), as shown above. Further, if this data was daily-updating and you wanted to find the difference with respect to **Today**, that is, the current date, then you could use the **Today()** function, and the calculation would update as shown here:

```
DATEDIFF('month', [Last purchase date], Today())
```

Customer Name	Last purchase date	
Aaron Bergman	11/10/2018	13
Aaron Hawkins	12/18/2019	0
Aaron Smayling	10/3/2019	2
Adam Bellavance	11/6/2019	1
Adam Hart	11/26/2019	1
Adam Shillingsburg	12/2/2019	0
Adrian Barton	11/19/2019	1
Adrian Hane	10/31/2019	2
Adrian Shami	11/19/2019	1
Aimee Bixby	11/19/2019	1
Alan Barnes	12/5/2019	0
Alan Dominguez	12/1/2019	0
Alan Haines	11/5/2019	1
Alan Hwang	12/24/2019	0
Alan Schoenberger	12/8/2019	0
Alan Shonely	6/21/2019	6
Alejandro Ballentine	7/17/2019	5
Alejandro Grove	3/27/2019	9
Alejandro Savely	12/11/2019	0
Aleksandra Gannaway	9/3/2019	3
Alex Avila	6/29/2019	6
Alex Grayson	12/22/2019	0
Alex Russell	9/10/2019	3
Alice McCarthy	12/2/2019	0
Allen Armold	12/11/2019	0
Allen Goldenen	9/7/2019	3
Allen Rosenblatt	8/27/2019	4
Alyssa Crouse	5/12/2019	7
Alyssa Tate	12/9/2019	0
Amy Cox	12/19/2019	0
Amy Hunt	5/14/2019	7
Andrew Allen	4/15/2019	8

Figure 7.50: A screenshot showing the final output of the Date calculation

In this exercise, you used the **DATEDIFF()** function to find how many months it has been since customers last made a purchase. In the next section, you'll see what to do when the value of data for a product is returned as null.

HANDLING NULL VALUES WHILE CREATING AND USING CALCULATIONS

Often, you might deal with data containing null values. These could be genuine entries in the data. For example, there may not be any **Sales** value to report against a particular product—even though it is part of the inventory, it may not have been sold yet. These nulls could also be because of some data entry errors. Most likely, you would identify and take care of these nulls at the data preparation stage. However, that may not always be the case. At times, you may need to tackle them within Tableau Desktop using calculations. Null values tend to pose a problem when used in calculated fields, simply because when doing arithmetic operations on fields, it may result in the output being null in Tableau. Refer to the following screenshot:

Figure 7.51 – A screenshot showing the Excel data and the output
of the calculation on fields with null values

The preceding screenshot is a quick mockup to show the Excel data on the left and the Tableau display on the right. You can see that both fields (that is, **Value of Product A** and **Value of Product B**) have *null values* in certain months. Now, when you want to find the total value in each month, you add the values of product A and product B. However, since both of these fields have null values in certain months, the calculated field only shows the output for months with values in both columns. For months where either of the values are missing, the calculated field gives null output. This is simply because you can't do math on null values without getting a null output.

To overcome this, you will use functions such as ZN, IFNULL, and ISNULL.

The data for this section is available for download using this link: https://packt.link/k59i9.

Refer to the **Handling Null Values in Tableau.xlsx** data file for this
section. Begin by connecting to this data in Tableau and creating a quick tabular view
showing **Month** and **Value of Product A** and **Value of Product B**. Create
a calculated field called **Value of Product A + B**. The formula is as follows:

```
SUM([Value of Product A]) + SUM([Value of Product B])
```

Add this calculated field to the view. It should update as shown in the
following screenshot:

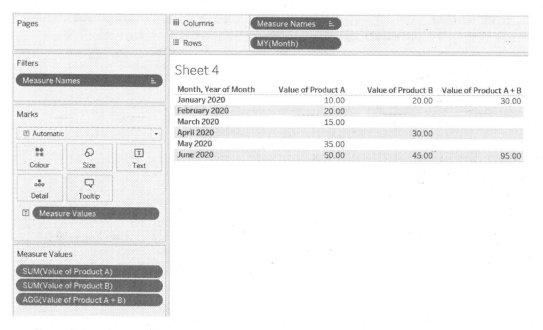

Figure 7.52: A screenshot showing the output of calculation on fields with null values

As you see, the calculated field needs some tweaking. The best way to handle these
null values when doing mathematical operations is to *convert them to zero*. You will
use either the **ZN**, **IFNULL**, or **ISNULL** function.

First, try the ~~ZN function. ZN~~ stands for *Zero if Null*, and that is exactly what this
function does; it *replaces the nulls with zero*. Since both fields contain null at some
point, you need to use the **ZN** function for both fields. Tweak your calculation to use
the following formula:

```
ZN(SUM([Value of Product A])) + ZN(SUM([Value of Product B]))
```

Once you update the calculation, your view will update as shown in the following screenshot:

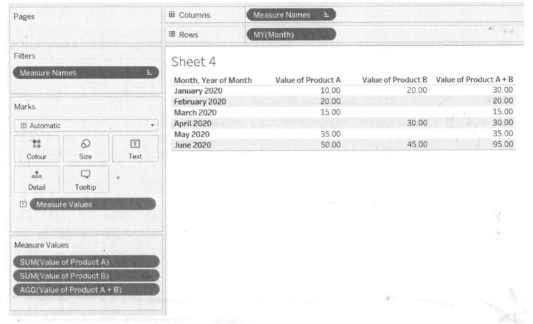

Figure 7.53: A screenshot showing the output of the calculated field using the ZN function

You now get values for every single **Month**, despite the *nulls* because Tableau is now *converting these nulls to zero* before adding them up.

You will now look at the IFNULL function. Amend your calculated field to *comment out* the formula using the ZN function, and instead use the **IFNULL** formula as follows:

```
IFNULL(SUM([Value of Product A]),0) + IFNULL(SUM([Value of Product B]),0)
```

Refer to the following screenshot:

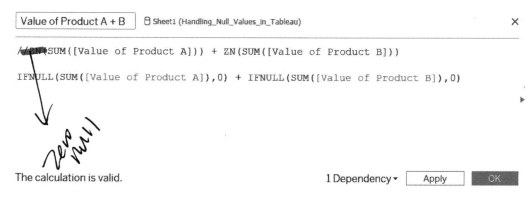

The calculation is valid.

Figure 7.54: A screenshot showing the syntax of the IFNULL function

Once you click **OK**, you will see that you still get output for each **Month**. The **IFNULL** function returns the expression if it is not null; otherwise, it returns the alternate expression that is defined: zero, in this case.

Now you understand the **ZN** and the **IFNULL** functions, you will look at the **ISNULL** function. The **ISNULL** function returns **True** if the expression contains a null value; otherwise, it returns **False**. In other words, the **ISNULL** function gives us a *Boolean output as either True or False*. If you wish to specify some criteria for when a null condition is **True**, you should use the **ISNULL** function with either a **CASE** statement or an **IF** statement. Edit your existing calculated field to comment out the **IFNULL** formula and use the following formula:

```
IF ISNULL(SUM([Value of Product A])) THEN 0 ELSE SUM([Value of Product
A]) END
+
IF ISNULL(SUM([Value of Product B])) THEN 0 ELSE SUM([Value of Product
B]) END
```

Refer to the following screenshot:

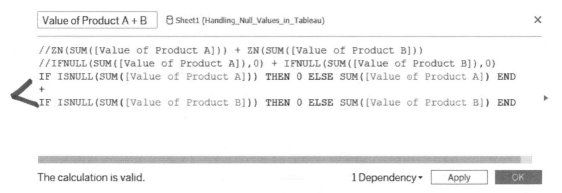

Figure 7.55: A screenshot showing the syntax of the ISNULL function

Once you click **OK**, you see that you still get output for each **Month**. The **ISNULL** function, when used in the **IF** statement, will return **Zero if it the Null condition is True**; otherwise, it returns the **False condition, which is the field that we have specified**.

CREATING CALCULATIONS ACROSS DATA SOURCES

In earlier sections of this chapter, you have seen how to create and use calculations, but all these calculations were done within the same data source. Having all your data in one source would be an idealistic scenario; however, that may not always be the case, and you may have to deal with data coming from multiple sources. This means you may have to compute calculations across data sources, too.

In this section, you will focus on how to create calculations across data sources using data blending. You will also look at how to create and use calculated fields to join data. You have already seen the data blending and join functionality in previous chapters, and you will use that knowledge to create and use calculations across data sources.

You will use the **Modified CoffeeChain** data along with **Budget Sales for CofeeChain.xlsx**. These can be downloaded at the following links:

- https://packt.link/EK3uu.

- https://packt.link/Pqpah.

Once downloaded, load the files into Tableau Desktop. Use the **Microsoft Access** option to connect to the *CoffeeChain Query* table from the **Modified_ CoffeeChain.mdb** data. Refer to the following screenshot:

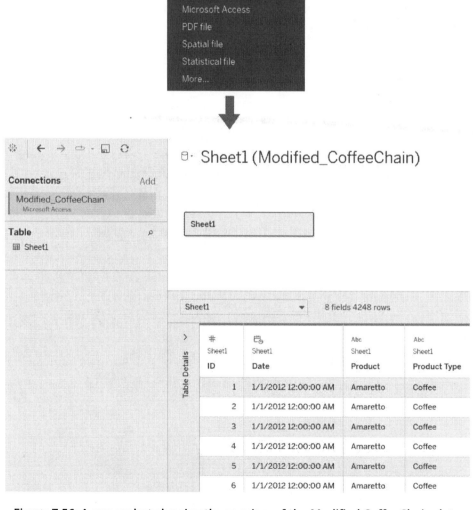

Figure 7.56: A screenshot showing the preview of the Modified CoffeeChain data

Look at this data preview. Notice that the **Date** field is of a **DATETIME** data type, even though the timestamp is 00:00:00. Once you familiarize yourself with this dataset, you will try to get the **Budget** data as well. To achieve this, click on the **Add** button in the left-hand side section of this data connection window and select the **Microsoft Excel** option to select **Budget Sales for CoffeeChain. xlsx**. This should create a cross-database join between the two. Refer to the following screenshot:

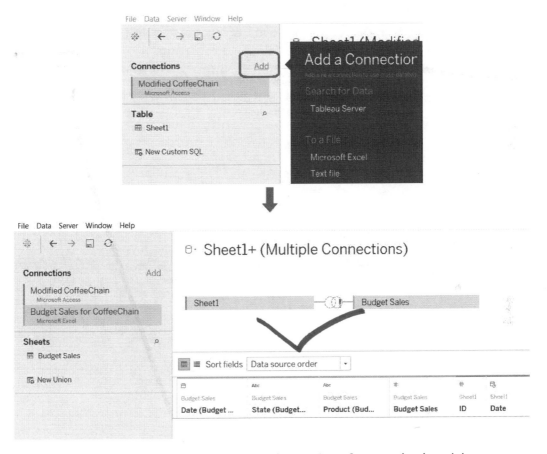

Figure 7.57 – A screenshot showing the preview of a cross-database join of CoffeeChain data and Budget Sales

Something has gone wrong with the join, indicated by the *red exclamation mark* and the lack of data to preview. This is because the **Date** field in the **Access** database is a **DATETIME** *field* whereas, the **Date** field in the Excel data is a **DATE** *field*. To use the **Date** field as a common linking field between both these datasets, it will have to be of the same data type. So, change the **DATETIME** field to a **DATE** field and then try to enable the join. Changing the datatype could be done in many ways; however, here, you will use the calculation method and will use this calculation to create a join between the two data sources.

Begin by clicking the *red exclamation mark* and then clicking the dropdown under the left column in the window where you are defining the join criteria. Select the **Create Join Calculation...** option. Refer to the following screenshot:

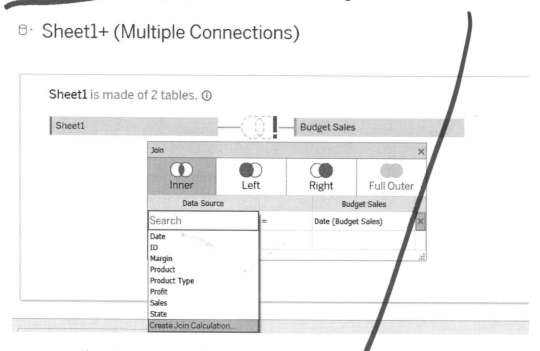

Figure 7.58: A screenshot showing the Create Join Calculation option

Type the following formula:

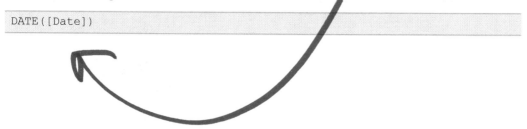

```
DATE([Date])
```

Refer to the following screenshot:

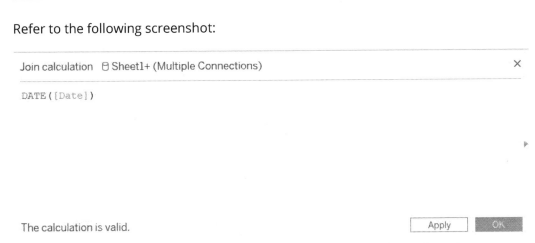

Figure 7.59: A screenshot showing the Create Join Calculation formula
for typecasting the Date field

Since the **Date** field in the Budget Sales data is already a **DATE** *data type*, select the
Date (Budget Sale) field from the dropdown. Refer to the following screenshot:

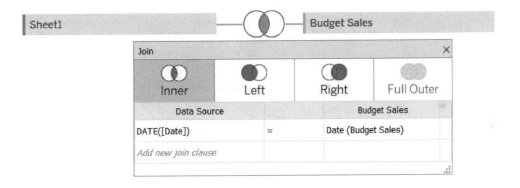

Figure 7.60: A screenshot showing the Date field in the Budget Sales data
being used for joining

You should see that the **Join** condition is resolved, and your dataset is now ready for use. The output of this join will be a single combined dataset and you can then create other calculations using this combined dataset.

You will now use a calculation across data sources using data blending, where you first connect to these datasets independently and then combine them on the fly as and when required.

So, you have the **Modified CoffeeChain** data and **Budget Sales for CoffeeChain** data, and you want to use these independently across your workbook. This won't present issues until you need to get data from both these data sources in one single sheet. For example, imagine you want to find the percentage of a target you have achieved across months of a year. You have the **Sales** field in the **Modified CoffeeChain** data and **Budget Sales** in the **Budget Sales for CoffeeChain** data; to find the percentage of the target achieved across those months, you need to create a new calculated field. Name this new calculated field **% Target Achieved**.

Begin by connecting to the **Modified CoffeeChain** data independently and then connect to the **Budget Sales for CoffeeChain** data. You should get two separate data sources in your **Data** pane. Refer to the following screenshot:

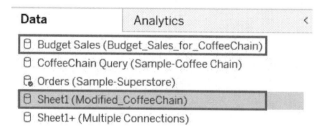

Figure 7.61: A screenshot showing Budget Sales and Modified CoffeChain as separate and independent data sources

Once you have both these data sources within Tableau Desktop, drag the **Date** field from the **Modified CoffeeChain** data into the **Rows** shelf, then drop the **Product** field from the same data source into the **Rows** shelf just after **YEAR(Date)**. Next, double-click on **Sales** from the **Measures** pane of the **Modified CoffeeChain** data. Then click on the **Budget Sales for CoffeeChain** data in the **Data** pane to enable the dimensions and **Measures** for that data source. You should now notice the blending link enabled for the **Date** field, as well as the **Product** field. Keep these links as is, then double-click the **Budget Sales** field from the **Measures** pane of the **Budget Sales for CoffeeChain** data. The view updates, as shown in the following screenshot:

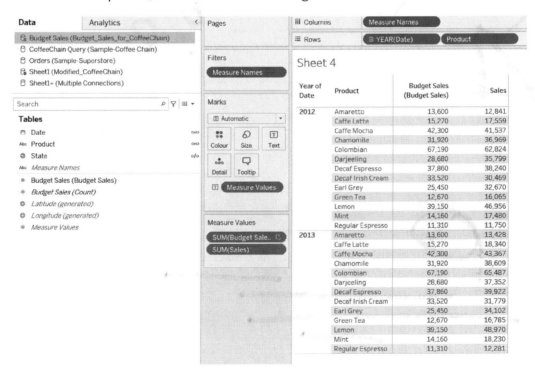

Figure 7.62: A screenshot showing the results of data blending

Now, create a new calculated field called **% Target Achieved** in your **Budget Sales for CoffeeChain** data. Drag the **Sales** field from the **Modified CoffeeChain** data into the calculation box and divide this by **SUM([Budget Sales])**. The formula is as follows:

```
SUM([Sheet1 (Modified CoffeeChain)].[Sales])
/
SUM(Budget Sales [Budget Sales])
```

Refer to the following screenshot:

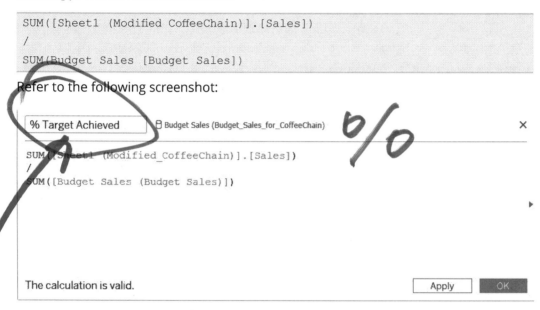

Figure 7.63: A screenshot showing the formula of the % Target Achieved calculation

The field **Sales** is shown as **[Sheet1 (Modified CoffeeChain)].[Sales]**, which shows that the field is coming from the **Modified CoffeeChain** data. Click **OK** and save this calculation. Change **Default Properties** to format this new field to show **Percentage with 2 decimals**. This can be done by using the **Default Properties > Number Format** option, which is available when right-clicking on the field in the **Measures** pane. Now, drop this new calculated field in the view and your view should update, as shown in the following screenshot:

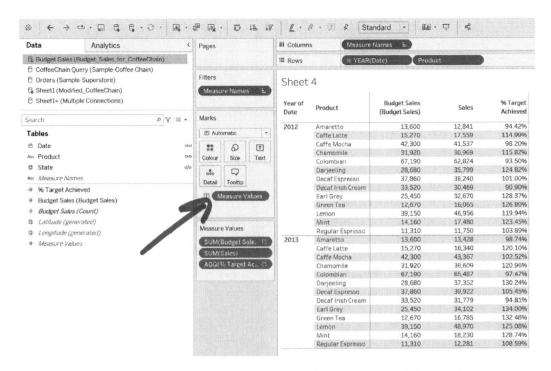

Figure 7.64: A screenshot showing the output of the % Target Achieved calculation

As you see in the preceding screenshot, there are some products where the %
Target Achieved is less than 100%, and there are certain products where the %
Target Achieved is more than 100%. You have now learned to create calculations
across data sources. A point to remember here, is that when you do this, the fields
you use always need to be aggregated.

You will now try some activities based on what you have learned so far.

> **NOTE**
>
> Now, even though we have tried to cover a lot of the Tableau functions, we
> still haven't been able to go through all the functions that Tableau has to
> offer. If you wish to know more about all the functions that Tableau has to
> offer, then you can look at the following links:
>
> https://help.tableau.com/current/pro/desktop/en-us/functions_all_categories.
> htm
>
> https://help.tableau.com/current/pro/desktop/en-us/functions_all_alphabetical.
> htm

ACTIVITY 7.01: CALCULATING THE PROFIT MARGIN

As a data analyst, you may encounter a scenario where you are required to compute profit margins using the **Profit and Sales** field and filter this **Profit Margin** below a certain threshold. The aim of this activity is to calculate the **Profit Margin**, which is computed by dividing **Profit** by **Sales**. Once you have the **Profit Margin** computed, you want to filter products and only display the **Profit Margin** for the **Xerox** product. Finally, you want to filter the **Xerox** products, and only look at those where the **Profit Margin** is more than 45%.

Steps for completion:

1. For this activity, use the **Orders** data from the *Sample-Superstore.xlsx* file.

2. Create a table/tabular view to show **Product Name**, **Profit**, and **Sales**.

3. Create a calculated field on **Product Name** to identify the **Xerox** products and group the rest of the products as **Others**.

4. Use this new calculated field to filter the table to show only the **Xerox** products.

5. Then create another calculated field to compute the **Profit Margin**, which will be derived by dividing the **Profit** values by the **Sales** values.

6. Add this new calculated field into the view and make sure to change the number format to show percentages with two decimals.

7. Use this new calculated field to filter the view to show the **Profit Margin** above 45% and sort the final output in ascending order of **Profit Margin**. Refer to the following screenshot:

Product Na.. ≐	Profit	Sales	Profit Margin ≐
Xerox 1980	15	34	45.00%
Xerox 222	61	135	45.00%
Xerox 1896	22	50	45.00%
Xerox 1920	40	90	45.00%
Xerox 1948	67	150	45.00%
Xerox 23	64	141	45.14%
Xerox 218	22	49	45.26%
Xerox 1915	1,262	2,789	45.26%
Xerox 1906	498	1,099	45.29%
Xerox 1940	279	616	45.36%
Xerox 1959	61	134	45.40%
Xerox 1968	75	166	45.48%
Xerox 1881	207	454	45.57%
Xerox 213	51	111	45.58%
Xerox 1956	41	90	45.60%
Xerox 1965	26	56	45.74%
Xerox 1889	236	517	45.74%
Xerox 188	98	213	45.74%
Xerox 1880	286	624	45.80%
Xerox 1952	45	98	45.92%
Xerox 1912	93	201	46.04%
Xerox 191	354	767	46.17%
Xerox 205	69	150	46.21%
Xerox 1993	68	148	46.32%
Xerox 1911	280	604	46.35%
Xerox 1894	79	170	46.41%
Xerox 1886	303	651	46.47%
Xerox 1996	82	176	46.47%
Xerox 226	156	334	46.59%
Xerox 1919	730	1,566	46.60%
Xerox 1950	23	50	46.63%
Xerox 1908	799	1,713	46.67%

Figure 7.65: A screenshot showing the expected output of Activity 7.01

NOTE

The solution to this activity can be found here: https://packt.link/CTCxk.

ACTIVITY 7.02: CALCULATING THE PERCENTAGE ACHIEVEMENT WITH RESPECT TO BUDGET SALES

As data analysts, you may often be required to compare actual sales with budgeted sales, to determine performance. In this activity, you will find out what percentage of budget sales targets have been achieved for the year 2012. You will use the *CoffeeChain Query* table from the **Sample-Coffee Chain.mdb** dataset. The data can be downloaded from the following link for this activity: https://1drv.ms/u/s!Av5QCoy LTBpnmkPL8Yx_0_2KtrG4?e=TrYFWQ.

1. Use the **Sample-Coffee Chain.mdb** data.

2. Create a bar chart to show **Sales** across **Products** for the year 2012.

3. Create a calculated field to find out the percentage **Achievement of Actual Sales** with respect to the **Budget Sales** for all the **Products** displayed in the view.

4. Color code the bars with respect to **% Achievement** in such a way that **Products** with less than 95% **Achievement** are called **<95% of Target achieved** (color-coded orange). Those with more than 100% **Achievement** are called **>100% Target achieved** (color-coded gray). Those between 95% and 100% **Achievement** are called **Between 95% to 100% Target** achieved (color-coded blue). Refer to the following screenshot:

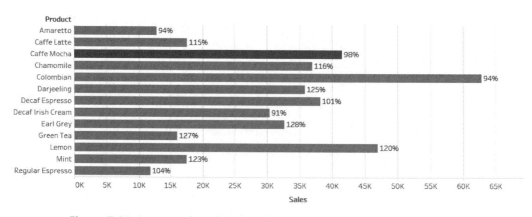

Figure 7.66: A screenshot showing the expected output of Activity 7.02

> **NOTE**
>
> The solution to this activity can be found here: https://packt.link/CTCxk.

SUMMARY

In this chapter, you explored some important aspects involved in creating and using calculations in Tableau and studied the difference between aggregate and non-aggregate fields. You looked at numeric, string, and date calculations, and learned to write logic statements and handle null values. Finally, you looked at how to use these calculations across data sources.

In upcoming chapters, you will move on to more advanced table and level of detail calculations, which will allow you to do even more with your data.

8

DATA ANALYSIS: CREATING AND USING TABLE CALCULATIONS

OVERVIEW

In this chapter, you will learn about the different types of table calculations in Tableau, their benefits, and how to use them effectively. The goal of this chapter is to improve your analytical skills using table calculations by looking at data through different views to understand the underlying patterns. By the end of this chapter, you will be well positioned to perform complex analysis on the data in your visualizations using table calculations.

INTRODUCTION

In any visualization, a virtual table is created based on the dimensions used in the view. This is added to the **Columns**, **Rows**, and **Marks** shelves.

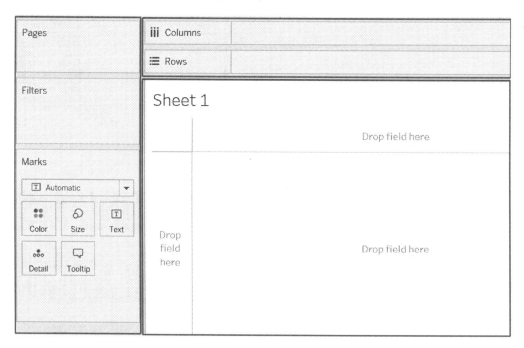

Figure 8.1: Virtual table in the view

The highlighted area in the preceding figure consisting of the **Rows**, **Columns**, and **Marks** shelves will make up your level of detail. The empty canvas outline for dropping fields contains the virtual table that will be affected by table calculations.

A table calculation is simply a calculation that computes results based on the table segment in scope. You will learn about segments and scope in detail in the following sections. For now, assume it is the entire empty canvas area. All table calculations will only be computed within the empty canvas outline or the virtual table.

In previous chapters, you learned about visualization methods that present data in a meaningful way. There may be times where you need to analyze a table, such as when you want to find the most profitable sub-category within a category. This is where table calculations come in handy.

In this chapter, you will learn about table calculations and their applications through various exercises. You will also learn about the functions that are a part of table calculations, and how to apply them. You will use the **Sample - Superstore** dataset throughout the exercises.

QUICK TABLE CALCULATIONS

Quick table calculations, as the name suggests, allow you to quickly apply frequently used table calculations to the view using the most typical settings for that calculation type. They save you the effort of using the column fields from data to create calculations. They have inbuilt logic , so you can use them directly in the view. Some of the most commonly used table calculations are as follows:

- **Running Total**
- **Difference**
- **Percent of Total**
- **Percent Difference**
- **Percentile**
- **Rank**
- **Moving Average**

You will start by learning how to apply quick table calculations, using the **Sample - Superstore** dataset. This file can be found by following the **Documents | My Tableau Repository | Data Sources** system path, and then opening the *Sample - Superstore.xls* file.

To begin, create a view that shows **Category** against **YEAR(Order Date)** and **SUM(Profit)**, as follows:

Figure 8.2: Initial view

Table calculations only work with measures, so you need a measure to add a calculation. To add a quick table calculation, first click on the measure dropdown, which is **SUM(Profit)** in this case.

Figure 8.3: Accessing the Profit drilldown

Navigate to the **Quick Table Calculation** menu.

Attribute		Running Total
● Measure (Sum)	▶	Difference
		Percent Difference
Discrete		Percent of Total
● Continuous		Rank
		Percentile
Edit in Shelf		Moving Average
△ Add Table Calculation...		YTD Total
Quick Table Calculation	▶	Compound Growth Rate
Total using (Automatic)	▶	Year Over Year Growth

Figure 8.4: Various quick table calculations

You can see that there are numerous quick calculations available, such as **Running Total**, **Percentile**, and **Rank**. You will now go through each of these in detail.

RUNNING TOTAL

Running Total, as the name suggests, is used to calculate the cumulative total of a measure across a specific dimension or table structure. It adds up the previous value with the current value to display that result in the current value's place in the running total. For example, consider that you are working on a project related to a car manufacturer. A common use case for this calculation, would be to calculate the month-by-month cumulative car sales for a year, to find out the total sales for that year. You can also further calculate it on a year-by-year basis to find out the overall car sales to date. The next exercise looks at this in detail.

EXERCISE 8.01: CREATING A RUNNING TOTAL CALCULATION

In this exercise, you will calculate the cumulative profit earned across different years for a particular category using the **Running Total** calculation. This allows you to view all years together for the profits earned, rather than individual years. The following steps will help you complete this exercise:

1. Load the **Sample - Superstore** dataset in your Tableau instance. In the **Connect** pane, click on **Microsoft Excel** and navigate to **Documents | My Tableau Repository | Data Sources**, and then open the **Sample - Superstore.xls** file.

2. Create a view that shows **Category** against **YEAR(Order Date)** and **SUM(Profit)**, as follows:

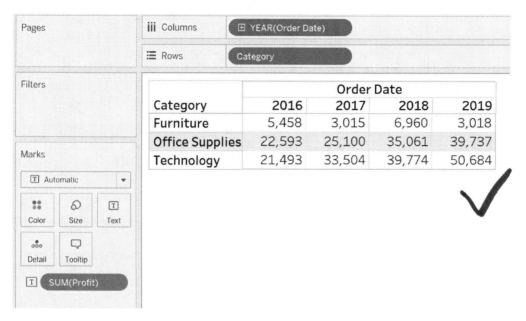

Figure 8.5: Running total initial view

3. Add a **Running Total** quick calculation to the view by selecting the following highlighted options:

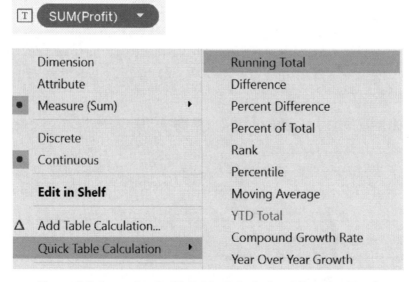

Figure 8.6: Accessing Quick Table Calculation | Running Total

4. The following view shows the final output:

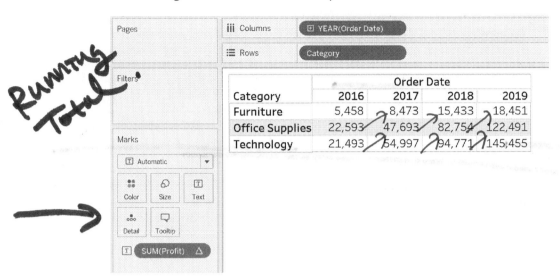

Figure 8.7: Final output

As you can see, by comparing the previous figure (final view) with the next one (initial view), the profit has been summed cumulatively by taking the previous year's profit, as well as the current year's profit. With **Furniture**, for example, the second value under the running total is computed using the previous value and the current value, that is, 5,458 + 3,015 = 8,473, and this is done similarly for other values.

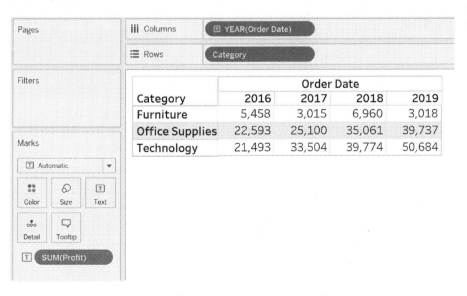

Figure 8.8: Initial view

This view is helpful for calculating the cumulative profit earned, year after year, for the different categories, as well as for identifying which category has been performing well and which hasn't. These insights can help you make important business decisions to understand which products can be used to generate higher profits.

Next, you will learn about the **Difference** table calculation.

DIFFERENCE

Difference, as the name suggests, is used to calculate the difference of a measure across a specific dimension or table structure from its previous value. Often, you may need to analyze how individual categories compare with their past performances, i.e. comparing product sales from previous quarters. Continuing with the car manufacturer example, a common scenario to apply this calculation, would be to compare the sales for the months of a year. This allows you to find out whether the total sales are greater or fewer, compared to the previous months. In the following exercise, you will learn how to apply a **Difference** table calculation to a worksheet.

EXERCISE 8.02: CREATING A DIFFERENCE CALCULATION

In this exercise, you will calculate the profit difference across years for a category. This will help you analyze whether that category is profitable or not:

1. Load the **Sample - Superstore** dataset in your Tableau instance.

2. Create a view that shows **Category** against **YEAR(Order Date)** and **SUM(Profit)**, as follows:

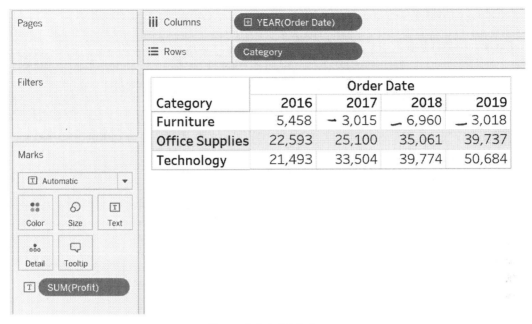

Figure 8.9: Initial view

3. Add the **Difference** quick calculation to the view, as shown in the
   following figure:

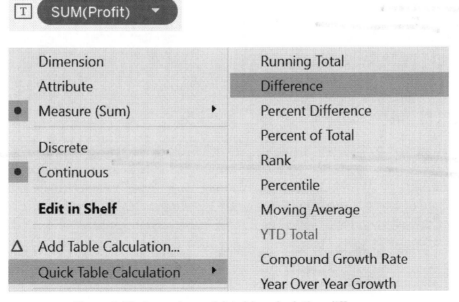

Figure 8.10: Accessing quick table calculation difference

The final view will be as follows:

		Order Date		
Category	2016	2017	2018	2019
Furniture		-2,443	3,945	-3,942
Office Supplies		2,506	9,962	4,675
Technology		12,011	6,270	10,910

Figure 8.11: Final output

As you can see, the result is the difference between the current year's profit and the previous year's profit; for example, for **Furniture**, the second value under **Difference** is computed using the previous value and the current value, that is, 3,015 – 5,458 = -2443. This is done similarly for the other categories. One thing to note here is the first year's value will always be blank, as there is nothing to compute the difference from.

In the next section, you will learn about the **Percent of Total** table calculation.

PERCENT OF TOTAL

A **Percent of Total** calculation is used to calculate the percent distribution of a measure across a specific dimension or table structure. For example, if you are analyzing a project that operates in multiple countries, you can calculate what percentage of the total revenue each country generates. This in turn can highlight underperforming countries, as well as the better-performing ones.

You will use this calculation in the next exercise.

EXERCISE 8.03: CREATING A PERCENT OF TOTAL CALCULATION

In this exercise, you will calculate the **Percent of Total** profits earned in different years for a category. By doing so, you can understand how each category has contributed to yearly profits. Perform the following steps to complete this exercise:

1. Load the **Sample – Superstore** dataset in your Tableau instance.

2. Create a view that shows **Category** against **YEAR(Order Date)** and **SUM(Profit)**, as follows:

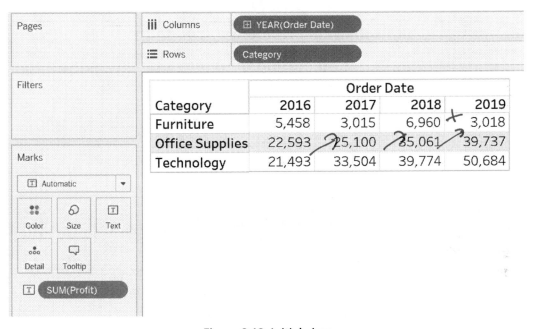

Figure 8.12: Initial view

3. Add the **Percent of Total** quick calculation to the view

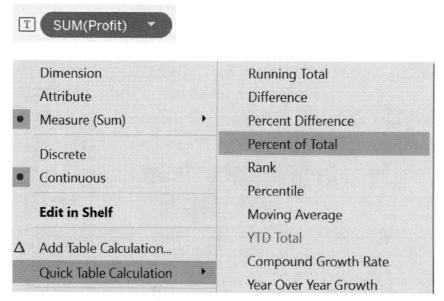

Figure 8.13: Accessing quick table calculation | percent of total

The following view is the final output:

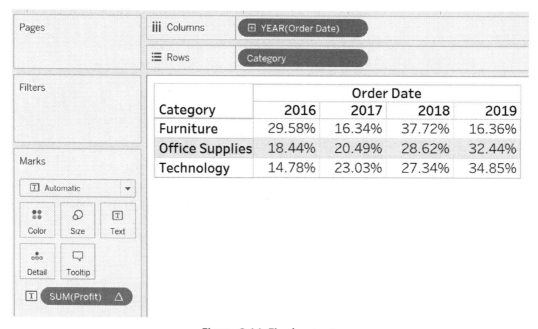

Category	Order Date			
	2016	2017	2018	2019
Furniture	29.58%	16.34%	37.72%	16.36%
Office Supplies	18.44%	20.49%	28.62%	32.44%
Technology	14.78%	23.03%	27.34%	34.85%

Figure 8.14: Final output

You can see that the profit has been converted to a percentage of the total, from all the years' profits. For example, for **Furniture**, you can first compute the sum of all the years' profits, which comes to 18,451. Then, divide each year's profits with this number. So, for 2016, you can compute it as 5,458 / 18,451, which is 29.58%.

This view helps find out which year has been better for generating profits for each category. The next step is to identify patterns indicative of higher profits in those years, and to try to replicate the patterns for the current year to generate similar or higher profits.

The next section looks at the **Percent Difference** table calculation.

PERCENT DIFFERENCE

Percent Difference, as the name suggests, is used to calculate the change in the percent distribution of a measure across a specific dimension or table structure. This calculation will first subtract a value from its previous value, and then compute the percentage change. As you may have noticed, this table calculation is a combination of the **Difference** and **Percent of Total** calculations. The reason for using a percentage is that absolute numbers do not always show the complete picture. For example, the sale of 10 Ferrari cars will generate more profit compared to 50 Honda cars. But if you compare this using actual numbers, the data will say that Honda is more profitable, even though Ferrari is actually more profitable.

You will learn more about using this calculation in the next exercise.

EXERCISE 8.04: CREATING A PERCENT DIFFERENCE CALCULATION

In this exercise, you will be calculating **Percent Difference** across the different years for a particular category. This will help you analyze, in terms of percentage, the profit difference for the various categories:

1. Load the **Sample – Superstore** dataset in your Tableau instance.

2. Create a view that shows **Category** against **YEAR(Order Date)** and **SUM(Profit)**, as follows:

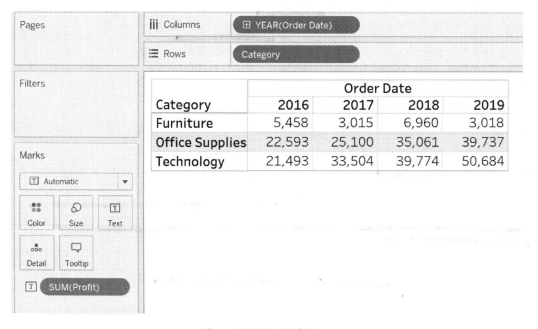

	Order Date			
Category	2016	2017	2018	2019
Furniture	5,458	3,015	6,960	3,018
Office Supplies	22,593	25,100	35,061	39,737
Technology	21,493	33,504	39,774	50,684

Figure 8.15: Initial view

3. Add the **Percent Difference** quick calculation to the view:

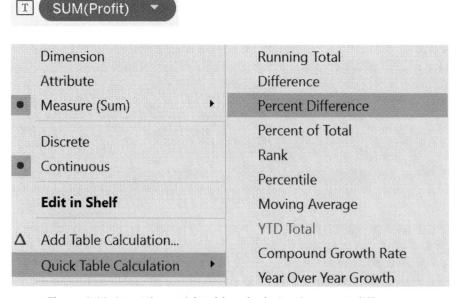

Figure 8.16: Accessing quick table calculation | percent difference

The following figure shows the final output:

	Columns	⊞ YEAR(Order Date)
	Rows	Category

Category	Order Date			
	2016	2017	2018	2019
Furniture		-44.8%	130.8%	-56.6%
Office Supplies		11.1%	39.7%	13.3%
Technology		55.9%	18.7%	27.4%

Figure 8.17: Final output

As you can see, the output shows the difference between the current value and previous values, divided by the previous value, for **Furniture**, the percent difference for 2016 is computed as 3,015 – 5,458 / 5,458, which comes to **-44.8%**.

This view helps to compare the individual category profits in terms of percent, and identifies how each category has performed compared to the previous year. This can help you understand whether the category did better (or not), compared to the previous year.You can further investigate the reason for performance differences, and act on the analysis accordingly.

Next, you will learn about the **Rank** and **Percentile** table calculations.

PERCENTILE AND RANK

Percentile, as you may have guessed, is used to calculate the percentile of a measure across a specific dimension or table structure. Similarly, **Rank** will rank the measure across a specific dimension or table structure. You will learn about these in detail in the next exercise.

EXERCISE 8.05: CREATING PERCENTILE AND RANK CALCULATIONS

In this exercise, you will calculate **Percentile** and **Rank** across different years for a particular category. This will help you understand how much profit various categories have generated in different years. Follow these steps to complete this exercise:

1. Load the **Sample – Superstore** dataset in your Tableau instance.

2. Create a view that shows **Category** against **YEAR(Order Date)** and **SUM(Profit)**.

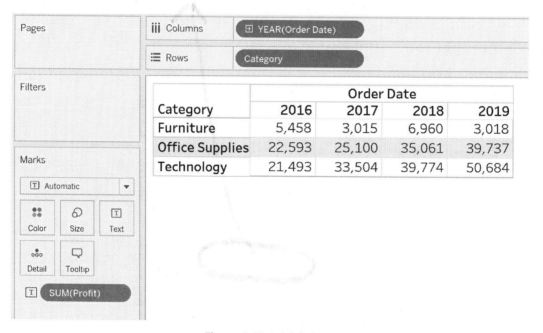

Category	Order Date			
	2016	2017	2018	2019
Furniture	5,458	3,015	6,960	3,018
Office Supplies	22,593	25,100	35,061	39,737
Technology	21,493	33,504	39,774	50,684

Figure 8.18: Initial view

3. Add the **Rank** quick calculation to the view, as shown in the following figure:

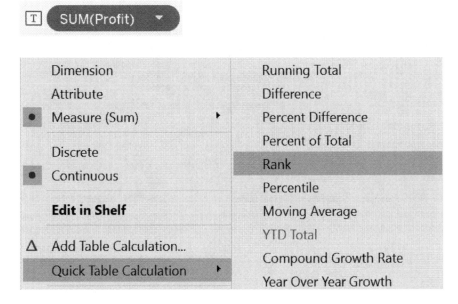

Figure 8.19: Accessing quick table calculation | rank

The following view will be the final output for **Rank**. The output is ranked based on the descending values of **SUM(Profit)**:

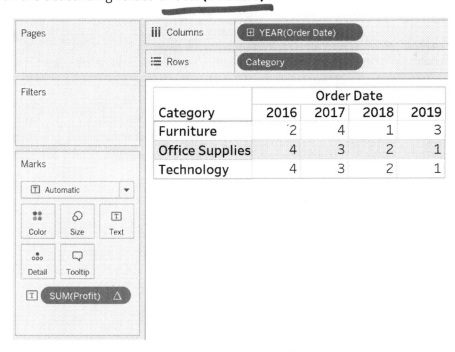

Figure 8.20: Rank output on selecting the Rank quick table calculation

4. Similarly, add the **Percentile** quick calculation to the view by selecting the **Percentile** quick table calculation. The following figure shows the final output for this:

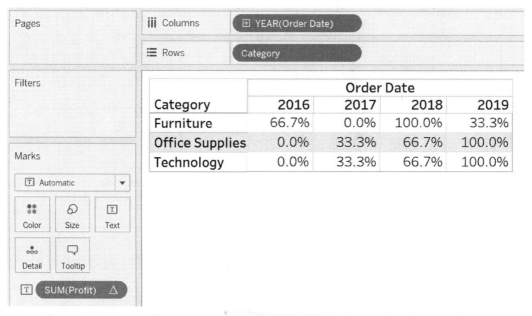

Category	Order Date			
	2016	2017	2018	2019
Furniture	66.7%	0.0%	100.0%	33.3%
Office Supplies	0.0%	33.3%	66.7%	100.0%
Technology	0.0%	33.3%	66.7%	100.0%

Figure 8.21: Percentile output on selecting the Percentile quick table calculation

With the **Rank** calculation, you ranked each year in a particular category based on the sum of the profits. The preceding figure shows the **Percentile** operation. For **Furniture**, the profit for 2016 is at the 0th percentile, which means that 0% of data is under $3,015. Similarly, for 2017, the profit is $6,960 at the 100th percentile, meaning that the profit for all other years is below this value. This view can help you do a year-by-year comparison for individual category profits in terms of percentile and rank, to identify how each category has performed compared to the previous year.

Next, you will learn about the **Moving Average** quick table calculation.

MOVING AVERAGE

Moving Average is used to calculate the average of a measure across a specific dimension or table structure in a dynamic range, rather than being static. The advantage of using a moving average is that more importance is given to the values of recent history, rather than using all historic data. Moving averages are commonly used for identifying trends of share prices, where you can analyze a 20-day moving average (last 20 days of share price), or a 50-day moving average (last 50 days of share price), to understand how the share price is moving. The next exercise looks at this in detail.

EXERCISE 8.06: CREATING A MOVING AVERAGE CALCULATION

In this exercise, you will calculate the moving average of profit earned across different years for a particular category. This will help you understand whether the average value is higher or lower than the previous year's profits:

1. Load the **Sample – Superstore** dataset in your Tableau instance.

2. Create a view that shows **Category** against **YEAR(Order Date)** and **SUM(Profit)**.

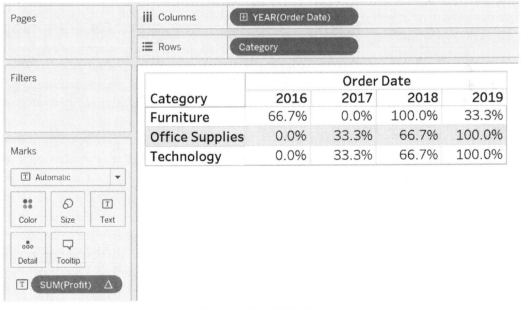

Category	2016	2017	2018	2019
Furniture	66.7%	0.0%	100.0%	33.3%
Office Supplies	0.0%	33.3%	66.7%	100.0%
Technology	0.0%	33.3%	66.7%	100.0%

Figure 8.22: Initial view

3. Add the **Moving Average** quick calculation, as shown in the following figure:

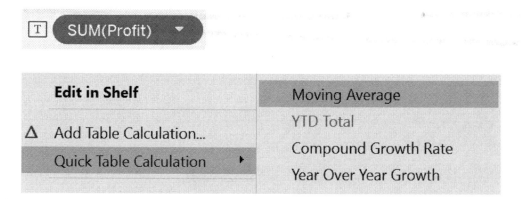

Figure 8.23: Accessing quick table calculation | moving average

This view will be the final output:

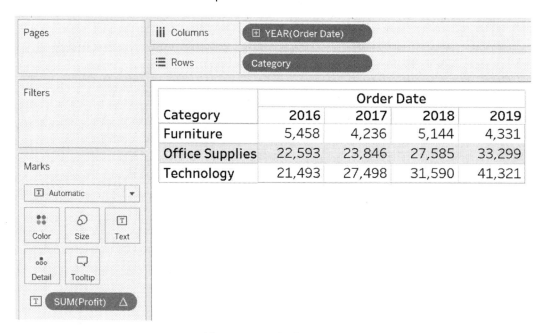

	Order Date			
Category	2016	2017	2018	2019
Furniture	5,458	4,236	5,144	4,331
Office Supplies	22,593	23,846	27,585	33,299
Technology	21,493	27,498	31,590	41,321

Figure 8.24: Final output

As you see, the profit has been averaged across the total from all the years' profits. First, the sum of all the years' profits is computed, and then, this number is divided by the number of years. For example, for 2017, the moving average comes to 8,473 / 2 = 4,236.

TABLE CALCULATION APPLICATION: ADDRESSING AND PARTITIONING

In the previous section, you learned about quick table calculations. But did you notice that all these calculations were working at the row level? What if you need to apply calculations at the column level? This is where the concept of addressing and partitioning comes into play.

Addressing means defining the direction of the calculation. A calculation can compute horizontally or vertically, depending on the option selected. Partitioning can be defined as the scope of the calculation; for example, you can partition a view into various years for different categories, or various categories for the same year.

In this section, you will learn about the following methods to address and partition data:

- `Table(across)`
- `Table(down)`
- `Table(across then down)`
- `Table(down then across)`
- `Pane(down)`
- `Pane(across then down)`
- `Pane(down then across)`
- `Cell`
- `Specific Dimensions`

You will continue working with the same example that you have been using in the previous exercises. First, you will explore the various ways of addressing data.

TABLE (ACROSS)

`Table(across)` performs a calculation horizontally across a table, and restarts after each row. For example, consider you have years on the `Columns` shelf for various product names on the rows, along with their sales. Here, `Table(across)` would perform the calculation for all the years' sales for an individual product, and then restart for the next product. The next exercise looks at this in detail.

EXERCISE 8.07: CREATING A TABLE (ACROSS) CALCULATION

Considering the example of car manufacturer sales, suppose you want to compare the sales for the various years. In this exercise, you will use a **Table (across)** calculation to find this. The following steps will help you complete this exercise:

1. Load the **Sample - Superstore** dataset in your Tableau instance.

2. Create a view that shows **Category** against **YEAR(Order Date)** and **SUM(Profit)**.

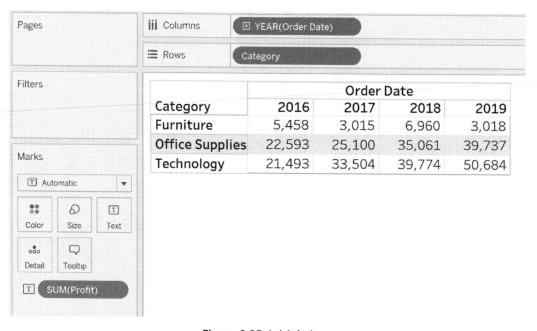

Category	Order Date			
	2016	2017	2018	2019
Furniture	5,458	3,015	6,960	3,018
Office Supplies	22,593	25,100	35,061	39,737
Technology	21,493	33,504	39,774	50,684

Figure 8.25: Initial view

3. Add the **Running Total** quick calculation to get the following view:

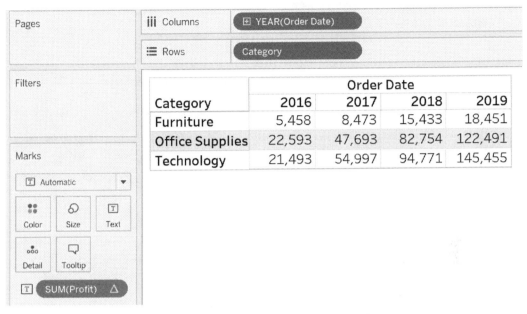

Figure 8.26: Running total for SUM(Profit)

4. Now, select **Compute Using** and then **Table(across)**, as shown in the following figure

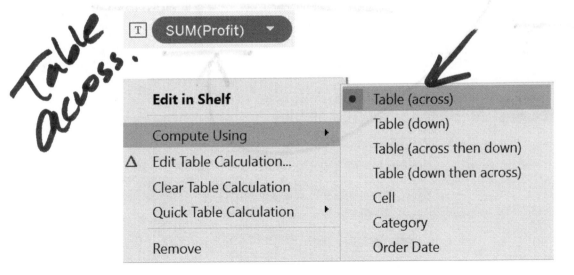

Figure 8.27: Selecting table (across)

The next figure shows the final view. You can see that the **Profit** table calculation is done for every **Category** (partitioning) across the different **Order Date** years (addressing):

| Category | | Order Date | | | |
		2016	2017	2018	2019
Furniture	Table (Across)	5,458	8,473	15,433	18,451
	Profit	5,458	3,015	6,960	3,018
Office	Table (Across)	22,593	47,693	82,754	122,491
Supplies	Profit	22,593	25,100	35,061	39,737
Technology	Table (Across)	21,493	54,997	94,771	145,455
	Profit	21,493	33,504	39,774	50,684

Figure 8.28: Final output

This view helps find the cumulative profit for the various categories over the years. This can help youunderstand how each category has been performing compared with other categories, over the years.

Next, you will learn about the **Table (down)** calculation.

TABLE (DOWN)

Table (down) computes the calculation vertically down the table, and restarts after each column. For example, consider that you have the various years on the **Columns** shelf for the product names (and their sales) on the rows. **Table (down)** would compute the calculation for all of a product's sales for an individual year, and then restart at the next product.

EXERCISE 8.08: CREATING A TABLE (DOWN) CALCULATION

For this exercise, you will compare the sales for various years, using the **Table (down)** calculation along years. This will help you compare the profits for the years, and help you understand whether the sales are improving or declining:

1. Load the **Sample – Superstore** dataset in your Tableau instance.

2. Create a view that shows **Category** against **YEAR (Order Date)** and **SUM (Profit)**.

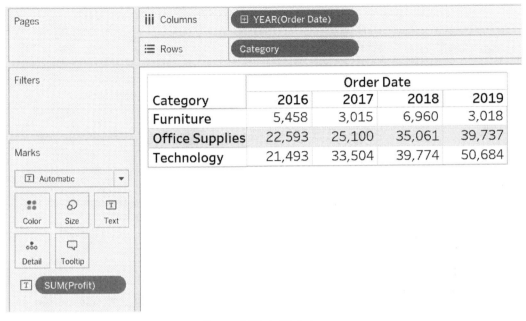

Figure 8.29: Initial view

3. Add the **Running Total** quick calculation to get the following view. This is the default, which is the across or horizontal direction:

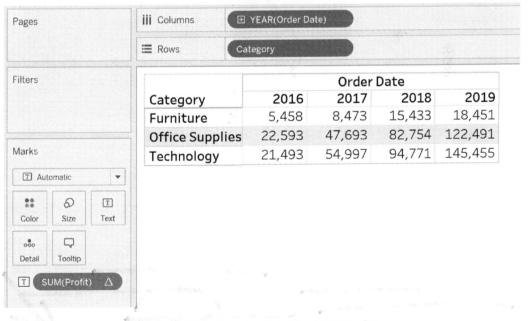

Figure 8.30: Running total for SUM(Profit)

4. Select **Compute Using** and then **Table(down)**, as follows:

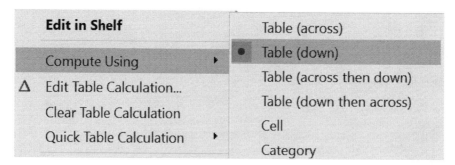

Figure 8.31: Accessing compute using | table (down)

5. The following figure shows the final view. You can see that the **Profit** table calculation is computed for every **Order Date** year (partitioning) for the three **Category** values (addressing):

Category		Order Date			
		2016	2017	2018	2019
Furniture	Table (Down)	5,458	3,015	6,960	3,018
	Profit	5,458	3,015	6,960	3,018
Office Supplies	Table (Down)	28,051	28,115	42,021	42,755
	Profit	22,593	25,100	35,061	39,737
Technology	Table (Down)	49,544	61,619	81,795	93,439
	Profit	21,493	33,504	39,774	50,684

Figure 8.32: Final output

This view can help you answer how each category has been performing based on profits across years. You could potentially make important business decisions based off these results.

Next, you will learn about **Table(across then down)** and **Table(down then across)** together. These are opposites. **Table(across then down)** computes the calculation horizontally across the table and adds the values at the end of each row to the first value of the next row. **Table(down then across)** performs the calculation vertically down the table, and adds the values at the end of each column to the first value of the next column.

In the **Table(down)** and **Table(across)** exercises, you treated the end totals for each column or row as separate values. So, you got a comparison for the different addressing results. For **Table(across then down)** and **Table(down then across)**, a value for the current row/column will be the result of the previous rows/columns along with the current row/column.

Considering the previous example of car manufacturer sales, suppose you perform **Table(down)** and then **Table(across)** for sales; Tableau would first compute the sales for the current year for all products, and then add that value to the next year's values. Hence, for the current year, you would get cumulative values for the previous years and the current year's sales.

EXERCISE 8.09: CREATING TABLE (ACROSS THEN DOWN) AND TABLE (DOWN THEN ACROSS) CALCULATIONS

In this exercise, you will continue with the example used in the previous exercises, and use **Table(across then down)** and **Table(down then across)** calculations. The following steps will help you complete this exercise:

1. Load the **Sample - Superstore** dataset in your Tableau instance.

2. Create a view that shows **Category** and **Sub-Category** against **YEAR(Order Date)** and **SUM(Profit)**, as follows. Filter on **Category: Technology** by placing **Category** on the **Filters** shelf:

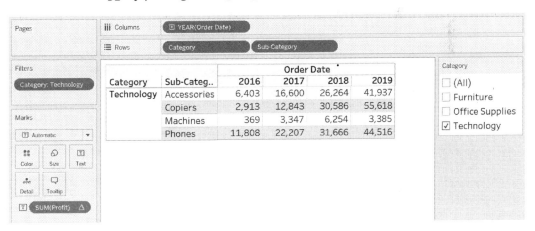

Figure 8.33: Initial view for table (across then down)

3. Add the **Running Total** quick calculation to get the following view. Here, you get the cumulative sum of profits for all the years for a sub-category. The default addressing would be **Table(across)**:

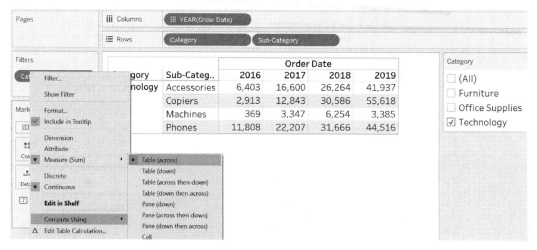

Figure 8.34: Running total for SUM(Profit)

4. Select **Compute Using** and then **Table(across then down)**.

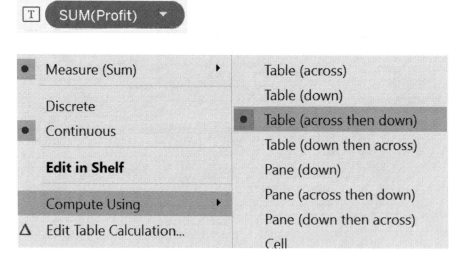

Figure 8.35: Accessing compute using | table (across then down)

The following is the generated view. You can follow the lines shown in the following figure to see how the computation is done:

Category	Sub-Categ..		Order Date			
			2016	2017	2018	2019
Technology	Accessories	Table (Across then Down)	6,403	16,600	26,264	41,937
		Profit	6,403	10,197	9,664	15,672
	Copiers	Table (Across then Down)	44,850	54,780	72,523	97,554
		Profit	2,913	9,930	17,743	25,032
	Machines	Table (Across then Down)	97,924	100,901	103,808	100,939
		Profit	369	2,977	2,907	-2,869
	Phones	Table (Across then Down)	112,747	123,146	132,606	145,455
		Profit	11,808	10,399	9,460	12,849

Figure 8.36: The working of table (across then down)

First, **Table(across)** is performed for **Accessories** (see the orange lines). Then, that total (**$41,937**) is computed by **Table(down)** (green line) with the profit of **Copiers** (**$2,913**) making it **$44,850**. This process is repeated until the table ends.

5. To change this to **Table(down then across)**, select **Compute Using** and then **Table(down then across)**, as follows:

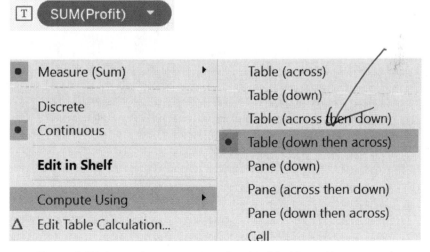

Figure 8.37: Accessing compute using | table (down then across)

This will be the generated view. Again, you can follow the lines to see how the computation is done. This is exactly the opposite of how **Table(across then down)** works:

Category	Sub-Categ..		Order Date			
			2016	2017	2018	2019
Technology	Accessories	Table (Down then Across)	6,403	31,690	64,661	110,443
		Profit	6,403	10,197	9,664	15,672
	Copiers	Table (Down then Across)	9,316	41,620	82,404	135,475
		Profit	2,913	9,930	17,743	25,032
	Machines	Table (Down then Across)	9,685	44,598	85,311	132,606
		Profit	369	2,977	2,907	-2,869
	Phones	Table (Down then Across)	21,493	54,997	94,771	145,455
		Profit	11,808	10,399	9,460	12,849

Figure 8.38: The working of table (down then across)

As you see, first the profits are added in a downward direction, then this sum is taken across to a different year. This process continues until the final year. This view can help you understand how the different sub-categories have been performing, based on profits summed together over the previous years.

Next, you will learn about panes. Table calculations can work down or across panes, depending on the calculation type. A pane can be defined as a combination of cells made up of fields on the **Rows** and **Columns** shelves, as in the following screenshot:

Category	Sub-Categ..	Order Date					Category
		2016	2017	2018	2019		☐ (All)
Furniture	Bookcases	-346	-2,755	212	-584		☑ Furniture
	Chairs	6,955	6,228	5,763	7,644		☐ Office Supplies
Pane 1	Furnishings	1,973	3,052	3,935	4,099		☑ Technology
	Tables	-3,124	-3,510	-2,951	-8,141		
Technology	Accessories	6,403	10,197	9,664	15,672		
	Copiers	2,913	9,930	17,743	25,032		
Pane 2	Machines	369	2,977	2,907	-2,869		
	Phones	11,808	10,399	9,460	12,849		

Figure 8.39: Panes

They can also be thought of as smaller tables within a bigger table. Table calculations can be performed on panes similar to how you did at the table level. The following is a list of the various pane-related computations:

- **Pane(across)**
- **Pane(down)**
- **Pane(across then down)**
- **Pane(down then across)**

You will start with **Pane(across)**.

EXERCISE 8.10: CREATING A PANE (ACROSS) CALCULATION

Pane(across) computes the calculation horizontally across the pane, and restarts at the next pane. Considering your previous example of car manufacturer sales, suppose you want to compare the sales for the various years, while also considering the different car segments, such as hatchback, sedan, and SUV. In this exercise, you will use the **Pane(across)** calculation to do this.

The following steps will help you complete this exercise:

1. Load the **Sample – Superstore** dataset in your Tableau instance.

2. Create a view that shows **Category** against **YEAR(Order Date)**, **QUARTER(Order Date)**, and **SUM(Profit)**, as follows:

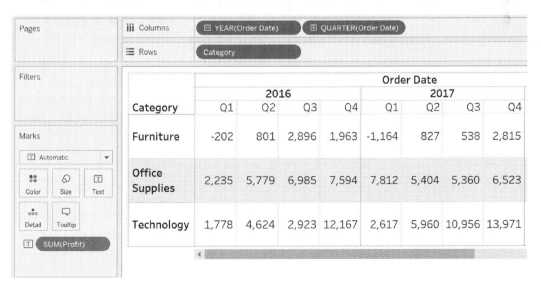

Figure 8.40: Initial view with a running total for SUM(Profit)

3. Filter on **YEAR(Order Date)** as **2016** and **2017**.

Figure 8.41: Adding a YEAR filter

4. You now have two horizontal panes. For a pane table calculation to be activated, you need more than one dimension in the rows or the columns. A pane here will be one row, per **Category**, per year; so you'll have six panes in the view. The first pane looks like this:

| Category | Order Date | | | | | | | |
| | 2016 | | | | 2017 | | | |
	Q1	Q2	Q3	Q4	Q1	Q2	Q3	Q4
Furniture	-202	801	2,896	1,963	-1,164	827	538	2,815
Office Supplies	2,235	5,779	6,985	7,594	7,812	5,404	5,360	6,523
Technology	1,778	4,624	2,923	12,167	2,617	5,960	10,956	13,971

Figure 8.42: Understanding pane (across)

5. Add a Running Total of Sum(Profit) and then select the **Pane (across)** option by clicking again on **SUM (Profit)**.

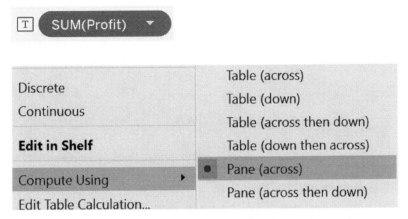

Figure 8.43: Accessing compute using | pane (across)

On selecting **Pane (across)**, you should see the following output:

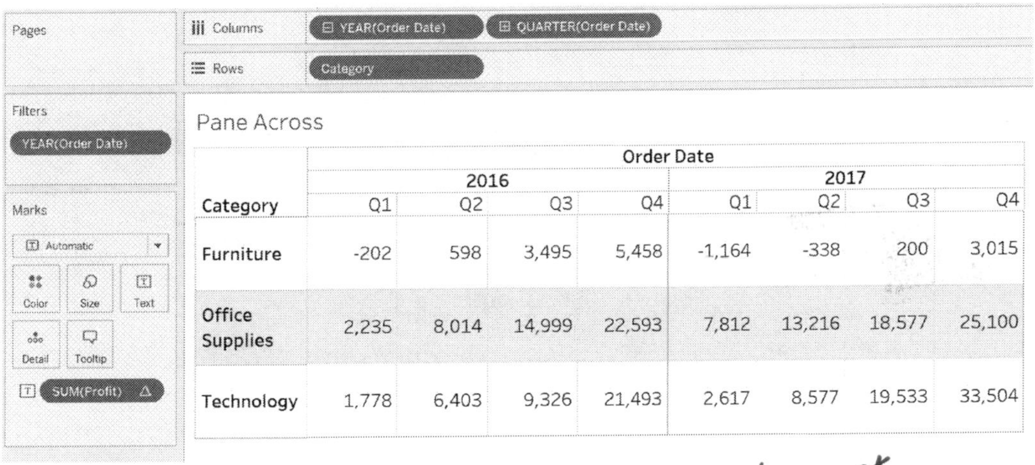

Pane Across

		Order Date							
		2016				2017			
Category	Q1	Q2	Q3	Q4	Q1	Q2	Q3	Q4
Furniture	-202	598	3,495	5,458	-1,164	-338	200	3,015
Office Supplies	2,235	8,014	14,999	22,593	7,812	13,216	18,577	25,100
Technology	1,778	6,403	9,326	21,493	2,617	8,577	19,533	33,504

Figure 8.44: Final output

[handwritten annotations: "No Pane down." and " More than 1 dimension of your view"]*

6. To understand this better, add **Profit** to another view and compute the result.

Category		Order Date							
		2016				2017			
		Q1	Q2	Q3	Q4	Q1	Q2	Q3	Q4
Furniture	Profit	-202	801	2,896	1,963	-1,164	827	538	2,815
	Pane (Across)	-202	598	3,495	5,458	-1,164	-338	200	3,015
Office Supplies	Profit	2,235	5,779	6,985	7,594	7,812	5,404	5,360	6,523
	Pane (Across)	2,235	8,014	14,999	22,593	7,812	13,216	18,577	25,100
Technology	Profit	1,778	4,624	2,923	12,167	2,617	5,960	10,956	13,971
	Pane (Across)	1,778	6,403	9,326	21,493	2,617	8,577	19,533	33,504

Figure 8.45: The working of pane (across)

As you see, each of the highlighted blue boxes just adds profits horizontally, and this restarts after each partition or pane horizontally. You can also validate the sum of profit by referencing the bottom table.

Category		Order Date							
		2016				2017			
		Q1	Q2	Q3	Q4	Q1	Q2	Q3	Q4
Furniture	Profit	-202	801	2,896	1,963	-1,164	827	538	2,815
	Pane (Across)	-202	598	3,495	5,458	-1,164	-338	200	3,015
Office Supplies	Profit	2,235	5,779	6,985	7,594	7,812	5,404	5,360	6,523
	Pane (Across)	2,235	8,014	14,999	22,593	7,812	13,216	18,577	25,100
Technology	Profit	1,778	4,624	2,923	12,167	2,617	5,960	10,956	13,971
	Pane (Across)	1,778	6,403	9,326	21,493	2,617	8,577	19,533	33,504

Figure 8.46: Final output analysis

This view can help you see how different categories have performed based on profits summed together over all different quarters across the two Order Date years. This can help you hone in on profits, to understand which quarters generated the highest profits.

Next, you will learn about **Pane (down)**. **Pane (down)** performs the calculation vertically down the pane, and restarts at the next pane.

EXERCISE 8.11: PANE (DOWN) CALCULATION

Considering the example of car manufacturer sales, suppose you want to analyze the sales of various car models sold per segment per year. Here, you can use **Pane (down)** addressing on the segment partitioning. The following steps will help you complete this exercise:

1. Load the **Sample – Superstore** dataset in your Tableau instance.

2. Create a view that shows **YEAR(Order Date)** and **Category** against **QUARTER(Order Date)** and the running total for **SUM(Profit)**, as follows:

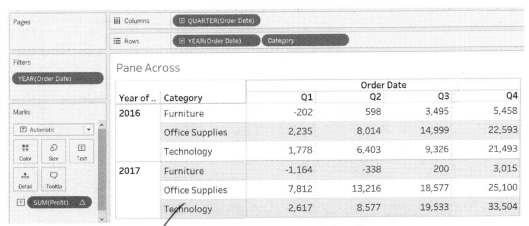

Figure 8.47: Initial view with the running total for SUM(Profit)

3. Filter on **YEAR(Order Date)** as **2016** and **2017**.

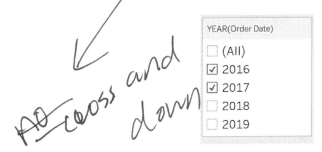

Figure 8.48: Adding a YEAR filter

4. Now, you will have eight vertical panes – four for **2016** and four for **2017** – based on the four quarters and two years.

Year of ..	Category	Q1	Q2	Q3	Q4
2016	Furniture	-202	598	3,495	5,458
	Office Supplies	2,235	8,014	14,999	22,593
	Technology	1,778	6,403	9,326	21,493
2017	Furniture	-1,164	-338	200	3,015
	Office Supplies	7,812	13,216	18,577	25,100
	Technology	2,617	8,577	19,533	33,504

(Order Date shown across Q1–Q4 columns)

Figure 8.49: Understanding pane (down)

5. Select the **Pane (down)** option by clicking again on **SUM(Profit)**, as follows:

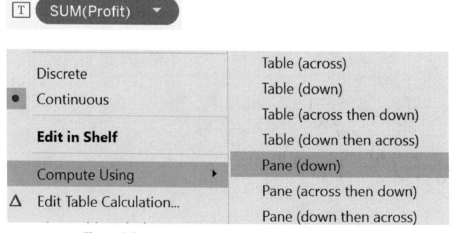

Figure 8.50: Accessing compute using | pane (down)

You will see the following output:

Pane Down

Year of ..	Category	Order Date			
		Q1	Q2	Q3	Q4
2016	Furniture	-202	801	2,896	1,963
	Office Supplies	2,033	6,580	9,881	9,557
	Technology	3,811	11,204	12,805	21,724
2017	Furniture	-1,164	827	538	2,815
	Office Supplies	6,648	6,231	5,898	9,338
	Technology	9,265	12,191	16,854	23,309

Figure 8.51: Final output

6. To understand this better, add **Profit** to the view and see the result.

Year of ..		Category	Order Date			
			Q1	Q2	Q3	Q4
2016	Profit	Furniture	-202	801	2,896	1,963
		Office Supplies	2,235	5,779	6,985	7,594
		Technology	1,778	4,624	2,923	12,167
	Pane (Down)	Furniture	-202	801	2,896	1,963
		Office Supplies	2,033	6,580	9,881	9,557
		Technology	3,811	11,204	12,805	21,724
2017	Profit	Furniture	-1,164	827	538	2,815
		Office Supplies	7,812	5,404	5,360	6,523
		Technology	2,617	5,960	10,956	13,971
	Pane (Down)	Furniture	-1,164	827	538	2,815
		Office Supplies	6,648	6,231	5,898	9,338
		Technology	9,265	12,191	16,854	23,309

Figure 8.52: The working of pane (down)

As you see, the values in each blue pane (highlighted) are summed in a downward direction, and this process restarts after every pane. Here, you can compare quarterly profits. For example, for **Q1 2016**, the total profit is **$3,811** and similarly, for **Q1 2017**, it is **$9,265**, which is approximately 2.5 times more profit. The same is cannot be said for **Q2** profits. Based on this, you can try to analyze the reasoning behind such differences, and use those insights to tweak business strategy.

Next, you will learn about **Pane(across then down)** and **Pane(down then across)**. **Pane(across then down)** is a combination of **Pane(across)** and **Pane(down)**; that is, it computes the calculation horizontally across the pane and combines the result with the values in the next pane. **Pane(down then across)** is the opposite of **Pane(across then down)**, as it performs the calculation vertically down the pane and combines the result with the values in the next pane. The next exercise looks at this in detail.

EXERCISE 8.12: CREATING A PANE-LEVEL CALCULATION

This exercise continues with the example of car manufacturer sales. Suppose you want the sales per segment per quarter for the different years together. Here, you can use the option of **Pane(across then down)** or **Pane(down then across)**. The result combines all detailed panes into a cumulative overall total. The following steps will help you complete this exercise:

1. Load the **Sample - Superstore** dataset in your Tableau instance.

2. Before creating the view, you must first create a combined field for **Category** and **Sub-Category**. This is required for the **Pane(across then down)** calculation, else Tableau will merge the sub-categories. Select **Category** and **Sub-Category** together, then, right-click and select **Create** and then **Combined Field**, as follows:

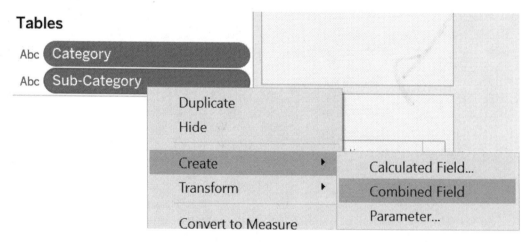

Figure 8.53: Creating a combined field

3. Create a view that shows **YEAR(Order Date)** and **QUARTER(Order Date)** against **Category**, **Sub-Category**, and the combined field. Also, add the running total for **SUM(Profit)**, as follows:

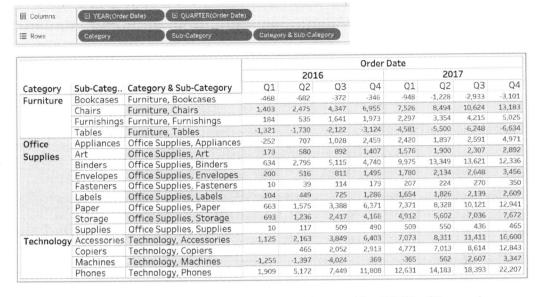

| | | | Order Date | | | | | | | |
| | | | 2016 | | | | 2017 | | | |
Category	Sub-Categ..	Category & Sub-Category	Q1	Q2	Q3	Q4	Q1	Q2	Q3	Q4
Furniture	Bookcases	Furniture, Bookcases	-468	-682	-372	-346	-948	-1,228	-2,933	-3,101
	Chairs	Furniture, Chairs	1,403	2,475	4,347	6,955	7,526	8,494	10,624	13,183
	Furnishings	Furniture, Furnishings	184	535	1,641	1,973	2,297	3,354	4,215	5,025
	Tables	Furniture, Tables	-1,321	-1,730	-2,122	-3,124	-4,581	-5,500	-6,248	-6,634
Office Supplies	Appliances	Office Supplies, Appliances	-252	707	1,028	2,459	2,420	1,897	2,591	4,971
	Art	Office Supplies, Art	173	580	892	1,407	1,576	1,900	2,307	2,892
	Binders	Office Supplies, Binders	634	2,795	5,115	4,740	9,975	13,349	13,621	12,336
	Envelopes	Office Supplies, Envelopes	200	516	811	1,495	1,780	2,134	2,648	3,456
	Fasteners	Office Supplies, Fasteners	10	39	114	179	207	224	270	350
	Labels	Office Supplies, Labels	104	449	725	1,286	1,654	1,826	2,139	2,609
	Paper	Office Supplies, Paper	663	1,575	3,388	6,371	7,371	8,328	10,121	12,941
	Storage	Office Supplies, Storage	693	1,236	2,417	4,166	4,912	5,602	7,036	7,672
	Supplies	Office Supplies, Supplies	10	117	509	490	509	550	436	465
Technology	Accessories	Technology, Accessories	1,125	2,163	3,849	6,403	7,073	8,311	11,411	16,600
	Copiers	Technology, Copiers		465	2,052	2,913	4,771	7,013	8,614	12,843
	Machines	Technology, Machines	-1,255	-1,397	-4,024	369	-365	562	2,607	3,347
	Phones	Technology, Phones	1,909	5,172	7,449	11,808	12,631	14,183	18,393	22,207

Figure 8.54: Initial view with the running total for SUM(Profit)

4. Filter on **YEAR(Order Date)** as **2016** and **2017**. Also, filter on **Category** by selecting **Furniture** and **Technology**, as follows:

Figure 8.55: Adding category and YEAR filters

5. You now have two horizontal **Year** panes and two vertical **Category** panes. Select the **Pane (across then down)** option by clicking again on **SUM (Profit)**.

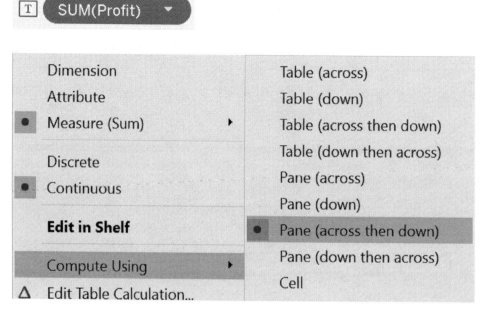

Figure 8.56: Accessing compute using | pane (across then down)

6. On selecting **Pane (across then down)**, the output generated is as follows:

Category	Sub-Categ..	Category & Sub-Category	Order Date							
			2016				2017			
			Q1	Q2	Q3	Q4	Q1	Q2	Q3	Q4
Furniture	Bookcases	Furniture, Bookcases	-468	-682	-372	-346	-602	-882	-2,587	-2,755
	Chairs	Furniture, Chairs	1,057	2,129	4,001	6,609	-2,185	-1,217	914	3,473
	Furnishings	Furniture, Furnishings	6,792	7,144	8,250	8,582	3,797	4,855	5,715	6,525
	Tables	Furniture, Tables	7,261	6,852	6,460	5,458	5,068	4,149	3,401	3,015
Technology	Accessories	Technology, Accessories	6,582	7,621	9,306	11,860	3,686	4,924	8,023	13,212
	Copiers	Technology, Copiers	11,860	12,325	13,912	14,773	15,071	17,313	18,914	23,143
	Machines	Technology, Machines	13,518	13,376	10,750	15,143	22,408	23,336	25,381	26,120
	Phones	Technology, Phones	17,052	20,315	22,592	26,951	26,943	28,495	32,706	36,519

Figure 8.57: Final output for pane (across then down)

7. To understand this better, add **Profit** to the view and calculate the result.

Pane Across then Down

Category	Sub-Categ..	Category & Sub-Category	Order Date 2016			
			Q1	Q2	Q3	Q4
Furniture	Bookcases	Furniture, Bookcases	-468	-682	-372	-346
	Chairs	Furniture, Chairs	-->1,057	2,129	4,001	6,609
	Furnishings	Furniture, Furnishings	6,792	7,144	8,250	8,582
	Tables	Furniture, Tables	-->7,261	6,852	6,460	5,458
Technology	Accessories	Technology, Accessories	6,582	7,621	9,306	11,860
	Copiers	Technology, Copiers		12,325	13,912	14,773
	Machines	Technology, Machines	13,518	13,376	10,750	15,143
	Phones	Technology, Phones	17,052	20,315	22,592	26,951

Sum(Profit)

Category	Sub-Categ..	Category & Sub-Category	Order Date 2016			
			Q1	Q2	Q3	Q4
Furniture	Bookcases	Furniture, Bookcases	-468	-214	311	25
	Chairs	Furniture, Chairs	1,403	1,072	1,872	2,608
	Furnishings	Furniture, Furnishings	184	352	1,105	332
	Tables	Furniture, Tables	-1,321	-409	-392	-1,002
Technology	Accessories	Technology, Accessories	1,125	1,038	1,686	2,554
	Copiers	Technology, Copiers		465	1,587	861
	Machines	Technology, Machines	-1,255	-142	-2,626	4,393
	Phones	Technology, Phones	1,909	3,263	2,277	4,359

Figure 8.58: The working of pane (across then down)

Notice the blue arrows, which indicate the profits being summed from the first to the last value in that row; the orange arrow indicates that the last value of each row is added to the first value of the next row. This process is repeated until the last row for each year. Once a year is completed, the calculation restarts for the next year. You can validate the numbers by looking at the **Sum(Profit)** values, as seen on the right side.

8. Change the calculation to **Pane (down then across)**, as shown in the following figure:

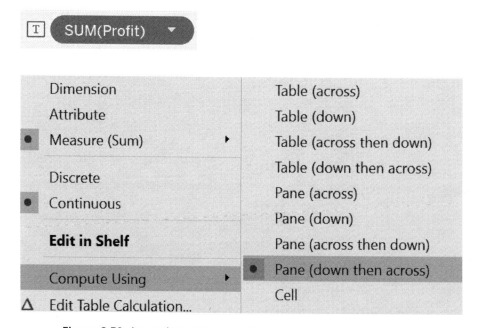

Figure 8.59: Accessing compute using | pane (down then across)

The output generated will be as follows:

Category	Sub-Categ..	Category & Sub-Category	2016 Q1	2016 Q2	2016 Q3	2016 Q4	2017 Q1	2017 Q2	2017 Q3	2017 Q4
Furniture	Bookcases	Furniture, Bookcases	-468	1,361	7,312	12,846	-602	1,173	6,534	19,565
	Chairs	Furniture, Chairs	935	2,433	9,184	15,454	-32	2,141	8,665	22,124
	Furnishings	Furniture, Furnishings	1,119	2,785	10,289	15,786	293	3,199	9,526	22,934
	Tables	Furniture, Tables	-202	2,377	9,897	14,784	-1,164	2,280	8,777	22,548
Technology	Accessories	Technology, Accessories	922	3,415	11,583	17,338	-494	3,518	11,877	27,737
	Copiers	Technology, Copiers	922	3,880	13,170	18,199	1,365	5,760	13,478	31,966
	Machines	Technology, Machines	-333	3,738	10,544	22,592	630	6,687	15,523	32,706
	Phones	Technology, Phones	1,576	7,001	12,821	26,951	1,453	8,240	19,733	36,519

Figure 8.60: Final output for Pane (down then across)

9. To understand this better, add **Profit** to the view and calculate the result for **2016**.

Pane Down then Across

Category	Sub-Categ..	Category & Sub-Category	Order Date 2016			
			Q1	Q2	Q3	Q4
Furniture	Bookcases	Furniture, Bookcases	-468	-> 1,361	7,312	12,846
	Chairs	Furniture, Chairs	935	2,433	9,184	15,454
	Furnishings	Furniture, Furnishings	1,119	2,785	10,289	15,786
	Tables	Furniture, Tables	-202	2,377	9,897	14,784
Technology	Accessories	Technology, Accessories	922	3,415	11,583	17,338
	Copiers	Technology, Copiers		3,880	13,170	18,199
	Machines	Technology, Machines	-333	3,738	10,544	22,592
	Phones	Technology, Phones	-> 1,576	7,001	12,821	26,951

Sum(Profit)

Category	Sub-Categ..	Category & Sub-Category	Order Date 2016			
			Q1	Q2	Q3	Q4
Furniture	Bookcases	Furniture, Bookcases	-468	-214	311	25
	Chairs	Furniture, Chairs	1,403	1,072	1,872	2,608
	Furnishings	Furniture, Furnishings	184	352	1,105	332
	Tables	Furniture, Tables	-1,321	-409	-392	-1,002
Technology	Accessories	Technology, Accessories	1,125	1,038	1,686	2,554
	Copiers	Technology, Copiers		465	1,587	861
	Machines	Technology, Machines	-1,255	-142	-2,626	4,393
	Phones	Technology, Phones	1,909	3,263	2,277	4,359

Figure 8.61: The working of pane (down then across)

Observe the blue arrows, which indicate the profits being summed from the first to the last value in the column. The orange arrow indicates that the last value of each column is added to the first value of the next column. This process is repeated until the last row for each year. Once a year is completed, the calculation restarts for the next year. Once again, you can validate the numbers by looking at the **Sum (Profit)** values, as seen on the right side.

CELL

Cell computes across the individual cells. The result is the same as adding the measure to the shelf directly, as shown in the following figure (the cell is highlighted using a box):

Cell

Category	Sub-Categ..	Category & Sub-Category	Order Date			
			2016			
			Q1	Q2	Q3	Q4
Furniture	Bookcases	Furniture, Bookcases	-468	-214	311	25
	Chairs	Furniture, Chairs	1,403	1,072	1,872	2,608
	Furnishings	Furniture, Furnishings	184	352	1,105	332
	Tables	Furniture, Tables	-1,321	-409	-392	-1,002
Technology	Accessories	Technology, Accessories	1,125	1,038	1,686	2,554
	Copiers	Technology, Copiers		465	1,587	861
	Machines	Technology, Machines	-1,255	-142	-2,626	4,393
	Phones	Technology, Phones	1,909	3,263	2,277	4,359

Figure 8.62: Computing using cell

The values are the same in both tables. **Specific Dimensions** computes using the dimensions you specify. You will learn about this in more detail in the following section.

CREATING, EDITING, AND REMOVING TABLE CALCULATIONS

Hopefully you now have a good understanding of quick table calculations, but what if you need to use some other calculation, such as ranking the rows in a table? Here, you can use the **Create** calculation window. Tableau supports many table functions besides quick table calculations. In this section, you will learn how to create, access, edit, and remove a table calculation.

CREATING A NEW TABLE CALCULATION

To create a table calculation, right-click on any measure value, and then click on **Create**, then **Calculated Field...**, as follows:

Figure 8.63: Creating a calculated field from Profit

Once you click on **Calculated Field...**, a calculation editor window will open up, as follows:

Figure 8.64: Calculation editor

Now, you can click on the dropdown and select the **Table Calculation** menu, as follows:

Figure 8.65: Accessing table calculation functions in the calculation editor

Next, the list of all the table calculations supported by Tableau appears, as follows:

Figure 8.66: Various table calculation functions

In Tableau, it's very easy to understand these table calculations. Each calculation is defined by specifying the syntax for use, the expected result from using the calculation, followed by an example.

You are already familiar with **RUNNING_TOTAL**, which is similar to **RUNNING_SUM**. The same calculation type can be used to do a variety of operations, such as sum, average, and finding the minimum and maximum values, which can be referenced under the table calculation menu.

EXERCISE 8.13: CREATING A TABLE CALCULATION USING THE CALCULATION EDITOR

In your projects, you might need to use one of the table calculation functions in the view. An example of this is the index function, which adds serial numbers to the rows in the view. You can do this by creating a table calculation. In this exercise, you will calculate the rank of **Sub-Category** based on **SUM(Profit)** across years. The following steps will help you complete this exercise:

1. Load the **Sample - Superstore** dataset in your Tableau instance. Use the combined field that you created earlier along with **YEAR(Order Date)**. Create a view as follows and also filter **Category** for **Furniture**:

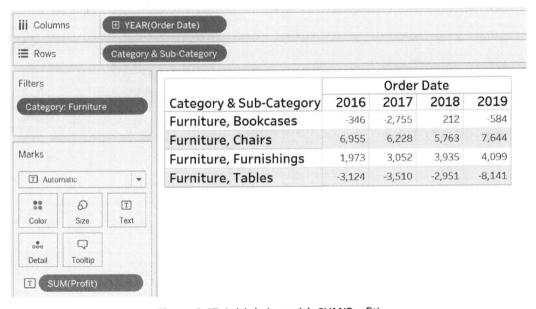

Category & Sub-Category	2016	2017	2018	2019
Furniture, Bookcases	-346	-2,755	212	-584
Furniture, Chairs	6,955	6,228	5,763	7,644
Furniture, Furnishings	1,973	3,052	3,935	4,099
Furniture, Tables	-3,124	-3,510	-2,951	-8,141

Figure 8.67: Initial view with SUM(Profit)

2. Now, create a RANK table calculation. Right-click on **Profit** in the data pane and select **Create | Calculated Field**.... This will open up the calculation editor.

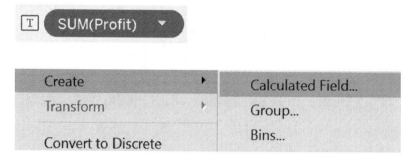

Figure 8.68: Creating a calculation using Profit

3. Add the following expression to the calculation editor:

```
RANK(SUM(Profit))
```

This is shown in the following figure:

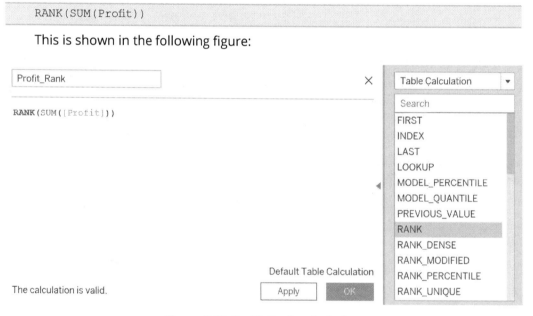

Figure 8.69: Profit_Rank calculation

4. Name it **Profit_Rank**.

5. Drag this onto the view on **Text**, as follows:

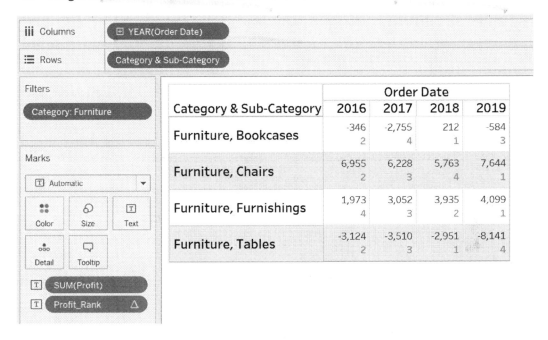

Category & Sub-Category	Order Date			
	2016	2017	2018	2019
Furniture, Bookcases	-346 2	-2,755 4	212 1	-584 3
Furniture, Chairs	6,955 2	6,228 3	5,763 4	7,644 1
Furniture, Furnishings	1,973 4	3,052 3	3,935 2	4,099 1
Furniture, Tables	-3,124 2	-3,510 3	-2,951 1	-8,141 4

Figure 8.70: Adding the Profit_Rank calculation to the view

6. Observe that the default is the **Table (across)** direction. Edit this and try to change the computation on specific dimensions in the view. Click on the **Profit_Rank** dropdown and select **Edit Table Calculation**... and then **Specific Dimensions**, as shown in the following figure:

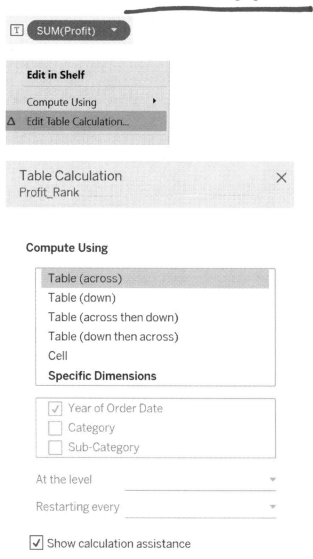

Figure 8.71: Accessing edit table calculation

Using these options, you can control how the table calculation is computed. It is important to understand the different options here:

- **At the level**: This determines the level at which the calculation is computed. The level here implies the different dimensions in the view, such as **Category** and **Sub-Category**. **Deepest** is the default if multiple dimensions are selected, which means the computation will happen at the lowest level of granularity, which is **Sub-Category** in your view.

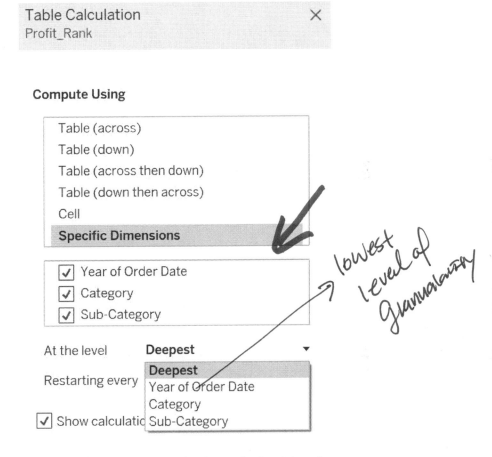

Figure 8.72: Various options under the At the level dropdown

- **Restarting every**: This option can be used to restart the computation based on the field selected.

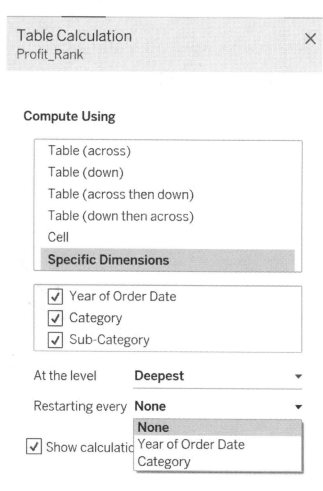

Figure 8.73: Various options under the Restarting every dropdown

- **Show calculation assistance**: This option highlights how the computation will work based on your selections. As the following figure shows, based on the selections, **Profit_Rank** will work in the downward direction (highlighted):

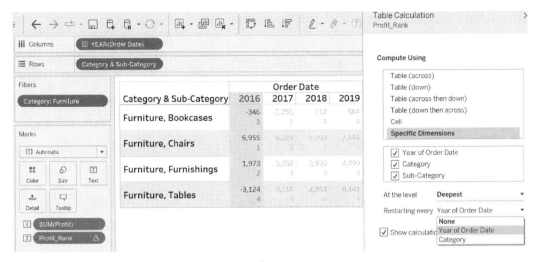

Figure 8.74: Using Show calculation assistance

This view showed how you can perform table calculations at different levels using the dimensions in the view.

REMOVING A TABLE CALCULATION

Once you have added a table calculation, you should also be able to remove it. This can be done by clicking on an existing quick table calculation and selecting the **Clear Table Calculation** option, as follows:

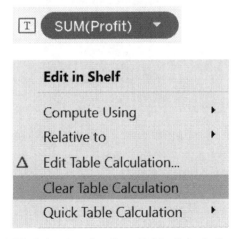

Figure 8.75: Selecting the Clear Table Calculation option

ACTIVITY 8.01: MANAGING HOSPITAL BED ALLOCATIONS

There may be scenarios where you need to use the historic value of a measure to compute its current value, for example, when finding the cumulative sum of sales for all quarters in a year.This can, in turn, help you visualize the entire year's sales, or the sales difference, compared to previous quarters. In such cases, a table calculation can be useful, as all logic is inbuilt, and you need only apply the calculation to the measure value.

In this activity, you will apply table calculations to a hospital-based project, to identify how many patients are currently admitted.You willconsider factors such as new admissions, discharges, and routine follow-ups, to check whether the threshold for beds is sufficient. By doing this, you can ensure the hospital will not run out of beds in the case of an emergency.

In the dataset, there is a date column indicating the current day, an Open column indicating the number of patients admitted, Discharges indicating the number of discharges, and Re-open indicating the number of patients getting re-admitted or following up for a previous admission. In addition, you also need to keep 100 of the total 900 beds free in case of an emergency. If the number of patients exceeds 600, it should be highlighted visually.

> **NOTE**
>
> The dataset used for this activity can be found and downloaded from
> https://packt.link/NNzlJ.

The following steps will help you complete this activity:

1. Open and connect the dataset for **Activity 1** in your Tableau instance.

2. Create a calculation named **current_patients** to find the number of patients currently admitted. This can be calculated after considering the **Open**, **Discharges**, and **Re-open** columns.

3. Once you have a bar chart view, display the date at the exact date level, along with the number of patients currently in the hospital, using the **current_patients** field created in the previous step. This view helps you view how many patients are admitted on a given day.

4. Add a **running_sum** table calculation to the **current_patients** table calculation in the existing view. This view helps you visualize the number of patients admitted on a given day considering all the previous days as well.

5. Create another calculation named Alert to indicate that the patient count is above 600. You need to use running_sum to identify the number of patients on a given day.

6. Now, you should be able to analyze the total number of patients admitted to the hospital, and see whether there are enough beds available.

7. The initial view is as follows:

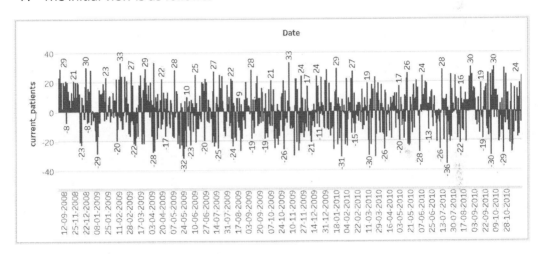

Figure 8.76: Initial view – activity

The final output is as follows:

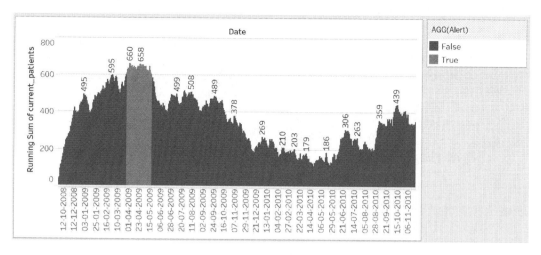

Figure 8.77: Final view – activity

Here, you can see that in 2009, there was a period when the number of patients was more than the number of beds. Although such incidents are rare, it is imperative that they are managed properly.

With this activity, you strengthened your knowledge of creating and using table calculations. This activity helped you see how you can use cumulative values to better analyze data, by highlighting anomalies or events that may have a significant business impact.

> **NOTE**
>
> The solution to this activity can be found here: https://packt.link/CTCxk

ACTIVITY 8.02: PLANNING FOR A HEALTHY POPULATION

In the previous activity, you created a visualization to indicate a drastic increase in the number of patients. As an analyst, you should also be able to use historic data, and identify patterns when the number of patients go up.

In this activity, you will use a range window to identify when the current admissions increase, and whether there is a specific observable trend. In this way, the hospital can be better prepared for the future. You will use the same hospital data used in the previous activity. The following steps will help you complete this activity:

1. Plot the window average of the **RUNNING_SUM** of **current_patients**, weekly. A window average takes the average of all values in the window, which in this case is the view.

2. Remove the average for the last 10-week range to check whether the count of currently admitted patients goes up or down. Create a parameter that can be used as input for the range; you can name it **Range_input**.

3. Use this **Range_input** parameter as the input for the **WINDOW_AVG** calculation named avg_admitted. You need to calculate the average from the last 10 weeks to the current week.

4. Use a dual-axis to show the **RUNNING_SUM** of current_patients and **WINDOW_AVERAGE**. Recall that a dual-axis is used to show two measures side by side in the same view. Right-click on the axis to enable this option after adding both measures.

5. Create an alert to compare the **RUNNING_SUM** of **current_patients** and **avg_admitted**. Highlight the weeks when the sum is more than the average.

6. The initial view would look like this:

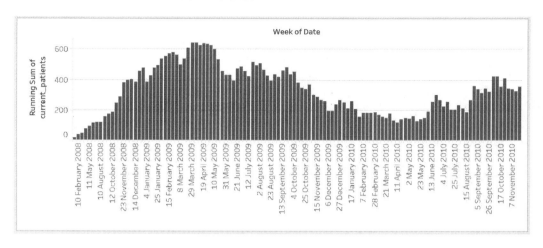

Figure 8.78: Initial view – activity

The final view should look like this:

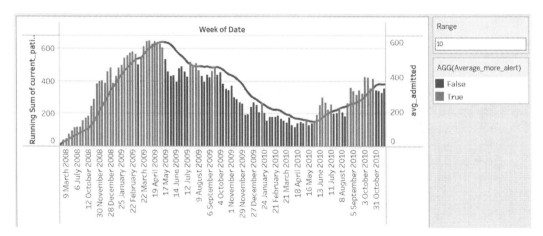

Figure 8.79: Final view – activity

You can now see when the current admitted patient count has gone higher than the 10-week average. The range can be changed based on the requirement by changing the input. An interesting observation is the month of July, which had a higher-than-average number of patients for the all of the previous 3 years, indicating thepossibility for a similar occurance for next July.

> **NOTE**
>
> The solution to this activity can be found here: https://packt.link/CTCxk.

SUMMARY

In this chapter, you learned about table calculations. You started by performing some quick table calculations, used to quickly apply commonly used table calculations in the view. Then, you explored ways to apply a table calculation using addressing and partitioning – how addressing defines the direction of the calculation, while partitioning defines its scope. Finally, you learned about creating a table calculation using the calculation editor, and about ways to address the view using specific dimensions.

In the next chapter, you will learn about **Level of Detail**, which is another powerful concept, used to control how views are displayed.

9

DATA ANALYSIS: CREATING AND USING LEVEL OF DETAILS (LOD) CALCULATIONS

OVERVIEW

This chapter introduces the concept of **Level of Detail** (**LOD**) calculations. You will learn about the different types of LOD calculations and the benefits of using them. The goal of this chapter is to improve your analytical skills using LOD calculations by looking at the data through different views to understand the underlying patterns. By the end of this chapter, you will be able to control the granularity of your data visualizations and perform comparative analyses using LOD calculations.

INTRODUCTION

For any visualization, dimensions determine the level at which measures are computed. As an example, consider the following view, in which the sum of profits is calculated based on **Country** and **Region**. These two dimensions form the details that are combined to determine the value of **SUM(Profit)**. Now, suppose you remove **Region** from the view. Then, **SUM(Profit)** would be re-computed, and would only consider **Country** in the view. Accordingly, the value of **SUM(Profit)** changes as the level of the computation changes, as can be seen from the following figure:

Level of Country and Region

Country	Region	Sum(PROFIT)
United States	Central	$39,706
	East	$91,523
	South	$46,749
	West	$108,418

Level of Country

Country	Sum(PROFIT)
United States	$286,397

Figure 9.1: Understanding LOD

LOD calculations help you control the granularity of visualizations. You can choose to view calculation results at a detailed level, or an aggregated level, based on the LOD function you use, LOD calculations require measures to be aggregated.

In this chapter, you will work with LOD calculations in Tableau.

Throughout these exercises, you will be working with the **Sample - Superstore** dataset, to learn about the different concepts related to LOD calculations.

EXERCISE 9.01: CREATING A LOD CALCULATION

You will now create an LOD calculation using the **Profit** measure in the **Sample - Superstore** dataset. The following steps will help you complete this exercise:

1. Load the **Sample - Superstore** dataset in your Tableau instance. Navigate to **Documents | My Tableau Repository | Data Sources**, then open the **Sample - Superstore.xls** file.

2. Once the data is loaded, in the data pane, right-click on **Profit** and select **Create | Calculated Field**..., as follows:

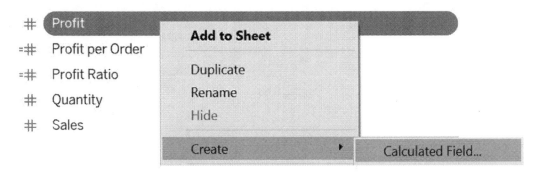

Figure 9.2: Creating a calculated field

3. In the calculation editor, select **Aggregate** from the dropdown to access the LOD calculations:

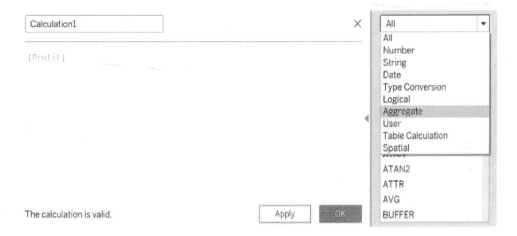

Figure 9.3: Calculated field editor

LOD calculations fall under the **Aggregate** set of functions. There are four LOD calculation types: **FIXED, INCLUDE, EXCLUDE,** and **Table-Scoped**. You will learn more about these as the chapter progresses. For now, hover over **FIXED**. Notice the calculation syntax, as can be seen in the following figure:

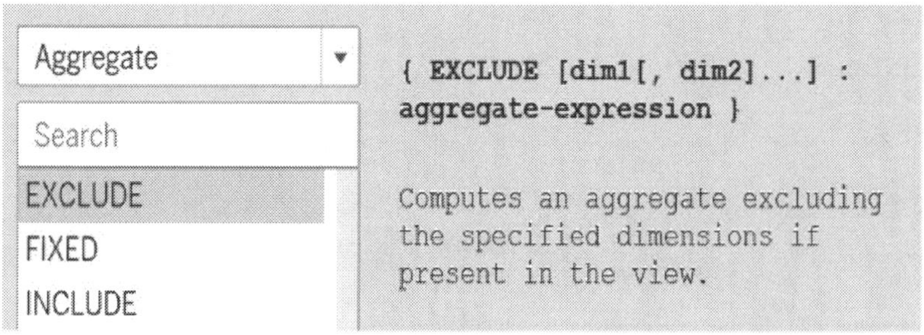

Figure 9.4: Various LOD types in Tableau

4. Click on **FIXED** and add it to the calculation editor. Add the **{FIXED : SUM([Profit])}** formula to the editor and click **OK**:

Figure 9.5: Creating a LOD calculation

LOD calculations require an aggregate measure. If you do not aggregate the measure, Tableau will show an error. Aggregation here means to use SUM, AVG, or similar types of calculation with a measure value, rather than using the measure directly, as with the SUM function previously.

5. For this calculation, compute **SUM(Profit)** at the highest level of granularity in the data, which is the **Country** level. Add this to the view, as follows:

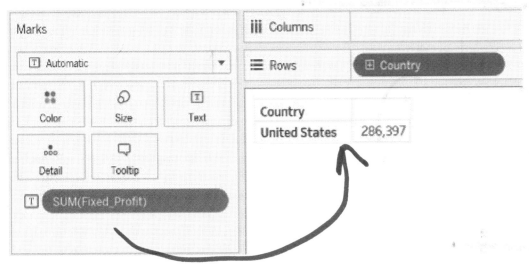

Figure 9.6: Initial view with country

Notice that the measure value does not change, irrespective of how many dimensions you add in the view:

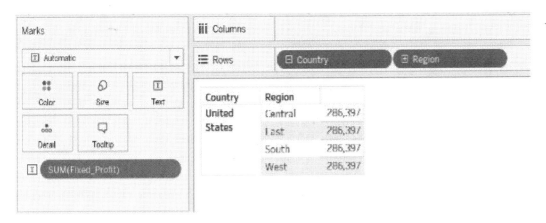

Figure 9.7: Initial view with region

In this exercise, you created an LOD calculation, by comparing how the **SUM(Fixed_ Profit)** aggregation behaves, based on various dimensions such as **Region**. You observed that the values of the output measure do not change, irrespective of the other dimension in the view, because you chose the **FIXED** LOD calculation.

Next, you will learn about the different types of LOD calculations.

TYPES OF LOD CALCULATIONS

In this section, you will learn about the various LOD calculations. There are four LOD calculation types:

- **FIXED**
- **INCLUDE**
- **EXCLUDE**
- **Table-Scoped**

You will now learn about each of these LOD calculations in greater depth. You will also learn their application in visualizations by performing an exercise for each.

FIXED

FIXED LOD calculations compute an expression using specified dimensions. An example would be identifying the top-performing product categories per region per country. This can easily be done using **FIXED** LOD calculations.

EXERCISE 9.02: CREATING A FIXED LOD CALCULATION

In this exercise, you will calculate **SUM(Profit)** fixed at a **Country** level. Suppose, as a country-level manager, you are only interested in the profits generated at country level, but occasionally would like to hone in on the **Region** level of that country. Now, you will compute a measure at a specific dimension level, rather than making calculations using all dimensions in the view.

> **NOTE**
>
> If you are using the local copy of **Superstore** that comes with Tableau, the field **Country** will have the label **Country/Region** instead. This will not affect the calculations.

Perform the following steps to complete this exercise:

1. Load the **Sample − Superstore** dataset in your Tableau instance.

2. Create a view that shows **Country** and **Region** along with **SUM(Profit)**. Currently, the view shows **SUM(Profit)** at the **Region** level, as follows:

Figure 9.8: Initial view with country and region

3. Create a **FIXED** LOD calculation:

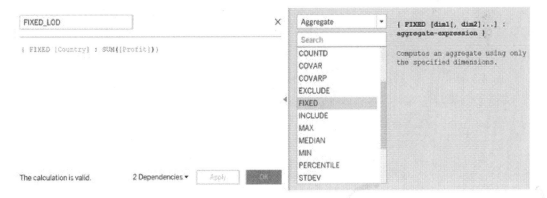

Figure 9.9: Calculation editor

4. You can use any number of dimensions in the expression before the colon (:).
   Note the expression on the right side of the colon (:) has to be an aggregation,
   or else you will get a syntax error:

Figure 9.10: Understanding the syntax of LOD calculations

5. Add this calculation to the view:

Figure 9.11: Comparing LOD and normal calculations

The second calculation in each row is the LOD calculation. Notice how the value remains constant irrespective of the **Region** dimension in the view.

In this exercise, you learned about the **FIXED** LOD calculation type and its application. You also saw how computation works when adding another dimension such as **Region** to the view. Next, you will learn about the **INCLUDE** LOD calculation.

INCLUDE

INCLUDE LOD calculations are used to calculate values based on the dimensions specified, along with those used in the view. This is useful when wanting to know results at a detailed level, but also want the view to be at a higher level. An example would be computing the average literacy rate at district level, but viewing it at state level. Here, instead of averaging it directly at state level, you would average it at district level, and then re-aggregate the results at state level. The next exercise covers this concept in detail.

EXERCISE 9.03: CREATING AN INCLUDE LOD CALCULATION

In this exercise, you will calculate **AVG(Profit)** using the **Customer** and **Region** dimensions. You will learn how to compute the average profit at a customer level, and then group it again by the **Region** dimension in the view. Perform the following steps to complete this exercise:

1. Load the **Sample - Superstore** dataset in your Tableau instance.

2. Create a view that shows **Region** along with **AVG(Profit)**, as follows:

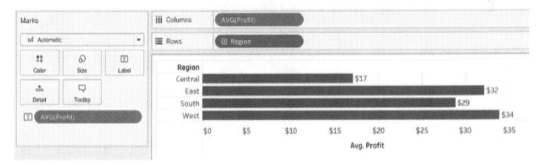

Figure 9.12: Initial view

3. Currently, the view shows **AVG(Profit)** at the **Region** level. Create an **INCLUDE** LOD calculation, and write the formula as given in the following figure:

Figure 9.13: INCLUDE LOD calculation expression

4. Use the average profit generated by a customer in that region to compute the overall average. Duplicate the preceding view, and add this calculation instead of **AVG(Profit)** to get the following:

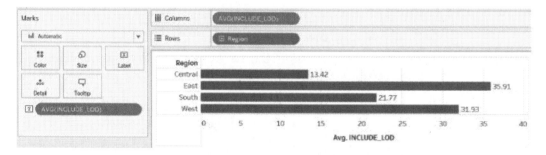

Figure 9.14: Adding the LOD calculation to the initial view

5. Check that the aggregation is set to average by clicking on the calculation dropdown and selecting the **Measure (Average)** option as **Average** on both the **Text** and **Columns** shelves:

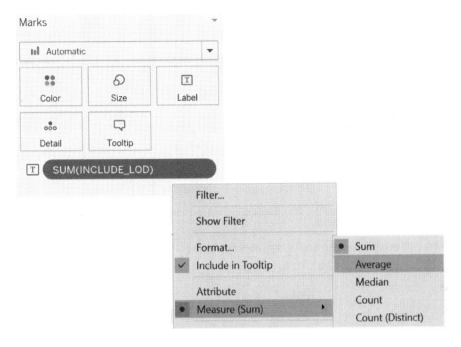

Figure 9.15: Changing a calculation aggregation format

Notice that the numbers are different in both views, despite the dimension being the same. You will now see how the computation is happening within Tableau.

6. At the **Region** level, to compute the average profit, add the profit across the region, and divide the sum by the total number of records , as follows:

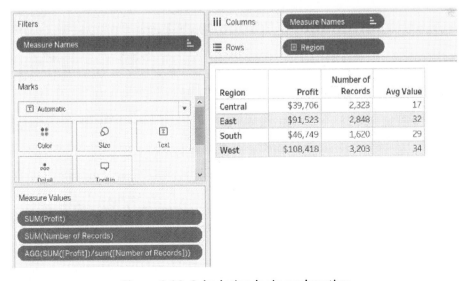

Figure 9.16: Calculation logic explanation

7. Now it is time to see how the customer-level computation works. Plot the average profit generated by each customer in **Central Region**. Once you have the average, sum all averages ($8,442), and divide the result by **Count (630)** to get the value of $13.42 per customer in that region. These values can be referred to in the **Summary** card, as follows:

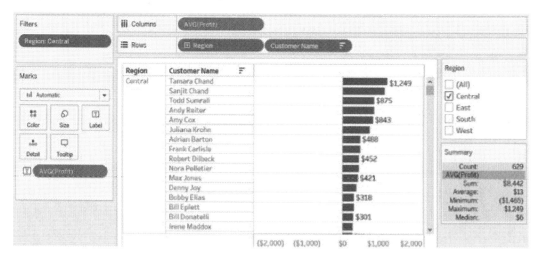

Figure 9.17: Customer-level computations

This kind of calculation is useful when you want to see the aggregations at different levels without using them in the view.

> **NOTE**
>
> You can perform a similar calculation at the **Segment**, ship mode, or any other dimension to understand underlying trends in data.

In this exercise, you learned about the **INCLUDE** LOD calculation type and how it can be applied to analyze trends at different levels of dimensions. Next, you will learn about the **EXCLUDE** LOD calculation.

EXCLUDE

An **EXCLUDE** LOD calculation declares dimensions to be omitted from the view LOD. It is the opposite of the **INCLUDE** LOD. In an **EXCLUDE** LOD, the calculation is computed excluding the specified dimensions in the expression; that is, the specified dimensions are ignored while computing the results. Continuing on with the previous example, you can add both the customer and product categories to the view, but can exclude the customer dimension when computing sales, and just calculate sales at a product category level. You will explore this in detail in the next exercise.

EXERCISE 9.04: CREATING AN EXCLUDE LOD CALCULATION

In this exercise, you will calculate **AVG(Profit)** using the **Customer** and **Region** dimensions, and will see how the **EXCLUDE** LOD calculation can be applied. This will help you learn how to compute the average profit only at the region level, despite having customer information in the view:

1. Load the **Sample - Superstore** dataset in your Tableau instance.

2. Create a view that shows the **Region** and Customer dimensions along with **AVG(Profit)**, as follows:

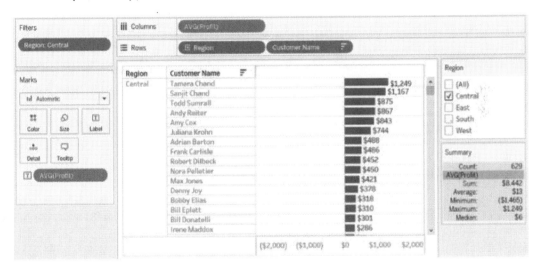

Figure 9.18: Initial view

3. Add a **Central** filter for **Region**. Here, you only view the **Customer** information for **Central Region**, along with the average profit.

4. Create an **EXCLUDE** LOD calculation to exclude the customer and re-compute the average profit, as follows:

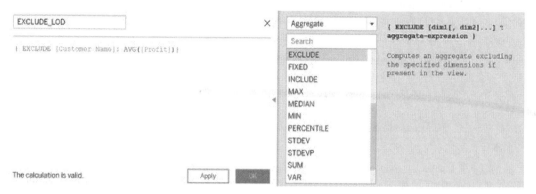

Figure 9.19: Exclude LOD expression

5. Add this calculation to the view, and you will see the following:

Figure 9.20: Adding exclude LOD to the view

6. Check that the aggregation is set to **Average**. Here, you have excluded the **Customer**-level profit, and have instead grouped it at a higher granular level of **Region**.

7. At a **Region** level, to compute the average profit, you can simply add the profits across the region and divide the sum by the number of records, as follows:

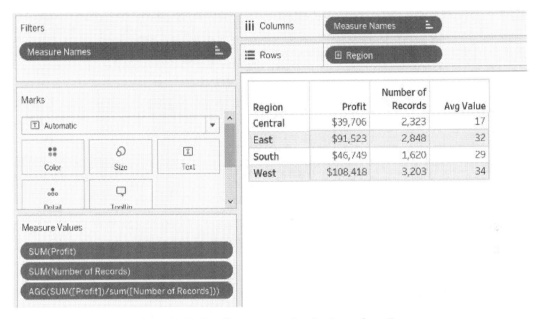

Figure 9.21: Profit computation logic explanation

This kind of calculation comes in useful when wanting to see aggregation at different levels without actually using them in the view. In this exercise, you learned about the **EXCLUDE** LOD calculation type, and how its application can help analyze trends at different levels of dimension. Next, you will learn about the **Table-Scoped** LOD calculation.

TABLE-SCOPED

Tableau provides a way to define an expression without using LOD functions such as **FIXED**, **INCLUDE**, and **EXCLUDE**. The following expression returns the minimum profit for the entire table:

```
Table-Scoped
```

```
{FIXED : MIN([Order Date])}

//similar to fixed with no dimensions
```

Figure 9.22: Table-scoped syntax

The **Table-Scoped** calculation is equivalent to a **FIXED** LOD calculation with no dimension declaration:

Figure 9.23: Comparison to the fixed LOD calculation type

Now you have learned about different LOD calculations, their syntax, and their applications, you can now see how Tableau categorizes LOD calculations and what canges are required in the worksheet view for the LOD calculation to give the right output.

LOD CALCULATIONS: DIMENSIONS OR MEASURES?

In the previous exercises, when calculating LOD calculations, you have always used a measure to give a numerical output. **FIXED** LOD calculations can show results in measures or dimensions, depending on the field used in the expression.

So, **MIN ([Order_Date])}** will be a dimension, because **[Order_Date]** is a dimension, and **{fixed Country: AVG([GDP])}** will be a measure, because **[GDP]** is a measure. In contrast, **INCLUDE** and **EXCLUDE** LOD calculations always show results in measures.

You will now learn how dimensions used in the view affect the LOD calculation's computation.

AGGREGATION AND LOD CALCULATIONS

In previous exercises, you computed **AVG(Profit)** per **Customer** at a **Region** level, but did not include **Customer** in the view. How did Tableau manage that?

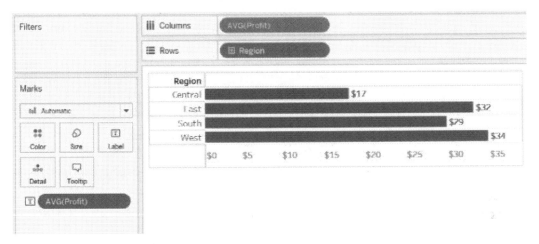

Figure 9.24: Understanding aggregations

The answer lies in how Tableau handles the level of aggregation. In this section, you will learn about the backend computation of LOD calculations in comparison to the LOD in the view in the following scenarios:

- LOD calculation is coarser than the view LOD.

- LOD calculation is finer than the view LOD.

- Nested LOD calculations.

You will now explore each of these in detail.

LOD CALCULATION IS HIGHER THAN THE VIEW LOD

Compared to the view, an expression provides higher-level detail for dimensions. For example, for a view that contains the **Region** and **Customer** dimensions, you can build a LOD calculation that uses only one of these dimensions:

```
{FIXED [Region]: SUM([Profit])}
```

Here, the expression provides a coarser LOD compared to the view. The value of the expression is based on one dimension (`[Region]`), whereas the view bases its view on two dimensions (`[Region]` and `[Customer]`).

The result, is that using the LOD calculation in the view causes certain values to be replicated,that is, to appear multiple times. Observe the measure values of each customer. This is what you saw in the **EXCLUDE** LOD exercise:

Figure 9.25: Similarity to the exclude LOD calculation output

LOD CALCULATION IS FINER THAN THE VIEW LOD

When referencing a superset of dimensions, an expression provides a finer LOD compared to the view. When this is used, Tableau aggregates results up to the view level. For example, the following LOD expression references two dimensions:

```
{FIXED [Region],[Customer]: AVG([Profit])}
```

When this expression is used in a view that has only **Region** as its LOD, the values must be aggregated. Here is what you would see if you dragged that expression to a shelf:

```
AVG([{FIXED [Region]], [Customer]] : AVG([Profit]])}])
```

This is exactly what happened in the **INCLUDE** LOD calculation exercise:

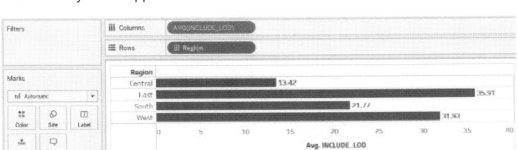

Figure 9.26: Comparing finer views with the include LOD output

When you calculated average profit at the customer level, and the view only had **Region**, all profits were first averaged at the customer level. The result of this was then averaged again at the **Region** level, which was the final output, as shown in the preceding figure.

NESTED LOD CALCULATIONS

In a nested LOD calculation, a LOD expression is used within another LOD expression, as follows:

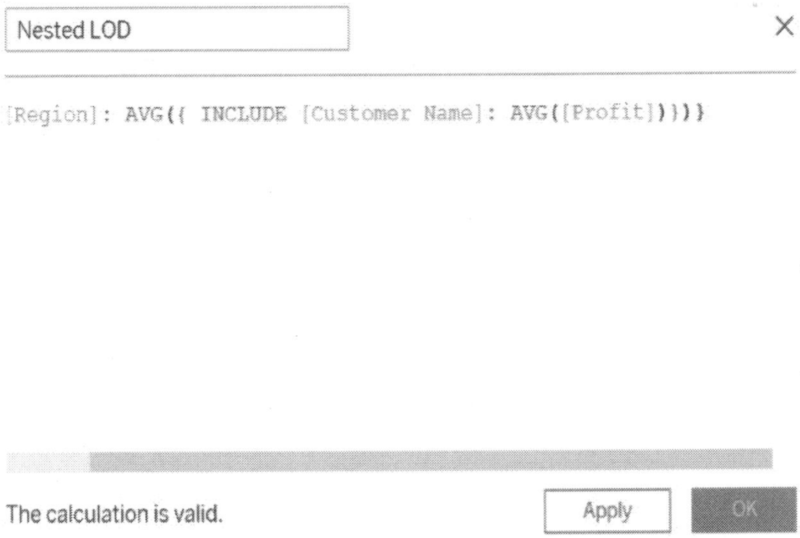

Nested LOD   ✕

```
[Region]: AVG({ INCLUDE [Customer Name]: AVG([Profit])})}
```

The calculation is valid.   Apply   OK

Figure 9.27: Nested LOD syntax

Here, an **INCLUDE** LOD is performed; that is, average profits are computed at the customer level, then this output is again averaged at the **REGION** level in the outer **FIXED** LOD.

When using nested LODs, the inner expression inherits its dimension from the outer expression. This means that you first calculate the average of the inner LOD, but also keep the level **Fixed** for **Region**. The output generated is as follows:

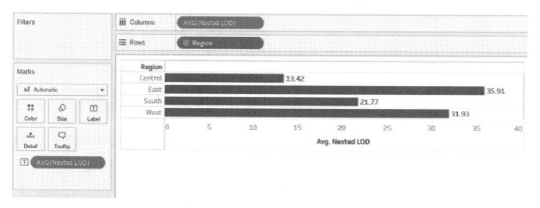

Figure 9.28: Nested LOD output

Can you identify which computation matches this result? It is the **INCLUDE** LOD calculation.

Nested LODs currently have limited use in a worksheet (depending on the complexity required), but are a powerful concept in Tableau.

Now you have familiarized yourself with the inner workings of LOD calculations, it is time to learn how different components within a workbook can affect the LOD calculation output. You will learn about filter applications, and some limitations of LOD calculations.

EFFECTS OF FILTERS ON LOD CALCULATIONS

There are different kinds of filters in Tableau. Since LOD calculations modify the aggregation levels based on the view, the filters applied in the view are executed based on the kind of LOD calculation applied. The following chart describes how filters are executed in the view:

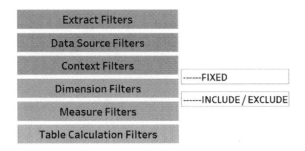

Figure 9.29: Order of filter execution

These are defined in greater detail below:

- **Extract Filters**: Extract filters are applied when you extract the data, as highlighted in the following figure:

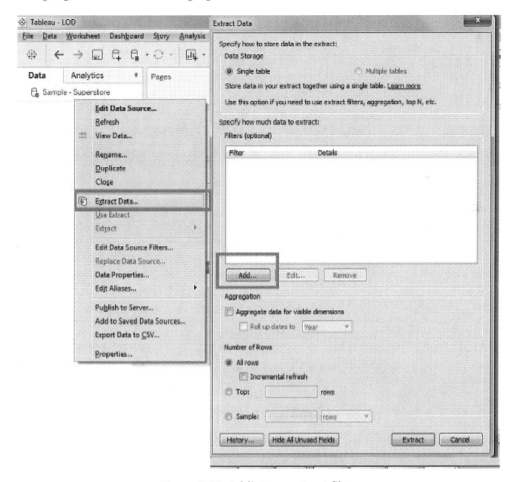

Figure 9.30: Adding an extract filter

Extract filters are executed before LOD calculations.

- **Data Source Filters**: These filters are applied when you add data in the Data Explorer tab, as highlighted in the following figure:

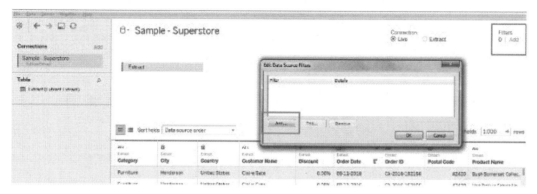

Figure 9.31: Adding a data source filter

Like extract filters, data source filters are applied before the LOD calculations execute.

- **Context filters**: A context filter is an independent filter type that dictates which values will be available in other filters in the view. It creates a data partition, that ensures the next filters are loaded with only the partitioned data, rather than the entire dataset's values. To add a filter on context, click the dropdown and select Add to Context, as follows:

Figure 9.32: Final filter to context

Context filters execute before LOD calculations. As good practice, to ensure that the LOD calculations work properly, make sure you add all filters to **Context**.

- **Dimension filters**: Dimension filters are related to dimensions added to the Filters shelf. Fixed LOD calculations execute before dimension filters. INCLUDE/EXCLUDE LOD calculations execute after dimension filters.

- **Measure and table calculation filters**: These two filters execute after all LOD calculations execute.

Now you have learned about the execution process of LOD calculations, you will also learn about some limitations of them. These are some of the major limitations of LOD calculations:

- Some data sources such as Microsoft Access, Microsoft Jet-based connections (connectors for Microsoft Excel, Microsoft Access, and Cubes) might not support LOD calculations.

- When using LOD calculations with data blending, the linking field from the primary data source must be available in the view before you can use LOD calculations from the secondary data source, or else it might not work.

- LOD calculations are not shown on the Data Explorer tab. Hence, you won't be able to add filters to these LOD calculations.

- When using a parameter inside a LOD calculation, you must reference it by the parameter name, and not by the value, else you may get an incorrect output.

Now you have learned about LOD calculations, it is time to work through some activities that may come up in real-world situations.

ACTIVITY 9.01: IDENTIFYING THE TOP-PERFORMING SALES EXECUTIVES

Imagine you are a data visualizer at the ABC Marketing company, and have been tasked with identifying the top performers in a segment. You have been provided with a dataset containing the details of all sales executives' names, the city and state they work in, and order details for sales, including the order ID and order date.

> **NOTE**
>
> You can find the dataset used for this activity in the GitHub repository for this chapter at https://packt.link/v7C3u.

To complete this activity, you must identify the sales representatives who have the highest sales values in each city. This activity serves to strengthen your knowledge of LOD calculations, and will give you the chance to apply what you have learned to real-world use cases.

The following steps will help you complete this activity:

1. Open the dataset in your Tableau instance.

2. The data should consist of **Order ID**, **Order Date**, the name of the sales executives, **State**, **City**, and the number of sales. You need to identify the top sales executives in each city using a **FIXED** LOD calculation.

3. Create a view consisting of **State**, **City**, **Sales Executive**, **Order ID**, and **SUM(Sales)**. Use the sorting option to sort this in descending order of **SUM(Sales)**. This view gives you an overall picture of the sales in different cities, along with order IDs, and the sales executive who sold that order.

4. Identify the sales executives who sold the order with the highest sale amount. To do this, create a **FIXED** LOD calculation to identify orders with the maximum sales value per city and state.

5. Once you have the maximum sales value, write another calculation to identify the sales executive who sold this order, using the preceding LOD calculation. Then, use this as a filter to show only the sales executives with the maximum sales value in the view. The final output should list all states and cities, along with the sales executive's name and sales amount.

   The initial view will look like the following:

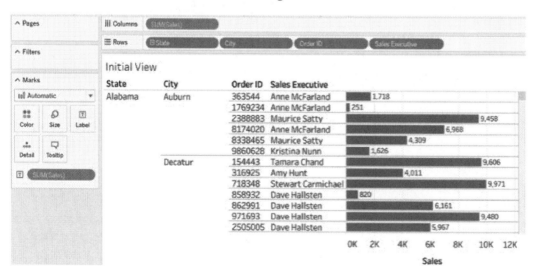

Figure 9.33: Activity 1 initial view

The final output will look like the following:

Figure 9.34: Activity 1 final view

In this activity, you identified the top sales performers using a **FIXED** LOD calculation. This activity emulates a real-world application, where you are required to identify top-performing instances in categories, such as top-selling products. By changing the dimensions in the LOD expression, you can change the way the view gets computed, thus reusing the same concept across various dimensions in the data.

> **NOTE**
>
> The solution to this activity can be found here: https://packt.link/CTCxk.

ACTIVITY 9.02: PERFORMING A COMPARATIVE ANALYSIS

Another common use case in any data visualization project, is to show comparisons based on parameters between different dimensions. For example, in a fast-food chain, some products sell more than others. By identifying such patterns, you can further analyze the reason for those sales, and strategize accordingly. This could mean introducing new products based on the best-selling ones, creating combo offers, etc. In the following activity, you will work on the food item dataset. You will perform a comparison between the cooking times for the various food items.

This activity serves to strengthen your knowledge of LOD calculations using comparative analysis. Before starting the activity, you must first understand the data. The data contains information about the food items such as name, diet (**veg** or **non-veg**), **cook_time**, flavor type (which contains sweet, sour, spicy, or bitter), and course type (such as starter, snack, main course, or dessert).

> **NOTE**
>
> You can find the dataset to be used for this activity at https://packt.link/le1Ta.

Follow these steps to complete the activity:

1. Open the dataset for this activity in your Tableau instance.

2. The data consists of the food dish name, diet, cook time, flavor type, and course type. Here, you need to compare the cooking time for different dishes. For this activity, you will only compare the cooking time for the desserts.

3. Create a view with the dish name and cooking time in a bar chart.

4. Create a parameter selection containing dishes in the dessert category. First, you need to create a calculation to check whether the dish is a dessert. If it is, keep the dish, else it can be discarded. Then, use this calculation as the input to the parameter.

5. Create an **EXCLUDE** LOD calculation to keep only the cooking time for the selected dish. If no dish is selected, the cooking time should be **0**. By doing this, you are creating a baseline with which to compare the other dishes' cooking times.

6. Create another calculation that gives the difference of cooking time of all other dishes compared to the selected dish. This calculation shows whether other dishes cook faster (or not) than the selected dish.

7. Add this calculation to the initial view. Now you can easily compare the cooking times of the selected dish against all the other dishes in the dataset.

The initial view will look like the following:

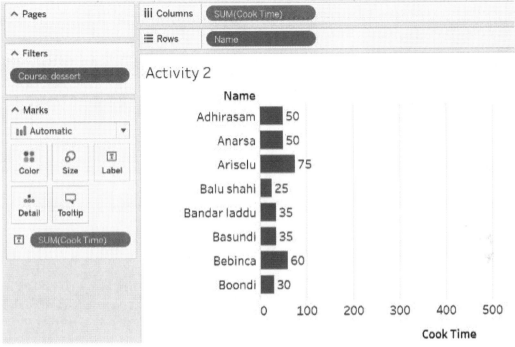

Figure 9.35: Activity 2 initial view

The final output should look like the following:

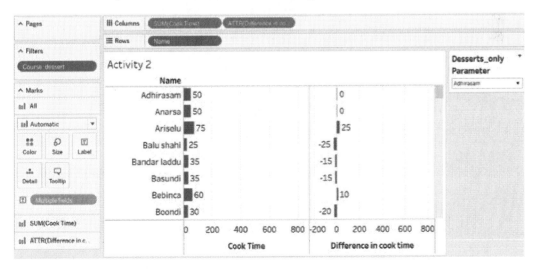

Figure 9.36: Activity 2 final view

In this activity, you compared the cooking time of various dishes using the **EXCLUDE** LOD calculation. This activity acts as a reference point to learn about real-world applications, where it is required to compare categories based on the various measure values associated with them.

> **NOTE**
>
> The solution to this activity can be found here: https://packt.link/CTCxk.

SUMMARY

In this chapter, you learned about the different types of LOD calculations. You learned how LOD calculations are executed internally, and saw how different components used in the view, such as filters, are executed, and how these affect the LOD calculation output.

The key benefit of LOD calculations is that they allow you to control aggregation levels in data without adding or removing components in the view. This can help identify trends at different levels of granularity within your dataset.

LOD calculations greatly enhance data analysis, and allow analysts to control the granularity of analysis or visualization. In the next chapter, you will combine all you have learned so far, and will begin to create storyboards and dashboards in Tableau.

10

DASHBOARDS AND STORYBOARDS

OVERVIEW

This chapter will teach you the processes for building Tableau dashboards and storyboards. You will learn about tools such as tiled versus floating objects, branding elements, and filter actions, as well as adding web pages to the dashboards. By the end of this chapter, you will be able to use these objects/elements to create highly interactive dashboards, communicate results, and create stories, providing important insights to end users. These are essential tools for every Tableau analyst and designer.

INTRODUCTION

Thus far, you have developed many core Tableau skills, including creating calculations, building and using filters, developing geospatial analyses, and many other core skills. In this chapter, you will use many of these skills to create dashboards that will enable your users to easily and effectively navigate complex datasets.

We will provide you with the essential skills for designing effective dashboards and storyboards using a variety of data sources. You will build on the many techniques and methods you have learned in previous chapters. You will learn how to effectively use filters, parameters, sets, and actions to make your dashboards and storyboards both powerful and flexible. Additionally, you will learn how to effectively design dashboards using data visualization best practices for color, spacing, interaction, design flow, and element sizing. All of this will be facilitated with hands-on exercises and activities.

By the end of the chapter, you will be well positioned to design highly effective, well-designed dashboards and storyboards to answer essential business questions.

THE WHO, WHAT, AND WHY OF THE DASHBOARD

Before you begin exploring how to best create dashboards in Tableau, it is equally important for you to answer some of the essential questions around building the dashboard: Why are you building the dashboard in the first place? What is your end goal and who is your target audience?

THE WHO: AUDIENCE

After years of building dashboards, one thing that most experienced Tableau users will agree upon is the fact that the kind of dashboard you build will depend on the seniority of the stakeholder that you'll be presenting it to. If you are building a dashboard for C-level execs or directors/VPs of the business, more often than not, you will need to create a holistic, high-level dashboard that presents a complete picture of the business data. By way of contrast, when you are building a dashboard for a business development manager or marketing manager, the dashboard needs to be a lot more granular and deeply detailed.

As you will see later in the section, the overall anatomy of the dashboard remains almost the same, but the granularity, as well as giving the end user the ability to "peel the onion" or dig deeper into the data, is what differentiates the target audience. Hence, before you start building the dashboard, it is important to narrow down your audience, consider their requests, and then start the process of framing the dashboard.

THE WHAT: BEGIN WITH THE END IN MIND

The next step in building the dashboard is to understand the end goal of the dashboard you are building. If you can answer these questions with relative ease, you already have a head start in the dashboard building process. Consider the following points before you start building your dashboard:

- Do you know how your audience will use this dashboard?

- Is there a specific point you want your audience to understand by looking at the dashboard?

- What are all the stakeholder questions your dashboard might have answers to?

- Does the dashboard provide contextual knowledge instead of just metrics?

Once you answer these questions, you should have a good end goal of what the absolute minimum your dashboard should have. After that, it is all about placing all the relevant worksheets and elements/objects in the dashboard for easy consumption of the data you want to share.

THE WHY: THE NEED FOR A DASHBOARD

The final question you should be asking is Why is the dashboard required in the first place? You can break that question down into multiple pieces as follows:

- What area of business is the dashboard concerned with? For example, a dashboard intended for the finance department would look different from the one for the digital marketing team.

- What kind of information/metrics does the end user want from the dashboard?

Once you've answered these questions, the process of building a dashboard will become a lot smoother, as you know the context for requesting this dashboard as well as how the dashboard will eventually be used.

DESIGNING A DASHBOARD

Dashboard design is one aspect of Tableau that is a bit subjective and relies on the design and visual skills of the dashboard designer. In this sense, there isn't a single correct end result, but there are general design principles that will make your dashboard easier to interpret and ultimately more useful. In this section, you will incorporate those principles within the Tableau framework to create an attractive dashboard that makes it easy for the end user to understand the underlying data.

Before you start on your dashboard design path, there are a few questions you should ask yourself and your users. These questions will help to guide you as you create the many elements that will eventually be used to populate the dashboard. Here are some potential questions:

- What are the critical metrics you should be measuring?

- How granular should your measurements be? Are you looking at data for hourly, daily, weekly, monthly, or annual intervals?

- Does location matter?

- Should you be aggregating the data to provide more useful insights?

- How much historical data do you need? Are historical trends pertinent to data analysis?

There are undoubtedly many more questions depending on the environment in which the business organization operates. Regardless of the specific questions, as a dashboard designer, you should have a sense of what's important to your end user and be able to prioritize and rank all the essential data. Going through this process will help when you start designing the dashboard and laying out the specific elements from most to least important.

Why is it important to design effective dashboards? The reason you spend so much time on building a powerful and easy-to-use dashboard is that it can be leveraged in multiple ways by multiple audiences. Unlike traditional reports often geared to a single metric for a single business unit and delivered on a fixed schedule, a dashboard can be used to engage users across the organization. An effective dashboard with a rich user interface and effective storytelling can serve the needs of many users without the need to create multiple versions of the same report.

In this chapter, you will illustrate effective dashboard principles using a coffee chain dataset that looks at sales, profit, expenses, and other metrics according to the following:

- Market size

- Market

- Product type

- Product

- State

- Area code (store location)

[handwritten: one piece of a dashboard is ~~just a one~~ visual that has multiple visualss inside that]

After a general overview of dashboard concepts, you will use this dataset in creating our dashboard, but before you do that, let's have a look at our finished dashboard so that you understand the end goal you are working toward.

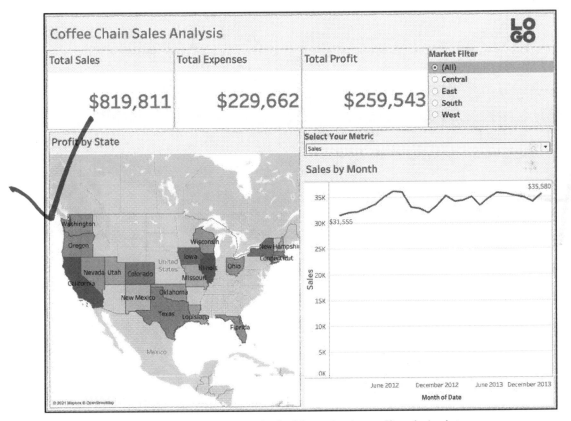

Figure 10.1: An example dashboard using coffee chain data

As you can see, the dashboard takes advantage of many Tableau capabilities, for example, chart types, titles, parameters, and filters. Each component of the dashboard content—the chart, map, and three calculated value panels—uses individual worksheets you have built from your dataset. This enables us to create a dashboard by inserting the selected worksheets and their related parameters, filters, and legends into a dashboard framework. Note also the symmetry in how the elements flow from top to bottom and left to right, with summary values at the top of the page followed by more detailed data as you move from top to bottom. Colors are harmonious and limited throughout, font sizes are consistent at each level, and element sizes within the graphs are minimized so viewers are not distracted by a lot of visual noise. The dashboard is very easy to read and navigate.

Contrast this with the following poorly designed dashboard using the same elements, but not maintaining best design practices.

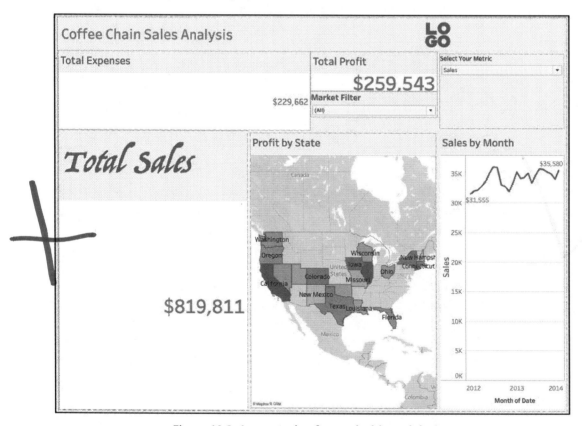

Figure 10.2: An example of poor dashboard design

Even though this version maintains the same top-to-bottom flow, it reveals multiple design flaws that make it more difficult to read while adding no additional value:

- The top level uses different font sizes across the two summary elements.

- The next level uses fonts that are too small to have an impact as well as inconsistent title formats.

- The chart is too small for the size of the dashboard to use it effectively.

This comparison should give you some ideas about the importance of good versus bad designs, and I am pretty sure that, as an analyst, you have probably seen worse dashboard designs, but this should give you some ideas on the importance of consistent and appropriate sizing, text, and color on a dashboard.

Now, let's move on to an overview of the design principles to follow for the creation of an effective and attractive dashboard.

THE BASIC LAYOUT

A Tableau dashboard is simple in concept; however, it can be challenging for new users to implement. Even experienced users find dashboard designing to be one of the more challenging aspects of Tableau. Designing a Tableau dashboard is not simply a matter of dropping elements on a canvas, shifting, and resizing them to fit perfectly on a page. Instead, you need to use a combination of objects, such as textboxes, images, horizontal/vertical objects, and web page objects (we'll often use the term containers) populated by worksheets you have created previously, combined with images, text, and other related elements. While there is a bit of a learning curve, the result is the ability to create dynamic, attractive dashboards filled with information and insights for our users.

In the design process, you can combine the best data visualization practices for spacing, sizing, layout, color, and user interaction with the many tools provided by Tableau to create powerful and intuitive dashboards. A helpful source for best practices can be found here: https://www.tableau.com/learn/articles/data-visualization-tips. In this section, you will first cover some best practices before moving on to using specific Tableau dashboard objects to display your information. Let's begin with general design practices.

DISPLAY SIZE

One of the first steps when designing a dashboard is to understand who the users are and how they will typically view the dashboard. You should understand whether our users will be working from a desktop machine, a laptop, tablet, or another mobile device. Think of display sizes as the size of the canvas that you have to decide on when building the dashboard; you should adapt your display size based on the expected use case of the dashboards – either on a laptop, desktop, or mobile device. If users have oversized monitors, you can potentially increase the size of individual items within the dashboard for better readability. Fortunately, recent versions of Tableau enable the designer to view a dashboard in multiple end user formats – you can see how your dashboard appears to both a laptop user as well as someone viewing from a mobile device.

POSITIONING

Positioning refers to the effective design of a dashboard layout, with related items grouped, and primary metrics given the optimal position on a dashboard (shown below in the next figure) typically at the top of the dashboard. For Western cultures, the flow is from left to right and top to bottom, as though the user is reading a book. To optimize our design, you should therefore place the most important metrics at the top of the page, with secondary measures placed below. Ideally, you can group supporting metrics on the same side of the page as a related primary metric so that the user can easily follow the flow of the dashboard.

This should read "left to right"

Western cultures read right to left.

Here's a general framework for how you want to position content on a page, using your final dashboard:

Figure 10.3: General structure of a dashboard

The idea is to have an informative title at the top of the dashboard while making efficient use of the valuable space on the page. This is typically followed by a section with summary metrics that an executive might be more likely to view. Detailed charts or tables come next; this is the section where regular users will need to be able to filter the data to understand more granular details. Finally, you will generally place your filters to the far right, an area where screen real estate is less valuable – or you can use a sliding panel to hide the filters until they are needed. Always remember that the most valuable visual space in Western culture sits at the top left of the page, so you should avoid cluttering that area with filters, images, logos, or detailed charts.

SPACING

One of the key considerations in dashboard design is to allow adequate whitespace for users. If dashboard elements are crowded together, users will have a difficult time understanding each element, and the overall impact will be less than optimal. Incorporating spacing using the Tableau Blank object (a blank container that gives you the ability to add spacing and/or other visual elements on the dashboard) can make a dashboard easier to read and ultimately more impactful. The Blank object can be found on the Tableau Objects tab adjacent to other elements such as vertical and horizontal objects.

Notice in the preceding example how elements can "breathe;" they do not run into one another or seem crowded at any point. This also helps viewers interpret the flow of the design, as they can easily navigate from top to bottom and left to right without any confusion.

COLORS

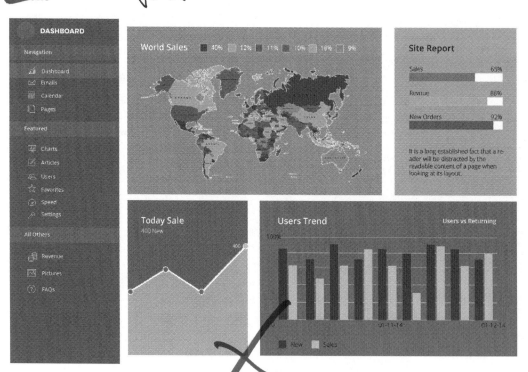

Figure 10.4: An example of a visually unappealing dashboard

As a dashboard designer, you need to resist the temptation to use too many contrasting colors (as pictured above), which can ultimately confuse or mislead the user. The human visual system has limitations on how many colors can be processed at a single time, so dashboards exceeding that level will look visually chaotic and lose their impact. Here are two useful references for working with color: http://www. perceptualedge.com/articles/visual_business_intelligence/rules_for_using_color.pdf and https://colorbrewer2.org. Ideally, our dashboard should use just three to four colors or brand palettes in a consistent fashion, making it easy for users to identify common elements across multiple charts. As we'll see in later examples, Tableau makes it very easy to change colors using one of the many available color schemes.

Our finished dashboard follows this principle by using a single primary color for the summary section, a second main color for the charts, and a consistent color scheme for the two maps. Overall, this provides a harmonious look and feel to the dashboard.

What happens when you try to use too many colors? Here's an example:

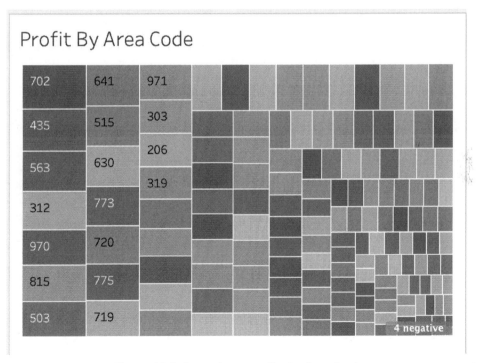

Figure 10.5: Excessive use of color in a chart

You now have a color for every area code in the area chart, but to what end? There are now 100+ colors, many of them repeated three or even four times. Even if you had a color palette with 100 unique colors, many would be difficult to distinguish from similar colors. All you have done is introduce more work for the viewer; instead of focusing solely on the distribution of the data points, the user will spend time attempting to decode what each color represents. It is important to remember that color should be used only when it adds to the story; in the preceding case, you could use five colors to highlight states at a regional level. This might show meaningful patterns without overwhelming the dashboard user, while also utilizing other chart types if possible.

SIZE

Given that dashboards have limited space, proper sizing is critical. Sizing is related to positioning as well; if you strive to size elements consistently, our user will see a natural flow to the dashboard and will focus on content rather than navigation.

Size can be thought of in two ways; the first refers to the size of individual elements (charts, summary numbers, and so on) in a dashboard. In other words, the physical footprint of each element composing a dashboard.

The second use of size refers to how you design individual items within a larger element. For instance, you need to decide how large chart titles will be, as well as labels, bar and line sizes, and other similar attributes. If these items are too large, our dashboard becomes cluttered, and the actual information may become overwhelming. If they are too small, the user may have a difficult time interpreting the information within each dashboard element. You need to strike a balance where information display is maximized and supported by the proper use of titles, labels, and other chart elements. Here are examples involving the proper and improper sizing of marks:

Market Size by Product by Sales

	Market Size				Market Size	
Product	Major Market	Small Market		Product	Major Market	Small Market
Amaretto	·	·		Amaretto	▪	▪
Caffe Latte	·	·		Caffe Latte	▪	▪
Caffe Mocha	·	·		Caffe Mocha	▪	▪
Chamomile	·	·		Chamomile	▪	▪
Colombian	·	·		Colombian	◆	▪
Darjeeling	·	·		Darjeeling	▪	▪
Decaf Espresso	·	·		Decaf Espresso	▪	▪
Decaf Irish Cream	·	·		Decaf Irish Cream	▪	▪
Earl Grey	·	·		Earl Grey	▪	▪
Green Tea	·	·		Green Tea	▪	·
Lemon	·	·		Lemon	▪	▪
Mint	·	·		Mint	▪	▪
Regular Espresso	·	·		Regular Espresso	▪	▪

Figure 10.6: Sizing marks is important for readability

While the marks on the left appear small, remember that they will appear larger when a worksheet is added to a dashboard due to the condensed sizing in a dashboard. The chart on the right already has marks that are so large that the result is the occlusion (overlap) of data points. When placed in a dashboard, these marks will appear even larger due to the reduced space given to the chart. The recommendation here is to make your marks small and then adjust their size once the chart has been added to your dashboard.

TEXT

How you use text in a dashboard is another important consideration. While the proper use of text may seem like a secondary consideration in a dashboard design, you need to recognize that poor use of text elements may discredit the rest of the dashboard. As with color, you want to minimize the number of fonts used, ideally limiting ourselves to two or three fonts per dashboard. Text style should be consistent across all individual chart titles and labels, and you might select a second font for titles or tooltips. The goal is to use a very legible font style and to have text support the information without being overwhelming.

Notice the use of font sizes in our dashboard example previously, and how they are sized consistently within each type of object. Also notice the relative sizes and how larger fonts are used for titles and summary metrics, while filters and legend text are much smaller.

EXERCISE 10.01: TEXT FORMATTING – WORKBOOK VERSUS WORKSHEET

In this exercise, you will review different text formatting options that Tableau offers by using the Sample – Coffee Chain dataset and exploring the formatting pane.

Here is the data download link: https://packt.link/zT15G.

1. Open Tableau and load Sample – Coffee Chain data into your Tableau instance.

2. Format at both a workbook level as well as at the level of individual elements. Navigate to **Format | Workbook** in the menu bar. Here is what you should get:

Figure 10.7: Format workbook options

This allows you to set global options for the workbook that also apply to your dashboard styling, making it a nice way to establish a consistent visual look.

3. Note that it is possible to override these options on any individual sheet or text object by selecting the **Format** menu command. Format an individual worksheet, which is a two-step process – first, right-click in your blank work area and select the **Format** option. This will open a tab to the left of the workspace, which is the second step for editing **Font**, **Alignment**, **Shading**, **Borders**, and **Lines** at the **Sheet**, **Row**, and **Column** levels.

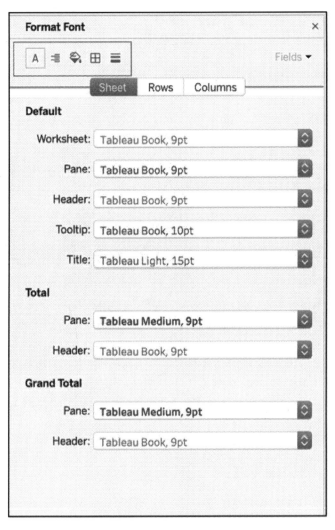

Figure 10.8: Object formatting options

These are the text formatting options at Workbook (complete report/dashboard) as well as Worksheet (individual sheet) level in Tableau. While this exercise was very limited in scope, it should have allowed you to gain some basic familiarity with text formatting before progressing to more complex elements in later sections, including Tableau interactions and objects you will use for your dashboard interaction.

Most dashboards require some level of interaction on the user end. Filters are a common means provided for user interaction, but you can also design using actions, tooltips, and highlighting to make a dashboard come alive. Tableau provides dashboard designers with multiple tools such as tooltips, actions, parameters, and more; the challenge lies in making them fit seamlessly so that they enhance the user experience. Here is a brief summary of these tools:

- Filters allow users to easily reduce or customize data displayed within a dashboard.

- Parameters often work like filters but can be customized by the dashboard designer to limit or direct user interaction.

- Actions are set up at the dashboard level to apply rules based on when and where a user clicks on an element in the dashboard.

- Legends can be used to provide context and allow users to highlight specific data elements.

- Highlighters may be used to show linked data elements across multiple charts or tables.

You want to keep these tools as unobtrusive as possible, leaving the primary canvas space available for the important content. Therefore, you will usually place them on the right side of a dashboard page, or even hide them on a sliding panel so you can maximize display space. You have covered these previous chapters, and this chapter, you will use the same interactive elements in dashboards.

DASHBOARD OBJECTS

Objects are Tableau elements used to build a dashboard and are typically found at the lower left of the dashboard window. You may consider them to be modular pieces that can be combined in endless ways to create a dashboard. Some will be used as containers for previously created Tableau worksheets, while others contain external or newly created content. Most can be used together to build a custom experience for the user. With objects, you can completely customize each dashboard you build.

Now let's consider each object type in detail.

VERTICAL OBJECTS

Vertical objects are frequently used containers designed to display one or more Tableau worksheets within a dashboard. They may be used as a standalone container within a tiled framework, or they may reside inside an existing vertical or horizontal container. In other words, they can be nested multiple times within a single dashboard, although there are practical limits to this approach, as we'll see soon. Vertical objects can also be used as floating containers, where the onscreen positioning is specified by the designer.

Use vertical objects to assist in laying out your dashboard from top to bottom; you can then easily add charts, maps, and other worksheet types inside each vertical container.

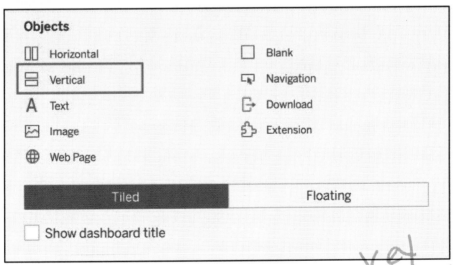

Figure 10.9: Selecting the vertical object

Vertical objects are likely to be the most used object type on many dashboards given their versatility, and their ability to nest multiple containers within a single master object. Our example dashboard uses vertical objects to contain most of our chart content. In most cases, our vertical containers will have a fixed set of coordinates (x, y, width, and height) based on their position within the dashboard, but you can use them as floating containers with a set of coordinates that allow the container to float outside of the dashboard structure. To set the floating option, right-click inside a vertical object and select the **Floating** menu option.

Figure 10.10: Creating a floating object

This will create a small window where you use the **Layout** tab to adjust the coordinates.

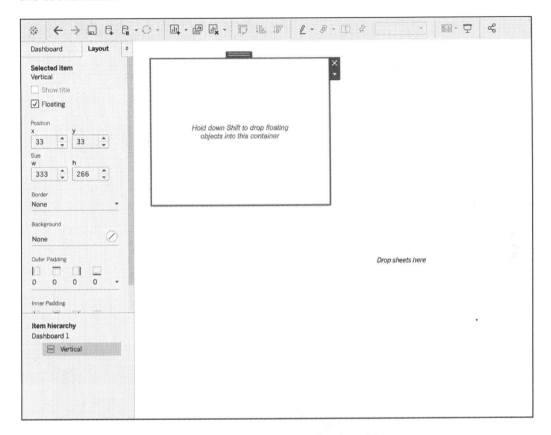

Figure 10.11: Positioning a floating object

Once the **x**, **y**, **w**, and **h** values have been set, the container will reside in that position, regardless of the positioning of the other non-floating objects. Be careful in how you use floating objects so that they do not interfere with the data display in your dashboard.

HORIZONTAL OBJECTS

`Horizontal` objects are frequently used containers designed to display one or more Tableau worksheets within a dashboard. They may be used as a standalone container within a tiled framework, or they may reside inside an existing vertical or horizontal container. As with vertical objects, they can also be used as a floating container, where the onscreen positioning is specified by the designer.

You often use horizontal containers to position dashboard elements from left to right within the dashboard. A typical use case might be to display three separate charts side by side inside of an existing vertical container. When used together, vertical and horizontal objects can help us to design dashboards that are symmetrical and balanced from top to bottom and left to right.

To add a Horizontal object, select the **Horizontal** icon from the **Objects** tab and drag it to the appropriate location in your dashboard.

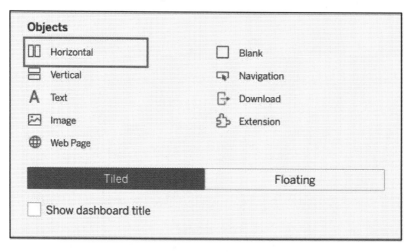

Figure 10.12: Selecting the horizontal object

Horizontal containers are used in much the same way as verticals and can also be nested multiple times. You can think of vertical containers being useful for laying out the north-south flow of the dashboards, with horizontals used for the east-west layout. Most complex dashboards will have both types in operation.

TEXT OBJECTS

Text objects are used primarily for fixed titles and Tableau workbook metadata such as the workbook name or sheet name. Text objects may also use parameters to create flexible titles or text within a dashboard. For example, a date parameter could be used to display the date range selected by a dashboard user.

To add a **Text** object to a dashboard, you again use the **Objects** tab, this time selecting the **Text** icon and dragging it to a specific location within the dashboard.

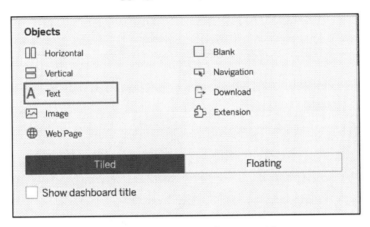

Figure 10.13: Selecting the text object

When a text container is dragged to a dashboard canvas, you will see the following (we've added some sample text here):

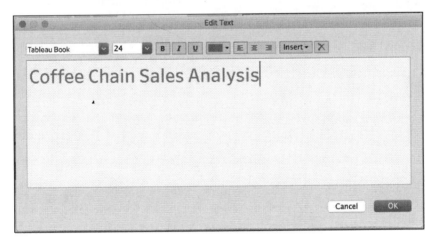

Figure 10.14: Viewing the text window

As you can see, the text can be fully styled by selecting a specific font, font size, style, and alignment from the menu bar in the text object window. These qualities make text objects more powerful than they first appear, as you can use them to customize our dashboards with additional notation or titles that are not bound to specific charts or other dashboard elements.

IMAGE OBJECTS

Image objects can be used to display nearly any popular image format within a dashboard. This is an easy way to insert logos, marketing materials, or other relevant visual content. Both local and web-based images can be inserted anywhere on a dashboard.

To add an image to a dashboard, go to the **Objects** tab and drag the **Image** icon to a spot in the dashboard.

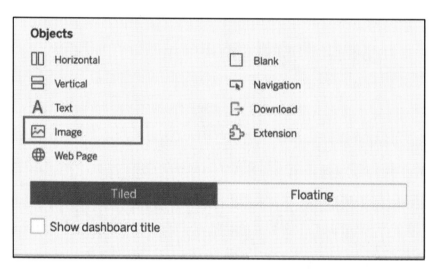

Figure 10.15: Selecting the image object

When an image container is dragged to a dashboard canvas, you will see the following:

Figure 10.16: Editing an image object

You may select a local image file by clicking the **Choose** button, or you can use a URL address to provide an image to the dashboard. In either case, it is possible to both fit and center the image inside the container to ensure it works well with the look and feel of the dashboard. Images can be used to display corporate logos, marketing slogans, or other relevant visuals.

WEB PAGE OBJECTS

A web page object makes it very easy to display web content y entering a URL address. This can be useful for displaying external content such as a landing page for a product or marketing campaign side by side with metrics from the page.

Once again, you navigate to the **Objects** tab to select the **Web Page** option, which can then be dropped inside the dashboard container.

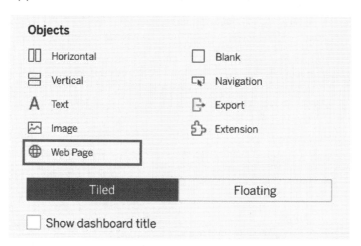

Figure 10.17: Selecting the web page object

When a web page container is dragged to a dashboard canvas, you will see the following:

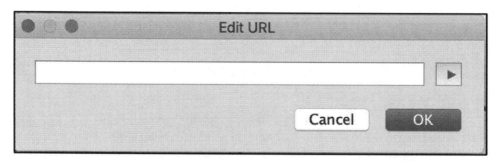

Figure 10.18: The URL window for a web object

Simply enter the URL link and your dashboard will have an embedded web page. This feature should be used with care, given the limited available space on a dashboard.

BLANK OBJECTS

Blank objects are used to create spacing within a dashboard, either between objects or around the margins. They prove highly useful for creating a dashboard where the individual elements can "breathe" due to the empty space surrounding them. This often has a positive impact on the readability of a dashboard. Blank objects are also useful for centering legends and helping to align margins between the chart elements.

To add a blank object, navigate to the **Objects** menu and drag the **Blank** icon to the dashboard container, typically placing it between charts or around the edges of the dashboard to improve spacing and readability.

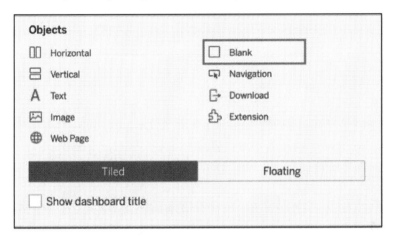

Figure 10.19: Selecting the blank object

In many cases, blank objects will have a fixed minimum width or height, depending on where they are inserted. Tableau defaults to 32 px, and this is the normal minimum whenever you drag an object onto the canvas, which turns out to be a nice size for providing space between elements on a dashboard. There are instances where you have full control over their width or height, depending on how they are used inside or between other objects. Blanks can be a bit tricky to use, so be patient and recognize the benefit they add to the appearance of your dashboard.

NAVIGATION OBJECTS

The navigation/button (Tableau 2020.3 and older) object is a recent addition to Tableau and can be used to facilitate easy navigation from the dashboard to another sheet or dashboard within the same workbook, or even to an external resource. Text or images may be used, allowing for a customizable experience using a logo or tagline. Note that this feature was first available in Tableau 2018.3; earlier versions will not have the `Button` object. You can find the Navigation/Button object icon on the `Objects` tab; drag it to your chosen location in the dashboard.

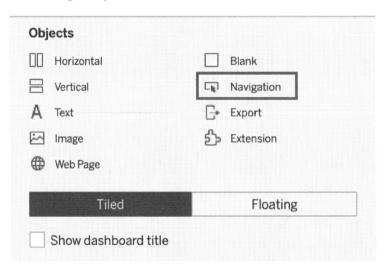

Figure 10.20: Selecting the button object

When a button container is dragged to a dashboard canvas, you will initially see a large arrow, but after selecting the `Edit Button` option, here's what appears:

Figure 10.21: Editing a Button object

This option can be a great way to customize a dashboard using carefully selected imagery and can also display a helpful tooltip to guide the dashboard user. You can also change the button image to add more design elements to your dashboard.

EXTENSION OBJECT

Extension objects are used to increase the functionality of a dashboard with third-party applications developed for Tableau. Note that many of these extensions will incur an additional cost based on the number of users and the duration of the license.

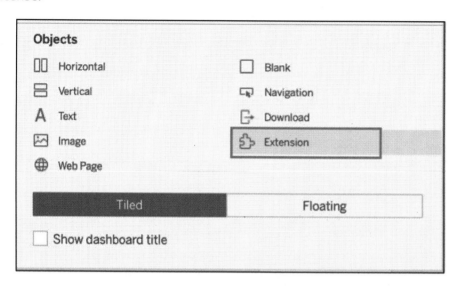

Figure 10.22: Selecting the extension object

You won't cover extensions in detail here, but they are worth exploring to find functionality that may prove beneficial for your dashboard. Many help integrate Tableau with data science functionality, while others extend Tableau data display options, enable geospatial integration, or allow custom scripting. More information can be found here: https://help.tableau.com/current/pro/desktop/en-us/dashboard_extensions.htm.

USING FLOATING OBJECTS

Before moving on, we'll briefly revisit the floating option for objects. In most cases, you will opt for the default tiled selection, but there are some use cases where floating containers make sense. Here are two potential use cases:

- Perhaps you wish to overlay some content in a specific location on the dashboard. While this can often be done using the traditional tiled approach, a floating container gives us complete positioning flexibility. You can set the x and y locations and specify the exact width and height of the object. This can also be useful for button objects, as you can place them discreetly in small sections of unused display space.

- You can also use floating containers (vertical or horizontal floating objects) to embed charts that can be controlled by a user through a parameter. This is useful in cases where you have more charts than a dashboard can reasonably hold. You can display the primary charts in a tiled format, and then leave some space for displaying a single chart based on a user selection. Each chart will have the same x-y coordinates and width and height attributes, so they are essentially stacked. However, only one can be displayed at any time, based on a parameter.

Take some time to explore the floating option, even though you might only use it sparingly. It has been valuable for each of the use cases above and many other such use cases.

EXERCISE 10.02: KPIS AND METRICS VIEW

You are the supply chain analyst of a coffee chain company, and you are required to build a high-level dashboard for the lead executive who wants to get a holistic view of sales, profit, and expenses by market and state, as well as understand the trends over the last 2 years.

You will now create three Scorecard worksheets, one line chart for each metric in a view, as well as a Profit by State geographical view. You will also add parameter metrics swapping, which you learned in the previous chapter, and use Filter Dashboard actions to filter the dashboard based on the state selected from the map view.

Worksheet 1-3: Total Sales and Other KPIs Worksheet View:

1. Open Tableau and load **Sample – Coffee Chain** data into your Tableau instance.

2. Create a new worksheet once the data has been loaded. Drag **Sales** to the **Text** marks card, as shown:

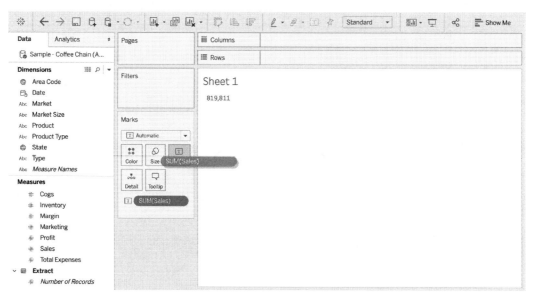

Figure 10.23: Dragging a measure to the Marks card

3. Now that the total sale is shown as text, format the text to make it look more like the scorecard you want. Right-click on **SUM(Sales)** under the **Marks** card and click on **FORMAT**, as shown:

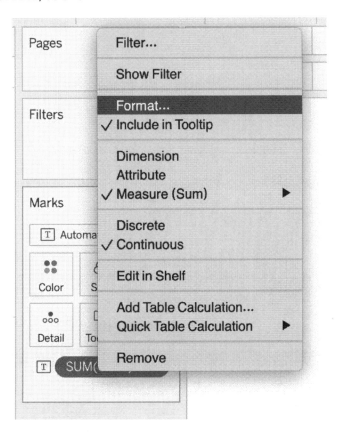

Figure 10.24: Formatting the measure

4. Change the font size to 28, the text format to bold, and use the color of your choice. The following screenshot will show what this would look like if you had opted for green:

Figure 10.25: Changing font sizes and color

5. Add a **$** currency sign to your KPI as you are talking about **Total Sales** in dollars. Right-click on **SUM(Sales)** under the **Marks** card to format the table and, in the format box, click on **Currency (Custom)** to add a $ sign, as shown:

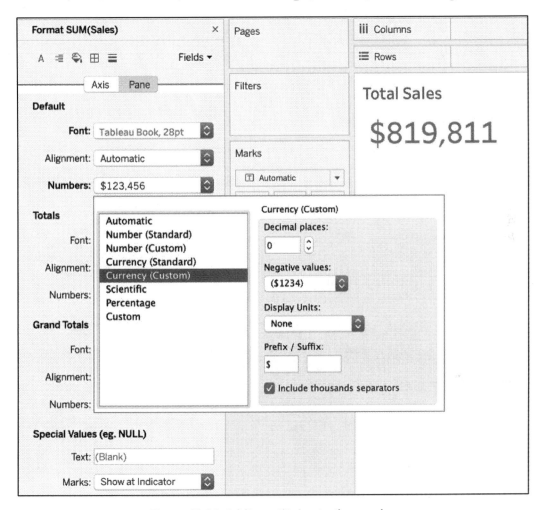

Figure 10.26: Adding a '$' sign to the number

6. Update the title from **Sheet 1** to **Total Sales** by double-clicking on the title, as shown here:

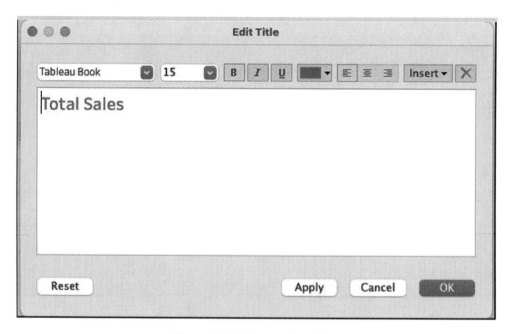

Figure 10.27: Formatting title

7. Since you will be creating a couple more similar worksheets, rename the worksheet to a more descriptive name, such as **Sales KPI** or something similar.

8. Duplicate the same worksheet and follow the same preceding steps to create Expenses KPI and Profit KPI worksheets, as shown here:

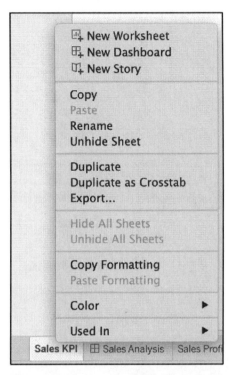

Figure 10.28: How to duplicate a sheet

9. The Profit KPI and Expenses KPI worksheets should look like the following screenshots:

Figure 10.29: Two other scorecard worksheets

In this exercise, you created Scorecard-driven KPI designs and individually formatted the KPIs to reflect the overall formatting of the dashboard you are in the process of creating (*Figure 10.3*). In the next section, you will create a couple of worksheets, including maps and a dynamic measure-switching worksheet with parameters.

EXERCISE 10.03: MAP AND PARAMETER WORKSHEET VIEWS

In this exercise, you will continue with the preceding example and create a couple more worksheets, including map view and parameter metric selection view worksheets.

Worksheet 4: Map Worksheet View:

1. Continuing from the previous exercise, now that you have created the KPI view, create a couple more granular worksheets. One of these will involve creating a map view by states and color them by total profits, while the second worksheet will utilize parameters to give end users the ability to select their own metric view from the options given in the **Parameter** dropdown. Open Tableau and load the **Sample – Coffee Chain** dataset if you closed the workbook previously.

2. Create a new sheet and double-click on **State** to create a map.

3. If the following view is not created automatically, select the **Marks** dropdown and switch **Automatic** to **Map**:

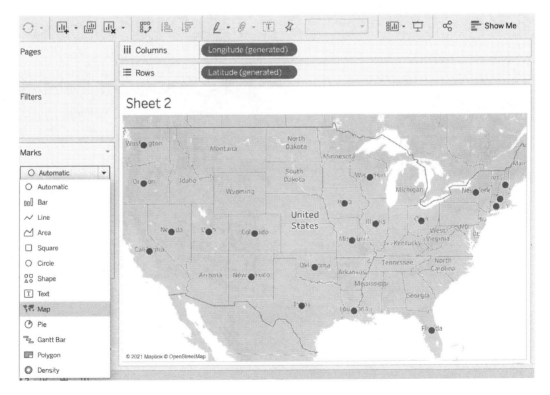

Figure 10.30: Converting the geo dimensions to a map

> **NOTE**
>
> For *Step 4*, your default view for maps may not be United States if you are not from the United States. To change the default country to United States, go to **Map** under **Menus** and click on **Edit Locations** and change your country to **United States**.

4. Drag **Profit** to the **Color** marks card and **State** to the **Label** marks card, as shown here:

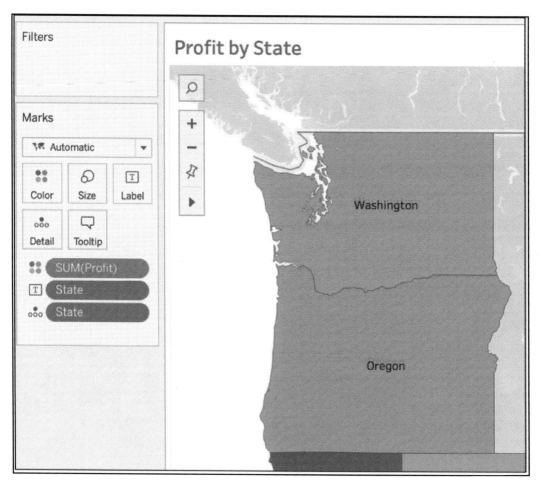

Figure 10.31: Filling the map by SUM(Profit)

Worksheet 5: Parameter Metric Selection Worksheet:

In the previous chapter, you created a similar parameter metric selection worksheet. You are going to create a similar worksheet here, wherein you will give end users the ability to select the metric the lead executive wants to view in the line chart/ trend chart.

1. Create a parameter by right-clicking on the data pane and selecting **Create Parameter**, name it **Select Your Metric**, and keep the data type as **String** and **Allowable values** as **List**, as shown here:

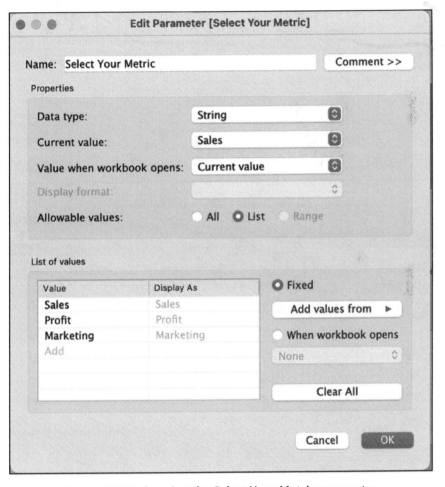

Figure 10.32: Creating the Select Your Metric parameter

2. To use the **Parameter selection** dropdown, use this parameter in a calculated field using an **IF ELSE** or **CASE WHEN** statement. Here, you'll use the **CASE WHEN** calculated field to display appropriate measures depending on the parameter that will be selected by your dashboard user from the **[Parameters].[Select Your Metric]** parameter you created previously. Now, create a calculated field by right-clicking on the data pane and using the following formula, where you are creating a **LOGICAL CASE** statement that, when **Sales** is selected as the parameter, will show **SUM(Sales)**, then do the same for **Profit** and **Marketing**.

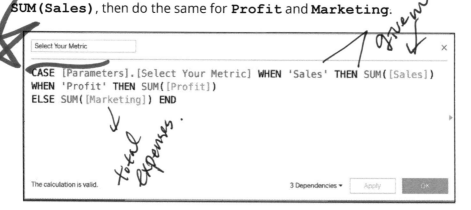

Figure 10.33: The Select Your Metric calculated field

3. Now, use these calculated fields and parameters in your new worksheet. Create a new worksheet and drag **MONTH(Date)** to the **Columns** shelf and the **AGG(Select Your Metric)** calculated field to the **Rows** shelf, as shown here:

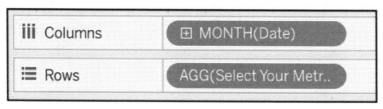

Figure 10.34: Adding date and select your metric calculated fields to the view

4. If your date dimension is a blue pill or a discrete dimension, right-click on the dimension and select **Continuous** from the dropdown.

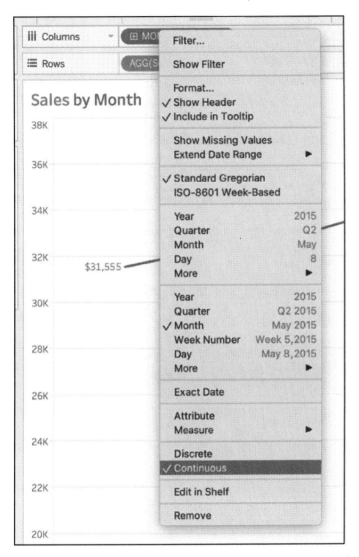

Figure 10.35: Changing the date to a continuous date

5. Next, show your parameter in the worksheet. For that, right-click on the **Select Your Metric** parameter in the data pane and click on **Show Parameter** as follows:

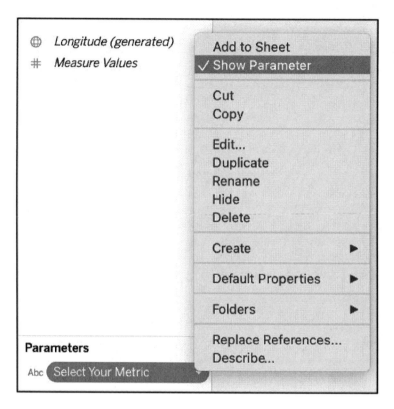

Figure 10.36: Show parameter

6. To make the worksheet more descriptive, use dynamic titles. Double-click on **Title** and either click on the **Insert** dropdown on the right and select **Parameters.Select Your Metric** or type the exact text, as shown here:

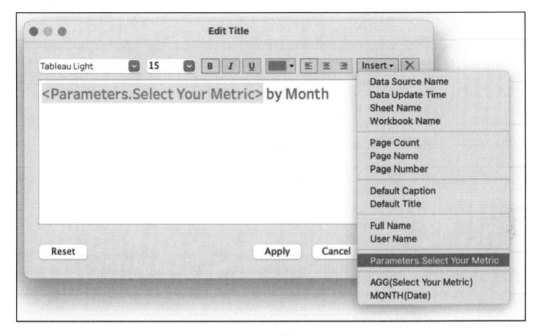

Figure 10.37: Inserting a parameter value into the title to make a dynamic title

7. Finally, add the **Select Your Metric** calculated field under **Label**. Click on the **Label** marks card and show **Select Your Metric** under **Line Ends**, as shown here:

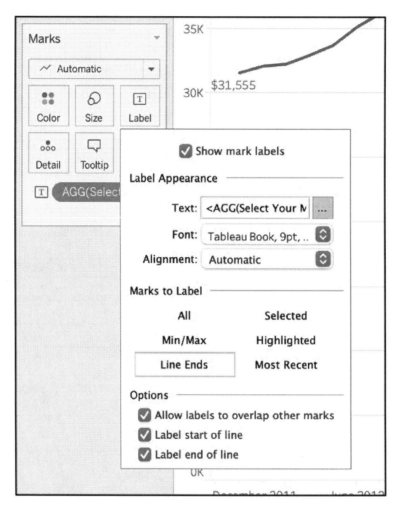

Figure 10.38: Showing labels only on line ends

The following screenshot shows what your final parameter metric selection sheet should look like:

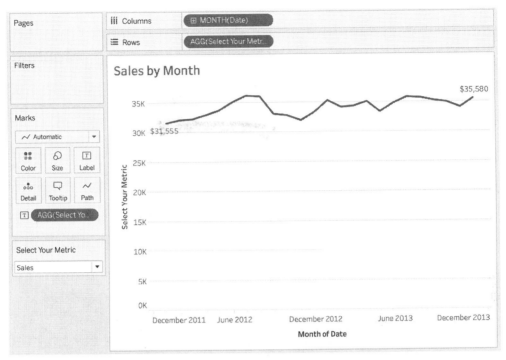

Figure 10.39: Trend analysis according to the metric selected

8. In your final dashboard, you also have a **Market** filter on your dashboard. Add that as a filter to this view and apply it to all worksheets using this data source, as shown here:

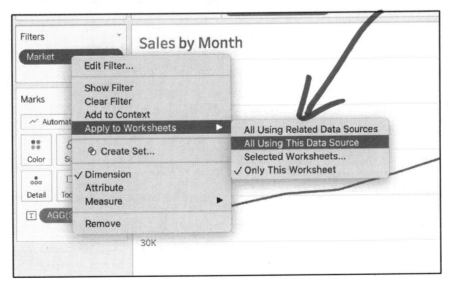

Figure 10.40: Applying the filter to all worksheets using this data source

This just about wraps up this section of creating individual worksheets. In the following exercise, you will start adding these worksheets to your Dashboard view, including additional elements to the dashboard, such as interactivity with the **Select to Filter State** dashboard action, dropdowns to filter the view, and adding your own branding elements.

EXERCISE 10.04: PUTTING IT ALL TOGETHER: DASHBOARDING

In previous exercises, you created all the required worksheets that you wanted for your dashboard. Now it's time to put all of them on the same canvas called **Dashboard** and format it accordingly.

Perform the following steps to complete this exercise:

1. Create the dashboard by clicking on the second icon at the bottom or navigating to **Dashboard** at the top menu bar and selecting **New Dashboard** as follows:

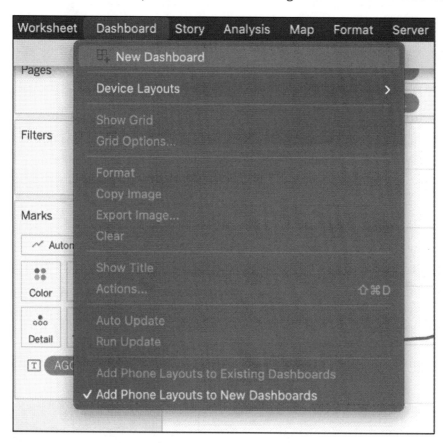

Figure 10.41: Creating a new dashboard

2. To create a dashboard, first select the size of the canvas/dashboard. It's recommended that you have a canvas with a width of at least 1000 and a height of 800 as most laptops and desktops are at least that size. Select **Desktop Browser 1000X800** as the canvas size but feel free to select the size that best suits your laptop/desktop.

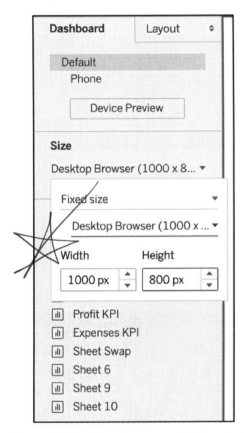

Figure 10.42: Choosing your dashboard size

Stick with tiled objects for the majority of the dashboard, unless you are in a situation where you need to add an object on top of another object or maintain a specific position for an object, which is not possible with Tiled objects. However, using tiled objects/canvases does allow you to control a lot of your objects and floating objects adapt to your screen size.

But before you start adding your worksheet to the view, it would be useful to start with a **Vertical** floating object overlayed by a **Blank** tiled object as it makes it relatively easy to place objects later, and the **Blank** objects also give you the buffer to place objects on the dashboard without moving other objects or messing up the dashboard altogether.

3. Drag a **Vertical** floating object to the canvas first, then change the position of the **Vertical** object to be **0 on X axis** and **0 on Y axis** and change the width and height to the size of the canvas. Also, add a thick border so that when you add a tiled **Blank** object on top of the **Vertical** object, you can differentiate between these objects, as well as adding a light green background to create the white and green contrast.

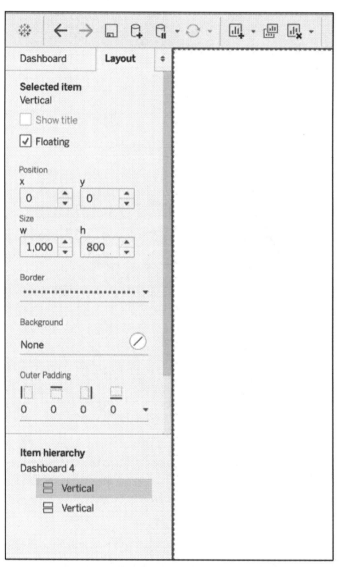

Figure 10.43: Formatting the vertical object, including position and size changes

[Handwritten annotation: Vertical assists in laying out the dashboard from top to bottom.]

NOTE

Vertical and horizontal objects are not required to create a dashboard, although they will make it much easier to build more detailed views. If you don't specify vertical and horizontal tabs in your design, Tableau will automatically arrange items in a Tiled hierarchy, unless you specify the object as floating.

[Handwritten annotation: Horizontal positions elements from left to right.]

4. Click on the **Tiles** section now and drag a **Blank** object to the view and add a thin line border as well as an outer padding of **15** to create spacing between objects.

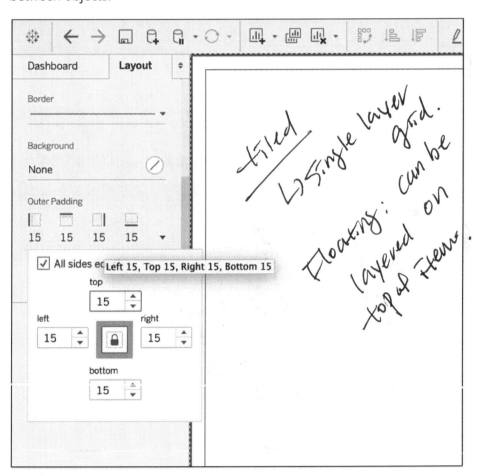

[Handwritten annotation: Tiled → Single layer grid. Floating: can be layered on top of them.]

Figure 10.44: Adding padding for differentiation

5. Now that the base is created, create your *Header and Branding* section. Your header is split into two sections: `Title` and `Logo`. To create these two sections, drag a tiled `Horizontal` object to the top of the view, add a border, place a `Text` object to the left of this newly created horizontal section, and name your dashboard `Coffee Chain Sales Analysis`, as shown in the following screenshot:

Figure 10.45: Adding a custom title to the dashboard

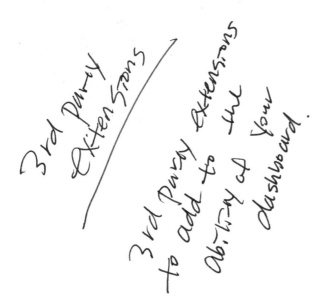

6. Next, to add a logo to your view, use a tiled **Image** object, place it to the right of the **Title** object, and select your desired logo, as shown here:

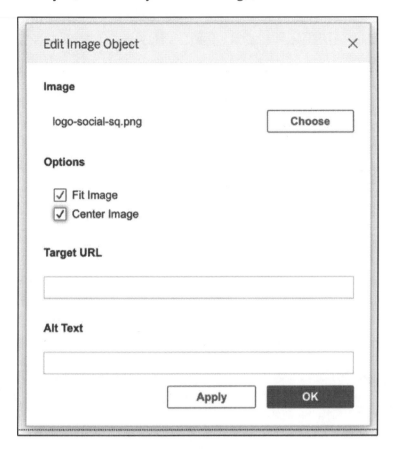

Figure 10.46: Adding a custom logo as a branding element

7. If the logo you've added is too big, you can double-click the double line at the top (see arrow). Select the parent layout containers and resize the window from the bottom.

Figure 10.47: Double-clicking on the double line selects the parent container

8. Now that the header section is ready, drag your Scorecards/KPI worksheets onto the view. But before that, you need to divide/create two sections for scorecards and charts later. Drag a tiled **Vertical** object right below the header section to create two sections for your use case.

> **NOTE**
>
> You have added red borders for descriptive and visibility purposes only. You will delete the border before finalizing the dashboard.

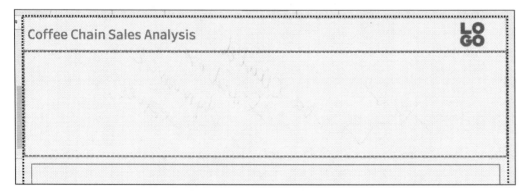

Figure 10.48: Scorecard section creation

9. First, drag the Sales KPI scorecard to the section, and then add the Profit KPI and Expenses KPI scorecards to the right, as shown here:

Figure 10.49: Adding scorecards to the view

10. But there is an issue with the scorecards above; there is too much whitespace remaining on the right. To fix that, select the parent container by double-clicking the double line, clicking on the **Options** dropdown, and selecting `Distribute Contents Evenly`.

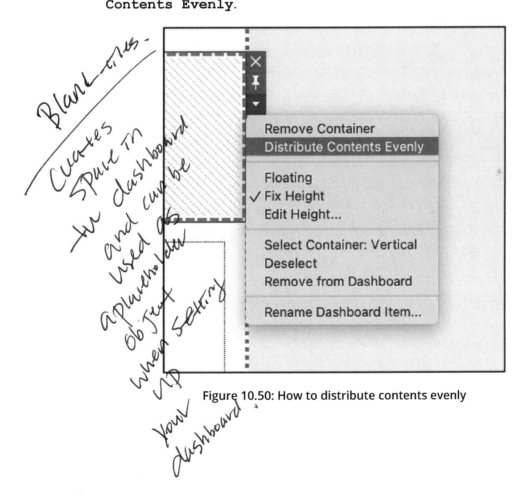

Figure 10.50: How to distribute contents evenly

11. There is still a lot more whitespace left in each of the scorecards, as seen in *Figure 10.50*. To fix that, click on the individual worksheet dropdown again and select **Fit** -> **Entire view**, as shown here:

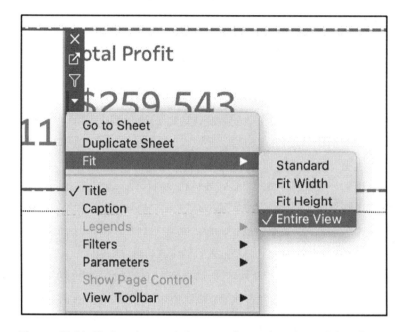

Figure 10.51: Fitting the worksheet to the entire view of the object

12. Lastly, for this scorecard section, add a thin border line to help us differentiate between the KPI sheets, as shown here.

13. Repeat *Step 10*, *Step 11*, and *Step 12* for the other two KPI sheets too, and this should be the result. Remove the bold red border from the parent layout container as the purpose of the border was served.

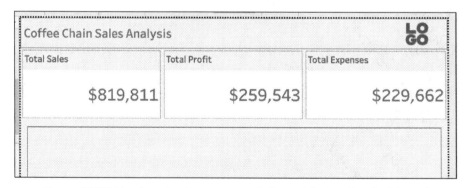

Figure 10.52: Header plus the scorecard view added to the dashboard

14. Next, add your **Map** view as well as a **Trends analysis** view to the dashboard by dragging the **Map View** worksheet from *Exercise 10.03* first and then dragging the **Parameter Metric Selection Sheet** sheet to the right of the map view. The result should look as follows:

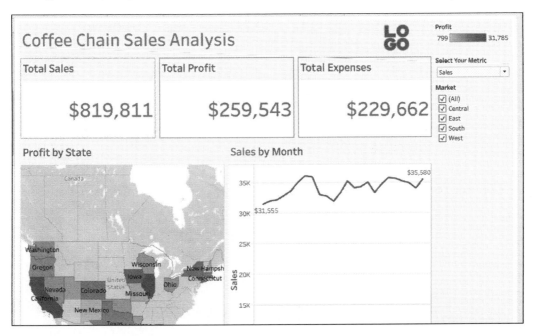

Figure 10.53: Adding another worksheet plus filters

Blank → Footer. → Title.

" " ⟶ (9)

I

Data Source

↓

Insert

Data Sorce name

as ← Data Update time

15. If you are not seeing any of the **Profit** color legends nor the **Select Your Parameter** parameter and **Market** filter, here is how to add them to the view:

    Click on the **Options** dropdown of the **Sales by Month** worksheet and select **Filter** -> **Market**.

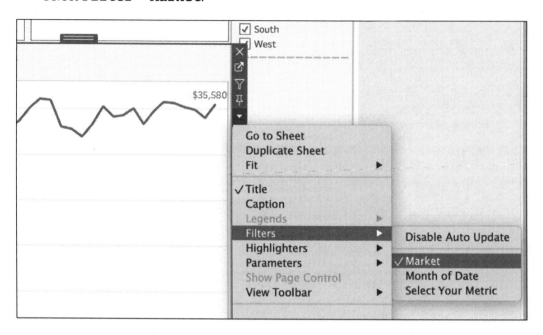

Figure 10.54: Manually adding filters to the dashboard

Add the **Parameter** dropdown by clicking on the **Options** dropdown of the **Sales by Month** worksheet and selecting **Parameter** -> **Select Your Metric**.

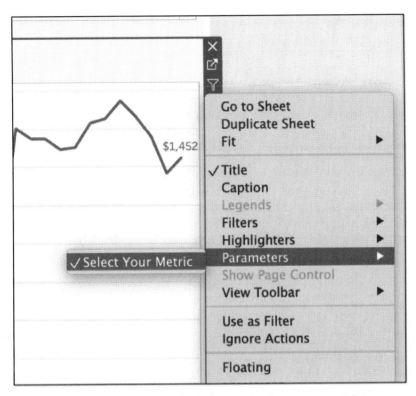

Figure 10.55: An example dashboard using education data

You don't require the Profit legend as part of the dashboard, so you can remove/delete that if it's already part of your dashboard.

16. If necessary, keep the filters/parameters as they are but move them to better positions for quick visibility as well as easier access.

    Drag **Select Your Metric** on top of the **Sales By Month** worksheet and resize the parameter/worksheet as required.

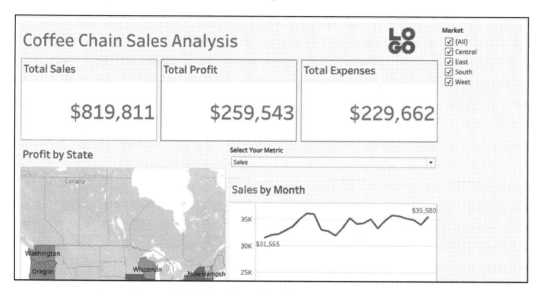

Figure 10.56: Dashboard without an action added

Drag the **Market** filter to the right of the **Total Expenses** worksheet to place it to the right. Next, add a thin green line border to the **Market** filter to match the formatting of other worksheets in that section.

17. Add a filter action to your map so that whenever your stakeholders click on a state on the map, all the other elements of the dashboard also get filtered. Navigate to the menu bar and click on **Dashboard** -> **Actions** or press *CMD + Shift + D* for Mac or *Ctrl + Shift + D* for Windows, as shown here:

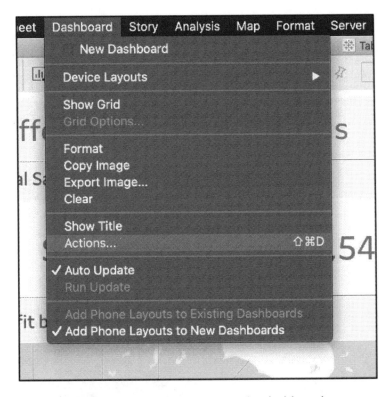

Figure 10.57: Adding action to the dashboard

18. Add a **Filter** action by clicking on **Add Action** -> **Filter**.

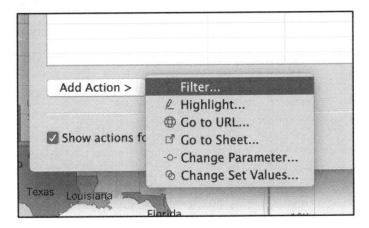

Figure 10.58: Selecting a filter action for the dashboard

19. Select your source sheet, which in this case is the **Map** worksheet, and run the action on **Select**. For **Target Sheets**, select all the worksheets and, from the **Clearing the selection will** option, choose **Show all values**, as you can see in the following screenshot:

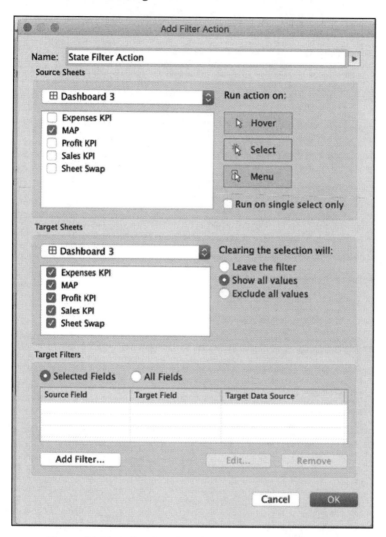

Figure 10.59: Selecting the filter action configuration

20. The final step is to add **State** as a field under **Target Filters**. For this, click on **Selected Fields** -> **Add Filter** and select **State** as the dimension to filter on, as shown, then click **OK**.

Figure 10.60: Selecting the fields in both the source and target sheets

This should be the final configuration for **State Filter Action**.

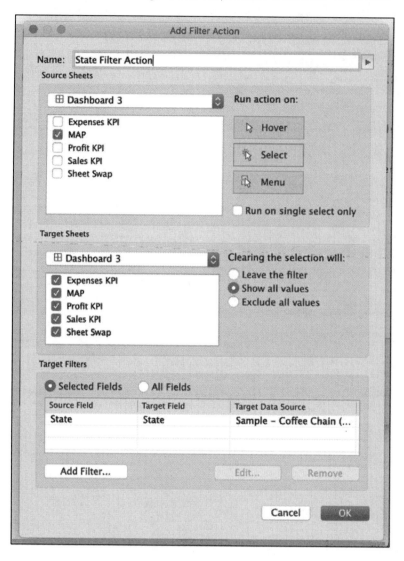

Figure 10.61: Final State Filter Action configuration

21. Test all the interactive elements of the dashboard. The following is a view of **West Market**, with **Profit** for **Select Your Metric** and **California** as the state:

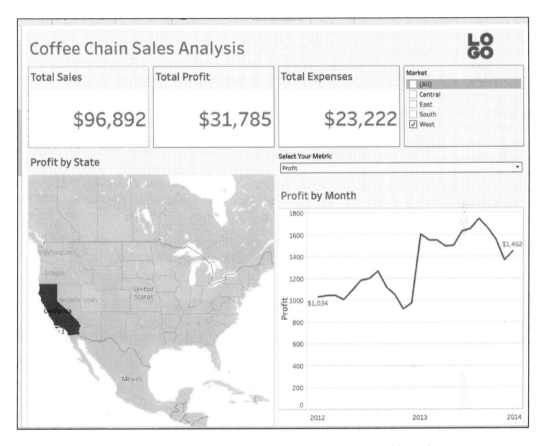

Figure 10.62: Final coffee chain sales analysis dashboard

That should conclude your first dashboard using Tableau. You added advanced interactivity to your view, including swapping metrics, using **State** action filters, and also used **Color**, **Size**, and **Branding** elements in our dashboard. Using the above view, you can infer that the total sales in California were $96,892, while $31,785 of those were profits. You can also easily identify the profit trend from the line chart, as shown above on the right.

CREATING STORYBOARDS

Storyboards differ from dashboards in a few different ways, but especially in one critical aspect – a dashboard is designed to display results for key organizational metrics (or similar measures), while a storyboard is designed to tell a pre-defined story. For example, a business user will use a dashboard to track a range of key metrics; the same user might use a storyboard to create a story based on very specific information found in the metrics (for example, showing how a single customer has grown over multiple periods, and a storyboard can help split those periods into multiple views).

To create a new story, you click on the **New Story** button on the menu at the bottom of the workspace. Selecting this button will give us a blank canvas with room for a single worksheet or dashboard. The next step is to drag a worksheet onto the canvas space; any related filters, parameters, and legends will automatically accompany the sheet. As with dashboards, you can adjust the screen size of the story and add text elements to accompany our chart. Storyboard text elements are designed to float on top of a chart; they can be used to add context to the displayed data.

One similarity between dashboards and storyboards is that both are built using existing worksheets, so you don't require a lot of additional effort to create a new storyboard. You simply need to find a story within the data, plan the sequence of storyboard slides, and add a title and text that walks the user through the story. Here's a very simple example where you have used a single chart with a different parameter selection for each tab in the story:

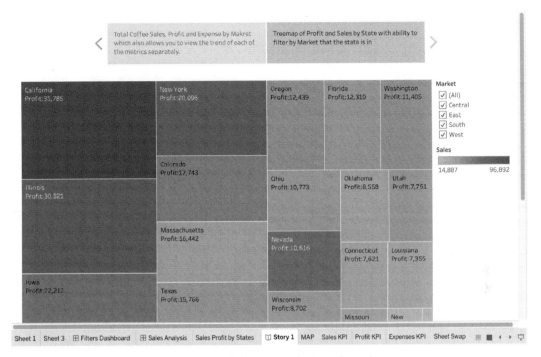

Figure 10.63: An example storyboard

Stories can be simple or complex, employing a single chart with changing filters or using many charts, maps, and summary worksheets to walk the user through something of interest. We'll use the next exercise to build the simple storyboard you see above.

EXERCISE 10.05: CREATING A SIMPLE STORYBOARD

You have created a dashboard previously. Now the manager wants to add another worksheet in a new page instead of adding more to the dashboard you built. In this exercise, you will create a treemap of states according to sales and profit and tell a story using the dashboard as well as the new Treemap worksheet:

1. Open the previously created dashboard again.

2. Create a new worksheet and drag **State** to detail under the **Marks** card. If longitude and latitude have been added to the **Column** shelf, remove them from the shelves.

3. Add **Profit** to **Size** and **Sales** to **Color**, as shown here:

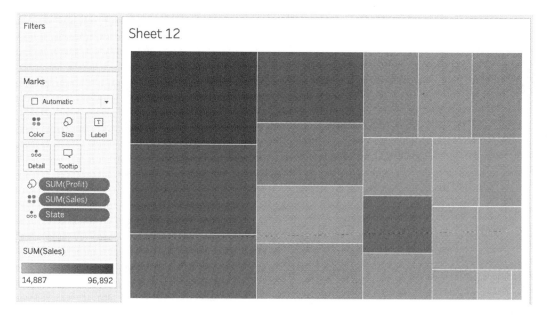

Figure 10.64: Treemap using Sales and Profit

4. Add more visual cues to the report, including **State** and **Profit** on the label, and update the title to **Sales/Profit by States**.

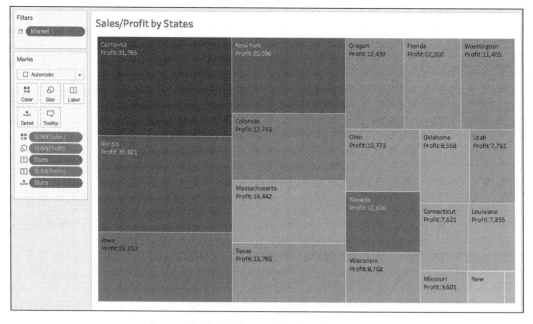

Figure 10.65: Adding a label to the treemap

5. You have one dashboard and one worksheet for your storyboard. Click on the **New Story** icon on the bottom toolbar. Rename it to **Coffee Sales by States** to update your story title.

6. Drag the **Coffee Sales Analysis Dashboard** (or the "dashboard name" you created previously) to the storyboard canvas. You should see this:

Figure 10.66: Adding a dashboard to the story point

7. The major difference between a storyboard and dashboard is that a storyboard can include multiple dashboards as well as reports in one view, and you can add captions for step-by-step insights into what the dashboard story is all about. The **Add a caption** option allows you to add interesting insights or story points to the dashboard. Click on **Add a caption** and write `Total Coffee Sales, Profit, and Expense by Market, which also allows you to view the trend of each of the metrics separately`, and also hide the **Story** title.

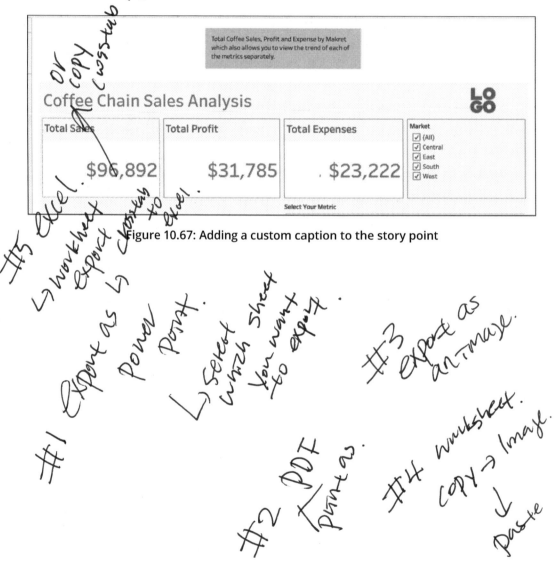

Figure 10.67: Adding a custom caption to the story point

8. Add another story point to the view by clicking on the **Blank** story point in the **Story** section.

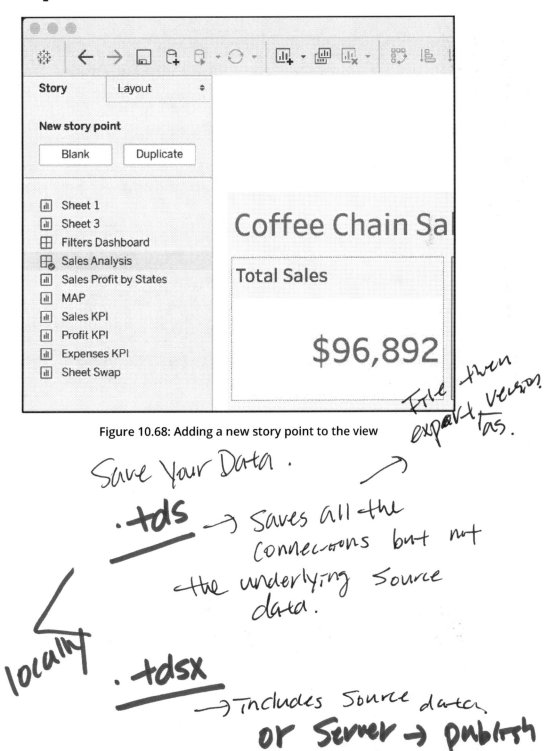

Figure 10.68: Adding a new story point to the view

[Handwritten notes:]

File then export version as.

Save Your Data.

.tds → Saves all the connections but not the underlying Source data.

locally

.tdsx → Includes Source data

or Server → publish

9. Drag **Sales Profit by States** (or the second dashboard you created earlier in the exercise) to the new story point and update the caption to read **Tree map of Profit and Sales by State with the ability to filter by Market that the state is in**.

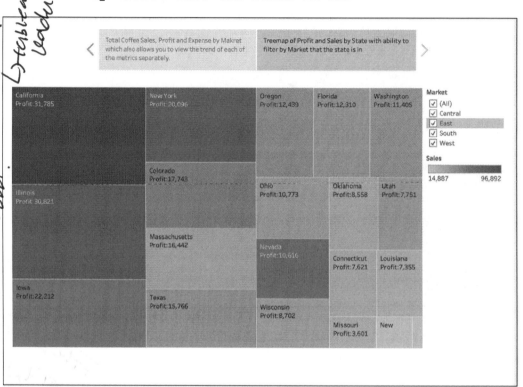

Figure 10.69: Final storyboard with the second story point with a custom caption

You have now completed a very simple storyboard and should be able to see the possibilities for more advanced stories. As you have seen in this basic example, storyboards can be very effective in walking a user through a focused narrative.

Let's finish this chapter by taking what you have learned and employing it to build a complete dashboard.

ACTIVITY 10.01: BUILDING A COMPLETE DASHBOARD

In this activity, you are an analyst working for the European Union looking to build a dashboard showcasing the 2014 versus 2015 growth in passengers across all European airports and also enable stakeholders to interact with the data.

You will create multiple scorecards and branding elements, as well as add a **Top N European Airports** parameters view to your dashboard. The final output should look as follows:

> **NOTE**
>
> You can find the dataset for this activity at the following link: https://packt.link/vyWvi.

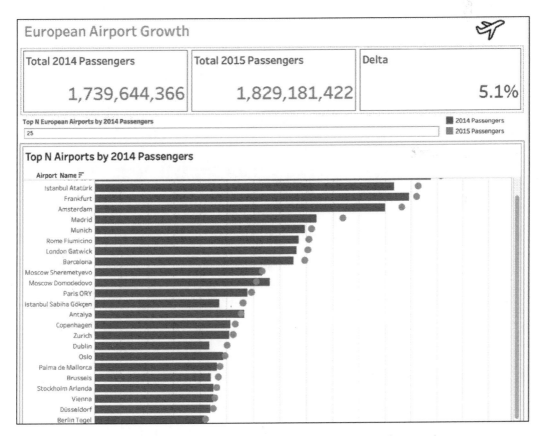

Figure 10.70: Final expected output using European airports data

The following steps will help you to complete this activity:

1. Open a new Tableau instance and load the European Airports 2015 data in the view.

2. Create three scorecard/KPI metrics: **Total 2014 Passengers**, **Total 2015 Passengers**, and **Passengers Growth/Decline**.

3. For **Total 2014 Passengers**, put **2014 Passengers** on the **Text** marks card and format the text as well as the title, as shown in the output. Do the same for **Total 2015 Passengers**.

4. For the **Passengers Growth/Decline** scorecard, create a new calculated field by using the following formula:

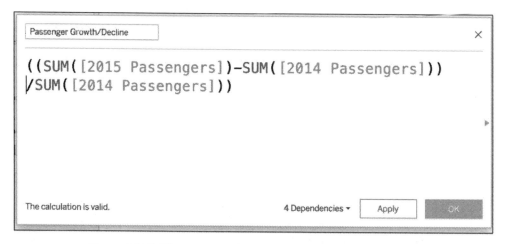

Figure 10.71: The passenger growth/decline calculated field

5. Using the **Passenger Growth/Decline** field, create a similar scorecard to the one you created for **2014 Passengers**.

6. Create a new worksheet and rename the worksheet **Top N Airports by 2014**.

7. Create a **Top N Parameter**, name your parameter **Top N**, select **Integer** as the data type, **10** for the current value, and then click **OK**.

8. Add **Airport Name** to the rows, and **2014 Passengers** and **2015 Passengers** to the **Columns** shelf, convert the two axes into a dual axis, and then synchronize the axis.

9. Under the **Marks** card, change one of the axes to the **Circle mark** type to create a **Bullet Chart** view that you want as your output.

10. To add the **Top N** parameter to the view, drag the name of the airport to **Filters**. Click on **Top** and filter the field by **Fields**. Then, select the parameter from the dropdown and add **2014 Passengers** as the field before clicking **OK**.

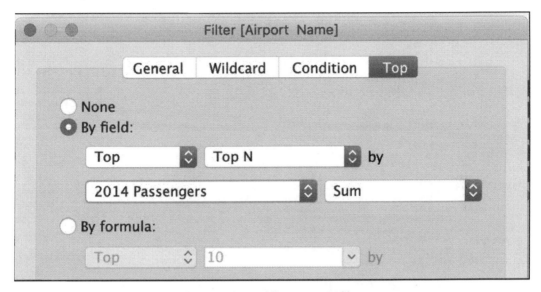

Figure 10.72: Adding a top N filter

11. Right-click on the **Top N** parameter in the data pane and click **Show Parameter**.

12. Add a couple of descriptive elements to the dual axis, drag **Passenger Growth/Decline** and **Country** to the Tooltip, and confirm whether **2014 Passengers** (**2015 Passengers**) are already part of the tooltip. If not, drag them to the **Tooltip** marks card as well.

13. Create a new dashboard and drag a **Vertical** tiled object. Start at the top with branding and work your way through the bottom.

14. Header: Drag a **Horizontal** tiled object, drag **Text**, and then call your dashboard **European Airports Growth**.

15. Next, download a hand airplane or an airline logo online and drag that using the **Image** tiled object to the right of the title of the dashboard.

16. Add another **Vertical** tiled object below the header and drag all three scorecards.

17. Next, drag another **Vertical** tiled object below the scorecards and put the **Top N Airports by 2014** worksheet in that section.

18. Align/realign the legends and parameters as per your requirements.

19. Your final output should look like this:

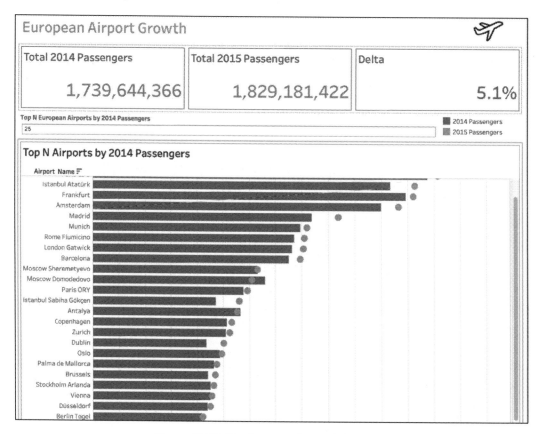

Figure 10.73: Final output for activity 10.01

> **NOTE**
>
> The solution to this activity can be found here: https://packt.link/CTCxk.

SUMMARY

This chapter covered the design and development of dashboards and storyboards, two essential tools for Tableau designers and users. Dashboards continue to be a critical component of the Tableau experience, with thousands of companies and organizations using them to communicate insights to executives, managers, and analysts.

Before you decided to create our first dashboard, you reviewed best practices for creating a dashboard and how size, color, and placement play an important role in dashboard development as well as the readability aspect of the dashboard. Later, you walked through each of the dashboard elements/objects and provided an example of how those objects work before you switched gears and started creating dashboards.

In our first **Coffee Chain Sales Analysis** dashboard, you used concepts learned previously to create the **Selecting Your Metric** parameter, learned how to divide your dashboard into sections, saw some tips and tricks for best placing the objects, and considered when to use tiled versus floating objects. You also formatted your dashboards and added your custom branding elements to the dashboard. Later, you walked through the creation of a storyboard and how that differs from a dashboard, and when to use a storyboard versus a dashboard. Finally, you concluded the chapter by walking through another unique dashboard using **European Airports** data and again used some of the advanced concepts that you have learned throughout the book, including the dual axis lollypop chart, the **Top N** filter using parameters, along with formatting the dashboard using best practices.

The knowledge gained here will allow you to create the dashboards and storyboards in the upcoming chapter. The dashboards and storyboards maximize the impact of each dataset that you encounter. The ability to integrate the power of Tableau calculations, filters, parameters, sets, groups, and actions into a single dashboard is a major step in developing your Tableau skills and providing essential solutions for your customers.

11

TABLEAU INTERACTIVITY: PART 1

OVERVIEW

This chapter will dive deep into the order of operations, filters, and sets and parameters in Tableau. We will also work through exercises on using groups and hierarchies in our views. Some of these features of Tableau give end users the ability to control the view. Finally, we will be discussing an activity that will utilize context filters, parameters, and sets on the World Indicator dataset to reinforce the skills you will gain in this chapter. By the end of this chapter, you will have gained the skills to create interactive reports, which give end users more control to slice and dice the data in the report.

INTRODUCTION

In this chapter, you will explore your options in creating reports/dashboards in Tableau, which allows you to arrange your data or report in a more comprehensible manner for your stakeholders/audience. Previous chapters have focused a lot on creating calculated fields, table calculations, and advanced calculations such as level of detail calculations. These types of calculations can help you go a long way in achieving desired results/views. However, you can also explore other ways of arranging, sorting, or grouping your data, adding another layer of interactivity to your reports, which in turn helps improve the ease of use of reports. This chapter will dive deeper into the order of operations, filters, and sets and parameters in Tableau from a conceptual as well as a practical perspective and discuss how to make the best use of these features in your reports/dashboards. In this chapter, you will review how to group data and hierarchy use cases and consider an interesting use case for parameters.

GROUPING DATA

The grouping of data is useful when you want to simplify or stack multiple dimension rows/members into one bigger bucket. For example, say you are working on a report on the population of countries in the world, and the standard data does not contain a custom grouping of all the South Asian countries. When you decide to create a custom grouping of all the South Asian countries by grouping countries such as India, Pakistan, Nepal, Sri Lanka, and so on, you will notice that a new dimension is added in your **Data** pane:

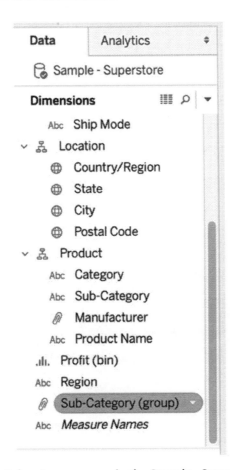

Figure 11.1: Sub-category group in the Sample - Superstore dataset

As is often the case with Tableau features, you can achieve the same results in multiple ways. You can use either of the following methods to create a group:

- Create a group from the worksheet view.

- Create a group from the **Data** pane.

You'll practice the both of these options in the following exercise.

EXERCISE 11.01: CREATING GROUPS

You are a retail analyst of XYZ group tasked to group multiple sub-categories so that it is easier for a sub-category manager to report on their KPIs of sales:

1. Open the **Sample - Superstore** dataset in your Tableau instance.

2. Create a bar chart of **Sales** across **Category** and **Sub-Category** as shown here:

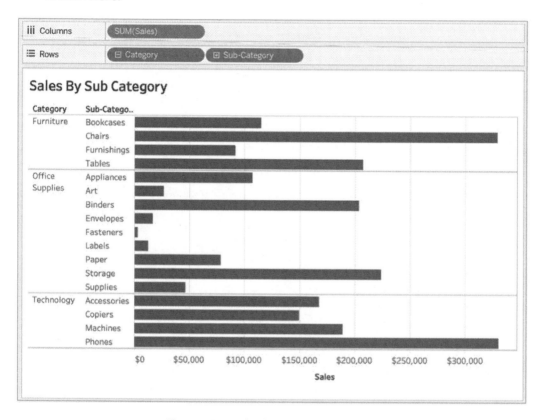

Figure 11.2: Sales by Subcategory view

Creating a Group from the Worksheet View:

3. Press *Ctrl* and select or press *Command*. Select the sub-category to select multiple **Sub-category** members in the view. Then, either right-click to group them or click on the group icon in the toolbar or within the tooltip as shown here:

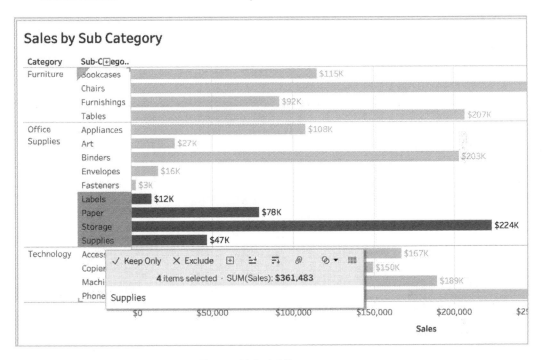

Figure 11.3: Adding groups

4. As you can see, a new **Labels, Paper, Storage, and Supplies** sub-category grouping is created. You can also rename the sub-category grouping by right-clicking and changing the alias name to be more descriptive, such as *Desk Stationery* if you desire.

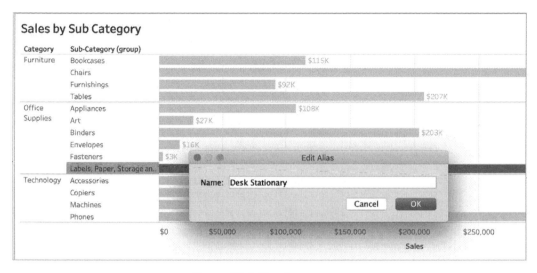

Figure 11.4: Naming groups

Creating a Group from the Data Pane

In the previous steps, you used the worksheet view to create a group. Now you'll create a separate group via the **Data** pane:

5. Create a new worksheet as you did in the steps above.

6. Create a bar chart of **Sales** across **Category** and **Sub-Category** as shown here:

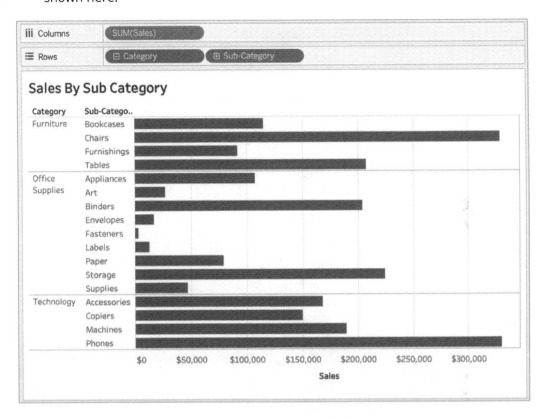

Figure 11.5: Adding groups from the data pane

7. Right-click on the **Sub-Category** dimension in the **Data** pane and hover over **Create**. Click on **Group...** from the sub-menu as shown in the following screenshot:

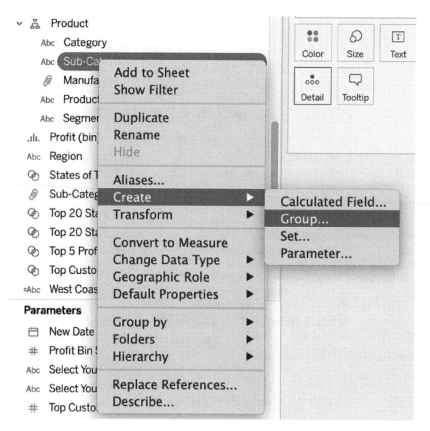

Figure 11.6: Creating a group from the Data pane

8. In the group pop-up window, change the field name to something more descriptive: **Papers Sub-Category(group)**.

9. Hold *Ctrl* or *Command* and multi-select the sub-categories that you want to group. In this case, group all paper related items in one group and click on the **Group** button:

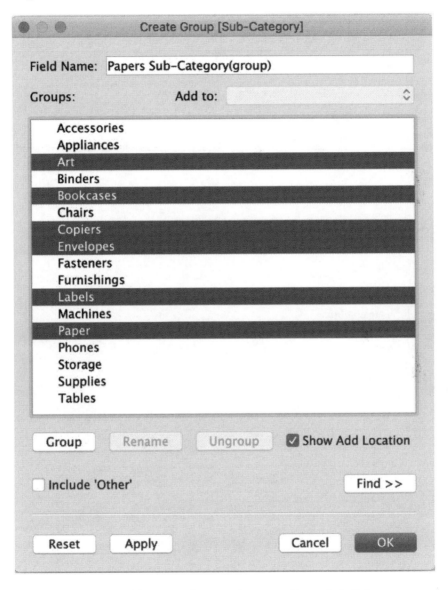

Figure 11.7: Adding members to the group Paper Sub-Category

10. Rename the selected items in the window to **Paper Items** for easier readability, as shown in the following screenshot. You can add or remove the items by dragging them in and out of the groups at your convenience.

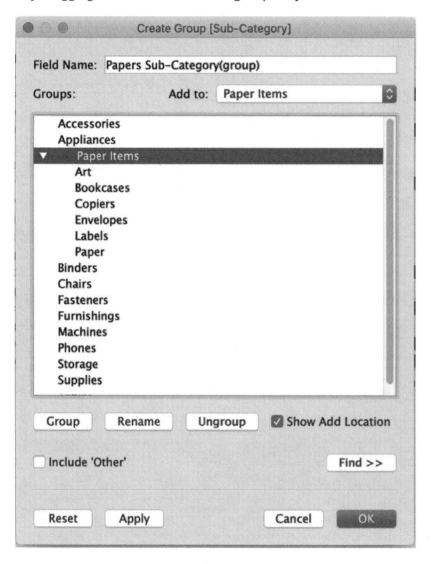

Figure 11.8: Editing a group

11. To check if your group is working the way you expect, drag the newly created group dimension **Paper Sub-Category(group)** to the **Rows** shelf and remove the **Category** as well as the **Sub-Category** dimensions from the view. You'll notice the group that you created in the previous step:

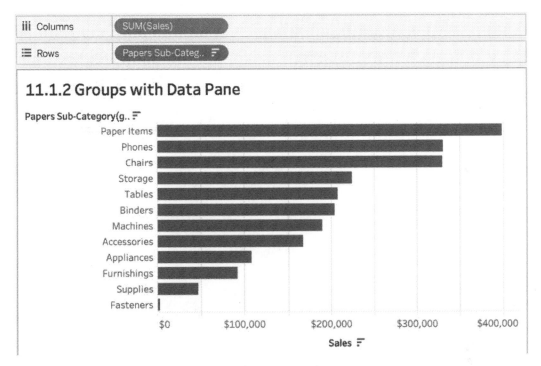

Figure 11.9 The groups sub-category

In this exercise, you explored two ways of creating groups: via the worksheet view and the **Data** pane. With your completion of this task, sub-category managers now have a way of looking at their KPIs for multiple grouped sub-categories.

> **NOTE**
>
> If you want to edit the grouping now or in the future, right-click on the new group dimension that was created (the dimension with the *clip* icon) in the **Data** pane and click on **Edit Group**. In the **Edit Group** popup, you can drag and drop to remove members or add new members to the group.

HIERARCHIES

Hierarchies are not specific to Tableau. As such, you have almost certainly used them previously, whether consciously or unconsciously. In a data context, when the relevant data is arranged logically based on its level of detail, it is called a **hierarchy**. In our **Sample - Superstore** dataset, you have already used hierarchies many times, including the **Location** hierarchy, which contains **Country/Region**, **State**, **City**, and **Postal Code**; the **Product** hierarchy consists of **Category**, **Sub-Category**, **Manufacturer**, and **Product Name**. Hierarchies grant you a comprehensive look into your data. For example, if you add the **State** dimension to your view, because of the hierarchies that were pre-created in your data, you can switch from state to city by clicking on the **+** icon in your shelf or go a level up by clicking the **−** sign as shown here:

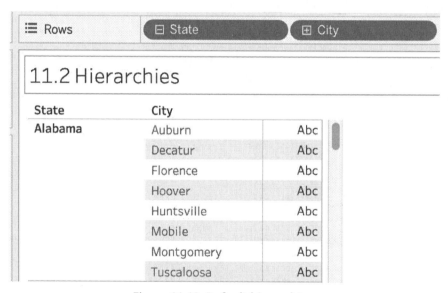

Figure 11.10: Default hierarchies

Take a look at how hierarchies can be created through the following short exercise.

EXERCISE 11.02: CREATING HIERARCHIES

As an e-commerce analyst of emzon.com, the product catalog manager wants to add **Segment** to the **Product** hierarchy. You will have to initially remove the original **Product** hierarchy and later create a new **Product** hierarchy by combining one of the existing ones.

> **NOTE**
>
> If you load the default **Sample - Superstore** dataset provided by Tableau in Tableau Desktop, you may notice that some fields are missing or new fields have been added. That is expected as Tableau constantly updates data files as per the requirements. If you want to avoid confusion, download the dataset from the official GitHub repository for this chapter, available here: https://packt.link/eLmSX.

1. Open the **Sample - Superstore** dataset in your Tableau instance, if it is not already open.

2. Follow *Step 2* and *Step 3* below only if your version of data has a **Product** hierarchy inbuilt. If not, proceed to step 4 directly. Assuming in your **Data** pane you find a **Decision Tree** icon(as shown below) attached to **Product** dimension, the decision tree signifies that the dimension is a hierarchy and can be drilled down in your view.

Figure 11.11: The hierarchy icon

3. Navigate to the **Product** dimension in your **Dimensions** data pane and right-click the **Product** dimension. Then click on **Remove Hierarchy**:

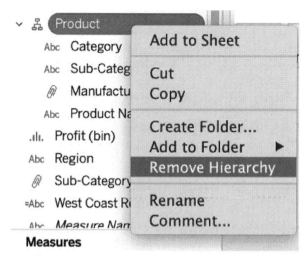

Figure 11.12: Removing the hierarchy

As soon as you remove the hierarchy, the **Decision Tree** icon is also removed and all the dimensions that were part of the hierarchy subsequently become their own dimensions. You will also be unable to drill them down as they are no longer logically arranged.

4. To re-construct the hierarchy that we just removed, multi-select dimensions by pressing *Ctrl* and selecting (for Windows) or *Command* and selecting (for Mac) all the dimensions that were a part of the product hierarchy. In this case, this will be **Category**, **Sub-Category**, **Manufacturer**, **Product name**, and **Segment**.

5. After selecting all the dimensions mentioned, right-click on any of the selected dimensions, hover over **Hierarchy**, click on **Create Hierarchy**..., and name the hierarchy **Product** as shown here:

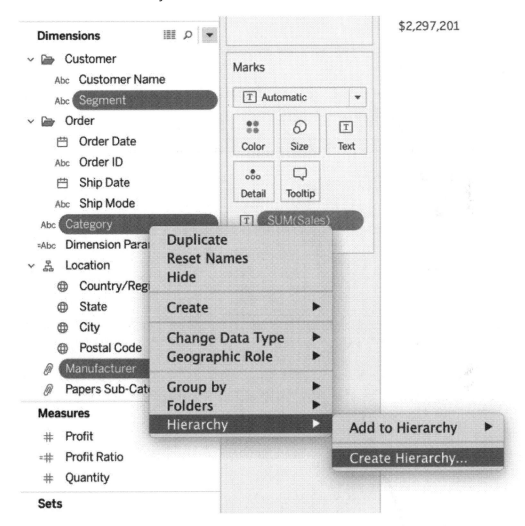

Figure 11.13: Creating a new hierarchy

Ideally, the order of multi-select in the previous steps should have allowed Tableau to select the level of your hierarchies. Unfortunately, Tableau levels them alphabetically, which is not the level you want:

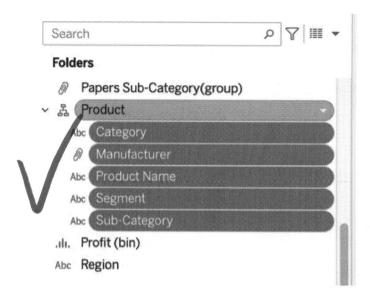

Figure 11.14: The newly created hierarchy

6. Before you create a hierarchy, you should have a good idea of the logical leveling of the hierarchy. In this case, these were **Category | Sub-Category | Manufacturer | Product name | Segment**. Drag your dimensions above or below depending on the level. For example, **Sub-Category** is below **Segment**, so drag **Sub-Category** above **Product Name** and **Manufacturer**:

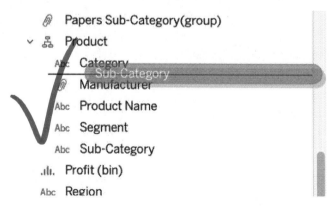

Figure 11.15: Dragging dimensions to change their logical order

7. Check if the hierarchy is working as expected. Drag the **Product** hierarchy to the **Rows** shelf and double-click on **Sales** to create a **Sales** report by **Product** hierarchy.

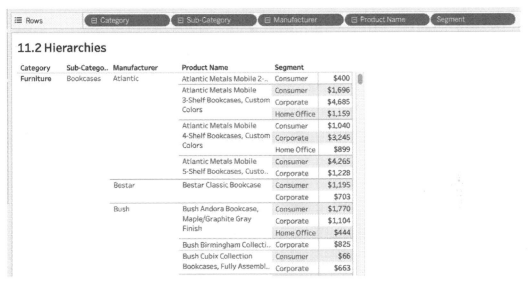

Figure 11.16: Final hierarchy

Like groups, hierarchies can be useful when you can logically arrange relevant data points based on their level of detail or granularity. You just removed as well as re-created a **Product** hierarchy in this exercise.

FILTERS: THE HEART AND SOUL OF TABLEAU

If you want to differentiate yourself from a casual Tableau developer, understanding the order of operations and the order in which Tableau manipulates and filters data is critical. In other words, to be a true expert in Tableau, you need to be able to determine when and where data was filtered and pinpoint the reason when the view doesn't produce the data you expect.

Think of the order of operations as the query pipeline. The order in which Tableau filters data is critical and Tableau follows a sequential order, as shown in the following chart.

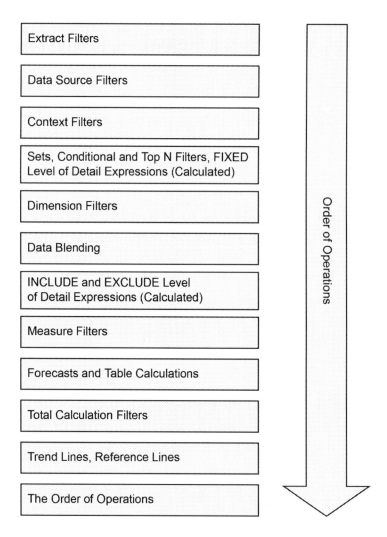

Figure 11.17: Tableau table of operations

When you create business dashboards in Tableau, you will have multiple filters, table calculations, and calculated fields to work with. As is the case with most programs, execution follows a set order/operation priority. The order of operations is just that. In the chart above, **Extract Filters** has the highest priority, followed by **Data Source Filters** and **Context Filters**, and **Trend Lines, Reference Lines** has the lowest priority. In the following sub-sections, we will try to explain most of the filters with an exercise to demonstrate the importance of this.

DATA SOURCE AND EXTRACT FILTERS

Data Source and Extract filters are the first in the order of operations in Tableau and take place before you create your first view or when you are loading your data into the Tableau instance. This type of filtering is useful when you don't want to load all the data from your server/source file into the Tableau instance. See this in practice in the following exercise.

EXERCISE 11.03: FILTERING DATA USING EXTRACT/DATA SOURCE FILTERS

As an analyst, you want to load only a sub-region of data into your Tableau worksheet to lower the load on the dashboard and limit the amount of data being downloaded into the worksheet. Create a view of **Sales** by **State** for the **East** region only.

1. Open the **Sample - Superstore** dataset in your Tableau instance if you don't have it open already.

2. Before creating a sample view, double-click on **Data Source** at the bottom-left of your screen.

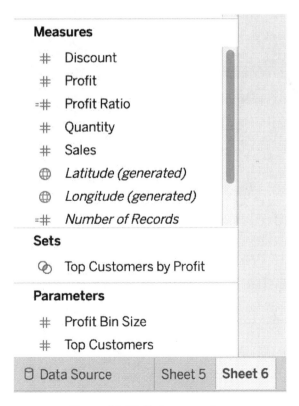

Figure 11.18: Data pane view

3. To import data for the **East** region only for your view, add that as a **Data Source Filter** here. On the **Data Source** page, click on **Add** in the **Filters** section at the top right of the view.

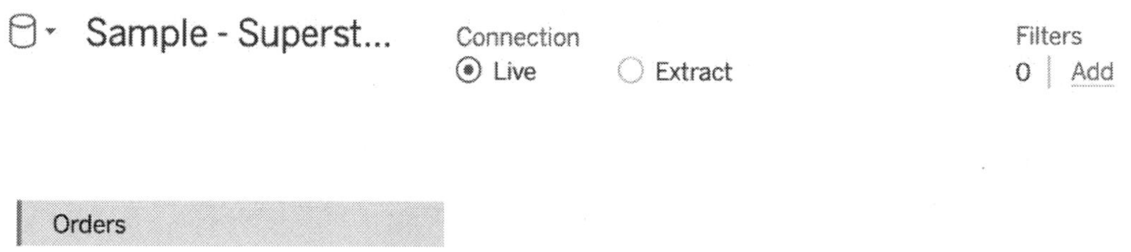

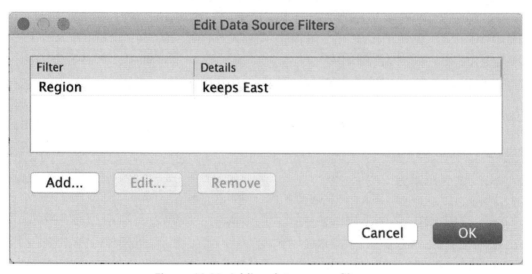

Figure 11.19: Data Source view

4. In the **Edit Data Source Filters** window, click the **Add...** button, select **Region**, and click **OK**. Just select **East** from the list and click the **OK** button. Click the **OK** button again to close the dialog box:

Figure 11.20: Adding data source filters

5. To confirm the working of the filters, create a new worksheet and review **Sales** by **State** from your data:

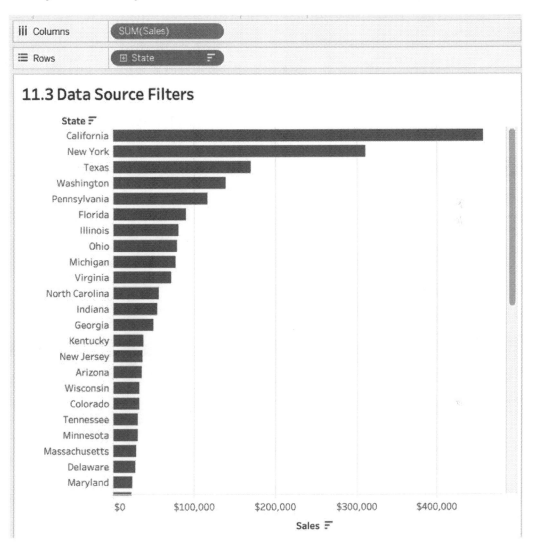

Figure 11.21: Data after adding a data source filter

You might not notice the difference in speed when loading any of the dimensions in your view because the data is not at gigabyte or terabyte scale. If you were working with large-scale data, utilizing data source filtering is one way to improve the speed and efficiency of your work.

When the data source you are importing contains more data than your report/dashboard requires, you can utilize data source filters to improve the efficiency and reduce the load on Tableau views. In this exercise, your goal was to improve the performance of your dashboard, and by using data source filters, you were able to limit the amount of data being loaded in the worksheet.

FILTERS USING VIEWS

These types of filters resemble how you group dimensions using views. In this type of filtering, you manually select one or multiple data points in the view to include or exclude from the view. In the following exercise, you'll perform these simple steps to create a filter in this way.

EXERCISE 11.04: CREATING FILTERS FROM THE VIEW

As an analyst, you have been given completely new data, and as part of the dashboard designing process, you want to do some **Exploratory Data Analysis (EDA)**. Creating filters using the view can be a great way of filtering data as you see the data in the worksheet.

Perform the following steps to complete this exercise:

1. Open the **Sample - Superstore** dataset in your Tableau instance if you have not already done so.

2. Create a bar chart of **Sales** by **State**. Drag and drop **State** to the **Rows** shelf and **Sales** to the **Columns** shelf. You should end up with the following view:

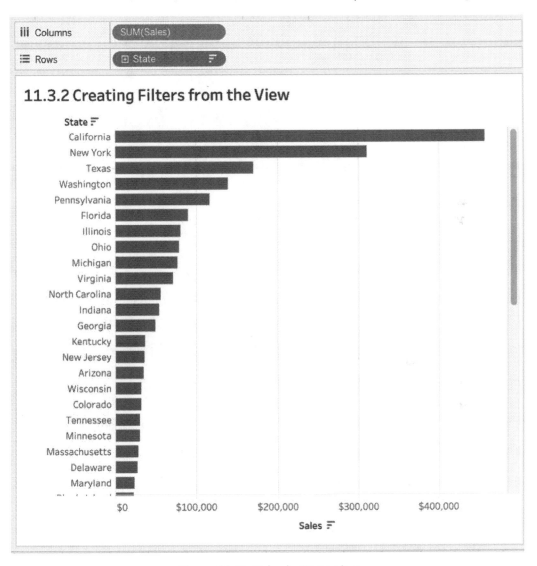

Figure 11.22: Sales by State view

3. Manually select your states/data points to include/exclude from your view. Click and drag a region to exclude the top five states by sales as shown here:

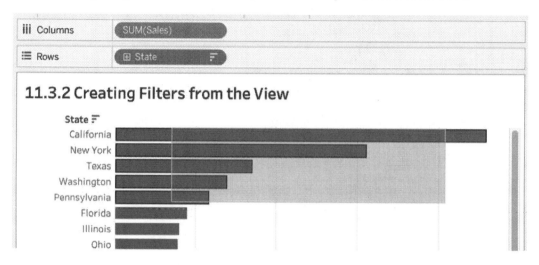

Figure 11.23: Dragging multiple data points to create a filter

4. If you hover your mouse over the selected region for a couple of seconds, a tooltip option pops up. From here, select **Keep Only** or **Exclude** for the selected states. You exclude these states, so click on **Exclude**:

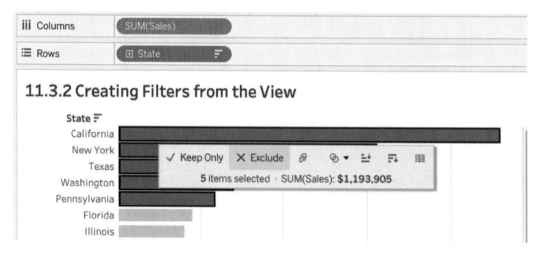

Figure 11.24: Include/exclude data points from the view

A **State** dimension filter will be added to the **Filters** shelf. In the next sub-section, you are going to dive deep into how to best use the **Filters** shelf, so hold on to your questions at the moment. Here is the final output:

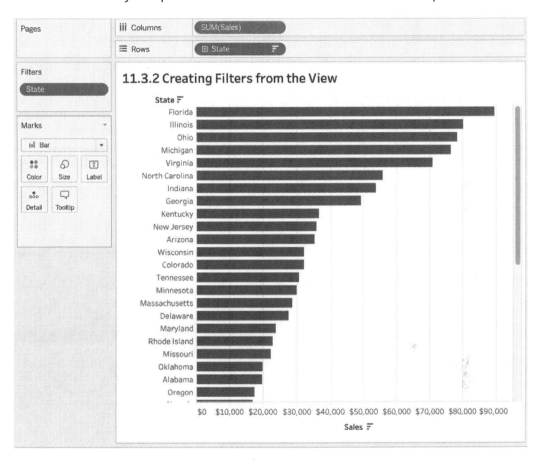

Figure 11.25: Final output after creating the filter from the view

In this exercise, you practiced manually selecting or dragging and selecting a subset of the view to include/exclude from the view. Creating filters using the view can be incredibly helpful when you initially conduct EDA, which is what all analysts start with when creating a new dashboard. Next, we will dive deep into how to best utilize the **Filters** shelf.

CREATING FILTERS USING THE FILTERS SHELF

In previous sections, we looked at filtering data either at the data source level or using views, but the right way to utilize filters in Tableau is via the **Filters** shelf. In this section, we will discuss how to use the **Filters** shelf for filtering dimensions, measures, as well as dates. But first, we will dive deep into the options of the **Filter** dialog box, which opens up when you drag any of the mentioned data types.

DIMENSION FILTERS USING THE FILTERS SHELF

Dimensions in Tableau are essentially categorical data. When filtering a dimension, you either include or exclude some part of this data from the view. The following dialog box opens up whenever you drag a dimension to the **Filters** shelf:

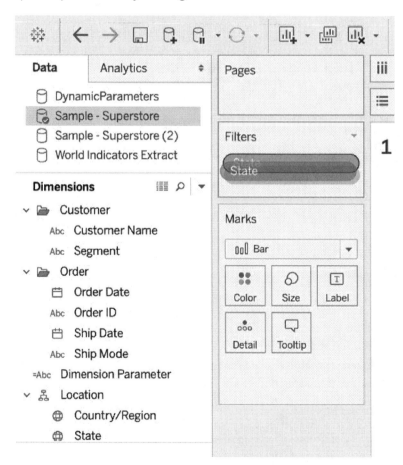

Figure 11.26: Dragging a dimension to the Filters shelf

The box has four tabs, as follows:

- **General**: You use this tab when to manually select the categorical data to include or exclude from the view. For example, if you wanted to filter **Sub-Category** on **Supplies** and **Tables**, you could manually select only two sub-categories to include, as shown below:

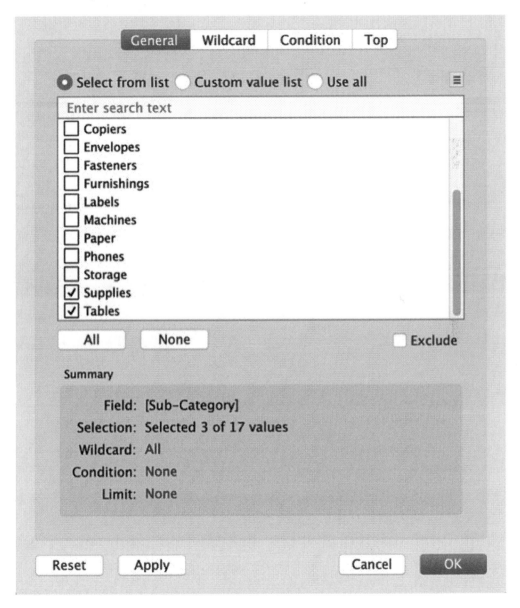

Figure 11.27: Filters shelf General tab

- **Wildcard**: The **Wildcard** tab is used to match a pattern of text to use the filter on. Say you had a column with thousands of URLs, which may or may not contain the term **football** in the URL. It would be quite tiring to use the **General** tab to manually select all the URLs that contain the term **football**, but using **Wildcard**, you can match the value by stating that the dimension either contains, starts with, ends with, or exactly matches the term **football** for your URL dimensions.

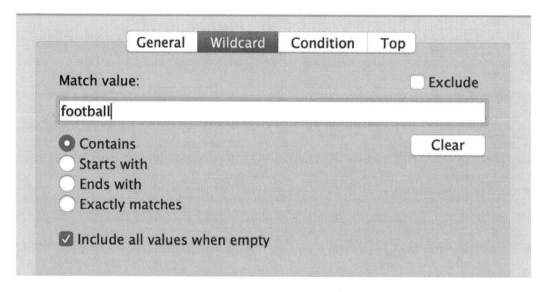

Figure 11.28: Filters shelf Wildcard tab

- **Condition**: In the **Condition** tab, you define rules or criteria for filtering the data. For example, you could also use the **Condition** tab to filter on those sub-categories that reported losses in your data. To do that, select **By field**, and in the dropdown, select **Profit** with **Sum** as aggregation and **< 0** as shown below:

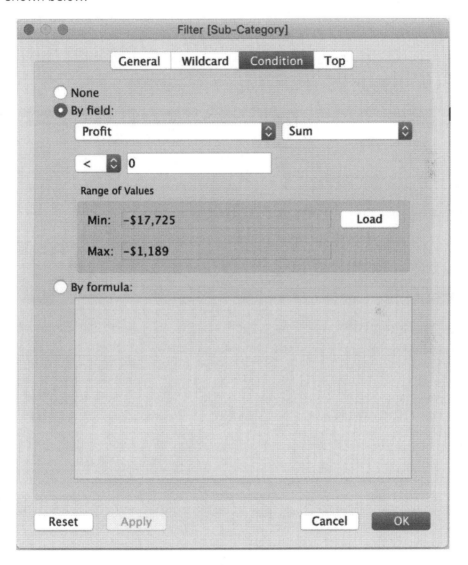

Figure 11.29: Filters shelf Condition tab

- **Top**: Use the **Top** tab in the **Filter** box when you want to compute the **Top** or **Bottom** N members of the view depending on the measure you want to filter the view on. In this example, you know that the **Bottom** three sub-categories are the rows with losses, so you can create a **Bottom** filter using these details, as shown here:

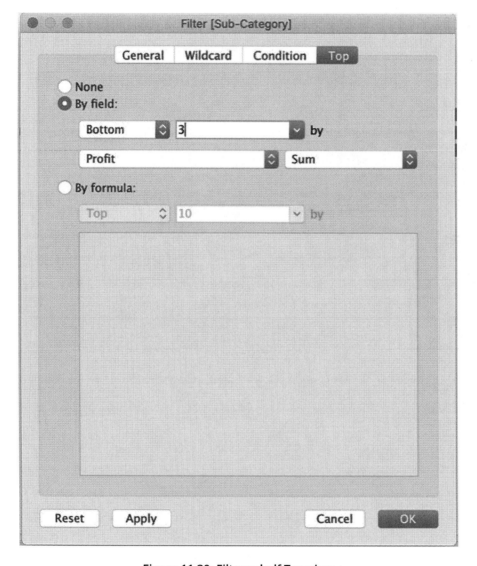

Figure 11.30: Filters shelf Top view

Next, you will utilize the **Filter** dialog box in an exercise.

EXERCISE 11.05: DIMENSION FILTERS USING THE FILTERS SHELF

The portfolio manager has been tasked with identifying a list of all sub-categories that are not making profit. You are tasked with creating a dynamic filter via the **Filters** shelf.

Perform the following steps to complete this exercise:

1. Open the Sample - Superstore dataset in your Tableau instance if you don't have it open already.

2. Create a **Profit** by **Sub-Category** bar chart and drag and drop **Sub-Category** to the **Rows** shelf and **Profit** to **Columns**. You should get the following view:

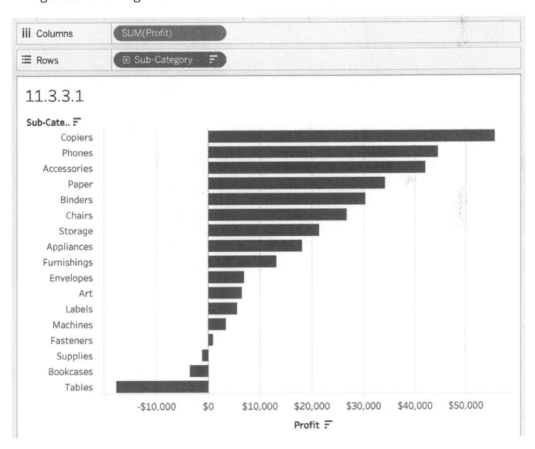

Figure 11.31: Profit by Sub-Category view

Note that there are three sub-cat egories (**Supplies**, **Bookcases**, and **Tables**) where the superstore made a loss. You want to include them in your view and exclude all other sub-categories. You can obviously manually select the sub-categories from the view itself, but go ahead and use the **Filters** shelf here, as instructed in the next step.

3. Drag and drop **Sub-Category** from the **Data** pane to the **Filters** shelf and a **Filters [Sub-Category]** dialog box opens up.

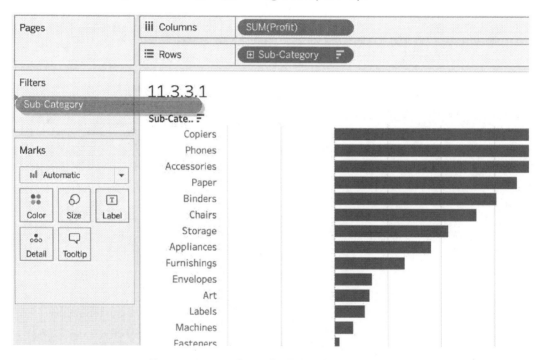

Figure 11.32: Only profitable sub-categories

4. In the dialog box, click on the **Condition** tab, select **By Field**, and filter on all sub-categories with **[Profit] <0**. You will get a list of all the sub-categories that are making losses for the business. Click on **OK** to filter the data.

5. You should get the following view showing a list of all sub-categories that are making losses:

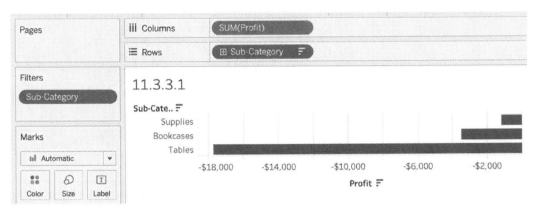

Figure 11.33: Only loss-making sub-categories

In your career as a data analyst, you will likely find yourself using the **Filters** shelf day in and day out as part of your job, making this an essential skill to have under your belt. In this exercise, you explored all the options Tableau has to offer in the **Filters** shelf for dimensions.

MEASURE FILTERS USING THE FILTERS SHELF

Measures are quantitative data, which means, unlike dimensions, filtering on measures involves selecting a range of numbers that you want to include/exclude from your view. Whenever you drag a **Measure** onto the **Filters** shelf, the **Filter** dialog box offers you four options to filter the **Measure** on. The following list will define these options in greater detail:

- **The Measure Filter Dialog Box**:

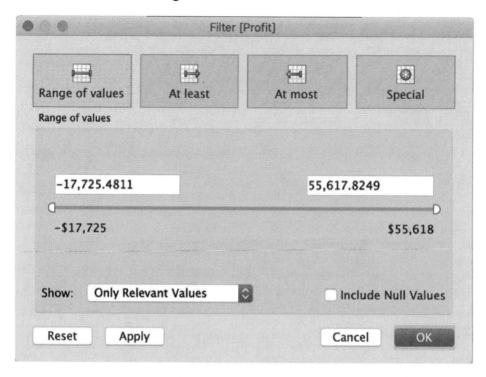

Figure 11.34: Range of values in the Filter window

- **Range of values**: In **Range of values**, you specify the range of values you want to filter on. In this use case, you only want profitable sub-categories, so your range will be from zero to the maximum as shown in the next screenshot *(Figure 11.35)*.

- **At least**: In `At least`, you specify the minimum value and all values greater or equal to the minimum value will be included in your view. This can usually be used when you don't have control over what the maximum for the column/data could be, and it is difficult to predict. In this use case, your minimum will be zero because you want only profitable sub-categories as shown here:

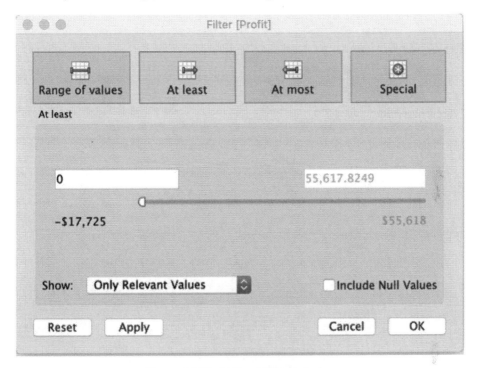

Figure 11.35: At least filter window

- **At most**: `At most` is the opposite of `At least` and is used when you want to include all values that are less than or equal to the maximum specified. This can usually be used when you don't have control over the minimum but know the maximum value that you want to be included in your view, which is exactly opposite to that of the `At least` tab. You cannot use `At most` for this use case identifying profitable sub-categories because all the negative values will also be included in the view, and you don't have control over them if you use `At most`.

- **Special**: As the name suggests, this filter is only used when you want to include either null values, non values, or all values. This tab is rarely used, but depending on the data, it may be required.

EXERCISE 11.06: MEASURING FILTERS USING THE FILTERS SHELF

The portfolio manager liked the work you did creating a view of loss-making sub-categories. Now he wants you to create a similar view, but instead of loss-making sub-categories, he wants a profit-making view this time. You will utilize **Profit** as a filter to create the view in the following steps:

1. Open the **Sample - Superstore** dataset in your Tableau instance if you have not already done so.

2. Create a **Profit** by **Sub-Category** bar chart, and drag and drop **Sub-Category** to the **Rows** shelf and **Profit** to **Columns**. You should be at the following view:

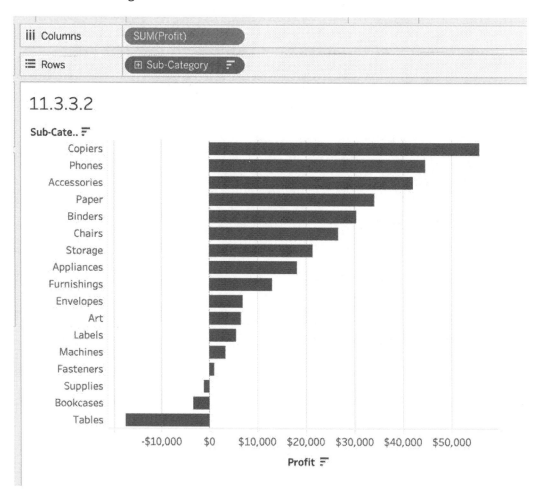

Figure 11.36: Profit by Sub-Category view

3. Drag **Profit** from the **Data** pane to the **Filters** shelf. The following dialog box opens up:

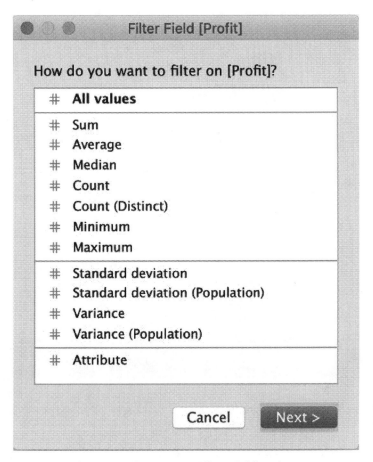

Figure 11.37: Measure Filter Field options

4. In the **Filter Field [Profit]** dialog box, select the aggregation for your measures. In this case, select **Sum** as you want to look at the sum of the profit.

5. **Range of values**, as well as **At least**, can be used for identifying profitable sub-categories. For this exercise, use **Range of values** to filter on profitable subcategories.

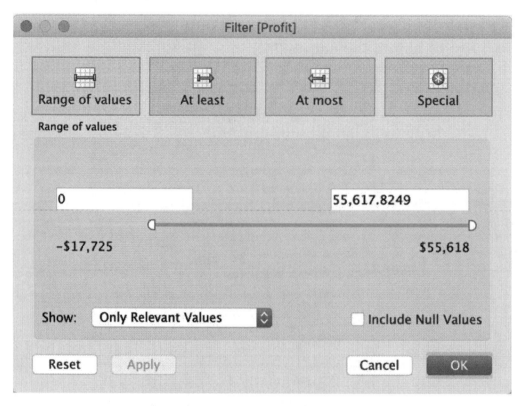

Figure 11.38: Range of values for Measure

6. Regardless of **Profit** option you decided to use, your final output should resemble the following:

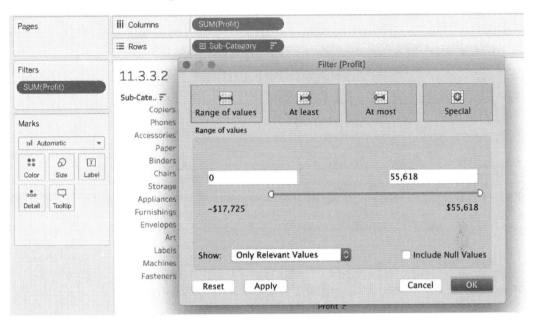

Figure 11.39: Measure filter final output

In this exercise, you utilized the **Measure** data type as a filter for the first time and explored all Tableau's corresponding options for this in detail. You used **Profit** to filter on only profitable sub-categories.

In the next section, you will explore date filters using the **Filters** shelf.

DATE FILTERS USING THE FILTERS SHELF

Dates are neither qualitative data nor quantitative data out of the box. We can filter dates either by **Relative Date**, **Range of Dates**, or filtering by discrete dates. Let's explore each one of the options and how they differ from each other, and in the exercise after the explanation, walk through a specific use case.

When you drag a **Date** dimension such as **Order Date** in your **Sample - Superstore** dataset, you are presented with the following window:

Figure 11.40: Date filter modal window

- **Filtering by relative dates**: If you choose to filter by a relative date, in the subsequent window, you can define the relative time-frame of your date and the dates will be filtered depending on the date on which the view was opened. Say you want to show only the last 12 months of data. In the **Relative Dates** dialog box, select **Months**, click on **Last**, and enter **12** months as shown here:

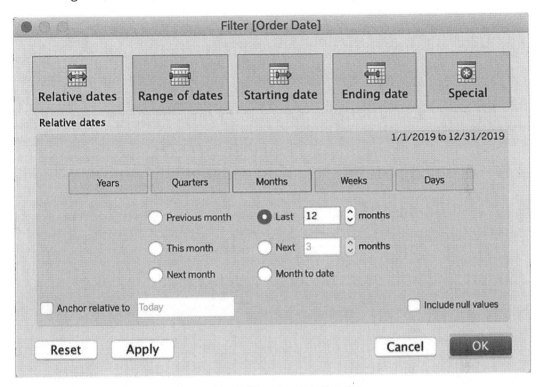

Figure 11.41: Filter by Relative dates

Relative dates are defined from the date the view was opened. If the data source only has dates till December 2019 and you are opening this in July 2020, the view will only include dates from August 2019 to the maximum date that is present in the data, which in this case is December 2019. Hence you will only see five months' worth of data. To change that, you can check **Anchor relative to** at the bottom left and enter the date as December 31, 2019, as shown here.

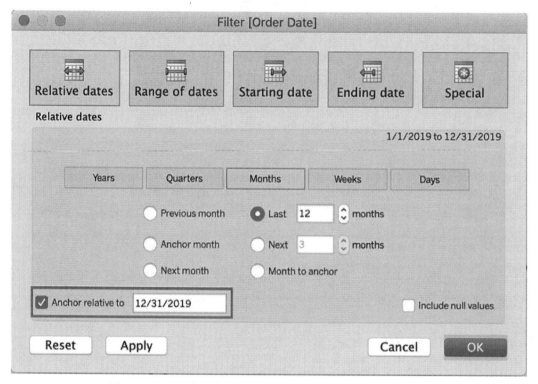

Figure 11.42: Filter by Relative dates with an anchor date

- **Filtering by range of dates**: You use this filter when you want your dates to have a fixed range. In this use case, you want 12 months of data relative to December 2019, so your range will be January 2019 to December 2019 as shown here:

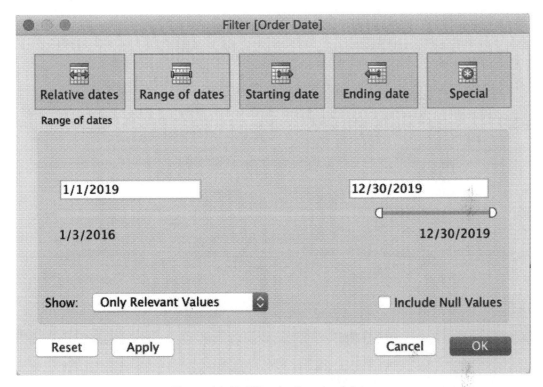

Figure 11.43: Filter by Range of dates

- **Filtering by discrete dates**: In the `Filter Field [Order Date]` dialog box, if you select discrete date values, you will filter on the entire date levels. For example, if you filter the discrete date on **Months** and select **January**, you will filter on **January** irrespective of the year. If you want to filter on a month and a year, select **Month / Year** from the `Filter Field` dialog box.

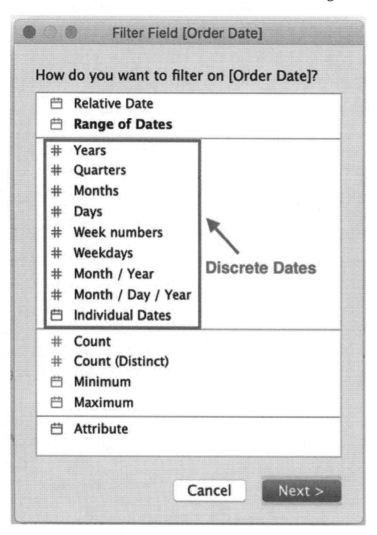

Figure 11.44: Filter by discrete dates

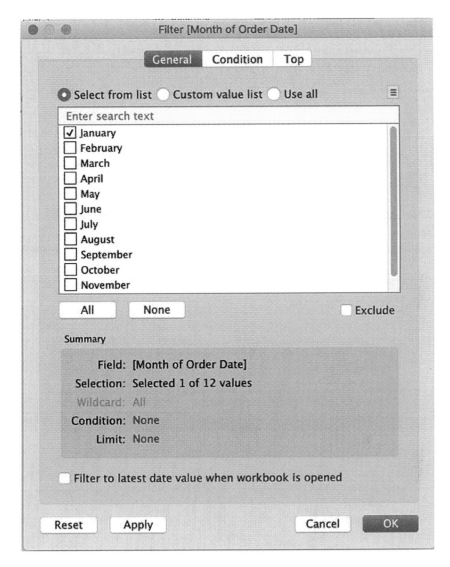

Figure 11.45: Filter by discrete month

In the following exercise, you will use the **Date** dialog box and create a time-series view to showcase the use of the **Date** filter.

EXERCISE 11.07: CREATING DATE FILTERS USING THE FILTERS SHELF

You are asked to create a time-series view of the sales of the last 12 months relative to the last updated date of the data. You will be using the **Sample - Superstore** dataset again in this exercise and utilizing relative dates, as well as anchoring relative to the options covered in the preceding section.

Perform the following steps to complete this exercise:

1. Open the **Sample - Superstore** dataset in your Tableau instance if you have not already done so.

2. Create a line chart of **Sales** by continuous **Month(Order Date)** as shown here:

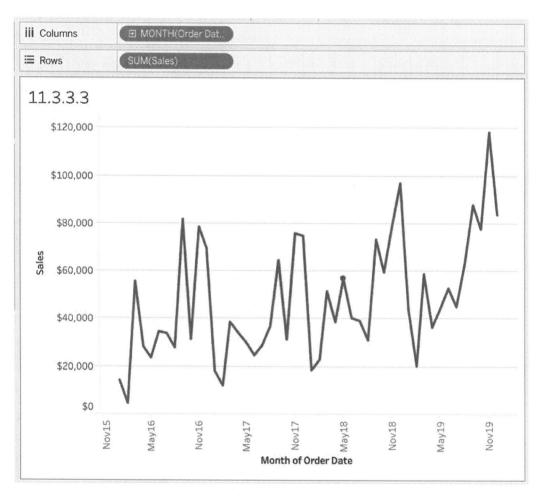

Figure 11.46: Time-series view after filtering on the last 12 months

You want the line chart to only show the last 12 months of data, so you will be using the **Filters** shelf to select only the last 12 months of data.

3. Drag and drop **Order Date** to the **Filters** shelf. In the **Filter Field [Order Date]** dialog box, filter the dates either by **Relative Date**, **Range of Dates**, or filtering by discrete dates.

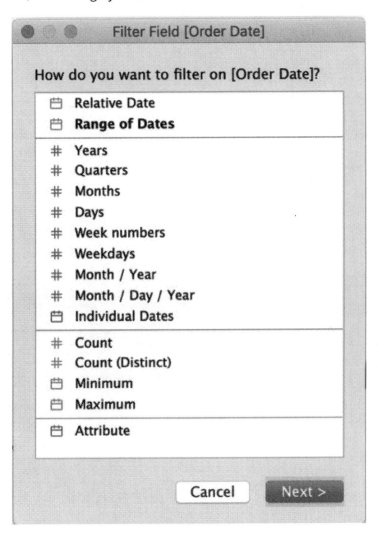

Figure 11.47: Date filter window

4. For this exercise, you will filter by **Relative Date** since you want your view to be dynamically updated in the future too, to only show the last 12 months of data. Click on **Relative Date** in the preceding dialog box and on the next screen select **Months** and enter **12**.

Figure 11.48: Relative dates date filter

This was discussed this in the **Note** section above. Since the **Sample – Superstore** dataset only has data till December 2019, and considering this book was written in July 2020, you will see only six checkmarks.

5. To change that, make use of **Anchor relative to** and enter the date as December 31, 2019, as shown here:

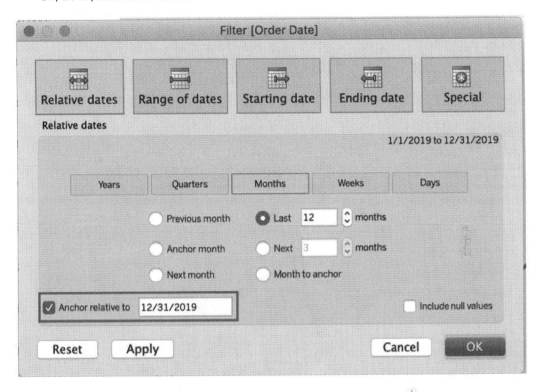

Figure 11.49: Relative dates with an anchor date

You achieved your goal of displaying the last 12 months' trends from the last date in the data using **Relative dates** with **Anchor relative** to December 2019. Here is what the final output should look like **(Month(Order Date)** has been added as a label in the **Marks** shelf for readability):

Figure 11.50: Time series to show the last 12 months relative to the anchor date

In this section, you were reviewed in relative detail the options that available for date filters and how to make the best use of them, and also how to make the best use of **Anchor relative to** and when to use it.

In the next section, we will look at how you can give the end user of your report/dashboard the ability to filter the report as per their requirements.

QUICK FILTERS

Thus far, you have been using filters on your data as a developer without giving end users the ability to filter on a view. One of the many reasons why Tableau is a beloved tool across the developer as well as the end user community is because it allows even end users to control the flow of data in a view. This reduces the back-and-forth with developers because the end user can use the filters to change the data and get the insights they desire. This type of end user filter control is achieved with quick filters.

There are multiple ways of showing your quick filters. The major differences between them are as follows:

Quick Filter Type	Use Case
Single Value (list)	Only select one value at a time in a list
Single Value (dropdown)	Only select one value at a time from a dropdown
Single Value (slider)	Only select one value at a time from a slider
Multiple Values (list)	Select one or multiple values at a time in a list
Multiple Values (dropdown)	Select one or multiple values at a time from a dropdown
Multiple Values (custom list)	Select one or multiple values at a time by searching
Wildcard Match	Wildcard matching of the dimension by specified search characters

Figure 11.51: Quick filter types

Each quick filter has a specific purpose and is widely used across pretty much every dashboard you will ever build. In the following exercise, you'll explore a specific example and review the exact steps to add quick filters to your view.

EXERCISE 11.8: CREATING QUICK FILTERS

Create a simple view of **Sales** by **State** and use **Region** as a quick filter, as regional managers will use the dashboard to filter on their specific dashboard. Use the **Sample - Superstore** dataset once again to complete this exercise.

Perform the following steps:

1. Open the **Sample - Superstore** dataset in your Tableau instance if you don't have it open already.

   You are going to create a cross table of **Sales** by **State** and use **Region** as a quick filter, but first you need to build the view.

2. Drag and drop **State** to the **Rows** shelf and, next, double-click on **Sales** to create the table of **Sales** by **State**. We will now add **Region** as a filter in our **Filters** shelf by selecting all values:

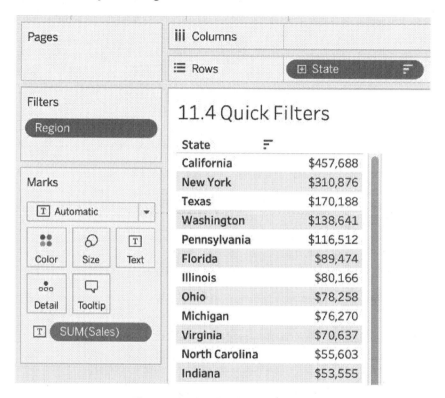

Figure 11.52: Sales by State view

3. Click the down-arrow or simply right-click the **Region** dimension in your **Filters** shelf and select **Show Filter**:

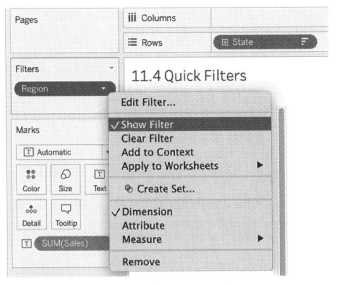

Figure 11.53: Show Filter step

4. Drag the **Region** quick filter from the right-hand side to the left-hand side just below the **Marks** shelf for ease of use. Tableau automatically created **Multiple Values (list)** as a quick filter. If you hover over and click on the arrow in the **Region** quick filter as shown here, you get the following options:

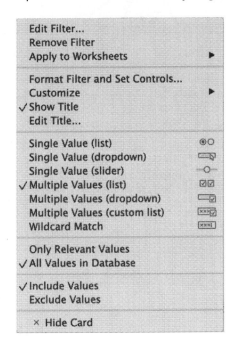

Figure 11.54: Quick filter type options

5. As a recap of all the quick filter types in Tableau, review the following:

Quick Filter Type	Use Case
Single Value (list)	Only select one value at a time in a list
Single Value (dropdown)	Only select one value at a time from a dropdown
Single Value (slider)	Only select one value at a time from a slider
Multiple Values (list)	Select one or multiple values at a time in a list
Multiple Values (dropdown)	Select one or multiple values at a time from a dropdown
Multiple Values (custom list)	Select one or multiple values at a time by searching
Wildcard Match	Wildcard matching of the dimension by specified search characters

Figure 11.55: Quick filter types (review)

6. In this use case, you want your end users to control the region that they want to view so that they are able to view one region or all regions at once. To do this, select **Single Value (list)**, change the quick filter type from **Multiple Values (list)** to **Single Value (list)**, keeping **Show "All" Value** from the **Customize** option checkmarked as shown here:

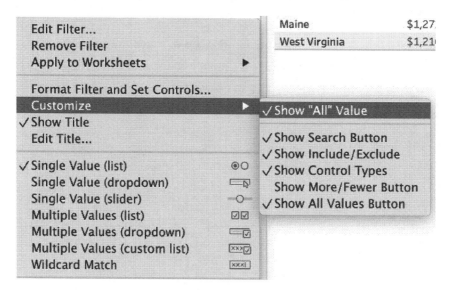

Figure 11.56: Quick filter Customize option

7. Select **East** for **Region** in our quick filter and the final output should resemble
    the following view:

Figure 11.57: Final output after adding a quick filter

Quick filters are why Tableau is such a powerful tool even for end users. In this
section, you have learned the major differences between the types of quick filters and
the best use cases for them. You then created **Sales** by **State** and used **Region** as
a quick filter.

APPLYING FILTERS ACROSS MULTIPLE SHEETS/MULTIPLE DATA SOURCES OR AN ENTIRE DATA SOURCE

When you add a filter to your view, it only applies to your current view. But there will be times when you want to apply the same filter across multiple selected, using the same or a related data source if there is a relationship between primary and secondary data. This section will examine the difference between each of these options and when to use them.

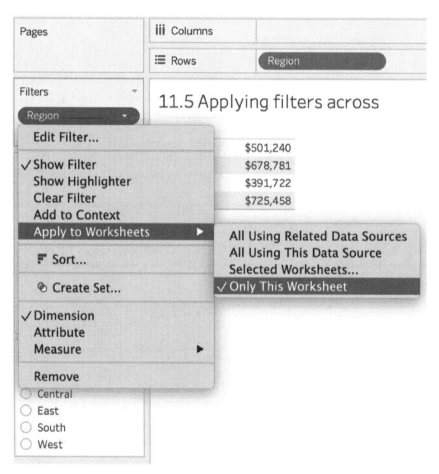

Figure 11.58: Apply to Worksheets options

- Applying a filter to **Only This Worksheet**: Here the filter(s) added to the worksheet is only applied to the worksheet to which the filter was added.

- Applying a filter to **Selected Worksheets...**: If you want your filters to be applied across multiple worksheets or even all of your worksheets, this option comes in handy. In the previous section, you created the **Region** filter. Say you want to use the same filter across a couple of other worksheets that are part of the Tableau workbook. You can do that as shown here:

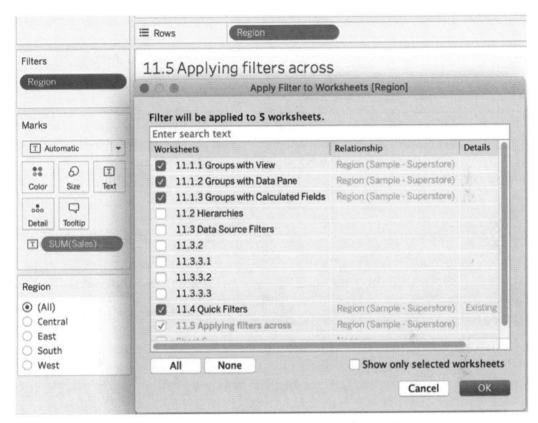

Figure 11.59: Apply a filter to the selected worksheets

- Applying a filter to **All Using This Data Source**: If you want to filter all worksheets that use the same **Sample - Superstore** dataset using the **Region** dimension, use this option. You can achieve the same result by selecting all worksheets in the **Selected Worksheets** option if the workbook only contains one data source.

- Applying a filter to **All Using Related Data Sources**: Choose this option when you want to use the filter from the current worksheet across multiple data sources. This feature was released in 2016, and when Tableau announced this feature release, the company mentioned that it was one of the most asked for features of all time.

This option only works when you create a relationship between a current or primary data source and a secondary data source. You do that by navigating to **Data** in the menu bar, then clicking on **Edit Relationships**. If Tableau does not automatically create some relationships between the data sources, you can create a custom relationship depending on the use case.

Custom Relationship comes in handy when the names of the common columns across the data sources don't match. Once you are able to create the relationship, you can select **All using Related Data Sources** for its magic to work. This option comes in handy when you are data blending, which was discussed in previous chapters.

CONTEXT FILTERS

When you add multiple filters into your Tableau view, each of these filters is calculated independently of the others. So, if you have two quick filters such as **Category** and **Sub-Category** in your view, when you select/deselect a filter, Tableau uses all of its data to show you the view.

If you want to limit the calculation across the whole data source and improve the performance of your report/dashboard (more on this in the exercise that follows), you'll want to use context filters. These help Tableau understand the context of the data and limit the amount of data filtering/loading that happens whenever you change a filter in your view.

In the Tableau order of operations, **Context Filters** has third priority. So when you set a filter as a context filter, you are essentially creating *one* independent filter and all other filters that are not context filters become dependent filters. This is because those other quick filters will process only the data that is first passed through the context filter.

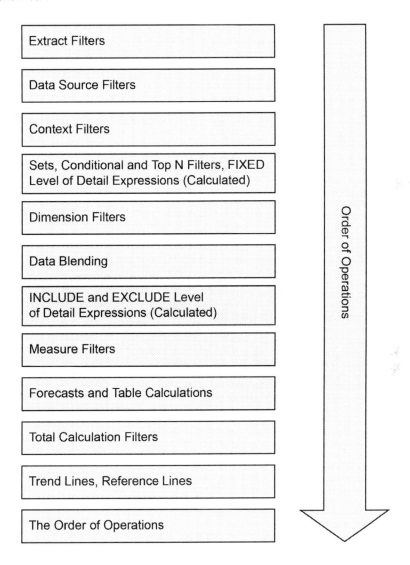

Figure 11.60: Tableau order of operations

An example of this in practice is detailed below.

EXERCISE 11.09: CREATING AND USING CONTEXT FILTERS

In this exercise, you will create and use context filters in an example use case with the **Sample - Superstore** dataset to see why mastering the Tableau order of operations is so beneficial.

1. Open the **Sample - Superstore** dataset in your Tableau instance if you don't have it open already.

2. Create a **Sales** by **Sub-Category** bar chart view, sort it descending by **Sales**, and add **Category** to the **Filters** shelf and show it as a quick filter. You should have the following view:

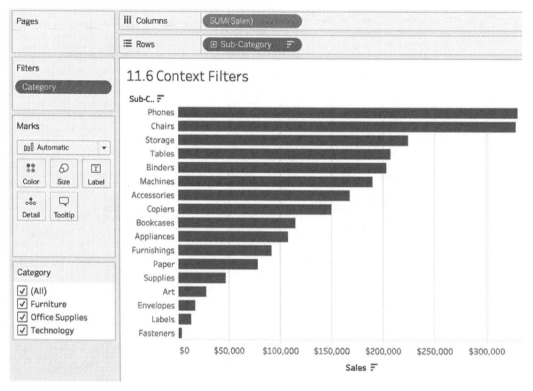

Figure 11.61: Sales by Sub-Category view

3. To show only the top five sub-categories by sales, add the sub-category in the **Filters** shelf, and using the **Top** tab, filter on the top five sub-categories by **Sum** of **Sales** as shown here:

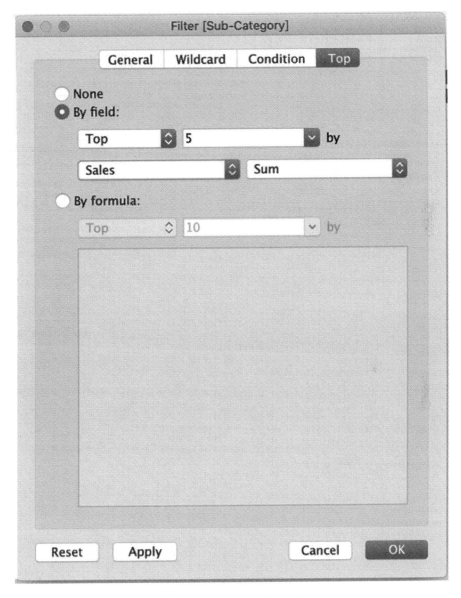

Figure 11.62: Top N filter view

4. Note that all the top five sub-categories in the view. However, if you start de-selecting some of the **Category** quick filters, you will notice that only some of the top five sub-categories remain in the view.

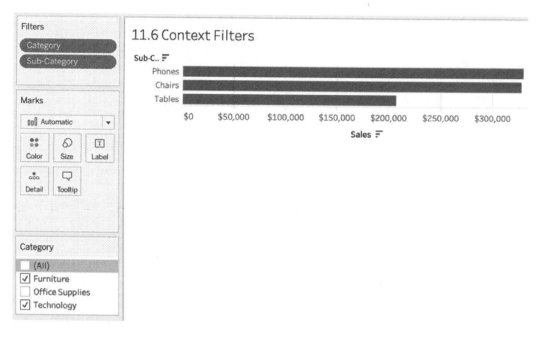

Figure 11.63: Need for context filters

The reason this happens (as you can see in the following figure) is that top N gets filtered first in Tableau operations before dimension filtering is applied to the view. Therefore, when you use the top N filter, Tableau has already calculated the top N for the dimension in the view; and when you use a secondary dimension for filtering, it gets filtered on the top N data and not the whole dataset.

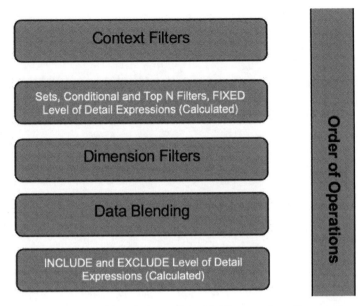

Figure 11.64: Sectional view of the Tableau order of operations

5. Use context filters to counter this since, in the order of operations, these are executed before top N filters, as seen in the preceding figure.

NOTE

Major benefits of context filters are as follows:

Performance Improvements: When working on a large-scale dataset and using a lot of filters, it is recommended that you limit the number of calculations required in the view. When you use context filters, Tableau creates a **TEMP** table with the context and subsequent filters in the order of operations after the context filter references the **TEMP** table for calculating. Say you have a Customer Order database with 100 million rows, and you want to only look at customers in California, which is 18 million rows. By using a context filter on **State**, you are limiting the querying of your whole dataset so that only a subset of the California data will be used for calculating all subsequent filters. This is extremely useful.

Top N Filters: As discussed above, if your view has top N filters, utilizing a context filter is highly recommended so that the filter works in the desired way of showing all the top N irrespective of the secondary filter selected!

6. To fix this issue, change your **Category** filter type to a context filter by right-clicking on **Category** and selecting **Add to Context** as shown here:

Figure 11.65: How to add a filter to context

7. If your filter in the **Filters** shelf turns into a gray dimension, the filter is being used as a context filter. Verify that the context filter is working as expected:

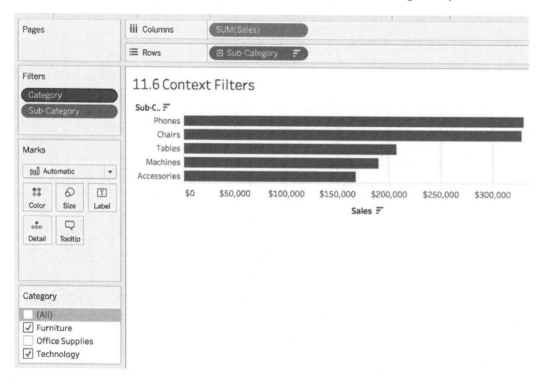

Figure 11.66: View after making Category a context dependent filter

As expected, after using **Category** as a context filter, the changes in **Category** quick filters are appropriately reflected in the view. **Category** becomes the dependent filter, where the top five sub-categories' filters become the independent filters that process the data that is passed through the context filter. It is now showing the top five sub-categories while using **Category** in context.

In this exercise, you explored why context filters are important and how the order of operations dictates how data is presented in the view. The context filter in this exercise was **Category**, which became the dependent variable, and the top N sub-category became the independent variable in our case.

SETS

Sets are custom-created fields used to define a subset of data based on pre-defined conditions or rules.

Think of sets as custom segments that are always binary: a data point is either in or out of the segment depending on whether the data point meets the criteria defined. Sets are created on dimensions, though your conditions can include measures if required. Sets can either be static or dynamic, and you can also combine multiple sets into one set in Tableau, which can be pretty useful, as you will learn from the following exercises. A set is identified in the **Data** pane by the field with a *Venn diagram* icon as shown here:

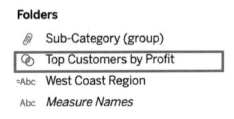

Figure 11.67: Venn diagram icon

STATIC SETS

As mentioned in the preceding section, sets can be either dynamic or static. In static sets, you define the set rules and create a fixed subset of the data, where the members of the set are not updated if the underlying data is updated with new data. For example, you create a Top City set manually, selecting New York, San Francisco, Mumbai, and London. The set members won't be changed even when new data is added or deleted. It's a static set. Dynamic sets can help counter this, but you will learn about dynamic sets in later exercises.

EXERCISE 11.10: CREATING STATIC SETS

In this exercise, you will create a view of the **Sample - Superstore** dataset where all products that contain **Envelope** as part of their name are grouped together as **In** while everything else is grouped as **Out**.

Perform the following steps:

1. Open the **Sample - Superstore** dataset in your Tableau instance if you don't have it open already.

2. Create a view of **Sales** and **Profit** by **Product Name**. Drag and drop **Product Name** to **Rows** and double-click **Sales** and **Profit** to get the following view:

Product Name	Profit	Sales
1.7 Cubic Foot Compact "Cube" Office Re..	$579	$2,706
1/4 Fold Party Design Invitations & Whit..	$23	$50
3-ring staple pack	$17	$42
3.6 Cubic Foot Counter Height Office Ref..	-$872	$2,946
3D Systems Cube Printer, 2nd Generatio..	$3,718	$14,300
3D Systems Cube Printer, 2nd Generatio..	-$468	$2,340
3M Hangers With Command Adhesive	$36	$108
3M Office Air Cleaner	$91	$260
3M Organizer Strips	$10	$83
3M Polarizing Light Filter Sleeves	$75	$216
3M Polarizing Task Lamp with Clamp Ar..	$570	$2,192
3M Replacement Filter for Office Air Clea..	-$20	$303
6" Cubicle Wall Clock, Black	$26	$125
9-3/4 Diameter Round Wall Clock	$183	$455
12 Colored Short Pencils	$3	$18
12-1/2 Diameter Round Wall Clock	$91	$551
14-7/8 x 11 Blue Bar Computer Printout P..	$173	$423

Figure 11.68: Profit and Sales by Product Name

3. Navigate to **Product Name** in the **Data** pane and right-click on it. Click **Create | Set...** as shown here:

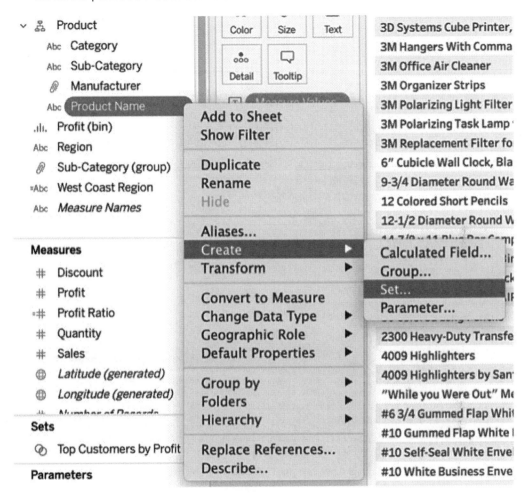

Figure 11.69: How to create a set

In the **Create Set** dialog box, you will notice there are three tabs (**General**, **Condition**, and **Top**), which are pretty similar to those of filters if you remember from the previous section.

4. Create a set for any product that has **Envelope** as part of its **Product Name**. Select the **Select From List** radio button, search for **Envelope**, and press the **All** button to select the list of all the products that contain **Envelope** as part of their name. Then, name your set **Envelope Product Set**, as shown below:

> **NOTE**
>
> The text search is not case-sensitive and, when you search text, it will search across the complete string and not find an exact match. Here, you searched for **Envelope** but your selected list also contains products with **Envelopes** in the name.

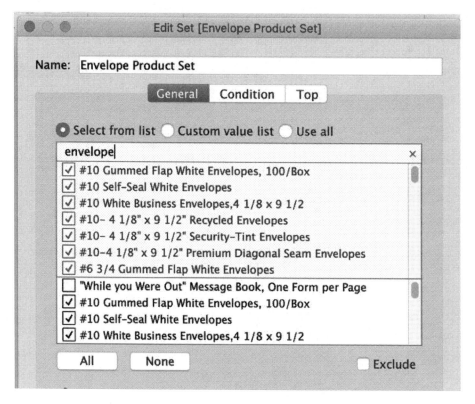

Figure 11.70: Manually adding members to the set

Before you click on the **OK** button, look at the **Summary** section in the `Create Set` dialog box and note that your set contains 48 out of 1,850 values. As mentioned previously, this way of manually selecting items for set creation is static, where the set members won't get updated if new records/rows are added to the data at a later date. You will see how to overcome this limitation in the next exercise.

5. Save the set by clicking on the **OK** button.

6. Check whether the set is working as desired. Drag `Envelope Product Set` to the **Rows** shelf. Consider the **In/Out** set here. If a product name meets the criteria that you set, that product will be **In** the set; and if the product does not meet the requirements, that product will be **Out**.

Figure 11.71: In/Out set view

7. Instead of **In/Out**, display the actual product name by right-clicking on **Envelope Product Set** and selecting **Show Members in Set**:

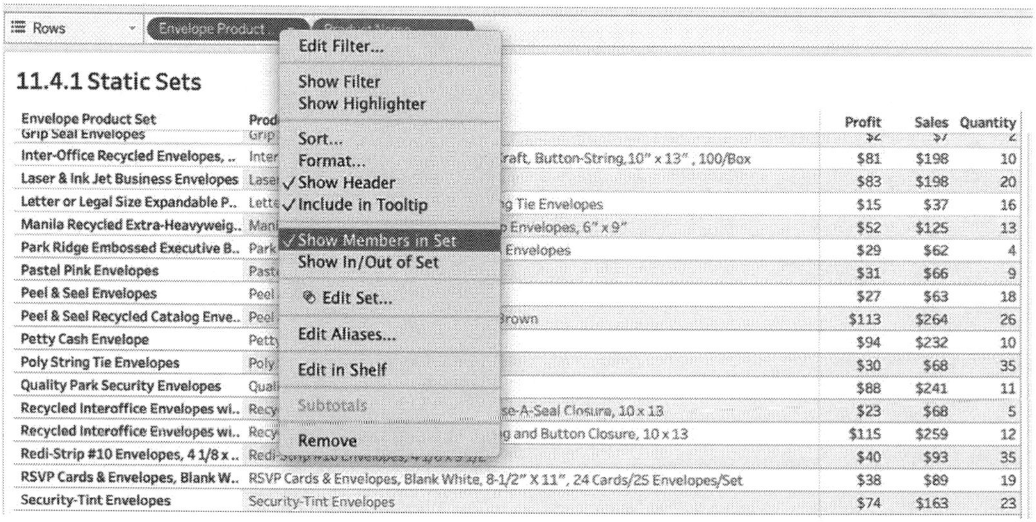

Figure 11.72: How to show members in a set

In this exercise, you encounterd sets for the first time and observed how static sets are used on dashboards. You also learned to show/hide members from a set and what the **Summary** tab in the **Create Set** dialog box means.

The next section will review dynamic sets and how they can overcome the shortcomings of static ones.

DYNAMIC SETS

In this section, you will learn why dynamic sets are preferred over static sets. You'll also practice using the two remaining tabs from the **Create Set** dialog box you encountered in the previous section. Dynamic sets use logic to dynamically update the members of the set, which means when the data changes, the set will be re-computed and the **In/Out** members can be added/deleted depending on the computation.

EXERCISE 11.11: CREATING DYNAMIC SETS

Though previous sets that you created were good, but the product manager responsible for all **Envelope** products has asked you to create a dynamic view of the groupings as he wants to update the **In/Out** groups whenever a new product name is added or deleted. You will be using the same view that you created in the previous exercise and extending that view to add dynamic sets.

Perform the following steps:

1. Open the **Sample - Superstore** dataset in your Tableau instance if you have not already done so.

2. Create a view of **Sales** and **Profit** by **Product Name**. Drag and drop **Product Name** to **Rows** and double-click **Sales** and **Profit** to get the following view:

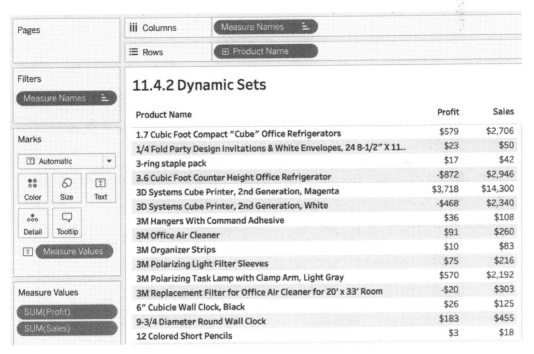

Figure 11.73: Profit and Sales by Product Name

3. Navigate to **Product Name** in the **Data** pane and right-click on it. Click on **Create | Set....**

4. Expand your previous set criteria. You want the top five profitable envelope product names that had more than $100 in sales. For this, use both the **Condition** and the **Top** tabs. Create the condition for at least $100 of sales first, as shown here:

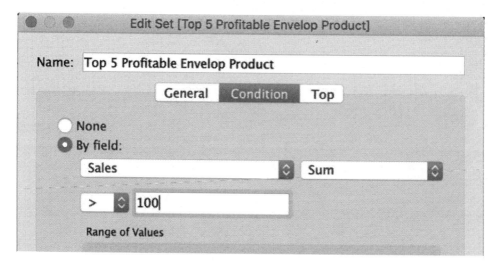

Figure 11.74: Conditional set definition

5. Add the criteria of top five profitable **Envelope** products in the **Top** tab, as shown here:

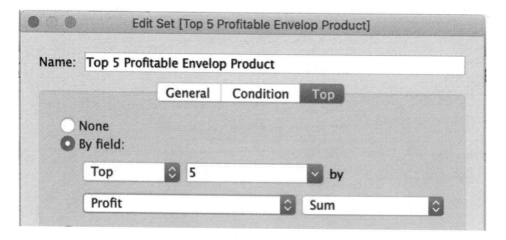

Figure 11.75: Dynamic set definition

6. You have not yet filtered for **Envelope** as you did for your static set, but if you use the same **General** tab to filter the **Envelope** products, your set won't be updated when new data is added. To ensure your future data is considered for the set, use the **Condition** tab and write a calculated formula to do this dynamically. Then, de-select **By field** and use **By formula** and write the following formula:

```
MIN(CONTAINS([Product Name],"envelope")) AND SUM([Sales])>=100
```

Edit Set [Top 5 Profitable Envelop Product]

Name: Top 5 Profitable Envelop Product

General | Condition | Top

○ None
○ By field:
    Sales | Sum
    >= | 100

Range of Values
    Min: Load
    Max:

● By formula:
```
MIN(CONTAINS([Product Name],"envelope"))
AND SUM([Sales])>=100
```

Reset | Apply | Cancel | OK

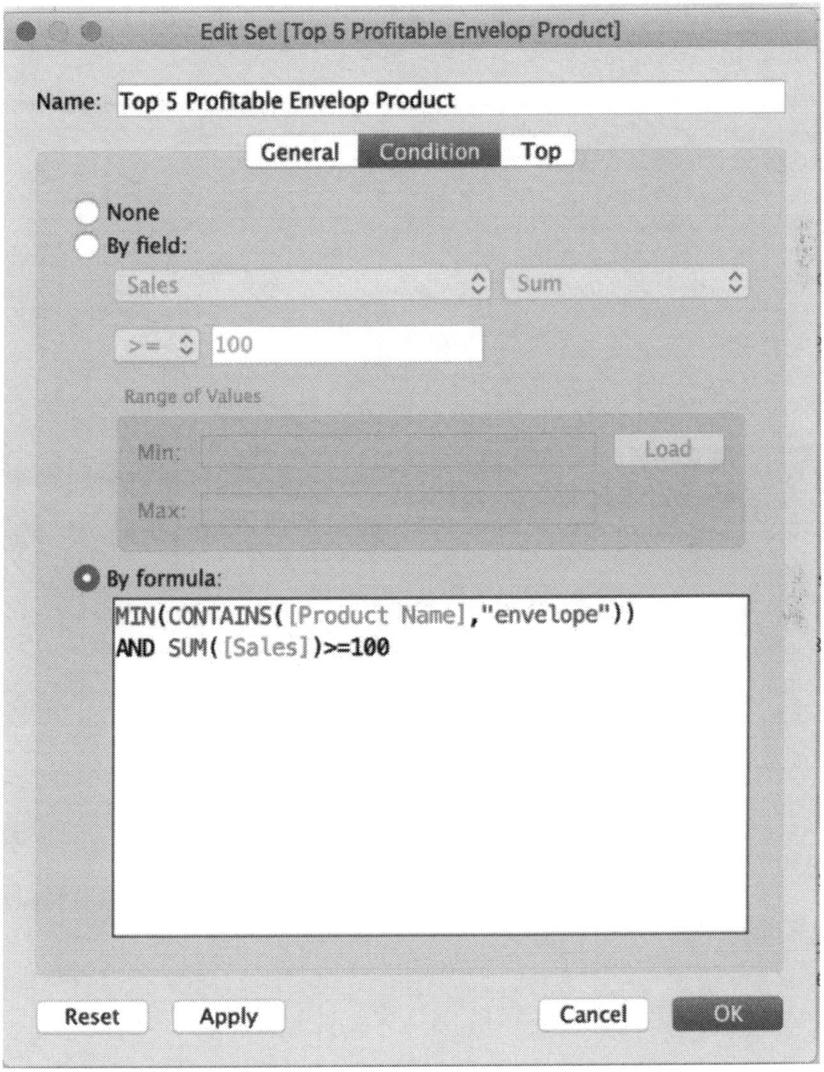

Figure 11.76: Formula-based conditional set

> **NOTE**
>
> You had to use **MIN** for **Product Name** because you cannot mix aggregate and non-aggregate in the calculated field without using aggregation for a non-aggregate dimension, as explained in previous chapters.

7. Before you do the spot check and saving the set, review the **Summary** section of the dialog box:

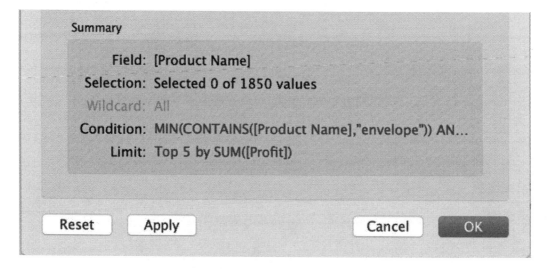

Figure 11.77: Summary box of sets

In the **Summary** section, your selection says **0** because you have not manually selected anything. **Condition** is the formula you used in your **Condition** tab, and **Limit** is the criteria in the **Top** tab.

8. Drag both sets you created in the last two exercises to your **Rows** shelf: You have the top five rows by profit in `Top 5 Profitable Envelope Product`, as seen. These five products are also part of the static set because these product names include `Envelope`.

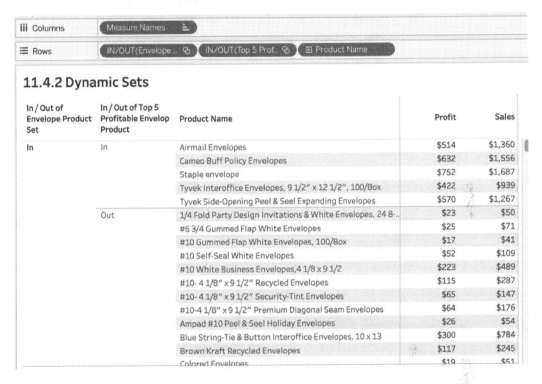

11.4.2 Dynamic Sets

In / Out of Envelope Product Set	In / Out of Top 5 Profitable Envelop Product	Product Name	Profit	Sales
In	In	Airmail Envelopes	$514	$1,360
		Cameo Buff Policy Envelopes	$632	$1,556
		Staple envelope	$752	$1,687
		Tyvek Interoffice Envelopes, 9 1/2" x 12 1/2", 100/Box	$422	$939
		Tyvek Side-Opening Peel & Seel Expanding Envelopes	$570	$1,267
	Out	1/4 Fold Party Design Invitations & White Envelopes, 24 8-..	$23	$50
		#6 3/4 Gummed Flap White Envelopes	$25	$71
		#10 Gummed Flap White Envelopes, 100/Box	$17	$41
		#10 Self-Seal White Envelopes	$52	$109
		#10 White Business Envelopes,4 1/8 x 9 1/2	$223	$489
		#10- 4 1/8" x 9 1/2" Recycled Envelopes	$115	$287
		#10- 4 1/8" x 9 1/2" Security-Tint Envelopes	$65	$147
		#10-4 1/8" x 9 1/2" Premium Diagonal Seam Envelopes	$64	$176
		Ampad #10 Peel & Seel Holiday Envelopes	$26	$54
		Blue String-Tie & Button Interoffice Envelopes, 10 x 13	$300	$784
		Brown Kraft Recycled Envelopes	$117	$245
		Colored Envelopes	$19	$51

Figure 11.78: Final output for dynamic sets

With this exercise, you are now able to create a non-static set that can update the set members depending on the changes made to the dataset or when new data is added or deleted from the set. Dynamic sets are usually preferred over static sets because they allow you to ensure new data is populated in sets in the future when you are not actively working on the dashboard.

ADDING MEMBERS TO THE SET

In both the previous sections, you created sets from scratch. In this section, we will address those cases in which you want to add more conditions to your set definition to add new members or delete them. Adding members to the set is more often done when stakeholders want to update the condition of the underlying set or the developer wants to experiment with complicated conditional logic.

The following exercise will guide through how to complete this task.

EXERCISE 11.12: ADDING MEMBERS TO THE SET

For the **Envelope Product Set** you created in the previous section, the product manager wants you to add a specific product to the set since they cannot add that product **IN** the set from their view and that product is not part of the top N sales or profit. As the dashboard developer, you are tasked with adding that specific product to the set.

Perform the following steps:

1. You will be reusing the view that you created in the previous exercise, but to demonstrate the workings of adding members to the set, remove **Envelope Product Set** from the view. Your view should now look as follows:

11.4.3 Adding members to Set

In / Out of Top 5 Profitable Envelop Product	Product Name	Profit	Sales
In	Airmail Envelopes	$514	$1,360
	Cameo Buff Policy Envelopes	$632	$1,556
	Staple envelope	$752	$1,687
	Tyvek Interoffice Envelopes, 9 1/2" x 12 1/2", 100/Box	$422	$939
	Tyvek Side-Opening Peel & Seel Expanding Envelopes	$570	$1,267
Out	1.7 Cubic Foot Compact "Cube" Office Refrigerators	$579	$2,706
	1/4 Fold Party Design Invitations & White Envelopes, 24 8-1/2" X 11" Cards, 25 Env./Pack	$23	$50
	3-ring staple pack	$17	$42
	3.6 Cubic Foot Counter Height Office Refrigerator	-$872	$2,946
	3D Systems Cube Printer, 2nd Generation, Magenta	$3,718	$14,300
	3D Systems Cube Printer, 2nd Generation, White	-$468	$2,340

Figure 11.79: Adding members to the set

2. To add members to the set, select the product name/row of data that you want to include in your view, and left-click the row to get the following:

11.4.3 Adding members to Set

In / Out of Top 5 Profitable Envelop Product	Product Name	Profit
In	Airmail Envelopes	$514
	Cameo Buff Policy Envelopes	$632
	Staple envelope	$752
	Tyvek Interoffice Envelopes, 9 1/2" x 12 1/2", 100/Box	$422
	Tyvek Side-Opening Peel & Seel Expanding Envelopes	$570
Out	3M Polarizing Task Lamp with Clamp Arm, Light Gray	$570
	1.7 Cubic Foot Compact	$579
	1/4 Fold Party Design Inv	$23
	3-ring staple pack	$17
	3.6 Cubic Foot Counter H	$872
	3D Systems Cube Printer, 2nd Generation, Magenta	$3,718

Options panel: ✓ Keep Only ✗ Exclude ⊞ ⊵ ⋤ ⊘ ▾ ▦
2 items selected · SUM of Measure Values: **2,762**
3M Polarizing Task Lamp with Clamp Arm, Light Gray

Figure 11.80: Include/exclude members from the set

3. Click on the *Venn diagram* icon in the options panel and select **Add to Top 5 Profitable Envelop Product (Sample – Superstore)** as shown in the following screenshot:

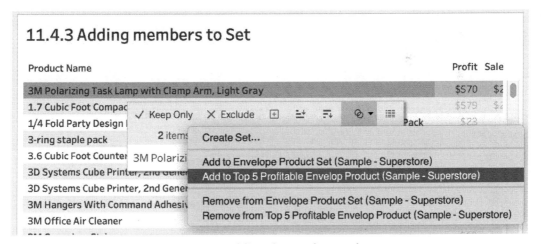

Figure 11.81: Adding the product to the set

4. As soon as you do that, the row **3M Polarizing Task Lamp with Clamp Arm, Light Gray** is moved from the **Out** set to the **In** set as shown here:

11.4.3 Adding members to Set

In / Out of Top 5 Profitable Envelop Product	Product Name	Profit S
In	3M Polarizing Task Lamp with Clamp Arm, Light Gray	$570
	Airmail Envelopes	$514
	Cameo Buff Policy Envelopes	$632
	Staple envelope	$752
	Tyvek Interoffice Envelopes, 9 1/2" x 12 1/2", 100/Box	$422
	Tyvek Side-Opening Peel & Seel Expanding Envelopes	$570
Out	1.7 Cubic Foot Compact "Cube" Office Refrigerators	$579
	1/4 Fold Party Design Invitations & White Envelopes, 24 8-1/2" X 11" Cards, 25 Env./Pack	$23
	3-ring staple pack	$17
	3.6 Cubic Foot Counter Height Office Refrigerator	-$872
	3D Systems Cube Printer, 2nd Generation, Magenta	$3,718
	3D Systems Cube Printer, 2nd Generation, White	-$468
	3M Hangers With Command Adhesive	$36

Figure 11.82: The product was added to the set

5. You would follow a similar process if you want to remove a data row from the set. Instead of adding, remove from the set options as shown here:

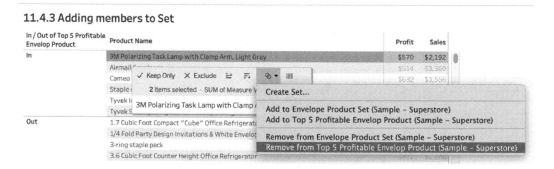

Figure 11.83: Removing a member from the set

Adding members to a set is pretty straightforward and can be incredibly helpful when you want to manually update the member set without editing the actual definition of the set.

COMBINED SETS

You have now created both static and dynamic sets. Individually, these sets work well, but you can also extend Tableau functionality by combining multiple sets to create a combined set. Using combined sets, you can perform additional analysis and compare and contrast multiple sets. When you create a combined set, you create an altogether new set that contains a combination of either all members from both sets, some members that exist in both sets, or a member from one specific set.

Complete the following exercise to see this in practice.

EXERCISE 11.13: HOW TO CREATE COMBINED SETS

Your regional manager wants you to create a view of states that are both in **Top 20 States by Profits** as well as **Top 20 States by Sales**. You will utilize combined sets for this, which will be created from two individual sets you'll make first: **Top 20 States by Profits** and **Top 20 States by Sales**.

Perform the following steps to complete this exercise:

1. Open the **Sample - Superstore** dataset in your Tableau instance if you don't have it open already.

Set 1: Top 20 States by Profits:

2. Create your first set with `Top 20 [States] by [Profits]` as shown here:

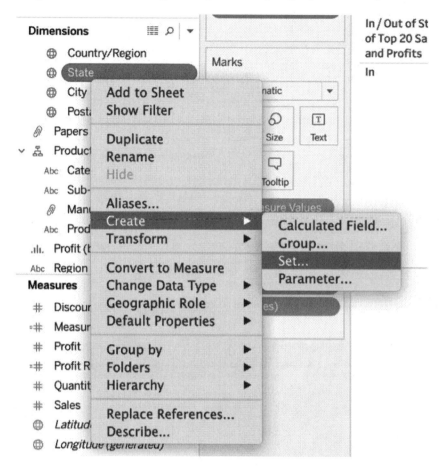

Figure 11.84: Creating the set

3. Name the set `Top 20 States by Profits`, select the `Top` tab from the window, and select `By field` and `Top 20 by Profit Sum` as shown below:

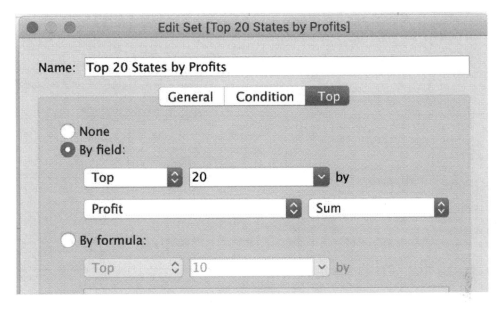

Figure 11.85: Top N members for the set

Set 2: Top 20 States by Sales:

4. Similarly, create your second set with **Top 20 [States] by [Sales]** as shown here:

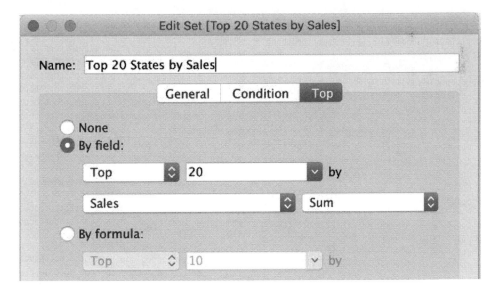

Figure 11.86: Top N members for the set -2!

5. Create a view by dragging **State** to the **Rows** shelf and adding **Profits** and **Sales** to the view as shown here:

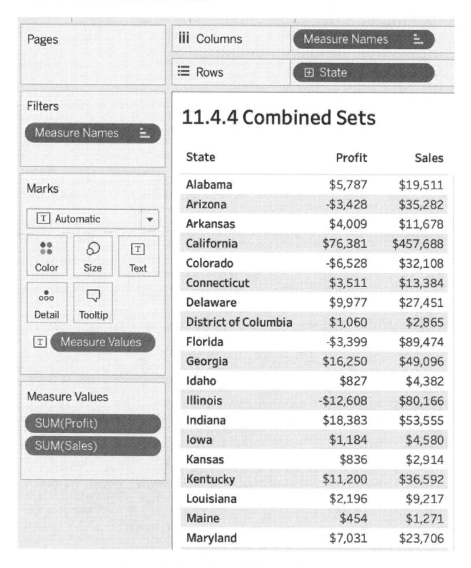

Figure 11.87: Profit and Sales by State view

6. Add both **Top 20 States by Profits** and **Top 20 States by Sales** to your view in **Rows** as shown here:

☰ Rows	IN/OUT(Top 20 St.. ⊘	IN/OUT(Top 20 St.. ⊘	⊞ State

11.4.4 Combined Sets

In / Out of Top 20 States by Sales	In / Out of Top 20 States by Profits	State	Profit	Sales
In	In	California	$76,381	$457,688
		Georgia	$16,250	$49,096
		Indiana	$18,383	$53,555
		Kentucky	$11,200	$36,592
		Michigan	$24,463	$76,270
		Minnesota	$10,823	$29,863
		New Jersey	$9,773	$35,764
		New York	$74,039	$310,876
		Virginia	$18,598	$70,637
		Washington	$33,403	$138,641
		Wisconsin	$8,402	$32,115
	Out	Arizona	-$3,428	$35,282
		Colorado	-$6,528	$32,108
		Florida	-$3,399	$89,474
		Illinois	-$12,608	$80,166
		North Carolina	-$7,491	$55,603
		Ohio	-$16,971	$78,258
		Pennsylvania	-$15,560	$116,512
		Tennessee	-$5,342	$30,662
		Texas	-$25,729	$170,188

Figure 11.88: Two sets view

The goal is to create a combined set from which you can get a list of all the states that are part of the top 20 by both profits and sales. For this, you want all **In** members of both of the sets you just created.

7. Press *Command* + multi-select both the sets for Mac or *Ctrl* + multi-select both the sets for Windows and click on **Create Combined Set...**:

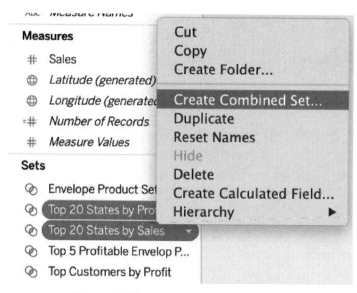

Figure 11.89: Creating a combined set

8. In the **Create Set** modal window, name your new set **States of Top 20 Sales and Profits**. You can also change the sets that you want to be part of the combined sets from the dropdown. There are four options for members in your combined sets, which are pretty self-explanatory. You want a list of all the states that are part of both the top 20 states by sales as well as profits, so use **Shared members in both sets** as shown here:

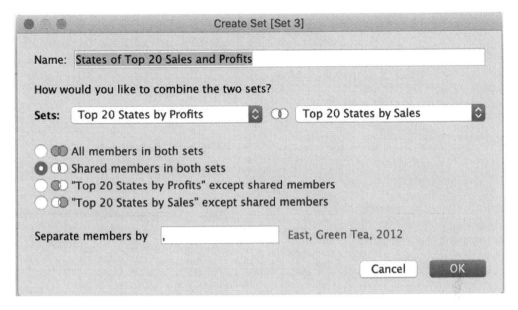

Figure 11.90: Combined set definition

Previous steps noted that you want your combined sets to contain all **In** members from both sets. In the following screenshots, you'll observe that the combined set has all the same states as the intersection of two individual sets.

In / Out of Top 20 States by Profits	In / Out of Top 20 States by Sales	State	Profit	Sales
In	In	California	$76,381	$457,688
		Georgia	$16,250	$49,096
		Indiana	$18,383	$53,555
		Kentucky	$11,200	$36,592
		Michigan	$24,463	$76,270
		Minnesota	$10,823	$29,863
		New Jersey	$9,773	$35,764
		New York	$74,039	$310,876
		Virginia	$18,598	$70,637
		Washington	$33,403	$138,641
		Wisconsin	$8,402	$32,115

Figure 11.91: In combined set view

Figure 11.92: States in the top 20 of both profits and sales

The final output will be as follows:

Figure 11.93: Combined Sets final output!

In this final section on sets, you learned how to use combined sets by walking through an example. The next will explore parameters.

PARAMETERS

Parameters are like variables/placeholders in Tableau, which give the end user the ability to control the view or data that is shown as part of the report. They allow you to customize your view, adding interactivity as well as flexibility to the workbook. Parameters are used to replacing a constant value from the view with more variable/ dynamic values, which are controlled by the end user. They can take any data type: strings, integers, floats, dates, or any varchars. They can easily be confused with filters but the major difference between parameters and filters is that, with filters, the data gets filtered from the view so that it only shows for the filtered values, whereas with parameters, the variables only act as a reference. Parameters control the value of the variable created instead of filtering on the data.

To use parameters in the view, there are four steps that you need to perform:

1. Create the parameters based on the requirements.

2. Show the parameter control to the end user, as we do for sets/filters.

3. Use the parameters either in the calculated field, filters, or reference lines.

4. Use the calculated field, filters, and reference lines in the view.

EXERCISE 11.14: STANDARD PARAMETERS

In this exercise, you'll create and use standard parameters. To observe the true essence of Tableau and parameters, you will create a more advanced view that allows your end users to select the dimensions as well as the measures that they want to see in the view.

In previous chapters, you have given users the ability to filter data, create groups, and create sets on pre-selected dimensions and measures, but you have not yet given users the ability to select/change the dimensions/measures as per their requirements. But there are many instances when stakeholders want the exact same view with different measures/dimensions. So, instead of creating 4-6 different views with different dimensions/measures combinations, letting users choose their own measures and dimensions is a more efficient way of handling the request while limiting clutter. This is the final view you are aiming for:

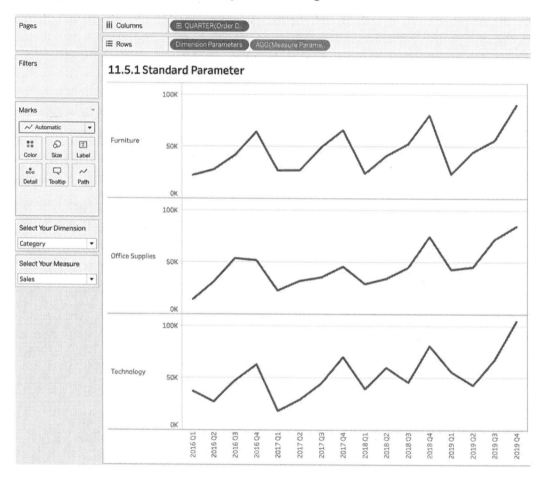

Figure 11.94: Final output for parameters

Perform the following steps to complete this exercise:

1. Open the **Sample - Superstore** dataset in your Tableau instance if you have not already done so.

   In this example, you will create a continuous line graph for the measure, selected by the end user, by quarter. As mentioned earlier, you want to give end users the ability to change the measures or dimensions.

2. There are four steps to using parameters. The first step is to *create a parameter*. Do this by either clicking on the arrow in the **Dimensions** pane and clicking on **Create Parameter...**, as shown in the following screenshot, or else right-clicking anywhere in the **Parameters** shelf and clicking on **Create Parameter...**:

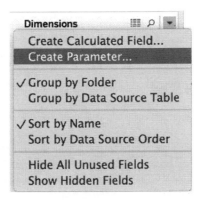

Figure 11.95: Creating a parameter

You will be creating two parameters in this exercise: one for selecting **Measures** and one for selecting **Dimensions**.

3. First, create a parameter for selecting **Measures**. In the **Edit Parameter** modal window, you have a choice of six data types: **Float**, **Integer**, **String**, **Boolean**, **Date**, or **Date & Time**. Since your parameter contains text, use **String** as the data type. For the **Allowable values** option, instead of all values, use **List** so that you can define the options available to the end user selecting the measure.

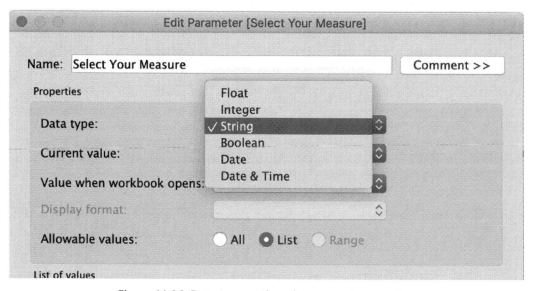

Figure 11.96: Data type options in parameter creation

When you select **List** for **Allowable values**, you are presented with **List of values** options. You then have to define your list, which will be the measure names that your users can select.

4. Manually add **Sales**, **Profit**, **Discount**, and **Quantity** to **List of values**. Your **Create Parameter** window should look something like this:

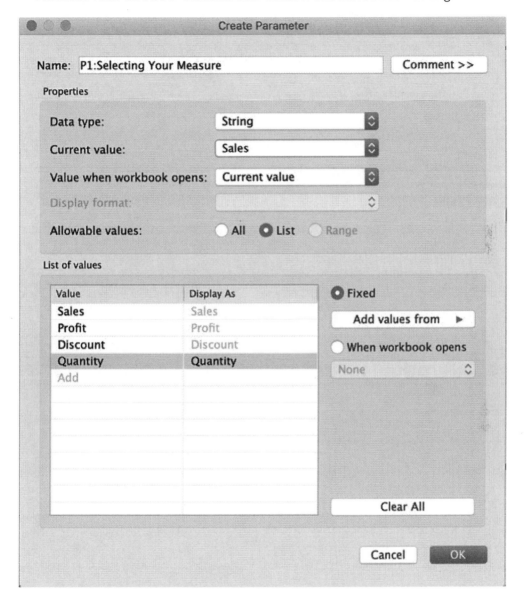

Figure 11.97: Adding measure options for the parameter

5. Repeat the same steps for **Select Your Dimension**. The **Create Parameter** modal window should look something like the following:

Figure 11.98: Adding a dimension option for the parameter

The next step is to use the created parameter in a calculated field. By default, parameters don't control anything unless you use the parameter either as part of a calculated field, reference lines, or filters. You will be using the calculated field to use the parameter, which acts as a placeholder substitution for dynamically populating the calculated field with the end user's selected measure/dimension.

6. Create a calculated field now, named **Measure Parameter**.

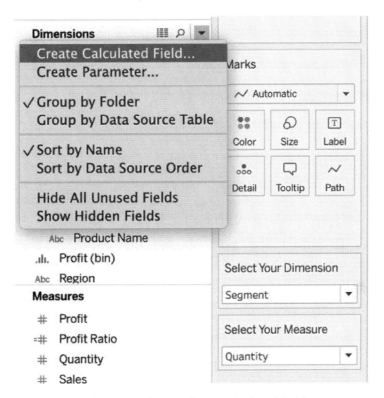

Figure 11.99: Creating a calculated field

7. Use the **CASE** statement so that if the user selects **Sales** measures in the parameter, your calculated field should show **SUM(Sales)** in the view. If the user selects **Profit** measures in the parameter, your calculated field should show **SUM(Profit)** in the view and so on. Here is the formula for the calculated field:

```
CASE [Select Your Measure]
WHEN "Sales" THEN SUM([Sales])
WHEN "Profit" THEN SUM([Profit])
WHEN "Discount" THEN AVG([Discount])
WHEN "Quantity" THEN SUM([Quantity])
END
```

| Measure Parameter | 🛢 Sample – Superstore | ✕ |

```
CASE [Select Your Measure]
WHEN "Sales" THEN SUM([Sales])
WHEN "Profit" THEN SUM([Profit])
WHEN "Discount" THEN AVG([Discount])
WHEN "Quantity" THEN SUM([Quantity])
END
```

The calculation is valid.   1 Dependency ▾   Apply   OK

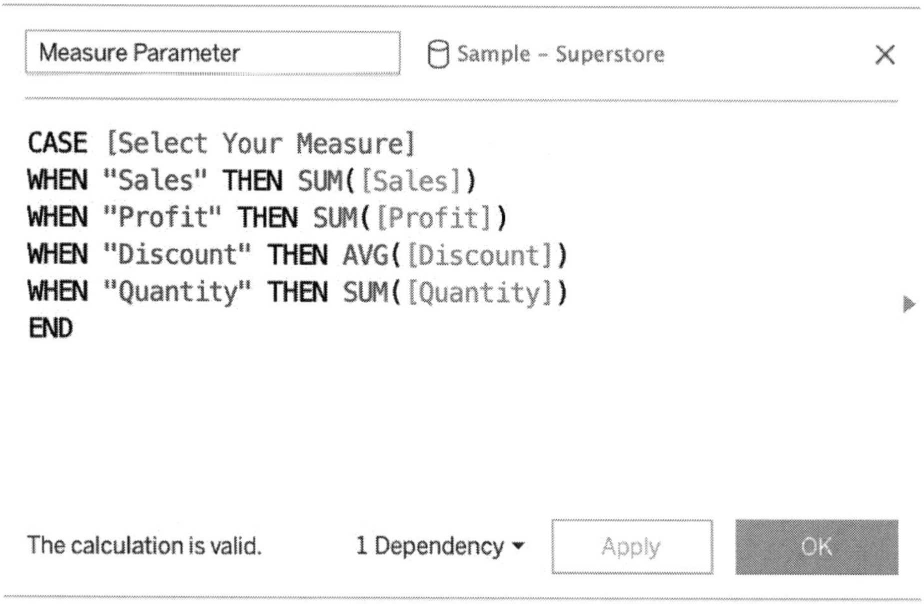

Figure 11.100: Case statement calculated field for the measure parameter

8. Repeat the same step for the **Dimension Parameter** calculated field with the following **CASE** statement:

```
CASE [Select Your Dimension]
WHEN "Segment" THEN [Segment]
WHEN "Category" THEN [Category]
WHEN "Sub-Category" THEN [Sub-Category]
WHEN "State" THEN [State]
END
```

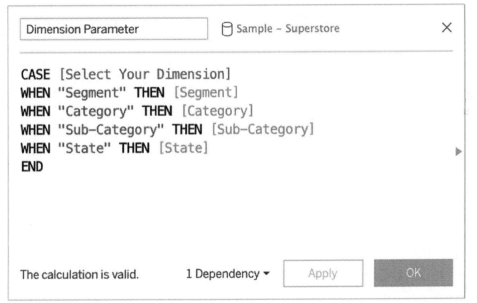

Figure 11.101: Case statement calculated field for Dimension Parameter

9. The next step is to create a view with calculated fields as well as using two of our parameters: Drag **Dimension Parameter** as well as **Measure Parameter** to the **Rows** shelf. Next, drag **Order Date** to **Columns** and change the date dimension to **Continuous** date by quarter. The view that you see is pre-selected based on the *current value* that you selected when creating the parameter. You had **Sales** for the **{Select Your Measure}** parameter and **Segment** for the **{Select Your Dimension}** parameter. So, your current view is the quarterly trend of **Sales** by **Segment**.

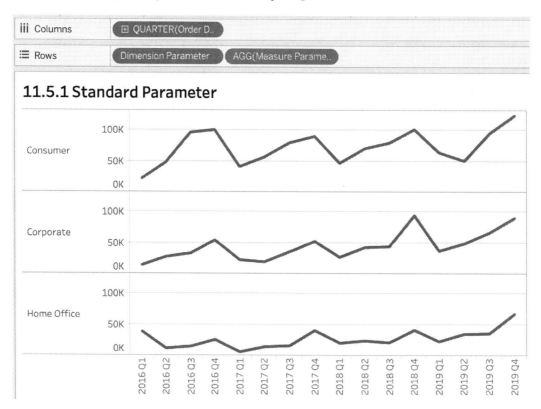

Figure 11.102: Parameter view with default parameters selected

10. The final step is to allow your end users to control the measure as well as the dimension in the view. Right-click on the parameter that you created and click on **Show Parameter Control**. Repeat the step for the other parameter:

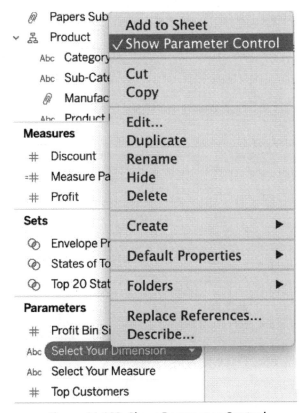

Figure 11.103: Show Parameter Control

11. Add the parameter control to your view, so that the end users have the ability to choose the dimension/measure of their choice. Here are two views with a different combination of dimensions and measures:

Profit by Category:

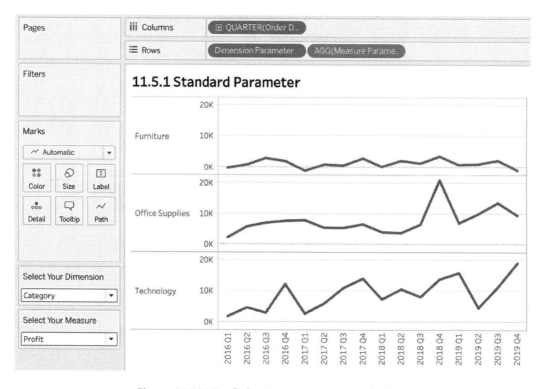

Figure 11.104 Profit by Category parametric view

Quantity by Segment:

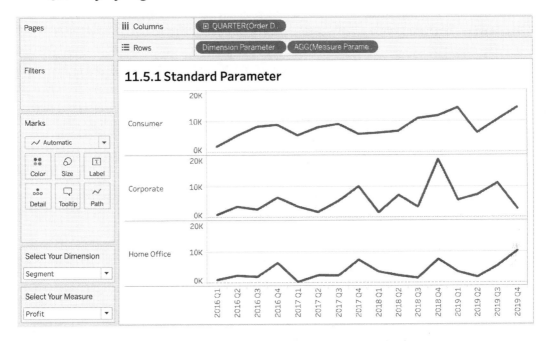

Figure 11.105: Quantity by Segment parametric view

As an end user, it can be confusing to look at different combinations because the line graph or graph view does not show which dimension/measure is part of the view. Though you have the dropdowns, to make it easier for end users, you can also include the callout in your title by creating a dynamic title that is updated along with the dimension in the view. Edit the title by double-clicking on the worksheet title and that opens up the **Edit Title** window as shown here:

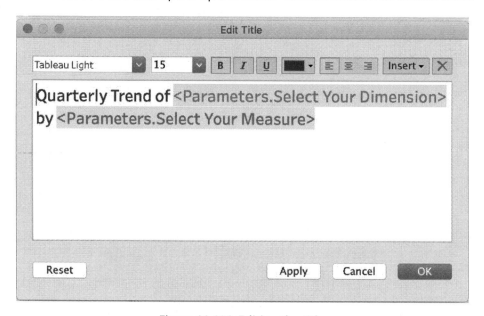

Figure 11.106: Editing the title

The preceding formula uses dynamic variables. In particular, **<Parameters. Select Your Dimension>** is dynamic such that, when you change the parameter from the dropdown in the worksheet, the title will be automatically updated. You don't have to type the exact variable; you can insert these variables by clicking on **Insert** in the top right-hand corner of the window as shown here:

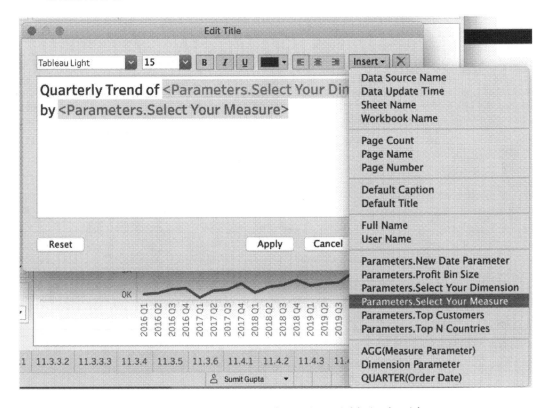

Figure 11.107: Inserting a dynamic variable in the title

Here is the final output that you aimed for:

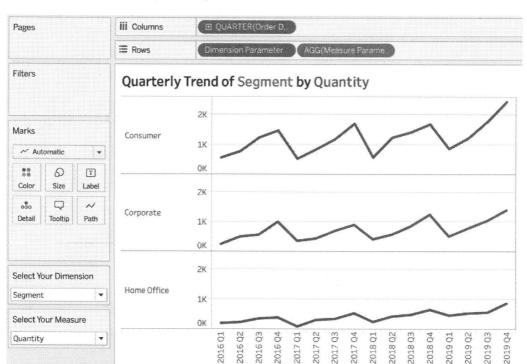

Figure 11.108: Parameter final view with parameter control

In this exercise, you learned what parameters are and how to use them in combination with calculated fields to create a dynamic worksheet where the end users have complete control over which dimension/measures they want the report view to be part of. The skills imparted in this section will go a long way toward growing your advanced knowledge and expertise in Tableau.

DYNAMIC PARAMETERS

Dynamic parameters was one of the most requested features in the Tableau Community forum, and the Tableau developers shipped the feature in the Tableau 2020.1 version in February 2020. Prior to Tableau version 2020.1, standard parameters had a specific limitation: When the data was updated with new entries (specifically dates), the parameters list/members were not updated. This meant that Tableau authors had to manually refresh the parameter list every time the data source was updated, which, depending on the frequency of the updates, could be very time-consuming. Dynamic parameters overcame that. With these, you can also allow your parameters to automatically choose the most recent date, which wasn't possible previously. Let's explore how this works with the help of an exercise.

EXERCISE 11.15: DYNAMIC PARAMETERS

In this exercise, you will be using new dummy data to see what parameters looked like in previous versions of Tableau (2019.4 or earlier). You'll then follow the steps outlined below to use the new parameters to automatically update the parameter list as and when the data source is updated.

> **NOTE**
>
> A screenshot of the previous version of Tableau has been included; however, you might not have that option. The goal is to communicate the point about static versus dynamic parameters, so you don't need to have two versions of Tableau installed. This exercise will stick with Tableau 2020.1 or later versions.

Perform the following steps to complete this exercise:

1. **Date parameters in Tableau 2019.1**: To create a parameter in an earlier version of Tableau, connect the **DynamicParameters.csv** file in Tableau. Create a parameter, and set **Data type** as **Date** and **Allowable values** as **List**, and instead of manually adding these dates, use **Add from Field** and the **Date** column to pre-populate the list of values as shown here:

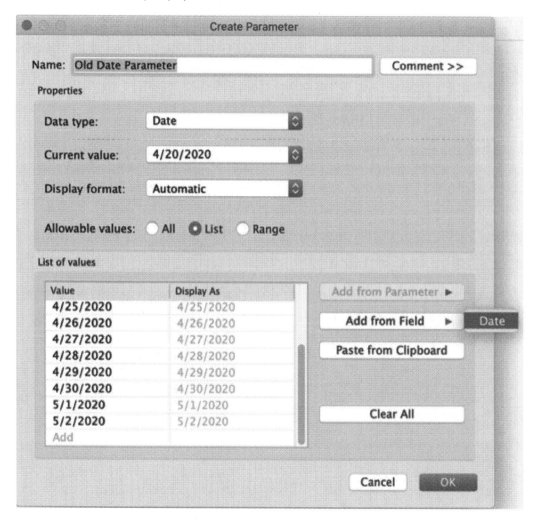

Figure 11.109: Dynamic parameters – adding from a field

This method, as discussed previously, is pretty static. If new data is added with new dates, the parameter won't automatically pre-populate **List of Values** to include the new dates as part of the updated data source, which was a limitation in previous versions of Tableau.

2. **Date Parameters in Tableau 2020.1**: Repeat the step with the same dataset but, this time, do so in the Tableau 2020.1 version. Connect the **DynamicParameters.csv** file in Tableau, create a parameter, and set **Data type** as **Date** and **Allowable values** as **List**. Note that, as soon as you select **List**, unlike previous versions of Tableau, Tableau 2020.1 has two options:

- **Fixed**: This is where you can pre-populate the list from a field as you did in the previous old date parameter.

- **When Workbook Opens**: This is dynamic option wherein the list will be pre-populated from the **Date** field, but instead of a fixed list, the list will get updated whenever new data is updated/added.

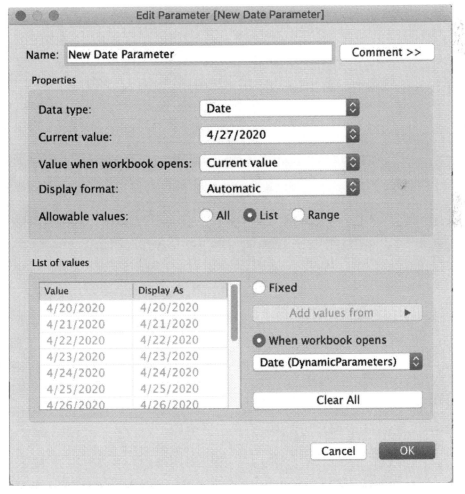

Figure 11.110: Dynamic parameters in Tableau 2020.1 and above

3. In the preceding screenshot, the last date is 5/2/2020. Open the **DynamicParameters.csv** spreadsheet in a tool of your choice (non-Tableau) and add a new row, **Date: 5/3/2020 and Sales: 80**. Save the file as shown here:

Date	Sales
4/20/20	98
4/21/20	97
4/22/20	98
4/23/20	88
4/24/20	53
4/25/20	95
4/26/20	5
4/27/20	60
4/28/20	67
4/29/20	41
4/30/20	41
5/1/20	48
5/2/20	15
5/3/20	80

Figure 11.111: CSV data from DynamicParameters.csv

4. To check whether the new date was added or not, close your Tableau workbook (make sure you save it first, though). Then, re-open the workbook and edit **New Date Parameter** to confirm whether the new date was appended to the list of values in the parameter. As you can see from the following screenshot, May 3, 2020, was automatically added to the list of values in the parameter.

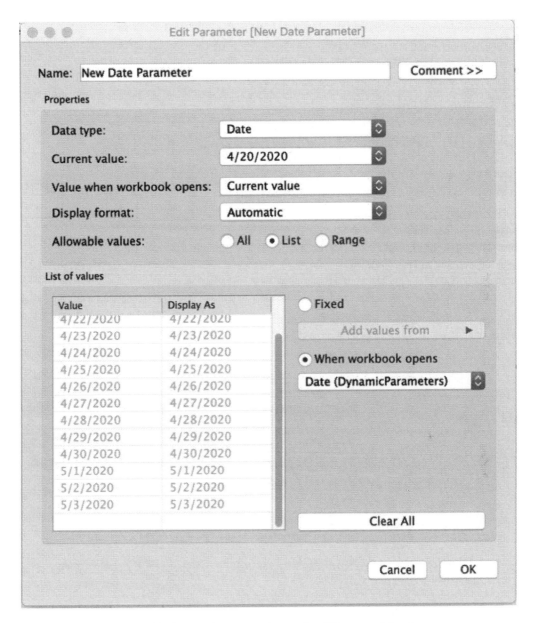

Figure 11.112: Dynamic parameters using When workbook opens

In this exercise, you reviewed the major differences between dynamic parameters and static parameters and saw how dynamic parameters automatically update the list of allowable values alongside the data source update.

In the last section of this chapter, you will put all you have learned about Tableau's advanced interactivity features into practice with a real-world scenario.

ACTIVITY 11.01: TOP N COUNTRIES USING PARAMETERS, SETS, AND FILTERS

As part of the annual hackathon in the company, each team is required to utilize the World Indicators dataset to showcase the top 5 countries according to certain metrics. You decide to show the top N countries by energy usage and also give end users the ability to change the N from 5 to 10, 15, or 20 for ease of use. You will create an interactive view of the World Indicators dataset using sets, context filters, and parameters in this activity.

By the end of this activity, you will have created an interesting view by utilizing all the major topics covered in this chapter, with a special focus on context filters and end user interactivity.

1. Connect to the **WorldIndicators.hyper** dataset downloaded from the project/book folder in Tableau.

2. Create a bar chart of **Country/Region** by **Energy Usage**.

3. Create a **Top N Countries** parameter with 5, 10, 15, and 20 as list values.

4. Create a set called **Top N by Energy Usage** and use the **Top N Countries** parameter for user interactivity.

5. Drag the **Top N by Energy Usage** set to the **Color Marks** shelf.

6. Show **Year[Year]** as a single drop-down filter.

7. Make sure the **Year** filter updates the list of *top N countries* by their energy usage. **Hint**: context filters.

8. Make the title dynamic, so when the **Top N Countries** parameter and the **Year** filter are updated, the title should appropriately reflect the changes. For example, if the user selects the top 10 countries for the year 2010, the title should be *Top 10 countries by their energy usage for the year 2010*.

The final expected output is as follows:

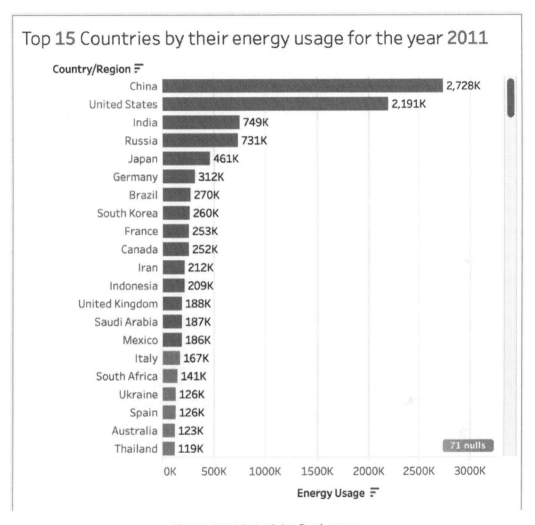

Figure 11.113: Activity final output

NOTE

The solution to this activity can be found here: https://packt.link/CTCxk.

SUMMARY

This chapter considered a number of advanced interactivity features in Tableau. We looked closely at the order of operations in Tableau, which is one of the most important concepts to master in Tableau if we want to create an efficient report for our stakeholders. We also discussed filters, sets, groups, and hierarchies, covered filters in depth, explored the difference between dimensions, measures, and date filters, and practiced using data source filters, which can be a great way to limit the data being loaded in your view.

Regarding sets, we reviewed static, dynamic, and combined sets, using the *Envelope* example to demo the concepts. In the section on parameters, we also defined the difference between static and dynamic parameters and learned one of the advanced use cases of parameters: dimension/measure swapping, which you can use to give end users the ability to choose the dimension/measures that they want to include in the view.

We wrapped up the chapter by working through an activity utilizing the World Indicators dataset. Here, you created a complex view using sets, context filters, and parameters, which in a way resembled a real-world scenario that you might face in your data job.

This concludes the print copy of this book, but it is not the end of your journey. Visit https://packt.link/SHQ4H for a further three chapters, covering such topics as tips and tools for increased interactivity (Part 2 of this lesson), dashboard distribution, and even a case study regarding the utilization of multiple data sources and the practical implementation of all the skills you learned throughout the course of this book.

INDEX